FAMILY, SELF, AND SOCIETY:

Toward a New Agenda for Family Research

FAMILY, SELF, AND SOCIETY:

Toward a New Agenda for Family Research

Edited by

PHILIP A. COWAN
DOROTHY FIELD
DONALD A. HANSEN
ARLENE SKOLNICK
GUY E. SWANSON
University of California, Berkeley

LEA LAWRENCE ERLBAUM ASSOCIATES, PUBLISHERS
1993 Hillsdale, New Jersey Hove and London

Lawrence Erlbaum Associates, Inc., Publishers
365 Broadway
Hillsdale, New Jersey 07642

Library of Congress Cataloging-in-Publication Data

Family, self, and society : toward a new agenda for family research / Philip A. Cowan . . . [et al.].
p. cm.
Includes bibliographical references and index.
ISBN 0-8058-0999-6
1. Family—Research—Methodology. 2. Family—Research—United States. 3. Family—Research—Japan. I. Cowan, Philip A.
HQ728.F3244 1992
306.85'072—dc20 92-28057
CIP

Printed in the United States of America
10 9 8 7 6 5 4 3 2 1

Contents

PART II: RETHINKING RESEARCH ON NUCLEAR FAMILIES

PART III: RETHINKING RESEARCH ON FAMILY NETWORKS IN MIDDLE AND OLD AGE

Preface

At the end of the 1980s the editors came together with a group of family scholars for 2 days to consider the current state of family theory and research and to look ahead to challenging issues likely to be raised between now and the beginning of the new century. Our gathering included sociologists, psychologists, psychiatrists, anthropologists, a theologian, and a historian. We presented and discussed critiques of family theories and research methods, struggled with tensions between levels of analysis (macro and micro), argued about the relative merits of pure and applied research, and returned to the endless task of integrating structural and functional analyses of family life.

Despite our differences, we agreed on a number of fundamental premises:

1. There are great struggles over the definition of what constitutes a family. The title is claimed by: nuclear mother-father-child groups; heterosexual, gay, and lesbian couples; single mother-child units; multigenerational households; and collectivities of unrelated but closely attached individuals. We agreed that we cannot assume that *nuclear* family arrangements will continue to be the only ones that are culturally approved. We came to consensus on the principle that, in specific social contexts, some family forms are more socially adaptive than others, but we did not agree on which contexts and which family forms were more adaptive, nor did we agree on the criteria that should be used to define adaptation.

2. Until recently, family researchers have focused primarily on White, middle class, contemporary Americans. In the face of a newly emerging interest in cultural diversity, family researchers must struggle more concertedly with the issue of whether it is possible to create general theories of family structure and

function that apply to families in specific social contexts. The issue of diversity is made more complex by the fact that families are always in a process of change; no single snapshot can adequately capture the nature of family life. We need to know much more about what it is that can be generalized and what must be qualified when we shift our focus from young parents and their 3-year-olds to aged parents and their middle-aged children. We must move away from a preoccupation with families who have minor children living at home to consider families as they define and redefine themselves across the lifespan.

Our understanding of family life today is heavily influenced by our perceptions of how families have changed across historical time. Based on some assumptions about what families were like more than 100 years ago, there is great concern about the fragmentation and decline of contemporary families over the last century. It is imperative to devote more time and energy to separating historical myths from historical facts.

3. Gender is, or ought to be, a central issue in the study of family life. The myriad of books on *parenting* reflect a new egalitarian ideology by addressing themselves to both mothers and fathers. But most of what we know from empirical research on parenting still comes primarily from studies of mothers and children. The issues of juggling work and family life have been studied in women but not in men. Furthermore, in the world of the oldest old, the survivors tend to be women. The data for family theories, then, have focused more heavily on female contributions to the atmosphere and quality of family life. And yet, in both two-parent and mother-headed households, men continue to have an impact on the family directly through the father-child relationship, and indirectly through their relationship with the child's mother.

4. No one has a monopoly on the appropriate methods to be used in family research. Researchers usually choose between qualitative, ethnographic, inductive methods and quantitative, laboratory-based, hypothesis-testing methods. The field of family studies desperately needs both approaches.

5. Researchers who study family dynamics tend to ignore the social and cultural context that provides meaning to individual lives. Conversely, researchers who study the impact of society on individuals rarely examine the mechanisms within the interior of family life that amplify or reduce the impact of society on family members and their relationships. Family research must always turn simultaneously inward to understand the individual views and interrelations of family members, and outward to understand the transactions between family systems and the larger social and cultural systems of which they are a part.

6. Descriptions of families tend to be interpreted as moral prescriptions. We must be careful to make explicit the values underlying the researcher's questions and methods, and to anticipate the problems inherent in comparative studies of families when *different* is translated to mean *better* or *worse*.

These points of agreement follow from a single general premise: Any agenda for family research in the 1990s must take seriously a *contextual* approach to the study of family relationships. The richness in family studies over the next decade, we believe, will come from considering the diversity of family forms—different ethnic groups and cultures, different stages of family life, different historical cohorts—as men and women attempt to raise their sons and daughters.

After the initial round of working papers and discussions at the conference held in February, 1989, we embarked upon this book. We asked authors not to play it safe by describing their old work, but to give us their new ideas and their new data. They did.

Our goal is to make more explicit how we think about families in order to study them and understand them. To illustrate the need for diversity in family studies, we present examples from new families, old families, majority families, minority families, American families, Japanese families, intact families, and divorcing families. This variety is intended to push the limits of our current thinking, not only for researchers but also for all who are struggling to live with and work with families in a time when family life is valued but fragmented and relatively unsupported by society's institutions.

Each of the first 4 sections of this volume contains a set of chapters focused on family theory, research, or methods of study, followed by one or two chapters discussing the general issues raised by the authors in that section. A 5th and final section contains a chapter by the editors outlining what we believe to be some of the major agenda items facing family theorists and researchers in the few years remaining until we enter the 21st century.

Part I

Every author in this volume assumes that people's being family or kin to one another constitutes a special kind of personal and collective project—kinship involves a set of tasks as well as relationships. Family projects are given direction and meaning by personal needs and by societal requirements. That is, what families are organized to do at any point in the life cycle is determined jointly by the demands of social institutions and by the interpretations of family members themselves. This *constructivist* outlook on families and kinship shapes the major grouping of our chapters.

The early chapters in Part I discuss how family relationships are created by individuals or societal groups to serve their requirements. Current theories and research on families are critically examined. Epistemological assumptions are raised and challenged. Eliane Aerts gives us an authoritative account and analysis of the conditions that led to the development of the Western family as we now know it; conditions that affirmed its institutional properties but changed the terms under which these could be embodied and fulfilled. Arlene Skolnick questions the existence of a mythical *golden age* of family life used as a standard to decry the current fragmented state of family life. Aerts and Skolnick rely on historical sources in drawing their conclusions.

The next three chapters are based on empirical methods widely accepted in the province of anthropology and psychology. Focusing on the context of the child in the school, Donald Hansen argues that we must move beyond traditional top-down theories focusing on how society influences parents who, in turn, influence children, and more recent bottom-up theories conceptualizing the individual as active shaper of self and society. He suggests that future concepts for this rethinking of the linkage between family, self, and society can be found by paying closer attention to the workings of time in both societal and individual life. Linda Burton and Carol Stack use an ethnographic approach to the study of multigeneration African American families in the United States to describe the dynamics of kin relationships in a framework that they argue is relevant to the study of the life course of mainstream families as well. George De Vos, drawing conclusions from both interview and psychological test data, shows that studies of Japanese family socialization point toward an interactional rather than an individual understanding of the development of the self.

Paula Fass places the theoretical chapters from Part I in historical perspective and discusses the dilemmas involved in obtaining reliable information about what families were like in different countries at different times. Annette Lawson draws together the theoretical issues raised by new transformations of old family myths, and points the way to the future of family theory-making.

Part II

The second section of the book focuses on nuclear families with young children. Their collective project involves family members arranging their relationships and their use of societal resources to meet the challenge of living together, or apart, as a family. These chapters offer vivid illustrations of the difficult requirements of such a project by looking at what it takes to change from a married couple to a family, and what it takes to continue *being a family,* despite the competitive demands of careers, despite the parents' personal limitations as organizers or familial arrangements, or despite the parents becoming divorced.

All of the chapters in Part II present new approaches to the analysis of family processes, including family formation, dissolution, decision making, and the maintenance of family ties across the lifespan. Philip Cowan, Carolyn Pape Cowan, and Patricia Kerig draw on data from their longitudinal Becoming a Family Project to enter the controversial territory of gender differences in development. They show that fathers, especially unhappily married fathers, tend to treat $3^1/_2$-year-old sons and daughters differently, and that some of the roots of differential treatment of boys and girls may lie in the process of becoming a family. Janet Johnston goes beyond the general finding that parental conflict and divorce cause problems for children to present a new model of the mechanisms by which marital conflict and divorce disorganize and reshape parent-child relationships. Using the Berkeley longitudinal data set, Guy Swanson examines how characteristics of wives' and husbands' personalities are related to the ways a family becomes organized. He goes on to examine when the family's organization is shaped by parents' personalities and when it is not, and to explore the connections between family decision making and children's intellectual abilities and ego defenses. Martha Moorehouse takes us from the oversimplified question of how mothers' employment affects children, to the more complex and interesting question of how women's employment and specific family processes associated with it affect specific domains of competence in young children. Susan Crockenberg's discussion of the chapters dealing with young families focuses on the need for greater understanding of the dynamics by which events, structures, and family interactions influence human development, and greater attention to the benefits as well of the costs of nontraditional variations in families.

Part III

In Part III we see the collective family project themes of Parts I and II played out again when the old–old, or the frail elderly, and their kin discover what they mean to one another in these changed circumstances. This setting is especially revealing of the nature of kinship, because in our society there are no clear normative patterns to guide these relationships. Rosemary McCaslin presents a new model emphasizing the societal-familial interactive nature of family relationships through the life course. We can understand individuals and families only when we know where they are in their family *careers*. Colleen Johnson, in an interview study, reports on the family ties of the oldest old—those aged 85 or more. Dorothy Field and Meredith Minkler, drawing on the longitudinal Berkeley Older Generation Studies, document both stability and change in the predictors of amount of activity and emotional involvement with family members. All three chapters make real the existence of self-activated kinship networks and the potential reorganization of kin ties as old people outlive their friends and customary organizational connections. Laura Carstensen's perspective on the chapters dealing with older families raises new questions about the way in which family theory and research must reconceptualize the family as an intergenerational system.

Part IV

In this section we illustrate collective family projects at different points in the family lifespan in several chapters containing four case histories, all but one drawn from the data sets of ongoing longitudinal research projects described in Part II. The first three family case studies include both fathers and mothers along with their child, and the fourth focuses on a man and his relationships with his family over much of his life. The case studies put living flesh on the bones of statistical analyses of group data. They also provide detailed portraits of the basic phenomena from which family theories are constructed.

Calvin Settlage and his colleagues Daniel Silver, Joseph Afterman, Kent Hart, and Kristin Nelson describe Walt at 18 and 21 months interacting with his parents. In their ongoing psychoanalytic study of separation-individuation, they describe the similarities and differences in the way aggression is regulated between Walt and his mother, and between Walt and his father. Isabel Bradburn and Joan Kaplan present the story of two families from the Becoming a Family Project, beginning with interviews with the couples during the third trimester of pregnancy, and extending until their first child completes kindergarten. By describing both similarities and differences between the two families, the authors provide illustrations of both central tendencies and variations within the quantitative data reported in the larger study. Using the Oakland longitudinal data set, John Clausen traces the life of Karl Schulz from childhood, through marriage, and into the experience of having grown children of his own, showing how the concept of planful competence helps us understand Schulz's life and family relationships.

Examining the family case studies, Nancy Chodorow points out that detailed descriptions of specific individuals and families can be used productively as qualitative illustrations of group trends from large data sets. She argues that case studies can and should also be used in a more inductive way to generate new theories of family functioning.

Part V

The single chapter in the final section of the volume proposes *an* agenda for family research during the remaining years of this decade. We do not claim to have created *the* agenda, because ultimately each researcher must develop his or her own. Rather, we propose and discuss six major items that we believe to be centrally important for the future of family research. These items incorporate the most salient questions, theoretical issues, and methods raised by the preceding theoretical papers, research reports, and case studies. As families change, as research questions change, so must our research models, methods, and theories. Our challenge is to do justice to understanding the increasing complexity of individual and family life as we approach the turn of the century.

Philip A. Cowan
Dorothy Field
Donald A. Hansen
Arlene Skolnick
Guy E. Swanson

I
RETHINKING OUR CONCEPTUAL MODELS

1 Bringing the Institution Back In

Eliane Aerts
University of California, Berkeley

Literature abounds on the incipient demise of the family in advanced industrial societies, but children continue to be born and raised by adult members of these societies. Somehow, then, the institution's function is fulfilled; families continue to exist. Why the pessimism? Clearly, the form families have taken and the constellation of values and roles centered on biosocial reproduction have undergone drastic transformation. The social consensus on what families are and ought to be, so strong in the 1950s and before, has weakened. If a stability of expectations around the social norms and roles relevant to any societal function is the hallmark of its institutionalization, then one can advance the view that the family as the institution concerned with the biosocial reproduction of society is in a state of flux. The reasons for this situation are multiple and complex. Among them are the changes in the social and economic position of women occasioned by the increase in women's level of education and employment and the liberalization of the laws on marriage and divorce, which have given women more freedom of choice in matrimonial and reproductive matters. But other cultural and demographic trends have contributed to the weakening of the social consensus on the values and norms sustaining family roles and prerogatives. My purpose here is to examine the impact of these wider social changes on the familial institution: to treat not only their effects on social understandings of what families are supposed to be but also on the understanding by real families and their members of socially acceptable familial roles and of the norms guiding their relationships and their lives as collectivities.

The decrease in the degree of institutionalization of the family is reflected in the uncertainty regarding its empirical definition. That leads some analysts to conclude that efforts to define the family are futile. These efforts were considered hopeless by a good number of the participants at the conference which gave birth to the present volume. But a proposal for bringing back an institutional approach to family studies cannot avoid the problem of defining its subject matter.

A useful definition must present the distinctive and general characteristics of this institution. Families are primarily the units of biological and cultural reproduction of societies. At the cultural level, the family institution "focuses on the regulation of the procreation and biological relations between individuals in a society and on the initial socialization of the new members of each generation" (Eisenstadt, 1968, p. 410). At the social level, in postindustrial societies, the family is

> a relatively small domestic group of kin (or people in a kinlike relationship), consisting of at least one adult and one dependent person, the adult . . . being charged by society with carrying out . . . the social function of procreation and socialization of children, provision of care, affection and companionship, sexual regulation, and economic cooperation. (Popenoe, 1988, p. 6).

For Malinowski (1962) the cross-cultural and diachronical multiplicity of family forms confirms the fundamental universality of the institution. His injunction to the typical anthropologist of his day is still relevant: "He must show where the family comes in, whence it draws its forces, how far it is inevitable and where it can be dispensed with" (p. 87).

The present-day diversity of family forms in the United States makes it more difficult to get on with Malinowski's task than does the diversity evoked by cross-cultural studies. This is so because, in the United States, a heterogeneity of family forms has developed in a situation where major cultural parameters and other institutions concerned with family life assume its uniformity. Governmental programs to help the family have foundered on this problem (Steiner, 1981), and it remains a stumbling block for all policies and studies regarding the institution at the societal level.

Popenoe's minimal operational definition of a family reflects the changes that have occurred in most Western countries in the last 20 years and covers the one-parent family as both the fastest growing form of socialization milieu and the most problematic. His approach was already adopted by policy makers in European countries in the 1960s (Kamerman & Kahn, 1978), and by scholars at the Royal Society of Medicine in London meeting to discuss the situation of the family in Britain in the early 1980s (Franklin, 1983). But such a minimalist definition of the family raises questions: Does it mean that, as a workable definitional and analytical tool, the family as a concept can dispense with the second adult who hitherto was included as a necessary biological and social component of the human institution? Can one safely assume that the functions fulfilled by what is called the "traditional" family can be and are fulfilled by this restricted group?

In order to address these questions, I shall systematically review the changes that have occurred since the 1950s, changes that have led to the need for a minimalist family definition. I choose the '50s because of the meaning of this decade both demographically and culturally, and also because it saw the publication by Parsons and Bales (1955) of the last major scientific analysis that fits the family into the larger societal system.

The "Traditional" Institutional Model

In the '50s and early '60s, many who did not read Parsons and who would not have recognized his name would have basically described the family and its functions in his terms. In Parsons' view, the family was a private enclave that needed protection from the encroachment of the public sphere in order to fulfill its role as a haven of psychic renewal for the breadwinner. His assessment of the nuclear family household composed of a working father, a homemaker mother and their children as the adaptive family form of the period after World War II, was correct for a time of economic expansion and high fertility. The generalization of the functionality of this family form for advanced industrial societies was questionable.

What is now called the *traditional* family was both the most frequent family form and the cultural ideal (Bianchi & Spain, 1986; Huber & Spitze, 1983; Van Horn, 1988). Parsons was criticized for seeing the family unit as isolated from other kin and primary networks (Kanter, 1977) but he was right in seeing that the nuclear family household was expected to be economically and emotionally self-sufficient. The consensus on what constituted a family and its place in society was so strong that scholars turned their attention to the inner functioning of family units and generally abandoned studies of the forms that families were taking in changing socioeconomic environments.

The rise in divorce and single parenthood since the '50s has rendered normative some forms of families that once were culturally and statistically deviant. The expansion of the service sector has increased the demand for female labor, thus opening up jobs for the increasing number of female heads of household. The economic slowdown and high inflation rates of the '70s have made double wage-earning mandatory for families to maintain their living standards or to reach the living standards of their families of origin (Van Horn, 1988). The strains that have occurred with regard to the place of the family in public policy decisions, and that have been denounced by countless scholars and politicians (Moynihan, 1986), are partly the result of the survival in public programs of the traditional view of the familial institution and of its relations to the society at large at a time of changed economic conditions.

As a case in point, I consider the Parsonian view of the role of the family in social stratification. This role is summarized by Mulkay (1971) in two points:

> 1. In America nuclear families are the main units of social ranking.
> 2. A family's rank depends primarily upon the husband's occupational role. (p. 84)

Point 1 is still mostly valid both culturally and as a matter of policy. The maintenance of the nuclear family criterion for allocation of benefits, services, and for taxation is one point of contention between policy makers and the social welfare agencies that deal with the consequences of redistribution of wealth. When only 28% of all households are constituted of nuclear families with children, and only 15% of homemaker mother and working father (Merrick & Tordella, 1988), the traditional model loses relevance as criterion for the assessment of economic needs and social placement. Nevertheless, nuclear families remain the point of reference for the assessment of economic progress, for the definition of compensatory programs, and for the evaluation of members' status.

In a curious, indirect way, Point 1 remains valid despite the disparity between reality and what this statement presupposes in terms of family forms to which a majority of people belong. It remains invidiously important to the extent that failure to belong to a nuclear family unit is very likely to entail a lower social ranking, all other things—such as race, religion, education—being equal. So, if one is not a member of a nuclear family unit, one tends to fall through the cracks twice: first because one is not counted as a member of a mainstream social category that serves as a basis for evaluating many other aspects of life, especially needs and resources; and second, serendipitously, because if one is not counted among those that are established mainstream members of society, one tends not to count when resources are allocated.

Point 2 of Mulkay's summary of Parsons' scheme is not valid anymore for the 23% of families which at any point in time are headed by women (Cherlin, 1988). But again in a subtle way, and because of the persistence of the validity of the first point in policy making, the *absent* husband's occupational role is an extremely potent indicator of a family's social rank. Of all families where a husband role is not fulfilled, over 50% are at or below the poverty level (Hacker, 1988). For most of these families, this placement results from downward mobility after the husband-father withdraws from the family unit. Thus, the persistence, despite considerable economic and social changes, of a Parsonian model of family life in public debate partly explains why previously "deviant" family forms are at a disadvantage in society. I think that these developments foster the misperception of an institutional decline of the family.

In the core of the paper I search for the meaning of basic institutional transformations through (1) examining change in crucial normative dimensions of family life; (2) assessing the social controls and levels of institutionalization of these changes; and (3) evaluating the functionality of *new* family forms.

INSTITUTIONAL TRANSFORMATIONS

Normative Dimensions

Recent demographic and cultural changes have affected three institutional aspects of the family: family definition, family boundaries, and family values.

Family Definition

An implicit assumption in social and academic circles is that people share the same sense of what makes up families. In fact, there is no consensus among social agencies or professionals or ordinary people on what currently constitutes a family (Grubb & Lazerson, 1988; Steiner, 1981). Current conceptions reveal disagreements concerning the number of people that need to be involved in a family, who they should be, and what determines the creation of a family and its boundaries. Some tend to define the family primarily as a place where a group of people share means of subsistence and tasks associated with producing them (Smith, 1968; Mintz & Kellogg, 1988). This approach conflates the concepts of household and family. Communes or live-in partnerships become families. Others define the family by its function but disagree on what this function primarily is: either the socialization of children or the psychological nurture of adults. Still others define the family strictly in terms of biological and legal bonds or of socioemotional bonds. The legal view relies on the biological and cognate ties between people, or legal adoption, to determine who belongs to a family and what that family is. The social view tends to extend familial status to groups formed by the sharing of responsibilities in the task of rearing children, whether or not the adults involved are biologically related or have legally adopted the children.

The task of defining the family comes recurrently to the fore of public debates because cultural changes have specifically affected people's notions of what is crucial in the institution. There are two aspects to the debates. The first is a matter of the empirical description of a domestic unit which will fall under the category of family for the purpose of ascribing social rights and benefits. The second, following on the first, is the identification of the basic function fulfilled by this unit which justifies its being considered a family (Allen, 1979; Stack, 1979). Both aspects are found in recent efforts to gain legal familial status or socioeconomic prerogatives by groups hitherto excluded from the traditional understanding of what families are:

Eliminating the Child. The claim that nonprocreative partnerships are families and should therefore benefit from the legal dispositions concerning the property, decision-making, and visiting rights of family members with regard to each other specifically highlights the current questioning of the social function of families. The issues are whether families are primarily legally sanctioned sets of relationships whose aim is the material and emotional well-being of adults or are groups organized around the bearing and rearing of children. (Note that a child adopted by a homosexual couple turns the relationship into a family under this latter understanding.)

The necessity of the presence of children or linked generations has hitherto been generally accepted for a family to exist. At an academic level, a discussion of whether the concept of marriage might be extended to homosexual forms of adult intimacy would be more meaningful than an extension of the use of family terminologies. The extension of the concept of family to permanent intimate relationships between adults would void it from analytical as well as descriptive usefulness. One would have to find a new concept that would describe units of procreation and socialization and the intergenerational transfer of property, and differentiate them from other intimate groups (Popenoe, 1988, pp. 6–7).

One of the arguments advanced by social welfare advocates in favor of public support for families with dependent children is that groups that are taking charge of the reproduction of society—the procreation and socialization of the next generation—deserve special societal consideration and some compensation for the financial burden of doing so. This crucial function which concerns society as a whole and in the long run affects all of its members cannot be left to fall exclusively on the resources of the discrete private groups that are *de facto* in charge of its fulfillment. A basic misunderstanding, willful or not, of the difference between the notion of the family as a social institution responsible for the reproduction of society and of the family as a private institution made of persons with all the rights and prerogatives of private individuals accounts for most of the fruitless debate in social policy between advocates and adversaries of supportive family programs (McCathren, 1981).

Eliminating the Second Parent. Less radical perhaps in its consequences for the transformation of the family than the disappearance of children from its definition is the disappearance of a second adult. Family agencies in Western Europe and some American social welfare advocates and scholars have found it productive to use a minimal operational definition of the family as made up of at least one adult and one dependent child. Scholars studying the family have followed suit. Relationships of consanguinity between adult and child are not assumed anymore; neither is the necessary presence of a second adult related to the first by bonds of sexual and emotional intimacy and playing a complementary parental role with regard to the dependent child.

One-parent families are not a novelty as a context for the socialization of children. It is a part of the biographies of many members of the older generation. The experience of widowhood in World Wars I and II, and of desertion by fathers during the Depression are not so very remote from society's experience (Thornton & Freedman, 1983). Women raising their children alone were one of the primary concerns of social reformers of the 19th century and the reason for the first welfare legislation in this century. Aid for Dependent Children, which became AFDC in 1961, was specifically designed to help World War I widows during the Depression (Leiby, 1978).

But there are significant differences between the single motherhood of the earlier decades of this century and that of current times. One difference consists in the frequently voluntary rather than accidental source of the single-parent family today; a second is to be found in the incidence of the single-parent experience in the life of new generations. A third difference is the extent to which the single-parent family of the past could rely on the larger kin groups and the community to provide surrogates for the absent parent. Currently, the remaining adult is expected to fulfill both parental roles unaided. Very few social mechanisms are in place to compensate for the loss of one parent. And this situation probably results in part from the perception that single parenthood is much more voluntary now than earlier.

As a final change affecting family definitions, advances in reproductive technologies have rendered optional the hitherto basic biological precondition for the creation of a family: a sexual relationship between two adults. The multiple forms of parental roles—biological, surrogate, adoptive—so generated are not, as yet, the subjects of a normative consensus.

This increased ability of adults to determine the form of the family they create, and the context in which they rear their children entails basic transformations in the institutional boundaries of the family, to which I now turn.

Family Boundaries

The transformations of family boundaries result principally from the increase in divorce and remarriage, and consequently in blended or reconstituted families. For the children of divorced and remarried parents, family and household become noncoincidental entities. The head of the household in which they live often does not have legal authority over them, nor is he or she legally required to insure the children's material well-being. The behavioral norms that apply to members of these reconstituted households are still very much undefined (Cherlin, 1978). Although familial roles are often adopted *de facto* by the new members vis-à-vis each other, the absence of sanctions for these roles leads to tensions that are very difficult to resolve (Pasley, 1987).

Joint custody decisions frequently create a situation where a child lives in two households, or at least spends enough of his or her time in the new paternal and maternal households to develop distinct homes and home habits in each of them.

This dual-household family experience for children is definitely new (Ahrons & Wallisch, 1987). The functionality of these multiple-household family forms as against the better analyzed multiple family household is discussed in section 3.

In-vitro fertilization, embryo transfer, and artificial insemination have created new sources of ambiguity for the determination of family boundaries. The newness of most of these technologies, or at least of their application, has as yet precluded an examination of the possible effects of such techniques and ambiguities for the offspring resulting from their use. (Implantation of a frozen embryo resulted in a live birth for the first time in 1984.)

These advances in reproductive technologies have created an artificial distinction between surrogate and biological motherhood at the level, at least, of social and legal considerations. A surrogate is a biological mother who has literally loaned her reproductive capacity to the biological father or to someone else by contract (Shannon, 1988). Problems have come from the biological surrogate mother's refusal to fulfill the contract and give up all claims on her infant, forcing courts to define the principles upon which their decision to attribute parental rights to the surrogate or contractual biological parent is based (Field, 1988).

Historically there have been cases where children were raised by multiple adults performing the roles of fathers and mothers. Utopian communities have provided socialization environments of this sort (Kanter, 1972; Zablocki, 1971, 1980). In such cases, biological and social parentage are not in question, and the prerogatives of parental roles are sustained and controlled by community consensus. But in the case of surrogacy, multiple parents may be in adversarial rather than cooperative relations with each other. The parties involved as well as the communities surrounding them tend to hold violently conflicting views on the principles that should apply in the legal settlement of the disputed parental rights. Most Western societies now recognize the rights of children to be informed about their biological origins, and consequently their right to decide for themselves where their primary filial allegiance should be placed. But contrary to adoption cases where the biological parent or parents voluntarily relinquish their child and renounce their rights, the conflicts between multiple parents on the question of legal parenthood in surrogacy cases can be expected to have very specific, perhaps destructive, consequences for the offspring concerned.

The ambiguous social significance of step, surrogate, and to a lesser extent, foster and adoptive parenting extends to the significance of lines of descent in society. Grandparents increasingly petition the courts to seek support of their rights to continue meaningful relations with their grandchildren after marital disruption or adoption (Thompson, Tinsley, Scalora, & Parke, 1989). These rights are by no means uniformly recognized across the different states. Simultaneously, the rights of inheritance from biological parents in adoption cases are recognized in several states. These differences in statutes regarding inheritance rights and grandparents' prerogatives existed well before this time. What has occurred, however, is an increase in the frequency with which courts are petitioned under these statutes. And the courts' decisions have received more publicity. The contradictory rulings resulting from these differences in statutes across the nation have contributed to the general impression of a progressive weakening of the familial institution.

Because there is a social consensus on the importance of feelings in family matters, and on the impossibility to legislate love and affection, family boundaries in cases of transformed family structures are ultimately decided by the members themselves on the basis of personal preferences rather than by legal sanctions and community consensus.[1] Since preferences do change, these boundaries are fluid and impermanent. And since they are decided by individual choice, members' definitions of these boundaries can and frequently do conflict.

Family Values

The social values that inform today's family life are the result of progressively narrow views of the essence of familial groups: from the community grounded Puritan family to the individual oriented family of the end of the 20th century. Historians have provided accounts of the values that informed familial realities in the past, and in so doing have given descriptions of the functioning of whole societies: Morgan (1966) of New England in the 17th century; Lewis (1983) of 18th-century Virginia; Levy (1988) of 17th- and 18th-century Pennsylvania; Ryan (1981) of the 18th and 19th centuries.

All these accounts of family life in Colonial and early republican times describe a tension between community and family resolved by a progressive privatization of family life (Wall, 1990). They also describe a progressive exclusion of "strangers" from the life of the group. At least in the Northern states, servants, where employed, were less and less likely to share the family's hearth over the years. This progressive privatization was accompanied by a progressive differentiation between the male and female roles both within and outside the household.

Accounts of the American family in the 19th century cease to ground it in the practices of a specific community or region. Family forms became diversified primarily along class and urban/rural lines during industrialization and the Western migrations. Differences between coexisting family forms, the frontier family

[1]Furstenberg (1987, p. 50) reports that in answer to a question regarding who divorced and remarried parents and their children include in their family, only 1% of parents did not include their biological children, while 15% of stepparents did not mention their stepchildren living in their household. Eight percent of children did not mention their biological parents (7% a mother and 8% a father), but 31% did not include stepparents. Moreover, members of the same group define its membership differently. Furstenberg and Spanier (1984) in their study of Pennsylvania parents found that contacts with grandparents on the noncustodial side was very much contingent on children's contact with their non-custodial parent.

versus the Chicago middle-class family for example, became compounded at the end of the 19th century by the influx of very diverse immigrant groups bringing with them the traditions and values of their mostly European origins.

The turmoil and changes witnessed in the United States during the 19th century and especially its second half almost preclude a systematic account of family values that would reflect a sufficiently general American view. Religious revivals strongly influenced the values of a significant part of the population (Johnson, 1978). Early feminist movements at times virulently decried the family behaviors and values of the middle class. This long period of political and social turmoil effectively ended the grounding of family values in the lives of communities.

The story of the family and therefore its history in the 20th century is one of paradox and exceptional trends. It is the story of homogenization of values in the face of ethnic diversity (Edwards, 1969), of extended public intervention in the face of privatization of family life (Pleck, 1987), of a move from family centeredness to self-centeredness (Rossi, 1987), of exceptional reversals in fertility behavior (Van Horn, 1988).

To what extent did family values change within these other trends? Family values *per se,* that is, the importance attributed to family life in American culture, has changed very little since the beginning of the century (Huber & Spitze, 1983; Yankelovich, 1981). The dominant picture of the ideal family is still that formed by heterosexual partners involved in a stable and caring relationship with each other and with their offspring, albeit that the ideal family size has returned to pre-baby boom levels. The central importance of the family in the life of Americans is perhaps most apparent in the outcry about family decline that becomes increasingly vocal as the end of the century draws nearer and empirical changes in family forms become more widespread in society. It is also apparent in the current unwillingness of public agencies to support new forms of families. Public policies that are seen as "encouraging" these new forms are violently decried by a substantial proportion of public opinion, and certainly by most current policy makers, as undermining "the" family (Murray, 1984; Peden & Glahe, 1986).

Nevertheless, there have been significant changes in values in the sense of standards of conduct (Williams, 1968) for men and women that practically equate to a different *valuation* of family life. Substantial changes have occurred in gender roles with the acceptability of instrumentality in women and expressiveness in men (Mason & Lu, 1988). Within families, these changes have found expression in the ideal of egalitarian family organization, the acceptance of mothers' gainful employment, and of fathers' active involvement in childrearing. Values in the sense of attitudes toward family-related behaviors have also changed (Mintz & Kellog, 1988). Divorce has become the normative way of dealing with enduring marital problems; college education is deemed as desirable for women as for men in any field of study; sexual activity in adolescence and premarital childbearing are not stigmatized, although not necessarily generally accepted (Jones et al., 1986, pp. 59–60). People who elect to remain childless are not inevitably perceived as selfish. (These kinds of family values are differentially adopted within American society, but a review of the position of specific ethnic and religious groups cannot be entered into here.)

Yankelovich (1981) made headlines with the results of an attitude survey that showed a predominant concern with the self among Americans. But in his book on the transition from materialist to postmaterialist values and attitudes in advanced industrial societies, Inglehart (1990) reveals U.S. opinion to be comparatively conservative in matters of family and sexuality. Except in one area, the necessity of motherhood for women's fulfillment, the number of Americans endorsing conservative views places the United States among the most conservative of seventeen Western industrial nations.

United States population trends in the 20th century have also been less *modern* than those of other Western nations (Rossi, 1987; Thornton, 1985). They have shown an amazing reversal of worldwide differences of fertility rates between prosperous and poor segments of the population. During the peak fertility years after World War II (from 1955 to 1960) upper-middle-class and lower-class fertility reached similar levels (Van Horn, 1988). Although fertility rates have dropped dramatically since then, birthrates in the United States are still higher than those of most advanced industrial nations. America trails other nations in matters of contraception and consequently is well ahead in the incidence of abortion and teenage pregnancy (Jones et al., 1986). Americans' preference for the married state paradoxically translates into higher divorce rates. This discrepancy at the societal level between values and outcomes suggests that the realities of social life may prevent people from adopting the behaviors that would permit them to achieve the goals they cherish. Such characteristics have prompted theorists to hypothesize a lack of integration of the familial institution in the political and economic fabric of society (Coleman, 1990).

The next section bears on this problem of integration at the macrosocial level. In it I examine how major social institutions interact and influence aspects of family life that strengthen or weaken the family institution.

Control and Institutionalization of Changes

Values and attitudes are important determinants of changes in specific behaviors relevant to family transformation. However, as we have already seen, values and behaviors can be quite discrepant at the aggregate level. Families as well as individuals are at times constrained to act in ways that contradict their preferences and ideals. Other factors must be found that explain the new features of family life. What or who ultimately controls what happens to families? Posing the question this way calls for a distinction between direct and indirect control. Direct control points to matters of authority: Who has the prerogative to decide in family matters, and who regulates and sanctions these decisions? Indirect control points to matters of influence and to social organizations and institutions whose self-serving policies entail definitions of the framework within which families can act.

Direct Control

Historians have traced the progressive independence of the nuclear family from the larger kin group over the centuries. This independence was well achieved in the middle class by the middle of the 17th century. Even in colonial times, American families were independent from larger kin groups, if not from communities. The changes in authority occurred *within* the family in the move from a patriarchal to an egalitarian authority structure from colonial times to today. Parental authority over children moved from the father to both parents in the 19th century. Mothers gained ascendancy in the case of young children by the turn of the century (Grossberg, 1988). But the courts have recently given some authority back to fathers in instances of child custody.

The increased legal recognition of children's and adolescents' rights has extended the scope of this egalitarian trend to the younger generation. Adolescents have gained the right, albeit precarious, of making unaided decisions about their sexual and reproductive life. The popular preference for an extension of nurturant rights—health care, quality education, equal pay for equal work—to children is slowly being superseded by the experts' advocacy of self-determination rights—choice of medical treatment, choice not to go to school, right to enter certain binding contracts (Rogers & Wrightsman, 1978)—at least for adolescents, and increasingly for children (Rodman, Lewis, & Griffith, 1984; Zimring, 1982). To the extent that self-determination rights are extended to the younger generation, the institutional prerogatives of the family are eroded. Although often justified in individual cases, the upholding of such rights in disputes between family members or between families and other institutions, such as school or health care organizations, weakens families' ability to function as socialization agencies in society.

The most significant overriding of family members' control over the definition and performance of their familial roles has occurred in the case of divorce (Jacob, 1988). Decisions in matters of direct control of property, in child-rearing arrangements, and financial provisions for different members pass in significant part in the hands of strangers. When parents disagree, the judge decides the fate of children, not only at the time of the divorce but for years afterwards when court approval has to be obtained by custodial parents for any move or decision that might affect the children's relations with the other parent. The freedom of action of parents can be radically curtailed, and the private lives of members severely invaded. The power of the judiciary to decide the fate of individual families, and the arbitrariness of the decision-making procedures involved, are both extensive (Glendon, 1987; Weitzman, 1985). Judicial precedents and the doctrine of "the best interests of the child"[2] have led to aberrant decisions when the best interests are decided in ignorance of the relationship that the child has established with a primary caretaker, and in ignorance of the importance of the stability, predictability, and permanence of this emotional bond for the child's development.

But divorce is not the only instance where the direct control of a family's life by its members comes to be overridden by outside agents and institutions. In practically all cases of family or child support provided by state or Federal agencies, family members' discretion in making major life decisions is curtailed (Ellwood, 1988). Among the decisions so constrained are those concerning where the parties can live, whom they can consult in health or other emergencies, and whether they can or must look for employment (even when raising young children). This intervention of outside agencies occurs for families receiving any form of public support: that is, for over 50% of families headed by single mothers, and about 10% of poor two-parent families. It affects between 20 and 25% of all children under age 18 (Bane & Ellwood, 1989).

Finally, in cases of use of artificial techniques of fertilization and embryo development, the control of reproductive functions is taken over by the medical profession. Parents usually have recourse to these techniques because of reproductive problems for which they are powerless. Nevertheless, the use of artificial techniques gives to specialists the control over otherwise natural processes (which embryo to select, when to start the procedures, and so on). The extent of external control over one's reproductive abilities come to the fore when disputes arise between parents during the lengthy course of the process.

Overall, periods of significant reduction of members' control over their own and their families' lives in favor of external agencies and institutions can be estimated to occur for over 50% of all families. This statistic represents a significant change in the institutional independence of the family from other social agencies earlier in this century. The rhetoric of public figures is, however, replete with injunctions to protect family privacy and independence from state intervention. Such a contradiction is probably a result of the absence of a familial law, that is, a corpus of laws protecting and sustaining families as entities and relationships, but a plethora of laws protecting the rights of individual family members as private persons rather than as incumbents of familial roles (Kay, 1969). Trends in law are ambiguous at this point. On the one hand, there is a strong support of the right to privacy in family, and especially in sexual, matters. This tendency is reflected in court decisions bearing on questions of contraception,

[2]The doctrine of the best interests of the child has a long legal history. The principle was enunciated in England in 1763, and used in 1849 by a New York judge in a custody case (Grossberg, 1988). Its definition and applications by the courts have been the object of critical scrutiny by Katz (1971) and Goldstein, Freud, and Solnit (1979), among others.

abortion, and sexuality between consulting adults (Dworkin, 1989a, 1989b; Hixson, 1987). On the other hand, the individualistic orientation of the law actually favors an increasing interference in private matters in cases where disputes arise between partners concerning the mode and results of their joint private actions and decisions (Thompson, Tinsley, Scalora, & Parke, 1989). Meyer et al. (1988) argue that an adversarial view of family relations develops as nations become more advanced and diversified economically and socially. Private issues become the object of public debate at the same time as family conflicts are more and more extensively decided on the basis of individual rights (Feshbach & Feshbach, 1978; Melton & Wilcox, 1989).

Family law varies considerably by state, but overall, legal sanctions supporting familial authority have weakened. The tendency has been general, even in Supreme Court decisions, for family members' rights as individuals to supersede those associated with the responsibilities of their familial roles (Sussman, 1988). To that extent the role of parents in socialization has weakened considerably, and the social recognition of the family as the fundamental institution for the transmission of human and civic values has lost institutional supports.

Indirect Control

The changes in laws and statutes on divorce, child custody, and reproductive techniques are themselves the result of a progressive influence of experts who have exercised considerable indirect control over the family since the last century.

The rise of the role of experts in family life has been reviewed by several historians in the context of studies of changes in family laws. Grossberg (1988, pp. 170–195) reviewed the influence of child-labor reformers, and of the medical profession in the regulation of paternal authority, contraception, and abortion in the 19th century. Pleck (1987) shows how medical and social work professionals invaded family life by setting the norms for judging parental competence and child abuse, and encouraging the reporting of deviance. Cases of deviance then justified expert intervention in family life. The 20th century saw the invasion of homes by specialists in health and hygiene, and child-rearing. The homes themselves became the target of home economists and architects in the name of family efficiency and economic frugality (Wright, 1980).

The media exercise an insidious control on family life when they introduce to mass audiences as "in," right, advanced, scientific, or sophisticated views espoused by particular, often privileged, groups. They also frequently present to American families distorted images of themselves. Popular academic authors do the same when they generalize to the American population very specific and limited examples of marriage, family, values and life course experiences.[3] Their

---

[3]The work of Sheehy (1977) on the female life course, of Rubin (1976) on working-class families, of Lasch (1977, 1979) on family and self-orientation of Americans, and of Bellah et al. (1985) can be criticized on these grounds.

writings introduce in public discourse and unfortunately often in public policy a referent image of familial reality which is claimed to be normative but is rarely more than a simplification of selective trends affecting selective populations. The media's use of these images and their amplification into revelatory discoveries about the life of ordinary people tends to transform these views into norms. Such a process constitutes an indirect but powerful control of family life by influencing the evaluation by family members and by interested institutions of familial realities against artificial norms. Costly policies and interventions are devised on the basis of assumptions generated by these distorted images. Family life in this way becomes constrained by unreal expectations and evaluations which prevent the unambiguous assessment of realities and the development of norms that reflect the range of experiences of real families.

The most influential indirect control of family life derives, of course, from the economic sphere of society, and particularly from the private policies of employers and the public policies of government. Taxation and welfare directly control the flow of resources from society to families, and, in so doing, set the parameters of individual family decisions in matters of matrimony, childbearing and child-rearing, education, residence, and so on. Huber and Spitze's (1983) and Van Horn's (1988) studies of changes in women's employment and fertility over the century support the view that these changes are to a significant extent the results of economic conditions and economic calculation on the part of young couples. Other indirect controls derive from the absence of family provisions and protections in the hiring and promotion of personnel in both public and private sectors. Parents, whether married or single, have to adjust their family's life and often their reproductive decisions to long-term employment or professional plans. Raising a family constitutes a serious career risk in America, especially for women. By extension, conflicting career and family demands create tensions in marital relations (Gilbert, 1985; Kline & Cowan, 1988; Spitze, 1988). Unemployment, financial difficulties, and occupational dissatisfaction are sources of strains most disruptive of marital relationships and family functioning (Liem & Liem, 1988, 1990). These strains are ultimately reflected in diverse forms of family disruption, from family violence to divorce.

The effect of economic conditions on families at the edge of poverty is of course significantly more direct and pervasive. Policies regarding the minimum wage, health insurance, and unemployment completely determine the ability or inability of nonskilled, two-wage-earner families to support themselves above the poverty line (Ellwood, 1988). Most of the time, the apparent freedom to act of these families, their independence and self-determination are negated by their inability, whatever they choose to do, to rise above poverty and economic insecurity. The meaningful economic parameters of their lives are defined at the national level and effectively control the most minute family decisions, extending to some very intimate matters indeed.

The disregard for family consideration inscribed in economic policies supported by the principle of free enterprise has created part of the problem faced by families today. Industry closures without provisions for employees and the resistance by politicians and industries themselves to the imposition of a minimum warning time before layoffs put a significant number of families at the mercy of forces quite often irrelevant to the sector of the wage earner's skills. Corporate buyouts which influence industry closings regardless of actual market conditions are sources of total unpredictability and total dependence for individual family members' lives. Information, education, occupational retraining cannot compensate for the consequences of the arbitrariness of these kinds of economic trends. They affect lives at all levels of professional competence (Newman, 1988). Policies in favor of parental leave and daycare support have been adopted by some states. But the fierceness of the debate on making such policies mandatory at the Federal level reveals the strength of the opposition to an "interference" of family considerations into the economic sphere.

Institutionalization of Change

An institutional approach to family changes focuses attention on the mechanisms by which other social spheres, such as politics and the law, influence and help to institutionalize transformations in family life. The link between the family and society is generally formulated and formalized in the regulation of family life emanating from that society's representatives: either in the legislature or the judiciary. But there are other very diffuse and indirect ways in which the family and society influence one another. The problem is to disentangle how these influences are actually operating. Formal codifications influence the ways in which individual members of society view themselves as potential marriage partners and as parents. Knowing that divorce is easily obtained and reasonably inexpensive probably changes people's attitudes toward the legal bond of marriage, toward courtship and its role, and toward bearing children. Such influences can only be inferred from attitude surveys, and people's responses across fairly long-term intervals marked by legal changes. The kind of publicity given to legal changes by the media also influence attitudes to an almost unknown extent. Ultimately, these influences crystallize into cultural changes in the place and role of marriage as a social institution. Changes in marriage in turn influence other social spheres, particularly the economic and educational, as women feel more and more the necessity to be trained for gainful employment and to hold well-paying jobs as an insurance against possible marital dissolution. We do not know the extent to which divorce legislation has influenced women's attitudes toward education and career. We only know that changes in the divorce statutes have preceded the drastic increase in young mothers' employment. These reciprocal influences existing between family and society have generated three crucial institutional transformations of the family that I briefly discuss next: the optional status of marriage, the legitimation of working motherhood, and the erosion of fatherhood.

The Optional Status of Marriage. Many changes in family-related behaviors have been integrated into American culture. Although some groups in society strenuously oppose these changes, the views of mainstream Americans are often tolerant, if not always supportive. Informal sanctions are rarely applied against individuals who have enacted new family behaviors, and formal—or legal—sanctions are absent. Divorce has become the normative way of dealing with enduring relational problems between spouses. Premarital sex and premarital child-bearing became more acceptable in the 70s. There is no significant social pressure exercised on women to get married if they become pregnant, and no strong social stigma attached to premarital motherhood (Thornton, 1989). Consequently, parents raising their children alone are not as often stigmatized, nor are they usually seen as in need of special consideration. These changes amount to one very important and institutionalized transformation: the disappearance of marriage as a normative precondition of family formation. This does not mean that marriage is not the favored status and context for bearing and rearing children, but rather that it is largely accepted as optional by increasingly large segments of the population.

The Legitimation of Working Motherhood. The second significant change is that of working motherhood. Sixty-two percent of women with children over 18 were in the labor force in 1983. This change is significant compared to the 50s (McLaughlin et al., 1988). For some parts of the population, mothers have had to seek employment well before the current period. But this employment generally led to elaborate family arrangements for the care of younger children (Hareven, 1982) and was almost exclusively found in working-class families and as temporary solutions to financial crises. The current situation is somewhat reversed, with better educated and higher status mothers more likely to be in the labor force than working- and lower-class mothers. The attitude change reflected in this situation is one of acceptable alternative life courses for women, with increased education and occupational involvement seen as desirable as family formation for young women, and career pursuit as a legitimate life goal.

The Erosion of Fatherhood. The corollary of this consolidation of women's position as economic providers is a concomitant weakening of the paternal role both within and outside the family (Furstenberg & Harris, 1990). There is much more normlessness and absence of institutionalization for the father's role and position in new family situations. Within the double wage-earner families, fathers have lost part of their power as breadwinners but have not compensated for this loss with a significant increase in their child-rearing role. There has not been a parallel acceptance and institutionalization of the homemaker fatherhood as there has been of the working motherhood. Fathers are still generally considered as more inept than mothers in matters of childcare and homemaking. Their trying to fulfill these roles is still more likely to be a matter of derision and criticism, not of admiration. At the societal level, the changes described earlier in reproductive technology, in the acceptability of single parenthood (usually motherhood), have had as a consequence to make the fathers' role expendable. Because fathers have been made expendable, there is much less support and agreement on what contemporary fatherhood implies.

The judicial system has significantly contributed to the erosion of fatherhood. Through most of the court decisions on reproductive rights, judges have favored female as against male progenitors. They have upheld the rights of women to abort fetuses without consulting the father, the maternal rights over embryos, and they favor biological mothers over biological fathers in contested surrogacy contracts. The principle of the best interests of the child still favors mothers in most cases of disputed custody. Child custody settlements in recent years have added up to taking away the rights but trying to enforce the responsibilities of paternity. Needless to say, it has led to disaffection from the role for many men confronted with the disintegration of the traditional family unit. Studies of paternal default in child support after divorce confirm that whenever fathers do not maintain a sufficiently involved relationship with their children that allows them to have some influence on the children's lives, they tend to neglect their obligations as providers (Seltzer, 1989; Seltzer, Schaeffer, & Charng, 1989). What has become of the paternal role in the transformed family? Is there a meaningful place for the father in the new familial institution? This question is a salient one for all of the new family forms analyzed below.

The conclusion that can be drawn at this point on the level of institutionalization of changes in family life is that it is change in the lives of women which has determined the changes in the family. Women have been disproportionately the initiators of divorce proceedings; they have rejected marriage as a necessity and have made singlehood and childlessness acceptable; they have set educational and occupational achievement rather than marriage and motherhood as indices of personal success. These changes have been institutionalized at the cultural level in part because women are also the arbiters of family values and family norms. And the last few decades have witnessed a strengthening of the position of women as definers of family forms.

These developments and the concomitant weakening of the paternal role bring us to the last part of this examination of the familial institution: to the consequences of these societal trends for the fulfillment of what remain as a family's least disputed functions—rearing and protecting children, preparing them for adult roles, and anchoring adult identities.

The Functionality of the Transformed Families

At a symposium on the family held in 1981 by the Royal Society of Medicine in London, Edmund Leach (1983) reminded participants of the importance of the social networks in which individual domestic units are embedded. For him, the weakness of the family in contemporary Britain is due to the lack of structural supports for that embeddedness and to the tendency of administrative practices to isolate families from each other and from communities. In the move from a macro to a micro institutional level effected in this section, I shall try, in necessarily brief analyses, to show the impact of families' environment on the strengths and weaknesses of new family forms in America.

The family's remaining functions are still very much as Parsons defined them: the care and socialization of children and the nurture and anchoring of adult personalities. Statistically, a majority of children are reared at least for a portion of their childhood in households with only one adult.[4] How do these conditions support the fulfillment of the basic institutional functions of biosocial reproduction? I first examine the most prevalent family forms, and perhaps the least problematic, and end up with the least prevalent but most problematic. Many adults and children move from one kind of situation to the other in the course of the childrearing years. Therefore the statistical distribution of family forms at any one time does not reflect the prevalence of some family experience in individuals' life courses.

Dual Wage-Earner Families

In its statistical importance, the dual wage-earner family has replaced the *traditional* family of the 50s and 60s. As in the recent past, the majority of family households with children (not of households in general) are made up of two adults and their dependent children who can be the offspring of one or both spouses (Santi, 1988). Therefore, this family system includes as a subset the reconstituted family made up of previously divorced partners and the children one or both had from a previous union. I shall examine the specific situation of reconstituted families later. In this part, I look only at families where both adults are employed, that is, where the breadwinner role is shared.

Currently, 62% of mothers of children under 18 are working. Among them, over 50% of working mothers have children under age 3 (Matthews & Rodin, 1989). This group is the fastest growing category of women entering the labor force. The trend in women's move to gainful employment is now followed by women regardless of their marital status and childrearing stage. Projections for

[4]The percentage of children who can be expected to live in one-parent families in the future is the object of controversy. The estimates vary quite widely for Whites, and a little less for Blacks. For example, Hofferth (1985) estimates that 70% of White and 94% of Black children can be expected to live some time in one-parent families by 1995, while Bumpass (1984, 1985) estimates these percentages to be lower, about 42% for Whites and 86% for Blacks. Hofferth (1987) justifies her estimates on methodological grounds: Her projections are based on cohort life table analyses of children born in 1980 while Bumpass' estimates are obtained from projections of past and present trends, regardless of the cohorts bearing the future.

the last decade of the century are that mothers' employment rates will reach if not surpass 75% (Hofferth & Phillips, 1987).

Dual wage-earning in two-parent families is unlikely to decrease significantly. It is fostered by the demands of a job market increasingly oriented to service employment where women have traditionally been favored employees, inflation trends that reduce the buying power of wages, women's increased education, and by cultural changes in women's values and expectations. All of these make the prospect of women's return to full-time motherhood unlikely. Children fare best in households free of tensions, whether or not the mother is working (Hoffman, 1987). One is tempted to conclude that men had better adapt to the situation and try to redefine their role within such households, and derive familial satisfaction from sources other than the traditional sole-provider role. Within couple relationships, nurture must be redefined as mutual help and caring. Sharing of tasks rather than complementarity of tasks becomes the crux of negotiated roles. Success resides in achieving equity rather than in the satisfactory performance of individual tasks (Gilbert, 1985). In other words, relationships rather than individual roles take priority as indices of achievement of family functions.

At this time, the burden of familial transformation in terms of identity and self-satisfaction is borne by men. When society does not value homemaking and parenting as highly as occupational achievement, the renegotiation of roles within dual wage-earner families requires of men that they relinquish a monopoly on the sources of the greatest prestige and pride and sharing in some lesser tasks. It is therefore unlikely that fathers will derive an enhanced self-fulfillment and satisfaction from their redefined roles. The strains of uncoordinated sources of gratification for spouses within dual wage-earner family systems are likely to maintain their susceptibility to dissolution in the foreseeable future.

Would an increase in outside support from social networks or institutions help relieve the strains? Studies up to this point do not evoke optimism. They suggest that the total amount of time actually devoted to household matters is not what counts in mothers' level of satisfaction with their family situation but rather their perception of an equitable contribution from their husbands to these tasks. More help with child-care, household tasks, more flexibility in working hours would not *per se* reduce tensions between spouses (Barnett & Baruch, 1987). Subjective feelings of who does more and who gets more are what count, and they are only remotely related to reality.

Thoits (1987) has cogently summarized the complexity of functional analyses of familial roles in dual wage-earner families, and summarized empirical results available at this time. Do families with two wage earners fulfill socialization and nurturing functions adequately? Do adults and children fare as well, better, or less well in them than in the traditional family? Thoits' review of research leads to the answer: It all depends. It depends on the members' expectations, on their ability to negotiate their multiple and shared roles, and to adapt to their partner's roles. It also depends on the existence of social structural support: child-care facilities, economic security, social network diversity.

Compared to the traditional family of Parsons' description, dual-career families have moved from parental role differentiation and complementarity to role similarity and competition. The internal dynamics of such a system of roles are much more likely to be influenced by subjective perceptions than by objective evaluations of role performance. To insure cooperation rather than competition, a sufficiently equitable reward system must exist for all roles performed.

Reconstituted Families

As a subset of the dual wage-earner family form, reconstituted families may belong to several different kinds of groups: those made up of two adults and the children of one of them from a previous union; or of two adults and their own offspring plus the children of either parent from a previous union; or two adults and their children from previous marriages. In this section I examine only the functionality of households where children do not share the same parents, or when the adults do not share the same children. The sources of strain come from the ambiguous status of the stepparent who legally has no parental authority over the minors who share his or her household, and to whose welfare he or she often significantly contributes.

For children, tensions result from having multiple parents, all of whom claim some loyalty and some influence in their lives. The anomic situation of stepfamilies has been underlined by Cherlin (1978). The functioning of these families shows perhaps the greatest variation of all new family forms. This is due to the interplay of several crucial variables, all possibly varying together: stepmother vs. stepfather vs. combined stepparent families; sex of stepparents' own children and sex of stepchildren; age of children when the family came into being; length of time the members have been sharing the same household; intensity of stepchildren's relations with their biological noncustodial parent (Clingempeel, Brand, & Segal, 1987). Putting together families differing in some or all of these characteristics would not be helpful in trying to understand their functioning. The variables enumerated above are likely to be sources of significant differences in family dynamics. That is perhaps the reason why systematic analyses of reconstituted families' functioning is lacking. And few studies exist that compare the ability of different kinds of reconstituted families to perform their basic socialization and nurturant functions. The conclusions we can draw at this point have to remain at a very general level.

Stepfather families, which form over 90% of all reconstituted families, seem to be problematic for girls, especially at adolescence (Hetherington, 1987). Part of the problem is due to the equivocal status of stepfathers which is manifested in the laws of incest across different states. In some states, sexual relations between stepparent and stepchildren are not prohibited, in others they are. This ambiguity of the sexual status of the stepparent-stepchild relationship is reflected in the increased rates of sexual abuse among stepparent-stepchild pairs (mostly stepfather-stepdaughter) compared to the rates of parent-child incest (Finkelhor, 1984; Gordon & Creighton, 1988).

Hobart (1988) shows that women are central in the functioning of stepfamilies whether as mothers or stepmothers. Stepmothers do parent their stepchildren living in the same household, while stepfathers see themselves first as husband to the mother, and through her, related to the children. Stepfathers tend not to get deeply involved in the paternal role with their stepchildren (Santrock, Sitterle, & Warshak, 1988). They are more likely to defer parenting to their wives. And their relationship with the children is contingent upon the quality of their relationship with their spouses. In that sense, they are less likely to feel committed to parental sexual norms with regard to their stepchildren, especially their stepdaughters. Claims of mother and daughter on the husband's attention carry more ambivalence in reconstituted families than in biological nuclear families, and mother-daughter rivalry is probably more likely to surface. These inherent sources of tension lead to a higher level of organizational rigidity in reconstituted than in biological nuclear families. Reconstituted families are more likely to assign tasks on the basis of stereotypical sex and age roles and to adhere to them more rigidly than biological families of similar socioeconomic status (Peek, Bell, Waldron, & Sorell, 1988).

Studies of families resulting from remarriage at this point suggest that marital disruption followed by remarriage does not result in children's developing meaningful relationships with multiple parents and relatives. Children who have biological and stepparents alive tend to develop meaningful emotional ties with only one or two of their parents, most often those with whom the child shares a household (Seltzer & Bianchi, 1988). The situation also does not result in meaningful accumulations of other relatives, aunts, uncles, grandparents. Although amicable relations are frequently developed with stepfamily members, these relations remain infrequent, superficial, and dissolve if any tension develops between the parents. They tend not to extend into help and support, or to endure after children have grown up.

The problem for reconstituted families becomes one of erasing as much as integrating residuals of past family experiences and starting anew as a nuclear household. However, the finding that stepfathers tend not to assume full paternal roles within reconstituted families suggests that such systems, even though they may try to reproduce the conditions of biological nuclear families, are never as complete and functional. The lack of legal sanctions for stepparental authority and the anomie surrounding the role fills the situation of the reconstituted families with ambiguity. Unless stepparents adopt their stepchildren, which is a very rare situation when biological parents are still alive, they generally do not have legal authority over their stepchildren, neither do they have any obligation of support. (Here again, statutes vary from state to state.) They are legally strangers to each other, especially in states where no sexual prohibition between stepparent and stepchildren exists. And this legal situation translates into insecurity and lack of commitment to the new roles and relationships created by stepparenting. Members do know they can rely only on each other's good will. The reconstituted family, as family, is basically an incomplete social system and a nonexistent legal entity (White & Booth, 1985).

Single-Parent Families

The origin of single parenthood must be considered before the family resulting from it can be examined. When the family results from divorce, desertion, or death, the family led by the single parent is a residual of experiences and assets built up during a period of nuclear family form. When single parenthood is the result of unmarried child-bearing, the family formed is genuinely based on only one parent. The parenting the children receive is that developed by a single adult who defines from the start a unique role encompassing the instrumental and expressive elements.

When single parenthood results from the departure from the household of the other parent, the role played by the remaining parent consists at least for a time of a combination of roles previously played by two people, neither of which can now be completely fulfilled. The children as well as the single parent experience a significant loss. The family structure is a result of a reorganization dealing centrally with the problem of compensating for that loss. In the case of unmarried parenthood, no such loss exists and the single parent role evolves naturally from the situation's demands.

In many cases of single unmarried parenthood, there is in fact another person, usually a sexual partner of the mother, in the household, if not permanently, at least frequently (Bumpass & Sweet, 1989). The sexual partner is a source of support for the mother, often contributes in material ways to the household, and interacts with the child or children. This case is closer to a nuclear household than to the household of a recently divorced or widowed mother. Thus, the empirical realities covered by the concept of single parenthood are quite diverse. As in the case of reconstituted families, the specific conditions of the family itself and of its environment are crucial components of its life and ability to function as a socializing and supportive milieu.[5]

---

[5]Remembering that 90% of single-parent households are headed by women, it is important to note the consequences of this family form for the socialization of the next generation. On the basis of most recent population surveys, McLanahan (1988) found that daughters living in single-parent households at some point during adolescence are more likely to become household heads and to go on welfare than offspring of two-parent families. But the difference in income between one- and two-parent families accounts for up to 25% of the difference in outcome. Similarly, Krein and Beller (1988) document the negative effect of single-parent households on the educational attainment of

The only statement that can be made with any confidence about single-parent families is that their functioning depends more than any other family forms on the supportive qualities of their environment. One adult in isolation can neither successfully perform paternal and maternal roles, nor satisfactorily fulfill adult emotional needs. The success of single-parent families depends on social structural support specifically aimed at helping the adult in his or her role as a parent, not only as a person. It also depends on the integration of the family in a supportive adult network that is in frequent if not daily informal interaction with *both* the single parent and the children. Institutions with specific individual targets such as schools or adult support groups do not function well as family supports because they address the needs of parents or of children as individuals isolated from one another. However, the presence of supportive social networks as well as the helpfulness of other institutions vary with families' ethnicity and socioeconomic status. Among nontraditional families, those with a single adult are most likely to fall under the jurisdiction of other social institutions, to become dependent on welfare agencies and to be regulated by judicial decisions (Bane & Ellwood, 1989; Hacker, 1988). Unfortunately, these institutions tend not to have a true "family" perspective from which to decide individual families' fate (Glendon, 1987; Grossberg, 1985, pp. 304–307; Kamerman & Kahn, 1978, pp. 420–475).

CONCLUSION: THE NEW FAMILY? AGENDA FOR POLICY AND RESEARCH

A wider diversity of acceptable family forms is already the rule in most Western postindustrial countries. Recent trends in marriage and fertility in the United States are not isolated phenomena; they repeat trends visible already for several decades in most European countries (Fletcher, 1988; Höhn & Lüscher, 1988; Popenoe, 1988). The major institutional change these trends reveal is the rupture between marriage and family formation in the sense that marriage is no longer a

children, especially males. They also found that the lower level of income in single-parent families accounts for part of the effect on offspring's educational levels. McLanahan and Bumpass (1988) determined, however, the crucial importance of socialization deficit as against economic problems or stress as the source of disruptions in the lives of children raised by single mothers. In their study of the effects of divorce on children's marital and educational careers, Keith and Finlay (1988) found that offspring of remarried mothers were even less likely than those of mothers who remained divorced to exceed their mother's education. Children of divorce who married at all tended to marry earlier than children of intact families, but more children of divorce forego marriage altogether. The reproduction of divorce works mostly along female lines, and slightly along male lines for lower SES groups. (See also the review of Demo and Acock [1988] of research on the effect of divorce on children.) Finally, despite the findings of Furstenberg, Brooks-Gunn, and Morgan (1987) that there is no *necessary* link between teenage childbearing of mothers and that of their daughters, single parenthood in the aggregate is reproduced from generation to generation.

socially sanctioned prerequisite of child-bearing. It means that men have, to some extent, lost the control of their progenitorial power. Women, more exclusively than at any time in the past, control the reproduction of the species, not only by using contraception and abortion to control the number of births, but also by the freedom they have to choose the men from whom they will draw for reproductive purposes, and by their ability to limit men's role in the process to their strict biological function. The rising rates of premarital birth and of divorce are the empirical consequences of these changes. Are these empirical consequences sufficiently drastic to justify the assertion that the family as a social institution is disappearing? Another way of asking the question is: Are blood ties between generation and biological coparenting still the object of value and the source of socially and culturally sanctioned rights and obligations? Some scholars' responses are pessimistic (Popenoe, 1988), others see in the current state a sign of the family's resiliency and its capacity to adapt to deeply changed cultural and economic circumstances (Fletcher, 1988; Spanier, 1989). Clearly, the institution has changed, but has it lost its functions?[6] Malinowski's question can help in sorting the elements of an answer.

Malinowski (1962) asked his fellow anthropologists studying the family to examine these points:

> where the family comes in, whence it draws its forces, how far it is inevitable and where it can be dispensed with. (p. 87)

These question, in today's situation, call for the answer to a preliminary question: Which family?

---

[6]Questions and hypotheses brought up in this concluding part are based on recent surveys of the United States population. These surveys of individuals and families reveal the heterogeneity of the life course and consequently of family experience among different ethnic groups. These differences are acknowledged here but many pages would be required to sort out the influence of the currents of cultural and economic changes on separate ethnic groups; Black and White experiences, converging for a brief period during the years of high economic prosperity of the late 60s are now diverging again (Farley & Bianchi, 1987). Although higher proportions of White women are now experiencing single motherhood, which has been a role performed for a long time by a majority of Black women, the discrepancies in proportions of women sharing the experience in different groups remain overwhelming. Birth to unmarried mothers were accounting in 1985 for 22% of all births, but 60% of all Black births, 28% of Hispanic births, and only 14.5% of White births (Zill & Rogers, 1988). Extended family arrangements as an economic solution continues to be adopted much more frequently within Black and Hispanic communities (Angel & Tienda, 1982). On the other hand, Indian children are more likely to live in traditional couple households than either Blacks or Whites but these households are much more likely to be poor than traditional households in either the Black or the White populations (Sandefur & Sakamoto, 1988). Nevertheless, despite differences in the proportions of different ethnic populations falling within diverse categories of family structure, and in the modes of adaptation to similar economic conditions, the trends bearing on institutional aspects of American family life transcend these ethnic particularities and will influence all ethnic groups, though certainly in different ways and degrees.

At this point it is safe to say that the *idea* of family remains very much valued, to the extent that individuals whose relations are not up to this point considered legitimate members of the social genus *family* want to join it and bear the obligations as well as the rights of familial roles. Fletcher (1988) even sees the increasing rates of divorce, the delayed childbearing, and the postponed marriages as signs of an unprecedented social valuation of the family. These relationships and roles are considered so important and so sacred that it does not do to enter into them unprepared, nor to remain in them if one fails to reach high expectations. Is the family killed by its success in being considered the ultimate human value? Not quite, I think. But it is true that there is a paradox in the cultural position of the family in Western societies, and of marriage as its basic component. Marriage as a lifelong commitment of a man and a woman to each other's care and happiness is widely endorsed as an ideal both at the societal and at the individual levels. But it is pragmatically accepted under compromised forms when it comes to reality, again both at the cultural and at the individual levels. In most Western European countries, family policies benefit non-legally sanctioned heterosexual partners and their children. Illegitimacy is not a source of social or economic exclusion, and divorce is now fairly easily granted. In the United States, the latter two conditions are found, and battles are drawn for the social sanctioning of the first.

Going back to Malinowski's questions, one can propose that the concept of family comes in any time the question of responsibility for the care and upbringing of children is brought up. The important change from the past is that the *family* does not come in before that point. Decisions to have a child, bear it to term, and legitimize its birth by marriage are left almost completely to the discretion of women. Many women still choose to make such a decision a family affair that involves the father and is the object of exchange with other kin. But strictly speaking childbearing is not a *family* question. The courts have progressively relegated the power to decide matters relevant to childbearing to the women concerned, and to them alone. They have given a minor the right to act on these matter without parental consent. Given these facts, the birth of a child creates a family only by establishing bonds of obligations for its care and of mutual dependency between one adult (usually the biological mother) and the child. The social sanctions and legal control for family relations start to apply from that point on. Hence, the minimal definition of family advocated here: one adult and one child dependent on that adult for its care and upbringing. *Family ties* may subsequently develop between the child and persons other than that adult caretaker: a father, grandparents, aunts, uncles, and so on. But it cannot be assumed any longer that significant, long lasting ties of this kind will develop and be sustained for a period long enough to make a significant impact on the child's socialization. Divorce frequently cuts short established ties, even with very close kin. The only family bond we can assume to be permanent is that between the child and its primary caretaker, that is, in 90% of the cases, with its mother.

Having answered Malinowski's first question in this manner, the answers to the next three are inevitable. Reduced to a minimum of two members, one being a dependent child, the family draws its force from its necessity in the process of social and biological reproduction. The child's acquisition of basic interactional and social skills depends on the existence of a strong early bonding between that child and the adult who is a permanent figure in his or her environment. The child's successful acquisition of skills for more specific adult roles and its functioning later in life can be traced to a large extent to the existence and the quality of that early family relationship. Therefore, it does not seem at this point that the *family* can be successfully replaced by institutions organized on the basis of a division of labor between the different tasks of caring for children that would preclude children's bonding with caretaking figures. Thus, the kind of minimal family I have described is *inevitable* and *cannot be dispensed with* for the performance of the basic functions of physical and emotional care of the younger generations.

At the other end of the life spectrum where renewed dependency occurs, Western societies have set in place the social and economic mechanisms permitting the family to be dispensed with. The obligations of care for dependent older adults have devolved to society. Whenever statutes regarding filial obligations exist, they tend not to be enforced (Sussman, 1988). Here, too, *family* relations have become voluntary.

However, families headed by a single adult have been found the most problematic in their ability to care for their members. Is it not a contradiction to posit the lone adult-child family form as normative within the institutional definition of the postindustrial family and to find at the same time that it is among the least able to fulfill its function of sociocultural reproduction?

This question underlines the fruitfulness of an institutional approach to the study of families. The minimal family form can be considered normative because it is the kind of family in which a significant percentage of children are raised at any point in time, and because it is and will be part of the family experience of *a large majority of all children* some time before they reach their 18th birthday. An institutional point-of-view directs attention to the societal conditions leading to the appearance of the minimal family forms within a cultural climate where the traditional two-married-parent form is highly valued. It points also to the causes of this minimal form's dysfunctionality. I here review two sets of causes, which have been empirically documented. First, the economic causes, which seem remediable if proper recognition and societal support are given to the transformed family. Second, the psychological causes, which are much more problematic and intractable, and bring up the most intriguing questions about the future of the institution: the weakening of the male role in socio-biological reproduction. This "question of the father" brings us back to the origins of the family.

The Economic Question

As at previous periods of radical economic upheaval, when there were basic changes in national economies (i.e., from agriculture and artisanal production to factories in the industrial revolution; from manufacture and industrial production to services in the postindustrial revolution), many family dysfunctions are related to economic hardship and uncertainties. New jobs require new skills and impose a reorganization of family life. The industrial revolution involved the work of women and children increasingly in mills rather than homes (Thompson, 1988). These new conditions were then seen as sources of destruction of the family as well as sources of criminality and social anarchy. The words of moral reformers of the period are echoed in an eerily familiar way by current conservatives whether or not of religious persuasion. The current postindustrial economic transition from secondary to tertiary economic sectors, which has lasted for the last 4 or 5 decades, has made its impact on the family by the large employment of women that such a shift favored, and by women's adjusting to their new economic role by a reduced fertility. These trends are not likely to reverse. One can, however, be realistically optimistic as to the family's survival, once society will have devised the means of compensating for their human costs. European countries have by and large accomplished the transition (Kamerman, 1984; Wilensky, 1990) by supporting families, that is, by integrating the rearing of children into the larger political and economic planning of their development. Since women are working and are needed as economic producers, services and supports must be in place in order to allow them to fulfill their reproductive function during a part of their economically productive years (Scarr, Phillips, & McCartney, 1989). In many countries, this support is given unconditionally on the basis of the social function performed—biosocial reproduction—rather than on the basis of individual needs, and therefore is available before the birth of the child. Women are, however, given a wide range of choices concerning that function: They have access to contraception, to abortion under certain conditions, and to different options for combining child-rearing and employment. These economic policies have not led to disproportionately differential birthrates among women of different socioeconomic status, nor led to undue demographic expansion. Immigrant populations in these European countries quickly reduce their fertility behavior and become similar to the population of the host country by the second generation. First generation immigrants already tend to be less prolific than the population they come from in their countries of origin (Höhn & Lüscher, 1989).

In the United States, many of the dysfunctions associated with new family forms and disruptions of nuclear families are found to be significantly attenuated when proper controls for differential economic resources are applied. Among these dysfunctions, one finds the reproduction of teenage pregnancy and childbearing across generations, and the lower educational achievement and higher rates of problem behavior for children in female-headed households (McLanahan, 1985, 1988; McLanahan & Bumpass, 1988; McLanahan & Booth, 1989; Miller & Bingham, 1989). Tensions in two-wage earner families could be reduced if work and careers of both husbands and wives were less vulnerable to family demands. With minimal provisions for maternity leaves and child-care the burden of equity between the daily tasks and work spheres of male and female wage earners could begin to be lightened. But the major achievement of economic support for families, that is, for the burden entailed by having and rearing children, would be the cultural and social validation given to the role, and its protection as a part of the future economic well-being of the society. The economy will need qualified men and women as producers of goods and services. But the benefits expected from the increased investments made by individuals in order to acquire such qualifications cannot be voided by their individual contribution to the sociobiological well-being of society. The two kinds of functions are too symbiotic in the long run to allow the maintenance of a high competitiveness and exclusiveness in the roles assuring their fulfillment. The family as an institution will survive, children will be born and reared in smaller or larger groups. The question is how well these groups will contribute to the genesis of the socioeconomic well-being of the society at large.

Part of the answer lies in families' being better integrated in societal planning and execution now. Women entered the labor force in ever greater numbers after World War II because there were jobs for them to take. At the level of the whole society, their contribution to the labor force is now economically indispensable. Contrary to the 19th century when the female labor force could sustain a high turnover without much economic cost, the work performed by women in today's economy requires training before and on the job which makes the stability of their employment a significant economic asset. (The unskilled jobs have largely moved to Third World and developing countries, and the emigration of such jobs continues.) It is costly for industries to lose trained female workers who begin their childbearing careers, and very costly for everyone not to benefit from women's increased education. As during the agricultural period, women's economic and reproductive functions are again much more closely enmeshed at all levels of society than they were during the established industrial period, but one of these functions has now moved from the household to the firm, and the ultimate control of the performance of both functions has consequently moved from the family to the political and economic decision makers. Many aspects of current family life and demographic trends—in marriage, childbearing, and divorce—are forms of adaptation to changed economic conditions and to the demands they put on people. The dysfunctional consequences of these adaptations for socialization and for the personal well-being of adults as well as children, which are decried as caused by the demise of the traditional nuclear family, can ultimately be traced back to a great extent to economic factors. Individual families, whatever their form, should have defrayed for them some of the economic costs of providing the current and future qualified manpower needed by the economy: the cost of childcare, education, and of retraining when acquired qualifications become obsolete. This would not be a transfer of means from the economy to the family but an integration and rationalization of a socioeconomic system where heavy costs are currently sustained because of the absence of such an integration.

The Father Question

Scientific and technological advances have permitted a radical disjunction between the two functions of *pater* and *genitor*. Although the recourse to artificial insemination of women with the sperm of total strangers remains extremely infrequent, the knowledge by men and women that fathers can be dispensed with is already having an impact on family life. It would be difficult to trace the effects of such advances in reproductive techniques on men's attitude and commitment to relationships and to families. Do they or do they not contribute to the flexibility men show in taking on new families and new children in remarriage, and to the ease with which they relinquish relations with their biological children (Furstenberg, Nord, Peterson, & Zill, 1983)? Men have always known that the authenticity of their progeny was in the hands of women, and they devised elaborate systems in order to prevent deceit. But now that paternity as well as nonpaternity can be determined, men have lost the initiative in selecting the partners with whom to breed. As persons they have become unnecessary to the reproductive process.

But the prevalent problem of fatherhood for new generations will be the loss of a father by children born in two-parent families. Although the father role is now seen as entailing a much more active involvement in child-rearing than in previous generations, the higher incidence of family disruption results in an overall decrease in the saliency of fathers in children's lives. The question of fathers' lasting responsibility for child support is not yet solved. Should one expect men who do not live in or otherwise influence the household in which their children are reared to provide for them in the absence of any other meaningful ties? Studies reveal that the only factor that seems to make a difference in the long run for the functioning of children of divorce is the material support that fathers provide. Other characteristics of father-child relationships, such as frequency of contact and psychological closeness, do not make a significant difference in children's behavior and emotional well-being (Furstenberg, Morgan, & Allison, 1987).

The introduction of a stepfather in the family does not compensate for the father loss through desertion or divorce. Girls fare less well in stepfather families than in families of single mothers. Boys seem to benefit after a while from the introduction of a male figure in the family, but whether it is because of the stepfather's behavior and interest in their stepsons, or whether it is because of the changes in the mothers' behavior and demands with regard to their sons after remarriage is not clear at this point. Furstenberg and Harris (1990) bring up the idea of "family swapping" as a sort of serial fathering, fathers taking on the care and support of the offspring of the women with whom they happen to have an enduring relationship, whether or not these offspring are also theirs. Fine (1989) suggests the need for legal reforms that would reflect and institutionalize the actual situation of fatherhood. He proposes the extension of paternal rights and obligations to stepfathers vis-à-vis the children who share their households. But would these changes in law really help to solve the ambivalent position of stepfathers with regard to their stepchildren, especially stepdaughters? Would changes in statutes resolve the sexual dynamics of stepparent families, and protect daughters from the tensions that can develop, even when no readily identified problems exist? The presence of stepchildren seems to be the factor that makes remarriages more unstable than first marriages (White & Booth, 1985). The research findings converge to suggest that reconstituted or blended family systems are psychologically unstable. The complexity and variety of individual cases are tremendous, and well-reflected in the clinical literature on blended families (Ganong & Coleman, 1987). But the best assessment of the problem of the father in new family forms from an institutional point-of-view still comes from studies of large samples that show differences in marital stability, prevalence of sexual abuse, adolescent delinquency, and premature sexual activity as well as low educational achievement in reconstituted families compared to first-time families with all relevant controls included.

The intriguing question that deserves much more systematic study is the difference found in the behavior of parents and stepparents with regard to children of different sexes and the differential effects of family disruption and stepfamilies on stepchildren (Morgan, Lye, & Condran, 1988; Hetherington, 1987; Wallerstein & Kelly, 1980; Needle, Su, & Doherty, 1990). Furstenberg and Harris's (1990) idea of serial fatherhood is somewhat undermined by the fact that stepfathers do not act, engage themselves, and respond to stepchildren as fathers do. Surrogate fatherhood is qualitatively different from biological or adoptive fatherhood in intact families, and much more so than biological motherhood is from stepmotherhood. Thus, one cannot really talk about serial fatherhood when only the fatherhood of biological or adopted fathers exercised within the household where the children live takes all the characteristics normatively associated with the role. Removed from the children's household, the biological father continues to act as a father only to the extent that his role remains complete, that is, involves extensive interaction and opportunities to influence, control, succor, and support the children (Seltzer, 1989). If these conditions are not fulfilled, the likelihood is great that fathers withdraw completely from their roles.

This chapter seems to conclude on a call for "bringing men back in." Studies of other postindustrial societies suggest that what we witness may be only an institutional transformation of fatherhood rather than its disappearance (Cherlin & Furstenberg, 1988; Furstenberg & Harris, 1990). When other social institutions—economic, legal, educational, religious—recognize the family as a set of relationships to be supported rather than of individuals to be freed or controlled, the family will show its resiliency and adaptability in the face of the sociocultural changes that accompanied the economic changes of the postindustrial revolution. In countries where cohabitation is more prevalent and nonmarital childbearing generally common, such as Sweden, paternal relationships with children all through their growing up years tend to be more stable than in cases of divorce and premarital birth in the United States. But father-child relations also benefit from more legal and economic supports and enforcements than in the U.S. Nevertheless, the return of fathers in the lives of their biological children may be more likely if formal and informal sanctions veer away from the enforcement of a nuclear family model.

Despite the possibility of a reaffirmation of the paternal role, the question arises whether current trends in marriage and male family behavior lead to a matriarchal family system that is more functional in postindustrial societies. Does the period of transition we currently witness lead to a reconstructed institutionalization of the family focused on women and children with a redrawing of family boundaries centered on women's relations with networks of support in fulfilling their reproductive and socializing functions? These relationships could be with a man (and more or less formalized), with one or more other women, or with kin—siblings, parents—or others. Trends in law and in the actual composition of families point in that direction. Men draw their significance in families and in the lives of children from their relations with women. Their biological ties are secondary to their socioemotional ties in defining their roles and their belonging to familial groups. Women are securing an increasingly important place as economic producers within society, and as providers for their offspring. The costs of these changes are still high, but social mechanisms are slowly being established which sustain the viability and functionality of single-parent households.

Conclusions on how satisfactory this normalization of a minimal woman-centered family form is, or can be, for adult identity and child development cannot be drawn at this time. Along with values and aspirations, people's adaptability changes. In view of the extent of the transformation of the basic institutional tenets of family life, and simultaneously of the cultural and economic contexts, both national and international, in which this transformation is taking place, the realm of the possible and acceptable has expanded so much that contradictory predictions can plausibly be advanced.

Although the question of whether the family has a future can confidently be answered in the affirmative, the question of its future within the political and social concerns of the nation is more doubtful. Research is needed at two levels.

First, the family's links with the legal and economic spheres of society need to be explicitly exposed. Statutes and economic conditions vary sufficiently from state to state to permit comparative studies of the consequences and effectiveness of different family regulations. The long-term effectiveness and the internal processes of new family forms must also be understood. The functioning of new families should be assessed free of the accompanying economic stresses that are usually associated with *deviant* family forms. What is the real effectiveness of the one-parent family when social supports are in place and economic survival is not a paramount concern? How do children reared by homosexual couples fare emotionally and cognitively in the long run? Do unmarried partners raise their family in ways similar to those of married parents? How stable are domestic partnerships compared with marriages when children are involved?

Second, the links between persons and parental roles must also be better understood. The father question specifically calls for in-depth research into psychological processes of commitment and alienation from parental roles. What external conditions are crucial, and which ones are secondary for the maintenance of fathers' commitment to their biological children? How do parents and children see themselves as family members?

The many questions in this concluding section are only a sampling of those that are important. They exemplify areas of investigation that would help us appraise the strengths and weaknesses of the transformed family, and help create the conditions in which children can grow and prosper.

REFERENCES

Ahrons, C. R., & Wallisch, L. (1987). Parenting in the binuclear family: Relationships between biological and stepparents. In K. Pasley & M. Ihinger-Tallman (Eds.), *Remarriage and stepparenting* (pp. 225–256). New York: Guilford Press.

Allen, C. M. (1979). Defining the family for post-industrial public policy. In D. P. Snyder (Ed.), *The family in post-industrial America—Some fundamental perceptions for public policy development* (pp. 21–36). Boulder, CO: Westview Press.

Angel, R., & Tienda, M. (1982). Determinants of extended household structure: Cultural patterns or economic needs. *American Journal of Sociology, 87,* 1360–1383.

Bane, M. J., & Ellwood, D. T. (1989). One-fifth of the nation's children: Why are they poor? *Science, 245,* 1047–1053.

Barnett, R. C., & Baruch, G. K. (1987). Mothers' participation in childcare: Patterns and consequences. In F. C. Crosby (Ed.), *Spouse, parent, worker* (pp. 91–108). New Haven, CT: Yale University Press.

Bellah, R. N., Madsen, R., Sullivan, W. R., Swidler, A., & Tipton, S. M. (1985). *Habits of the heart—Individualism and commitment in American life.* Berkeley: University of California Press.

Bianchi, S. M., & Spain, D. (1986). *American women in transition.* New York: Russell Sage Foundation.

Bumpass, L. (1984). Children and marital disruption: A replication and update. *Demography, 21,* 71–82.

Bumpass, L. (1985). Bigger is not necessarily better. *Journal of Marriage and the Family, 47,* 797–798.

Bumpass, L., & Sweet, J. A. (1989, January). *Children's experience in single-parent families: Implications of cohabitation and marital transitions.* Paper presented at the meetings of the American Association for the Advancement of Science, San Francisco.

Cherlin, A. (1978). Remarriage as an incomplete institution. *American Journal of Sociology, 48,* 634–650.

Cherlin, A. (1988). *The changing American family and public policy.* Washington, D.C.: The Urban Institute Press.

Cherlin, A., & Furstenberg, F. F., Jr. (1988). The changing European family. *Journal of Family Issues, 9,* 291–297.

Clingempeel, W. G., Brand, E., & Segal, S. (1987). A multi-level multivariable developmental perspective for future research on stepfamilies. In K. Pasley & M. Ihinger-Tallman (Eds.), *Remarriage and stepparenting* (pp. 65–93). New York: Guilford Press.

Coleman, J. S. (1990). *Foundations of social theory.* Cambridge, MA: Harvard University Press.

Demo, D. H., & Acock, A. C. (1988). The impact of divorce on children. *Journal of Marriage and the Family, 50,* 619–648.

Dworkin, R. (1989a). The great abortion case. *New York Review of Books* (Vol. 36, June 29), pp. 49–53.

Dworkin, R. (1989b). The future of abortion. *New York Review of Books* (Vol. 36, September 28), pp. 47–51.

Edwards, J. N. (Ed.). (1969). *The family and change.* New York: Alfred Knopf.

Ellwood, D. T. (1988). *Poor support—Poverty in the American family.* New York: Basic Books.

Eisenstadt, S. (1968). Social institutions. *International Encyclopedia of the Social Sciences* (Vol. 14, pp. 409–429). New York: Macmillan Co. and The Free Press.

Farley, R., & Bianchi, S. M. (1987). *The growing racial difference in marriage and family patterns.* Ann Arbor, MI: Population Studies Center, University of Michigan, Research Reports No. 87–107.

Feshbach, S., & Feshbach, N. (1978). Child advocacy and family privacy. *Journal of Social Issues, 34,* 168–178.

Field, M. A. (1988). *Surrogate motherhood: The legal and human issues.* Cambridge, MA: Harvard University Press.

Fine, M. A. (1989). A social science perspective on stepfamily law: Suggestions for legal reform. *Family Relations, 38,* 53–58.

Finkelhor, D. (1984). *Child sexual abuse.* New York: The Free Press.

Fletcher, R. (1988). *The shaking of the foundations.* London: Routledge.

Franklin, A. W. (Ed.). (1983). *Family matters—Perspectives on the family and social policy.* Oxford: Pergamon Press.

Furstenberg, F. F., Jr. (1987). The new extended family: The experience of parents and children after divorce. In K. Pasley & M. Ihinger-Tallman (Eds.), *Remarriage and stepparenting* (pp. 42–61). New York: Guilford Press.

Furstenberg, F. F., Jr., Brooks-Gunn, J., & Morgan, S. P. (1987). *Adolescent mothers in later life.* New York: Cambridge University Press.

Furstenberg, F. F., Jr., & Harris, K. M. (1990, April). *The disappearing American father? Divorce and the waning significance of biological parenthood.* Paper presented at the Conference on the American Family, State University of New York at Albany.

Furstenberg, F. F., Jr., Morgan, S. P., & Allison, P. D. (1987). Paternal participation and children's well-being after marital dissolution. *American Sociological Review, 52,* 695–668.

Furstenberg, F. F., Jr., Nord, C. W., Peterson, J. L., & Zill, N. (1983). The life course of children of divorce: Marital disruption and parental conflict. *American Sociological Review, 48,* 656–668.

Furstenberg, F. F., Jr., & Spanier, G. B. (1984). *Recycling the family: Remarriage after divorce.* Beverly Hills, CA: Sage.

Ganong, L. H., & Coleman, M. (1987). Effects of parental remarriage on children: An updated comparison of theories, methods, and findings from clinical and empirical research. In K. Pasley & M. Ihinger-Tallman (Eds.), *Remarriage and stepparenting* (pp. 94–140). New York: Guilford.

Gilbert, L. A. (1985). *Men in dual-career families: Current realities and future prospects.* Hillsdale, NJ: Lawrence Erlbaum Associates.

Glendon, M. A. (1987). *Abortion and divorce in Western law: American failures, European challenges.* Cambridge, MA: Harvard University Press.

Goldstein, J., Freud, A., & Solnit, A. J. (1979). *Beyond the best interests of the child.* New York: The Free Press.

Gordon, M., & Creighton, S. J. (1988). Natal and non-natal fathers as sexual abusers in the United Kingdom: A comparative analysis. *Journal of Marriage and the Family, 50,* 1, 99–105.

Grossberg, M. (1985). *Governing the hearth—Law and the family in 19th century America.* Chapel Hill: University of North Carolina Press.

Grubb, W. N., & Lazerson, M. (1988). *Broken promises—How Americans fail their children.* Chicago: University of Chicago Press.

Hacker, A. (1988, October 13). Getting rough on the poor. *New York Review of Books,* pp. 12–17.

Hareven, T. K. (1982). *Family time and industrial time.* Cambridge, England: Cambridge University Press.

Hetherington, E. M. (1987). Family relations six years after divorce. In K. Pasley & M. Ihinger-Tallman (Eds.), *Remarriage and stepparenting* (pp. 185–206). New York: Guilford Press.

Hixson, R. F. (1987). *Privacy in a public society—Human rights in conflict.* New York: Oxford University Press.

Hobart, C. (1988). The family system in remarriage: An exploratory study. *Journal of Marriage and the Family, 50,* 649–661.

Hofferth, S. L. (1985). Updating children's life course. *Journal of Marriage and the Family, 47,* 93–115.

Hofferth, S. L. (1987). Recent trends in the living arrangements of children: A cohort life table analysis. In J. Bongaarts, T. K. Burch, & K. W. Wachter (Eds.), *Family demography: Methods and their applications* (pp. 168–188). Oxford: Clarendon Press.

Hofferth, S. L., & Phillips, D. A. (1987). Child care in the United States, 1970–1995. *Journal of Marriage and the Family, 49,* 559–571.

Hoffman, L. (1987). The effects on children of maternal and paternal employment. In N. Gerstel & H. E. Gross (Eds.), *Families and work* (pp. 362–395). Philadelphia: Temple University Press.

Höhn, C., & Lüscher, K. (1988). The changing family in the Federal Republic of Germany. *Journal of Family Issues, 9,* 317–335.

Huber, J., & Spitze, G. (1983). *Sex stratification—Children, housework, and jobs.* New York: Academic Press.

Inglehart, R. (1990). *Culture shift in advanced industrial society.* New Jersey: Princeton University Press.

Jacob, H. (1988). *Silent revolution—The transformation of divorce law in the United States.* Chicago: Chicago University Press.

Johnson, P. E. (1978). *A shopkeepers' millenium—Society and revivals in Rochester, New York, 1815–1837.* New York: Hill and Wang.

Jones, E. F., Forrest, J. D., Goldman, N., Henshaw, S., Lincoln, R., Irosoff, J., Westoff, C. F., & Wulf, D. (1986). *Teenage pregnancy in industrialized countries.* New Haven, CT: Yale University Press.

Kamerman, S. (1984). Child care and family benefits: Policies of six industrialized countries. In R. G. Genovese (Ed.), *Families and change—Social needs and public policies* (pp. 60–67). New York: Praeger.

Kamerman, S., & Kahn, A. J. (Eds.). (1978). *Family policy—Government and family in fourteen countries*. New York: Columbia University Press.

Kanter, R. M. (1972). *Commitment and community—Communes and utopias in sociological perspective*. Cambridge, MA: Harvard University Press.

Kanter, R. M. (1977). *Work and family in the United States*. New York: Russell Sage Foundation.

Katz, S. N. (1971). *When parents fail—The law's response to family breakdown*. Boston: Beacon Press.

Kay, H. H. (1969). The outside substitute for the family. In J. N. Edwards (Ed.), *The family and change* (pp. 260–270). New York: Alfred A. Knopf.

Keith, V. H., & Finlay, B. (1988). The impact of parental divorce on children, educational attainment, marital timing, and likelihood of divorce. *Journal of Marriage and the Family, 50,* 797–809.

Kline, M., & Cowan, P. A. (1988). Rethinking the connections among "work" and "family" and well-being. *Journal of Social Behavior and Personality, 3,* 61–90.

Krein, S. F., & Beller, A. H. (1988). Educational attainment of children from single-parent families: Differences by exposure, gender, and race. *Demography, 25,* 221–234.

Lasch, C. (1977). *Haven in a heartless world—The family besieged*. New York: Basic Books.

Lasch, C. (1979). *The culture of narcissism: American life in an age of diminishing expectations*. New York: W. W. Norton.

Leach, E. (1983). Are there alternatives to the family? In A. W. Franklin (Ed.), *Family matters: Perspectives on the family and social policy* (pp. 3–18). Oxford: Pergamon Press.

Leiby, J. (1978). *A history of social welfare and social work in the United States*. New York: Columbia University Press.

Levy, B. (1988). *Quakers and the American family—British settlement in the Delaware Valley*. Oxford: Oxford University Press.

Lewis, J. (1983). *The pursuit of happiness—Family and values in Jefferson's Virginia*. Cambridge, England: Cambridge University Press.

Liem, J. H., & Liem, G. R. (1990). Understanding the individual and family effects of unemployment. In J. Eckenrode & S. Gore (Eds.), *Stress between work and family*. New York: Plenum.

Liem, G. R., & Liem, J. H. (1988). Psychological effects of unemployment on workers and their families. *Journal of Social Issues, 44,* 87–105.

Malinowski, B. (1962). *Sex, culture, and myth*. New York: Harcourt, Brace, and World.

Mason, K. O., & Lu, Y.-H. (1988). Attitudes toward women's familial roles: Changes in the United States, 1977–1985. *Demography, 25,* 39–57.

Matthews, K. A., & Rodin, J. (1989). Women's changing work roles—Impact on health, family, and public policy. *American Psychologist, 44,* 1389–1393.

McCathren, R. R. (1981). The demise of federal categorical child care legislation: Lessons for the '80s from the failures of the '70s. In H. C. Wallach (Ed.), *Approaches to child and family policy* (pp. 101–143). Boulder, CO: Westview Press.

McLanahan, S. (1985). Family structure and the reproduction of poverty. *American Journal of Sociology, 90,* 873–901.

McLanahan, S. (1988). Family structure and dependency: Early transitions to female household headship. *Demography, 25,* 1–16.

McLanahan, S., & Booth, K. (1989). Mother-only families: Problems, prospects, and politics. *Journal of Marriage and the Family, 51,* 557–580.

McLanahan, S., & Bumpass, L. (1988). Intergenerational consequences of family disruption. *American Journal of Sociology, 94,* 130–152.

McLaughlin, S. D., Melber, B. D., Billy, J. D. G., Zimmerle, D. M., Winges, L. D., & Johnson, T. R. (1988). *The changing lives of American women*. Chapel Hill: University of North Carolina Press.

Melton, G. B., & Wilcox, B. L. (1989). Changes in family law and family life. *American Psychologist, 44,* 1213–1216.
Merrick, T., & Tordella, S. J. (1988). Demographics: Peoples and markets. *Population Bulletin, 43,* 1–48.
Meyer, J. W., Ramirez, F. O., Walker, H. A., Langton, N., & O'Connor, S. M. (1988). The state and the institutionalization of relations between women and children. In S. M. Dornbusch & M. H. Strober (Eds.), *Feminism—Children and the new families* (pp. 137–158). New York: Guilford Press.
Miller, B. C., & Bingham, C. R. (1989). Family configuration in relation to the sexual behavior of female adolescents. *Journal of Marriage and the Family, 51,* 499–506.
Mintz, S., & Kellogg, S. (1988). *Domestic revolutions—A social history of American family life.* New York: The Free Press.
Morgan, E. S. (1966). *The puritan family—Religion and domestic relations in seventeenth-century New England* (rev. ed.). New York: Harper and Row.
Morgan, S. P., Lye, D. N., & Condran, G. A. (1988). Sons, daughters, and the risk of marital disruption. *American Journal of Sociology, 94,* 110–129.
Moynihan, D. P. (1986). *Family and nation.* San Diego: Harcourt, Brace, Jovanovitch.
Mulkay, M. J. (1971). *Functionalism, exchange and theoretical strategy.* New York: Schoken Books.
Murray, C. (1984). *Losing ground: American social policy, 1950–1980.* New York: Basic Books.
Needle, R. H., Su, S., & Doherty, W. (1990). Divorce, remarriage, and adolescent substance use: A prospective longitudinal study. *Journal of Marriage and the Family, 52,* 157–169.
Newman, K. S. (1988). *Falling from grace—The experience of downward mobility in the American middle class.* New York: The Free Press.
Parsons, R., & Bales, R. F. (1955). *Family, socialization, and interaction process.* New York: The Free Press.
Pasley, K. (1987). Family boundary ambiguity: Perceptions of adult stepfamily members. In K. Pasley & M. Ihinger-Tallman (Eds.), *Remarriage and stepparenting* (pp. 206–224). New York: Guilford Press.
Peden, J. R., & Glahe, F. R. (Eds.). (1986). *The American family and the state.* San Francisco: Pacific Research Institute for Public Policy.
Peek, C. W., Bell, N. J., Waldren, T., & Sorell, G. (1988). Patterns of functioning in families of remarried and first-married couples. *Journal of Marriage and the Family, 55,* 699–708.
Pleck, E. (1987). *Domestic tyranny—The making of American social policy against family violence from colonial times to the present.* Oxford: Oxford University Press.
Popenoe, D. (1988). *Disturbing the nest—Family changes and decline in modern societies.* New York: Aldine De Gruyter.
Rodman, H., Lewis, S. H., & Griffith, S. R. (1984). *The sexual rights of adolescents—Competence, vulnerability, and parental control.* New York: Columbia University Press.
Rogers, C. M., & Wrightsman, L. S. (1978). Attitudes toward children's rights: Nurturance or self-determination. *Journal of Social Issues, 34,* 59–68.
Rossi, A. S. (1987). Parenthood in transition: From lineage to child to self-orientation. In J. B. Lancaster, J. Altmann, A. S. Rossi, & L. R. Sherrod (Eds.), *Parenting across the life-span: Biosocial dimensions* (pp. 31–81). New York: Aldine De Gruyter.
Rubin, L. B. (1976). *Worlds of pain—Life in the working-class family.* New York: Basic Books.
Ryan, M. P. (1981). *Cradle of the middle-class—The family in Oneida County, 1780–1865.* Cambridge, England: Cambridge University Press.
Sandefur, G., & Sakamoto, A. (1988). American Indian household structure and income. *Demography, 25,* 71–80.
Santi, L. L. (1988). The demographic context of recent changes in the structure of American households. *Demography, 25,* 509–519.

Santrock, J. W., Sitterle, K. A., & Warshak, R. A. (1988). Parent-child relationships in stepfather families. In P. Bronstein & C. P. Cowan (Eds.), *Fatherhood today—Men's changing role in the family* (pp. 144–165). New York: Wiley.

Scarr, S., Phillips, D., & McCartney, K. (1989). Working mothers and their families. *American Psychologist, 44,* 1402–1409.

Seltzer, J. A. (1989, January). *Relationships between fathers and children who live apart.* Paper presented at the annual meetings of the American Association for the Advancement of Science, San Francisco.

Seltzer, J. A., & Bianchi, S. M. (1988). Children's contact with absent parents. *Journal of Marriage and the Family, 50,* 663–677.

Seltzer, J. A., Schaeffer, N. C., & Charng, M. (1989). Family ties after divorce: The relationships between visiting and paying child support. *Journal of Marriage and the Family, 51,* 1013–1032.

Shannon, T. A. (1988). *Surrogate motherhood—The ethics of using human beings.* New York: Crossroads Publishing Co.

Sheehy, G. (1977). *Passages: Predictable crises of adult life.* New York: Bantam Books.

Smith, B. T. (1968). Family—Cooperative structure. In *International Encyclopedia of the Social Sciences* (Vol. 5, pp. 301–313). New York: Macmillan Co. and The Free Press.

Spanier, G. B. (1989). Bequeathing family continuity. *Journal of Marriage and the Family, 51,* 3–13.

Spitze, G. (1988). Women's employment and family relations. *Journal of Marriage and the Family, 50,* 595–618.

Stack, C. (1979). Extended familial network—An emerging model for the 21st century family. In D. P. Snyder (Ed.), *The family in post-industrial America* (pp. 49–62). Boulder, CO: Westview Press.

Steiner, G. Y. (1981). *The futility of family policy.* Washington, D.C.: The Brookings Institution.

Sussman, M. B. (1988). Law and the legal system: The family connection. In S. K. Steinmetz (Ed.), *Family and support systems across the life span* (pp. 11–34). New York: Plenum Press.

Thoits, P. (1987). Negotiating roles. In F. J. Crosby (Ed.), *Spouse, parent, worker* (pp. 11–22). New Haven, CT: Yale University Press.

Thompson, F. M. L. (1988). *The rise of respectable society—A social history of Victorian Britain, 1830–1900.* Cambridge, MA: Harvard University Press.

Thompson, R. A., Tinsley, B. R., Scalora, M. J., & Parke, R. D. (1989). Grandparents' rights—Legalizing the ties that bind. *American Psychologist, 44,* 1217–1222.

Thornton, A. (1985). Changing attitudes toward separation and divorce: Causes and consequences. *American Journal of Sociology, 90,* 856–872.

Thornton, A. (1989). Changing attitudes toward family issues in the United States. *Journal of Marriage and the Family, 51,* 873–893.

Thornton, A., & Freedman, D. (1983). The changing American family. *Population Bulletin, 38,* 1–44.

Van Horn, S. H. (1988). *Women, work, and fertility, 1900–1986.* New York: New York University Press.

Wall, H. M. (1990). *Fierce communion: Family and community in early America.* Cambridge, MA: Harvard University Press.

Wallerstein, J., & Kelly, J. (1980). *Surviving the break-up: How children and parents cope with divorce.* New York: Basic Books.

Weitzman, L. J. (1985). *The divorce revolution.* New York: The Free Press.

White, L. K., & Booth, A. (1985). The quality and stability of remarriages: The role of stepchildren. *American Sociological Review, 50,* 689–698.

Wilensky, H. L. (1990). Common problems, divergent policies: An 18-nation study of family policy. *Public Affairs Report, 31,* 1–3.

Williams, R. (1968). The concept of values. In *Encyclopedia of the Social Sciences* (Vol. 16, pp. 283–287). New York: The Macmillan Co. and The Free Press.
Wright, G. (1980). *Moralism and the model home—Domestic architecture and cultural conflict in Chicago, 1873–1913*. Chicago: Chicago University Press.
Yankelovich, D. (1981). *New rules—Searching for self-fulfillment in a world turned upside down*. New York: Random House.
Zablocki, B. D. (1971). *The joyful community*. Baltimore: Penguin.
Zablocki, B. D. (1980). *Alienation and charisma—A study of contemporary American communes*. New York: The Free Press.
Zill, N., & Rogers, C. C. (1988). Recent trends in the well-being of children in the United States and their implications for public policy. In A. Cherlin (Ed.), *The changing American family and public policy* (pp. 31–115). Washington, D.C.: The Urban Institute Press.
Zimring, F. E. (1982). *The changing legal world of adolescence*. New York: The Free Press.

2 Changes of Heart: Family Dynamics in Historical Perspective

Arlene Skolnick
University of California, Berkeley

. . . families constitute responses to cultural and historical predicaments.
—C. C. Harris (1983)

In 1939, an interviewer from the Berkeley Guidance study observed that the home of one of the study children seemed a much calmer place than it had been on earlier visits. The mother's morale seemed much higher. Mrs. M.[1] told the interviewer that her troubled marriage had recently improved, and her husband had become less abusive. A number of things helped to account for the changes, including an improvement in her health. But one of the biggest factors in her life, she explained, was the recent opening of the Bay Bridge. Along with a friend, she had been exploring the delights of the newly available city of San Francisco. It had helped to make her more interested in life, more independent, and more able to hold her own with her husband.

Mrs. M's story illustrates how a relatively small historical event in the world outside the home can have a significant impact on the emotional dynamics inside. The point is obvious, yet not one often taken into account in family research. Although researchers in recent years have recognized the importance of social context, the significance of social history is often overlooked. Yet just as individuals and families are constantly changing, so is the surrounding social context, particular in urban industrial societies.

Sociohistorical change is an ongoing process that takes a number of forms. Most broadly, it includes shifts in "the plate techtonics of society" (Yankelovich,

[1]Not her real name. Thanks to Betsy Wolfe, who developed this narrative from the archival records.

1981)—fundamental changes in technology, economics, and demography—such as the shift from agrarian to urban industrial society. It also includes the endless historical alteration of good times and bad, periods of relative calm and well-being, and periods of war, famine, depression and other calamity. Historical change can also take the form of social, cultural, and political trends, such as increasing levels of education, shifts in attitudes and values—sex role traditionality for example—and the expansion of political rights to formerly excluded groups. It also includes smaller but significant changes like the invention of the automobile, the telephone, anaesthesia, the birth control pill—or even, in the example cited earlier, the opening of a road or bridge. This chapter argues that whether or not we examine in our own work the impact of social change on the lives of the people we study, it is an aspect of family life and individual development across the life course that researchers need to take into account.

Understanding the links between social history and family life has several distinct uses for family researchers as we approach the end of the 20th century. One use, obviously, is to examine the impact of social change on the lives of the people we study. The intersection between social history and family experience does offer rich possibilities for research. But even for the researcher who does not pursue these issues directly, an historical perspective on family life is an essential part of the background assumptions we bring to our work. A knowledge of how family life has changed in the past can help us to make sense of current family changes, clarifying some of the social structural roots of the kinds of emotional predicaments faced by contemporary families.

We cannot really understand families in the present or make projections about the future without some understanding of family life in the past. Over the past 3 decades, dramatic changes in divorce rates, women's labor force participation, in the proportions of single parent families, and the like have given rise to anxieties that the family as an institution is in decline or even about to disappear. Much discussion about the current family crisis proceeds in the absence of any historical perspective, or worse, is based on assumptions about the past that are often at odds with historical evidence.

I begin with a brief overview of some main approaches and themes in recent research on the family. Next, I discuss the theme that has perennially preoccupied family sociology as well as many recent historians—the transition from the traditional to the modern family, and the implications of earlier transformations in family life for understanding the current crisis of the family. Finally, I discuss the implication of these findings for research on contemporary families.

THE NEW HISTORY OF THE FAMILY

In recent years the history of the family has become a multidisciplinary enterprise, including not just historians but also sociologists, anthropologists, demographers, economists, and even a handful of psychologists. As a result, the bulk of what is known about family life in past centuries was gained in the past 2 decades. Many gaps remain, along with disagreement about various matters among researchers. Still, enough has been learned to clarify the major outlines of family change over the past several centuries, and to dispel many myths about earlier family life.

Stimulated by new research methods, and a turn towards the study of ordinary people—history "from the bottom up"—the new history of the family uses a number of approaches. Much of the new research on early families has been demographic. For example, the use of census data and parish records have enabled historians to analyze household size and structure, age at marriage, frequency of remarriage, rates of fertility, and mortality. Some historians are more directly concerned with psychological quality and cultural meanings of family life; others have focused on how households function as economic and social units.

An early landmark was Philip Aries' (1962) book *Centuries of Childhood,* which advanced the novel idea that the concept of childhood was a relatively recent cultural invention. Aries argued that in premodern Europe, children entered the world of adults as soon as they left infancy. Childhood as a distinct stage of life emerged only in the past several centuries. The discovery of childhood was part of the emergence of the modern family.

Since Aries wrote, historians and others have challenged some of his methods and conclusions, but not his basic insight: that the family, and the stages of life we take for granted—childhood, adolescence, adulthood—are not timeless entities built into human nature, but aspects of the human condition that have been reshaped with historical change. Whether or not children were regarded as "small adults," it is clear that the concept of childhood was far less elaborated in the premodern era that it came to be later. Further, children's roles were much less differentiated from adult roles than in urban industrial society; from an early age, children historically have worked alongside adults, and were thought to be capable of serious intellectual training. (Vinovskis, 1978) Aries' most controversial claim—that parents were not always closely attached to their infants, has survived a major challenge on sociobiological grounds (Bellingham, 1988; Pollack, 1983). There may indeed have been large numbers of loving parents in the preindustrial past, but evidence suggests there has been a sea change in attitudes towards infants and in their actual treatment. Practices shocking to modern sensibilities were widespread. For example, it appears that a major source of Europe's population explosion in the 18th century was a massive decline in infanticide. In Europe and colonial America, well-to-do families often "put out" their newborn infants to wet nurses for a year or two, increasing already high rates of infant mortality. In general, then, the conditions surrounding childbearing in past times could often be "murderous to the children" (Flandrin, 1979, p. 216).

In recent years, historians have examined the emergence of later stages of the life course—adolescence, old age, middle age, or adulthood. The historical "discovery" of new life stages does not mean that there was no awareness of the changes that occur between birth and death; rather it refers to their cultural recognition and institutionalization. In our own time, as large numbers of people are living into their 80s and beyond, we have witnessed the creation of new stages of life—"mid-life," the "young-old" versus the "old-old."

A related line of research is the study of the life course. Used more as a sociological than a psychological concept, "the life course" refers to the sequence of culturally defined roles a person occupies through life. Focusing not on stages, but transitions such as starting and leaving school, marriage, and child-bearing, the life course perspective examines the interplay between three kinds of time—individual development, stages of family development, and historical time. For example, it examines the timing of individual transitions such as marriage and leaving home in relation to the family as a collective unit as well as to the historical period.

Many of the most significant changes in family life can be traced to shifts in the length and patterning of the life course. The twentieth century has witnessed most of the increase in longevity that has occurred since prehistoric times. It has also experienced most of the great decline in fertility in the West that began in the 1800's. Until the early decades of this century, parents were faced with the substantial probability that any child would die before reaching adulthood. The two or three child family that became the norm in America in the 1920s was a product of a new confidence that children would survive. Because they had shorter lives and more children, our great grandparents rarely remained alive long enough to experience the empty nest stage of parenthood. For the first time in history, the average couple has now more living parents than it has children. Ours is also the first era when most of parent-child relationship takes place after the child is an adult.

Many of the troubling family changes of recent years can be seen as shifts in the life course, rather than changes in basic family structure. In the 1950s, for example, young adults entering their 20s moved quickly, en mass, into marriage and parenthood—a pattern not seen in any other decade of this century, or earlier. Today, young people in their twenties are likely to live alone or to live together unmarried. These arrangements have turned to be not permanent substitutes for marriage, as many feared in the 1970s, but as part of an altered life course (Modell, 1989).

THE WORLD WE HAVE LOST

One major reason for applying an historical framework to contemporary family life is that much research and theorizing about the family is based on assumptions about the family in past times and not supported by actual historical evidence. The overall implications of the first decades of the new field can be summed up as "the discovery of complexity" (Elder, 1981). There is no such thing for example, as "the French family" of the 17th or 18th century (Flandrin, 1979), the "English family," or "the American family." At any particular time, a society will contain multiple kinds of families rather than a single type, varying with social class, region and occupation, and other aspects of social life. This is especially so in America, where diversity has been a fact of family life since before the constitution. Further, family change does not take place evenly; at any one time, some families may resemble those of the century past, while others are living in ways that may not become common until a century into the future.

Much of today's discourse about the family is shaped by what historian Peter Laslett (1976) calls a "world we have lost syndrome"—a tendency to draw a sharp contrast between a golden vanished *past* of stable, supportive families and an unhappy *present* when the family has "fallen apart" and family bonds eroded. Yet historians have identified no period in the past that could qualify as a golden age of family relations. They have found that family disruption by death, premarital sexuality, illegitimacy, marital and generational conflict, and what would today be considered the maltreatment of children were common in the family life of past times. Every generation on record seems to have believed it was witnessing "the decline of the traditional family" (Hareven, 1982). Above all, the new history demonstrates the point quoted earlier, that family life is embedded in the demographic, economic, and social contexts of particular times and places.

One of the earliest casualties of the new social history was what William J. Goode (1963) has called "the classical family of Western nostalgia"—the assumption that the typical Western family just before industrialization was a large extended family consisting of parents, children, and grandparents, and assorted aunts and uncles. Industrialization, according to this view, dissolved the harmonious multigenerational household, and pared the family down to "the isolated nuclear family." Historical demography has shown that this description is wrong. Industrialization did not lead to the decline of the extended family household, because these were no more common in the past than now.

One of the strongest unwritten—indeed, undiscussed—norms of Western culture is that households should be "neolocal"—that is, that couples after marriage should set up their own residence, and not live with inlaws (Laslett, 1984). Most households in Western Europe in past centuries contained nuclear families—parents and children—and no other relatives. Even in some rural parts of Europe where an elderly parent might be expected to live with a married child, few people lived long enough to make the three generation household a common arrangement. Further, such households when they occurred were typically based not on sentiment, but on contracts spelling out what each party owed the other (Berkner, 1972). Of course, kin relations do not depend on living together under one roof. Although it is methodologically more difficult to track relationships between households, the existing evidence does not suggest that kin relations were any more extensive in the preindustrial Western Europe than they are today. Of course other parts of the world—China and Japan, Southern and Eastern Europe—have had classical extended families as part of their cultural tradition.

Families in the agrarian past were not as geographically stable as they were assumed to have been; mobility was common as people moved in search of land, work, and opportunity. Inheritance practices forced sons who were not heirs to leave after they married (Mitteraur & Seider, 1982). And before the age of the telephone, the automobile, and jet planes, separated kin were less likely to stay in contact than now (Laslett, 1979). Recent studies of contemporary kinship have documented the persistence of kin ties in contemporary society, whether or not families are geographically displaced (Fischer, 1982).

Although early American households were not filled with large numbers of extended kin, families have changed in profoundly significant ways since the founding of the country. Households before the 20th century were larger than they are today, partly because of the higher number of offspring per couple. In addition, preindustrial households typically included nonkin, such as servants, apprentices, hired hands, boarders, orphans, and other dependents from the community. Above all, the preindustrial household was an economic unit, and its need for labor determined how many people lived together under one roof. Families often brought in older children and young adults as servants and apprentices, and sent out their own children to work in other households if they were not needed at home.

Over the course of time, the family shifted from being a "public" to a "private institution" (Flandrin, 1979; Laslett, 1973). During the 19th century, and well into the 20th, for example, the practice of boarding and lodging persisted, in the middle as well as working class. This custom not only provided income for the household, but an alternative form of family living for young people and others not living with families of their own. Boarding and lodging declined dramatically in the first half of the 20th century—as standards of living rose, and as household privacy norms shifted. Tamara Hareven (1982) observes, ". . . the most important change in American family life has not been the breakdown of the three generation family but rather, the loss of flexibility in regard to taking strangers into the household" (p. 449).

Popular myths about a golden age of family relations in past times obscure some of the most striking historical facts—especially, the harsh demographic realities of life before the 20th century. High mortality rates across the life course made untimely death a common family experience. It was only during this century that a majority of the population could expect to live out a normal life course—growing up, leaving home, marrying, and surviving to age 50 with one's spouse. For most people in the past death came before one's last young adult offspring left home.

The gain in longevity we enjoy today is fairly recent; it is only since World War II that grandparenthood has become a distinct and nearly universal part of the life course (Cherlin & Furstenberg, 1986). But mass longevity has a dark side—the historically unprecedented problem of caring for a vast population of frail elderly. Even countries, like Japan, with a long tradition of parents and married children living together, have been strained by the 20th century phenomenon of the four and five generation family (Plath, 1980).

It has become clear that family change is a complex and ongoing process. Further, changes in family life seem not to be driven by a single force, such as economic development, but by complicated interplay among economic, technological, demographic, political, and cultural factors. Although the core structure of the Western family preceded industrialization, the most crucial step in the making of the modern family was the shift of work outside the home that occurred with the rise of an increasingly commercial and market oriented society. In the rest of this chapter, I examine alternative ways of looking at the restructuring of family life that took place with this shift, and its implications for understanding contemporary family arrangements.

PARSONS REVISITED

During the 1950s and 1960s the dominant interpretation of family in modern society was the brand of sociological analysis known as functionalism. Talcott Parsons (1955, 1965) was perhaps *the* major sociological theorist in America as well as the leading theorist of the family. A structural-functional theorist who saw the family as a vital element in the larger social system, he defined the framework within which family, childhood socialization, and gender relations were analyzed during the 1950s and 60s. Although his work has been severely criticized, and despite its limitations, his writings contain valid insights into the family's functions in modern society, as well as its strains. Parsons' work represents an ambitious attempt to place the wider social context of family life, the emotional dynamics of the family as a group, and the psychological development of the child into the same equation.

Parsons took issue with those who argued that with the coming of modern industrial society, the family had lost its functions and was facing dissolution. He argued that the family was changing, but that it was not in decline. With the rise of industrialism, the family had indeed "lost" its function as a unit of production. But its remaining functions had made it no less and possibly *more* important than it had been in the past. The modern family, structurally "isolated" from kin and the economy, had become a more specialized institution, dedicated to the socialization of children and the emotional stabilization of the adult personality. Borrowing a term from evolutionary notions of adaptation, Parsons referred to this process as structural differentiation.

Parsons' model of the modern family has been criticized on a number of grounds. Early critics argued that he was empirically wrong about the *isolation* of the nuclear family. Parsons emphasized the *structural* isolation of the nuclear family from kin—that is, the separation of the family from the economy in industrial society. But he and his followers did tend to see the nuclear family as somewhat socially isolated also. Since the 1950s however, numerous studies have shown that kin ties are much more extensive and important in industrial societies than implied in Parsons' model. Not only have extended family relations persisted among those Americans with roots in the classical extended family systems of Southern and eastern Europe and Asia, but a modified form of extended family is generally widespread in modern industrial societies. Further, these researchers argued, contrary to Parsons, that this "modified extended family" (Litwak, 1965) is more "functional" than the isolated nuclear family.

While critics of the isolated nuclear family concept argued that Parsons had misrepresented social reality, others objected that his theorizing relied too heavily on current practices. Thus, Parsons seemed to endorse the prevailing gender patterns of the 1950s, arguing that the man specializing in the "instrumental" breadwinner role, and the woman in the "expressive" homemaker role, was an unchangeable functional necessity in modern industrial society. Another criticism was that Parsons' model of internalization ignored the possibility of conflict between the individual and society, resulting in an "oversocialized" view of human nature (Wrong, 1961). Also, Parsons assumed, optimistically and wrongly, that the society itself was a smoothly working, self-correcting system.

In fact, however, another, less optimistic theory of the modern family lurked in Parsons' writings. He painted a somber portrait of the internal sources of strain in the "structurally differentiated" nuclear family. One source of strain, he observed, was that the housewife mother role was a "pseudo-occupation," a hard job that was not considered a job in a society in which work was defined as something done in the outside world that produced a paycheck. Parsons also saw as problematic in a system in which childhood was extended, and emotional relations between parents and children were intense and prolonged, yet the young adult offspring had to achieve independence in adulthood. Nevertheless, Parsons did not see in these tensions a challenge to the main thrust of his theory. Nor did he see them leading to change.

Along with most American social scientists of the time, Parsons believed that structural change and social conflict had virtually come to an end in modern societies. Thus, Parsons' theory lost credibility as result of the upheavals of the 1960s, especially the student revolt and the youth counterculture. Widespread dissent on the part of the educated young was exactly what was not supposed to happen, according to the theory. Neither were the family changes that began to be apparent in the 1970s. The concept of the instrumental breadwinner and the expressive housewife and of the smooth integration of young people into the social system may have reflected the social realities of the 1950s, but seemed antiquated when reality changed.

Nevertheless, the questions Parsons raised still represent vital issues for the social sciences. Recently, there has been a revival of interest in his work as the "macro-micro issue" becomes the focus of theoretical concern in sociology (Alexander, Geisen, Münch, and Smelser, 1987). His basic model of the interconnectedness of family life with the larger society, and with the emotional dynamics of individuals remains useful. (For a similar view of Parsons' contemporary relevance, see the chapter by Donald Hansen, this volume.)

Figure 2.1 represents an attempt to put Parsons theory in motion by adding the dimension of change through time, and by making the causal arrows between society, family, and individual run both ways. The triangle at left represents Parsons' original model of the family in modern society. In Parsons model, the

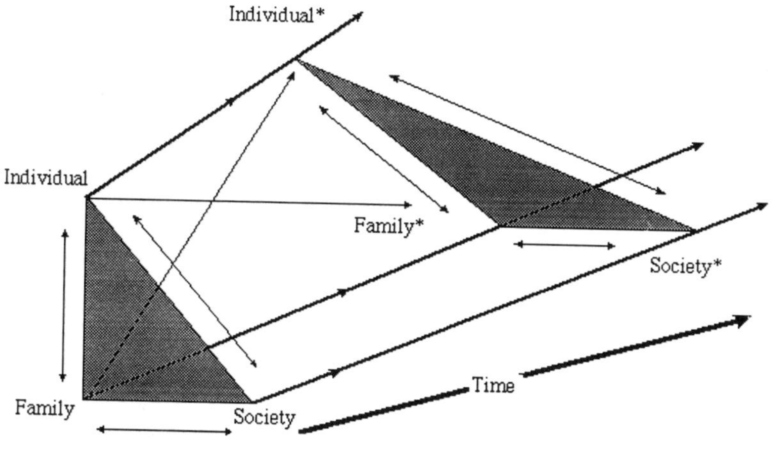

Three dimensions are proposed (Individual, Family, and Society) that operate along a fourth dimension of Time. The shaded areas in the diagram are planes that depict interactive relations among the three dimensions for any fixed value of Time. These dimensions also influence themselves and each other across Time. For example, between the shaded areas are two unidirectional crossing arrows that represent influences along Time, of Family on Individual, and of Individual on Family (asterisks denote transformations of the dimensions in Time). Also proposed, though not shown, is the influence along Time of any interaction on Individual, Family, and Society.

Because this diagram is schematic and not a testable model, it should be noted that the shaded areas can assume any form. Further, any relations among Individual, Family, and Society are not necessarily linear.

*Thanks to Diana Baumrind and Wayne Shoumaker who collaborated in devising the model.

FIG. 2.1. A revised Parsonian Model.*

arrows would only go in one direction, from society to the parents, who act as transmitters of the culture to their children, who then internalize cultural roles and norms. Thus, the macro-world of social structure shapes the processes of family socialization to produce individuals who will internalize social norms and values, and grow up to take their place in, and thereby reproduce, the social structure.

We can solve some of the problems of the original model by making the arrows go both ways. We need not assume that each one has the same strength, but only to recognize that each one has some effect. Thus, families and individuals devise strategies to cope with economic and social conditions, children influence parents, and are capable of learning from society directly.

Finally, Parsons' essential insight into the role of the family in modern society remains correct: Despite the social upheavals of recent years, the family is "not in any general sense less important, because the society is dependent *more* exclusively on it for the performance of *certain* of its vital functions" (Parsons, 1955, pp. 9–10). Indeed, a number of social scientists since Parsons time assert that family ties have become more significant as a source of identity and social and emotional support. Whether the family can satisfy the burdens that are structurally imposed on it is another matter.

STRUCTURAL CHANGE, FAMILY STRESS, CULTURAL CRISIS

Parsonian functionalism was basically ahistorical; it had little to say about the process by which modern family arrangements came into being. Since the 1960s, a great deal has been learned about families in the transition to urban industrial society. In contrast to the functionalist paradigm, more recent scholars view families and individuals as active agents in responding to economic change, and in shaping the kind of societal and family arrangements that ultimately result from them. Further, culture and ideology are conceived to be important autonomous factors in the process of change, reflecting a strong new interest in culture throughout the social sciences (Alexander & Seidman, 1990).

Between the 1790s and 1850, economic, political, and social transformations shattered the world that colonial Americans had known. The early 19th century witnessed, as one historian puts it, perhaps "the climactic era of modernization" in America (Howe, 1976). The political revolutions of the late 18th century, along with a complex of economic social demographic change ushered in the modern age.

Before the 19th century, the family was a public institution whose members were bound together in a common economic enterprise. In the colonial period especially, the family was conceived to be a part of society; the distinction between public and private, so basic to modern life was scarcely made. The prevailing cultural ideology defined the family as an integral part of a hierarchically organized, patriarchal society. The authority of a father, his expectations of obedience and respect, were part of a great chain of authority descending from God through the King down to the household. Fathers continued to exercise control over their children in adulthood. The primacy of the father in the colonial family was reflected in the law, which gave fathers absolute rights to custody of their children and legal control of the family's resources, as well as in childrearing manuals which were addressed to fathers, not mothers (Mintz & Kellogg, 1988).

Individuals and families were subject to the demands of the community; neighbors and formal authorities closely supervised family life, and intervened to promote order in the home. Local officials might compel an estranged couple to remain together, a battered wife to remain with her husband, or parents to exercise greater discipline over their children. While colonial society valued happiness in marriage, it insisted on stability. The tensions that resulted from the close involvement of family and community helped to prepare the way for new forms and new ideas of family life (Wall, 1990).

The colonial model dominated and defined American life until the middle of the 18th century. After that, a variety of changes altered the practical realities and assumptions that had sustained it. Populations became larger and more diverse. Free land enabled young men to escape dependence on their fathers. Individuals and families became resistant to the constraints of community supervision over domestic life. Family life was implicated in the intellectual and cultural shifts that occurred with the American Revolution. As historian Jay Fliegelman (1982) has argued, in a society in revolt against patriarchal tyranny, there were deep ideological connections between domestic and political life. A growing literature on the family emphasized companionship and mutual affection in marriage, and rejected the earlier emphasis on unquestioning obedience as the chief goal of childrearing.

The spread of the new concept of the family as a private institution was closely linked to a set of rapid social and economic changes that took place in America in the early 19th century. Although the changes were part of the process of industrialization, major shifts in family functioning began to appear even before factories grew significantly. By the 1820s, America was in transition from an agrarian society to a commercial urban and industrial one. Urban growth was especially explosive—the cities were expanding at a faster rate than at any later period in the century.

These changes led to a profound alteration in the functions and cultural meaning of family life, in the roles of men, women, and children inside and outside the household, as well as in the relations between family and society. With the industrial revolution, work and family work was no longer based in the home. As men left home to work in offices, stores, and factories, family roles were restructured. Further, the new household functions and the new roles within the family were elaborated in a compelling and pervasive belief system that has been labeled the "cult of domesticity" or the ideology of "separate spheres." The glorification of motherhood, and the notion that "women's place is in the home" were born in this era. With men leaving home to work, the contrast between home and the outside world became a contrast between woman and man. Family came to mean a distinct social unit consisting of a working man, a homemaking woman, and their children. The household was transformed into the *home,* a term that acquired a host of cultural and psychological meanings it did not have earlier—intimacy, love, privacy, comfort, protection from the world at large. The middle class home in the 19th century was the embodiment of a new way of family life and the new ideology of domesticity. And although it was a middle class creation, the domestic ideal eventually came to dominate American culture (Hareven, 1982; Ryan, 1981).

The early decades of the 19th century, before the new ideology took hold, were a time of cultural ferment and confusion—a period of "unprecedented change for which—the traditional society of the time was institutionally, ideologically and psychologically unprepared" (Rorabaugh, 1979). The consumption of alcohol reached an all-time high and America appeared to have become a "nation of drunkards." It was also a period of cultural upheaval, marked by a major religious revival—the Second Great Awakening, and a host of social movements. The new ideology of family life was an important part of the new social order that crystallized around the middle of the century. The new American family was conceived to be a "haven in a heartless world," not only a refuge from the larger society, but a repository of moral values that the larger society was abrogating. In a time of unbridled change, the family became a symbol of stability and an idealized lost past, the only place where market values gave way to love and care.

The 19th century middle class domestic ideal embodied a concept of family that had emerged in the 18th century in the upper classes of England and America. The Victorian version of the private, companionate family contained a greater emphasis on order, control, and polarized gender roles than did the earlier model. Historian Lawrence Stone (1977) describes this as "the nineteenth century reversal." The sexual prudery we associate with the term "Victorian," although not all Victorians were as passionless as the stereotype assumes (Degler, 1980; Gay, 1984) nevertheless did reflect a wider preoccupation with self-discipline. For example, efforts to stamp out masturbation in children and young men became a cultural obsession in the Victorian era (Smith-Rosenberg, 1985).

The restrictiveness of the Victorian family ideology may have been part of the cultural struggle to come to terms with the family's new structural attributes. The doctrine of separate spheres and the cult of true womanhood legitimized and glorified the roles to which women were being structurally assigned. Along with Stone, Smelser and Halpern (1978) suggest that Victorian prudishness may be understood as a form of social control in a time of rapid change—"an exercise in 'over-control' of a new institution that was unfamiliar and appeared to be dangerously fragile" (p. S308).

One of the most significant products of the new self-consciousness about the family was its underlying sense of crisis—"a conspicuous and persistent public obsession with the well-being of the American household" that fueled numerous reform movements and the passage of new laws to govern the home (Grossberg, 1985). The realities of family life were more complicated than portrayed in Victorian imagery. The process of change was rapid in some parts of the country—upper New York State was the California of the 19th century—and gradual in others. Working class, rural and immigrant families continued to be economic units, with wives and children working as well as men. Middle class families, who most closely approximated the domestic ideal, were not always the preserves of perfect happiness and harmony. The contrast between image and reality was a constant source of public concern. Even if actual behavior departed from the ideal, people still defined it as proper and legitimate, and used it to justify their actions.

As Tamara Hareven (1982) points out, the impact of the ideology could be seen in declining rates of married women's labor force participation across the 19th century, despite the fact that employment opportunities were increasing. The ideals of the urban middle class came to influence working class and immigrant families in the 20th century. As immigrants became Americanized, especially in the second and third generation, they embraced the domestic ideal.

Along with the shift in gender roles and relations, a new perception of childhood emerged with the modern family, along with a profound change in the conditions of child development. Looked at economically, the development of industrial society reverses the flow of wealth in the family; in agrarian society, wealth flows from children to parents, in modern societies, the flow reverses (Caldwell, 1982). The advent of urban industrial society leads to a general shift from "quantity" to "quality" as a reproductive strategy; agrarian parents, under conditions of high mortality, have many children, for economic returns in the form of child labor and support in old age. In contrast, the modal parents in urban industrial society bear few children, provide lengthy and attentive care, including support through years of education, all without expecting a direct material return. Instead, modern parents define their commitment in emotional and moral terms. The "economically useful child," therefore, became one who is "economically useless" but "emotionally priceless" (Zelitzer, 1985).

Early in the 19th century, middle class urban families began to follow this reproductive strategy, controlling the number of births with whatever means available. This need to control fertility may have been a direct source of Victorian prudery (Fass, 1977). With young people no longer inheriting their occupations from their families, occupational identity had to be achieved individually. Middle class families organized themselves to provide a proper education for sons and guidance towards a career, and the preparation of daughters for desirable marriages. For working class families, transformation in the value of children is a long-term trend that was not completed until the virtual end of child labor in the 20th century.

MODELS OF SOCIAL CHANGE AND THE FAMILY

In recent years, research on 19th-century family life in the transition to urban industrial society has burgeoned. In addition, scholars from a number of disciplines have developed highly similar general models of the process by which societal change affects families, and families and individual family members in turn respond to change. For example, historian William McLoughlin (1978), in a study of America's major religious revivals, draws on anthropologist Anthony Wallace's (1970) studies of cultural transformation in so-called "primitive" peoples and applies it to social change in America's complex, pluralistic, and literate society. Although McLoughlin and Wallace focus on wider aspects of cultural reorientation, they grant family as a central institution, a key role in the process of change. Historian Carroll-Smith Rosenberg (1985) applies the McLoughin–Wallace model more specifically to family, gender, and generational change in the 19th century. The model of change most focused on the family is the one developed by sociologists Smelser and Halpern (1978).

The foregoing scholars agree that major social and cultural transformation seems to unfold through the following stages:

1. *Individual and family stress.* As the world changes, prevailing cultural norms and understandings and practices are disrupted long before new ones have taken shape. Ongoing practices, and the beliefs that justify and sanctify them, form cultural narratives, or what Clifford Geertz (1973) has called "blueprints for experience"—ways of understanding and reacting to the world. When significant change occurs, and the old blueprints no longer fit everyday social reality, people become confused. Existing norms become unsettled. Cultural strain shows up early in the family, as daily experience departs from the existing paradigm of family life. Starting with a few individuals who appear as deviants, growing numbers of people show signs of psychological stress—personality disturbance, drinking and drug problems. Whether or not they show signs of disturbance, young people in transition to adulthood are particularly sensitive to the impact of socioeconomic and cultural dislocations; reworking the rules inculcated in them as children, they also serve as the principal agents of cultural transformation.

2. *Cultural struggle* (Smelser & Halpern, 1978). In the second stage, personal problems become public issues. As consensus breaks down, social and political conflict increases. Competing definitions of the situation are offered by jour-

nalists, religious leaders, academics, and others who comment on society. Some social groups view the changes as dangerous, and call for a return to the old ways. Others, especially those disadvantaged in the older social order—youth, women, minorities—welcome change. Each group seeks to validate its own view of the world by selecting from the culture's array of cherished but competing values. New religious leaders and sects emerge. Eventually, the cultural struggle may turn into a political one, as social movements emerge to press for some change in line with their own definitions of the situation. The social movement may take the form of moral crusade, an attempt to pass a law, or set up a new institution.

3. *Restabilization.* The third period is one of adaptation to change. A new consensus forms in which older values are reconciled with the new realities. The old institutions and cultural blueprints are restructured. New ways of doing things become the new norms, and the society enters a period of relative stability, until the next accumulation of change.

THE CONTRADICTIONS OF DOMESTICITY

While external changes—economic, technological, political—constantly impinge on family life, tensions inside families, and at the border between family and society also add fuel to the process of family transformation. Although the 19th century middle class Victorian family, now defined as "the traditional family" is still regarded by many today as the ideal pattern of domesticity, historians have identified a distinct set of strains within it. This does not necessarily suggest that it was a more flawed form of family organization than the colonial family. The close involvement of the community in the family in colonial times led to one set of strains, the separation of private and public life in the 19th century another. Each historical era is like a different cultural system, adapting to different economic and demographic realities, with a different set of costs and benefits.

The domestic ideology of the Victorian era burdened the family with an extravagant load of expectations. Each of the new family roles, and the family itself, contained the potential for difficulty and disappointment. Nineteenth-century Americans looked to the family for both personal fulfillment and as the foundation of social order. Kirk Jeffrey (1971) has argued that in many ways the 19th century domestic ideal portrayed the family as a utopian community, analogous to the communes that reformers developed during the same decades that the new concepts of family were being designed. The same three utopian themes pervaded both sets of writings—retreat from urban chaos, careful design to physical surroundings of everyday life, and perfecting the quality of human relationships.

Victorian notions of gender and domesticity subjected married women to heavy burdens. The restricted, demanding role of the middle class Victorian housewife contrasted with the relative independence of young women before marriage. Although courtship and engagement were often a happy period, the transition to marriage and its responsibilities was often difficult; many experienced what has been called a "marriage trauma" (Mintz & Kellogg, 1988).

Maintaining a 19th century household—cooking, cleaning, mending and darning, and caring for the sick was hard work even for most middle class women, yet it was not recognized as such; housework was pastoralized (Boydston, 1991), seen as an expression of women's selfless, spiritual nature, not as work. The task of making the home both perfect and perfectly happy was ultimately impossible; to the extent that women took this literature seriously, and there is evidence they did—the discrepancy between image and reality may have given rise to feelings of guilt and futility. There is a good deal of evidence that large numbers of women suffered from a host of psychological and psychosomatic maladies that enabled them to drop out of domestic roles (Smith–Rosenberg, 1985). Further, rising divorce rates after the middle of the century testified to the dissatisfactions that were a byproduct of raised expectations for marital happiness.

For children and adolescents, the shift away from the family economy created new discontinuities in growing up. The separation of home and work in the industrial era had eroded the material basis of parental authority. Children and adolescents no longer took part in the work they would be doing as adults; parents could no longer prescribe or ever assure the occupational futures of their children. Displaced from the family economy, many young people found no place in the world of work either. "Idle youth" were perceived to be a threat to the social order, propelling the development of public schools (Smelser & Halpern, 1978).

For many middle class children, the transition to adulthood over time became longer, lonelier, and more problematic. Identity was no longer given at birth, but became a developmental task, something that had to be worked out for the young by themselves—although with the support of their parents. By the late 19th century, adolescence became for many middle class young people, a time of "soul-searching" and "struggle for self" (Baumeister & Tice, 1986).

A related source of difficulty in middle class families was an emotional structure based on intense emotional bonds in infancy and childhood, with the opposing demand for a high degree of autonomy and independence in adulthood. Parsons had noted this discontinuity in the modern family, but saw it as functional in an economic system that worked in isolation from the kinship system. Thus, he observed, the modern family had less father and more mother than the traditional arrangement, leading to more intense Oedipal feelings in sons, but the resulting emotional force would propel sons away from the family, which the economy required anyway. In contrast to this functional view, however, more direct historical evidence suggests that discontinuity in parent child relations towards the end of the 19th century led to an increase in family conflict and the intensity of adolescent problems (Baumeister & Tice, 1986).

For parents, the new arrangements brought the dilemma of increased responsibility and lessened control. Middle class parents concentrated financial and emotional resources in caring for and educating a small number of children, keeping them as dependents for longer periods of time. No longer economic assets, children came to represent the family's emotional future. By adulthood, these children would reward or betray the hopes and sacrifices of the parents. The possibilities of both upward and downward mobility were great during this period—especially downward (Coontz, 1988). All of this heightened the sense of individual and parental responsibility for success or failure.

REMAKING DOMESTICITY

By the 1880s and 90s, another wave of social and economic change began to unsettle the seeming stable social order established by the Victorian middle class. Divorce rates climbed steadily after the Civil War, reaching 100,000 in 1914. Birth rates of the White middle class dropped still further, leading President Theodore Roosevelt to warn that Americans were committing "race suicide"; preachers, journalists and academics lamented the breakdown of the family. Victorian gender roles and sexual norms came under challenge from younger generations of middle class women, now more likely to be educated and employed than in the past; the suffrage movement, the advocates of birth control, as well as younger generations of middle class intellectuals added fuel. The youth revolt of the 1920s represented the culmination of these trends (Fass, 1977).

Despite the fears of the older generation in the 1920s, college youth of the era were not revolting against the family or rejecting the domestic ideal. Rather, the "companionate" concept of marriage was an extension of Victorian themes (Fass, 1977; Griswold, 1982). The sexual side of marriage became newly important as part of a more intimate personal relationship between husband and wife. Although the Victorian ideal of marriage also promised intimacy and affection, this goal was impeded by prudery and the need to avoid pregnancy. Reliable contraception resolved that contradiction, permitting the "sexualization of marriage" (Fass, 1977, p. 262). Dating and petting, the inventions of 1920s young people that shocked the older generation, were part of the new pattern of marriage, enabling young people to explore their compatibility with a variety of partners. The new patterns of courtship reflected the emergence of a modern youthful life course that became normative in the middle class for both males and females; extended schooling, including at least some high school, an extended period of dating, early marriage for romantic reasons, some postponement of parenthood after marriage (Modell, 1989).

MODERN IN A NEW WAY

What does all this too sketchy overview of family change imply for our understanding of American family life today? It seems likely that future historians will look back on our own era as a third period of family transformation (Cherlin & Furstenberg, p. 45), prompted by a continuation of the same broad economic, demographic, and social trends that affected the United States since the end of the 18th century.

Indeed, we are in the midst of world-wide revolution in family patterns. Every other advanced industrial country, and much of the rest of the world, is experiencing the same transformations of family life we have lived through over the past several decades: women flooding into the workplace, rising divorce rates, more single parents, blended families, shifting gender roles and sex norms. In other countries, however, the disruptions of changes have been cushioned by social policies aimed at guarding the well-being of children and families: child allowances, prenatal care, parental leave, child care.

There is no question that the changes over the past 3 decades have been dramatic and disturbing. But the main question is whether these changes represent a breakdown of the family, the end of the family as we have known it, a move to no families, or a shift to alternative family forms such as the single parent family. Commentators have tended to divide into pessimists, who believe the family to be "in decline" and optimists who argue that the family is "here to stay" (Bane, 1976), and simply adapting to change. In recent years, the pessimists have greatly outnumbered the optimists. But each position possesses some validity. To argue that the family is simply adapting to change is to underestimate the degree of individual and family stress that occurs during periods of rapid social change when family life is being restructured. But to argue that Americans in general are fleeing family marriage and family ties is to exaggerate the extent of change in both behavior and values; although there is a greater tolerance for divorce, single living, and alternative life styles, the overwhelming preference, expressed in both survey data and demographic statistics, over 90% of Americans marry—giving us one of the highest marriage rates in the world. Virtually everyone who marries plans to have children.

Most family scholars recognize that rising divorce rates do not reflect a flight from marriage so much rising expectations for satisfaction in marriage, thus an increased likelihood of disappointment. Today most people are no longer willing to tolerate the kind of noncompanionate, *utilitarian, disenchanted,* or *empty shell* marriages that were rampant in the marital research of the 1950s and 1960s. As Griswold (1982) argues: "What emerged in the twentieth century was less a repudiation of Victorian marriage than an elaboration of its central assumptions."

Despite diversity, change, and trouble in the family, there is little evidence that America is becoming a society of unattached individuals. Even those who divorce are not in flight from intimacy and commitment. Summing up the findings from their study of divorcing families, Mavis Hetherington and her colleagues concluded that divorced men and women wanted "sustained, meaningful relationships and were not satisfied with a series of superficial encounters." . . . They wanted "lasting intimate relations, involving deep concern and a willingness to make sacrifices for the partner. . ." (Hetherington, Cox, & Cox, 1977, p. 42).

Even without raised expectations for marriage and the changes in women's roles, marriage in the late 20th century would have been transformed from what it had been in the past simply by changes in fertility and mortality rates. As late as 1900, at least one of the spouses would probably have died before all the children left home. Today active parenting occupies only a relatively small part of our longer life spans. Lifelong marriage now implies two people spending a third of a century or more alone in a household together (Kain, 1990).

This same reduction of the proportion of the life span devoted to parenting has contributed to the massive influx of women into the paid labor force over the past few decades. The two-worker family has become a dominant family form, although as always, there is great variation in family patterns. A considerable number of families with young children still maintain the "traditional" breadwinner–homemaker arrangement. Although women still bear the major burden of housework and childcare, cultural ideals have shifted towards a more "symmetrical" egalitarian arrangement (Goldscheider & Waite, 1991).

While women's roles have reversed the Victorian pattern, trends with regard to children have intensified themes already present in the 19th-century family. Control over fertility has increased, fertility rates have reverted to long-term downward trends, and children have become even more "emotionally priceless." New birth technologies such as artificial insemination, surrogate motherhood, and in vitro fertilization, as well as the demand for adoption testify to the high emotional and symbolic value of children.

Meanwhile, the transition to adulthood has become still longer and more difficult. The stable and reasonably well-paying blue collar jobs that used to be available to young men with little education have virtually disappeared. Even those young male workers who are well educated are at far greater economic risk, and earn lower incomes, than their counterparts in the 1950s and 60s. For the middle class, success in a highly competitive, technological economy is more demanding than it used to be. For many middle class families, the result of these changes are downwardly mobile offspring, the re-filled empty nest, and the "ILYA syndrome"—incompletely launched young adults (Schnaiberg & Goldenberg, 1989).

Despite the dramatic changes of recent years, however, the dominant cultural ideal of family life in America remains the companionate or nuclear family, minus the polarized gender roles of the 1950s. Also, there is increasing recognition that families do not have to fit the pattern of the 1950s family to be warm, supportive companionate environments. Further, vertical family ties and kin networks may be more important than they were, as women, the traditional "kin-keepers" are living longer, and as marital and economic instability lead people to turn to kin for material and emotional support. In sum, there has been continuity, as well as change and diversity.

RESEARCH IMPLICATIONS

This chapter aims to sensitize family researchers to the implications of recent historical research in understanding contemporary family life. I have argued that an historical perspective supplies an essential corrective to view society and family life as static entities, "reproducing" themselves from one generation to the next. The history of American family life suggests that change—and diversity—has been a constant. I now examine the implications of historical change for the research enterprise itself.

Family research is itself embedded in an historical context that affects our work in two different ways. First, by affecting our findings; second by affecting us—the kinds of questions we ask, the kinds of theoretical frameworks we adopt, the kind of tacit assumptions we bring to our work. I offer one example of the first kind of effect: One study of the Berkeley longitudinal subjects found a correlation, in women, between intellectual competence and the number of children they had (Livson & Day, 1977). Nevertheless, this was not a generalizable finding of a link between intelligence and fertility, but historically specific to one cohort of women—the mothers of the postwar baby boom. The existence of such a link was easily refuted; in older and younger women correlation between IQ and was negative (Retherford & Sewell, 1988).

But other findings may be culturally and historically specific in ways we don't know about. For example, much of our knowledge about personal and social development across the life course is based on people who experienced the Great Depression, World War II, Korea, the postwar era of prosperity, the baby boom, the feminine mystique, and the Cold War. They raised their children in the baby-boom era or the turbulent 1960s. Most of the families we study, if the parents are in their 30s, were part of the baby-boom generation who grew up in affluent times, encountered the Vietnam War, the hopes and turbulence of the 1960s, the malaise and economic stagnation of the 1970s. It is possible to elaborate similar profiles for every cohort of parents and for children.

Periods of rapid change have their own dynamic, as we have seen earlier. The years from about 1965–1975 appear to have been a period of cultural turbulence comparable to the 1920s and early 19th century. Norms, attitudes, and behavior were in a state of flux; statistical indicators of family life—marriage, birth, and divorce rates veered sharply away from the trends of the 1950s. If the family is amidst a wave of social transformation like those in past, the recent level of family uncertainty and instability may be temporary. Indeed, since the late 1970s, many of these trends have leveled or even reversed—birthrates have risen markedly since the late 1980s—and we have entered a time of restabilization. Some demographers find evidence of a "return to family"—not to the family patterns of 1950s, but the more symmetrical pattern of two-earner families. There is even evidence that men are increasing their share of household responsibilities (Goldscheider & Waite, 1991).

Another sociohistorical factor that may be affecting our research findings is that the majority of American families, especially young families, have been under economic stress for almost 2 decades. Since 1973, Americans have been living through a "quiet depression" that has been masked by a conspicuous but highly uneven prosperity (Levy, 1987; Phillips, 1990). Changes in the wage and salary structure have been pushing the country towards a two-class society. The upper fifth of the population has enjoyed great prosperity during the 1980s and early 90s. Meanwhile, many families are living through a replay of the Great Depression, enduring severe economic loss. Many more families are struggling simply to maintain a middle class standard of living. These economic shifts have had a strong yet scarcely noticed effect on families, especially young families. Since the 1970s, people entering adulthood have coped with the decline in economic opportunity by delaying marriage, postponing childbearing after marriage and keeping both spouses in the workplace.

Yet typically, psychological researchers present their findings as if they were transhistorically valid—as if the research subjects "might have lived anywhere, anytime" (Caspi & Bem, 1990). When they have considered historical change, it has been in the form of cohort effects—nuisance variance to be controlled and explained away. Ignoring the possible effects of social history not only affects the generality of research findings, but represents a missed opportunity to pursue a variety of significant questions about family process in a period of rapid social change.

Some sociologically oriented researchers have been examining the effects of economic and other kinds of social change on the emotional dynamics of family life. Katherine Newman (1988) has been studying the impact of sudden downward mobility due to job loss. A study mentioned earlier examined impact of shrinking economic opportunity on young middle class adults in the process of leaving home (Schnaiberg and Goldenberg, 1989). More recently, some child development researchers have begun to report research on the effects of economic stress on families and children (McLoyd & Flanagan, 1990).

The most significant sustained effort to link social change to individual and family lives is the Glen Elder's ongoing research (1974, 1979, 1987). In *Children of the Great Depression,* (1974) Elder drew on the archives of the Oakland Growth study to pose new questions about the effects of economic loss on young people who were adolescents in the 1930s. In a later study, using another, younger, Berkeley longitudinal sample—the Guidance Study—he found that the developmental stage at which children encounter major, dislocating events is an important factor in shaping the impact of that experience (Elder, Caspi, & Van Nguyen, 1986). His later work on the effects of military experience in World War II continues the same themes.

Beyond investigating the impact of particular historical events, Elder has always been concerned with developing a more general analysis of the links between historical time, the individual life course, and family processes. Nevertheless, Elder has had too few imitators, even though he has supplied guidelines that could be applied to other historical events: translate the historical event into family processes, look at the differential effect of the event on members of same cohort, consider the age and point in the life course at which individuals experienced the event, consider how characteristics of persons and families before the event may have mediated or moderated responses to it.

More recently, Stewart and Healy (1989) have proposed a promising model for linking individual development to historical change. Briefly, the model proposes that historical events like wars and depressions, as well as shifts in social trends, affect people differently at different stages of life. Thus, events and conditions experienced in childhood may influence fundamental values and basic assumptions about the way the world works; events in early adulthood influence life choices and identity; events in adulthood may influence behavior, but not necessarily attitudes and values. For example, a "traditional" wife may go to work in wartime, but may not become less traditional in her concepts about gender roles.

Stewart and Healy suggest that discrepancies between worldviews and behavior may lead to internal conflicts, and complicate the process of socialization; for example, the employed mother whose basic assumption was "women's place in the home" would be sending a complex message to her offspring, making it difficult for researchers to determine what a child is internalizing. The model they propose makes it possible to predict for any cohort, the degree to which parents or peers influence identity, the degree of internal conflict a cohort will experience about central roles in their lives.

Another form of historical effect is on our own work. We are influenced by the same socioeconomic, cultural, and historical factors as the people we study. This influence is most easy to see in earlier eras. Parson's (1955, 1965) work clearly reflects the neo-Victorian family patterns of the 1950s, as well as the continued influence of Victorian notions of separate spheres. The preoccupation of many psychological researchers in the 1950s with the effects of infant training regimes—breast vs. bottle feeding, early vs. late toilet training—now seems to have reflected the confluence of a temporarily fashionable version of Freudian theory with a general interest in infant care during the baby boom. The preoccupation with self theories in the 1970s seems to reflect the historical circumstance of that time—a large generation of younger and older adults for whom identity became problematic in a time of rapid, disorienting change. This is not to suggest our theories are necessarily wrong. Nor does it suggest that we can lift ourselves by our epistemological bootstraps and rise above the constraints of living in our own slice of historical time; the best we can do is be aware that such constraints may, and probably do, exist.

One likely candidate for obsolescence is the paradigm that views family norms and practices, and the social systems of which they are part, as static, and equates change with disturbance or breakdown. This model, Parson's theory being the prime example, has been largely replaced in sociological theory by a new paradigm in which historical change and human agency play more central roles. In this view, change is constant, and human institutions are always in the process of being remade by the people involved in them, and especially by successive generations. One way of thinking about this alternative paradigm uses the image of the dance; Norbert Elias (1978) suggests that society and its institutions are like a continuously re-patterned social dance.

Over 2 decades ago, John Edwards (1967) argued that family research suffered from a "nuclear family bias" that confused family structure with family functioning: "We desperately need an alternative model of normal development. . . Crucially, it would delineate the components of well being and the patterns of 'healthy' families, regardless of the structural configurations" (p. 508). More recently, Blechman (1982) has made a similar point; she argues that researchers tend to inspect only one side of an issue, looking for harmful effects of departures from the traditional nuclear family structure and failing to consider the positive features of alternative patterns. As Martha Moorehouse's chapter shows, the same bias in favor of traditional norms affects the study of working mothers and their families.

In the end, the most important use of history may be to sensitize researchers to the social sources of the dilemmas that families confront. In a recent book on family therapy, Deborah Lupenitz (1988) argues that knowledge of the social history of the family should be part of the sensibility of the clinician:

> Adding the historical picture to the clinical one, she writes, "is like combining the views of the right and left eyes. Through the clinical eye one sees the behavior of parents in terms of 'pathology,' 'error,' 'dysfunction,' or even what has been called the 'dumb cruelty' of families. Through the historical eye, one sees people acting on a stage designed by political and economic process. . . To paraphrase Marx, . . . although families do create their own problems, they do not create them 'just as they please.' " (pp. 145–146)

REFERENCES

Alexander, J. C., Geisen, B., Munch, R., & Smelser, N. J. (1987). *The micro-macro link*. Berkeley: The University of California Press.

Alexander, J. C., & Seidman, S. (Eds.). (1990). *Culture and society: Contemporary debates*. New York: Cambridge University Press.

Aires, P. (1962). *Centuries of childhood: A social history of family life* (R. Baldick, Trans.). New York: Knopf.

Bane, M. J. (1976). *Here to stay: American families in the twentieth century*. New York: Basic Books.

Baumeister, R. F., & Tice, D. (1986). How adolescence became the struggle for self: The historical transformation of psychological development. In J. Sulls & A. Greenwald (Eds.), *Psychological perspectives on the self* (Vol. 3). Hillsdale, NJ: Lawrence Erlbaum Associates.

Bellingham, B. (1988). The history of childhood since the "invention of childhood": Some issues in the eighties. *Journal of Family History, 13,* 347–358.

Berkner, L. K. (1972). The stem family and the developmental cycle of the peasant household: An eighteenth century Austrian example. *American Historical Review, 77,* 398–418.

Blechman, E. A. (1982). Are children with one parent at psychological risk: A methodological review. *Journal of Marriage and the Family, 44,* 179–195.

Boydston, J. (1991). The pastoralization of housework. In L. K. Kerber & J. Sherron De Hart (Eds.), *Women's America: Refocusing the past* (pp. 148–161). Oxford, England: Oxford University Press.

Caldwell, J. (1982). *Theory of fertility decline*. New York: Academic Press.

Caspi, A., & Bem, D. J. (1990). Personal continuity and change across the life course. In L. A. Pervin (Ed.), *Handbook of personality* (pp. 549–575). New York: The Guilford Press.

Cherlin, A., & Furstenberg, F. F., Jr. (1987). *The new American grandparent*. New York: Basic Books.

Coontz, S. (1988). *The social origins of private life: A history of American families 1600–1900*. London: Verso.

Degler, C. (1980). *At odds: Women and the family in America from the revolution to the present*. Oxford/New York: Oxford University Press.

Elder, G. H. (1974). *Children of the Great Depression*. Chicago: University of Chicago Press.

Elder, G. H. (1979). Historical change in life patterns and personality. In P. B. Baltes & O. G. Brim, Jr. (Eds.), *Life span development and behavior* (Vol. 2, pp. 117–159). New York: Academic Press.

Elder, G. H. (1981). History and the family: The discovery of complexity. *Journal of Marriage and the Family, 43,* 489–519.

Elder, G. H. (1987). Families and lives: Some developments in life course studies. *Journal of Family History, 12,* 179–199.

Edwards, J. N. (1967). The future of the family revisited. *Journal of Marriage and the Family, 38,* 505–511.

Elias, N. (1978). *The civilizing process*. Oxford: Blackwell.

Fass, P. (1977). *The damned and the beautiful. American youth in the 1920's*. Oxford/New York: Oxford University Press.

Flandrin, J. L. (1979). *Families in former times*. Cambridge, England: Cambridge University Press.

Fliegelman, J. (1982). Prodigals & Pilgrims: The American Revolution against patriarchal authority 1750–1800. Cambridge, England: Cambridge University Press.

Gay, P. (1984). *The bourgeois experience: Victoria to Freud*. New York: Oxford University Press.

Goldscheider, F. K., & Waite, L. J. (1991). *New families, no families*. Berkeley: University of California Press.

Goode, W. J. (1963). *World revolution and family patterns*. New York: The Free Press.

Griswold, R. (1982). *Family and divorce in California, 1850–1890*. Albany, NY: State University of New York Press.

Grossberg, M. (1985). *Governing the hearth: Law and family in nineteenth century America*. Chapel Hill: University of North Carolina Press.

Hagnal, J. (1965). European marriage patterns in perspective. In D. V. Glass & D. E. C. Eversley (Eds.), *Population in history: Essays in historical demography* (pp. 101–143). London: Arnold.

Hareven, T. K. (1982). American families in transition: Historical perspectives on change. In F. Walsh (Ed.), *Normal family processes* (pp. 446–466). New York: Guilford Press.

Harris, C. C. (1983). *The family and industrial society*. London: George Allen & Unwin.

Hetherington, M., Cox, M., & Cox, R. (1977). Divorced fathers. *Psychology Today*, April, p. 42.

Howe, D. W. (1976). Victorian culture in America. In D. W. Howe (Ed.), *Victorian America*. Philadelphia: University of Pennsylvania Press.

Jeffrey, K. (1972). The family as utopian retreat from the city: The nineteenth-century contribution. In S. Teselle (Ed.), *The families, communes and utopian societies*. New York: Harper & Row.

Laslett, B. (1973). The family as a public and private institution. *Journal of Marriage and the Family, 35*, 480–494.

Laslett, P. (1976). Societal development and aging. In R. H. Binstock & E. Shanas (Eds.), *Handbook of aging and the social sciences* (pp. 87–116). New York: Van Nostrand.

Laslett, P. (1977). *Family life and illicit love in earlier generations*. Cambridge, England: Cambridge University Press.

Laslett, P. (1989). *A fresh map of life: The emergence of the third age*. London: Weidenfeld and Nicolson.

Leupnitz, D. (1988). *The family interpreted: Feminist theory in clinical practice*. New York: Basic Books.

Levine, R. A., & White, M. (1987). Parenthood in social transformation. In J. B. Lancaster, J. Altmann, A. S. Rossi, & L. R. Sherrod (Eds.), *Parenting across the life span: Biosocial dimensions*. New York: Aldine De Grueyter.

Levy, F. (1987). *Dollars and dreams: The changing American income distribution*. New York: Russell Sage Foundation.

Litwak, E. (1965). Extended kin relations in an industrial democratic society. In E. Shanas & G. F. Streib (Eds.), *Social structure and the family: Generational relations*. Englewood Cliffs, NJ: Prentice-Hall.

Livson, N., & Day, D. (1977). Adolescent personality correlates of completed family size. *Journal of Youth and Adolescence, 6*, 311–324.

McLoughlin, W. (1978). *Revivals, awakenings, and reform*. Chicago: University of Chicago Press.

McLoyd, V. C., & Flanagan, C. A. (Eds.). (1990). Economic stress: Effects on family life and child development. *New Directions for Child Development, 46*(whole issue), Winter. San Francisco: Jossey-Bass.

Mintz, S., & Kellogg, S. (1988). *Domestic revolutions: A social history of American family life*. New York: The Free Press.

Mitterauer, M., & Sieder, R. (1982). *The European family*. Chicago: University of Chicago Press.

Modell, J. (1989). *Into one's own: From Youth to Adulthood in the United States 1920–1975*. Berkeley: University of California Press.

Newman, K. S. (1988). *Falling from grace: The experience of downward mobility in the American middle class*. New York: The Free Press.

Parsons, T. (1955). The American family: Its relations to personality and the social structure. In T. Parsons & R. F. Bales (Eds.), *Family socialization and interaction process* (pp. 3–21). Glencoe, IL: The Free Press.

Parsons, T. (1965). The normal American family: Its relations to personality and the social structure. In S. M. Farber, P. Mustacchi, & R. H. L. Wilson (Eds.), *Man and civilization: The family's search for survival* (pp. 31–50). New York: McGraw-Hill.

Phillips, K. P. (1990). *The politics of rich and poor: Wealth and the American electorate in the Reagan aftermath*. New York: Harper Perennial.

Plath, D. (1980). *Long engagements: Maturity in modern Japan*. Stanford, CA: Stanford University Press.

Pollock, L. (1983). *Forgotten children: Parent-child relations from 1500–1900*. Cambridge, England: Cambridge University Press.

Retherford, R. O., & Sewell, W. H. (1988). Intelligence and family size reconsidered. *Social Biology, 35,* 1–40.

Rorabaugh, W. J. (1979). *The alcoholic republic*. New York: Oxford University Press.

Ryan, M. (1981). *Cradle of the middle class: The familyin Oneida County, New York, 1790–1865*. Cambridge, England: Cambridge University Press.

Schnaiberg, A., & Goldenberg, S. (1989). From empty nest to crowded nest: The dynamics of incompletely-launched young adults. *Social Problems, 36*(3), 251–269.

Smith-Rosenberg, C. (1985). *Disorderly conduct: Visions of gender in Victorian America*. New York: Knopf.

Stewart, A. J., & Healy, J. M., Jr. (1989). Linking individual development and social changes. *American Psychologist, 44,* 30–42.

Vinovskis, M. A. (1978). An "epidemic" of adolescent pregnancy? *Journal of Family History, 6,* 205–230.

Wrong, D. (1961). The oversocialized conception of man in modern sociology. *American Sociology Review, 26,* 183–193.

Yankelovich, D. (1981). *New rules: Searching for self-fulfillment in a world turned upside-down*. New York: Random House.

3 The Child in Family and School: Agency and the Workings of Time

Donald A. Hansen[1]
University of California, Berkeley

> When and if we pass beyond the unspoken despair in which we are now living, when we feel we are again able to control the race to destruction, a new breed of developmental theory is likely to arise. . . . I think that its central technical concern will be how to create in the young an appreciation of the fact that many worlds are possible, that meaning and reality are created and not discovered, that negotiation is the art of constructing new meanings by which individuals can regulate their relations with each other. Jerome Bruner (1986)

One of the most difficult challenges facing family research today is to recognize something we already know: that the doors and windows of the family do not keep the rest of the world outside, nor do they keep the family members in. We know this in our everyday lives, yet in our research and theory we continue to view families as if they are separated from the world outside by a skin that is at most semipermeable. This research strategy has paid off well, contributing importantly to the understandings we have gained into family roles, relationships, and dynamics.

Through most of the century, this selective perception has carried a reasonable price. Today, however, the price is rising rapidly, as family members confront increasing demands on their time, attention and effort from the workplace, marketplace, school, community, and a multitude of other constituted orders, as well as their more fluid and informal relationships. To continue to ignore the interpenetrations and tensions of these multiple involvements in our methods of inquiry is to invite trivialization and irrelevance in our research and theories.

---

[1]I am especially indebted to Guy E. Swanson and Philip A. Cowan for their comments and suggestions on an earlier draft of this paper.

Opening our methods to the outside world unleashes a flurry of questions—about the intersections of individual, intimate group, society, culture, and history—that are fundamental to our understandings of family life. In this chapter, focusing on the child in family and school, I consider two of the most basic and frustrating of these questions. The first concerns the child's agency in home and school: Can the individual act purposefully, and to any important degree independently of the compulsions and constraints of the immediate situation and of the larger sociocultural orders? The second concerns the influence of family and school on one another: How and to what degree are the individual's experiences in one social setting and time imported into another setting and time?

The questions appear deceptively simple. Of course the child is able to act intentionally, and helps shape the situations he or she is in. And clearly the child at times comes home from school angry or excited, just as parents may take their work home with them. As the essay unfolds, however, so do the complexities of the questions, revealing the difficulties they present to our methods of research.

In another essay (Hansen, 1988) I have argued that the dominant metaphors of family research and theory—social roles and social systems—needlessly restrict our ability to deal with such questions. Loosening the integumentation assumptions, that essay explores the abilities of these metaphors to represent the influences of the child's school stressors on family stability, change, and development.

The current chapter extends this argument, exploring the workings of time—the temporal spread of experience—in the exercise of agency. The explorations further loosen the integumentation assumption, specifying the processes whereby the child's experiences in home and classroom interfuse.

THE CHILD AS ACTIVE AGENT

In conventional research wisdom the family has been seen as the locus of intense socialization in the first few years of life, and then as supportive or disruptive of the school's efforts to complete the socialization and education of the growing child. In recent years, that view has been somewhat modified, to accommodate the understanding that many parents continue through the school years and beyond to be important role models (positive and/or negative) and active influences on the development of the child. Yet even in this elaborated view the child as a thinking, feeling, intending person is remarkably absent.

Somehow, in the course of our systematic efforts to understand the interactive influences of the families and schools on such things as motivation, self-esteem, responsibility, and social functioning, children are lost as recognizably active agents in their own lives. Concern for the development and well-being of the child clearly motivates much of our research, yet our methods for addressing that concern tend to lead us into the implicit assumption that children are simply responsive to the everyday practices in home and school that influence their development.

In our own family lives most of us would find this assumption nonsensical. We know our children as active participants in these practices, at times staunchly defending established routines and normalcies (especially those that constrain and define their parents), at times actively involved in deliberate negotiative strategies for changing the ways things are done and what is expected (especially those routines and expectations that constrain the children), even helping reshape the "normal" order and their place and possibilities in it. We recognize our children, as ourselves, as at times passive recipients of other influences, but at times as active agents in their own lives and the lives of those around them.

Consider Kimberley.[2] Any of the 250 individuals my colleagues and I have followed over the past decade might serve as well to illustrate the demands that are placed on our methods when the initiating focus and continuing interest is on the individual family members actively confronting the constitutive orders of the lived-in world. Indeed, many stories of our other subjects are more dramatic than Kimberley's, drawing us into the numbing experiences of alcoholic and abusive homes or the stresses of growing up in ethnic or linguistic communities that suffer the prejudice and discrimination of the mainstream society. But Kimberley has grown up in a comfortable middle-class environment, and the relative simplicity of her story is less distracting and thus more challenging to our conceptions of agency and time.

When Kimberley's relationship with her 6th-grade teacher suddenly deteriorated in the middle of the school year, we wanted to find out why. We had followed Kimberley through her 5th grade in a quiet suburban elementary school, and into her 6th grade in the more robust ambience of middle school. A bright, attractive child, Kimberley dresses somewhat differently from the others, often wearing long and rumpled dresses that seemed too old for her, reminding her teacher of a "neglected waif." Kimberley thinks she is "sorta like in style and in fashion," but even her best friend calls her clothes "dorky."

She is unusually oriented toward adults, never failing to acknowledge the entry of either of the two researchers in our project or of other teachers or visiting parents who came and went during the day. Earlier in the year she would often stay after school to try to chat with the teacher or ask for help with Math or some other assignment. She had done this throughout the previous year, and we knew it was partly because no one would be in her home until early evening. Recently, however, she stopped staying after school, and began to openly defy her teacher's requests and question her authority.

Mrs. Thorncliff is a strong and capable teacher, and Kimberley's behavior

[2]I am indebted to JoEllen Fisherkeller for her persistent sensitivity in the study from which this narrative draws. Throughout the narrative, all names are fictitious.

frustrates and angers her. It does not confuse her, however. She is convinced that it is a response to her persistent demands for better work, and especially homework. Kimberley is bright, but she lacks focus. In the new middle-school, with its increased lesson demands and heightened confusions of peer relations, Kimberley seems to think she can resist the teacher and assignments whenever she wants. However competent the child may be cognitively, she is incompetent in attitudes and self-control; she needs strong and consistent demands, close monitoring, and tight control from the teacher.

Mrs. Thorncliff's view is clearly reflected in Kimberley's report cards through that year. Her grades in subject areas drop from a B average in the first grading period to C− in the fourth, while the teacher's evaluation of Kimberley's efforts falls from G (Good) in the first period to G/N (Needs Improvement) in the second and to a pure N in the third and fourth. Mrs. Thorncliff believes that her evaluations are fair, accurately representing an uncontrolled and at times rebellious student.

Kimberley's record in earlier grades appears to support the view that she has trouble with work demands. Her grades in elementary school were erratic, in contrast to her consistently advanced scores on standardized tests. At the beginning of her second year, she was reading at a 6th-grade level and her report cards in the first and second grades were filled mostly with the highest of grades—"outstanding effort." Through elementary school her test scores continued to rise, while her grades declined, erratically. To Mrs. Thorncliff this combination of inconsistent grades and consistent scores is the record of a capable but poorly controlled individual.

Kimberley's trouble, the teacher believes, is located in Kimberley herself, but its source is in the child's home environment. Aware that Kimberley's parents had divorced a few years earlier, the teacher concludes that with only a working mother, the entire family lacks control, allowing Kimberley to do more or less whatever she feels like doing at any time, even to the point of ignoring or resisting her mother's inconsistent demands.

This location of Kimberley's "problem" appears reasonable within Mrs. Thorncliff's framework of understanding. But we had known Kimberley for almost a year and a half and had witnessed a dramatic change the year before, as she moved through the 5th-grade year. When we first started our study, about 2 months into the school year, her 5th-grade teacher, Mrs. Sobol, confided that Kimberley was "on a downward plunge." But Kimberley clearly was emotionally attached to the teacher, a bright, sensitive woman about the age of Kimberley's mother.

Mrs. Sobol, too, knew that Kimberley's parents were divorced, and she was aware of Kimberley's erratic record in earlier years. But, in contrast to Mrs. Thorncliff, she believed that in coping with her frustrations and uncertainties at home Kimberley was seeking strong, consistent, and supportive adult contact. The teacher worked carefully to provide that supportive strength, and through the year Kimberley rallied. We saw her quietly grow in poise and confidence and, correspondingly, less hungry for the attentions of every adult who entered the classroom. By the end of the year "outstanding effort" evaluations again dominated her report, and it was clear that Kimberley had earned the grades and her teacher's respect. Having witnessed this reversal, we were uneasy with Mrs. Thorncliff's location of "Kimberley's problem" so fully within Kimberley and her home life. Whatever Kimberley's personal troubles, and whatever was going on at home, it was clear that Kimberley is highly responsive to her classroom situations.

Mrs. Thorncliff's construction appeared indifferent to the reflective, self-aware person we knew Kimberley to be. Over the year, we often saw this indifference to other students' subjective sensibilities, as she explained, with sociological acuity, the accomplishments and failures of her students in causal and antecedent statements, that turned on the phrase "because of."

Mrs. Thorncliff's disinterest in her students' own "in order to" motives parallels the implicit assumptions, familiar in both family and educational research, that the child is a passive/resistant recipient of adult instruction, direction, and control. Some researchers, particularly those concerned with socially situated motivation (e.g., Covington, 1983; Rueda & Mehan, 1986; Weinstein, 1985) have persistently avoided this implicit denial of child agency, but it continues to dominate research and theory that link families and schools.

It is tempting to argue that this situation reflects no more than a concession to organizational reality, that the researchers' focus remains fixedly set on those areas most open to change and intervention: parents, teachers, administrators, and their negotiative context. But the traditions of family and educational theory—shaped in large by the conventional wisdom of the time and cultures they shared and by the problematics they embraced—suggest that far more is involved.

The neglect of childhood agency is, in fact, rooted in Western traditions of thought and socialization practice. Those traditions pervade the formative theories in sociology and social psychology that continue to inform family and school research. In largest part, the neglect of childhood agency reflects the workings of objectivism, which has so powerfully dominated the behavioral and social research on which family-school inquiry must draw. The constraints of those ideational traditions are far reaching and severe, urging restrictions on the use of the researcher's own competencies and capacities, excluding all but rational constructs and/or empirical data available to the senses of sight, sound, and touch. They also constrain the researcher's attentions to the subject—the child/student, parent, teacher, administrator—restricting us to indices that can be treated "objectively" for purposes of research.

And they constrain the procedures we employ to cope with the enormous complexities of our subjects, systematically delimiting the variants admitted and the logics of their relationships. The pursuit of rigor in methodological procedures also forces further constraints on situational and empirical variants, and on the range of admissible variation in social, cultural, and temporal scope. In the priorities placed on objective rationality, empiricism, and methodological rigor, the capacities to recognize human agency are often severely and unnecessarily diminished.

Our thinking reaches for coherence and completeness, and we begin to assume the answers to research questions before the evidence takes form. Often the unfinished—and hence explorative—question is rushed to completion, in order to finish a project, to meet a deadline, to answer critics, or simply to be done with a task that seems to be never-ending. In that tendency toward completeness the question of agency often suffers in facile assumptions that deny or exaggerate its possibilities.

And, often, answers to the question of agency are assumed even before the research question is posed.

AGENCY AND STRUCTURAL PROBLEMATICS

Assumptions that effectively deny or ignore the workings of agency often are made intentionally, as a means to win workable coherence and manageability from the complex and obscure world the researcher addresses. In the fundamental assumptions about what is most meaningful to human inquiry, that is, the question of agency may be seen as expendable.

It is this difference in the sense of what is coherent and significant—in those assumptions and principles that determine what is to be admitted and what is to be denied as meaningful questions—that most importantly distinguish approaches to research and theory from one another. And it is in the context of these differences that the validity and utility of the disparate data, facts, and generalizations must be established.

These fundamental organizing ideas and presuppositions are commonly referred to as the problematics of an inquiry. In this sense of the word, problematics refers to the field of concepts that organizes a particular field of inquiry. This field of concepts presents a general sense of significance and coherence within which sense can be made of particulars.[3] The problematics not only permit some kinds of questions to be asked while suppressing others, they also allow a restricted range of ways of asking those questions while disallowing others.[4] By necessity, we approach and organize our inquiries within these more

[3]The term problematics is often used to refer to the problems addressed in a field or study. In this sense, the term as used here is itself somewhat problematic. Nonetheless, I have employed it here, rather than further confuse the dialogue with another constructed term, which itself would require definition.

[4]This inclusion and exclusion is in itself neither good nor bad; it is simply a necessity of systematic inquiry, the researchers' response to the "great buzzing confusion" of human life. So-

or less explicit fields of concepts, even though we may not always be aware of those fields. Some disciplines are more self-consciously concerned than others with their problematics, and the acuity of that concern may change even over brief periods of time. The level of concern may reflect disciplinary and organizational insecurity, as seems to have been the case in sociology—a relative newcomer to university life—compared to its parental disciplines, philosophy and history, or even to its older siblings, such as psychology. Nonetheless, as Johnson (1979) argues, even in history "the organizing ideas and presuppositions may lie very deep. They none the less exist" (p. 201).

In their most ambitious forms objective problematics exclude the very possibility of appreciable individual or collective agency. These methods draw on the natural sciences, seeking law-like operations that are independent both of individual experience or interpretation and of historical-cultural circumstances.

To appreciate this exclusion, briefly consider one of the 20th century's most influential examples of objectivist problematics, the functional systems theories of Talcott Parsons. It may at first seem strange that I turn to Parsons for this example—rather than those of a contemporary researcher/theorist who has focused more persistently on family-school research. Who, after all, reads Parsons these days? But, like Freud, Parsons profoundly affected the cultural understandings we bring to our work, and the methods he crafted continue their profound influence on the diverse areas of substantive inquiry from which family-school research draws.

In its most familiar sociological form, the question of human agency is located in the tensions between individual effort and the social order, tensions expressed in the aged Hobbesian problem of a rational order of free individuals: If all pursue their own rational interests, how can order be maintained? The question assumes an openness to considerable variability in situated order as well as individual subject.

The history of sociology is in many ways defined by the puzzle of this relationship. For those whose problematic assumes the constitutive efficacy of human action, it is a history of frustrated efforts to rescue intentionality and efficacy from the insistent domination of the historically constituted social system. Possibilities of human agency are persistently reintroduced, only to dissolve in the confusing complexities of political, economic and organizational constraints.

---

ciolinguistics have made commonplace the recognition that this selective inclusion of admissible "reality" begins with language itself, and that both language and reality are situationally specific, and in constant turmoil and change. Nor is it possible with final certainty to determine that any given problematic is superior to another. We can with self-satisfied comfort assume that the problematic of primitive witch doctors is altogether wrong-headed, compared to the rationality of modern medical schools. Those who have left their hospital beds following the ministrations of modern shamans, acupressurists and faith healers may question our comfortable certainty, however.

This frustration is poignant in Max Weber's writings. The sweep of his inquiries across time and place—probing the common-sense knowledge of everyday life in Calvinistic England and Colonial America, in ancient Judaism and Confucianism, and then in the medieval city—was breathtaking, bringing a new coherence to the questions of consciousness, agency and order within the constraints of European academic thought in the emerging 20th century. In Weber's theories of social action, "The whole vast ambiguity of our century was held for one brief moment in a desperate synthesis" (Hughes, 1958, p. 209).

The synthesis was indeed desperate, for at every turn Weber himself saw that his insistence on "verstehen"—understanding human activity as meaningful to "suffering, striving, doing" actors—seemed to reveal the relentless domination of functionally rational organization. The subjective insistence of Weber's problematic led him to the dispiriting conclusion that the future held only a nightmarish life, dominated by an iron cage of functional rationality. His inquiries into diverse societies and times seemed to repeat the dismal theme: Human agency itself creates its own bondage.

Weber's social action theories, and to a lesser degree the theories of Durkheim and Marx, serve as the central underpinnings of the single most influential problematic in 20th century sociology, Talcott Parsons' functionalist systems theories (1951; Parsons & Bales, 1955). Parsons' strategies of functional analysis, however, transform Weber's informing problematic.

For Weber the study of societies past and present offered insight into tendencies, probabilities, options, and possibilities of life in an industrializing world. He foresaw the iron cage as the fate of civilization, but it was only a probable—and not inevitable—fate. Nor was it a response to the functional necessities of social development. Rather, it was the persistent trend of human organization based on principles of functional rationality. It appeared to be the emergent future, but only if men and women chose to ignore their possibilities for organizing through action based on different principles. In Parsons' problematic, these possibilities and probabilities mutate into responses to functional imperatives.

Weber's insistence on the open-ended and multiplex nature of social change tends to fade in Parsons' ambitious theories, in favor of teleological assumptions that order and change are due to the functional roles they serve. Intentional action tends to be subordinated, to the point of irrelevancy, to the functional requirements of evolving structures. Weber's insistence on meaningful, goal directed action tends to be forgotten as attention fixes on the functional responsiveness of social roles to culturally-mediated systemic processes. Human action may be meaningful, in the Weberian sense, but only within the binding social norms and institutionalized values of the system.

Parsons, of course, was aware of the need to deal with the tensions between functional imperatives and individual agency—to show how functional requirements come to be met through the workings of intentional choice and action. The awareness shows in his comments in specific areas, for example: ". . . many of the framers of the Constitution had legal training. Even though they provided for only one Supreme Court . . . they did lay the foundations for an especially strong legal order" (Parsons, 1971, p. 93).

In passages such as this, Parsons seems to simply emphasize the primacy of social institutions and systems, rather than their functional determinacy. Such an emphasis, of course, is compatible with the recognition that role-playing individuals—not only the founding fathers of a society, but also children and less eminent adults—provide linkages between systems and institutional orders, including the family and education.

In most of his work, however, Parsons, as many functionalist and systems theorists who followed, went beyond an emphasis on the primacy of social institutions. Rather, he sought to establish that individuals adopt and perform their roles in response to the functional requirements of those systemically related institutions.

The details of his analyses of transformations of the family in the industrial revolution, for example, appear familiar: Home and work are separated, and the intimate family group is structurally isolated. In historical accounts these developments are seen as but common themes amidst countless variations as individuals, families, communities and political activists reconstituted their lives and relationships within the range of options open or openable to them. But in Parsons' treatment, the functional necessities of modernism *required* these changes in the family, altering role demands and norms. Children and their parents simply complied.

The fundamental process in this response to functional necessities is the socialization function, which effects the internalization of the commitments and capacities in children that are essential to their future role performances:

> Commitments may be broken down in turn into two components: commitment to the implementation of the broad values of society, and commitment to the performance of a specific type of role within the structure of society. . . . Capacities can also be broken down into two components, the first being competence or the skill to perform the tasks involved in the individual's roles, and the second being "role-responsibility" or the capacity to live up to other people's expectations of the interpersonal behavior appropriate to these roles. (Parsons, 1959, p. 298)

Schools, too, respond to the functional necessities of the system, articulating the socialization function with the allocative function of selecting and allocating manpower. Parsons, of course, was writing about overall patterns of socialization and differentiation in the social system, and acknowledged that individual cases could vary considerably within the functional patternings of the social system. These variations might be due to idiosyncratic failures, but even these often could be seen as responses to the strains and contradictory imperatives of systemic transformations and adjustments.

Parsons demonstrated the utility of functionalist perspectives in substantive analyses that were often penetrating. A notable example is his discussion of the indifference and rebellion of school children of "relatively high ability but low family status" as a response to contradictory role expectations. In these comments, Parsons anticipated the ethnographic interpretations of Willis' (1977) now classic study of the way working class "Lads" in Burmingham come to take working class jobs. This indifference and even overt revolt, Parsons noted, is often taken to arise from alienation from cultural and intellectual values:

> I would suggest exactly the opposite: . . . Those pupils who are exposed to contradictory pressures are likely to be indifferent; at the same time the personal stakes for them are higher than for the others, because what happens to them in school may make much more of a difference for their futures than for the others, in whom ability and family status point to the same expectations for the future. In particular for the upwardly mobile pupils, too much emphasis on school success would pointedly suggest 'burning their bridges' of association with their families and status peers. (Parsons, 1959, p. 312)

Functional problematics, then, do allow important questions to be raised about the linkages of family and school, despite their implicit denial of agency. A functional analysis, for example, helps specify and extend Mrs. Thorncliff's location of Kimberley's problems in her home life. For Kimberley's family can be seen as buffeted by a social system in fundamental change, in which the structural differentiations of sex-roles are losing their previous clarity and the locus of socialization is shifting away from the parent-child relationship. These *systemic* changes introduce pervasive but uneven strains throughout society, and Kimberley's family suffers more than most.[5]

Kimberley has grown in a home in which a single parent has for years attempted to play both the *instrumental* and *expressive* roles, which in *traditional* families differentiate fathers and mothers. Even before her parents divorced some years ago, her father was instrumentally ineffective, and his expressive behaviors were too unpredictable to allow the children to identify with him as a person or with the roles he played within or outside the home. Although her mother's on-again off-again fiance has been living with the family casually for about 3 years he has resisted taking on a parental role. Kimberley resents his inconsistent interventions, which she feels are "very bossy" and insensitive. Thus, the *power* function of family is also uncertain and inconsistent.

The role confusion of Kimberley's home life has made it difficult for her to internalize both the commitments and capabilities that her teacher demands. Clearly, she identifies with the *particularistic* norms her mother represents, but she does not identify with the parenting role her mother presents. Although we

[5]In this and the following three paragraphs, terms in italics are Parsons'.

have not been able to detail the qualities of her various teachers in the earliest years of elementary school, it appears that she did her best work with those teachers who, like her warm and supportive 5th-grade teacher, tempered their roles in applying *universalistic norms* and the *differential reward of achievement* with a quasi-motherliness.

Middle school curricula, however, more clearly reflect a systemic strain toward increased specialization. This accentuates the school's function in selecting and allocating, increasing pressure toward academic achievement and independence. With these pressures it is increasingly difficult to temper the instrumental role of teacher with expressive motherliness—and Mrs. Thorncliff was not the kind of person who would try. In Parsons' functional analyses, Kimberley's family is thus seen as a rather distressed system for the child's internalization of the role commitments and capabilities required for functional participation in the differentiating and allocative processes of schools.

Drawing on Parsons' ambitious and diverse publications, the analysis could be continued with considerable subtlety and detail, but even to this point their utility, particularly in linking societal to sociopsychological processes, should be undeniable clear.

So, too, should their limitations. For in these perspectives on Kimberley, Weber's thinking, striving, doing individual is turned into a complicated puppet, with no identifiable possibilities other than adequately or inadequately responding to the needs and constraints of the system, as they are presented in home and school.

Although some of the empirically suspect aspects of Parsons' constructs—notably his functionalist theory of social evolution—have been abandoned, his functionalist strategies of explanation have been widely adopted in social inquiry, particularly in what are known as "Social Systems" theories. The vision endures, often unarticulated, of transcending variations in historical circumstance and human subjectivity in the identification of objective and universal structures.

Functionalism is only one variety of the many structuralist problematics that—at least at the level of macro analyses—effectively deny or diminish the possibilities of agency. The closely related structuralism of French anthropology, notably in the work of Claude Levi Straus, similarly allows little possibility for the effective play of intentionality or agency. Even Michelle Foucault—who denies the structuralist label—argues that although the belief systems of any society are always in "perpetual transformation," such changes are not the outcomes of anyone's conscious strategies or intentional agency; they are "anonymous and without a subject."

From one perspective, the work of Foucault and the structuralists, and of Noam Chomsky and other sociolinguists of his period, represent cultural correctives to the monolithic dominance accorded social structure by Parsons and other macrosociologists. In their work, agency may be rescued from the functionalist bias, but it is lost again to the workings of direct speech acts, deep structures, or other formal and independent cultural determinants.

Similarly, in Louis Althusser's structural Marxist problematic "history is a process without a subject." The impression that men make history is superficial, for the individual is made by the existing society. Thus there is an autonomy of the political, often linked to economic determinism. Parallel assumptions are also seen in Bowles and Gintis' (1976) otherwise radical analyses of the reproduction of social inequality in the service of capitalistic interests.

As in the case of Piaget's developmental structuralism and in the more social-psychological structural role theory (cf. Hansen, 1988), the constructs developed within this macro-level problematics are of undeniable, but delimited relevance to family-school research. It is sometimes useful to collapse large-scale institutional relations and processes into mechanistic, structural, or organismic metaphors that simplify otherwise overwhelming complexities. Such metaphors can sensitize inquiry, if their limitations are recognized. But there is a price to be paid for the methodological constraints of macro-deterministic approaches, with their relatively static conceptions of the interplay of individual and social order, and their indifference to the spatially and temporally situated variation that is crucial to the identification of human agency and possibility.

AGENCY AND THE SUBJECTIVIST INSISTENCE

In recent decades, the monolithic dominance of structuralist problematics and methodologies in social and behavioral research has begun to come apart.[6] A disarray of correctives has surfaced, first in philosophy, then in socio-cultural disciplines, then in psychology. Many are concerned with structuralist tendencies to treat research subjects as objects, some with restrictions in research methodologies and substantive foci, some with the suppression of the researcher's own human capacities. They also vary in degree and ambition, as well as clarity and coherence. Some present alternatives or complementarities to the structuralist problematics. Others reach for broader conceptions of the relationship of the individual to socio-cultural structurings and to the "intersections of biography and history" (cf. Mills, 1959).

The most persistent of the correctives and the most far-reaching in their

[6]I realize the phrase "has begun to come apart" may sound inadequate to some who have witnessed the retreat of objectivist problematics over recent decades. At the metatheoretical level, the objectivist monolith today finds few articulate defenders, and in most enclaves of research intersubjective and even hermeneutical methodologies are accepted as complements, if not alternatives to more quantitative procedures. Nonetheless, in research training, practice and politics, objectivist traditions continue to constrain research thought and constrict the range of recognized possibilities in the design and conduct of social and behavioral research. Examination of current textbooks in research methods will help confirm this point.

implications demand an end to the methodological constraints on the subjective meanings and intersubjectivities of both the research subjects and the researcher. Resonating especially the seminal work of Alfred Schutz, Marin Heidegger, and George Herbert Mead, these correctives vary in substance and detail, but share an understanding that the everyday and extraordinary experiences of human life are often hidden from empirical inquiry. To truly study human life, we have no choice but to address the objectively unknowable workings of the human mind and heart.

This subjective sensibility begins with Weber's insight (which Parsons embraced, then increasingly neglected) that the linkage of subjective meaning to social action is critical to understanding social order and human agency. Weber's verstehen directs attention to the impotence of empirical regularities and correlations, when they are isolated from the meanings and constructs acting individuals use in making sense of their own social experience.

This is but the beginning of a subjective sensibility, however. It immediately demands recognition of the interplay of multiple realities in everyday life, a multiplicity implied but not addressed by conventions of linking social roles: The child/student is at once a son or daughter, a grandchild, an heir, a student, a friend, an enemy, and a multitude of other relationships. However useful these familiar conventions they fail to express the intersubjectivity of the multiple realities, inviting the assumption that the interlinkages are firmly located within the individual role player. To insist on the intersubjective locus of these multiple realities is to reveal otherwise hidden possibilities of individual agency.

The subjective sensibility goes to an even more pervasive level of human life, suggested in what is often called the "linguistic turn" in philosophy. The gathering of this turn is seen in Mead's (1934) inquiries into self and society, which self-consciously move from subjectivists' traditional emphases on consciousness and phenomenology to an emphasis on language and communicative reflexivity. This turn brings to the center of attention the interplay of language and social practice in the constitution of both individual and societal life.

The linguistic turn was acutely sharpened in Heidegger's hermeneutic understanding that meanings are neither objectively fixed nor arbitrary. The hermeneutic understanding thus locates itself directly in that realm of controversy between objectivist and subjectivist, in a sense embracing both and siding with neither. In the hermeneutic understanding, both the relativity and the givenness of language are the result of interpretation.

But interpretation, clearly, must be subject to constraints or shaping influences, or else we would live in total incoherence. The question is, where are the loci of these constraints? Functionalists would place them in the social system or structure, and many recent sociolinguists have sought them in some kind of formal constraint—such as Chomsky's deep structures—which is independent of both individual and society.

In the hermeneutic understanding, by contrast, the constraints are situational:

> . . . We are never not in a situation. Because we are never not in a situation, we are never not in the act of interpreting. Because we are never not in the act of interpreting, there is no possibility of reaching a level of meaning beyond or below interpretation. But in every situation some or other meaning will appear to us to be uninterpreted because it is isomorphic with the interpretive structure the situation (and therefore our perception) already has . . .
>
> . . . [Constraints on meaning inhere] not in language but in situation, and because they inhere in situation, the constraints we are always under are not always the same ones. Thus we can see how it is neither the case that meanings are objectively fixed more that the meanings one constructs are arbitrary. To many these have seemed the only alternatives, and that is why the claims for objectivity and subjectivity have been continually discussed. (Fish, 1979, pp. 250; 265)

Hermeneutics insists that we attend the intersubjective constituting of "reality" and "normalcy," and the centrality in this of the individual's "concerns" and "projects" (cf. Heidegger, 1927; MacIntyre, 1984). In this perspective, agency is no longer seen simply as an expression of one's will. Rather, it is "concerned engagement" with one's project, interplaying within the unfolding continuities and "normalcies" of moment-to-moment living.[7]

> To be concerned is to be involved and absorbed in the world in a particular way, with a particular manner or style that comes from adopting a project as one's own. The project in turn is best viewed as a practice directed towards its own intrinsic good. . . Thus concerned, one understands the situation in terms of the project that engages one. . . A concern is a structured involvement in the world that seeks particular ends, that organizes the world in a coherent way, that provides a way of understanding both self and situation. It is a way of thinking and seeing, but first of doing. (Packer & Scott, 1992)

Kimberley's side of the story is no less self-serving than Mrs. Thorncliff's, but it is far more subtle and reflective. She had been "extremely embarrassed" one day when Mrs. Thorncliff called the entire class to attention to read a phone message from Kimberley's mother, asking her to pick up her younger brother and sister after school and take care of them through the evening. But Kimberley insists that isn't what brought on the trouble. The next day Kimberley told Mrs. Thorncliff that she had been embarrassed, and asked her to never do that again. Two weeks later Mrs. Thorncliff read a similar note aloud. Now, Kimberley says, she doesn't care anymore what "that teacher" wants.

Kimberley and her teacher see the note incidents quite differently. To Mrs. Thorncliff reading notes from home to the entire class is "only routine," and she can't understand why it would bother anyone so much. But after the second note

---

[7] I am indebted to my colleague, Martin Packer, for sharing his theoretical and research work in progress, and specifically for turning my attention to Heidegger's conception of agency as concerned management.

incident she recognized how emotional Kimberley could get, and she plans to give any further notes to her privately, even though this risks the impression that she is playing favorites.

To Mrs. Thorncliff the notes "were" simply events of the recent past; to Kimberley they "are" a continuing threat to her most central concerns in the classroom. Her private problems at home have been publicly revealed, in a way that is surely being distorted by the other kids, and especially by Brenda and Gloria. The notes tell them that her home life is somehow different from theirs, more limited in money, time, and other resources. Her parents are divorced, her mother has a demanding job, and Kimberley is expected to do things that demean her age and status. While her peers can enjoy their independence and maturity after school, she is forced to remain in the role of mother's little helper.

In her incisive "because of" explanations, Mrs. Thorncliff fails to recognize that Kimberley's focal day-to-day concern in the classroom is not doing her lessons, but rather winning the respect and admiration of her peers. Painfully concerned about her presentation of self in front of her classmates, day after day Kimberley closely monitors her own behavior and words in light of theirs. Plagued with thoughtful contradictions, she thinks she knows herself "pretty well," but she also says, "I don't like to believe myself sometimes." Her words suggest an awareness that cannot be spoken, understanding that cannot be put into words, the realm of what Polanyi calls "tacit knowledge," what we know but cannot tell.[8] In this realm takes place the work in finding the believability of one's self, the deeper work in what Haan calls the "life-long enterprise of making self-consistent sense" of one's self in the world (cf. Haan, 1977).

As others of her age and time, Kimberley is focally concerned with making sense of herself in her world, most importantly in seeing herself through the eyes of others, in a reflexive awareness of self-and-other. More than most of her peers, however, she has not yet found this satisfying sense of the world, or of herself in the eyes of those few others who are sufficiently important to her. Through the years of our research visits, Kimberley's self-and-other monitoring continued to be intense and continual, compared even to others in this uncertain age and milieu. Yet she remained one of the more socially isolated of the children in her class.

In the first months of our observations, it seemed that her overt actions toward others—teachers as well as students—were often surprising and unpredictable. As we came to know her better, however, we were able to recognize that this volatility expressed a persistent concern, not simply with gaining acceptance and intimacy, but acceptance with respect and admiration. She explains her lack of

[8]Giddens (1984) calls it the "practical consciousness," which lies between unconscious motives and the "discursive" consciousness that can be put into words. "Practical consciousness involves recall to which the agent has access in the durée of action without being able to express what he or she thereby 'knows' " (p. 49).

popularity and her difficulties with peers in terms of her maturity, in essence telling herself that she deserves their respect, but they are too young to realize it. When she answers correctly in class, she feels sometimes "very superior: I feel like I deserve a lot more than the other kids in the class—like a queen." But other times, when she gives the wrong answer, "I feel like everybody's ganging up on me . . . to humiliate me." She even throws herself into her lessons, at times, so her on-again off-again friends "won't be able to think I'm so upset I can't do my work."

In the 5th grade, Mrs. Sobol had been a critical resource in Kimberley's many projects that served this persistent concern with statusful acceptance. Herself the object of Kimberley's admiration, Mrs. Sobol consciously worked to build Kimberley's self-confidence by acknowledging and praising her ideas and abilities. But Mrs. Thorncliff was sparing in her praise of anyone, and Kimberley quickly identified herself as someone who was particularly undeserving. From the first days of the school year, Kimberley had known that Mrs. Thorncliff would be of little help in her efforts to win acceptance and esteem.

In reading the notes, Mrs. Thorncliff not only violated Kimberley's assumptions about their impoverished relationship, but also about the authority of adults, and most pervasively about what Kimberley's took to be the classroom "normalcy."[9] "That teacher" no longer had the right to order her around as if she were her mother, for her mother would never be so insensitive to a child's requests, nor so blind to a child's concerns. Her mother's life is difficult, and she needs the help, and when she sends those notes they are for Kimberley alone, not for the entire class. But Mrs. Thorncliff is mean and insensitive. Maybe it was O.K. to read a note from home in front of the class when she was in school, but she didn't understand or even care what it was like to be young now. Far from a resource, Mrs. Thorncliff is now seen as a threat to Kimberley's most important identity projects and concerns.

Family normalcies and relationships, heavy with burdens of past days and years, thus infuse Kimberley's present reality in the classroom as she shapes her projects, living into what she is becoming, what she could be, what she should be. Kimberley is no exception: Human life is not lived in an isolated "present," but in a present that is at once past and future and spatially fluid. We recognize this multitude of perspectives in our own daily lives. Often in our inner conversations and explanations to others our "prospectives" are among the most salient of these perspectives, as we tell ourselves that we did or will do such-and-such "in order to" accomplish or gain this or that.

Teachers and students clearly know this in themselves and often can readily identify at least some of the perspectives that help shape their own moment-to-moment behavior. And often they know this in others, using the prospectives of

---

[9] For a discussion of normalcy in family and classroom, see Hansen, 1988.

their own everyday lives and their remembered pasts to interpret one another's behavior. This capacity flourishes in gifted teachers, and is often seen, in varying degrees, in students.

Over a half-century ago, George Herbert Mead explored the workings of this "specious present" in individual and social life. Although Mead's more general arguments have informed family research for decades, his ruminations on time and space—which underlie many of the constructions developed in *Mind, Self and Society*—have been little noted.

Their neglect by social researchers is not surprising. Abstract and obscure in argument, they are couched at a "cosmological" level of applicability in which human life is illuminated not only by the spatio-temporalities of other animals, but also those of plants and organic matter. When I confronted them as a graduate student some decades ago, I was disappointed. After *Mind, Self and Society* they appeared tedious and precious, and of little relevance to sociological theory. The problem, I now recognize was mine. Yet it was not mine alone, for my response reflected the prevailing problematics of social inquiry at that time, in which even Mead's duality of self and society (rather than a dualism) was only just admissible. Times and cultures change, however, and today Mead's explorations into the interplay of past, present and future in the continuity and change of living forms can be seen to be closely pertinent to our contemporary theories and research on the child in family and school.

Mead (1938) insisted that experience "always has a bit of the future in it" (p. 413), as well as the past:

> The temporal spread of the experience includes that which is later and that which is earlier, and there is determination in both directions. We call it a present, though some of the past and future is included within it. . . . The future comes in terms of the act, the past in terms of the field of the act. Where they merge in the process, we have the present. (pp. 339–340; 348)

The temporal spread of experience into the past—what we might call the "present past"—is a familiar theme in both family and school research and theories, such as those that trace the shaping influences of past relationships to self esteem, academic confidence, achievement motivation and classroom conduct. In these interfusions of past and present, however, human life tends to be portrayed as little more than responsive to the press of necessity, the endpoint of a causal series or complex of antecedent conditions in which the individual could not have done otherwise.

Yet even in the most extreme conditions of necessity—as when facing unavoidable death—human experience cannot escape the future. Mead (1938) writes:

> The necessity is one that comes from behind. That which has taken place falls into an order in which alternative possibilities play no part. . . And yet there remain

> these alternatives. . . . The inevitableness of death does not carry with it the determination that it will be a death of resignation, or protest, or triumph. Whatever is, is necessary; and whatever is, goes on into the future. (649–650)

The idea of a present future may appear somewhat unfamiliar, yet in a limited sense it is a commonplace of both statistical and interpretive efforts to predict conditions at one time with conditions identified at an earlier time. It is implicit in the hundreds of studies of aspiration and achievement motivation, and in analyses of short- and long-term trends in achievement scores. It is also familiar in discursive essays, such as Coleman's (1988) analysis of the deterioration of socialization within family and school in the context of societal transitions to a service-based economy. The sense of present futureness is less familiar in social and behavioral analyses, but it can be seen clearly in Allport's (1960) psychology of "becoming," in Vygotsky's vision of teaching to the child's emerging "zone of proximal development" (see Tharp & Gallimore, 1989).

In Mead's social philosophy, sensitive to the human capacities for language, abstraction, reflective thought and interpretation, as we shall see later, the interpenetrations of past, present and future grow far more subtle and complex than even Allport and Vygotsky represent. Long-past childhood nurturances and pleasures interplay with images, dreams and fears of what is going to be, what could be, resonating in the student's perception of the teacher's demands, encouragements and mannerisms, in ways that help constrain or compel the student's present response.

AGENCY AND DURÉE: BEYOND STRUCTURALISM AND SUBJECTIVISM

As we have seen, structural problematics and methodologies tend to underplay or ignore those qualities associated with human agency, such as intentionality, purposeful behavior, and self-reflexivity. Interpretive and hermeneutic problematics tend to reverse this bias, underplaying the shaping and constraining influences of power and rationality—of social structure and culture—as well as long-term historical process.

Recent decades have seen an increasing number of concerted efforts to move beyond this unrepentant dualism of objectivism and subjectivism. Notions abound of some kind of *dialectic* of empirical and interpretive methods. A few go even further, arguing that we must search for entirely new methods that have shaken free from the false dichotomy of objectivism and relativism (notably, see Richard Bernstein, 1983).

Many of these efforts turn to the day-to-day activities in families and/or schools to develop and demonstrate their emerging constructs. One of the earliest attempts was mounted by Basil Bernstein (1971) in England, who attempted to locate the pivotal issues of social theory in linguistic codings which were both constituted by and constitutive of social interactions.

Pierre Bourdieu, in France, touches directly on issues concerning family-school relations in his persistent attempt to rise beyond both the objectivist and the neo-structuralist problematics, particularly of those of Foucault. Bourdieu's concern for the interplay of objective knowledge and the legitimation of power has yielded, among many others, the concept of "cultural capital" (Bourdieu, 1977). The concept is familiar to many family-school researchers, who are also frequently advised that Bourdieu's problematic is insufficiently sensitive to the workings of individual purpose and rationality (Mehan, 1989).

As the hermeneutic insistence brings psychology into the realms of the social, it demands incorporation of ethnographic-like procedures into sociological analyses. As anthropologists move from distant villages into contemporary urban settings they also move toward sociological sensibilities. And emerging attention to the workings of temporality in both individual and social life undermines many of the distinctions that sociologists and historians have crafted to protect their own disciplinary identities.

History, too, is changing, as Abrams (1982) points out: "Social change is made by people doing new things. As the acknowledged masterpieces of the discipline of history become increasingly theoretically explicit . . . the unity of theoretical method between history and sociology becomes thereby steadily more obvious" (p. 300). Thus one of the best works recent works in the recent sociology of education is not the work of a sociologist but of a social historian, who refuses to be held captive by the traditional disciplinary distinctions.

Fass' *Outside In* (1989) ranges over the 20th century in analysis of the processes of educating "outsiders"—immigrants, Blacks, Catholics and women (Fass, 1989). But this is not history in its traditional sense, the rich but selective traditions of narrative history—with its attention to the settings and circumstances within which individual agents act and the intricate webbings of causal influence. Nor is it a history of *ad hoc* explanations based on individual agency, which resists appeal to structure and social theory.

But neither is Fass' work an analytical history which, much like structural sociology, places priority on causal influences that are beyond the actors involved. In emerging forms of historical inquiries represented by Fass, agency and structure interplay, much as they do in the structuration theories of Giddens. Thus, in discussing the education of immigrant children in New York City schools of the 30s and 40s, Fass (1989) traces the interplay:

> . . . between social definitions, school policies, and student experience to describe how the schools were re-created in the context of their pluralistic populations. But it was not schools alone that were changed. The changes in the schools and the

> effect they had on students altered the culture in general. In this sense, the transformation of the schools was not only the product of social change, but also affected the nature of Twentieth-century social life. (p. 6)[10]

Of modern social theorists, Anthony Giddens has dealt most systematically with problems of agency and time. His "structuration theory" has attracted considerable attention from both adherents and critics. Drawing on Goffman's dramaturgical constructs, it indirectly reflects many of Mead's seminal ideas, shaped over a half century earlier.[11] But where Mead—as have so many other intersubjective theorists—attempted to extrapolate his acute interpersonal theories to larger matters of social order and change (Mead, 1932, 1934, 1938), Giddens more self-consciously attempts to develop a theory that from its outset is sensitive to both the hermeneutical and the organizational qualities of human life.

Giddens (1987), in essence, takes the hermeneutical understanding an important step further, in his attention to the neglected problems of time and space. Like Mead and Heidegger, he questions the dominant Kantian conceptions of time as a flow of events running from past to present, and hence indivisible from space:

> When asked 'where' time comes from and 'where' it goes, most people in modern societies have no difficulty in either in thinking of time in a spatial manner, or in indicating its direction. Time is pictured as running along a line beginning behind the body and extending out in front. . . Such a picturing of time is surely associated with our typical view of history, which sees the past as 'behind' us and the future as 'in front.' . . . Those living in cultures in which tradition is a primary medium of organizing time experience do not seem to portray time in this way. (p. 143)

Giddens (1987) argues that we must think of time not as this sort of environment for the lapsing of events, but rather as "constitutive of forms of social activity. Space, then, might be understood as "the settings of interaction." Time is thus not simply linear; it is also "reversible": "Reversible time is time as

---

[10]Although the family does not come to central focus in Fass' (1989) analyses of schooling, it is implicit in the background:

> "Whatever else they have achieved, schools in the Twentieth century have succeeded in interposing between parents and their children, for longer and longer periods, they authority of a public and state-controlled agency. . . . While historians have recently been attracted to the belief that public life has been on the decline since the early nineteenth century, a close look at the schools would suggest an equally potent and parallel trend as more and more aspects of private life—and among them some of the most intimate—have increasingly become a matter of public and state interest. One of the most significant of these has been childhood, over which parental authority has been systematically eroded." (pp. 189–190)

[11]Not surprisingly, then, much of Gidden's thinking is compatible with Berger's forays into the social construction of reality (Berger, 1963; Berger & Luckman, 1966), which also draws heavily on Mead as well as phenomenology.

repetition, temporality as reproduction. . . . For however much a culture might be dominated by modes of strict time-regulation, day-to-day life remains geared to the repetition of events and activities" (p. 143–144). For Giddens (1984) three forms of temporality interlace in all moments of social life. One is the *durée* of day-to-day life, or the ordering of social activities—their structuration—through their repetition from day-to-day:

> The terms 'social reproduction,' 'recursiveness' and so on indicate the repetitive character of day-to-day life, the routines of which are formed in terms of the intersection of the passing (but continually returning) days and seasons. Daily life has a duration, a flow, but it does not lead anywhere; the very adjective 'day-to-day' and its synonyms indicate that time here is constituted only in repetition. (p. 35)

Although Giddens (1984) does not use the term it is clear that day-to-day durée is the structuration of the assumed "normalcy," discussed earlier. At every moment this durée intersects with the durée of the life span of the individual, which is experienced as irreversible time, an inevitable movement from birth to death. The durée of day-to-day life and the *durée* of the life span of the individual interweave with the third form of temporality in social life, the durée of institutions, in which patterns of continuity and change carry on "well beyond the life spans of any particular generation of individuals" (p. 35).

For Giddens (1987), this neglected element of social theory—durée, the temporal spread of experience—allows repair of the rift between objectivism and subjectivism, avoiding the presumption of causal priority in either social institutions or in subjectivite intention. The constitution of agents and structures are not two independent sets of phenomena, a dualism, but represent a "duality of structure." To understand this duality, however, it is necessary to move beyond the conceptions of "structure" that rest on visual analogies:

> English-speaking social scientists . . . see structural properties of institutions as the girders of a building, or the anatomy of a body. . . . If we conceive of structure in this fashion, it is not surprising that action appears to be limited by structural constraints . . . although it may be that within those limits—so one would have to presume—the agent is capable of acting freely. According to the notion of the duality of structure, by contrast, structure is not as such external to human action and it is not identified solely with constraint. Structure is both the medium and the outcome of the human activities which it recursively organizes. Institutions, or large-scale societies, have structure properties in virtue of the continuity actions of their component members. But those members of society are only able to carry out their day-to-day activities in virtue of their capability of instantiating those structural properties. (pp. 60–61)

Within a classroom, then, student and teacher interact within differential sanctions and structural constraints that reflect the continuing structurations of education and the larger political economy. Each experiences and understands these sanctions and constraints differently, and each finds in them differing enablements and possibilities. As they interact, each refers to their common involvements in those structures, at once employing and affirming languages and collective values. And in this, they are constrained and enabled by those structures, even as they help to reconstitute them.

Not long after the note incidents, Mrs. Thorncliff reported another instance of Kimberley's open defiance. Walking up to the teacher's desk, Kimberley told Mrs. Thorncliff that the assignment she had given the class had "confused everyone," because she had not explained it correctly. When the teacher asked why the others didn't speak up for themselves, Kimberley said, "I have to do this, because they are too scared of you. I'm the one who has to stand up for people in this room, because they are afraid of you." Mrs. Thorncliff then asked the class who was confused. No one responded, confirming her belief that Kimberley was simply being defiant. Kimberley confirms the story, insisting that the others were too scared to answer, yet she was clearly upset about the lack of support from those she was trying to help.

Kimberley's attack surprised the teacher. Mrs. Thorncliff sees the challenge to her authority as another instance of Kimberley's "resistance" to the demands for harder and better work. But in her focus on because of explanations, the teacher again fails to see that Kimberley's acts express more important concerns, and the teacher's new role in her projects. If the discredited teacher can not be used as a resource, she can serve as a foil in Kimberley's project to gain admired acceptance.

The teacher also fails to recognize how threatening the note incidents are for Kimberley. They have disrupted the day-to-day durée of Kimberley's classroom life, the assumed normalcy that had provided a coherent base for Kimberley's identity projects. They also threaten Kimberley's life-span durée, as her now incoherent day-to-day durée interweaves with the retrospective past and prospective future of her life course. When she was in 3rd and 4th grade it was O.K. to do such things as baby sit her brother and sister. Now she is more mature and, like her peers, needs more time for her own life, to nurture the beautiful young woman she is willing herself to become.

She sees herself on course toward college, career, and the full life that she knows so well from family dramas on TV. She admires her mother, and expects to have a career and a family, but not quite as her mother has done. She wants to go to the same prestigious university that her mother went through, but then on to a higher status career instead of just a job, and she will find a better husband and have a better family life. She sees her schooling as an all-but certain progression toward those life-course concerns, knowing that she must "do well" to get into college, but confident that she can rally whenever it is necessary. Thus this long-term project—the durée of her life-span—interweaves (though with a secondary importance) with her day-to-day life in the classroom, which is dominated by her concern for statusful acceptance.

Kimberley's challenge to the teacher also reveals that she knows a great deal about the structurations of her school. She has had first-hand experience with the administrative authority in her school, which she believes Mrs. Thorncliff has unfairly used against her. When students are late they are supposed to bring a written excuse from home. But Kimberley's mother leaves for work early, and Kimberley must get herself off to school. Mrs. Thorncliff knows this, yet she sends Kimberley to the vice-principal, knowing she'll get detention because she doesn't have the note from home.

Kimberley is aware of many other expressions of large-scale structurations in her day-to-day life, as well. She recognizes that she is caught in structural contradictions of home and school—a mother who must work, young children who need care, an insensitive and demanding teacher who controls grading, school rules that are written for traditional and intact families. She sees her mother's vulnerability in the working world, the stress of long hours, hears her complain about the burdens of responsibility with too little authority, her fears of losing her job, her constant worries about money and the future. And she knows that opportunities are opening for women, assumes that they will continue to expand, and believes that it will be easier for her than it was for her mother. But Kimberley does not yet fully recognize that within the structurations of schooling and the corporate workplace formal records and informal impressions and typifications persist across time and space, to open or delimit future possibilities.

Kimberley's mother shares many of these expectations for the future and her understandings of the durée of day-to-day life they share. Both Kimberley and her mother refer to her as a "latchkey kid." To Kimberley this means little more than that she must leave an empty house in the morning and return to its loneliness after her day in school. Her mother more clearly sees that this difficult arrangement is simply their best choice, given the realities of today's world. She knows the importance of parental support, and she believes that she is doing the best she can to help Kimberley gain from school what she will need in later life. She tries to help with homework whenever Kimberley asks, and she lets Kimberley know that she expects a lot from her. Often she tells her daughter how bright, mature, and beautiful she is, and that she can "be" anything in life she wants to be.

Her perception of the structural constraints, stresses, and enablements in each of their lives is more acute than Kimberley's, but she, too, shows only a vague understanding of the long-term sociocultural changes that are expressed in her life story, or in the routines and regularities of her day-to-day living. She feels fortunate that it is now possible for a single woman to support three children, yet worries that she can't do all she would like. Aware of Kimberley's difficulties with her teacher and her peers, she does "the best she can" to help her work through her pains and problems. But, in the durée of her own life span, she is not greatly concerned with Kimberley's day-to-day problems, for she remembers that she was "alot like that" as a child, too.

Thus we see three individuals—a dedicated and competent teacher, a knowledgeable and involved mother, and an intelligent and self-perceptive student—all working toward Kimberley's academic success in her 6th-grade year. But their actions, often insensitive or indifferent to one another's day-to-day and life span projects and concerns, and entwined within changing structures of social relations of which each is only partially aware, have the unintended consequence of resuming the "downward plunge" that Kimberley had pulled herself from the year before.

Whatever the accomplishments and shortfalls of Gidden's work to date, he has with unusual clarity and certainty shaken free from many of the preconceptions that are built not only into objectivist problematics, but into our cultural traditions. To those who are closely familiar with the life work of George Herbert Mead there is something basically familiar about Giddens' arguments, just as there is a basic familiarity to the subjective sensibility or the hermeneutic insistence.[12]

Mead's seminal influence on hermeneutic and interpretative problematics is clear. His constructs in *Mind, Self and Society*—demonstrating not only that self awareness and society are reflexively constituted, but also that reflexivity itself is constituted reflexively—are directly represented in a wide array of contemporary understandings of the social constitution of reality.[13] Although Giddens only occasional references Mead's basic ideas, his work resonates with Meadian themes. His conception of the duality of individual and order, in which each expresses and constrains the other, essentially elaborates and extends the basic arguments of *Mind, Self and Society*. Further, Giddens' focal concept of durée is anticipated in Mead's attention to the "temporal spread of experience."

Giddens has far more acutely attended the interfusions of this duality at the structural level, in the durée of institutions. There is a fundamental theme of critical importance in Mead, however, that is not yet seen in Giddens' work. The absence of this theme reflects another of the prevailing traditions of our culture that bear on the question of agency: an inattention to the *workings* of "the future." Here, then, is reason to return to Mead, for more than documentation of his seminal influence. For in this case, Mead's seminal contributions have yet to be incorporated into contemporary social and behavioral theory.

---

[12]Mead, like Weber, wrote before the hermeneutic insistence had become familiar part of social and behavior thought. Although the hermeneutic sensibility is evident throughout his writings, like Husserl, Mead is of interest on these points simply as a seminal influence on the more immediately relevant and complete work crafted by Heidegger.

[13]See, for notable examples, the eloquent works of Blumer (1969), Berger (1963; Berger & Luckman, 1966) and Goffman (1959, 1977), and the constant comparative methodologies of Strauss, Glaser, and Schatzman (Glaser & Strauss, 1967; Strauss, 1959).

AGENCY AND THE WORKINGS OF TIME

For Mead (1938), agency is inherent, as the individual lives into the future:

> The living being acts to reach a certain result in the future, the realization of its act. In this action it may be said to select its own time system and the space that this involves. It thus determines the world within which it lives. Its determination, however, is a selection, and a creation only in the sense of a reconstruction. (p. 417)

In this basic conception of "the act" we see the nub of what Giddens calls the "reproduction" of social forms, as well as the duality of structure and structuration. Mead (1938) detailed these ideas in collections of lecture notes and written "fragments," published in *The Philosophy of the Act* and *Philosophy of the Present*. In these, he identified three distinct modes in the actor's situated organization of past, present, and future. Each of the three differs from "necessity," described before, in their perceived "possibilities of conduct" (p. 649).

Although Mead's discussion is far more complex and abstract, these differences involve varying uncertainty in the organization of experience. In "necessity," as we have already seen, the given past seems to determines the present perception of future possibility, yet room is left for doubt. Thus a "giveness" of history—virtually a causal necessity—plays a part in human life, but even in this giveness there is a degree of uncertainty in the face of the future.

That uncertainty enlarges as the individual entertains alternate possibilities of conduct. The "distance" of the referent future makes a difference, however. In perceptive organization, the possibilities of the future are immediately present and recognizable. The act "awaits" only its selection from the familiar field of conduct provided by past experience—even though "the result is bound as a new experience to be different from what has occurred" (Mead, 1938, p. 415). Perceptive organization, then, essentially expresses Giddens' durée of day-to-day life, in which social activities are ordered "via their repetition" or "routine" qualities.

As the future grows more distant or uncertain "reflection" replaces perception. As in perceptive organization, the act awaits only a selection, but in reflective organization that selection is delayed. The future is in doubt, yet we maintain an "attitude of assurance" that the future will emerge from our more-or-less stable image of the past. Moving from one perspective to another, we speculate on the uncertain possibilities, we form hypotheses and plans. These anticipations of the future are grounded in the field provided by the "stable" past, and yet they simultaneously change that past. Mead (1938) asserts:

> . . . the world that we see about us extends before us in various futures, and answering to each there is a past which is in some respects different from any

> other. . . . The past is always necessary, but the past which is there is not necessary, i.e., is dependent upon the future which determines the present and its interpretation. (pp. 608; 616)

Still, we are undisturbed in our assurance that "the novel experiences that are coming will appear in a world that is relatively unchanged." We are able to form an abstract idea of the form the future will take, selecting from the field of alternatives provided by the past. Mead (1938) states:

> If we are to meet a new personage, or one whom we know under entirely new conditions, we find ourselves rehearsing the secure elements of that which is to take place. A certain social structure is given. Certain common standards and interests are involved. A certain common past experience belongs to all concerned. In terms of these given elements we construct a form which the coming interview must take. . . . But this form does not determine the content that will arise. The assurance with which we step into the future . . . is not a prevision of the unique experience that will appear. (pp. 417–417)[14]

Reflective organization thus leads to tendencies to act in ways selected from past experience, but controlled by an abstract future. The future thus does more than pull the individual toward desired possibilities, it becomes active in structuring the present. In the most profound sense, the present future is recognized as constitutive and potentially creative.

Although rare, some recent studies implicitly recognize the play of this present future in the complexities of present behavior. A notable example is Suarez-Orozco's (1988) study of Hispanic immigrant students from the war-torn countries of Central America. These youth somehow survive the vibrant and troubled inner-city schools, despite the many messages of discouragement and discrimination that plague Hispanic immigrants from rural areas. Suarez-Orozco, in a brilliant display of the possibilities of psychological anthropology, identifies the motivations of this persistence in the young immigrants' pursuit of their dreams of "being somebody," a dream that is fired by a desire to be worthy of the sacrifices made for them by their parents.

In Giddens' constructs, this dream presumably involves the durée of the life span—the youth envision themselves as successful young adults, while the working-class Lads in Willis' *Learning to Labour* (1977) see a future that is "flat," only "more of the same." For Giddens the life span is experienced as

---

[14]The separation of time and space, which is of central importance in Giddens' duality of structures, is also treated closely in this work. In reflection, as alternative possibilities appear, the future more clearly influences action. And the more distant these possibilities, the greater the spatial spread of their influence. Time is separated from space as the individual holds to temporally future possibilities as controlling influences on present conduct, and under some conditions the individual may experience a "timeless space."

irreversible time, moving from birth to death. But in Mead, the interfusions of past, present and future are more subtle. That dream is a present future in the day-to-day conduct of these youth, and the compelling pull of the dream reaches into and shapes their constructed past.[15]

Mead's third mode of organization arises when there is conflict between future-oriented tendencies to act in ways provided by the past. Action is inhibited, and past as well as future are in doubt. In animals this conflict of tendencies leads to random or displacement behaviors and, if the conflict is continuing and severe, to flight. Humans, however, attempt to resolve the conflict through formulating hypotheses or experiential perspectives that are consistent with the competing tendencies. In the process, "the act awaits not only a selection but also an organization of the field" (Mead, 1938, p. 351). The past, that is, must be rewritten, and when the field involves self-and-other relationships this means, in the most profound sense, that one's sense of self must be reestablished.

Mead did not pursue the implications of this mode in any systematic detail, but clearly they are profound. McHugh (1967), for example, has demonstrated the effects of continuing relativity, by giving subjects in a problem-solving situation random responses of agreement or denial. Some individuals eventually questioned the system itself, withdrawing from further participation. Others, continuing to accept the reality of the situation, moved from active coping to eventual psychological withdrawal, reporting feelings of powerlessness and normlessness.

The interplay of these forms of organizing past, present, and future in experience offers further possibilities for understanding the processes involved in both reproduction and change of individual and social forms. Both stability and change—structurations—are indicated in the interplaying processes of perceptive, reflective and relative modes. The relevance of this for curricula development, teaching and parenting is immediate and of considerable import.

The interplay suggests details in the interlacings of Giddens' constructs of the three forms of durée. It also suggests that Giddens and others who have responded to the hermeneutic insistence—emphasizing the centrality of repetition, routine and normalcy in the durée of day-to-day life—have yet to consider some of those very moments of living in which agency may be most actively exercised, and most constitutive of alternative structurations of both self and society.

---

[15]Another, more speculative display of this sensitivity to the interplay of past, present and future is McLeod's (1987) interpretation of the "Brothers," a Black gang who—in contrast to the predominantly White "Hallway Hangers"—held to visions of possibility despite the many discouragements of everyday living in inner-city communities and schools. Although McLeod's attention to family life was not as close as the rest of his study (a lapse which, with hindsight, he regretted), his data point to the importance of past and present parental controls, expectations and aspirations. He speculates that these influences interplayed with the historical moment, in which the future of Blacks in America appeared (at least to the Brothers) to have abruptly changed. The apparent successes of the Civil Rights Movement and of affirmative action allowed them the hope that the opportunities denied their parents (and which their parents urged them toward) would in fact be open to them.

To Mrs. Thorncliff, Kimberley's insistence that she really wants to learn is contradicted by her performance. Not only does she neglect her homework, even in class she lacks focus and drive, evading her assignments. Her 5th-grade teacher, Mrs. Sobol, had seen the same thing: "She'll sit and look at a plain sheet of paper for half and hour, and then she'll raise her hand and say 'I need a book' [or something like that]. And then she'll sit for another half and hour. [And when I finally look at her work] she's written two sentences in two days!" But Mrs. Sobol also saw something that Mrs. Thorncliff missed: that Kimberley's performance expresses a desperation and helplessness that is closely tied to her home life.

In Mead's terms, Kimberley's experiences of her world are conducted to an unusual degree through "relativity" modes of processing, in which sense of self and world are ever in doubt. She struggles to establish and maintain emergent understandings, in which the present uncertainties dissolve into the comfort of a familiar and valued past that is flowing into a desired future. But as her efforts to find admiration and acceptance in the eyes of others are once more frustrated, her attention again rivets on the apparent contradictions of the present situation.

As we came to know Kimberley, we learned more about the many ways she carries her family into the classroom, and the ways she takes her life in school home with her. For Kimberley's mind, emotions, and judgments—her self—are rarely in only one time and place. When asked for an example of being humiliated in class, she shifts focus to her family, complaining that they laugh at her when she makes a mistake, even in games like Trivia. Kimberley is being hurried into assuming the parent surrogate figure, replacing a working mother and an ambivalent father figure in the care and control of her younger brothers. Her mother knows it is hard for Kimberley to take on so much responsibility for the home, usually caring for the younger children until early evening, often cooking dinner, almost always making her own breakfast, helping with the cleaning. And the mother knows how hard the divorce situation has been on all of them, especially while she's been trying to work through the possibilities of another marriage. But she is proud of Kimberley at the same time, knowing that many 11-year-olds would be unable to do what Kimberley does, especially without getting into some kind of trouble.

When Kimberley was on her "downward plunge" in 5th grade, her teacher reported that "She's always on the edge of tears," and told us of a talk they had had a day before:

> She doesn't feel that she deserves anything, and her mom is wonderful and great and does everything she should do. When I asked her, "Does she love you," she said "Yeah," and I said "Does she love you alot?", and she said "I don't know." I said, "Does she tell you that she loves you?" She said, "No, not very often." . . . "How does she show you [that she loves you]?" And then she started to cry, and

she said "When I bring my good work home she always says the exact same thing, "Real nice, good work Sweetie."

At home and in the classroom, every interaction is a potential confirmation and a potential threat to her emerging awareness of self-and-other and her understandings of a sensible world, and she searches urgently to make sense once again of her self and her world. She frets over real and imagined slights, redefines the meanings of past interchanges and relationships, reconstructs images of what she is becoming and might become, revises lists of friends and enemies, shapes plans to repair the damage the teacher or a spiteful classmate has done.

Rather than evading her lessons, then, Kimberley is "actively dissembling" (cf. Hansen, 1989): accepting their importance and acting as if she is doing them, at times even half-way convincing herself that she is doing them, frustrated at her inability to resolve the turmoil within so she can turn to the tasks in front of her. However much she wants to learn and to do the assigned tasks, at times she cannot maintain focus as she struggles once again to reestablish coherence. It is as if she is on trial, never quite certain of what she has done or hasn't done, tacitly aware that she herself is helping to make the indictments against herself, searching, at times frantically, for evidence that she is a better and more complete person than she "knows" herself to be deep down. And in all this, agency is inherent as she struggles to make sense of this classroom and to protect her self from further injuries.

CONCLUSION: ITEMS FOR THE RESEARCH AGENDA

The spatio-temporal interfusions of family and school in the life of the child strain our methods of family research and theory in three directions simultaneously. In one direction, we realize the limits of our current conceptualizations of the child as an active agent in the practical everyday living of organized society. In the second, we recognize the limits of our conceptualizations of the ways sociocultural structures and processes shape and are shaped by everyday living, as well as extraordinary events. In the third, we realize the limits of our conceptualizations of the child's intersubjective "realities," as unique expressions of a specific socio-historical time, in which past, present, and future fluidly interpenetrate and alter one another.

The special tensions of the child/student today offer rich possibilities for exploring those limits, enlivening our understandings of the interpenetrations of multiple constituted orders in everyday living. Every family member is involved in these interpenetrating orders—corporations, service settings, schools, families and churches, to name only a few—which compete for the individual's energies, attentions, and loyalties. The tensions experienced by the child/student are particularly compelling, however, for they are exceptionally intense and volatile.

In particular, compared to young and middle-aged adults, the child/student experiences relatively dramatic and abrupt developmental changes within researchable spans of time, negotiating often intense and volatile changes in family and peer involvements, generally in a gradual but undulating movement from family and toward peers. The individual and family tensions of these changes may reveal intra- and interpersonal qualities normally hidden from the researcher. Further, the striking variations, from child to child and family to family, present opportunities for comparative inquiry, linking individual, interpersonal, and situational variables, again within researchable spans of time.

Further, the child articulates these developmental, familial, and peer dynamics within an exceptionally demanding and constraining organization. The demands and constraints of the school—imposed with and largely justified through an implicit appeal to the child/student's "future"—are more severe than most organizations in which other family members are involved, and they involve broader ranges of the child/student's current and anticipated activities and relationships. And all this takes place within a context of inconsistencies, tensions, ambiguities, and elusive possibilities—not only within the school organization, but also in its inter-institutional relations with the rapidly changing worlds of family, work, and popular culture.

As we open our research and theory to the many facets of childhood agency, we run into confusion and ambiguity in the concept of agency itself. The term invariably interlinks intention, action, and consequence, but its various usages differ strikingly in focus and implications. Its most general and popular use is in reference to the "shakers and movers" in social and programatic change. Here the distinguishing quality of agency is efficacy: The agent is one who is able to achieve intended outcomes.[16] Thus, the student activism on American campuses in the 60s and the massive resistance of Chinese students in Tinneman Square in the 80's both lacked the necessary "agency" to win the sweeping social and cultural transformations that were envisioned.

This confounding of human agency with efficacy invites the conclusion that agency is but an illusion. Individuals and collective movements appear unable to resist, much less direct, the relentless structurings of power. Further, intentional action invariably precipitates unintended consequences, as was seen when the student activism in the early 60s helped entrench the power of Ronald Reagan. The intentional effort to change unleashes unanticipated consequences that eclipse even the greatest intended outcomes. In this usage, then, the agency of

---

[16]Similarly, the failure of radical visions of education in the 70's has been laid by one of its leading theorists to the naive belief that enlightened and self-selected teachers could be the agents of change, with scant regard given the organizational and cultural constraints that they faced (cf. Young, 1988).

the child in family and classroom is of only periodic interest, for the child's efficacy is severely delimited by the ideologies and structures of adult domination. Expressions of intention and purpose tend to take the form of resistance, rebellion, and willful negotiation from a disadvantaged position, and even successful demands are gained only at considerable cost.

In more subjective usages, by contrast, the concept of agency centers on human purpose, intrasubjective intentions, goals, and plans, with the understanding that these plans may be imperfectly expressed in action, or even suppressed by situational constraints. Essentially reversing the delimitations of those that focus on efficacy, these usages minimize the problem of unintended consequences, in essence assuming that they are the result of suppressed, conflicting, or inadequately conceived or coordinated plans. In this usage, the powerless child in the family or classroom may be seen as an agent even though the agency is never expressed in action. Again the question of agency appears trivial, fixing attention on intrapsychic phenomena and correspondingly neglecting familial and classroom and relationships.

In this chapter, by contrast, the term agency centers in *doing,* in situated, self-aware, and reflective activity. Focus is not on intention or outcome, but rather on self-referenced acting. Max Weber clearly established the distinction between intentional "action" and "behavior"—the nonintentional, conforming response to the constraints and enablements of the situation. To be sure, this conception of behavior is valid for a great deal of day-to-day activity, which contributes to the maintenance and reproduction of established relationships and structures. But the distinction between the agency of change and behavioral conformity ignores a great deal of our day-to-day activity in which intentional and self-aware actors strive to maintain and renew their constitutional orders and their place within them.

In short, to deal with the child in family and school—or more generally with the interpenetrations of family life with other constituted orders—we must attempt to see individuals as at times intentional, self-aware agents of change, at other times as nonintentional, "drifting," and compliant, and at others as self-aware participants of established routine and order. And we must attempt to recognize how they are rarely if ever in only one time and place. Fluidly changing pasts and futures interplay in the child's classroom life, and so do families, TV dramas, playgrounds, and multiple other real and fantasized places and relationships. We must go beyond the immediate time and place of any situation—family, classroom, playground, or Saturday night party—if we are to fully study the child and to recognize the possibilities of agency in that child-in-structuration.

In this effort, we will find both resources and constraints in the theories and methodologies that inform family and school research. For the child that we confront in the classroom, in the families we study, or in our own homes, is far more vibrant and complex than the neglected child of our academic disciplines.

In the most general terms, what is required is that in our research we accord the growing child the full measure of humanity we recognize, tacitly as well as rationally, in ourselves. This also demands that we attend more closely to the ways our own sense of self and possibilities is shaped and constrained by the language we use, the "problematics" we accept, and the culture we endorse, as well as the organizations and structures in which we act. And it demands that we confront the interfusions of our own everyday activity, sociohistorical structurings, and intersubjective/cultural processes.

In research and theory that today stretch the traditions of their disciplines, we see diverse searchings for new methods of inquiry that are more adequate to the complexities of contemporary life. And at the center of these searching—the core that gives the study of families and schools its meaning—is Kimberley, the societal individual. From structural perspectives—including the role theories that pervade family research—she is both a victim and an achievement of her times, her family, her schooling, a reasonably functioning and conforming member of society, as it is expressed in her home and classroom. These structural perspectives have many important things to say about Kimberley. But there is more to say—about the ways the social construction of meanings and normalcies interfuse with the workings of time and place in individual and institutional life, linking Kimberley not only to the constraints and enablements of structure but also to its constituting structurations. When we find workable ways to say these things, we will see future Kimberley's quite differently, as unique sociohistorical expressions, as captives of routine and defenders of everyday normalcies, and as intentional, concerned, constitutive selves for whom many worlds are possible.

REFERENCES

Abrams, P. (1982). *Historical sociology*. Ithaca, NY: Cornell University Press.

Allport, G. (1960). The open system in personality theory. *Journal of Abnormal Social Psychology, 61*, 301–310.

Berger, P. L. (1963). *Invitation to sociology*. Garden City, NJ: Doubleday-Anchor.

Berger, P. L., & Luckman, T. (1966). *The social construction of reality: A treatise in the sociology of knowledge*. New York: Doubleday.

Bernstein, B. (1971). *Class, codes and control*. London: Routledge & Kegan Paul.

Bernstein, R. J. (1983). *Beyond objectivism and relativism: Science, hermeneutics, and praxis*. Philadelphia: University of Pennsylvania Press.

Blumer, H. (1969). *Symbolic interaction: Perspective and method*. Englewood Cliffs, NJ: Prentice-Hall.

Bourdieu, P. (1977). *Outline of a theory of practice*. Cambridge, England: Cambridge University Press.

Bowles, S., & Gintis, H. (1976). *Schooling in capitalist America: Educational reform and the contradictions of economic life*. New York: Basic Books.

Bruner, J. (1986). *Actual minds, possible worlds*. Cambridge, MA: Harvard University Press.

Coleman, J. (1988). Families and schools. *Educational Researcher, 16*(6), 32–38.
Covington, M. (1983). Strategic thinking and the fear of failure. In S. F. Chipman, J. Segal, & R. Glaser (Eds.), *Thinking and learning skills: Current research and open questions, Vol. 2.* Hillsdale, NJ: Lawrence Erlbaum Associates.
Fass, P. (1989). *Outside in: Minorities and the transformation of American education.* New York: Oxford University Press.
Fish, S. (1979). Normal circumstances, literal language, direct speech acts, the ordinary, the everyday, the obvious, what goes without saying, and other special cases. In P. Rabinow, & W. Sullivan (Eds.), *Interpretive social science: A reader.* Berkeley: University of California Press.
Giddens, A. (1984). *The constitution of society: Outline of the theory of structuration.* Berkeley: University of California Press.
Giddens, A. (1987). *Social theory and modern socioloty.* Stanford, CA: Stanford University Press.
Glaser, B., & Strauss, A. (1967). *The discovery of grounded theory.* Chicago: Aldine.
Goffman, E. (1959). *The presentation of self in everyday life.* Garden City, NJ: Doubleday-Anchor.
Goffman, E. (1975). On face-work: An analysis of ritual elements in social interaction. In A. Lindesmith, A. Strauss, & N. Denzin (Eds.), *Readings in social psychology.* Hinsdale, IL: Dryden Press.
Haan, N. (1977). *Coping and defending: Processes of self-environment organization.* New York: Academic Press.
Hansen, D. A. (1988). Schooling, stress and family development: Rethinking the social role metaphor. In J. Aldous & D. Klein (Eds.), *Social stress and family development.* New York: Guilford Press.
Hansen, D. A. (1989). Lesson evading and lesson dissembling: Ego strategies in the classroom. *American Journal of Education, 97,* 184–208.
Heidegger, M. (1927). *Being and time.* New York: Harper and Row.
Hughes, H. S. (1958). *Consciousness and society.* New York: Vintage Press.
Johnson, R. (1979). *Three problematics: Elements of a theory of working class culture.* London: Hutchinson.
MacIntyre, A. (1984). *After virtue: A study in moral theory.* Notre Dame, IN: University of Notre Dame Press.
McHugh, P. (1967). *Defining the situation.* Indianapolis: Bobbs-Merrill.
McLeod, J. (1987). *Ain't no makin' it: Leveled aspiration in a low-income neighborhood.* Boulder, CO: Westview Press.
Mead, G. H. (1932). *Philosophy of the present.* Chicago: University of Chicago Press.
Mead, G. H. (1934). *Mind, self and society.* Chicago: University of Chicago Press.
Mead, G. H. (1938). *The philosophy of the act.* Chicago: University of Chicago Press.
Mehan, H. (1989). *Understanding equality in schools: The contribution of interpretive studies.* Meetings of the American Sociological Association, San Francisco.
Mills, C. W. (1959). *The sociological imagination.* New York: Oxford University Press.
Packer, M. J., & Scott, B. (1992). The hermeneutic investigation of peer relations. In T. Winegar & J. Vaalsiner (Eds.), *Social development in context.* Hillsdale, NJ: Lawrence Erlbaum Associates.
Parsons, T. (1951). *The social system.* New York: The Free Press.
Parsons, T. (1959). The school class as a social system: Some of its functions in American society. *Harvard Educational Review, 29*(4), 297–318.
Parsons, T. (1971). *The system of modern societies.* Englewood Cliffs, NJ: Prentice-Hall.
Parsons, T., & Bales, R. (1955). *Family, socialization and interaction process.* Glencoe, IL: The Free Press.
Rueda, R., & Mehan, H. (1986). Metacognition and passing strategic interactions in the lives of students with learning disabilities. *Anthropology and Education Quarterly, 17,* 75–82.
Strauss, A. (1959). *Mirrors and masks.* New York: The Free Press.

Suarez-Orozco, M. (1988). *Central American refugees and U.S. high schools*. Stanford, CA: Stanford University Press.

Tharp, R., & Gallimore, R. (1989). *Rousing minds to life*. New York: Cambridge University Press.

Weinstein, R. (1985). Student mediation of classroom expectancy effects. In J. B. Dusek (Ed.), *Teacher expectancies*. Hillsdale, NJ: Lawrence Erlbaum Associates.

Willis, P. (1977). *Learning to labour*. New York: Columbia University Press.

4 Conscripting Kin: Reflections on Family, Generation, and Culture

Linda M. Burton*
The Pennsylvania State University

Carol B. Stack
University of California, Berkeley

People do not necessarily do what they are supposed to do for kin, but they know what they are supposed to do, when they should do it, and that kin will summon them to do family labor. This chapter presents a framework for examining how families as multigeneration collectives, and individuals embedded within them work out family responsibilities. We introduce kinscripts, a framework representing the interplay of family ideology, norms, and behaviors over the life span. Kinscripts encompasses three culturally defined family domains: kin-work, which is the labor and the tasks that families need to accomplish to survive from generation to generation; kin-time, which is the temporal and sequential ordering of family transitions; and, kinscription, which is the process of assigning kin-work to family members.

The kinscripts framework is derived in part from the family life course perspective (Aldous, 1990; Elder, 1987; Hagestad, 1990; Hareven, 1982, 1986), studies of kinship (Aschenbrenner, 1975; Di Leonardo, 1986, Hinnant, 1986; Stack, 1974), and literature on family scripts (Byng-Hall, 1985, 1988; Steiner, 1974). The principal basis of kinscripts, however, is our ethnographic research conducted between 1968 and 1990 with urban and rural, low-income, multigenerational, Black, extended families in the northeast, southeast, and mid-west portions of the United States. Case history data on families involved in these ethnographic studies are used to illuminate components of the kinscripts framework where appropriate.

The kinscripts framework was developed to organize and interpret qualitative observations of (a) the temporal and interdependent dimensions of family role

---

transitions; (b) the creation and intergenerational transmission of family norms; and (c) the dynamics of negotiation, exchange, and conflict within families as they construct the life course. This framework is based on the premise that families have their own agendas, their own interpretation of cultural norms, and their own histories (Hagestad, 1986a; Reiss & Oliveri, 1983; Tilly, 1987). Families assist individual members in constructing their personal life courses, but in the process, families as collectives, create an agenda of their own (Watkins, 1980).

The kinscripts framework can be applied across race, ethnicity, social class, and to the range of family forms existing in contemporary American society. Typically, the conceptual frameworks used to interpret the life course of kin are derived from explorations involving White, middle class families. Kinscripts, in contrast, is an example of a framework that is derived from the study of low-income Black families but offers insights for study of mainstream families as well.

KINSCRIPTS

Family Scripts

The concept of scripts as used in the family therapy literature is an integral part of the kinscripts framework. Family scripts prescribe patterns of family interaction (Byng-Hall, 1988; Ferreira, 1963). They are mental representations that guide the role performances of family members within and across contexts.

The kinscripts framework extends the notion of scripts to the study of the family life course. Specifically, kinscripts focuses on the tensions that are produced and negotiated between individuals in families in response to scripts. These dynamics are discussed in context of three culturally defined, family domains: kin-work, kin-time, and kinscription.

Kin-work

Kin-work is the collective labor expected of family-centered networks across households and within them (Di Leonardo, 1986). It defines the work that families need to accomplish to endure over time. The family life course is constructed and maintained through kin-work. Kin-work regenerates families, maintains lifetime continuities, sustains intergenerational responsibilities, and reinforces shared values. It encompasses, for example, all of the following: family labor for reproduction; intergenerational care for children or dependents; economic survival including wage and nonwage labor; family migration and migratory labor designated to send home remittances; and strategic support for networks of kin extending across regions, state lines, and nations.

Kin-work is distributed in families among men, women, and children. Samuel Jenkins, a 76-year-old widower in Gospel Hill, provided his own interpretation of kin-work. After Samuel's oldest daughter died, his granddaughter, Elaine, moved in with him along with her three children, a 6-month-old baby, a 2-year-old and a 3-year-old. Samuel is raising these children. Elaine, he says, is running the streets and not providing care. When asked why he is parenting his grandchildren, he said:

> There ain't no other way. I have to raise these babies, else the service people will take em away. This is my family. Family has to take care of family else we won't be no more.

Janice Perry, a 13-year-old pregnant woman from Gospel Hill, described her rather unique kin-work assignment. Her contribution to the family, as she understood it, was through reproduction. She states:

> I'm not having this baby for myself. The baby's grandmother wants to be a "mama" and my great-grandfather wants to see a grandchild before he goes blind from sugar. I'm just giving them something to make them happy.

Janice's mother, Helen, comments further:

> I want this baby. I want it bad. I need it. I need to raise a child. That's my job now. My mama did it. It's my turn now.

Samuel Jenkins, Janice Perry, and Helen Perry have clear notions of kin-work within families. While their individual family circumstances are different, kin-work for each one of them is tied to providing care across generations and maintaining family traditions and continuity.

Kin-work is the consequence of culturally constructed family obligations defined by economic, social, physical, and psychological family needs. Henry Evans, a 38-year-old resident of New Town (Burton & Jarrett, 1991), a northeastern Black community, provided a very clear profile of his assigned kin-work. He noted that his kin-work emerged from the physical and psychological needs of his family members. Henry was the only surviving son in his family. His mother had given birth to 11 other sons all of whom were stillborn or died shortly after birth. At the time of his interview, Henry was providing care for his father, who had recently suffered a heart attack, his 36-year-old sister who was suffering from a chronic neuromuscular disease, and his 40-year-old sister and her four children. When asked about his family duties, he remarked:

> I was designated by my family as a child to provide care for all my family members. My duties read just like a job description. The job description says the

> following: (a) you will never marry; (b) you will have no children of your own; (c) you will take care of your sisters, their children, your mother and your father in old age; and (d) you will be happy doing it.

Henry went on to discuss how his commitment to the family life course took precedence over his personal life goals:

> Someone in my family must be at the helm. Someone has to be there to make sure that the next generation has a start. Right now, we are a family of co-dependents. We need each other. As individuals, my sisters and father are too weak to stand alone. I could never bring a wife into this. I don't have time. Maybe when the next generation (his sister's kids) is stronger, no one will have to do my job. We will redefine destiny.

The life situation of Henry Evans is not an unfamiliar one. Hareven (1982) in a detailed historical analysis of families who worked for the Amoskeag Company in Manchester, New Hampshire provides poignant examples of how, for many individuals, the demands of kin-work superceded personal goals (Hareven & Langenbach, 1978). Comparable evidence is noted in Plath's (1980) indepth interview study of contemporary Japanese families. In each cultural context, across historical time, kin-work was described as self-sacrificing hard work—work designed to insure the survival of the collective.

Kin-time

Kin-time represents the temporal scripts of families. It is the shared understanding among family members of when and in what sequence role transitions and kin-work should occur. Kin-time encompasses family norms concerning the timing of such transitions as marriage, childbearing, and grandparenthood. It includes temporal guides for the assumption of family leadership roles and caregiving responsibilities. The temporal and sequencing norms of kin-time are constructed in the context of family culture. Consequently, for some families, these norms may not be synonymous with the schedules of family life course events inferred from patterns assumed to exist in larger society.

Stack's (in press) ethnographic study of the migration of Black families to and from the rural south provides an example of the relationship between kin-time and kin-work. Two aspects of kin-work are highlighted—reproduction and migration. The timing and sequencing of reproduction and migration is such that young adults first have children and then migrate to the North to secure jobs and send money back home. Their young children are left behind in the South to be reared by grandparents or older aunts and uncles. After an extended period of time, the migrating adults return to the South and for some, their new young-adult children repeat the cycle—they bear children and migrate North.

The temporal sequencing of reproduction and migration in these families reflects a scripted family life course involving cooperative action among kin. Family members must be willing to assume economic and childcare responsibilities according to schedule. Individuals in families, however do not always adhere to kin-time. A young adult may chose not to migrate, another may leave home but fail to send remittances, and yet others may return home sooner than expected. These individuals are considered insurgent by kin and may create unexpected burdens that challenge family resilience.

Kin-time also demarcates rites of passage or milestones within families, including the handing down of familial power and tasks following the death of family elders. For example, in the Appalachian mountains in southeastern United States, older women proclaim those few years after the death of their husbands, when they alone own the family land, as the time they have the most power in their families. The grown children and nearby community members observe, in a timely fashion, the activities of these elderly rural women. It was still common lore in the 1980s that the year these older widowed women announced plans for planting their last garden is the last year of their life. That year kin vie for their inheritances. Thus, the life course of families, which involves a scripted cycle of the relegation of power through land ownership, continues to unfold.

Kin-scription

It is important to understand how power is brought into play within the context of kin-time and kin-work. The question this raises is summed up in the tension reflected in kin-scription. Rather than accept the attempts of individuals to set their own personal agendas, families are continually rounding up, summoning, or recruiting individuals for kin-work. Some kin, namely women and children, are easily recruited. The importance women place on maintaining kin ties and fostering family continuity has been assiduously documented (Dressel & Clark, 1990; Gilligan, 1982; Hagestad, 1989b). Placing preeminent emphasis on kin-keeping—the undertakings necessary to keep kin connected and family traditions transmitted—women often find it difficult to refuse kin demands.

The life course of a young woman, Yvonne Carter, who lives in Gospel Hill, offers an example of the interplay of power, kin-scription, and the role of women. When Yvonne's first love died 14 years ago, she was 21. At 35, she recounted how the years had unfolded:

> When Charlie died, it seemed like everyone said since she's not getting married, we have to keep her busy. Before I knew it, I was raising kids, giving homes to long lost kin, and even helping the friends of my mother. Between doing all of this, I didn't have time to find another man. I bet they wouldn't want me and all my relatives anyway.

How relatives collude to keep particular individuals wedded to family needs: a chosen daughter in Japan (Plath, 1980), a chosen son in rural Ireland (Scheper-Hughes, 1979), confirm Yvonne Carter's suspicion—she has been recruited for specific kin-work in her family.

Recruitment for kin-work is one dimension of power in kin-scription. Exclusion from kin-work is another, as this profile of Paul Thomas, a 36-year-old resident of Gospel Hill illustrates.

Paul Thomas, down on his luck, out of sorts with his girlfriend, and oldest of 7 children had just moved back into his mother Mattie's home when he was interviewed. Eleven of Mattie's family members live in her two-bedroom apartment. The family members include Paul's two younger brothers, one who returned home from the service and moved in with his new wife and child, an unmarried sister, a sister and her child, and a pregnant sister with her two children. Paul reported finding his move back home, the result of repeated unemployment, particularly difficult under these living conditions.

After Paul moved back home, Mattie characterized Paul's history within the family as follows:

> Paul left this family when he was thirteen. I don't mean leave, like go away, but leave, like only do the things he wanted to do, but not pay attention to what me or his brothers and sisters wanted or needed. He took and took, and we gave and gave all the time. We never made him give nothing back.

In Mattie's view, her son Paul abandoned the family early on, claiming rights, but not assuming responsibilities. On a later visit to Mattie's apartment, family members gathered in the living room were asked a rather general question about doing things for kin. Paul stood up to speak. Addressing the question, with anger and entitlement in his voice, he said:

> I come back only for a little while. I am the outsider in the family. The black sheep. I belong, but I don't belong. Do you understand what I mean? I am only important because my mother can say, I have a son, and my sisters can say, I have a brother. But it doesn't mean anything. I can't do anything around here. I don't do anything. No one makes me. My sisters know what they have to do. They always have. They know their place! Now that I'm getting old I've been thinking that someway I'll make my place here. I want Ann (his sister) to name her baby after me. I'm begging you Ann. Give this family something to remember that I'm part of it too.

Renegade relatives such as Paul attest to subtle dynamics that challenge their places within families. These relatives may inadvertently play havoc with family processes while simultaneously attempting to attach themselves to family legacies.

When kin act out or resist procedures to be kept in line, families have been known to use heavy-handed pressures to recruit individuals to do kin-work.

However, kin may be well aware that family demands criss-cross and that it is impossible for the individual summoned to do kin-work to satisfy everyone. In particular, those family members assigned to do kin-work cannot be in two places at once. Adults, and even children under such circumstances, may be left to choose between conflicting demands. Stack's study of family responsibilities assumed by children in the rural, southeastern community of New Jericho, provides an example of competing demands placed on adolescents as they are recruited for family tasks.

In New Jericho, multiple expectations are transmitted to children whose parents migrated from the rural south to the northeast. It is not unusual for adolescents, skilled at child-care and other domestic activities, to be pulled in a tug-of-war between family households in the North and South. Kin at both locations actively recruit adolescents to move with them or join their households. Parents in the North, and grandparents in the South are the main contenders. Children find themselves deeply caught in a web of family obligations. At 11 years-of-age, Jimmy Williams was asked to move to Brooklyn to help his parents with their new baby. But, his grandmother needed his help in rural North Carolina. Jimmy responded by saying:

> I think I should stay with the one that needs my help the most. My grandmother is unable to do for herself, and I should stay with her and let my mother come to see me.

In this example, Jimmy was conscripted by two households within the family network. The decision Jimmy made to remain with his grandmother punctuates the leeway given to children to make judgments in the context of personal and family interests. In a similar situation young Sarah Boyce said:

> I'll talk to my parents and try to get them to understand that my grandparents cannot get around like they used to. I want to make an agreement to let my brother go to New York and go to school, and I'll go to school down here. In the summer, I will go and be with my parents, and my brother can come down home.

Children are conscripted to perform certain kin tasks that are tied to the survival of families as a whole. Definitions of these tasks are transmitted through direct and indirect cues from family members. Jimmy and Sarah responded to the needs of kin, taking advantage of the flexibility available to them in negotiating the tasks. That same flexibility is not always available for adults. The life situation of Sandra Smith provides an example.

Sandra Smith, married and a mother, found herself pressed between the demands of kin in her family of origin and her in-laws in Gospel Hill. She states:

> I'm always the one everybody comes to take care of children. My mother expects me to raise my sister's three kids. My mother-in-law calls upon me to mind my

> nieces and nephews while she takes it easy. She expects me to kiss her feet. I won't do it, none of it, everybody can go to hell.

Sandra, in fact, did refuse to kin-work. When asked what impact her choice would have on her situation in the family, she said:

> It means I won't have nobody. But so what, they need me more than I need them.

Pressed between opposing sets of demands and resentments that build up over the years, refusal to do kin-work is a choice some individuals opt for. Refusal, however, may be costly, particularly for those individuals who are dependent on the economic and emotional resources of kin.

DISCUSSION

The examples of kin-work, kin-time, and kin-scription provided in this discussion are drawn primarily from our ethnographic studies of low-income, multigenerational Black families. The examples illuminate extraordinary situations of individuals embedded in families that have scripted life courses. All families, unlike those described here, do not have such well-defined family guidelines. The family guidelines that exist for those who live in Gospel Hill, New Jericho, and New Town emerge out of extreme economic need and an intense commitment by family members to the survival of future generations.

The kinscripts framework is useful for exploring the life course of the families highlighted in this discussion, but it can also be applied to families that construct their life course under different circumstances. Kinscripts is particularly suited to exploring the effects that certain individuals within families have on the life course of kin. In all families across racial, ethnic, and socioeconomic groups there are individuals who cannot be counted on to carry out kin tasks; who leave the family fold for reasons of personal survival; who remain as dependent insiders within families making excessive emotional and economic demands on family members; and who return to the bosom of kin because of personal experiences such as unemployment, homelessness, divorce, or widowhood. From each angle, and in a diversity of family systems, the life course of kin through kin-work, kin-time, and kin-scription are affected by the personal agendas of family members.

Consider, for example, how the kinscripts framework might be used in exploring the life course of a kin network in which one of its members is experiencing divorce. Divorce is a fairly common experience in mainstream American families (Anspach, 1976; Hagestad & Smyer, 1982; Norton & Moorman, 1987). Under such circumstances, an adult child with dependent children may return to the home of his or her parents. The return home may put the scripted life course of kin in disarray, necessitating that collective family notions of kin-work, kin-time, and kin-scription be reconstructed. In terms of kin-work, grandparents, who, in the past may have assumed a less active role in the rearing of their grandchildren, may now be expected to take on a more formal surrogate parent role (Johnson, 1988). With respect to kin-time, family members may delay certain transitions in response to the divorce. For example, an older parent might put off retirement for a few years to generate enough income to help their adult child reestablish themselves financially. Kin-scription may also be revised. The adult child experiencing the divorce may have been the family kin-keeper—that is, the person in the family charged with organizing family reunions, documenting family history, and negotiating conflicts between relatives. Given the change in this kin-keeper's life course, these duties may have to be reassigned to another family member.

Kinscripts can also be applied to explorations of the relationship between broader social conditions, unemployment, and the life course of kin. Under ideal conditions, unemployed family members are absorbed by kin as best they can. Given severe socio-economic conditions, however, tensions between individual needs and kin-work, kin-time, and kin-scription may emerge. Again, the family life course may have to be redesigned. For example, low-income families attempting to absorb down and out kin members, or homeless mothers and children, find that sometimes in the face of economic cutbacks and emotional crisis they must, however reluctantly, "let go" of family members who cannot pull their weight. When public welfare support decreased in the 1980s, it produced a remarkable increase in families with these experiences. Stressful economic conditions decrease both individuals' and families' ability to perform effectively. Certain economic and political changes can disrupt kin-time delaying family milestones such as childbearing and adding complexity to family timetables, and inhibit kin-work and kin-scription, thereby increasing tensions between the individual and family life course. The kinscripts framework, drawing on the life course perspective, is attentive to exploring these issues in the context of social change.

Another application of the kinscript framework is seen in the study of family members who leave the fold of kin. Under certain circumstances, particularly in the case of a dysfunctional family, an individual may temporarily disassociate himself from kin as a means of personal survival and then return to the fold having learned new family skills. Within the context of the kinscripts framework, several questions might be addressed: (a) What implications does the individual's exit from the family have on kin-work, kin-time, and kin-scription? (b) How does the individual negotiate reentry to the kin network? (c) What affect does that individuals reentry have on the family's restructuring of the life course?

In summary, our contention is that kinscripts can be a useful framework for research in which the basic questions concern how families and individuals negotiate, construct, and reconstruct the life course. The utility of this framework is found in observing the interplay of three culturally defined family domains—kin-work, kin-time, and kin-scription.

CONCLUSION

This chapter suggests a way of thinking about the life course of individuals embedded within the life course of families. The kinscript framework was proposed. Kinscripts is conceptually grounded in the life course perspective, studies of kinship, and the literature on family scripts. As such, many of the ideas outlined in kinscripts are not new. What is new, however, is the union of these various perspectives in the domains of kin-work, kin-time, and kin-scription.

In addition to describing three domains of the family life course, kinscripts represents an attempt to use knowledge generated from the study of Black multigeneration families to formulate a framework that can be useful for the study of families in general. Minority families have historically experienced issues that mainstream families have only recently been attentive to. Examples of issues include: the juggling of work and family roles for women, single-parenthood, extended family relationships, and poverty. Important lessons can be learned through exploring these issues in the context of the life course of minority families. These lessons can provide critical insights on the life course of the variety of family forms existing in contemporary American society.

ACKNOWLEDGMENTS

The research reported in this paper was supported by grants from the National Science Foundation (RII-8613960), the Brookdale Foundation, the Center for the Study of Child and Adolescent Development, The Pennsylvania State University, a FIRST Award from the National Institute of Mental Health (No. R29MH46057-01), a William T. Grant Faculty Scholars Award to the first author, and a Rockefeller Foundation grant to the second author. This paper was partially prepared while the authors were Fellows at the Center for Advanced Study in the Behavioral Sciences. We are grateful for financial support from the John D. and Catherine T. MacArthur Foundation, the Spencer Foundation, and the Guggenheim Foundation. We also wish to thank Robert Weiss, Gunhild Hagestad, Ann Crouter, Jean Lave, Blanca Silvestrini, Judy Stacey, Brad Shore, Jane Ifekwunigwe, Cindy Brache, and Caridad Souza, for their helpful comments on an earlier draft.

An expanded version of this chapter appears in the *Journal of Comparative Family Studies,* Volume XXIV.

REFERENCES

Aldous, J. (1990). Family development and the life course: Two perspectives on family change. *Journal of Marriage and the Family, 52,* 571–583.

Anspach, D. F. (1976). Kinship and divorce. *Journal of Marriage and the Family, 38,* 323–335.

Aschenbrenner, J. (1975). *Lifelines: Black Families in Chicago.* New York: Holt, Rinehart, and Winston.

Byng-Hall, J. (1985). The family script: A useful bridge between theory and practice. *Journal of Family Therapy, 7,* 301–305.

Byng-Hall, J. (1988). Scripts and legends in families and family therapy. *Family Process, 27,* 167–179.

Burton, L. M., & Jarett, R. L. (1991). *Studying African-American family structure and process in underclass neighborhoods: Conceptual considerations.* Unpublished manuscript. Pennsylvania State University.

Di Leonardo, M. (1986). The female world of cards and holidays: Women, families, and the work of kinship. *Signs: Journal of Women and Culture in Society, 12,* 440–453.

Dressel, P. L., & Clark, A. (1990). A critical look at family care. *Journal of Marriage and the family, 52,* 769–782.

Elder, G. H., Jr. (1987). Families and lives: Some developments in life-course studies. *Journal of Family History, 12,* 179–199.

Ferreira, A. J. (1963). Family myth and homeostasis. *Archives of General Psychiatry, 9,* 457–463.

Gilligan, C. (1982). *In a different voice.* Cambridge, MA: Harvard University Press.

Hagestad, G. O. (1986a). Dimensions of time and the family. *American Behavioral Scientist, 29,* 679–694.

Hagestad, G. O. (1986b). The aging society as a context for family life. *Daedalus, 115,* 119–139.

Hagestad, G. O. (1990). Social perspectives on the life course. In R. K. Binstock & L. K. George (Eds.), *Handbook of aging and the social sciences* (3rd ed.). New York: Academic Press.

Hagestad, G. O., & Smyer, M. S. (1982). Dissolving long-term relationships: Patterns of divorcing in middle age. In S. Duck (Ed.), *Personal relationships, Vol. 4: Dissolving personal relationships.* London: Academic Press.

Hareven, T. K. (1982). *Family time and industrial time: The relationship between the family and work in a New England industrial community.* New York: Cambridge University Press.

Hareven, T. K. (1986). Historical change in the social construction of the life course. *Human Development, 29,* 171–180.

Hareven, T. K., & Langenbach, R. L. (1978). *Amoskeag.* New York: Pantheon.

Hinnant, J. (1986). Ritualization of the life cycle. In C. L. Fry & J. Keith (Eds.), *New methods for old age research.* MA: Bergin and Garvey.

Johnson, C. L. (1988). Active and latent functions of grandparenting during the divorce process. *The Gerontologist, 28,* 185–191.

Norton, A. J., & Moorman, J. E. (1987). Current trends in marriage and divorce among American women. *Journal of Marriage and the Family, 49,* 3–14.

Plath, D. (1980). *Long engagements.* Stanford, CA: Stanford University Press.

Reiss, D. (1981). *The family's construction of reality.* Cambridge, MA: Harvard University Press.

Reiss, D., & Oliveri, M. E. (1983). The family's construction of social reality and its ties to its kin network: An explorations of causal direction. *Journal of Marriage and the Family, 45,* 81–91.

Scheper-Hughes, N. (1979). *Saints, scholars, and schizophrenics.* Berkeley, CA: University of California Press.

Steiner, C. M. (1974). *Scripts people live: Transactional analysis of life scripts.* New York: Grove Press.

Stack, C. (1974). *All our kin.* New York: Harper & Row.

Stack, Carol. (in press). Call to home: African American's reclaim the rural south. New York: Basic Books.

Tilly, C. (1987). Family history, social history, and social change. *Journal of Family History, 12,* 320–329.

Watkins, S. C. (1980). On measuring transitions and turning points. *Historical Methods, 13,* 181–186.

5 A Cross-Cultural Perspective: The Japanese Family as a Unit In Moral Socialization

George A. De Vos
University of California, Berkeley

As an anthropologist as well as a psychologist I would like to call attention to the ethnocentrism that is still implicit in western derived social science as it addresses itself to the self as a concept and the family as an institution. We have more generally considered a cross-concept of the self elsewhere (De Vos, 1985; De Vos & Suárez-Orozco 1990).

Here, from a cross-cultural perspective afforded by Japan I shall consider the **family unit** as basic to moral socialization, and consequently to make a plea for us in subsequent research to better pursue an **interactional** as well as our more customary **individualistic** approach to the nature of the self. There is frequent mention of the gains to be made by examining interactions or transactions as units of analysis in social science. If one examines actual practice, however, the units or categories of analysis comprising the self remain in the individual and avoid feelings of the sacred as essential to social meaning. The self is extricated from being a member of a group or inhabiting a role. Religious experiences of awe, reverence, and gratitude as part of something larger than ourselves are neither examined nor considered as inextricable from "meaning." Morality as essential to a social self is considered separable from first experiences in some form of family life.

Morality as part of the self in family or social group membership, as I suggest, is true whether we consider the Confucian tradition of some Asian societies or the family heritage in past or present versions of the Judeo-Christian heritage of the west. In this presentation, taking the point-of-view of the Japanese cultural tradition, I shall try to be dispassionate, avoiding too much intrusion of my own cultural biases or strongly held values.

Running implicitly through this chapter, and a dominant theme in Hansen's chapter is the anticipated future as part of self and part of group membership, whether in the form of achievement motivation, or in the moral consideration of the future consequences of present acts.

THE MORAL IMPLICATIONS OF CAUSALITY

Both the Christian and Confucian traditions had a world view that started with a moral universe. The development of positivism in western science to a great degree freed the natural world from divine intentionality as an ordering principle. As applied to the social sciences positivism initiated abiding points of view that see sociology or human history as explainable in materialistic terms, governed by natural laws that can ultimately applied to human thought as well.

The Universe as now described by Western science thus is *not* a moral universe, for it is no longer homocentric. There is therefore, within contemporary Western thought a tendency to grant the impersonal in nature priority over personal awareness. This was the perceptive suspicion of Confucianist scholars when first confronting western thought.[1] There is an absolutist tendency in Western thought to push toward an ultimate unitary explanation in mechanical terms. An Asian concept of balance would seek better to delineate how the appearance of self-consciousness in a life form makes intentionality a new causative motive force influencing the natural world (De Vos & Sofue, 1986).

Religion and science, or, moral and rational thought, are parallel developments within the human mind. From their earliest appearance, however, they are so intertwined that they never become completely analytically separable in the inner experience of most individuals.[2] Magic is the expression of an instrumental need for control employed to ward off fears engendered by an unpredictable environment. Magical beliefs and practices derivative of an early psychosocial developmental stage in human thought sometimes remain in the realm of the sacred, not subject to examination; other times they themselves become treated somewhat more "scientifically." For example, the practices of alchemy in the Middle Ages gradually were objectified into the explanatory regularities of chemistry—but not until alchemy first became generally free of magical attributions as explanatory. With difficulty, and never completely, the magical precausality of childhood becomes objectified, detached from human desire, and is transmuted into instrumental rational-scientific thought.[3] But what is the relationship between mechanical causality and intentional causality?

---

[1]See De Vos, Confucian Thought in Tokugawa Japan nd.

[2]In several contexts I have already referred to this interpenetration of experience of will and mechanism psychodynamically in complex causal explanations (see especially De Vos & Suárez-Orozco 1990, chapter 3).

[3]Suffice it to say that a need for control remains a motive in both magic and science. Humans have successfully implemented a search for both understanding and control over nature. In world

Human volition is, by its very nature, moral. That is to say, one who possesses intentionality knows that human intentional behavior, or even intentional thought, whatever its form, has consequences: it is causal. Morality, then is most simply considered knowledge of intentional causality, cause and effect in human behavior, that is, knowledge of the consequences of behavior within a reflexive self. To understand the determinative effects of human moral development, and why *religious* thought is inescapable in one form or other in human society, is to know that moral-social considerations cannot be superseded or supplanted by morally neutral scientific observation.

As neutral observers, however, let us turn again to some psychological discussion of psychosocial development as explanatory of human moral nature. This will help explain why Confucian thought, organized around the family as the basic social unit, regardless of its total or relative exclusion of the supernatural, is nevertheless, deeply religious in so far as it sees moral development as central to the development of the self and the maturation of human knowledge—the maturation of moral considerations of behavior. Confucianism is also interested in the ***entire life course***—from childhood through sagehood in old age—a continuous progressive self development, never perfected, but ending only by death.

THE EXPERIENCE OF DIVINE INTENTIONALITY

Curiously, when comparing the western tradition of morality with that of The Confucian influenced countries of China, Korea, Japan, and Vietnam (Slote & De Vos, in press) one notes that morality in the Western tradition is most often represented as inextricably interwoven with concepts of *supernatural* power and divine forces governed by love or wrath intervening in the human social world. The Confucian moral universe doe not deal with any such divine intervention as the basis of personal morality. For this reason and others, many scholars, my opinion to the contrary, would deny Confucianism to be a religion, even though admitting it to be an ethical system built around the family as a primary unit of society. Let us explore this as we seek out how the family role is basic to the sense of moral self in traditional Japanese.

A religious sense of intentional power can be represented in various forms. Causal interference in the sequence of human events can be attributed to a single deity, or manifest through the actions of different deities. Humans employ a variety of personalized representations of the intentionally directed consequences of supernatural power. Even in popular Buddhism there has been developed a pantheon of beings with various representations of a hell and a personalized

society as a whole there is increasing awareness of our awesome control over mechanisms of destruction as well as our capacity to disturb the ecological balance of our planet. How can we control ourselves?

afterlife. These were historical additions to atheistic Buddhism, allowing for popular representations of power in divinity.

As the present head monk at Mt. Hiei expressed it to me, most adherents of religious sects are, though reassuring *belief,* seeking for personalized external succor and assistance. For some few others however, true religion is seeking inner *enlightenment,* a realization of inner capacities as well as limitations. The *power* of God sought outside is rather to be sought as actualization of the force of intentionality within.

Reestablishing a fusion with some form of external power is a primitive, universally utilized, psychological mode of coping with a need for security. Satisfaction is, at least momentarily, gained through attempts at anaclitic attachment to, or introjection of, outside power (Blatt, 1974). A fear of possible separation becomes a significant part of parental interaction paralleling some maintenance of a defensive belief that it is one's own vocalization and gesture that influences the outside to provide needed security. Moral transactions for some start as, and remain, negotiations for succor.[4]

Separation can result in overwhelming anxiety because it often occurs regardless of volition. An intense feeling of helplessness begins to alternate with a still continuing optimism that one's internal intentionality may still bring on satisfaction. One is powerless to prevent loss, but the infant comes to experience and define his own separateness as assuageable by social reattachment. With physiological maturation, body motility is sensed as progressively coming under one's voluntary or "willful" control. There is also sensed selective outside approbation and disapproval of efforts to move about, and outside appraisal of how one uses one's body. Indeed, the outside intentional beings even require and force certain forms of internal muscular control into what will later be perceived as patterns of motoric propriety, the morality of body movement.[5]

As the boundaries of separateness become increasingly evident, the infant especially senses the horror of isolation from the source of pleasure, protection,

---

[4]There is both command and fearful supplication in the act of crying. When the initial separation of the self comes to be more harshly experienced, power must be sought from projected external, intentional willful beings, and potentially destructive anger must be avoided. To the extent that one comes progressively to experience the "reality" of inner helplessness one seeks benign engulfment—reattachment—or one can come symbolically to seek or "ingest" power. Acts of commensual communion, are found in religious ritual enactments cross-culturally (De Vos & Suárez-Orozco, 1987).

[5]There may result a battle of wills. The anal sphincter can become symbolically in Western culture not only an erogenous focus of positive and negative feelings, but also a symbol of conformity and submissiveness or defiance and rebellion. In infancy the awesome realization that pleasure and security is subject to the will of another intentional individual can be devastating because the "other" does indeed "go away," potentially leaving one helpless. The experience that this outside source can be destructive and/or the fear of losing this "almighty" source of goodness, constitute the first sense of true human horror or overwhelming "separation anxiety," as discussed by Freud (de Grazia, 1948).

and comfort. As the child experiences that the source of comfort is not solely within himself but is shared with his parents, they then become omnipotent. They *are* intentional power.[6] Yet the early stage of omnipotent intentionality, located within, leaves profound residual dynamics in the human mind.

As the boundaries between the developing self and the external world make the sense of separateness evident, the child projects into the external universe his own life, animation, and tendencies, which often continue to interparticipate with his own wishes, thoughts, and gestures. The infant who once experienced the cosmos as an intimate continuity, now as child animistically endows it with life and intent that still can be controlled through the manipulation of proper formulae.

Human thought during early childhood is characterized by a continuing lack of precise differentiation of internally stimulated intentionality as distinct from the outer mechanical energies of the external world.[7] Mechanism and intention, either in the self or in other living beings, can only be separated from one another after further maturation, given the available cultural forms of conceptual thought making such separation possible. There remains a tendency in contemporary Western science, religion, and philosophy no matter how well developed, to fuse these forms of causality or subordinate one to the other.

An essential aspect of all thought is interaction, a dynamic flow of interchange which is conceptualized as causality—whether between beings or objects. Many experiences of causality are temporal in that the flow is from prior conditions to subsequent ones. Other experiences of causality are interactive in spatial as well as temporal dimensions. Intentional causality is subjected to moral evaluation, that is, it is constructive, benign, harmonious in intent, or is it destructive or malevolent?

Adults as well as children alternate subjectively between experiences of power and powerlessness. As the child grows, he begins to establish his own separated position in the complex world of natural forces and human social events.

In Jean Piaget's (1930, pp. 237–305) elegant analysis of the development of causality in the child, early thought is characterized as being permeated by the "realism of perception." Early on, subjective perceptions are taken as given. The perceptual distortion that the moon "moves" as he or she does, is indeed, taken very seriously; the universe as animate and participating with his own actions, thoughts, wishes, and gestures. During the sensorimotor stage (approximately

[6]Satisfaction (the breast that brings food, the body that brings warmth and protection), which was experienced earlier as intimate and inseparable, with the increasing sense of separateness, begins to be experienced as subject to an outside, sometimes hostile intentionality demanding obedience—even a complete capitulation of "will"—the conative in human experience. These go into the intentional causality of the supernatural experienced as religious

[7]The early, perceptive work of Piaget (1930) attests to the various forms of precausal thought in children that intertwine intentionality and mechanism.

the first 18 months-of-life), the infant's thinking is dominated by egocentric perceptions rooted in an incapacity to precisely judge from where causality is empowered, whether part of the self or part of the outside world. Thinking remains "animistic" as well as "magical." Rocks move because they are "alive." The child who experiences his own musculature in movement, projects it into the inanimate world, endowing it with life. Japanese can readily turn their sense of reverence and awe out onto nature. Inchoate Shinto beliefs continue to endow nature with vitality and soul. Mt. Fuji is awesome and treated with reverence.

Thus a sense of awe and reverence about power may find both natural as well as human exemplars that become objects of worship (De Vos & Sofue, 1986). The Japanese concept of "*Kami*" in some respects resembles what has been described as "*Mana*" elsewhere in Polynesia (Firth 1940; Levy 1973, pp.154ff). In some cases it directly adheres to individuals. Some humans such as Sugawara, the Heian period courtier-calligrapher are enshrined. The Kitano Shrine in Kyoto is to this man-become Kami, whose moral wrath became feared as a cause of pestilence and other disasters after his wrongful exile and subsequent death.

Piaget discusses how in primitive psychological precausality, thinking itself is powerfully "efficacious." The initial confusion between the self and the external world gives the child the illusion that a great source of power remains located within the self. What is *not* discussed in Piaget's writings is the awesome, possibly traumatic nature of the sense of power which remains part of magical and/or religious representations in adults in all cultures. There are potential psychopathological traumas that can be rigidified into a future neurosis as the child senses that his or her own ideas cause hurtful things to happen. Should an accident happen during a period of enmity, the child's inner experience as part of the stage of "realism" in thought might be that an evil wish (which can be conscious or unconscious) might have caused a parent or a sibling to be hurt. Such early "egocentric" experiences are not easily undone in the development of a sense of guilt over one's own destructive wishes. Thoughts, gestures, or wishes of a sexual as well as destructive nature might prove so morally devastating that they create profound propensities for guilt, which can be later represented in religious imagery in relation to a potentially wrathful supernatural force.

One can seek to influence, or to alter divine will by being "pleasing" to a deity. One also learns from childhood various culturally available notions of negotiation used as means of interacting with a powerful external being should help be needed. Concepts of early social negotiation in childhood, as well as later forms which can be observed as occurring between adults, remain as paradigms for influencing action in others. This very human perception of negotiation with the supernatural is most evident in various forms of ritual sacrifice (De Vos & Suárez-Orozco, 1987).

A sense of volitional control *within* starts very early in the human infant. To be able to name is to be able to control.[8] If one learns the right word one gains control over the named object.[9]

There may not be any immediate moral involvement in the desire for control. A moral sense becomes evoked only later when one develops awareness of the social consequences of one's desire to control or to destroy. At first, there is a split between good and bad outer objects (Kernberg, 1975). What is experienced as "bad" also tends to be projected outward. "Good" as best as possible is kept within. Only when there is developed a capacity to take conscious inner "responsibility" does the moral necessity to anticipate the consequences of behavior manifest itself.

The development of a human *conscience* or *superego,* which allows one to assume responsibility for one's intentionality, is part of the phylogenetic evolution of the human forebrain. The forebrain frees us from being bound to the immediate present. Increased storage capacities and complex networks allow us to draw on memory input as in a computer. We can predict the future. The human brain extends us in *time* and space without having to move close physically. We can quickly test out the consequences of alternative paths before taking action. The results of pursuing a given desire become visible ahead of time. As we come to know *sin,* in hurting another by our willful behavior, or collectively, by using science to create new capacities for destruction, we become responsible for anticipating the future.

With the maturational growth of a "self," the source of power begins to be more precisely and discreetly located either in the intentional energy of powerful humans, in nature, in the belief in supernatural intervention, or in the control exercised over one's own body by directed thought. One's culture instructs one in how to envision power in moral harmony with those of one's own group.

There continues into adulthood the experiential context of the child's own musculature in which power has been experienced. There is continual progressive experiential observation of the body and the growing self, as well as the natural world. Because the experience of power and the attribution of power, in most instances, is mediated through some social context, the perception of a moral universe as it is envisioned in Confucianism is quite understandable. It is not simply the product of childish adherences visible in adult thought.

For some groups, nature continues to be considered as having intentional qualities. For some, nature is benevolent and nurturant; for others, harshly directed toward humanity rather than impartial. As man worships aspects of

---

[8]As Piaget (1930) described it in his earlier writings, the word *adheres* to the object named.

[9]In many groups, as in the case of the Jews, the name of one's tribal god was kept secret. Should one's enemy learn the sacred name, the god could be controlled, and the group vanquished (Graves, 1952). Such institutionalized forms of early prelogical thought are patently magical in nature. In them, proper magical use of words is an instrumental extension of subjectively experienced volition out into the social world.

nature, they are sometimes imbued with intentional force. Thus thunder may come to either to punish or bring needed rain; the arrival of spring is given to man and can excite a sense of gratitude for the new life springing from the earth and the care of fruitfulness bestowed each yearly cycle. In this sense, nature itself can be perceived as divine. Divinity is seen by man as a source of blessing. Reverential gratitude is a basic religious feeling that needs outlet, that needs objectification in some symbolic representation.

Among the Japanese reverence and gratitude also can continue to be expressed religiously **within** the family system, or toward a *"sensei,"* one "born before" a role model who guides one's efforts toward mastery. Objects of revered benevolence remain the person of the mentor, as well as the mother and father. A supernatural image may not be necessary. The sense of deep gratitude need not be attributed to a figure such as Jesus or a nurturing Virgin Mary

The figures of Amida and Kannon, derivative of popular Buddhism, have been used by some Japanese as objects of gratitude, but others with the same emotions to express do not transcend their own family unit. The fact that the deepest gratitude need not be expressed toward a supernatural object can be related to the preempting of such emotional states by Confucian teachings in which the focus remains in the immediate social world. Such feelings of gratitude are not diverted out onto a realm of supernatural benefactors. Yet they are what I consider to be religious in experience. Gratitude is diffused throughout human social transactions. The ultimate virtues to be cultivated in feeling good about life are all directed toward humanity, not divinity. They are *gen* or in Japanese *gi,* propriety, wisdom, good faith, and righteousness.[10]

This moral centrality of the family role in the realization of self in the confucian tradition contrasts with the cultivation of an individualistic perception of morality among contemporary westerners. Most children are consciously dissatisfied with some of the moral as well as other personal limitations of parents. Most can no longer pretend to themselves that parents are near-perfect role models to be emulated. Unlike the Japanese situation, American perception of parental roles and role playing behavior do not cloak the manifest deficiencies of those who are supposed to be moral exemplars. It is more readily evident to the young in America that those who become parents have individual goals more salient than family harmony, or the sacrifice of the individual aspect of self for family betterment. A large percentage of Americans find divorce an available

---

[10]Bellah (1957, p. 77) in studying Tokugawa religion, also directly includes Confucianism as a religion. It is a religion for Bellah, as it is, in my judgment, because what can be termed spiritual cultivation brings a person to oneness with the universe in sensing a suffusion of goodness. Two main types of *religious* action according to Bellah, as well as myself, are the deep reverence with which a Japanese Confucianist returns *on,* or gratitude, and the dedication to self-cultivation in social interaction as a continuing goal of human life. Many Japanese Confucians were vigorous in practicing activism and attacking the quietism that could remove a person from responsible participation in society.

way out of mutually irreconcilable wishes and expectations. The sense of self increasingly is not sought in the habitation of a not to be broken family role.

In Reisman, Denny, and Glazer's (1958) use of terms, religious ideals around the family were more frequently internalized in the older Christian "inner directed" Western tradition. In the contemporary West moral patterns are more often sought for outside the family in some forms of social purpose. "Other directed" Americans, characteristically refer to peer standards to replace directives for behavior espoused, but not actualized by parents.

PROPRIETY, SITUATIONAL SENSITIVITY AND FUTURE ORIENTATION IN JAPANESE SOCIALIZATION

Obedience vs. Propriety

Starting from a western cultural perspective in psychoanalysis, interpretations concerning the so-called "anal period" in childhood development have been too focused upon the control of defecation and the ensuing battle of wills occurring between parent and child. When the vicissitudes of this period in early childhood are approached cross-culturally and normatively, rather than clinically in terms of problems that may arise in any culture, one finds it more generally to be a period of the developing of "will" or conation, a period when one learns a social balance between inner guided motor control and response to outside social cues.

Early on, highly dependent, one learns to take cues from the outside to guide behavior. One begins to make judgments on the basis of outside cues and to draw upon these in governing one's own behavior in a social context. As I have noted, a period of learning control is a period during which one seeks, albeit magically, to maintain intentional volition. In other terms, a child seeks, to some degree, to maintain a locus of control within the self, and gradually develops some confidence about being able to use one's own body, as well as one's thoughts, to judge outside events. Depending on prevailing practices of parenting, and an increasing capacity for mastery, there can be progressive shifts in balance between outer and inner regulation, finally, from heteronomy toward autonomy.[11]

During World War II some psychological anthropologists attempted to understand patterns of behavior suggesting psychological rigidity and self-righteousness prevalent among the Japanese (Gorer, 1943; Le Barre, 1945). Their efforts were ill-founded, as later evidence proved. These earlier attempts at describing a "national character" had directly applied Western derived psycho-

[11]Examined clinically, there are a number of rigidified imbalances resulting in what are usually termed neuroses, which result from particular psychosexual disturbances occurring at critical periods in development. So called "character traits" can be set; there can develop strong rebellious propensities, or overly compliant attitudes. Rigid defenses can occur both motorically and/or conceptually.

analytic theory heavily dependent on Western clinical observations. They were not based on sufficient observation of actual Japanese socialization practices.

The general consensus resulting from direct studies (e.g., Lanham, 1956) is that toilet training in Japan was never imposed with any of the rigor characteristic of some groups observed in traditional Western child rearing. In Japan, what is controlled very early by direct manipulation of the body, rather than any use of guiding words, is proper bowing and other deference behavior directed toward important outsiders. There is a continued sensitivity aroused from early on about properly controlled motoric behavior. We can relate this part of early childhood experience in Japan to a moral sense located in the musculature as I attempt to do next.

Social relationships are symbolized in proper posture, which is as important as the verbal deference also practiced from early on. A Japanese mother's concern with social compliance, or with other consequences of a child's behavior, is not about obedience or disobedience, but about how a child may hurt the feelings of others and hence do poorly socially. If behavior is too directly aggressive the child will be isolated (Lanham 1956, 1962).

Obedience for itself is not the desired goal, but what is sought for is an awakening in a child of an awareness of the potentially negative consequences of behavior (cf. Miyake et al., 1986). The potential for hurting one's family, not only oneself, is learned fairly early. Behavior can cause collective harm a long time distant. Vigilance becomes part of a future time orientation while the child's sense of self remains embedded within his family. There is a socialization of achievement motives not individualistically, but collectively defined (De Vos, 1973). Social or occupational failure produces guilt for hurting those deserving gratitude (De Vos, 1960). The parent becomes the sacrificial figure rather than a more distant divinity (De Vos, 1984).

Maternal discipline when well exercised in Japan avoids a test of wills. Japanese mothers are more likely to appeal to a child's awareness of consequences (Azuma, Kashiwagi, & Hess, 1981). The child is made aware of his potential for injuring objects as well as people. This is a form of moral inculcation, rather than a tempering of contentious wills as is parent-child interaction the U.S.

Japanese children are quickly made sensitive to their capacity to arouse negative feelings in others. As compared in systematic studies by developmental psychologists, American mothers are more apt to make desired behavior, whether toilet training or other forms of compliance, a question of obedience to the will of the mother (Azuma et al., 1981). The Japanese mother avoids any such confrontation. She "gets with the child" and uses her closeness to move the child toward compliance with her wishes without making them a direct issue. Taking a Piagetian perspective, motoric training of early behavior precedes comprehension. It is preparatory to a sensitivity to the intentionality of others in the actual social world. In the West there is institutionalized in religious training an immutable set of requirements divinely ordained, codes of behavior in regard to sexual and aggressive behavior set down by a potentially wrathful or suffering deity. Hence from a Western religious perspective Japanese moral thought has been considered more socially situational rather than based on universalist absolute principles. Further, it is usually directed toward persons with whom one has actual social contact. In the traditional culture one could avoid moral responsibility for those outside one's social network, although today one notes a widening of concern with universalizing of the concept of human rights being taught in Japanese schools.[12]

Field Dependence vs. Field Independence

There are considerable numbers of cross-cultural studies of the cognitive development of children related to school performance (De Vos, 1982). One such series of inquiry concerns itself with whether in making perceptual judgments a child is "field dependent" or "field independent." There is a developmental progression from field dependent judgments toward field independent ones (Witkin, 1967; Witkin & Berry, 1975). To explain the meaning of these terms and the type of observations on which they are made, one can cite one task given to subjects placed in a dark room. They are shown a rod in a frame that is lit up at one end of the room. The frame can be tilted slightly, or the rod may be placed in other than a vertically upright position. The subject is asked to judge when the rod is upright, and when it is not.

Subjects can be separated into those who tend to judge the upright position in terms of the frame in which it is placed, and those who use their own body posture sitting on a chair as the basis for judging the rod. This test and other test results were correlated and differentiated between Mexican-American children who do relatively poorly in school and "Anglo"-American children who do relatively better in their studies (Kagan, 1974; Kagan & Buriel, 1977). Mexican children tend to remain more field dependent while Anglo children become more quickly field independent. Conversely, Mexican children tend to be more cooperative and socially sensitive, whereas the Anglo children tend toward individualistic competitive behavior (Madsen, 1967, Madsen & Shapira, 1973). More recently, Vaughn (1988) comparing students of six Japanese secondary schools in Japan with six in the bay area found Japanese to be far more field independent than their American counterparts.

Drawing on related studies with Black and Mexican ethnic minorities in the United States, there is a tendency in the resulting discussions to see traits of cognitive independence and social compliance as inversely related. Traits emphasizing social compliance are considered to be due to patterns of child training

---

[12]With this emphasis on behavioral consequences rather than abstract principles, Japanese moral training is potentially more "legislative" and negotiable. Indeed rather than concern with statutes, equity plays a much more important role in Japanese legal practice and in court decisions.

emphasizing authoritarian forms of discipline and hierarchical status positions in the family. The locus of power remains prevailingly external in such individuals. Heteronomous fear of authority remains, not to be superseded by a more internalized superego.

Cues for acceptable behavior are part of a sensitivity to the norms of "significant others" or a dominant reference group (see discussion of role of peer reference groups in ethnic minorities in De Vos, 1978). Such individuals are "other directed" (Riesman et al., 1958). Inferentially, they cannot use their own bodies with confidence for perceptual verification.

However, how are we to consider the fact that Japanese children tend to be field independent on the one hand, but socially sensitive and compliant on the other, brought up in families emphasizing hierarchy in both language and social gestures? Japanese in the cognitive, perceptual realm confound generalizations made on the basis of American studies, just as generalizations in American psychology (McClelland, 1961) about "need achievement" being inverse to affiliative and nurturant needs are confounded by the more family oriented definitions of achievement found in the fantasies of Japanese when they are tested with the same tests given American subjects (De Vos, 1973; Vaughn, 1988).

Most field dependent compliant children remain present oriented. The time dimension of many Mexican children is relatively brief and present oriented (Kluckhohn, 1953). They do not develop the extended future time orientation so evident in the Japanese. Anglo children show a future time orientation, but they are less constrained by it, for they do not envision that possibly contentious or openly competitive behavior will be damaging to future goals. They are less disciplined toward social sensitivity to guide their behavior than are Mexican or Japanese children.

I have discussed in more detail elsewhere (De Vos, 1982), when considered comparatively, Japanese children manifest in their cognitive development forms of field independence that indicate on a cognitive level, as least, they maintain a locus of power within. In Japanese this is consonant with the internalization of moral directives emphasizing forms of family responsibility depending on social sensitivity and social compliance. In the Japanese context, cognitive independence is coupled with compliant receptivity to teachers or other mentors allowing for better adaptive learning. In the American pattern cognitive independence is coupled with social and psychological competitiveness and individualistically oriented internalizations. Lower class American children not interested in formal learning feel psychologically free to more or less openly defy the teacher in the school situation.

American children generally are not compliant at school. In fact, the amount of defiance and disrespect displayed toward teachers has produced a present crisis in the public schools. A good number of teachers are leaving the profession, not due solely to the relatively low salaries provided teachers (itself a symptom of social disrespect), but due the direct physical as well as status violence directed toward them in the classroom. One observes that such irreverent behavior toward a teacher is very rarely in evidence among Asian-American children who continue to treat a teacher with respect. Generally teachers complain that the parents of many of their pupils do not support their efforts. Attendance at PTA meetings in Japan are close to 80–85% compared with very sparse attendance in most American school districts.

In Japan at present there are some signs of unrest in the schools, but by and large, Japanese internalization still appears to emphasize a type of socialization that stresses an anticipation of the consequences of behavior to family as well as self. Compliance is not simply on the basis of obedience to a potentially frightening authority. Japanese children show more immediate social sensitivity and concern with the opinion of others, but they also manifest *an awareness of behavior consequences in a future time orientation* that can envision alternative future consequences resulting from present behavior.

In other words, Japanese children are socialized toward present social sensitivities, but these are to be understood in the context of a future time orientation. They are socialized toward group compliance, but not by stern measures instilling a fear of authority, rather through a form of maternal guidance that instills a reverence for authority reinforced ritualistically by verbal and physical gestures of deference. On a cognitive level there is less frightened repression of consciousness, but behavior restraint. Constraint in behavioral expression demands the *suppression* of thought and affect rather than severe *repression* of either. Many Japanese children do not become cognitively blocked, although some do. More characteristically, there is no retardation of an internalized potential for self-guided cognition that can continue to be used from an inner locus of control From childhood on, Japanese learn *severe behavioral constraint maintained for social purpose*. There is a compliant intake of knowledge imparted by hierarchical figures acting in the status of parent. The American pattern of egalitarian self-assertion includes defiant attitudes to parents. One finds much less of this in Japan.

AGE GRADING AND A SENSE OF MASTERY

There are two points to consider in comparing the social behavioral implications of the Japanese family emphasis placed on present compliance for future mastery as compared with American learning patterns.

Rote Learning vs. Verbal Explanation

First, as has been noted, a Japanese cultural mode of socialization is the direct use of the child's body by the parent in patterning expected behavior. In more extreme cases there can be a molding of the child in an emotional closeness to the mother that gratifies dependency as a means of maternal control.[13] From the very beginning Japanese mothers when compared with their American counterparts communicate through close body contact (Caudill & Weinstein, 1966). American mothers treat their infants as independent objects; verbal communication is emphasized from early on. In Japan, "proper" motoric learning instilled early enough, as already discussed, maintains an inseparable aesthetic and moral component that tends to remain implicit in feelings about body comportment throughout life. This was a culturally consistent pattern with the later learning of aesthetic traditions through the manipulation of the body by the teacher or "sensei."

A motoric stage in both cognitive and moral perception is implicitly acknowledged in Japanese concepts of training, whether in social comportment or in artistic skills. A child or an apprentice is expected to learn through pliant behavior before understanding what is being done or why.[14] A recent example of such a method of training is the Suzuki method of teaching children the violin. There are certain elementary pieces where everyone plays together from the youngest on up. The more adept are not excused from the elementary exercises, they play along with the little tots. There is a participatory togetherness that creates willingness to practice in those less skilled and stimulates an optimism about being able to reach the next difficult level of behavioral performance playing next to those who have already done so. So, basic learning is social and behavioral, not individual and conceptual.

Rote repetition and memorization as well as behavioral participation in ritual have been used in a number of traditions to inculcate sacred scriptures. Note that such a pattern seems to be appropriate in the imparting of a literate religious tradition because it is not the expectation that children are to examine critically the beliefs derived from sacred sources.

Secularized scientific investigation is based on the contrary notion that all present knowledge is based on theory that must receive continuous critical examination with a willingness to doubt current orthodoxy. The current arguments in pedagogy are about how much is to be imparted first before the learner becomes sufficiently equipped to be able to start to use a critical approach with merit.

It was incomprehensible to Western observers who visited premodern schools in China or Japan, how learning could take place through rigorously applied rote methods. Learning would be instilled by group recitation of what was to be learned without any attempt to explain what one was reciting. Comprehension was not an immediate goal. One would learn the meaning of the words later.

---

[13]One can note some lack of development of clear ego boundaries separating mother and child when such dependent bonds are maintained (Doi, 1973). Considered from a clinical standpoint one can see how such a continuing dependent relationship may cause a number of psychological disturbances. Suffice it to say that excessive attachment to a controlling mother can be a source of considerable personal malaise in Japan, as elsewhere.

[14]This is very apparent when one looks at traditional patterns of apprenticeship in Japan. It also appears in the learning of the martial arts.

Such forms of recitation are now only practiced in sacred or semisacred contexts in western settings. In all schools from early childhood one learns to recite The Pledge Of Allegiance to the American flag in a rote manner.[15]

It has been equally baffling to Western observers how the "imitative" Japanese, who started modernizing by emulating Western industrial patterns exactly and rigidly, could ever hope to compete successfully in modern manufacturing. Again, they were doing first and comprehending later. In the learning of an artistic tradition from a teacher, comprehension was supposed to come eventually from the continual exercise of correct behavior. One comprehends eventually what one is doing. This form of learning is contrary to the American principle in education to explain everything so that the learning individual knows what he is doing. This "intellectualizes" learning. The "grace" of proper doing is not considered.

The traditional Japanese modes of instruction remained more moral and aesthetic and even magical. Langdon Warner (1958) describes how the master swordmaker learned and imparted the art of properly tempering steel through ritual acts that measured the proper timing to be used.

Emotions engendered ritually, first within the family, could be experienced without being totally understood. Reverence and awe were to be encouraged in the teaching situation. Everlasting gratitude was the feeling to be experienced in the teacher-student relationship. The moral authority of the teacher was reinforced by the transference of respect already engendered toward parents. The family, instills a sense of reverence for the "sensei"—the one born before.

A *practicing* member of a religion is behaving as well as thinking in religious terms. There is deep expressive gratification to be realized in ritual, and perhaps for some others, there is a sense of malaise engendered in failing to follow prescribed forms of ritualized or routinized behavior. For example, some Japanese are truly workaholics. They feel uneasy during the weekends.

Motoric learning from very early childhood on creates patterns, that when followed, produce a reassuring sense of morality. Following specified patterns ritualistically can impart a sense of aesthetic rightness and also a moral satisfaction of orderliness, ultimately giving the individual a sense of general orderliness and predictability. Proper gestures can be magical gestures insuring a controllable, predictable world.

Ability to believe in an orderly predictable world, which can be improved to run even more properly, is one of the deepest needs that an ideology or a religious system seeks to satisfy. Security is not only found in belief, but in the proper

---

[15]In Catholic schools in the United States during my childhood, the "Our Fathers" and "Hail Marys" as well as the "Apostles Creed" were recited without any attempt at explanation of the words. During my early years of Catholic education I never learned in school what was meant by "Blessed is the fruit of thy womb, Jesus." The words were sacred and were to be repeated—not to be comprehended.

motoric behavior necessary to insure belief. Strict adherence to politeness, still practiced in the proper bringing up of Japanese children, continues to perpetuate patterns of propriety that have moral tone even though the direct ideological or religious referents to Confucian dogma are no longer used consciously. Being critical of proper family authority, gesturally or verbally is a breach of the unquestioned sacred as much as reviling God would be to a Western believer.

In understanding traditional plastic and dramatic art forms in Japan, one must note how rote behavior continues on the long road taken toward eventual mastery. There is no presumption that every practitioner will eventually come to full comprehension.[16] Lack of knowledge, or even lack of belief, does not exclude someone from becoming part of a group created around a tradition. This is especially true for religious organizations. This is in contrast to the West where those seeking to become a convert to a religious body are to be tested to see whether they have proper comprehension and proper adherence to the essential beliefs of the group before they are formally admitted. Helen Hardacre (1985) describes how she was asked to join Reiyuukai, a new Japanese religion she was studying. She demurred that she did not share the beliefs of the participants. This was of no matter she was told. By doing things together socially she would come to understand and to comprehend.

Age Grading and Optimism in Future Oriented Confucian Societies

A second basic difference from American concepts of learning is the force of an age grading system that emphasizes compliance for future mastery throughout the life trajectory. In considering authority and social status among adults, contemporary American society has not worked out a comfortable distinction between vertical relationships that are temporary as in age grading, and those that are due to status differences of a more permanent nature. Present day Western societies in their efforts at democratization are progressively attempting to do away with concepts of seniority among adults, regardless of age. In the United States this effort has been extended to "children's rights" within the family as something to enforce legally, especially should parents be considered too authoritarian.

In contrast, much emphasis in deference behavior in Asians starting in the

[16]Francis Hsu (1985), has written with considerable insight into the continuity in art due to the tradition of the [*iemoto*]. An *iemoto* is the sole unchallengeable master of a tradition. Upon death this tradition is passed on to a successor. He is the only one who can modify or change anything. All others, trained or being trained, are subject to his final authority. Religious and philosophical traditions as well as Noh drama, Kabuki, schools of flower arrangements, all have *iemoto*. In the Noh tradition, for example, only an experienced true master knows the meaning of the cryptic codes that describe the state of mind to attain in attempting a particular role. The master doesn't attempt to impart such knowledge or secrets except to his immediate successor.

family is related to age graded offices. Such age graded deference behavior causes less social resentment than that related to social class or ethnic differences. It is difficult for a contemporary American, looking at social hierarchy in a Confucian society, to understand the emotions attached to age grading and its continuing complex relationship to both mastery and dependency as well as morality. For Americans deference behavior readily demeans the adult. It is interpreted as submissiveness and possible weakness of character, or a form of deviousness. It would seldom be considered as marking a future time framework, a form of nondemeaning patience informed by an optimistic consideration of future possibilities.[17]

To properly understand age grading one must examine more fully the concept of self-development in traditional Confucian family education, especially when it is transferred to that of an artisan apprentice, a would-be artist, or scholar. An anticipation of future power is the heart of the concept of apprenticeship in Japan as elsewhere (De Vos, 1975). Theodore Reik (1941) analyzing "moral masochism" makes an excellent description of the mentality of the apprentice, who by submission, gains eventual mastery. One doesn't submit to comply; one submits to gain power. This is the essence of early identification around family roles experienced by the child.

A sense of endurance itself may become pleasurable in enhancing an internal sense of "being able to take it," furthering the anticipation of one's future goals. "Patience" is not passive in nature, rather the individual is already actively engaged in a future purpose of eventually attaining a dominant role.

Patience is an instrumental virtue not demeaning to those who practice it. Others recognize it as a legitimate deferment of future goals. The Japanese could submit to the American occupation without losing all sense of honor. They could outlast it. When one knows that one has kept one's inner capacities despite tribulation, there is assurance that the proper energy will be there to realize one's goals at a future time. Things are going to change if one can hold on and endure.

If we look at the localization of the sense of power, the sense of causality experienced within Confucianism, we must **not** assume that functioning in a social hierarchy creates a sense of powerlessness in the individual. On the contrary, the Japanese sense of pleasure in accomplishment comes out of the ability to exercise ones role to the optimum regardless of one's relative status in society.

In our interviews in Arakawa, Wagatsuma and I were impressed with the number of individuals in lowly positions who nevertheless experienced a moral

[17]I shall not enter into the topic of the problems of continuing manipulative dependency [*amae*], well discussed by Doi (1973), practiced by subordinates toward their superiors. Note that dependency in Japanese does not lead to any general social passivity, but may be related in some instances to vigorous social striving and occupational success (De Vos, 1975; Vogel, 1965). Nor are dependency and deference congruent concepts. One refers to the continuing receptive need for gratification from some one in a position to bestow benefits, the other, is an expression of respect, even reverence to someone superior in status.

sense of themselves as doing their job well. They identified with their work rather than being alienated from it.[18] The sense of propriety in role delivers to the individual certain forms of pleasure in accomplishment and the realization of self that is hard to understand by people imbued with an egalitarian philosophy that says that those beneath are failures, and the only way to realize oneself whether man or woman is to become a relative economic success in a competitive striving society.

Moreover, an emphasis on social role does not make the individual fatalistic, because embodied in the Confucianist tradition, as Tu (1985) has well explained in his writings, is a sense of continuous self-development so that the older individual has a greater sense of accomplishment in this regard than do those who are more youthful. The reverence for age in a Confucian society deals with the fact the individual has had more time toward a sense of self-realization with greater wisdom.

It is our egalitarian concept that constrains us to see that the only way to feel or to sense one's self in lowly status positions is to feel a frustration of an inner sense of power. This is a reading into others, a projection, of how we would feel if we are imbued with an egalitarian philosophy and we would find ourselves in a hierarchical situation. We would perhaps have less capacity to examine the pleasures of accomplishment to be realized within such a constrained role.

The Japanese best seller several years back, *Kokotsu No Hito,* would be almost incomprehensible for an American readership. In this work, a woman comes to devote herself entirely to an irascible, childish, demanding, senile father-in-law. The ultimate degradation is that this demanding unpleasant old man has to have his diapers changed when he becomes incontinent. What is hard for a Western reader to comprehend is how any woman would turn herself into a voluntary slave to such a person. The idea of voluntarily taking on this burden oneself, but more than that, finding a sense of self-realization in it, is incomprehensible to us. Mother Teresa in India is a saint, not a role model.

It is the subtle sense of self in social role, related to the moral performance, albeit sometimes in a ritualistic way, that is the greatest difficulty for Western understanding. One finds even in those of the newer generation of Japanese increasing incomprehension of this type of attitude. In the search for *[shiawase],* happiness, the Japanese is giving up his understanding, and on various levels, the religious meaning of endurance.[19]

---

[18]According to Marx, alienation is a consequence of becoming a worker in an industrialized exploitative society. Contrary to this, we found that many individuals, rather than thinking of themselves as being constrained or pushed into a lowly position, were able in some way to actualize themselves despite their lowly positions. Therefore, the sense of powerlessness that is often attributed to individuals of lowly positions, or to women vis-á-vis men in hierarchical gender situations does not necessarily become the inner experience of the person with a confucian sense of self.

[19]As I have indicated in the psychoanalytic literature, the discussion that comes the closest, in my judgment, to the understanding of how in the past self-sacrifice could become a central meaning is to

What does body propriety have to do with an inner sense of power or powerlessness? I submit that constraint and propriety enhances a sense of moral ascendency. This sense of self-worth can be relatively independent of external social status. Those in lowly positions, by doing their job the best way possible, preserve a sense of personal worth. They may not have any social power, but they maintain a sense of self-regard. If one does one's own assigned job well, some self-satisfaction is possible. This is hard to comprehend by members of some minority groups who refuse jobs because they are considered demeaning.

The Asian minorities in the United States could not be demeaned by the work assigned them within the host society as immigrants. They maintained their sense of personal worth within their family relationships. Respect within the family sustained them against outside discrimination. They could not be alienated in a Marxian sense. Their work did not become purposeless or without meaning. They were sustained by a religion of the family.

In the past, farm families apprenticed their children to merchants and artisans in the city. Second sons and third sons were sent in from the rural countryside. First sons succeeded to the farms. A dynamic population flow in Tokugawa society was based on this continual urbanization into the townsmen culture by eager new arrivals (Wagatsuma & De Vos, 1984). The apprentice worked very hard for little pay. An apprentice worked up to 14 hours without any right to complain. Maids were their feminine counterparts. Young girls were in this sense apprenticed to learn domestic duties in a higher status household. A complainer, male or female, would be sent home in disgrace, where the family would berate the "failure." An apprentice knew if he worked hard enough he could even have a "Noren wake," symbolically a splitting of the entry cloth designed with a house emblem that was strung across the doorway of a traditional establishment. The boss would "split" functions with him, making him a branch or a subsidiary master, or if he was quite successful, he might even marry the boss's daughter.

In such a system of thought one is tempering oneself to overcome future obstacles. The moral muscles are being exercised to strengthen oneself to triumph over future competition. The lifting of daily burdens strengthens the spirit, even if the flesh must be sacrificed. This is the Japanese virtue of endurance (Wagatsuma & De Vos, 1984). This virtue is exercised by both men and women. Children experience it as it was exercised by their young mothers at home. Younger fathers practice it in their occupational roles.

---

be found in Theodore Reik's (1941) discussion of masochism. The pleasure to be derived from pain is in the anticipation of the ultimate triumph. In Christianity it is the reassurance that "the meek shall inherit." The act of endurance is almost an eroticization of the future—taking on of certain roles whether it is that of a nun totally devoted as a "bride of Christ" or a Japanese mother totally devoted to a child. For the individual, so seeking meaning from these roles can become a total avowal and a course of gratification to sacrifice the self for a larger cause. Among religious practitioners in the West, only among those considered would-be saints does one find equally tolerated, or equally espoused, such a seeking of a meaningful sense of accomplishment in dedication.

The young man is in no better status than is the young bride. In entering a company at the bottom or in becoming an apprentice, one must submit to a system to be rewarded only with time. Today there are wage scales and about 45 hours a week officially, but often one is required to work overtime. The young man either as a worker or a member of management is still required to work very hard for relatively little pay. Wage labor has eroded this tradition in Japan without completely doing away with the concept of age grading in modern industry.

In sum, in considering hierarchy in a Confucian social context one must emphasize that ideally, at least, the system is not demeaning to those in lower or younger positions. The optimistic inner religious message of Neo-Confucianism is one of self-development through the better progressive exercise of one's social or family role.[20] Rather than an emphasis that in changing status one becomes a greater success the message points toward achieving personal satisfaction through the life span separated into male and female paths.[21]

Mentorship: The Role of the Sensei

For the Japanese, mentorship is quasi-religious. The Confucianist derived sentiments of reverence and gratitude that are supposed to be expressed to the yet living previous generation can only be understood in terms of the sacred. Being made into an object of veneration or gratitude can be discomforting for a contemporary Westerner. Such behavior is sometimes decried by secularized Japanese as well, who prefer "dry" to "wet" emotional attachments, as it is phrased. The actual benefits bestowed do not explain the intense symbolic value of mentorship. One can almost consider some adolescent Japanese, like ducklings, going through a phase wherein they can become "imprinted by a teacher, or "sensei"—a person "born before." Some retain throughout their careers a veneration for a master. There remains for many a romanticized image of the sensei, somewhat akin to the youthful image of a first love.

An American agricultural specialist, Clark, visited Hokkaido during the time when Hokkaido University was being established as a pioneer institution specializing in modern agriculture and fishing. After a visit of several months, he casually remarked when leaving, "Boys, be ambitious." He forthwith became a symbol for the zeal felt by this first generation of students. They built a statue to

[20]There is no such assurance in American society. There is no security in aging. On the contrary, one faces the problem of Willie Loman in Death of a Salesman, that at some future time one will be dispensed with when no longer useful. This implicit message is explicit when one looks at contemporary sports or in the entertainment world. During the period of peak success one is rewarded but one is quickly discarded when injuries or infirmities make the individual no longer useful or attractive.

[21]Within the family, therefore, the mother does not try to compete with the role of father because it is seen as a higher role. The goal is to become the mother of successful children.

him and took his words as the school motto. They embodied the undying gratitude felt toward "Clark sensei."[22]

Mentorship is a two-way relationship. In its Confucian context it is as important to the sense of self-dignity and accomplishment of the master as it is to the pupil. Erik Erikson (1959) in describing various stages of the life cycle, sees a successful aging process as involving a sense of generativity turned toward continuity into the next generation. Many aging Japanese are as concerned with such a successful bestowal, as they were with receiving when young, from parents or from a mentor.

A sense of continuity is deeply felt in all religions, whether it is contained in a belief in the personal continuity of one's individual soul as in the Christian and Muslim traditions, or as a belief in the continuity of a family lineage or occupational tradition as is fostered in Confucian thought. The sense of continuity demonstrates that an individualistically oriented self experience is concerned with *individual* continuity, while *a self-as-member* is concerned with the continuity of something more than the individual body or essence.

Basic to Japanese Confucian inspired religious thought seeing the family as a unit of morality is respect and gratitude. There is a gratefulness for what is received and a need to return the gratitude by some acts on one's own part, be they morally defined in terms of good and bad action, materially in terms of a bestowal upon others, or as an ascetic sacrifice of pleasure to achieve greater purpose. Some form of responsible behavior is deemed repayment for what is received. Japanese concepts of *On* therefore seem to be consonant with, if not derived from, Confucian thought. *On* as benevolent giving from elders to be repaid came to be heavily imbued with this reverential sense of something so precious and, indeed sacred, that it can never be totally repaid. In the west this is only accorded to God or Jesus.

Generational continuity is found in the occupational world in Japan as a direct transcendence for the nurture that was supposed to be given as parents to children. The emotional tone between older and younger is what makes a sense of hierarchy bearable, even desirable, for those raised within a Confucian family wherein role harmony ideally reigns. In this cultural atmosphere equalizing relationships is not a goal. One equalizes basically only with friends of the same age.

There is present day mythology in Japan about the ideal company president. He is a folk hero who exemplifies the ideal exercise of power and control for the

[22]Being accepted into a mentoring situation is considered very important for one's career by young Japanese. The contemporary sense of alienation felt by many Japanese college students attending large classes is intense. The sought-for direct contact with a teacher cannot be realized. Radical students quickly change their ideology once they are taken into an organization after graduation and put into the hands of older members of the organization for in-house training.

benefit of his workers, as well as producing a product that will benefit the populace at large. The purpose of gaining power as head of a company is to become a benevolent figure. Power is not for its own sake but to help others. Realizing ambition is not an individualistic achievement; it is to be able to bestow favors on others. One becomes a boss or "*kacho*" to be a "sage" advising the younger people coming up through the firm (cf. description of nurturant fantasies elicited by T.A.T. pictures in De Vos, 1973). In Japanese fantasy, older men are not only teaching younger men, but taking care of them. What is to be bestowed, and the manner of bestowal, in the perception of Americans would be considered a kind of "maternal-like" benevolence.

There are indeed those who seek to actualize this cultural shared fantasy. There is gratification to be derived from playing a membership role. It is a repetition of an idealized family setting in which parents take care and provide, even to the point of self sacrifice, for their children. The biggest gratification to be attained is to make enough money to be a philanthropist in the original meaning of the word. There are periodically such figures to be found in Japanese industry. Beliefs in this pattern are thereby reinforced.

Contrary to the emphasis that is put by some observers on the situational ethic of Japanese, actual ethnological observation of an urban community convinced Wagatsuma and myself (1984) how much public service is present in some urban Japanese communities. Many older Japanese do get beyond immediate concern with their own family. They do get involved with social causes. We were examining community activities related to delinquency in Arakawa Ward in Northwest Tokyo, a district of petty artisans and merchants. We found that there were a plethora of voluntary organizations joined both by men and women.

One such activity will illustrate. A number of men over 55 became *Hogoshi,* voluntary probation officers, (somewhat resembling the "big brother" program found in some American cities) looking after from two to four delinquent youth remanded to their charge by the formal probation officer. This was not simple surveillance; sometimes a mentor-like relationship was established. The recidivism rate of youth working with *Hogoshi* was relatively low. Because these *Hogoshi* came from the same ward as their charges, they knew their life pattern and could closely interact with them.

Leisure time for many older Japanese is utilized for such social causes as neighborhood betterment. The social atmosphere constrains one to join a number of organizations. In fact we are of the firm impression that Japanese today are greater joiners than middle class mainstream Americans.[23] Among so called

---

[23]Roger Barker (1968), completed a very detailed study comparing a Mid-west town in the United States with a town of the same population in Britain. He examined all the voluntary organizations, whatever their purpose, and found that Americans are greater joiners than English. If someone did a similar systematic present day comparison of the United States and Japan, I am certain that the Japanese would be found to spend more time on community activities than their middle-class American counterparts.

"salary men," it is mainly their housewives who are so occupied. In the merchant and artisan groups men are also drawn in. It is obvious in some instances it is the network that forces them to enter a number of these "voluntary" groups. The Japanese too, have their "Rions" and they roar together with their fellow boosters as Lions do in the United States. Kiwanis cosponsors exchange programs for youth. The Japanese, even in large city neighborhoods, have local organizations resembling small town America.

Collectively, volunteers are bestowing some good on the community. This development in Japan may not be directly Confucian in origin, but is important to consider the type of family-like self-actualization related to responsible status that engenders such activities.

Compared with the United States, the Japanese family and local community are maintaining better coordination, despite the individuating and socially isolating features of modern mass society everywhere.[24]

Vicariousness and Generational Continuity in Women

I have already touched on how social sensitivity is engendered in Japanese primary socialization. Related to this quality of sensitivity is how a capacity for vicarious cross-gender identification is further developed as part of a women's role, whereas men, while remaining dependent upon women, in contrast, are not supposed to identify, openly at least, with women who inhabit the inferior gender role.

But, as also noted above, in age graded situations there can be vicarious male identification with inferiors by superiors; a maternal-like nurture from older to younger. Instrumental contracts bind lower class labor to middle class management in the West. Hierarchical exploitation can breed alienation as Marx well described it. However, in Japan there are mitigating features in age graded social inequality that prevent such class alienation from becoming a primary social concern. Whatever the objective situation, subordinates tend to identify with the success of the company to which they belong rather than feeling exploited by others who achieve wealth and status at their expense.

Women are before all else members of a family. As entering brides they are constrained to belong to a new family and to seek gratification by joining in family success. The capacity to endure subordinate status in order to succeed, and to experience success through some form of vicarious identification reaches its apotheosis in Japanese mothers. Success is experienced jointly in the family unit as part of the complementarity of family roles between men and women.

[24]There are many difficulties increasingly faced by the aged in Japan which we cannot here consider, but the Confucian concepts of the past have prevented the isolation of the aged apparent in modern urban America. Respect for the aged has not completely disappeared, but indeed problems are increasing.

Vocational success is role aim of the man. Aiding this accomplishment is the successful exercise of the role of the wife-mother.

I have written elsewhere (De Vos, 1975) how the boy's success gives pleasure to the mother. Supposedly, the husband's success also gives pleasure to the wife and should be sufficient for her. This varies with the individual woman, but whatever the inner feelings they are not to be displayed in the course of role performance within the family. Individualized goals would be immoral when not subordinated to family goals. This moral sense is conveyed from mother to children in the attitudes expressed as part of their supervision. Japanese women are superb role performers on the stage of domestic life.

There was however, an inescapable underlying tension in the Japanese family in wife-mother-in-law relationships. The mother-son tie is often maintained into adulthood and marriage. As a consequence the younger wife is frustrated in gaining reciprocal intimacy from her husband and resigns herself to seeking fulfillment as a nurturant mother rather than as a companionate wife. She turns more to her children than to her husband in self-realization within a marriage. In many contemporary families in Japan women are not too apt to feel gratified as wives of salary men husbands who are running on a treadmill. As mother, she turns to the education of her children as her hope for a future accomplishment that will outdistance that of her husband. Simple continuity of family occupation is being replace by a growing anomic discontent one witnesses in some wives of those in the business or professional world. The father's role is receiving less idealization. Vocational achievement, however remains a moral imperative in the maternal attitudes imparted to children.

In American society vicarious identification is most readily pleasurably satisfied in those who follow team sports. They feel enhanced by the victory of their team. They gain physical empathic excitement in watching their team play. Within the American family, however, while parents do feel gratification when children succeed, they indulge children toward their realization of what have been personal rather than family goals. The degree of complementary empathic involvement between spouses as a family unit with common moral-vocational purpose is much less. The ideal marital relationship is supposed to be mutually companionate rather than the complementary performance of family roles. The ideal is horizontal intimacy rather than the harmonious maintenance of gender and age graded hierarchy dedicating the family to the realization of future family goals.

CONCLUSIONS: SOME CULTURAL CONTRASTS IN APPROACH

In American psychology we start with the individual as unit of analysis of behavioral motivation. Although the validity of an interactionist approach is acknowledged, it is seldom practiced. This is surely true in the study of moral development. In the foregoing, I have argued that our perspectives change when we look at the family unit in assessing moral experience in any individual. This is indeed a valid point from which to assess moral development of those growing up with an East Asian cultural heritage.

If the unit of judging behavior is the family, morality for some may be developed situationally or contextually rather than in accord with some universal principles. It is questionable whether we can say that such development is less or more mature in creating a universally applicable psychosexual sequence that remains valid cross-culturally.

A second contention of the foregoing discussion is that one cannot separate religion and morality, or at least, certain experiences that are usually termed "religious" in nature. Feelings of awe, reverence, and gratitude in the West are seldom explored except in what is seen as a religious context. In the present day they are seldom envisioned as part of the continuing experience of interpersonal family life.

Again, is it not ethnocentric to consider that such experiences as reverential gratitude are only appropriate when directed toward supernatural figures such as Jesus Christ or the Virgin Mary? I have not seen any studies of moral development that make any examination of how religious beliefs that include attitudes of reverence or gratitude are to be judged when related to moral imperatives. Yet we know that for many individuals moral tonicity is maintained in the context of a sacrificial savior.

A third related comparative contention is that there are cultural differences in guilt formation that must be considered in understanding moral development. American psychology tends to be limited in its empirical approach to parental sanctioning as it induces internalization and the experience of guilt. The forms of parental sanctioning usually considered are physical punishment, isolation, or deprivation. The sacrificial suffering of parents is usually not considered as having a determinative effect on the moral development of a child. The human empathic capacity to feel compassion for the suffering of others starts early. It has not been tested empirically, except in those experiments where the individual is some how induced to inflict pain on another. The witnessing of pain is related to feeling responsible for the pain inflicted. Studies of attendant guilt appear in the psychoanalytic literature in clinical studies of guilt, but it does not appear in systematic studies of internalization or normal moral development. Yet we do observe that acts of religious conversion in the Christian tradition often involve the experience of being loved by a sacrificial deity who relieves us of our sins. A sacrificial Christ elicits gratitude and, for some, the inner strength to forego further destructive or other forms of "immoral" behavior. In such a situation moral tonicity cannot be judged solely as taking place *within* the individual, but in the context of an individual's *interaction* with his or her[25] god.

---

[25]The readiness to feel guilt is related to the readiness to feel gratitude in an interactional "interpersonal" process defined in religious terms whether the actors concerned are in the family or in the Church. Our acts are karmic: morality is the inner experience of intentional causality.

REFERENCES

Azuma, H., Kashiwagi, K., & Hess, R. (1981). *The influence of maternal teaching style upon the cognitive development of children.* Tokyo: University of Tokyo Press.

Barker, R. (1968). *Ecological psychology: Concepts and methods for studying the environment of human behavior.* Stanford, CA: Stanford University Press.

Blatt, S. (1974). Levels of object representation in amaclitic and introjective depression. *The psychoanalytic study of the child.* (Vol. 29). New York: Norton.

Bellah, R. (1957). *Tokugawa religion.* New York: The Free Press.

Caudhill, W., & Weinstein, H. (1966). Maternal care and infant behavior in Japanese and American urban middle class families. In R. Koning & R. Hill (Eds.), *Yearbook of the international sociological association,* Switzerland: Broz, entire issue.

de Grazia, S. (1948). *The political community: A study of anomic.* Chicago: University of Chicago Press.

De Vos, G. A. (1960). The relation of guilt toward parents to achievement and arranged marriage among the Japanese. *Psychiatry, 23*(3), 287–301.

De Vos, G. A. (Ed.). (1973). Role narcissism and the etiology of Japanese suicide. *Socialization for achievement: Essays on the cultural psychology of the Japanese.* Berkeley: University of California Press.

De Vos, G. A. (1975). Apprenticeship and paternalism. In E. Vogel (Ed.), *Modern Japanese organization and decision making.* Berkeley: University of California Press.

De Vos, G. A. (1978). Selective permability and reference group sanctioning. In N. Yinger & S. Cutler (Eds.), *Major social issues:* New York: The Free Press.

De Vos, G. A. (1982). Adaptive strategies in American minorities. In E. E. Jones & S. Korchin (Ed.), *Minority mental health.* New York: Praeger.

De Vos, G. A. (1984). *The incredibility of western prophets.* Amsterdam: University of Amsterdam Press.

De Vos, G. A. (1985a). Dimensions of self in Japanese culture. In A. Marsella, G. De Vos, & F. Hsu (Eds.), *Culture and self: Western perspectives* (pp. 139–184). London: Methuen.

De Vos, G. A. (1985b). Introduction: Approaches to the self for a psychocultural perspective. In G. A. De Vos, A. Marsella, & F. Hsu (Eds.), *Culture and self: Asian and western perspectives.* London: Methuen.

De Vos, G. A. (1986). Confucian family socialization: The religion, morality, and esthetics of propriety. In W. Slote (Ed.), *The psycho-cultural dynamics of the Confucian family: Past and present.* International Cultural Society of Korea (ICSK) Forum Series No. 8.

De Vos, G. A. (1992). Confucian hierarch versus class consciousness in Japan. *Social cohesion and alienation: Minorities in the United States and Japan.* Boulder, CO: Westview Press.

De Vos, G. A. (in press-a). Confucian thought in Tokagawa Japan. In W. Slote & G. A. De Vos (Eds.), *Confucianism and the family.* London and New York: Cambridge University Press.

De Vos, G. A. (in press-b). Confucian family socialization: The religion, morality, and esthetics of propriety. In W. Slote & G. A. De Vos (Eds.), *Confucianism and the family.* London and New York: Cambridge University Press.

De Vos, G. A., & Ross, L. R. (1982). *Ethnic identity.* Chicago: University of Chicago Press.

De Vos, G. A., & Sofue, T. (1986). *Religion and the family in East Asia.* Berkeley: University of California Press.

De Vos, G. A., & Suarez-Orozco, M. M. (1987). Sacrifice and the experience of power. *Journal of Psychoanalytic Anthropology.*

De Vos, G. A., & Suarez-Orozco, M. M. (1990). *Status inequality: A psychocultural approach to the self.* Newberry Park, CA: Sage.

Doi, T. (1973). *Anatomy of dependence.* Tokyo: Kodansha.

Erikson, E. H. (1959). Identity and the life cycle: Selected papers. *Psychological Issues, 1*(1), 1–171.

Firth, R. (1940). The analysis of Mana: An empirical approach. *Journal of Polynesian Society, 49,* 483–510.

Gorer, G. (1943). Themes in Japanese culture. *New York Academy of Science, 5,* 106–124.

Graves, R. (1952). *The white goddess.* London: Faber and Faber.

Hardacre, H. (1984). *Kurozumi, kyo.* Princeton: Princeton University Press.

Hsu, F. L. K. (1985). The self in cross-cultural perspective. In G. A. De Vos, A. Marsella, & F. Hsu (Ed.), *Culture and self: Asian and Western perspectives.* New York: Tavistock Publications.

Kagan, S. (1974). Field independence and conformity of rural Mexican and urban Anglo-American children. *Child Development, 45,* 765–771.

Kagan, S., & Buriel, R. (1977). Field dependence-independence and Mexican-American culture and education. In J. Martinez (Ed.), *Chicano psychology.* New York: Academic Press.

Kernberg, O. (1975). *Borderline conditions and pathological narcissism.* New York: Jason Aronson.

Kluckhohn, F. (1953). Dominant and variant value orientations. In C. Kluckhohn, H. A. Murray, & D. M. Schneider (Eds.), *Personality in nature, society, and culture.* New York: Knopf.

Lanham, B. (1956). Aspects of child care in Japan: Preliminary report. In D. Haring (Ed.), *Personal character and cultural milieu.* New York: Syracuse University Press.

Lanham, B. (1962). *Aspects of child-rearing in Kainan, Japan.* Unpublished doctoral dissertation. Syracuse University.

La Barre, W. (1945). Some observations on character structure in the Orient. *Psychiatry, 8,* 319–342.

Levy, R. I. (1973). Tahitians: Mind and experience in the society islands. Chicago: University of Chicago Press.

Madsen, M. (1967). Cooperative and competitive motivation of children in three Mexican subcultures. *Psychological Reports, 20,* 1307–1320.

Madsen, M., & Shapira, A. (1973). Cooperative and competitive behavior or urban Afro-American, Anglo-American and Mexican village children. *Developmental Psychology, 9,* 16–20.

Marsella, A., De Vos, G., & Hsu, F. (1985). *Culture and self: Asian and western perspectives.* New York and London: Tavistock.

McClelland, D. (1961). *The achieving society.* Princeton, NJ: Van Nostrand.

Miyake, K., et al. (1986). Infant temperament, mother's mode of interaction, and attachment in Japan: An interim report. In I. Bretherton & E. Waters (Eds.), *Monographs of Society for Research in Child Development.* Sapporo, Japan: Hokkaido University.

Nakane, C. (1970). *Japanese society.* Berkeley: University of California Press.

Piaget, J. (1930). *The child's conception of causality.* London: Routledge and Kegan Paul.

Piaget, J. (1932). *The moral judgment of children.* London: Routledge and Kegan Paul.

Reik, T. (1941). *Masochism in modern man.* New York: Grove Press.

Reisman, D., Denny, R., & Glazer, N. (1958). *The lonely crowd: A study of the changing American character.* New Haven: Yale University Press.

Suenari, M. (1986). The religious family in central Taiwan. In G. De Vos & Sofue (Eds.), *Religion and the family in East Asia.* Berkeley: University of California Press.

Tu, W. M. (1985). Selfhood and otherness in Confucian thought. In A. F. Marsella, G. A. De Vos, & F. L. K. Hsu (Eds.), *Culture and self: Asian and Western perspectives.* New York: Tavistock Publications.

Tu, W. M. (1986). On neo-Confucian and human relatedness. In G. A. De Vos & T. Sofue (Eds.)., *Religion and the family in East Asia.* Berkeley: University of California Press.

Vaughn, C. (1988). *Cognitive independence, social independence, and achievement orientation: A comparison of Japanese and U.S. students.* Unpublished dissertation, University of California, Berkeley.

Vogel, E. (1965). *Japan's new middle class.* Berkeley: University of California Press.

Wagatsuma, H., & De Vos, G. A. (1984). *Heritage of endurance: Family patterns and delinquency formation in urban Japan.* Berkeley: University of California Press.

Warner, L. (1958). *The enduring art of Japan.* New York: Grove Press.

Witkin, H. A. (1967). Cognitive styles across cultures. *International Journal of Psychology, 2,* 233–250.

Witkin, H. A. (1969). Social influences in the development of cognitive style. In D. A. Goslin (Ed.), *Handbook of socialization theory and research.* New York: Rand McNally.

Witkin, H. A., & Berry, J. W. (1975). Psychological differentiation in cross-cultural perspective. *Journal of Cross-Cultural Psychology, 6,* 4–87.

Witkin, H. A., & Goodenough, D. (1977). Field dependence and interpersonal behavior. *Psychological Bulletin, 84,* 661–689.

6 Perspectives on Family Theory: Families in History and Beyond

Paula S. Fass
University of California, Berkeley

These five chapters suggest the expanding intellectual universe within which we live and the expanded context within which researchers on the family are newly challenged to operate. That universe includes anthropological relativism wherein the "traditional" western family is only one form among many (Stack and Burton, De Vos); the historicity of the contemporary family (Skolnick); the problematic reflexivity whereby we are confronted by the social consequences of our theories (Aerts); and the vast terrain of epistemological and ontological questions in which our traditional modes of inquiry (objectivist and positivist) has been questioned and assaulted (Hanson, De Vos). Thus the methods of our inquiry, the nature of our judgments and evaluations, and the societal consequences of our theories are in the process of acute and complex investigation.

This situation was predictable since research on the family is part of a wider process of intellectual reassessment taking place within and outside the academy. But predictable or not the result of this process of reevaluation is that we are now in a period of acute uncertainty, an uncertainty that is intellectual, social, and deeply moral. While the involvement in contemporary intellectual currents is therefore tonic, it also comes with some real costs. These costs are seen in the declining willingness to provide normative definitions of what the family is and our consequent unwillingness to judge family forms.

All of this turmoil is largely the result of the decline and fall, for that is what it amounts to, of the once prevailing Parsonian model. In each of the papers in Part I, this issue is either central or lurking very close to the surface. I suggest that until we free ourselves of the tyranny, not of Parsons, but of our disillusionment with Parsons, most family research will be struggling with problems of definition, rather than with creating new theories.

The best way for me to indicate the large dilemmas to which our inquiries have led us is to begin with Arlene Skolnick's chapter which seeks to use the literature on family history to illuminate aspects of family research and intervention in the 1990s. She has read widely in the historical literature on the Western family and very ably discusses several basic issues: the distinction, often large, between family ideals (including prescriptive norms) and actual families in the past; the significance of the life course and its analysis for historical and contemporary problems; and the immense complexity of family forms not just in the past as a whole but at any single point in the past. Having thus theoretically liberated herself from the illusion of a simple past from which the confusing present is counterpoint, she proceeds to reconstruct a picture of the "traditional" American family which often ignores or elides these distinctions. And she ignores them for some very sound reasons. First, the historical literature upon which she draws is often based on research in prescriptive literature that defined what families should be like and/or is based on demographic reconstructions of small groups of avant-garde families (in the early 19th century context, this meant urban, White, middle class). Second, Skolnick latently defines families and charts family change in structural (Parsonian) terms. Thus, the salient issues that define "traditional" families are questions of gender differentiation, family size, and function. She distinguishes historical periods according to whether families were nuclear or extended, urban or rural, economically functional or units of sentiment and affection. While she has removed the romantic haze surrounding past families she has not brought them out of Parson's shade. Above all, she reconstructs a model of a past "traditional" family which is surprisingly homogeneous and familiar—men and women's spheres are distinct; families are private and nuclear; the home is the repository of moral order and social poise. Although beset by problems and not altogether functional for its members, this traditional family is nevertheless familiar as at once the forerunner of Parson's norm and as the departed model (either yearned for or despised) that lies in our imagined past.

In fact, as Skolnick is fully aware, even during periods of so called traditional family hegemony, there is no reason to believe that families actually conformed to these highly schematic and largely White, urban middle-class patterns and every reason to see multiplicity of family types—farm families (dominant throughout most of the 19th century of expanding frontiers); immigrant families of vast variety (between 1830 and 1860, there were proportionately more immigrants in the United States than at any other time before or since); African American families in slavery and freedom. Add to this the enormous differences among even White, urban natives (Moravians for example, or childless couples) and one can begin to sense the problem with the schema proposed by Skolnick. She is obviously aware that diverse realities frequently underlay prescriptive models, but is nevertheless eager to describe a specific configuration as more or less congruent with particular historical circumstances. She knows that Parson's model is both prescriptive and historically limited and yet she needs to use his categories to construct the ideal "traditional" family. Skolnick's postmodern self-consciousness has made her wary of past foibles but not well equipped to deal with historical change. How does one describe change without first constructing a "norm" that disciplines the undulating reality of the past? How does one anchor a phenomenon as slippery as the family without adopting some basic referents? It is not surprising that Skolnick adopts Parson's lingering structural beams even though she has overthrown the house he built and its explicit evaluations.

A genuinely historicized version of the past (understood in its own terms and not as a fixed point of departure) would begin by taking these various past families seriously, and invest them with historical significance and historical consequences. It would be far less likely to generalize about past families on the basis of "ideal" types. Most historical generalizations about the family over the past 200 years are usually just that, broad generalizations based, more often than not, on definitions provided by research on selected secure, White, middle-class families who, while they were far from dominant in number, are assumed somehow to define the standard. This implicit functionalism, which concentrates on a single family form as better suited than others to particular historical circumstances has defined much of the dominant historiography and lingers in Skolnick's review. It is true, as Skolnick properly observes, that some groups are norm-givers and by their power and influence create conscious standards with which others must wrestle, but this is a matter of the politics of the family not its culture or sociology. In fact, historical generalizations about past families often provide us with little more than a foil whose lesson is, to misquote Tolstoy, all past families seem pretty much the same, only contemporary families are different in their own ways. Of course, Skolnick knows that all past families were not alike, but in trying to escape from the evaluations inscribed in Parsonian norms, she adopts a kind of historical model that makes some families seem in step with the times, while other family forms are largely ignored.

Just as problematic from the point-of-view of contemporary concerns is the limited range of families Skolnick uses as an anchor for her history. In developing a historical model of the traditional family, Skolnick relies exclusively on the literature about Western European families. But the history of the West European family is, after all, not the context of meaning for many, perhaps most, of contemporary American families. If the extended family is the family of Western nostalgia, that is true largely for theorists and scholars. For many Americans today their nostalgia (and sense of change) is for families whose historical roots are in Asia, Africa, Central and Southern Europe, Latin America, and emphatically not Western Europe. When they remember extended kin as a real basis for succor and complex kin networks they may in fact be correct, and we have tossed out the extended family and its real history much too hastily (also a Parsonian inheritance). Is it really relevant that in France in the 17th century, or even in the United States in the 19th century, most households were nuclear, when contemplating the changes experienced by Chinese Americans in the course of two or three generations? In seeking to provide a historical context for present multicultural concerns, family theorists will have to extend their field of vision. Tracing the evolution of the present-day American family is much trickier than summarizing the history of the Western family.

I suggested earlier that family research is now subject to all the epistemological uncertainties of our time. Family history is no exception. Skolnick is clearly aware of many of the pitfalls but, as a sociologist eager to draw contemporary lessons from historical research, she relies on the conclusions provided by historians rather than something often more valuable—their assumptions and approach. Skolnick views the family largely as a passive institution and the life course as created largely by external historical forces. In fact, the most exciting historical work [Greven (1978); Ryan (1981); Fliegelman (1982)] has proposed a much more dynamic picture of the relationship between families and social change. In this sense, historians have moved beyond Parsonian functionalism and adopted more developmental models to suggest that family life can re-create other institutions (church, politics), both through the specific psychological training of the young and because theories about families and values centering on families can influence other social and political policies (Rothman, 1971). By looking at family culture and the family as part of culture, rather than at family structure (even dynamic structure as in life course analyses); at how life course issues created other institutional responses (in schooling, for example) [Fass (1977, 1989)]; at how definitions of family constrain social values; and at how the very language of family influences politics and other cultural expressions, historians have come to see family as a force in history. I think theorists of the family will have to take these insights much more seriously as we move through the decade of the 90s and beyond.

As we eagerly seek to leave Parsons behind, sociologists have been the hardest pressed to fill the breech in definitions. Elaine Aerts had the most difficult task of any of the five contributors for to her fell the direct challenge of proposing an alternative to the Parsonian model, an alternative based on actual contemporary families. Like the others, Aerts wants to avoid attaching stigmas of deviancy to those families who do not fulfill Parsonian norms, but as an excellent social theorist she hopes to be able to generalize and not dissolve into the despair of merely observing the extraordinary fragmentation to which we have now become accustomed in our research. Aerts's paper is a model of broad research and systematic clear thinking as she moves toward defining the female-headed household as a new family norm. But in her determination to replace Parsons with something equally comprehensive (perhaps an unnecessary challenge) her paper is beset by its very virtues. Among these I would place its strenuous systematization—the very urgency of her need to replace Parsons with something more realistic. This, together with contemporary statistics (which *seem* so different than the "traditional" historical family), has pushed her too quickly to adopt a female-headed alternative without completely considering the implications clearly embedded in her discussions.

One of the great strengths of Aerts's paper is her recognition of how theory has influenced policy. In this concern, I think she is articulating the latent consciousness of all the contributors, but her systematic examination makes clear why so many theorists have been pushed to depose Parsons: What we say in our theories matters and it matters in ways that make us increasingly uncomfortable. But should her alternative really make us more comfortable? What she is proposing is that the state take the place of the male parent, providing not only assistance but, in effect, taking on the social placement role usually provided by males in traditional families. Aerts has presented a lucid, if brief, analysis of the basic historical dynamic of family life in the past 150 years, a dynamic which can be summed up as increasing privatization together with great and growing social anxiety and concern. She also sees, but does not connect with this the fact, that auxiliary institutions which developed from this concern—social work and psychiatry, education and family assistance programs—have systematically eroded family privacy.[1] As this has happened the impersonal state (not the community) has subverted family autonomy so that privacy in families, especially in dependent families, is more and more a fiction. Her new definition of the family together with her suggestions about increased state services erases this fiction. It raises as a norm, and therefore potentially as an ideal, a new definition with chilling implications. That norm is a female-headed family in active partnership with the state. The solution cries out for a gender-based interpretation: The female-headed family is now to be completed, controlled and made whole by the male state. I think before we rush to rid ourselves of the deviancy inscribed in Parsonianism we ought to be extremely wary of proposing a potentially even more fearsome engine of oppression to women, children, and the future. If we remember that what we say the family is will increasingly define what the family ought to be we should become extremely careful in outlining possibilities.

Aerts tried to provide a more "realistic" definition in a post-Parsonian world. Is it possible to define the family? I think that the answer is yes, although it may be useful to understand that all theories have their costs. Perhaps our theories must begin by being more modest. Perhaps too, we must be less afraid in adopting our theories to "objective" realities to make judgments and to reject those tendencies in real life we find problematic. The first task is to recognize that theory and reality will never coincide exactly, and that the grander the theory the less exact the fit, and that there is no necessary virtue in making our theories more apparently "realistic."

I think Donald Hansen's paper has a lot to teach us about the nature of theory

[1]The fact that families have increasingly "yielded" their social functions to other institutions has traditionally been viewed as part of the process of privatization, that is families have been left with emotional functions only. But this Parsonian view which optimistically reconstructed families around affection remains highly questionable. It is quite as likely that families have become less private in the very process of becoming less and less in control of various social functions.

itself that may be absorbed into these observations. Relying heavily on our contemporary poststructuralism, Hanson argues for the subjective dimension of research as well as for the complexity that inheres in individual experience. Human beings, as Hanson shows in the case of children, are always enmeshed in a continuous process of interpretation, of making sense of their universe, and of trying to influence it so that their actions are never simply reducible to the large environmental forces acting upon them. Hanson's paper is at the other extreme from Aerts's. Where she wants to construct systematic theory, Hanson wants to subordinate theory to the multiplicity of individual based experience. Where she wants to generalize across cases, regions, classes, Hanson wants to focus on thick interpretation and to show the individual as something more than the socioeconomic forces operating upon him/her. Where Aerts sees families reacting to a very large universe of social forces, Hanson wants to make the individual an active willing constituent of that universe. Where Aerts is willing to have female-headed families the passive recipients of state assistance, can we not propose alternatives? Aerts is easier to summarize, Hanson takes some time to digest.

In many ways, Hanson has seen what historians have come increasingly to appreciate—the unpredictable, active, and interactive nature of reality and the individual as a lively part of that process. This returns historians to the original wellspring of their discipline, to the idea of past events as discrete and nonrepeatable. This new historicity is not easy for historians to relearn, but it is perhaps that which historians can be most influential in teaching. It was, of course, Max Weber, above all, whom Hanson rightly admires, who made historians aware that historical evidence could be examined in a more global fashion and it is, in part, the Weberian thrust that is now being scrutinized and reassessed. I think Hanson's essay is an important balance to Aerts and it will be necessary to carry his insights with us as we proceed with our thinking about the family, perhaps above all to free us from views that stress inevitability and render us passive in judgment and action. But, it is very difficult to generalize from his almost novelistic sensibilities since those emerge from a milieu whose payload is the deconstruction of theory. Hanson can help us to focus on the individual and on individual families as much of the best psychology can do and it will make us continually aware that families, as Burton and Stack also make clear, are complex functioning processes, not just social atoms or institutions.

It is to Carol Stack and Linda Burton's credit that they have tried to adopt a dynamic, process-oriented view in their concept of kinscripts. I am not at all sure that one can generalize from the specific rituals they describe in rural, African American families as they propose to do, but their paper has two great virtues from the point-of-view of post-Parsonian theory. First it avoids the contamination of normative evaluation by seriously adopting the values of the families they study. Instead of judging these families by governing theories of what the family should be like, they examine how real families have created strategies for mutual succor and social survival. Rather than defining them as deviant according to a trans-social and trans-temporal norm, Stack and Burton judge the success of these families in their own terms.

Second, as they get closer to the actual families under study, Stack and Burton continue to judge and discriminate among them—some families are more successful than others according to their own requirements. This is not a normless universe. I think this last point is very important. As we move beyond Parsons, it is extremely tempting to opt for a kind of evaluative promiscuity where anything and everything is equally a family. Everything is as good as everything else. This retreat from judgment comes in recoil from a period of overly gross prescription. In fact, however, it is a mistake to abandon judgment and its results for family theory and family life can be devastating. I think it will be necessary for family theorists to continue to have operative definitions, definitions based not on some vast mechanical system but flexible and pragmatic definitions that do not avoid clear statements of value. These values need not be either ideals of complete families or deeply gendered (as in Parsons); they can concern issues like cognitive success, mental well-being, or the prevention of drug addiction, etc. Finally, Stack and Burton make clear that the view that families have moved in a linear direction toward greater affective individualism (as Skolnick suggests) is questionable. As we become more intimately familiar with actual families today and in the past, we may seriously begin to question this view which is as much a prescriptive and normative ideal as anything in Parsons.

One of the great values of Parsons' model of the family was that he persuaded us that the family mattered—to individual development *and* to the manner in which the society functioned. Parsons had been deeply influenced by a half century of social theory which began with anxieties about family disorganization—a view best exemplified in W. I. Thomas and Florian Znaniecki's (1927) study of the Polish peasant. Parsons transcended that anxiety, heavily lodged in studies of poor immigrant populations in inner cities, by enmeshing the family in ideal types and in what we today recognize was an overschematic and inflexible functionalism. In transcending past anxieties, Parsons continued to emphasize structure, much as his predecessors did, largely ignoring aspects of dynamic process. But, it was the valorization of the family that was the key to historians' initial absorption in reconstructing family life in the past. In our quest to reject Parsons I am deeply concerned that we may also be rejecting that basic understanding that the family matters and that it mattered in the past and continues to matter today.

It is in that context that De Vos's paper on the Japanese family is so important. As an anthropologist De Vos wisely rejects rigid notions of trans-social norms either of the structural or psychological variety, but as a psychologist he instinctively recognizes that family relations are basic constituents of individual and social life. The brilliance of this intersection between psychology and anthropology allows him carefully to attend to how family relations interpenetrate wide circles of belief and behavior, in religion as well as politics and education, affecting gestures as well as actions, patterns of cognition as well as belief. De Vos's paper is a necessary auxiliary to Stack and Burton's. Where the latter ask questions about subjective meanings and intrafamilial expectation, De Vos embeds these meanings in a large universe of social act and cultural belief. But as in so many theories that try to connect different planes of social experience, De Vos is forced to abstract in ways that make us more and more uneasy. Since my own knowledge is largely of the American family I draw my examples from his descriptions of the American scene. For example, De Vos is surely correct to note the large distance between Japanese norms that are fundamentally familial and American norms that are individualistic and therefore potentially very stressful to family harmony. In the West, at least since the 18th century, the family has flowed more ambiguously into the society. Still, I think he may be exaggerating the unitary normative character of American individualism, certainly among subgroups in the population as Burton and Stack make clear, but even among middle-class leaders. To use one cultural identifier among others, rote learning was familiar to any 19th century school child. It may be useful to remember that John Dewey's revolution in education (and he was neither the first nor last "radical" in this regard) was to reject this form of learning.

In fact, De Vos appears to be far more sensitive to the nature of Japanese culture than to American, and he often uses the American family as little more than a foil for the Japanese. My own experience as an American historian has led me to question the gross generalization which equates America with individualism not only because I am alert to the multitudinous complexities of American ethnicity (surely Jewish-American mothers take as much pleasure in their son's success as Japanese mothers), but because American theorists have always *worried* so much about individualism. (Much as he rejected rote learning Dewey equally rejected unrestrained individualism in deference to a much denser community ideal and these two were related in his theory.) This is only to say that comparative perspectives often suffer from inadequately nuanced comparisons. If De Vos wishes us to appreciate the multiple significances of family life culturally, he has surely succeeded, and it is probably in this wider attention to how families fit into culture generally that the future of family studies lie, certainly for historians. But as this evolves, it will require far more attention to the complexities, ironies, contradictions and conflicts within the culture than De Vos allows.

Throughout the 20th century Americans have worried about family life. In fact one could see this as a fundamental cultural expression. Indeed, as far back as the late 17th century, Massachusetts towns began to appoint special officers to oversee family life as part of their growing concern that rigid Puritan norms were often abrogated. Today, of course, we imagine that Puritan families, entwined in rich communities and connected to God's laws, were always cohesive and mutually supportive, that children were obedient and parents responsible. We look nostalgically to the past to heal the wounds of the present. But this is historical mythologizing, not history. The history of families in the American past has been messy, only its theories have been neat. One of the great strengths of the chapters before us is to reject the neatness of theory as a measure for present realities. In that sense, Parsons has been deposed. But, as I look to the year 2000 I hope to find much more than an anti-Parsonian chorus. I would like us to take seriously the idea of past and present complexity in family forms, the heterogeneity of cultural sources for family experience, and the salience of family life for all aspects of culture.

Does this mean that we give over theory entirely and opt for a pragmatic acceptance of fact? I think not, as this would be neither possible nor desirable and very much the wrong knee-jerk reaction to Parsons. There are no facts without theories because the very questions we ask are theoretically, or at least conceptually, informed. More significantly, as moral beings who interpret our experience, questions of evaluation must and should shape our work. That moral passion is present in each of these chapters, even in the seemingly most objective. Aerts cares as deeply about social policies as Hanson cares about the children of his studies. Burton and Stack lovingly recreate meanings and obligations among kin, and De Vos worries about neuroses. And Skolnick hopes history will allow us to accept rather than define as delinquent the present family forms. When Americans measure present families against the past they are making moral statements, whether these statements are aimed to create a more perfect future (as is often the case in feminist literature) or flay the present as measured against a better past (Lasch, 1977). If our theories have become less schematic so too has our morality. Above all, we like our forebears continue to worry about family life. That is a good sign.

REFERENCES

Fass, P. S. (1977). *The damned and the beautiful: American youth in the 1920's*. New York: Oxford University Press.

Fass, P. S. (1989). *Outside in: Minorities and the transformation of American education*. New York: Oxford University Press.

Fliegelman, J. (1982). *Prodigals and pilgrims: The American revolution against patriarchal authority, 1750–1800*. Cambridge, England: Cambridge University Press.

Greven, P. Jr. (1970). *Four generations: Population, land, and family in colonial Andover, Massachusetts*. Ithaca, NY: Cornell University Press.

Greven, P. Jr. (1978). *The Protestant temperament: Patterns of child-rearing, religious experience, and the self in early America*. New York: Knopf.

Lasch, C. (1977). *Haven in a heartless world: The family besieged*. New York: Basic Books.

Rothman, D. J. (1971). *The discovery of the asylum: Social order and disorder in the New Republic*. Boston: Little, Brown.

Ryan, M. P. (1981). *Cradle of the middle class: The family in Oneida County, New York, 1780–1865*. Cambridge, England: Cambridge University Press.

Thomas, W. I., & Znaniecki, F. (1927). *The Polish peasant in Europe and America*. 2 vols. (2nd ed.). New York: Knopf.

7 Perspectives on Family Theory: New Myths From Old

Annette Lawson
University of California, Berkeley

Long ago at the beginnings of my discipline of sociology in the mid- to late-19th century in Europe, its procreators had no doubt that they were engaged in a moral enterprise. Suffering human beings constrained by history into class formations or by collective values and a division of labor, by the very facticity of social institutions, were essentially determined. Social actors might dream of a future in which they were themselves creative participants who could learn from their own and the larger pasts in which they were embedded, but this was *but* dreaming. Dreams were not the stuff of sociology, nor their understanding and interpretation accessible through the methods of science. This despite the later arrival on the social science scene of Freud. But the future of humankind could be dreamt about by the social scientist: and utilizing the tools of proper observation and analysis, truths would be unraveled, enabling expert advice to be offered to the leaders—politicians, educationists, health reformers, and others who would follow this with legislation and the development of appropriate institutional strategies. Thus would human society progress and human suffering lessen.

Even after World War II and the Holocaust, a belief in the steady progress of humankind persisted and in the heady excitement of building the new society, the tradition of social science as a moral science continued to flourish. In Britain, there was always a struggle between the theorists and the empirical researchers but work on the family was often carried out in multidiscipline teams. In Bethnal Green Michael Young and Peter Willmott (1957, 1973), Peter Townsend (1957), and Peter Marris (1958) mapped community change, in Nottingham, the Newsons (1963) examined child-rearing by interview and at the London School of Economics, the Medical Research Council was persuaded by David Glass, the demographer and sociologist, to fund the first major longitudinal study of a nationally drawn population. (This study had been begun in 1946 in an attempt to quantify the costs of maternity for the new Health Service.) Under the direction of a medically qualified person (J. W. B. Douglas), both large scale quantitative analysis of the influence of class on the development of children and small scale observational and interview studies were carried out. A psychiatrist, several psychologists, and I worked together from 1962–1968 to develop ways to study children in their home settings and understand why it was that when they arrived at the school gate at the age of five, class differences were already so disadvantageous. There was no question that this was a moral enterprise; our questions were directed to solving social problems and playing our own part in a genuinely brave new world.

Then, as history unfurled, progress was far from assured and public leaders were not ready to listen, sociologists engaged in a range of strategies directed more to enabling the discipline to flourish in the academy, to developing theory or methods (or, if not developing them, at least persistently worrying away at them like a dog with a bone), and to redefining the problems with which they were primarily concerned. In Britain, empiricism flourished for some time but in the late 1960s and 1970s as new Universities were founded and sociologists became professors running large departments, entire subdisciplines turned away from the State and redefined themselves. The best example of this process was the development of criminology into a sociology of deviance—a process that began at a conference in Cambridge with Stan Cohen and Laurie Taylor held at the Institute of Criminology in 1971. But Cambridge University, itself, still has no degree in Sociology, nor does Oxford. These bastions, despite the appointment of distinguished professors such as Anthony Giddens in Cambridge or Stephen Lukes in Oxford, have resisted the youngest social science. From the continent of Europe and from those Americans who eschewed massive numbering or Parsonian theory, the British departments took subjectivity, participant observation, and interactionism. But it was not sociologists, by and large, who examined families. This turf was left rather to the psychologist studying the urban west and to the anthropologist elsewhere.

In America, the history of sociology has followed a different path and the discipline is much more strongly established and has had (or so it seems to me) a stronger influence on at least some administrations. But its place as a moral enterprise has perhaps been less than clear.

Now, in the late 20th century we seem to have come full circle and are permitting ourselves—indeed demanding of ourselves—that we learn from our original and later thinkers, that we make the boundaries we have set about ourselves more permeable and less high—and make them, perhaps, not of barbed wire that wounds and reminds us of militaristic moments (even recent glories are best forgotten here) but of soft, ecologically sound, wooden, climbable fences through which one can see what is on the other side, not in order to say the grass is greener, but to invite the anthropologist, psychologist, or historian who works there to visit who will in turn reciprocate the invitation.

Each of these chapters reflects this desire. Our century is growing old even as it paradoxically is overwhelmed with the new—technology and ideas driving and swooping in the florid pluralism of the western world while in other regions there is a desperate attempt to run before walking, both in response to the urgently insistent demands of the west and in a desire to catch up. Yet our age shows: We are tired at century's end of studies that do not move us on, that factorize the individual without linking her or him to a social context, or that focus only on context and cannot accept an acting person at the heart. We do not learn, we think, from an acceptance of social problems predefined often by political expediency and media interest as the proper locus of our research beam. We know, too, that we are ourselves actors in this drama and responsive to and responsible for such definitions. We must, we argue, look to the past in order to reach for the future and give up the comforting blankets that have sustained us each in our separate development within each discipline. It is thus, not enough simply to state without further understanding or elucidation that we must deal with process, not moments only; that we need to link historical moment with cohort effects; that we must build various dimensions of experienced time and place into our research agenda, and open our ethnocentric vision to a comparative analysis. No. It is not enough. We need to recommend specific subjects for research and spell out the ways to incorporate these pious but, to my mind, also lofty and exciting hopes.

My pleasure in reading all of these remarkable essays has grown with reflection on the contribution of each because every one, while criticizing in appropriate ways past mentors and thinkers, carefully selects those debts of thought that not only might but, since we are engaged in a moral enterprise, *ought* to be included in our thinking now. Why lose our babies (or Talcott Parsons) as we regenerate? Rather, enable their growth and take their mature thinking with us. In addition, each of these authors brings in an imaginative future. The subjects of research here are seriously accepted as actors in large and smaller scale dramas so that the notion of script is moved on to become more useful in our research agenda. Time is integrated also so that each essayist wants to look not only back and forward in a linear way but also to develop more complex notions of what Hansen calls the "present-future."

Finally, each essay is not circumscribed by a particular disciplinary tradition. Skolnick is a psychologist but writes of history and social forms while an anthropologist (Stack), and a sociologist (Burton), employ participant observation and the idea of kin in modern America. De Vos, a psychoanalytically oriented psychologist and anthropologist (to which he, himself draws attention at the opening of his essay) uses a cross-cultural as well as interdisciplinary approach to examine the Japanese family as a moral enterprise.

Let me point to certain other commonalities. Each of these contributors accepts the plurality of family forms in the same instance that they acknowledge a generally held deep, emotionally important understanding that each lay actor has of *family*. Elaine Aerts tackles the problem head on and, utilizing the idea that families "are primarily the units of biological and cultural reproduction of societies" (p. 4), she determines the basic unit is the adult and dependent child. Cowan has pointed to the central importance of feminism for family research and Aerts demonstrates this with her definition, for since the adult is normally the mother, the father's role is instantly problematized. Citing Malinowski's injunction to "show where the family comes in, whence it draws its forces, how far it is inevitable and where it can be dispensed with" (p. 4), Aerts uses classical and careful analysis of its changing social forms, policy development and its impact, and changes in reproductive technologies, especially artificial insemination, to demonstrate with each paragraph the links between social institutions and family lives as well as values held about *the* family and suggests as Ferdinand Mount has in the UK (1982) that the family is resistant to coercion though not able to avoid poverty. Her plea to bring back the *institution* is developed into a close argument that enables specific and urgent policy-directed questions for research to be posited. For, if it is accepted that the basic unit (both in a structural and a meaning-situated sense) is the mother and dependent child, then the widespread acceptance of the working mother, the role of father and the functionality of new family forms, including reconstituted families, all become urgent problems for investigation. Indeed, this changing structure highlights the interplay of legislative and executive changes on the minutiae of daily life in families.

Despite the difficulty in talking of *the* family, Arlene Skolnick shows both its emerging, discontinuous, and stable forms in America. Hers is part of a grand tradition in sociology that debunks modern common sense. She shows that in each generation there have been fears of the decline in family values. But we can accept the hegemony of an ideational family as concrete as any actual formation statistically measurable through census returns. And she does argue, despite her belief that the nuclear family household and marriage for love predated industrialization, for the emergence of a family that had a different emotional center—both as between spouses and in relation to children in terms of the reasons for having them and in the ways they were reared. Her essay begins, as centuries should end, with a plea for history and an insistence on a deeper understanding of social change as not only impacting families and individual members of families but as an integral part of family development itself.

Central to Skolnick's argument is an acceptance of the constructivist role of the researcher, for she points out that there was a virtual silence on the history of the family until the last two decades when historians (led by Philip Aries' pathbreaking *Centuries of Childhood*) have developed it into a veritable industry. This was triggered by a movement to social and away from traditional history. It was probably also deeply influenced by the new women's history—the writing of women's past lives. Part of feminist scholarship, historians in this field fit firmly into the debunking mode themselves but they have also enabled a completely new social analysis. Topics such as the private and public domains, sexuality, the division of labor, slavery, and domestic economy are now (or should be considered) essential aspects to a rounded picture of families. I will return to the need for such a rounded picture.

In common with most other authors in this section, Skolnick also returns to Talcott Parsons, again pointing to the construction of thought and topic as being in important ways formulated by social scientists. Parsons set the ways in which until now we have thought about the family, and especially about the interplay between family roles and external influences. Indeed, his way of thinking became what "everyone knew"—that fathers were instrumental and mothers expressive and that children were best reared by mothers at home and that young persons, having been socialized appropriately and having internalized social values, would be readily integrated into the society. Research questions could not even be thought, and certainly therefore not formulated outside this frame of reference. There is still a daily struggle for women as they attempt to reconcile their out-of-home and paid working lives with the demands of this ideal. Although Skolnick accepts the problems in Parsons of an optimistic functionalism in the family of male-breadwinner, female home-keeper, and child-rearer, she notes and can utilize his appreciation of the female role as a "pseudo-occupation" and this family form as containing severe "structurally-differentiated" strain (pp. 50–52).

But Parsons did not see such acknowledged strains as leading to change. Hence the disappointment that followed when the 1960s upset everyone's expectations of solid Darwinian development along a progressive line. Skolnick wishes to rescue Parsons, however, and develops a schema as an analytic tool. She proposes that this is done against a background of "structures of conflict" in which when something new of importance such as a technological shift or a new primary school, is introduced, family arrangements may alter in a way that is not consistent with current values, producing further cultural conflict. Such an approach makes room for economic recession and increasing unemployment on the one hand or the introduction of the personal computer into homes on the other.

In the 1990s we certainly would be naive indeed to see the world as in conditions other than struggle. We need to understand that longevity and lower fertility means that for the first time in history we spend more time now as adult offspring of our own parents than we do as parents of dependent children. Not having any ready made models to follow—narrative structures or scripts to pursue and finding ourselves in a present and future that is confusing, conflict is likely. Social scientists have already developed cultural constructs to deal with these facts—mid life, old-old and young-old, for example.

These are the kinds of changes that fundamentally alter family patterns, family time, family tasks, and as Carol Stack (an anthropologist) and Linda Burton (a sociologist) would argue, *Kinscripts*. Before moving to a discussion of this chapter, which is a first class example of how research should be done, I turn to Donald Hansen's spectacular synthesis of social theory. Like Skolnick, Hansen remembers Parsons and like her, he also notes how useful elements of the functionalist problematic remains. Again, like Skolnick, Hansen's problem is to bring home to the researcher visiting from *outside* what we already know but too often do not integrate into our research plans: that Parsons was wrong in his separation of the home from this *outside* world. The case of the little girl, Kimberley, as she progresses through elementary and middle school illuminates his elaboration of a situated and, paradoxical though it may seem, behavioral, Meadian approach. Hansen shows us the different meanings ascribed by Kimberley and her teacher to the same objective activity—reading out loud a note from her mother—experienced as normal by the teacher and as profoundly embarrassing by the child whose normalcy is actually threatened by this act. Various essential ingredients shape Hansen's thinking:

First, the actor is granted human agency in a serious way. Hansen is not simply denying a *tabula rasa*, he is insisting that even the relatively powerless child is able to act upon the world, to change her own and the experience of others. And he achieves this in understanding one child's slide down the social ladder of achievement at school—a topic of thousands of very differently constructed studies that would leave us knowing what was associated with what and even, perhaps, understanding something of the feelings of those involved but not really understanding how grades fell, why they fell and why they picked up. Here Weber is Hansen's ancestor.

Second, the actor acts in various dimensions of time—what Giddens has called the *durée*—of day-to-day time—repetitive or reversible therefore; of the time of an individual's life-span; and of the institution that continues after death.

Third, the individual has a continuing concept of the future—a generalized and specific own future that is also made up of the past and the present moment. Hansen refers to the "present future." This is the most exciting part for this reader. The imagination of the actor enters into the behavior exhibited and can be accessed through observation and appropriate questioning and also inferred and interpreted through an empathetic understanding. Furthermore, Hansen's ideas about agency and time are close in many senses to the Stack and Burton essay.

Wanting to understand patterns of early (or "out of time") teenage childbearing in certain Black communities, Burton conducted ethnographic and participant observation studies in various comparable Black communities. She needed an explanatory system that could encompass difference at the community level as well as similarity. In a tradition pursued by Glaser and Strauss (1967), these authors produce grounded theory, not from White middle-class America but from Black extended families. In a practical way and citing Glen Elder (1978) and Dennis Hogan (1978), Stack and Burton take on the task of "weaving together sociological perspectives of the life course and anthropological studies of kinship and the developmental life-cycle of families."

In this chapter three culturally defined family domains are examined: kin-work, kin-time, and kin-scription. The first refers to those tasks undertaken by kin as part of the work of maintaining family structures, the second to the timing of these tasks, and the last to the creation, alteration, and setting of the work and its timing together with sanctions for breaches in the script. One small example helps to give the flavor of a beautifully crafted analysis. In one community there is a powerful script that requires chosen young girls to bear babies out of wedlock and early. These babies are to be reared by grandmothers, not too old to be able to keep up with the toddler and not too young because they are needed both to care for their own grandmothers and to support the whole family economically. The concept of mothering simply becomes grandmothering. "I'll be to old to be a grandmother," is said by the 35 year-old-woman, "if that granddaughter of mine (aged 13) doesn't get on and have that baby" (not a direct quote but see Chapter 4 for the actual words used). There are clearly powerful norms in conflict with those of a hegemonic White middle-class culture and perhaps in conflict with the desires of individuals to live a different script. A later section of this essay deals with just such a rebellion.

A major advantage, then, of this analysis is that it can be applied to any family form and, although functionality is retained, it suggests no absence of conflict.

Finally, George De Vos, in an old tradition, appropriately returns us to the moral enterprise. He also, because he works from an inner world, enables us already to appreciate the interplay of theory and therapy. From the similar and universal experience of infants—of, for example, the stone crawled over, handled and mouthed, different understandings of the nature of the world and its forces are taken in. In particular the locus of power and control and the need to express gratitude are worked out in particular cultures in different ways. "For some groups, nature continues to be considered as having intentional qualities" (p. 121) but in Japan de Vos tells us, a divinity is not necessary. Rather, "the ultimate virtues [. . .] are directed towards humanity." (p. 122). This essay develops the interplay between cultural values (in Japan for present compliance for future mastery) and family experiences. In Japan, Neo-Confucianism appears to have integrated some of the individualistic values of modern America for self-fulfillment but this is through the better progressive exercise of one's social or family role. In common with other authors here, de Vos works to integrate the social and the individual.

What then can we take from these essays for our research task? What should be our script for family research?

- The nature of the research we now need accepts the thinking of the ancestors but incorporates that of the feminist, insisting on gender as pivotal in understanding family functioning or that of individuals. Any question now posed, therefore, at the least must ask whether gender is material and delineate when and why and in what ways.
- There must be no hard boundary between the family, however structured, and other worlds. Both Hansen's study of Kimberley and Stack and Burton's of

Gospel Hill demonstrate that. It is not overwhelming when one sees the work accomplished in this way.

• The link in our story-line lies with the imagination. Kimberley is not only at school when she is physically present there but also at home. These multiple realities—multiple roles—may be played only in certain appropriate settings or by breach in the "wrong" settings, but they are present in the heads and hearts of the actors we study. They must, as long ago C. Wright Mills (1959) recommended, be in ours.

• We must be aware of our power to structure the very problems we seek to unravel by using language in such a way that it precludes the questions we need to pose. Techniques and approaches drawn from clinical psychology, education, anthropology, and interactionism have taught us to listen to the actors in order to formulate such problems in appropriate language, and there are new techniques to do so, again drawn from the range of fields open to the social scientist. For example, a current research project in the UK examining the division of domestic labor in couples with young children has drawn from an adult education program in Bolivia used with illiterate peasant women. Couples are asked to place cards describing a range of tasks and responsibilities on a chart in five columns headed according to whether they are wholly carried out by one or the other, with help from each other, or equally. The actual mapping is engaged in with enthusiasm and the discussion taped for further analysis. It appears to be an elegant way of short-circuiting the diary and the interview, may obtain better quality data, and enables the couple to examine their own arrangements.

• Ancestors taught us we could not be "value-free" but "value-relevance" can still be achieved and we should work to retain that as part of our script.

• Such basic ordering of our script does not imply any need to abandon the turning of meaningful statements into numbers. Rather, it should ensure the numbers remain, when aggregated, possible to retranslate back into meaningful statements.

• We do, however, need to beware the too concrete. We do all experience the power of the social fact. As a woman I may not enter certain portals, such as many of the clubs of old London except through certain doors and under strict limitations as to my rights. My school enables or constrains me by what it offers and what it forecloses as well as by the way a particular teacher acts. But, as Giddens has explored, social structures are not actually buildings, just as the body is not actually a machine. Deconstructing those images will help us utilize permeable boundaries.

• Postmodernism need not frighten us. Rather, take the example of Judith Stacey's (1990) *Brave New Families,* a sociologist using participant observation and interview (or conversation) to examine the lives of just two Silicon Valley families in their complexity and diversity. In daily life and in the construction of meaning, these families find creative ways to manage economic disorder and gender conflicts.

• The subject matter—the focus of our work—needs to take on the urgent problems that arise as a result of new family formations. One absence is curious and should be ended. Sexuality is surely embedded in family lives but none of these authors confronts it as part of our problematic. It is, it seems to me, a perfect example of a topic written out by larger societal scripts, by the need for social scientists to raise funds and gain tenure and by traditional concerns. I recall giving my first paper on my adultery study in 1980 or thereabouts and the psychologist, Liam Hudson, complaining that I appeared to be concerned with myth and not sex. That surely was strange in such a study. Indeed, I found myself writing out sex and my respondents almost invariably doing the same. I had to develop breaching strategies in interviews to bring it back. In such ways are we constrained by our own society's values and boundaries to social intercourse.

I use the term *myth* or *mythologies* to describe the narrative structures in culture that can be pursued by individuals, albeit not unconstrained (Lawson, 1988). The terms are helpful because they capture not just present and new stories but narrative structures from long past and can be interpreted to include the unconscious and the *tacit*—that knowledge we have but do not speak, as Hansen reminds us. A myth is also open to new developments and story lines that emerge to deal with present difficulties, contradictions and solutions. I suggest the elements I have listed here might form a basic structure to our end of century mythology.

I can do no better than end by quoting from this volume with only slight modification to spread its utility, from one of ourselves. Here is Hansen (p. 100):

> In the most general terms, what is required is that in our research we accord the (subject) the full measure of humanity we recognize, tacitly, as well as rationally, in ourselves. It also means we attend more closely to that recognition of humanity, not only in the (subject) but in ourselves, attempting to recognize how our sense of self and possibilities are both shaped and constrained by the language we use, the "problematic" we accept, and the culture we endorse, as well as the organizations and structures in which we act.

REFERENCES

Elder, G. (1978). *Children of the great depression: Social change in life experience*. Chicago: Aldine.

Hogan, D. (1978). *Transitions and social change: The early life of American men*. New York: Academic Press.

Glaser, E. G., & Strauss, A. L. (1967). *The discovery of grounded theory*. Chicago: Aldine.

Lawson, A. (1988). *Adultery: An analysis of love and betrayal*. New York: Basic Books.

Marris, P. (1958). *Widows and their families*. London: Routledge and Kegan Paul.

Mills, C. W. (1959). *The sociological imagination*. Oxford: Oxford University Press.

Mount, F. (1982). *The subversive family*. London: Jonathan Cape.

Newson, E., & Newson, J. (1963). *Patterns of infant care in an urban community*. London: Allen and Unwin.
Stacey, J. (1990). *Brave new families*. New York: Basic Books.
Townsend, P. (1957). *The family life of old people*. London: Routledge and Kegan Paul.
Young, M., & Willmott, P. (1957). *Family and Kinship in East London*. New York: The Free Press.
Young, M., & Willmott, P. (1973). *The symmetrical family*. London: Routledge and Kegan Paul.

II RETHINKING RESEARCH ON NUCLEAR FAMILIES

8 Mothers, Fathers, Sons, and Daughters: Gender Differences in Family Formation and Parenting Style

Philip A. Cowan
Carolyn Pape Cowan
University of California at Berkeley

Patricia K. Kerig
Simon Fraser University

For the past 17 years, we have been studying families in the process of development. Beginning with couples during their first pregnancy, we have followed their families until their first children finished Kindergarten (Cowan & Cowan, 1990; Cowan, Cowan, Heming, Garrett, Coysh, Curtis-Bowles, & Bowles, 1985; Cowan, Cowan, Schulz, & Heming, in press), investigating the family factors associated with the couple's adaptation to parenthood and the first child's adaptation to school. Although we did not initially plan to concentrate on gender issues, our longitudinal findings make it clear that we cannot describe *parents* without knowing whether we are talking about mothers or fathers, nor can we discuss *children* without specifying whether we are talking about boys or girls. We have come to believe that it is not possible to understand family processes without paying attention to the particularities of husband-wife, father-son, father-daughter, mother-son, and mother-daughter relationships—at least in the early phases of family development.

Discussions of the role of gender in family life and child development (e.g., Parsons & Bales, 1955) tend to raise controversy. In the psychological literature of the 1970s a major disagreement erupted between Maccoby and Jacklin (1974), who claimed that developmental differences between boys and girls were comparatively few, and Block (1976a, 1976b, 1983, 1984), who documented differences between boys and girls in almost every aspect of their development. Our interpretation of the research of the 1980s (e.g. Block, 1983; Ervin-Tripp, O'Connor, & Rosenberg, 1984; Fagot, 1985; Kerig, 1989; Maccoby & Martin, 1983; MacDonald & Parke, 1984; Siegal, 1987) is that Block's view is closer to the mark, but the outcome of the controversy is still under discussion (e.g., Lytton & Romney, 1991).

Previous arguments about whether there are developmental or personality differences between boys and girls tend to center on sampling issues and on the adequacy of the particular studies that reviewers include in their "box score" summaries of research trends. We have several additional methodological concerns. First, in disputing Maccoby and Jacklin's claim that parents generally treat boys and girls similarly, Block argued that most researchers through the 1970s studied mothers *rather than fathers;* the findings were misleading because in comparison with mothers, fathers tend to show more differential treatment of boys and girls.

Second, the search for gender differences usually focuses on counts of behavior frequencies or global ratings of parents' or children's behavior, cumulated or averaged across a laboratory session or home visit. However, dynamic socialization theories would suggest that the important events affecting gender differentiation are more likely to be revealed in *microanalyses* of parents' *contingent* responses to specific child behaviors. For example, it may not be how parents react in general that shapes the development of gender-linked differences in their children, but how they react when their children behave in ways that they consider appropriate or inappropriate to their sex—for example, when little boys play with cut-outs or little girls engage in roughhousing (Fagot, 1978).

Third, investigators have been so concerned with proving or disproving the existence of gender effects in parenting patterns that they have paid little attention to variations among families. Recent studies suggest that in some families mothers or fathers may be highly reactive to the gender of their children whereas in others, both parents may treat sons and daughters similarly.

In her influential book on gender in the family, Nancy Chodorow (1978) linked the origins of gender differentiation in children with the gendered allocation of parents' roles in childbearing. Women do most of the work of rearing both sons and daughters. Because boys are inherently different from, and girls inherently similar to, their primary caretakers, boys and girls are faced with qualitatively different developmental tasks as they attempt both to establish emotional connectedness and to separate from their important attachment figures. In Chodorow's formulation (see also Chodorow, 1989), family arrangements stimulate development along gendered lines, but consistent with Freud (1964), the mechanisms of gender differentiation are located primarily *within the children* as they attempt to develop and individuate from their parents. In this process, Chodorow argues, girls are more likely than boys to grow up ready to take on nurturing family roles, thus creating a generational pattern of maintaining traditional masculine and feminine roles through the "reproduction of mothering."

The hypothesis we propose here does not contradict Chodorow's analysis, but shifts perspective from the intrapsychic mechanisms of the child to the dynamics of the family system as they unfold during the transition to parenthood. We have amassed considerable evidence in the course of our longitudinal research to support the contention that one key source of gender-differentiated parenting is inherent *in the process* by which men and women make their transition from couple to family. The transition appears to heighten the existing differences between men and women, which, in turn, amplifies the tendency of mothers and fathers to treat their sons and daughters differently.

Consistent with an emerging body of theory and research, we focus on the *marital relationship* as an important context in which parent-child relationships develop (Belsky, 1984; Cox, Owen, Lewis, & Henderson, 1989; Crockenberg & Covey, in press; Goldberg & Easterbrooks, 1984; Heinicke & Guthrie, in press; Howes & Markman, 1989). We show that as partners become parents, the tendency toward husband-wife differentiation in the marital relationship amplifies a tendency toward gender-linked interactions with their children during the children's early development. Moving beyond the usual question of *whether* gender is salient in parent-child relationships, we attempt to illuminate the fact that families vary markedly in the extent to which parents treat boys and girls differently. We test the hypothesis that the more husbands and wives diverge during the transition to parenthood and early months of childbearing, and the greater their level of marital distress, the more we will find that gender affects their styles of interacting with their preschool-aged children.

HOW THE TRANSITION TO PARENTHOOD AMPLIFIES DIFFERENCES BETWEEN MOTHERS AND FATHERS

We have described in a number of reports what happens to men, women, and marriage as partners become parents (e.g., Cowan et al., 1985; Cowan & Cowan, 1992). In general, Jessie Bernard's (1972) aphorism suggesting "two marriages in every marriage—his and hers"—extends to the process of becoming a family. Men and women follow different schedules in preparing for parenthood, and experience the impact of the transition at different times in different ways.

A Five-Domain Structural Model of the Family

In an attempt to synthesize previous conceptual schemes (e.g., Belsky, 1984; Heinicke & Guthrie, in press; Parke & Tinsley, 1982), we developed a 5-domain model of family structure to examine interrelated aspects of new parents' adaptation:

1. the characteristics of each individual in the family, with special emphasis on self-concept and self-esteem;
2. the husband-wife relationship, with special emphasis on their division of labor and patterns of communication;
3. the relationship between each parent and the child, including parents' ideas about parenting, parenting style, and parenting stress;

4. the intergenerational relationships among grandparents, parents, and children;

5. the relationship between nuclear family members and other individuals or institutions outside the family, with special emphasis on friendships, work, and the balance between life stresses and social supports.[1]

Each of the five domains describes a different level of system organization; individual, dyad, triad, three-generational, and the larger societal context in which the family develops. Our interest lies not only in what happens within each domain, but on how the domains are interconnected. For example, fathers' or mothers' self-esteem can be affected by their relationships with their parents, their children, their coworkers, and their spouses. Our model suggests that a *combination* of what is happening in each domain influences satisfaction/dissatisfaction and adaptation/distress for the individuals, the couple, and the family as a whole. In contrast with family approaches that focus either on individuals *or* on the system (cf. Grotevant & Carlson, 1989; Walsh, 1980), we assume that individual, dyadic, triadic, three-generational, and extra-family domains each contribute important and *unique* information to our understanding of family functioning. Our model is consistent with Bronfenbrenner's (1979) ecological approach, in which we are trying to understand family development and dysfunction in the larger context of the family's life.

Description of the Study

In the Becoming a Family Project, we assessed 72 expectant couples with interviews, questionnaires, and observations: 48 of the couples completed interviews and questionnaires in late pregnancy and an additional 24 completed questionnaires after birth only. Then, all of the couples were reassessed when their children were 6, 18, 42, and 66 months old. In the last two assessments, when the children were approximately 3½ and 5½ years, we added videotaped assessments of the individual child and of parent-child and whole family interaction in our laboratory at the Institute of Human Development. At the kindergarten follow-up we also obtained teacher ratings of the child in the classroom and individual assessments of the child on the Peabody Individual Achievement Test.

As the couples entered the study, a randomly chosen one-third of the 72 expectant couples were offered an opportunity to work with us in a preventive intervention program—couples groups with trained leaders that met every week for 6 months, from late pregnancy through the first 3 months of parenthood (see Cowan & Cowan, 1987; C. Cowan, 1988). Because we expected couple relationships to change over time regardless of the partners' status as parents, we

[1]It is necessary to consider a sixth domain, sibling relationships, once the first child is joined by a brother or sister.

followed a comparison sample of 24 childless couples who had not yet decided whether to have a baby over a comparable period of time.

The total sample ranged widely in socioeconomic circumstances, and ethnic background, with 85% of the participants Caucasian and 15% Black, Asian-American, or Hispanic. They lived in 28 communities in the greater San Francisco Bay Area, and ranged in age at the beginning of the study from 21 to 48 years: the mean age of the men was approximately 30 years, and the women's average age was 29 years. The partners had been together for an average of 4 years, with a range extending from 8 months to 12 years. Their total family incomes averaged $22,500, with a range extending from $7,000 to $72,000 in 1979 dollars.

Increasing Gender Differentiation During the Transition to Parenthood

The new mothers and fathers in our study experienced more change, and more negative change, than couples not having a baby in each of the five family domains that we assessed in pregnancy and at 6 and 18 months postpartum (Cowan et al., 1985).

1. *Gender differences in identity as a parent.* On an instrument we call *The Pie* (C. P. Cowan & P. A. Cowan, 1990a), men and women listed various aspects of themselves (partner, parent, worker, son, friend—as many or as few as they wished) and divided a circle 4″ in diameter to represent the psychological size or salience of each piece, not the hours spent in that role. Both men's and women's "parent" identity increased significantly during the transition to parenthood. Women's "parent" piece increased from 10% in late pregnancy to 34% (1/3 of *The Pie*) at 6 months after birth, whereas men's psychological involvement in their "parent" identity increased from 5% to 21% (1/5 of *The Pie*). During the same period, women's partner/lover aspect of self declined from 34% to 22% while men's sense of self as partner/lover declined from 35% to 30% of *The Pie*. We interpret these statistically significant trends to mean that compared with their husbands, new mothers become even more psychologically involved in their identities as parents and even less involved in their identities as marital partners. As we see below, new mothers also become much less involved in their identities as workers or students.

It is interesting to us to find that although there were marked differences between men and women in their self-descriptions on *The Pie,* their descriptions of their personality traits related to gender—masculinity and femininity—on the *Adjective Check List* (Gough & Heilbrun, 1980) revealed no systematic changes over time, either in the new parents or the childless couples. That is, the changes in identity and roles that are associated with becoming a family are *not* reflected in gendered personality changes during the early childbearing years, at least as assessed by parents' self-reports.

2. *Gender differences in the marital relationship.*

(a) Family roles. We investigated behavioral changes in family roles using a *Who Does What?* questionnaire (C. P. Cowan & P. A. Cowan, 1990b), in which men and women described their *relative* involvement at each assessment period in household, decision-making, and childcare tasks. Husbands' and wives' family work roles, on the whole, became more specialized and less shared during the transition to parenthood (P. A. Cowan & C. P. Cowan, 1988). Although both men and women had reported in pregnancy that they expected the women to do the bulk of the baby care, mothers were doing even more of the baby care at 18 months postpartum than either partner had predicted. Not surprisingly, both spouses' satisfaction with the family division of labor declined during the transition to parenthood, with wives even more dissatisfied than husbands at each assessment period.

(b) Marital satisfaction. Of 15 studies with pre- and posttransition measures of marital quality, including our own, all but 2 report significant declines in marital satisfaction during the transition to parenthood (P. A. Cowan & C. P. Cowan, 1988). In our study, marital satisfaction scores (Locke-Wallace, 1959) in new mothers and fathers declined significantly from late pregnancy to 6 months after birth, with another drop from 6- to 18-months postpartum. This decline is especially noteworthy given that assessments of the nonparent couples over a comparable period revealed essentially stable marital satisfaction.

Even though both fathers and mothers were moving in the same downward direction, they did so on different timetables. Women showed most of their decline in satisfaction with marriage at the 6-month postpartum assessment, whereas men's marital disenchantment occurred primarily during the next year when their babies were between 6- and 18-months-of-age. Thus, particularly at the 6-months-after-birth follow-ups, husbands and wives reported feeling very differently about their marriage.

3. *Gender differences in ideas about parenting.* From pregnancy to 18 months postpartum, wives filling out our Ideas About Parenting Scale (Heming, Cowan, & Cowan, 1990) agreed increasingly with statements that child care should be done almost entirely by parents, whereas husbands reported feeling even more strongly that other child care resources were acceptable.

4. *Gender differences in intergenerational relationships.* We do not have quantitative data on this point, but it is our impression that despite the fact that both men and women become involved in renewed or more frequent contacts with their parents during their own transition to parenthood, the new mother's relationship with her own mother takes on even more salience and intensity. This is reflected in most couples' reports of emotional discussions about whether or when her mother or both parents should come to meet and help with their new grandchild.

5. *Gender roles outside the family.* In addition to all of the differential changes for new fathers' and mothers' lives and relationships inside the family

we found different shifts in men's and women's relationships with work and friends outside the family. As women accepted more family responsibilities, they gave up their involvement in their jobs or careers, at least temporarily. All of the women in our study were employed or involved in training or schooling during pregnancy, and all took some time off during the first postpartum year. By 18 months after the birth of their first child, 43% of the women were still at home with their children full-time. The mothers who returned to work or school tended to do so on a reduced schedule. Full-time employment for women meant working up to 40 hours per week, whereas full-time work for men often exceeded 50 hours per week. Consistent with their actual involvement in work, women's psychological involvement in their work identity declined significantly on *The Pie*.

Women who worked outside the home had husbands who did more of the housework and childcare than did women who were full-time housewives (Cowan & Cowan, 1992). Yet, even full-time working women came home to a "second shift" (Hochschild, 1989) in which they took the major responsibility for running the home and caring for the child. As Hochschild has shown vividly, this gender role imbalance in the allocation of family work, and the discrepancy between husbands' and wives' concern about it, takes a high toll, particularly on women's feelings about themselves and their marriages.

Gender Differentiation and the Quality of the Couple's Relationship

Almost all investigators who report an overall decline in the quality of the couples' relationship attribute it to the negative changes and disequilibration associated with this major life transition. However, in the couples in our study there was virtually no correlation between the amount or direction of change in any of the five domains of family life and the decline in men's and women's marital satisfaction. We must find alternative explanations for new parents' declining marital satisfaction in the first year and a half of parenthood.

Our interviews with couples suggested that the growing *differences between the partners'* experiences might be contributing to their feelings of disenchantment with their relationship as a couple. To measure increasing differences between partners over time we constructed *a composite difference index* (Cowan et al., 1985), using one or two measures selected from each of the five family domains described earlier. We examined differences between his and her:

1. size of the "parent" piece of *The Pie*
2. satisfaction with *Who does what?* and perception of positive change in their sexual relationship
3. ideas about parenting

4. descriptions of their families of origin (Family Environment Scale; Moos, 1974) and
5. balance between life stress and social support.

We calculated the absolute difference between his and her score on each measure, transformed it into a standard z-score, and added up the 6 difference scores to yield an overall difference index for each couple.

We then entered men's and women's marital satisfaction scores during pregnancy as Step 1 in hierarchical multiple regressions predicting marital satisfaction at 18 months postpartum. Subsequent entries in the equation could then be interpreted as accounting for *change* in marital satisfaction during the transition to parenthood. As we expected, increasing differences between the spouses from pregnancy to 6 months postpartum accounted for a significant 6% (women) or 10% (men) of the overall change in marital satisfaction from pregnancy to 18 months after the birth of their first child. The more different partners became, the more change in their marital satisfaction, most often in a downward direction.[2] Not surprisingly, the between-partner difference that carried most of the weight in predicting their decline in marital satisfaction was the increasing discrepancy in the size of his and her identity as parent on *The Pie*.

Furthermore, the more different partners became, the more likely they were to report increased marital conflict between pregnancy and 18 months after the birth of their first child. Over and above partner differences, this increasing conflict accounted for an additional 5% of the women's and 12% of the men's decline in marital satisfaction.

Step 1		*Step 2*		*Step 3*		*Dependent variable*
Pregnancy Marital Satisfaction	→	Increase in Gender Differentiation	→	Increase in Conflict and Disagreement	→	18 months postpartum Marital Satisfaction

In total, the variables from Steps 1 through 3 accounted for 37% of the variation in women's satisfaction with marriage and 42% of men's marital satisfaction by the time their children were 1½ years old.

We have additional evidence from the intervention results that gender differentiation during the transition to parenthood is implicated in men's and women's increasing dissatisfaction with marriage. We found that couples groups randomly offered to one-third of the expectant parents helped those partners avoid some of the decline in satisfaction with marriage experienced by the parents with no

---

[2]The correlations between absolute change and decline in marital satisfaction from pregnancy to 18 months postpartum were very high— $r = .83$; $df = 45$; $p < .001$ for men and $r = .94$; $df = 45$; $p < .001$ for women. These findings justified interpreting Steps 2 and 3 of the regression equation as exploring marital satisfaction *decline*.

intervention (Cowan & Cowan, 1987; C. Cowan, 1988). At the 18-months postpartum follow-up, all couples who had participated in the intervention were still in intact marriages whereas 12.5% of the nonintervention couples had already separated or filed for divorce.

If, as we believed, marital differences were directly implicated in declining marital satisfaction, then the couples group intervention should have an impact on differences between spouses. Analyses comparing patterns in new parent couples with and without the intervention revealed that the scores of fathers and mothers who had participated in a couples group showed *less divergence at the 6-months-after-birth follow-ups*. That is, spouses who had worked with us on their relationship issues as they were becoming parents described their experiences and their lives more similarly than husbands and wives without the intervention—in the size of their *Pie* pieces labeled "parent"; in their satisfaction with *Who does what?*; in their level of paid work outside the home, and in the balance of life stress and social support. On the total difference index, the group participants showed significantly less of the traditional gender differentiation in identity and roles than the nonintervention spouses reported.

In sum, our preventive intervention designed to help couples focus on their marital relationship during the transition to parenthood helped to increase spouses' tendency to view their identities and roles in a similar light and to reduce their tendency to feel more disenchanted with their marriage. We cannot be sure that the attenuation of partner differences accounted for the positive effects of the intervention on the marriage. It seems clear, however, from the multiple regression predictions of marital decline, *and* from the contrast between the couples with and without an intervention, that differences between partners play a role in how spouses feel about their overall relationship—at least during the family formation period.

LINKS BETWEEN BECOMING A FAMILY AND GENDERED PARENTING

We turn now to the connections among gender differences, the process of gender differentiation during the transition to parenthood, and gender-linked parenting. We describe briefly some of the discrepancies we observed between mothers' and fathers' behavior with their 3½ year-old children. We show how these discrepancies are anticipated by differences that existed between the parents before the birth of their child, and we demonstrate that the more husbands and wives differ in parenting style, the more likely their parenting is affected by whether their child is a girl or a boy.

We acknowledge at the start that the ideal study to answer questions about gender-differentiated parenting has yet to be done. Given a family with a mother, father, 4-year-old son and 2-year-old daughter, parents might treat their children differently because of birth order (they learn from the first child what not to with the second), age, or gender. In order to isolate and study the impact of gender within families, unconfounded with birth order and age, we would need a longitudinal study of male-female twins. Alternatively, we could select large numbers of families with different combinations of male and female children and follow them over the life course. Given the constraints of time and the constellation of families available to most researchers, we and other researchers have compared families with girls to families with boys of the same age. We made inferences about *within-family* dynamics from *between-family* data. Although this approach is reasonable, it is not fool-proof. Thus, when we learn that fathers of sons treat their children differently than fathers of daughters, we assume that the fathers of sons would behave differently *if* we could see them with daughters, and that the fathers of daughters would behave differently if we could observe them with their sons.

The Research Context

When the children in our study were 3½, each family visited our project playroom on three occasions. During the first 1½ hour visit, the child worked at some tasks and games with a male-female team of experimenters for 45 minutes. Then, with a second male-female experimenter team, the child worked and played with one parent for 45 minutes. This process was repeated with the other parent during a second visit. On a third occasion, the whole family spent 45 minutes to 1 hour working and playing together at a number of structured and unstructured tasks. All of these sessions were videotaped and the separate teams coded the child's and the parents' styles of interacting (For more detail, see Cowan & Cowan, 1990; Pratt, Kerig, Cowan, & Cowan, 1988).

During the parent-child and whole-family visits, the 3½ year old was presented with tasks that were difficult for preschool children to do alone. The parents were asked to be as helpful as they typically would at home. We told them that we were not as interested in how well the child performed as we were in how children and parents of this age work and play together.

Recall that as part of the study design, 48 couples were given full pre- and post-baby questionnaire assessments and an additional 24 couples were assessed only after birth. At the preschool period, 34 of the 48 couples with full prebaby assessments had remained in intact marriages *and* completed interviews, questionnaires, and laboratory assessments at all four assessment points. An additional 12 of the 24 couples who were assessed after birth only had remained in intact marriages and completed all of the preschool assessments. Thus, there were 34 families available for pregnancy-to-preschool predictive analyses and 46 available for concurrent analyses of the links between family functioning and gender differences in parenting style.

Observational Ratings of Parents' Behavior

Based on rating scales developed by Jack and Jeanne Block (1980) and modified by Donald Rahe at the University of Minnesota, our colleagues Linda Kastelowitz and Victor Lieberman developed a global rating scheme for parenting behavior over the course of each interaction session. An innovative aspect of this system was that raters evaluated both the highest and the typical level of 15 dimensions of parenting behavior. These ratings factored into 6 scales: warmth, responsiveness, structure, limit-setting/maturity demands, engagement, and creativity. We combined the first 5 of these scales into 2 composite indices that were designed to assess Baumrind's key concepts of *authoritative* parenting style (parents provide structure and limit setting with warmth, responsiveness, and engagement) or *authoritarian* parenting style (parents provide structure and limit setting with cold, angry, disengaged responses).

With simple t-tests we determined whether parents tended to treat preschool sons and daughters differently on any of the 6 parenting style scales or on the composite authoritative or authoritarian indices. Recall that these are between-family comparisons of families with first-born sons and families with first-born daughters. Consistent with many of the studies we have cited earlier, our data reveal no differences between the behavior of mothers of sons and mothers of daughters on any of the measures of parenting style in our preschool laboratory visits. However, fathers of sons were rated as significantly more responsive ($t = 1.81$; $p < .05$), engaged ($t = 2.87$; $p < .003$), and creative ($t = 2.60$; $p < .006$)[3] than fathers of daughters.[4] In the composite indices of parenting style, fathers of girls were observed to be marginally less authoritative ($t = -1.50$; $p < .07$), and significantly more authoritarian ($t = 2.26$; $p < .01$), than fathers of sons.

Our strategy for understanding why fathers but not mothers show gender-differentiated parenting shifts briefly to *within*-family analyses. We look first at the discrepancies that occur *when two parents treat the same child differently*. We attempt to identify the source of these differences between mothers and fathers by examining two related hypotheses which, to the best of our knowledge, have not been tested in earlier studies:

1. Parenting style discrepancies between mothers and fathers of 3½ year-old children are predictable from differences between the parents assessed before the child's birth (in pregnancy).

2. Parenting style discrepancies between mothers and fathers of preschoolers tend to be greater when the parents have become increasingly different from one another during the transition to parenthood.

---

[3]Degrees of freedom for statistical tests were 44 unless otherwise noted.

[4]Analyses are based on 23 families with girls and 23 families with boys. Parenting style measures were standard z-scores for each factor or composite, based on the sample of 46 fathers or mothers.

We then shift back to *between-family* analyses to test two additional hypotheses:

3. Differences between fathers' treatment of sons and fathers' treatment of daughters occur primarily in families in which the parents have different parenting styles.

4. Differences between fathers' treatment of sons and father's treatment of daughters occur primarily in families in which the parents have high marital conflict and disagreement.

Creating a Parenting Style Discrepancy Score

In social science research, difference or discrepancy scores are usually regarded with caution because a measure of difference created by subtracting one score from another risks cumulating the errors of measurement that are inherent in each score taken alone. A further difficulty can arise when differences based on scores at the ends of the distribution of each variable have different meaning than differences based on intermediate scores. Our dilemma was that we could not avoid some kind of difference score calculation because discrepancies between husbands' and wives' parenting behavior were exactly what we were interested in. Our provisional solution was to begin by calculating husband-wife differences in authoritarian parenting style—the composite score that reveals gender differences more clearly than authoritative parenting style. We created the difference score from his and her composite scores rather than adding up the absolute differences between partners on each of the scales included in the composite (warmth, structure, etc). The composite score, we reasoned, would be less subject to measurement error than the sum of its components because idiosyncratic errors in each component would tend to cancel each other out.

Second, the authoritarian scale score was transformed to a standard z-score before calculating the husband-wife difference so that the numbers had similar meaning all along the continuum of fathers' and mothers' ratings. High scores on authoritarian parenting reflected parents who were cold, angry, not sympathetically responsive to the child, structured, and demanding. Low scores described parents who were warm but laissez-faire (i.e., permissive).

Deal, Halverson, and Wampler (1989) have argued that parents who are similar in attitude or behavior generally tend to be effective parents, whereas couples with high discrepancies are more likely to be ineffective parents. Analyzing our mother-child and father-child interaction sessions, we found no significant correlations between the magnitude of partner discrepancies in authoritarian parenting and ratings of *mothers'* warmth or structure. However, *fathers* in couples with more discrepant ratings of authoritarian parenting style tended to be less warm ($r = -.44$; $p < .001$), less responsive ($r = -.50$; $p < .001$), less engaged ($r = -.35$; $p < .01$), and less structuring ($r = -.50$; $p < .001$) with their preschoolers than fathers in couples with similar parenting style. When couples are discrepant in parenting style, then, fathers tend to be on the authoritarian side of the continuum (r = .30; $p < .05$).[5]

Predicting Discrepancies Between Parents in Authoritarian Style

Is it something about their 3½-year-old child that brings out differences between parents, or do parenting differences reflect discrepancies between the parents that were already evident before the child was born? To see whether differences between the partners in late pregnancy predicted different parenting styles four years later, we examined the 6 measures of partner difference that we had used to predict declines in marital satisfaction, and we added three measures that we expected to be relevant to later parenting style (see Table 8.1). The measures, obtained from 34 couples (see p. 178), include *differences in adaptation or well-being* (self-esteem, marital satisfaction, role satisfaction, life stress/social support balance), *differences in experience* (size of "partner" piece of *The Pie,* descriptions of one's family of origin), *differences in family roles* (extent to which child care tasks are specialized rather than shared), and *differences in beliefs* (disagreements in ideas about parenting). Parents' scores were first converted to standard z-scores separately for husbands and wives. Absolute husband-wife differences were then calculated for each of the 9 pairs of scores.

As we expected, parents who were very different in their level of authoritarian behavior with their 3½ year-old already differed during pregnancy in their psychological involvement as "parent" (r = .46; df = 32; $p < .003$), in their predictions of more gender-differentiated responsibilities of child care (r = .32; df = 32; $p < .05$), in their ideas about parenting (r = .42; df = 32; $p < .007$, and in their overall satisfaction with their family division of labor (r = .37; df = 32; $p < .05$).

The husband-wife differences in pregnancy that centered around child-related issues predicted parenting differences during the preschool period. Differences between the expectant parents' descriptions of the more general aspects of their well-being—self-esteem, marital satisfaction, positive changes in the sexual relationship, the climate in their families of origin, and the balance between life stress and social support—did *not* predict discrepancies between the parents in authoritarian parenting style 4 years later.

We then tested the hypothesis that *increasing* differences between parents from pregnancy to 6 months postpartum contributed to differences in parenting style during the preschool stage. For each of the 4 child-related measures (parent pie piece, sharing of childcare, overall satisfaction with family tasks, and ideas

[5]Actually, as we will see, this statement holds primarily for fathers and daughters. Fathers in more discrepant couples were marginally *less* authoritarian with sons (r = .29; df = 21; $p < .10$) and significantly *more* authoritarian with daughters r = .68; df = 21; $p < .0001$).

TABLE 8.1
Variables and Instruments Used in Creating Husband-Wife Difference Scores

Domains	Variables and Measuring Instrument
Individual:	Self-esteem (adjective Check List; Gough & Heilbrun (1980). Size of Pie piece labled "partner" (C. P. Cowan & P. A. Cowan, 1990a).
Couple:	Marital satisfaction (Locke & Wallace, 1959). Perception of positive change in the sexual relationship. Overall satisfaction with the Who Does What? arrangements of household tasks, decision-making, and childcare. Extent to which husbands and wives describe differentiated roles in child-care tasks on Who Does What? (C. P. Cowan & P. A. Cowan, 1990a).
Parent-child	Ideas about parenting (Heming, Cowan, & Cowan, 1990)
Three-generations:	Descriptions of the quality of warmth, cohesion, and conflict in the family of origin (relationship scales from the Family Environment Scale (Moos, 1974).
Outside the family:	Balance between life stress and social support (see Cowan et al.,1985).

about parenting) we calculated the increase or decrease in husband–wife differences between the pregnancy and 6-month postpartum assessment periods. The differences were converted to standard scores and summed to create a single measure of increasing discrepancy between husbands and wives. This index of parents growing more different from each other during the early phase of the transition to parenthood showed a substantial correlation with authoritarian parenting style discrepancies when the children were 3½ ($r = .53$; $df = 32$; $p < .001$).

In sum, discrepancies between husbands and wives during pregnancy *and* increasing differences between the spouses during the transition to parenthood predicted greater differences in parenting style, as observed when the children were 3½-years-old by coders blind to any other family data. This suggests that when two parents treat their preschool child differently, it is not simply a product of the relationship between the child and each of the parents. Rather, parents' differences in parenting style emerge from the earlier differences between them—before the child arrives on the scene and before the sex and temperament of the child are known.

Discrepancies Between Parents and Gender-Differentiated Parenting

Let us begin to weave the threads of our argument together to show how gender-differentiated parenting is amplified by the dynamics of the couple relationship within the family. We turn to a test of our third hypothesis that differences between how fathers of sons and fathers of daughters treat their children occur primarily in families in which the parents have discrepant parenting styles.

We keep our focus on authoritarian parenting style, the tendency of parents to be demanding, structuring, and cold or hostile during the mother-child or father-child visits to our laboratory playroom. The question is whether (a) the sex of the child, (b) discrepancies between the parents' styles of parenting explain variations in authoritarian parenting, and (c) the interaction between the two variables explain additional variance in parenting style. In light of our findings that fathers tend to treat daughters more negatively than sons, the specific form of the interaction we are predicting is that discrepancies in parents' styles will be associated most strongly with authoritarian parenting in fathers with daughters.

Given the relatively small number of subjects (46 men and 46 women), and our desire to examine the full continuum of parent differences, we used a multiple regression approach rather than an analysis of variance strategy in which the sample would be divided into four cells—couples with high and low parenting discrepancies who are parents of girls or parents of boys. In separate hierarchical multiple regressions on mothers' or fathers' authoritarian parenting, we entered the child's sex (boys = 0; girls = 1) on Step 1 of the equation, the difference between the parents on authoritarian parenting on Step 2, and the interaction term (child sex × couple difference) on Step 3 (see Table 8.2).

There are no significant main or interaction effects for mothers. That is, mothers of sons showed no more and no less authoritarian behavior than mothers of daughters according to our laboratory observations. Differences between the parents did not explain variations in mother's parenting style. Furthermore, mothers in couples with more discrepant parenting were no more likely to treat boys and girls differently than mothers whose styles were similar to their husbands'.

By contrast, for fathers, the child's sex, the discrepancy between the parents in authoritarian behavior, and the interaction between sex and discrepancy all contributed significantly to a combined 35% of the variance (adjusted R-squared) in father's authoritarian parenting of their children. Fathers were generally more

TABLE 8.2
Child's Sex, Parenting Discrepancies, Couple Conflict, and Fathers' Authoritarian Parenting Style

Step	*Variable*	*R*	R^2	R^2 *Change*	*F Change*	*p*	*Betaln*	*r*
1	Child sex	.35	.12	.12	5.58	.02	.35	.35
2	Discrepancy between parents in authoritarian parenting style	.44	.19	.07	4.69	.04	.30	.30
3	Interaction: child sex x parenting discrepancy	.63	.39	.20	13.66	.001	.88	.60
	Adjusted R^2		.35					

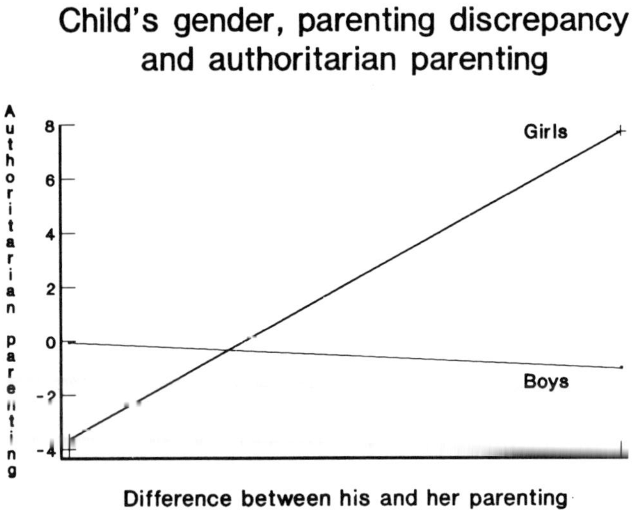

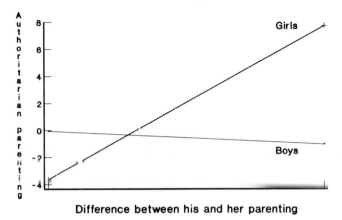

FIG. 8.1. The interaction between child's sex and parenting discrepancy effects on fathers' authoritarian parenting.

authoritarian with daughters, especially if their parenting styles were different from their wives' styles. Most important for our purposes, a plot of the regression lines supports Hypothesis 3 (See Fig. 8.1). Fathers whose first-borns were boys were at or below the mean of the distribution of authoritarian parenting, whether they were in low or high parenting discrepancy couples.[6] Fathers whose first-borns were girls and whose parenting was similar to their wives' were somewhat below the mean of the distribution toward the permissive end of our parenting style index. However, the more discrepant the husband-wife parenting styles in families with girls, the more likely the fathers were to be rated as high on the authoritarian index when they worked and played with their 3½-year-old daughters.

Based on our findings, the general conclusion of many reviewers of the research on gender—that fathers tend to treat boys and girls differently—requires some modification. The finding we reported before, that fathers of sons were more responsive, engaged, and creative in the parent-child laboratory sessions than fathers of daughters, *was attributable primarily to men who differed from their wives in parenting style.* It is possible that some of the controversy about whether there are gender differences in the parenting of young children results from lack of comparability between samples in terms of husband-wife differences in the quality of their relationships with their children.

What do we know about the couples who showed more discrepant parenting

---

[6]Because the measure of authoritarian parenting was transformed to z scores, the mean of the sample was 0.

styles? First, as we already reported, our observations of discrepancies between the parents when the child was 3½ were predictable from differences between the parents on child-related issues before the baby was born. Second, differences in parenting style were more likely to occur in couples whose differences had increased over the transition to parenthood. Hypothetically, the developmental pathway from partner differences in pregnancy to gender-differentiated parenting should look like this:

Partner differences in pregnancy	→	Increasing partner differences	→	Parenting style differences between partners	→	Differences between fathers of boys and fathers of girls

The Role of Marital Quality in Gender-Sensitive Parenting

To what extent is the quality of the parents' marriage implicated in gender differentiated parenting? A provocative finding emerged from our analysis of correlations between the quality of husband-wife interaction and parents' interaction with their 3½ year olds. When parents were more discrepant on our authoritarian parenting style scale during their separate parent-child visits, they were observed to be significantly less positive and more negative *toward one another*—showing less couple warmth and less praise ($r = -.36$; $p < .01$) and more conflict and criticism ($r = .32$; $p < .02$)—in the triadic mother-father-child sessions. In other words, when there were large differences between the parents on how authoritarian they were in their separate interactions with their preschooler, we observed more conflict and criticism *between them* when they worked and played with the child together.

It was also the case that the greater conflict between the parents during the family session when the child was 3½ was predictable from some of the same pregnancy measures that predicted discrepancies in parenting style 4 years later. Expectant parents' initial differences in parenting ideas ($r = .29$; $p < .05$) and self-esteem ($r = .34$; $p < .01$), and increasing discrepancy over time in the size of their "parent" aspects of self ($r = .34$; $p < .01$), satisfaction with their role arrangements ($r = .57$; $p < .001$), and declining satisfaction with the overall marriage between pregnancy and 18-months postpartum ($r = .43$; $p < .01$), predicted more conflict between the parents in the whole-family visit during the preschool period.

In hierarchical multiple regression equations with mothers' or fathers' authoritarian parenting style as the dependent variable, we entered the child's sex on Step 1, observed couple conflict on Step 2, and the interaction between child sex and couple conflict on Step 3. The results are similar to those in the analysis of parenting differences. None of the variables accounted for statistically significant amounts of variance in *mothers'* authoritarian parenting. For fathers, how-

TABLE 8.3
Multiple Regression: Child's Sex, Couple Conflict, and Fathers' Authoritarian Parenting Style

Step	*Variable*	*R*	*R^2*	*R^2 Change*	*F Change*	*p*	*Betaln*	*r*
1	Child sex	.35	.12	.12	5.58	.02	.35	.35
2	Couple conflict	.47	.22	.10	5.42	.03	.32	.33
3	Interaction: child sex x couple conflict	.60	.36	.14	8.5	.006	.59	.49
	Adjusted R^2		.31					

ever, all three variables contributed significantly to the equation, accounting for a total of 31% (adjusted R-squared) of the variance in fathers' authoritarian parenting style (see Table 8.3). When we plot the regression lines that represent the statistically significant interaction term (see Fig. 8.2), we can see that higher levels of couple conflict amplify the differences between fathers of sons and fathers of daughters. Fathers tended to show average levels of authoritarian behavior with preschool age sons but above average authoritarian treatment of daughters, increasingly so *as marital conflict increased.*

Because between-parent discrepancies in parenting style showed a low but significant correlation with marital conflict in the presence of the child, we wanted to know whether the parenting differences and couple conflict made separate and independent contributions to our understanding of gender dif-

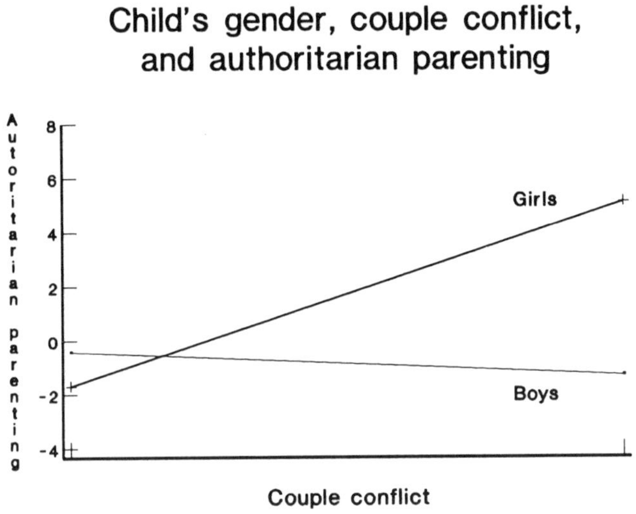

FIG. 8.2. The interaction between child's sex and couple conflict effects on fathers' authoritarian parenting.

TABLE 8.4
Child's Sex, Parenting Discrepancies, Couple Conflict, and Fathers' Authoritarian Parenting Style

Step	*Variable*	*R*	R^2	R^2 *Change*	*F Change*	*p*	*Betaln*	*r*
1	Child sex	.34	.12	.12	4.83	.03	.32	.32
2	Discrepancy between parents in authoritarian parenting style	.44	.20	.08	3.83	.057	.28	.29
3	Couple conflict	.51	.26	.06	3.27	.08	.26	.33
4	Interaction: child sex x parenting discrepancy	.67	.45	.19	12.94	.001	.86	.60
5	Interaction: child sex x couple conflict	.71	.51	.06	4.57	.04	.41	.49
	Adjusted R^2		.44					

ferences in authoritarian parenting style. In a third multiple regression equation, we found that the sex of the child, the interaction between the child's sex and mother-father parenting discrepancies, and the interaction between the child's sex and the parents' marital conflict, all accounted for statistically significant amounts of variation in parenting style in the preschool period (see Table 8.4).[7] Our interpretation of this finding is that parenting differences and marital conflict each contribute independently to amplify the tendency of fathers to treat daughters in an authoritarian manner. The variables in this regression equation account for 44% of the variance in fathers' authoritarian parenting.

Our findings present us with pieces of a puzzle, but certainly not the complete picture.

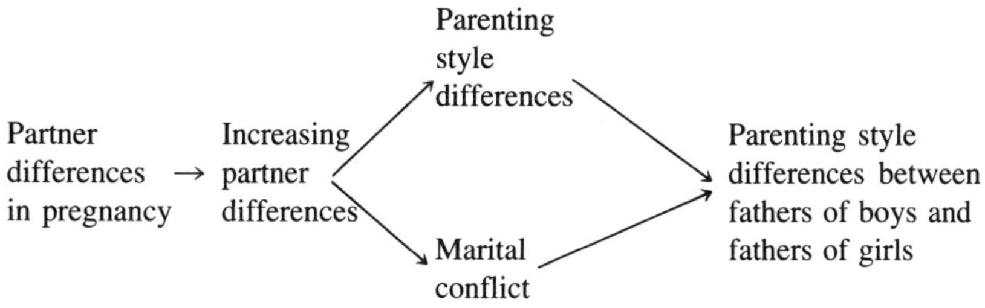

Husbands and wives are different from each other when they come into a marriage and after they conceive a child. The process of becoming a family appears

[7]Table 8.4 shows that the main effect contributions of couple conflict and parenting discrepancies are marginally significant, while their interactions with gender are both significant.

to heighten the differences between the spouses, increasing the tendency for more conflict and criticism between them. This, in turn, is associated with greater discrepancies between husbands and wives in how they work and play with their child during the preschool period. While correlational data do not provide us with *proof* of causal connections, we suspect that as husbands and wives become fathers and mothers, initial and growing differences between them foster the potential for more marital conflict and differences in how they handle their first child.

Along with higher levels of marital difference and conflict, one parent may enjoy a more positive relationship than the other parent does with the child, a state of affairs that may serve to increase their conflict as a couple and differences in how they respond to the child. As differences and strain in the husband-wife relationship and in a parent-child relationship increase, gender may become a more salient organizing principle for all of the relationships in the family.

Why Are Fathers the Carriers of Gendered Parenting?

Although the theoretical model we have proposed suggests that conflict and differences between the spouses provide a major source of the discrepancies in men's and women's parenting style, our data indicate that this pattern holds only for father's parenting behavior. These results are consistent with the work of several researchers who report higher correlations between observed marital quality and parenting for fathers than for mothers (Belsky, Gilstrap, & Rovine, 1984; Goldberg & Easterbrooks, 1984). Brody, Pellegrini, and Sigel (1986) found few husband-wife differences in teaching styles in couples who were maritally satisfied, whereas in highly distressed couples, fathers were more negative and mothers were more positive in teaching their 5- to 7-year-olds. None of these studies examined the possible impact of the child's gender on these patterns.

Adding to our findings based on the global ratings of parent-child interaction, Patricia Kerig (1989, 1991a, 1991b) conducted microanalytic analyses of the dyadic interactions between parents and children in the Becoming a Family Project. Kerig's data showed strong links between marital quality and negative relationships with daughters *for both parents,* but the effects for mothers were more subtle, perhaps explaining why they did not show up in the global analyses. Using emotion-based codes for *each* behavior of parent and each behavior of the child, Kerig was able to document systematic patterns of parents' responses to specific behaviors shown by their children. She showed that girls were negated more often than boys were by both of their parents. The parents of girls were more often rejecting, critical, challenging, controlling, and protesting, refusing their daughters' requests and reprimanding them. Maritally dissatisfied fathers were even more negating of their daughters than were maritally dissatisfied mothers. The mothers who were unhappy with their marriages tended to negate their daughters *when the daughters asserted themselves,* but the unhappily married fathers were more negating regardless of what their daughters did.

At this point, we can only speculate about the dynamics of the links between marital and parenting quality for mothers and fathers of sons and daughters. The implications of these trends for children's development are compelling, especially in terms of what daughters of parents with less happy marriages may be learning in their interactions with their parents. From their fathers they receive a high level of negating messages no matter what they do. From their mothers they learn that assertive behaviors are not acceptable. Perhaps these mothers are training their daughters in an interactional style that they themselves use with their husbands. Whatever the rationale, the pattern is an important one because of the negative implications of the authoritarian parenting style for children's development (Baumrind, 1979, 1991).

Tinsley and Parke (1987) argue that the impact of marriage on parenting may be greater for fathers than it is for mothers because the paternal role is less well defined than the maternal role. In their uncertainties about intimate relationships, men may look toward their wives, especially for clues about how to behave with their daughters. It is also the case that fathers spend less time directly involved in working and playing with their children when they are young. This may help account for the fact that the tone of their relationships with their daughters—but not with their sons—tends to mirror the quality of their relationships with their wives. If there is less psychological distinction for men between the roles of "husbanding" and "fathering," this may increase the likelihood of spillover from marital distress to a more negating style of parenting. Conversely, women may be able to keep their maternal and spousal roles in separate compartments (Johnson, 1988). The fact that women are socialized to play socially well-defined and psychologically distinct roles of mother and wife may tend to protect their relationships with their children from the effects of a troubled marriage.[8]

We have been asking why daughters receive the fallout from their fathers' difficult marriage, but let us focus on the issue of gender from another perspective. Parents in highly conflictful relationships showed colder, more critical, authoritarian parenting styles in three of the four gender combinations: mothers with sons, mothers with daughters, and fathers with daughters. What prevents the spillover from marital distress to parenting style for fathers of sons?

Although most parents spontaneously mentioned that they would be equally happy to have a son or a daughter, several facts support our hunch that boys are still very special for fathers (Cowan & Cowan, 1992).

1. Although there were no differences in the self-descriptions of prospective fathers of sons and daughters before their babies were born, 2 years later,

---

[8]As Kerig's microanalyses suggest, the protection is not complete. Marital difficulties do tend to spill over into mother's relationships with their daughters in reaction to specific behaviors.

men who had sons used significantly more of the favorable items on the Adjective Check List to describe themselves than men who had daughters.[9]

2. If their first child was a girl, couples were more likely to have a second child by the time the first was 18-months-old.[10] Although there may be many reasons for this phenomenon, it means that many families with first-born girls are coping with a second transition to parenthood sooner and are subject to more strain than families whose first-borns are boys.
3. In the first 4 years of our study, couples were more likely to separate if their first child was a girl. This is consistent with the results of a much larger study of a national sample by Morgan, Lye, and Condran (1988) and of two in-depth family studies by Jeanne and Jack Block (Block, Block, & Gjerde, 1986) and Mavis Hetherington (Hetherington, Stanley-Hagan, & Anderson, 1989). What we may be seeing in our study is that the effect of gender on parent-child relationships found in families of divorce are present in intact families as well, although we are not suggesting that the effects of divorce and of marital discord in intact marriages are identical.
4. Mothers and fathers perceive boys as more vulnerable than girls during a separation or divorce: Mothers feel that boys are difficult to rear alone, and a marital split usually deprives sons of having their fathers available on a regular basis. Our tentative hypothesis, then, is that both parents make active efforts not to let marital and other family difficulties erode the quality of the relationship between father and son. Unfortunately, unhappily married men do not generally make the same efforts to safeguard their relationships with their daughters. Fathers tend to treat their young sons fairly well, regardless of how the marriage feels, but when the marriage is in difficulty, their relationships with their daughters are troubled.

In sum, maritally dissatisfied fathers tend to treat their daughters the way they treat their wives. Men's dissatisfaction with their wives seems to be reflected in their more negative treatment of their daughters—at least when the girls are young. Because this spillover from the marriage to the parent-child relationship does not happen as regularly in families with sons, our statistical analyses reveal differences in fathers' treatment of sons and daughters by men in highly conflictful or discrepant couples.

This line of reasoning does not address the issue of why mothers tend to treat sons and daughters similarly, regardless of the level of conflict with their hus-

---

[9]Boys were coded 0; girls were coded 1. Correlation between sex of child and favorable items for fathers describing themselves on the Adjective Check List: r = .32; df = 44; $p < .05$.

[10]Correlations between having a girl and having a second child before the first was eighteen months old: r = .25; df = 44; $p < .05$.

bands or the amount of discrepancy between their own and their spouses' parenting behavior.[11] We believe that one of the key determinants of mothers' similar treatment of sons and daughters may be their daily involvement in their children's care. As we have seen, mothers' involvement in the parenting role reflects the fact that parenting is more closely linked with their identity than it is for fathers. Over the long haul of days and weeks, issues raised by young sons and daughters are probably more similar than they are different. Even mothers who work full time may be able to keep their relationships with their children emotionally separate from their feelings about their husbands. (If this is so, it may be this ability of women that leads their husbands to feel shut out.) It would be important to study families with primary care or highly involved fathers to see whether the tendency toward gender differentiation in fathers' behavior would be less in these families, even when marital distress or parenting differences are high.

CAVEATS AND CONCLUSIONS

Limitations of this Study

The data we report here are concerned primarily with authoritarian parenting and its components. Although the dimensions of parental warmth/responsiveness and demandingness are central to the understanding of family socialization (Baumrind, 1979), we are under no illusion that a single index of the composited global ratings, based on 40 minutes of interaction in a laboratory setting with parents and their 3½ year-olds, adequately encompasses all that there is to be said about how gender influences the relationship between parents and their children. Nevertheless, these measures are good predictors of children's adaptation to school 2 years later (Cowan, Cowan, Schulz, & Heming, in press). There are other measures at different levels of analyses in different contexts that must be explored in order to develop a more comprehensive view of the role of gender in family relationships. What we have provided here, we hope, is a family systemic way of thinking about how the role of gender in the family might be investigated.

The Direction of Effects

We recognize that our explanations of gendered parenting all focus on contributions made *by the parents*. The fact that within-family discrepancies between the parents are predictable, in part, from prebaby husband-wife differences, and that they occur primarily when marital differences and conflict are high, certainly

---

[11]Despite Kerig's findings that maritally unhappy mothers *do* negate their preschool-age daughters when the girls are being assertive, mothers of girls and mothers of boys make many fewer gender-related distinctions in their interactions with their children.

support the hypothesis that gender differences in parenting are not attributable solely to the characteristics of the child. And yet the child certainly contributes to the salience of gender in the family. For example, Kerig (1991a, 1991b) found that daughters were more responsive to fathers who were maritally satisfied and less compliant to fathers who were maritally distressed. We speculate that in addition to fathers making a special effort to maintain positive relationships with their sons despite stormy relationships with their wives, sons may make a special effort to keep their fathers involved when the atmosphere between the parents is charged with conflict.

Our results raise some questions about the general tendency to focus on the *mother*'s role in gender socialization. It was maritally distressed fathers, after all, that tended to give their daughters such a difficult time. It seems clear that the blame that researchers and family scholars have directed at mothers for high levels of family distress needs to be shared by fathers as well.

The *final* model of how gender operates in the family will likely involve a bidirectional theory of social/psychological construction. Parents' and children's intrapsychic construction of gender, as well as their interpersonal styles and responses to one another, cumulated over time, result in a more or less gender-sensitive, gender-differentiated pattern of relationships.

The quality of the parents' marriage provides a context for gender development by influencing the kinds of relationships boys and girls experience directly with their mothers and fathers and by providing models of intimate relationships, which children observe as their parents relate to one another. These constructions of self-in-relationship may have consequences for the kinds of relationships children will form with others outside the family—most significantly the relationships they develop with their own intimate partners. Beyond Chodorow's reproduction of mothering, then, we have the "reproduction of relatedness." The chain of development proceeds from one's experience of being a daughter/son, to being a female/male, to becoming an intimate partner, to becoming a mother/father who carries gendered expectations about marriage, parenting, and child development into the next generation.

Society, Culture, and Gender Differences

By focusing in so tightly on family dynamics, we have not given cultural forces in gender differentiation the importance they deserve. Gender stereotypes are not invented anew within each individual or family. Societal prescriptions for men's and women's roles and the status they carry influence the choices husbands and wives make about how they arrange their lives inside and outside the family. Definitions of so-called gender-*appropriate* personality characteristics for men and women also have some influence on what men and women actually do.

Beyond the specific descriptions and prescriptions concerning gender, differential treatment of men and women has direct and indirect effects through the institutions that affect couples' work patterns and child care arrangements when children are young. Women and men do not receive equal pay for equal work. That places pressure on couples to keep women at home and men at work full-time once a child comes into the family. The lack of high quality, affordable child care adds to the pressure on both parents, with the result that women feel strain when they limit their paid work roles to stay home, and conflict when they are at work about what is happening at home (Cowan & Cowan, 1987, 1992).

Once children move from the family into the school system, the impact of differential treatment of boys and girls is played out in a new arena. Maccoby (1990) has made a cogent argument for looking outside the family to the child's sex-segregated peer groups as primary influences on the development of gender-linked roles and personality. At present, in most Western countries at least, societal forces work in concert with biological forces and family processes to reproduce and maintain differences between men and women, between boys and girls, and between parents and children.

We have discussed cultural forces as if they act from the outside on passive family members.

Society ⟶ Family ⟶ Individual

As we have argued, family arrangements in which mothers do the majority of parenting create a cycle in which men and women are more likely to move toward social roles, personality traits, and styles of emotional expression and regulation that perpetuate societally sanctioned gender stereotypes.

Society ⟷ Family ⟷ Individual

Furthermore, the findings we have reported here indicate substantial between-family variation in the occurrence of gender differentiation in roles and behavior. The fact that marital quality may increase or decrease parents' tendency to treat male and female children differently indicates that family dynamics help to determine what is selected from cultural stereotypes and enacted within the home.

Although men tend to adopt parenting styles that respond to the gender of their child more often than women do, fathers' sex-stereotypic parenting does not occur when they are in marriages that are satisfying to them. What we need to know is whether the marital relationship somehow provides an environment in which negative treatment of young girls is less likely, or whether men with certain family histories and personality styles tend to establish more positive relationships with their wives and daughters.

Future Research

Regardless of how we draw the ultimate path diagram linking society and culture with family dynamics and the development of gender identity, gender roles, gender personality, and sexuality in individual family members, one conclusion is clear now. Theory and research on gender development must adopt a systems point-of-view. Not all boys differ from all girls in all domains. Not all parents (not all fathers), show gender-related parenting styles, and even when they do, not all children conform to these socialization pressures. In order to understand the form and quality of father-son, father-daughter, mother-son, mother-daughter relationships, we must take into account the quality of the relationship between the parents as it unfolds over the course of family formation and development. And, to understand how marital quality shifts over time, we must take a closer look at the societal supports and barriers that affect how couples arrange their families and create a balance between work and family life.

We have not yet explored the potential *consequences* of gender differences in parenting for parents or their children. We are concerned that many of the gender differences we observed in families that purport to be sensitive to the stereotypes of gender continue to promote boys' autonomy and discourage girls' assertiveness and independence. There will likely be both costs and benefits for children's development of this differential treatment by parents. Sons get encouraged to be independent and powerful, possibly at the cost of overcontrolling their affect and distancing themselves from intimacy. Since we know that boys tend to be overrepresented in the psychopathologies involving aggression and other externalizing behaviors (Asher & Coie, 1990), we must take these patterns seriously. Daughters get rewarded for being compliant and for establishing close and intimate relationships, possibly at the cost of achieving autonomy and control over their choices. This may be reflected in the fact that girls tend to be overrepresented in the psychopathologies involving depression (Weissman & Klerman, 1977) and internalizing behavior.

The emerging field of developmental psychopathology (Cicchetti, Toth, Bush, & Gillespie 1988; P. Cowan, 1988; Rutter & Garmezy, 1983) is based on the premise that the identification of the causal mechanisms in adaptation and dysfunction requires that we trace the pathways between girls' and boys' early experience and their later developmental outcomes. We believe that a central question in this endeavor, rarely asked so far, is what role gender differentiation plays in shaping developmental outcomes for boys and girls all along the continuum from childhood to adulthood.

We have focused here on intact two-parent families although we are well aware that this arrangement represents a declining proportion of the family population in many countries. We would argue that this kind of general family system formulation is needed when we study families of divorce too; conflict between the parents is a key factor in the quality of post-divorce parenting behavior and children's adjustment (Hetherington & Camara, 1984; Johnston, this volume; Wallerstein & Kelly, 1980). Future research must pay more attention to single mothers' and single fathers' intimate relationships with new partners and the impact of these relationships on the quality of the interaction between each parental figure and the child. The research on contemporary nuclear families suggests that fathers contribute much more than mothers do to gender-differentiated parenting. If fathers are not present in the home, do mothers become more reactive to the gender of their children, or do they still treat sons and daughters similarly? If mothers are not present in the home, do fathers become less reactive to the gender of their children?

Children are reared in a variety of households, some that include several generations of women and no men (e.g., Burton & Stack, this volume; Kellam, Simon, & Ensminger, 1982). We believe that it is useful to examine the quality of intimate relationships among the adults in the household, and the potential impact of differences and conflict between the adults on (a) the quality of adult-child relationships, and (b) the tendency of caretakers to amplify or minimize the significance of gender in their patterns of family interaction (e.g., Vaughn, Egeland, Sroufe, & Waters, 1979). This is a special case of the more general issue of exploring how three-generational relationships influence the role of gender in shaping parent-child interactions.

Finally, ethnicity is a central personal and societal force that shapes the relation between culture, family, and individual development. Studies of how gender plays out in families from different ethnic groups will enrich our understanding of how family dynamics amplify or reduce the tendency for boys and girls, men and women, to develop along different pathways.

Male-female differences are present at birth but that is not the whole story of gender effects in development. The process of becoming male and female begins at birth and continues throughout the adult years. Different gender-related shifts (e.g., personality, roles) occur at different times and in different ways for men and women. Most theories of gender development focus on how biological, psychological, or cultural forces affect individuals or dyads. We believe that more comprehensive explanations of gender differences will require longitudinal analyses of the key aspects of the family system over time in order to understand how those parts of family life operate in some families to produce differential treatment and differential development of sons and daughters.

ACKNOWLEDGMENTS

This study has been supported throughout by NIMH grant MH 31109. We also want to acknowledge major contributions to the longitudinal study by members of the research team: Gertrude Heming served as data manager throughout the study, and Dena Cowan, Barbara Epperson, Beth Schoenberger, and Marc Shulz, processed the immense data set. Ellen Garrett, William S. Coysh, Harriet

Curtis-Bowles, and Abner Bowles III were the other two couples who followed the families over time and led intervention groups; Laura Mason Gordon and David Gordon interviewed couples in the last three years. Sacha Bunge, Michael Blum, Julia Levine, David Chavez, Marc Schulz, and Joanna Cowan worked with the children in the study; Linda Kastelowitz, Victor Lieberman, Marsha Kline, and Charles Soulé worked with the parents and children together. We are grateful to Jack Block, Joan Kaplan, Nancy Chodorow, Michael Pratt, and Daphne deMarneffe for their comments on an earlier draft of the chapter.

REFERENCES

Asher, S. R., & Coie, J. D. (Eds.). (1990). *Peer rejection in childhood,* Cambridge, England: Cambridge University Press.

Baumrind, D. (1979). The development of instrumental competence through socialization. In A. D. Pick (Ed.), *Minnesota symposia on child psychology* (Vol. 7). Minneapolis: University of Minnesota Press.

Baumrind, D. (1991). Effective parenting during the early adolescent transition. In P. A. Cowan & M. E. Hetherington (Eds.), *Advances in family research* (Vol. 2). Hillsdale, NJ: Lawrence Erlbaum Associates.

Belsky, J. (1984). The determinants of parenting: A process model. *Child Development, 55,* 83–96.

Belsky, J., Gilstrap, B., & Rovine, M. (1984). The Pennsylvania infant and family development project, I: Stability and change in mother-infant and father-infant interaction in a family setting at one, three, and nine months. *Child Development, 55,* 692–705.

Bernard, J. (1972). *The future of marriage.* New York: World.

Block, J. H. (1976a). Debatable conclusions about sex differences. *Contemporary Psychology, 21,* 517–522.

Block, J. H. (1976b). Issues, problems, and pitfalls in assessing sex differences: A critical review of *The psychology of sex differences. Merril-Palmer quarterly, 222,* 283–308.

Block, J. H. (1983). Differential premises arising from differential socialization of the sexes: Some conjectures. *Child Development, 54,* 1335–1354.

Block, J. H. (1984). *Sex role identity and ego development.* San Francisco, CA: Jossey-Bass.

Block, J. H., & Block, J. (1980). The role of ego-control and ego-resiliency in the organization of behavior. In W. A. Collins (Ed.), *Minnesota Symposia on Child Psychology* (Vol. 13). Hillsdale, NJ: Lawrence Erlbaum Associates.

Block, J. H., Block, J., & Gjerde, P. F. (1986). The personality of children prior to divorce: A prospective study. *Child Development, 57,* 827–840.

Brody, G. H., Pellegrini, A. D., & Sigel, I. (1986). Marital quality and mother-child and father-child interactions with school-aged children. *Developmental Psychology, 22,* 291–296.

Bronfenbrenner, U. (1979). *The ecology of human development.* Cambridge, MA: Harvard University Press.

Chodorow, N. J. (1978). *The reproduction of mothering.* Berkeley, CA: University of California Press.

Chodorow, N. J. (1989). *Feminism and psychoanalytic theory.* New Haven. Yale University Press.

Cicchetti, D., Toth, S. L., Bush, M. A., & Gillespie, J. (1988). Stage-salient issues; A transactional model of intervention. In E. Nannis & P. Cowan (Eds.), *Developmental psychopathology and its treatment. New directions for child development* (No. 39, pp. 123–146). San Francisco: Jossey-Bass.

Cowan, C. P. (1988). Working with men becoming fathers: The impact of a couples group intervention. In P. Bronstein & C. P. Cowan (Eds.), *Fatherhood today: Men's changing role in the family*. New York: Wiley.

Cowan, C. P., & Cowan, P. A. (1987). A preventive intervention for couples becoming parents. In C. F. Z. Boukydis (Ed.), *Research on support for parents and infants in the postnatal period.* Norwood, NJ: Ablex.

Cowan, C. P., & Cowan, P. A. (1990a). *The Pie*. In J. Touliatos, B. F. Perlmutter, & M. A. Straus (Eds.), *Handbook of family measurement techniques* (pp. 278–279). Newbury Park, CA: Sage.

Cowan, C. P., & Cowan, P. A. (1990b). *Who does what?* In J. Touliatos, B. F. Perlmutter, & M. A. Straus (Eds.), *Handbook of family measurement techniques* (pp. 447–448). Newbury Park, CA: Sage.

Cowan, C. P., & Cowan, P. A. (1992). *When partners become parents: The big life change for couples*. New York: Basic Books.

Cowan, C. P., Cowan, P. A., Heming, G., Garrett, E., Coysh, W. S., Curtis-Bowles, H., & Bowles, A. J. (1985). Transitions to parenthood: His, hers, and theirs. *Journal of Family Issues, 6,* 451–481.

Cowan, P. A. (1988). Developmental psychopathology: A nine-cell map of the territory. In E. Nannis & P. Cowan (Eds.), *Developmental psychopathology and its treatment. New directions for child development* (No. 39, pp. 5–30). San Francisco: Jossey-Bass.

Cowan, P. A. (1991). Individual and family life transitions: A proposal for a new definition. In P. A. Cowan & E. M. Hetherington (Eds.), *Family transitions: Advances in family research* (Vol. 2, pp. 3–30). Hillsdale, NJ: Lawrence Erlbaum Associates.

Cowan, P. A., & Cowan, C. P. (1988). Changes in marriage during the transition to parenthood: Must we blame the baby? In G. Y. Michaels & W. A. Goldberg (Eds.), *The transition to parenthood: Current theory and research* (pp. 114–154). Cambridge, England: Cambridge University Press.

Cowan, P. A., & Cowan, C. P. (1990). Becoming a family: Research and intervention. In I. Sigel & G. Brody (Eds.), *Methods of family research, Vol. I* (pp. 1–51). Hillsdale, NJ: Lawrence Erlbaum Associates.

Cowan, P. A., Cowan, C. P., Shulz M., & Heming, G. (in press). Prebirth to preschool family factors predicting children's adaptation to kindergarten. In R. Parke & S. Kellam, (Eds.). *Exploring family relationships with other social contexts: Advances in family research* (Vol. 4). Hillsdale, NJ: Lawrence Erlbaum Associates.

Cox, M. J., Owen, M. T., Lewis, J. M., & Henderson, V. K. (1989). Marriage, adult adjustment, and early parenting. *Child Development, 60,* 1015–1024.

Crockenberg, S. B., & Covey, S. L. (in press). Marital conflict and externalizing behavior in children. In D. Cicchetti (Ed.), *Rochester symposium on developmental psychopathology. Vol. 3.* Hillsdale, NJ: Lawrence Erlbaum Associates.

Deal, J. E., Halverson, C. F. Jr., & Wampler, K. S. (1989). Parental agreement on child-rearing orientations: Relations to parental, marital, family, and child characteristics. *Child Development, 60,* 1025–134.

Ervin-Tripp, S., O'Connor, M. C., & Rosenberg, J. (1984). Language and power in the family. In C. Kramarae, M. Schulz, & W. M. O'Barr (Eds.), *Language and power*. Newbury Park, CA: Sage.

Fagot, B. I. (1978). The influence of sex of child on parental reactions to toddler children. *Child Development, 49,* 459–465.

Fagot, B. I. (1985). Beyond the reinforcement principle; Another step toward understanding sex roles. *Developmental Psychology, 21,* 1097–1104.

Freud, S. (1964). Some psychical consequences of the anatomical distinctions between the sexes. In J. Strachey (Ed. and Trans.). *Standard edition of the complete psychological works of Sigmund Freud* (Vol. 19, pp. 243–258). London: Hogarth Press.

Goldberg, W. A., & Easterbrooks, M. A. (1984). The role of marital quality in toddler development. *Developmental Psychology, 20,* 504–514.

Gough, H. G., & Heilbrun, A. B., Jr. (1965/1980). *The adjective check list manual.* Palo Alto: Consulting Psychologists Press.

Grotevant, H. D., & Carlson, C. I. (1989). *Family assessment: A guide to methods and measures.* New York: Guilford.

Heinicke, C. M., & Guthrie, D. (in press). Stability and change in husband-wife adaptation and the development of the positive parent-child relationship. *Infant Behavior and Development.*

Heming, G., Cowan, P. A., & Cowan, C. P. (1990). Ideas about parenting. In J. Touliatos, B. F. Perlmutter, & M. A. Straus (Eds.), *Handbook of family measurement techniques* (pp. 362–363). Newbury Park, CA: Sage.

Hetherington, E. M., & Camara, K. A. (1984). Families in transition: The process of dissolution and reconstitution. In R. D. Parke (Ed.), *Review of child development research: The family* (Vol. VII). Chicago: University of Chicago Press.

Hetherington, E. M., Stanley-Hagen, M., & Anderson, E. R. (1989). Marital transitions: A child's perspective. *American Psychologist, 44,* 303–312.

Hochschild, A. (1989). *The second shift: Working parents and the revolution at home.* New York: Viking Penguin.

Howes, P., & Markman, H. J. (1989). Marital quality and child functioning: A longitudinal investigation. *Child Development, 60,* 1044–1051.

Johnson, M. M. (1988). *Strong mothers, weak wives: The search for gender equality:* Berkeley: University of California Press.

Kellam, S. G., Simon, M. B., & Ensminger, M. E. (1982). Antecedents in first grade of teenage drug use and psychological well-being: A ten-year community-wide prospective study. In D. Ricks & B. Dohrenwend (Eds.), *Origins of psychopathology: Research and public policy.* New York: Cambridge University Press.

Kerig, P. K. (1989). *The engendered family: The influence of marital satisfaction on gender differences in parent-child interaction.* Unpublished doctoral dissertation. University of California, Berkeley.

Kerig, P. K. (1991a, April). *Marital and gender effects in parent-child interaction.* Poster presented at the meetings of the Society for Research in Child Development. Seattle, WA.

Kerig, P. K. (1991b, August). *Sequential analyses of parent-child interaction: Marital and gender effects.* Poster presented at the meetings of the American Psychological Association, San Francisco, CA.

Locke, H., & Wallace, K. (1959). Short marital adjustment and prediction tests: Their reliability and validity. *Marriage and Family Living, 21,* 251–255.

Lytton, H., & Romney, D. M. (1991). Parents' differential socialization of boys and girls: A Meta-analysis. *Psychological Bulletin, 109,* 267–296.

Maccoby, E. E. (1990). Gender and relationships: A developmental account. *American Psychologist, 45,* 513–520.

Maccoby, E. E., & Jacklin, C. N. (1974). *The psychology of sex differences.* Stanford, CA: Stanford University Press.

Maccoby, E. E., & Martin, J. A. (1983). Socialization in the context of the family: Parent-child interaction. In E. M. Hetherington (Ed.), P. H. Mussen (Series Ed.) *Handbook of child psychology: Vol. 4. Socialization, personality and social development,* 4th ed. (pp. 1–101). New York: Wiley.

MacDonald, J., & Parke, R. D. (1984). Bridging the gap: Parent-child play interaction and peer interactive competence. *Child Development, 55,* 1265–1277.

Moos, R. H. (1974). *Family Environment Scale.* Palo Alto: Consulting Psychologists Press, Inc.

Morgan, S. P., Lye, D. N., & Condran, G. A. (1988). Sons, daughters, and the risk of marital disruption. *American Journal of Sociology, 94,* 110–129.

Parke, R. D., & Tinsley, B. (1982). The early environment of the at-risk infant: Expanding the social context. In D. D. Bricker (Ed.), *Intervention with at-risk and handicapped infants.* Baltimore, MD: University Park Press.

Parsons, T., & Bales, R. F. (1955). *Family, socialization, and interaction process.* Glencoe, IL: The Free Press.

Pratt, M. W., Kerig, P. K., Cowan, P. A., & Cowan, C. P. (1988). Mothers and fathers teaching three year-olds: Authoritative parenting and adults' use of the zone of proximal development. *Developmental Psychology, 24,* 832–839.

Rutter, M., & Garmezy, N. (1983). Developmental psychopathology. In P. Mussen (Ed.), *Handbook of child psychology* (Vol. IV). New York: Wiley.

Siegal, M. (1987). Are sons and daughters treated more differently by fathers than by mothers? *Developmental Review, 7,* 183–209.

Tinsley, B. J., & Parke, R. (1987). Grandparents as interactive and social support agents for families with young infants. *International Journal of Aging and Human Development, 25,* 261–279.

Vaughn, B., Egeland, B., Sroufe, L. A., & Waters, E. (1979). Individual differences in infant-mother attachment at twelve and eighteen months: Stability and change in families under stress. *Child Development, 50,* 971–975.

Wallerstein, J., & Kelly, J. (1980). *Surviving the breakup.* New York: Basic Books.

Walsh, F. (Ed.). (1980). *Normal family processes.* New York: Guilford.

Weissman, M. M., & Klerman, G. L. (1977). Sex differences and the epidemiology of depression. *Archives of General Psychiatry, 34,* 98–112.

9 Family Transitions and Children's Functioning: The Case of Parental Conflict and Divorce*

Janet R. Johnston
Stanford University

It is now generally acknowledged that parental conflict is a serious risk factor that predicts child disturbance. This has been found both *within intact families* (Block, Block, & Gjerde, 1988; Block, Block, & Morrison, 1981; Emery & O'Leary, 1982; Johnson & Lobitz, 1974; Johnson & O'Leary, 1987; Porter & O'Leary, 1980; Whitehead, 1979) and *within divorcing families* (Hetherington, Cox, & Cox, 1982; Jacobson, 1978; Johnston, Gonzalez, & Campbell, 1987; Rutter, 1971; Shaw & Emery, 1987). Recent attention to the children of marital violence has identified the more severe and overt forms of parental hostility and aggression as placing children at greater risk, although the parental violence is often linked with other stressors in these very troubled families (Hershorn & Rosenbaum, 1985; Jouriles, Barling, & O'Leary, 1987; Rosenbaum & O'Leary, 1981; Shaw & Emery, 1988; Wolfe, Jaffe, Wilson, & Zak, 1985). Exposure to parental conflict, together with affective distress and psychological disorders within parents (usually the caretaking mother), is a greater hazard to children than are many other stressful events associated with divorce, including acute loss due to separation from a parent (usually the father). (See Rutter's early epidemiological studies, 1971; and extensive reviews by Emery, 1982; and Grych & Fincham, 1990; Cherlin, Furstenberg, Chase-Lansdale, Kiernan, Robins, Morrison & Teitler, 1991).

---

*Some of the data in this chapter has been previously published in an article entitled "Role Diffusion and Role Reversal: Structural Variations in Divorced Families and Children's Functioning." *Family Relations, 39*(4), pp. 405–413. Copyright (1990) by the National Council on Family Relations, 3989 Central Avenue N.E., Suite #550, Minneapolis, MN 55421. Reprinted by permission.

One of the problems with previous work in this field is the manner in which conflict has been conceptualized and measured. The notion of marital conflict, although an intuitively compelling idea, can mean different things. In fact it is a multifaceted phenomenon. It has a content dimension and can refer to disagreements over a series of issues such as finances, child discipline, division of household tasks, and marital fidelity. It has a tactics dimension and can refer to ways of handling disagreements such as verbal reasoning, verbal aggression, and physical aggression. It has an attitude component as well, referring to negative emotional feelings about another person or event (Straus, 1979). The duration of conflict and its patterns over time are also important. In the above mentioned studies, conflict has been equated most crudely with divorce, or with various measures of marital dissatisfaction, mixed with items about hostile attitudes and physical aggression. It is important to make clearer distinctions about what kinds of conflict have a negative impact on children and under what conditions.

It has long been recognized that some form of conflict is endemic in families and social groups and, indeed, can have the positive function of signaling to families when they must adapt and change in order to meet the needs of individual members (Simmel, 1955). It is not the existence of conflict per se that is the issue here. Rather, the issue is whether the family has mechanisms for managing or resolving conflicts. Recent findings indicate that long-term marital satisfaction is associated with a certain level of openly expressed conflict (disagreement) in the marriage, as long as it occurs in the context of a couple relationship that is relatively respectful and appreciative (Gottman & Krokoff, 1989). On the other hand, sustained negative emotional feelings towards one another and expressed aggression in the form of verbal and physical abuse between parents are generally perceived as predicting poor marital quality and problematic child outcomes (Patterson, 1980). Hence the conceptions of marital conflict of interest are *felt hostility* and *expressed aggression*.

Additionally, a major issue that, to date, has been examined too simplistically is which specific areas of children's functioning are affected by parental conflict. From a series of studies on children of marital discord and divorce, the preponderance of evidence is that parental conflict is associated with problems of undercontrol (aggression, conduct disorder, and delinquency) in children, with more severe effects occurring from longer exposure to the conflict (Block et al., 1981; Emery & O'Leary, 1982; Hershorn & Rosenbaum, 1985; Hetherington et al., 1982; Rutter, 1971; Wolkind & Rutter, 1973). There have been only a few studies indicating that parental conflict is associated with disorders of overcontrol in children, including anxiety, depression, and withdrawal (Block et al., 1981; Whitehead, 1979). However, there is recent evidence that children of marital violence are more likely to be clinically disturbed in both internalizing and externalizing dimensions (Jaffe, Wolfe, Wilson, & Zak, 1986a, 1986b; Shaw & Emery, 1988; Wolfe, Zak, Wilson, & Jaffe, 1986).

This dichotomous distinction between externalizing and internalizing may not be particularly useful or informative when considering the population of children triangulated by parental conflict. Our own observations are that many of these children present with unfamiliar patterns, some of which look like nascent character disorders. The patterns of their disturbance are perhaps better understood from an ecological perspective. In order to survive in fragmented and potentially dangerous family relations, these children appear to be developing adaptive and defensive modes of response which, if not corrected, consolidate and become incorporated into their repertoire of characteristic coping behaviors. Some of these responses are positive, prosocial adaptations such as acutely heightened empathy. Most responses, however, are maladaptive, with a mixture of emotional constriction, withdrawal, interpersonal manipulativeness, and aggressive, antisocial behavior. Failures to defend and adapt are indicated by anxiety and stress responses, including somatic symptoms (Emery, 1989; Johnston et al., 1987).

Another issue that needs to be studied is the relative extent to which children are psychologically damaged by parental conflict. A surprising aspect of these general findings is that although a large and growing body of evidence indicates a robust (consistent) connection between parental conflict and child disturbance, there is a relatively modest association between these two factors, especially in nonclinic populations (Emery, 1982). It may be that a large number of children escape symptomatic response to, or are only slightly affected by, parental conflict. We have been intrigued by a wide range of outcomes in children of divorced parents, despite often very conflictual coparental relationships. Whereas some children seem to recover their normal developmental stride, for others development is accelerated. Moreover, some children become more resilient and develop considerable interpersonal competence. A worrisome percentage, however, become enmeshed in the conflict, remain emotionally distressed, and manifest stress symptoms and behavior problems (Johnston & Campbell, 1988).

Within this broad context, the immediate focus of this research agenda was on what makes for these different outcomes in children. What individual and family factors buffer them from distressed parental relationships or provide catalysts for their prosocial development? As yet we know very little about what intervening variables protect children from parental discord, although a few have been identified. For instance, a good relationship between the child and the primary caretaking parent has been found to shield the child from parental discord or parental psychopathology (Hess & Camara, 1979; Hetherington et al., 1982; Rutter, 1979). Second, individual characteristics of the child are important. In particular, in almost all the foregoing studies, boys have been found to be more vulnerable and girls more immune to family discord. Third, family composition is important. We have found that only children and the eldest child appear to be more negatively affected (Johnston & Campbell, 1987; Kline, Tschann, Johnston, & Wallerstein, 1989).

Rutter (1987), however, has questioned the usefulness of identifying specific environmental factors as buffers and particular characteristics of children as markers of resilience, as if they are inherently fixed attributes of the situation or individual. Note that being a boy may be protective in one situation and impose more stressful demands in another. Also, a factor such as cognitive maturity can act as a buffer in one situation by helping the child understand and cope better, whereas in another situation, it may be too stressful for an intelligent child to grasp what is happening in his family. Consequently, Rutter proposes that we identify *protective mechanisms* that shield children and *processes which lead to greater resilience* in children.

A number of very recent longitudinal studies of family and child development, including our own, imply that the effects of the spousal relationship upon the child are likely to be mostly indirect and mediated by the quality of the parent-child relationship. These studies indicate that marital distress and poor individual adjustment of a parent can be associated. Both of these factors are likely to lead to a deterioration in parental functioning, which in turn leads to more problematic parent-child relationships. Children's social and emotional adjustment appears to be an outcome of both the parent-child relationship and individual characteristics of the child.

Reporting on a sample of 72 couples followed from pregnancy until their first child was 3-years-old, Cowan and Cowan (1988) found that the pre- and post-birth couple relationship as well as the parents' individual functioning influenced parenting styles, which in turn were related to the preschooler's cognitive and social-emotional adjustment. The link between harmonious coparenting and better parent-child relationships was more true for girls than for boys. Easterbrooks (1987) followed 33 married couples with first-born infants over a 2-year period and found that initial marital harmony was associated with more sensitive, positive, and affectionate parent-child relationships, and with toddlers who were more compliant and less temperamentally difficult. Howes and Markman (1987), in a study of 20 families, found that premarital conflict and poor communication predicted highly dependent mother-son relationships and low dependence between mothers and daughters, which in turn was associated with less sociability in children aged 1- to 3-years. Caspi and Elder (1988) assessed four generations of families (N_{min} = 84) and found that personality difficulties among the subjects were associated with marital conflict which in turn predicted more rejecting, arbitrary parenting and subsequent undercontrolled behavior in offspring. This was more true for women than for men.

In a sample of 178 children, aged 1- to 18-years, we found that verbal and physical abuse between spouses prior to divorce, predicted postseparation parenting that was more problematic, in that it involved using the child in the conflict and for emotional support, less modeling and expecting ego control, less warmth and empathy, and more rejection and distancing. These dimensions of the parent-child relationship were associated with more problematic emotional and behavioral adjustment in the children at the time of the separation (Tschann et al.,

1989). Two years after the divorce, the same sample of children were assessed again and it was found that prior marital conflict continued to cast a long shadow over the children's postdivorce adjustment. It not only had direct effects on the children but also indirect effects because it was linked to mothers' less effective coping, greater emotional maladjustment, and less warm, empathic, and ego-controlled relationships with their children (Kline, Johnston, & Tschann, 1991).

In sum, there is a growing body of consistent empirical observations which indicate that marital conflict in some way shapes and transforms the parent-child relationship, and this consequently places children more at risk for emotional and behavioral disorders. What has not yet been theoretically and empirically clarified is precisely how parent-child relationships change in response to marital/parental discord and how these changes relate to the vastly different array of observed outcomes, both positive and negative, for children.

One of the more common and straightforward behavioral explanations for the negative impact of parental discord is that children observe and model the aggressive tactics of their parents (Bandura, 1977). This hypothesis, while distinguishable from the notion of "identification with the aggressor" in psychoanalytic theory (Anna Freud, 1966), shares some elements with it, and implies that marital conflict has a direct effect on the child. However, this is an incomplete explanation because it does not accurately reflect the wide array of effects observed in children of conflictual parents, particularly their internalizing symptoms and the consolidation of attitudes that reflect their developing moral sense and personality structure.

The expression of aggression is usually constrained by a set of affective and status, or dominance, structures within the family, with related rules of conduct that guide behavior. Whether and to what extent aggressive models are internalized is influenced by how the family is organized as a working unit, the affective relations between the members, and whether the child is a boy or girl. For instance, there is evidence that children identify with a more dominant parent when that parent rates high on warmth. They also tend to identify with the parent of the same sex. Hence children with a dominant, warm parent of the opposite sex and a disparaged parent of the same sex, are likely to have complex partial identifications with both parents, resulting in anxiety, low self-esteem, and other internalizing or neurotic symptoms (Gassner & Murray, 1969; Hetherington, 1965; Hetherington & Frankie, 1967; Klein, Plutchik, & Conte, 1973; Schwarz & Getler, 1980). It is the nature of the power/authority structure in the family, and the quality of the emotional relations generated between members, as well as the gender and individual characteristics of the child that will be important determinants of how children will be affected by parental disputes.

Recently, Swanson (1988) has provided a promising theoretical orientation which incorporates many of these determinants. He argues that the collective level of development of the family (or conversely, its state of disorganization) will have a direct bearing on the development of the children's ego defenses. The basic question Swanson asks is, what are the structural bases on which family members are interacting with one another?

At very primitive levels, family relations are ambivalent, tenuous, easily replaceable, and essentially egoistic. Other members are acknowledged only when they meet one's own needs. All members fend for themselves, fighting or fleeing to protect their own interests. There is no coordinated functioning of the family as a group, no central purpose, no recognized or consistent authority or leader. Extrapolating from this description, I suggest this quality of family relations is probably typical or borderline or psychotic parents in regressed states. At the next, rudimentary stage of collectivity, family members are organized as an interdependent network in which they make deals or exchanges among themselves. The implicit rule is, "If you do this for me, I'll do that for you." Since there is still no central coordination of function and no agreement as to purpose, method, or procedure, frequent conflicts of interest can arise because meeting one member's needs will hurt or hinder another. Hence there is fragmentation, and stable or unstable splits and alignments occur within the family, typically across generations.

The next level of collective development of the family involves the formation of a charismatic center, wherein one or more members assume a prototypical leadership function by virtue of the faith and trust invested in them by others. Normally, one expects parents to assume this charismatic function, especially for young children, but aberrations can occur. Some children are placed in the role of providing central purpose and emotional sustenance for the adult members.

A fourth level of collectivity, the work group, is considered important for children's ego development. At this level, leaders fulfill executive functions in coordinating and guiding the family group according to more rational, though often not explicit, rules. Other members are assigned roles in fulfilling both individual and collective needs. Generally, it is expected that parents will assume coleadership functions and the roles children play will be developmentally appropriate ones.

Swanson's main point is that children's defenses are developed to enable them to justify and preserve their family relationships and so, their level of ego functioning will correspond to the level of the family's structural organization. While his hypothesis is a bold and controversial claim that needs much more theoretical development and empirical confirmation, Swanson's overall thesis suggests a new way of conceptualizing the impact of parental conflict on children. Marital discord and divorce are likely to erode the level of collective development of family life, exposing the children to a more primitive ecological environment, to which their internal models of relationship and adaptive and defensive styles of relating are closely linked (Bretherton, 1985; Main, Kaplan, & Cassidy, 1985).

The question, then, becomes whether the family has mechanisms for managing or resolving conflicts of interest. Does it have an organizational or decision-making structure that allows the individuals' needs to be recognized and provided for? Does it have effective leadership and a network of cooperative role relations that allow it to function as a collective unit when necessary? If so, are these roles assigned appropriately with respect to the developmental capacities of family members? Hence, in the theoretical reformulation that follows, I argue that structural aberrations in the family as an organizational entity, especially failed leadership and inappropriate assignment and diffusion of roles, will have patterned consequences for children's developing styles of interpersonal relations and for the expression of their emotional and behavioral problems.

THEORETICAL FORMULATION

Drawing upon a widely varied body of literature in developmental psychology, socialization, divorce, clinical models of family systems, and family sociology, I propose a process model of the way parental conflict changes the structure and functioning of the family as a working group and changes the affective relations between the family members, thereby exposing the children to more problematic relationships with their parents (see Fig. 9.1). As is shown, the connections hypothesized in this model have varying amounts of empirical support and much of this support is implied rather than directly evident.

Spousal Conflict and Breakdown in the Parental Alliance

Spousal conflict is likely to disrupt the leadership functions of parents, changing their authority and power within the family. Put another way, marital conflict is likely to lead to a deterioration in the parental alliance, defined as the parents' support of and respect for each other in their executive roles within the family.

Early studies often treated marital conflict, divorce, and parental discord and disagreement over the children as synonymous concepts and indeed, the results indicate that they generally have similar effects on children (e.g., Block et al., 1981; Rutter, 1971). More recent studies of shared parenting after divorce have questioned the assumption of a high correspondence between spousal conflict and coparental conflict. Ahrons (1981), Steinman (1981), and Steinman, Zemmelman, and Knoblauch (1985), for instance, have pointed out that some parents can remain angry or actively dislike each other as spouses but still maintain respect for and support of each other in their capacity as parents, to the apparent benefit of the children. Hence, although the parental alliance is likely to be negatively affected by marital conflict, this is not an assured outcome.

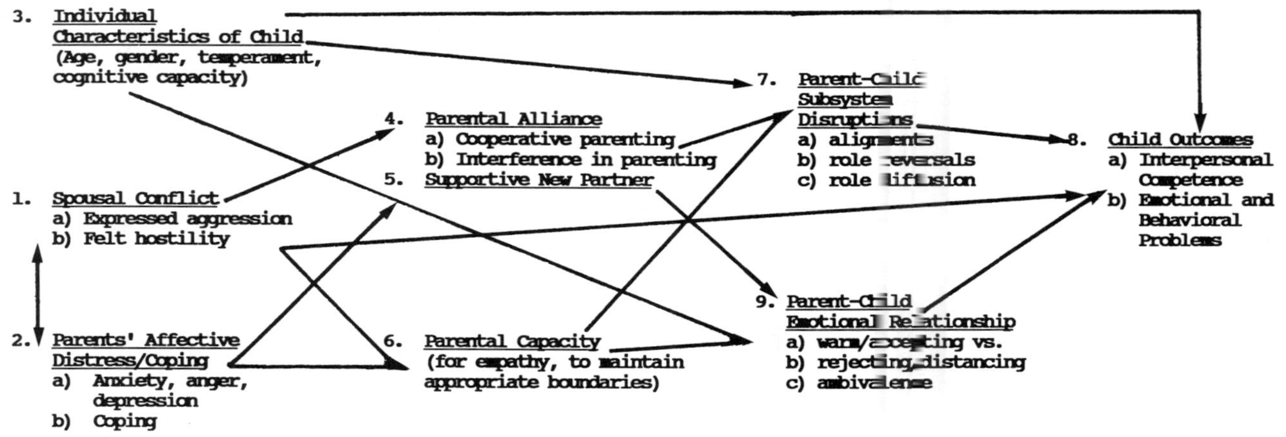

FIG. 9.1. Theoretical model proposing how parental conflict and divorce affect children.

Spousal Conflict, Parental Distress, and Capacity for Empathy

Spousal conflict is likely to be associated with parental anger, distress, or depression. (I will beg the question as to which is the prior element.) Emotional distress is likely to change parents' responsiveness to children and diminish their capacity to maintain boundaries between their own and their children's needs. In this sense, their capacity for empathy and nurturance is limited.

Although there is not sufficient evidence to document the claim that the spousal relationship is the most important social support, and that it enables a parent to maintain appropriate boundaries and sensitivity to the child's needs, there is considerable evidence, at a more general level, that a warm, harmonious, and confiding coparental relationship is associated with better parenting (Brody & Pellegrini, 1986; Cowan & Cowan, 1988; Easterbrooks, 1987; Goldberg & Easterbrooks, 1984; Jouriles, Pfiffner, & O'Leary, 1988; Pederson, 1982; Quinton, Rutter, & Liddle, 1984). Earlier research has drawn particular attention to the parents' diminished capacity for warmth and empathy towards the child in the acute stages of marital separation, during which time there is considerable interspousal hostility, expressed aggression, anger, and depression. All of these disturbances are related to parents' being preoccupied with their own problems and therefore less sensitive to and less able to respond to their children's needs. It is also not uncommon for parents to have fantasy wishes, sometimes acted upon, of abandoning their children (Wallerstein & Kelly, 1980).

Breakdown in Parental Alliance, Diminished Parenting Capacity, and Parent-Child Role Changes

When the parental alliance breaks down and parents are less able to distinguish their own needs from those of their children, the children are often induced to assume inappropriate roles or attempt to fulfill spousal/parental functions. For example, some children align with one parent against the other, and some assume the role of confidant(e), peer, or mentor to a distressed parent, as well as *parent* to their siblings. Such phenomena have generally been referred to as *role reversal* between parent and child.

Of course, other family members such as grandparents or a new spouse may assume parenting functions, both supporting a distressed parent and sparing the child that burden. However, if no one is able to fulfill the nurturing functions, the family unit remains disorganized and the members act unilaterally in their own individual interests, or in the interests of subgroups of the unit. This family disorganization is referred to as *role diffusion*.

These structural changes in the way in which the family is organized as a task group (role reversal and role diffusion) are particularly relevant in divorced families, where marital distress has resulted in a permanent split in the family unit. Previous research has identified some long-term changes that can take place in the parent-child relationship after divorce, whereby the parent becomes profoundly dependent upon the child, and the child, in turn, monitors, nurtures, and guards the parent's well being. At one level, the parent may turn to the child to satisfy specific needs, which may range from having a sympathetic listener or playmate to obtaining sexual gratification. At another level, the child can become a displacement figure for the parent's fantasy needs for care and protection and hence the parent becomes extraordinarily dependent upon the child for nurturance and direction. Some children become a displacement figure for the ex-spouse and are therefore perceived as the enemy. In extreme cases there can be a total fusion of parent and child, with a loss of psychological boundaries, and a true symbiosis can develop. Moreover, these disturbances in relationship can be highly focalized and encapsulated around specific, significant issues, becoming activated at certain stressful times, or they can be diffuse and general features of the parent-child relationship. Wallerstein (1985a, 1985b) has termed this phenomenon as the syndrome of the "overburdened child," and Johnston and Campbell (1988) have noted that it is especially likely to occur in high-conflict divorced families.

For several decades, structural family theorists have argued that breakdown of the parental subsystem is likely to result in inappropriate alliances across generational boundaries, role reversals, and role diffusion, all of which place children at risk for increased stress, scapegoating, and symptom formation (Isaacs, Montalvo, & Abelsohn, 1986; Lidz, Cornelison, Fleck, & Terry, 1968; Minuchin, 1974; Vogel & Bell, 1968). However, the attention of family therapists has been captured by the way in which the symptomatic child is an expression of the aberration or breakdown in family life, and little attention has been given to the child as an interdependent actor or agent in this process.

Although many of these phenomena have been richly described in family theory and clinical practice, structural changes in families and their consequences for children have been virtually neglected by developmental psychologists interested in socialization influences. Hence, they have not been empirically investigated, and the theoretical formulations have not shed light on the developmental implications for the child. It is particularly important to understand the conditions under which children cope with the unusual responsibilities and emotional burdens thrust upon them and even, in some cases, appear to benefit by becoming more resilient, empathic, and interpersonally competent children. It is, of course, equally pressing to understand the conditions that overwhelm them.

Parents' Affective Distress, Diminished Parental Capacity, Parent-Child Role Disturbance, and Emotional Relationships Between Parent and Child

Consequent upon the breakdown of the parents' capacity for empathy, the emotional relationships or affective bonds between parents and children are likely to change. Some children feel more angry and rejecting towards the ungiving, nonsupportive parent. Other children, in response to threats of rejection or emotional abandonment inherent in the parent's self-absorption or anger, seek to merge with the emotional experience of their distressed parent. Hence, boundaries between their own and their parent's feelings become unclear. There is considerable evidence for these claims.

Parents who are less sensitively attuned to children's capacities and to the developmental tasks they face are less likely to be warm, nurturant, and affectionate (Belsky, 1984). The relationship of depressed, self-absorbed mothers with their children is more likely to be disrupted, mutually hostile, and rejecting (Bond & McMahon, 1984; Colletta, 1979; Greist, Wells, & Forehand, 1980; Orvaschel, Weissman, & Kidd, 1980). Negative cycles of coerciveness and rejection can occur between parents and children in families characterized by marital conflict, where mothers are depressed, irritable, and punitive (Hetherington et al., 1982; Johnson & Lobitz, 1974; Olweus, 1980; Patterson, 1980).

However, children who successfully fulfill important protective functions for a parent—those who become the confidant(e) who provides emotional support and advice, who act as coconspirator or comrade in arms against the other parent (or against the world), and who indirectly or expressly gratify a parent's sexual needs—can be the recipient of conditional warmth and acceptance from that parent (Johnston & Campbell, 1988; Wallerstein, 1985a, 1985b). The efficiency and competency with which a child supports a parent and provides needed emotional reassurance has important implications. Clinical observations have revealed that children who fail to meet a parent's expectations in these respects, those who are unstable allies, or those who actively ally with the hated other parent can be precipitately rejected and abandoned, psychologically if not physically (Johnston & Campbell, 1988). Hence, the functions that the child performs with respect to the parent are reciprocally related to the quality of the emotional relationship between parent and child, and can lead to a rejecting, negative relationship, a warm, accepting one, or an ambivalent relationship with elements of both acceptance and rejection.

The Contribution of the Child to the Parent-Child Relationship

I hypothesize that the extent to which the child assumes unusual functions as a result of family subsystem boundary changes, and the extent to which the child loses emotional boundaries and becomes enmeshed in the parent's distress and anger, will depend on the child's age and gender as well as on other individual differences of temperament, intelligence, or history of preexisting vulnerability in psychological functioning. To date, these hypotheses have not been addressed in any systematic manner except with respect to parent-child alignments.

A recent study has shown that in high conflict divorces, the extent and kind of alliance that a child makes with one parent against the other depends to a great extent upon the child's cognitive development, as indicated by age (Johnston & Campbell, 1987). In that study, very young children (2- to 4-years) had temporary reactions of distress and clinging to one parent in response to observed parental fights, whereas children aged 4- to 7-years often made temporary allegiances, with first one parent and then the other, with respect to the concrete issues under dispute, reflecting their cognitive capacity for a unilateral perspective (i.e., they could assume only one parent's perspective at a time). When the children developed the capacity for self-reflexive thinking and could simultaneously appraise both parents' opposing views (6- to 9-years), they understood better the enduring hostile feelings of the parents towards each other and the insolubility of the conflict. Consequently, they became vulnerable to acute loyalty conflicts, which later seemed to be partly resolved by the children making a sustained alliance with one parent and rejecting the other. Alliances were common among children 9- to 12-years in these chronically high-conflict families. These findings have been corroborated by observations of children during the acute phase of conflict (at the time of divorce) in a more *normative* population (Kelly & Wallerstein, 1976; Wallerstein & Kelly, 1976).

Apart from age and gender, other individual characteristics of the child, such as temperament and cognitive capacities, have been found that modify the parent-child relationship. Temperamentally difficult infants who are irritable, slow to adapt to change, irregular in their biological cycles, and subject to negative mood states produce more negative and avoidant responses in their mothers (Campbell, 1979; Milliones, 1978; Rutter, 1971). Children who are perceived as defective in some way—those who are weaker, more dependent, or less attractive—are more likely to be used as scapegoats (Vogel & Bell, 1968) and can even be the targets for abuse and neglect (Belsky, 1980).

On the other hand, intelligence has been found to be a strong asset in children, predicting their engagement in tasks and school competence, which in turn affects self-esteem (Garmezy, Masten, & Tellegen, 1984). Anthony (1987) has drawn particular attention to the "representational capacity" of children—that is, their ability to test reality, understand what is going on about them, maintain psychological separateness, and use creative thought to symbolically manage stressful experiences. Children who can do this seem to have a greater capacity to assimilate and master such extreme stressors as living with a psychotic parent. These same capacities may enhance a child's ability to cope in the midst of parental conflict, and may safeguard good outcome.

Some preschool children in chronically conflictual families are able to use fantasy and play to reconstruct and reorder their world and hence maintain a psychological distance from parental disputes, whereas other young children, whose play is constricted or continually disrupted by their anxieties and fears, do not seem to be able to symbolically master the family chaos (Johnston & Campbell, 1988). Among latency-age children, we have observed specific individual styles of adapting to or protecting themselves from intense parental disputes, which seem to depend on two factors: the degree of psychological separateness or differentiation from a parent, and their cognitive style of either assimilation or accommodation in response to the family's conflicting demands. Well differentiated children who assimilate parental demands have been found to maneuver actively between their parents and to maintain a critical, distanced attitude; they often develop a "trickster" mode of coping. Differentiated children who accommodate to parental demands suffer more severe loyalty conflicts, but try to manage their emotions and remain fair and equidistant to both sides. Undifferentiated children who accommodate act like chameleons with both parents, or become involved in strong alliances with one parent. Undifferentiated children who try to assimilate their parents' opposing demands may become diffusely disturbed and emotionally and behaviorally symptomatic (Johnston, Campbell, & Mayes, 1985).

Parent-Child Relationships and Child Outcomes

Finally, although both short- and long-term child outcomes are considerably complex as a consequence of these family processes, I venture some tentative predictions, at least in the short term. There is a growing body of findings within the socialization literature that substantiates the connection between the quality of parent-child relationships and particular patterns of social, emotional, and behavioral adjustment in children.

Children who have conflictual, mutually coercive, and rejecting relationships with their parents are likely to be aggressive and to exhibit conduct disorders (Hetherington et al., 1982; Johnson & Lobitz, 1974; Patterson, 1980). In younger children, lack of parental interest is associated with disruptions in attachment (Egeland & Sroufe, 1981), and in older children it is associated with aggression, noncompliance, impulsivity, moodiness, and low self-esteem (Block, 1971). Conversely, a warm, nurturing parent-child relationship, in which the parent exerts sensitive control and places appropriate limits, is associated with high self-esteem, assertiveness, and affiliative behavior in children (Baumrind, 1971).

There is little empirical evidence about the effects on children of assuming *inappropriate* functions or roles with respect to their parents. In general, family therapists have associated this with psychosomatic disorders, especially eating disorders (Minuchin et al., 1975; Minuchin, Rosman, & Baker, 1978; Selvini-Palozzoli, 1974), and with psychotic disorders in intensely enmeshed families (Bowen, 1978; Lidz et al., 1968; Wynne, Rykoff, Day, & Hirsch, 1968). Others, such as Weiss (1979), have suggested that when a child successfully fulfills important functions in the family, he or she acquires increased self-esteem, a sense of independence, and early social maturity. Although this appears to be true for some competent children, we have found that developmentally inappropriate role reversals can overburden many children who sense that their acceptance by the parent is contingent upon meeting the parent's needs. Children can become covertly resentful and angry that their own needs are ignored, but at the same time feel compelled to continue taking care of the parent lest they be abandoned or rejected (Johnston & Campbell, 1988; Wallerstein, 1985a, 1985b). An overinvolved, dependent parent-child relationship often has elements, also, of covert hostility and ambivalence, which in turn are associated with anxiety, withdrawal, and emotional constriction in children (Coolidge & Brodie, 1974; Johnston et al., 1987; Waldron, Shrier, Stone, & Tobin, 1975).

Hence, one can propose several paths to particular short-term outcomes with respect to children's postdivorce functioning, depending upon the parent-parent and parent-child relationships in combination with the nature of the child. First, positive outcomes, defined as interpersonal competence and the relative absence of disabling emotional and behavioral symptoms, will be predicted for children where the interparental conflict has been resolved or contained within a successful coparental alliance, and where parental warmth and family role structure remain intact or are restored following divorce. Where parental functioning has collapsed, but other family members (including new spouses and older siblings) have successfully assumed these functions, children will be more protected. Better outcomes will also be predicted for children with more personal resources. These include older children and girls, and those children who have more adaptive temperaments, fewer prior psychological difficulties, and greater capacity to master stressful family situations cognitively, through language and play. Second, children who assume the burden of emotional care for parents and siblings can be expected to develop overly responsible, controlling, and pseudo-adult styles of relating to others, with less awareness of their own emotional needs and diminished pleasure in social and emotional relations with peers. It is expected that these children will be involved in more ambivalent relationships with parents, and although they will manifest withdrawal and emotional constriction, they will not be identified as having emotional and behavioral problems. Third, children of all ages and both genders, in families marked by failed leadership, diffusion of roles, and rejecting relationships, are expected to have self-preoccupied (narcissistic) interpersonal styles in which their own needs and wants take priority over the needs of others. Fourth, negative child outcomes, indicated by emotional and behavioral problems and somatic symptoms, will be predicted by negative and rejecting parent-child relationships and by family subsystem boundary diffusion among those children who have fewer personal resources.

SAMPLE AND METHODS

In a preliminary empirical test of these ideas, only a core piece of the rather complex process was evaluated, as represented in Fig. 9.2. Individual characteristics of the child were limited to age and gender. Characteristics of parents

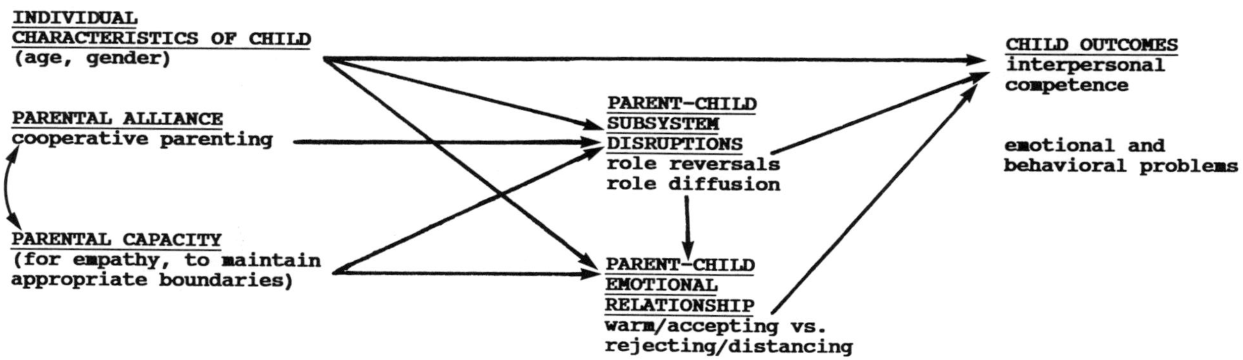

FIG. 9.2. Partial theoretical model of family process and children's functioning.

comprised their capacity to maintain a coparental alliance as a divorced couple and their ability to maintain parental boundaries as an individual parent. The level of family collective development was captured by two concepts: role reversal (measuring appropriateness of role assignment) and role diffusion (measuring role disorganization). Affective relations between parents and child was a bipolar concept measuring warmth and acceptance versus rejection and distancing. Two broad outcomes of child functioning were examined as a consequence of these family processes, namely, interpersonal competence and emotional and behavioral problems.

The sample of divorced families used for this study was selected from an archival data base that focused on processes within families, especially parent-child relationships, studied within 12 months of filing for divorce/custody (baseline) and again between 1 and 2 years later (follow-up). The total data base consisted of 312 families with 523 children. To reduce some of the complexity in family structure and process generated by family size and composition, and age of child, further selection criteria were applied. First, because family relationships are probably more salient during middle childhood (compared to late adolescence, when peers become very important), children ages 4–12 at baseline were selected. Second, to decrease the complexity due to family composition, only children or the eldest child in two-children families were selected. Third, because the aim was to examine the effects of coparental functioning after divorce, families were selected in which both parents maintained contact with the child on the average of 1 day every month during the 2-year follow-up period. Finally, to avoid assessing the families during the upheaval of the divorce itself, in this study only the follow-up data were utilized, averaged from the one-to-two-year ratings. Since parental separation had occurred on the average 14 months prior to being seen at baseline, this is a concurrent study of family relations and child outcomes between 2 and 3 years after the final separation.

The final sample consisted of 133 children (64 boys and 69 girls). Their average age at baseline was 7.43 years (s.d. = 2.66). On the average, children saw the noncustodial parent (or, in joint custody, the least-seen parent) 8.26 days per month (s.d. = 5.70). The majority of children (80%) were White and the remainder (20%) were Black, Hispanic, Asian, Pacific Islander, or Native American. Average length of parents' marriage was 10.6 years (s.d. = 5.03), and average length of separation was 14.03 months (s.d. = 19.99) at baseline. Median income range for fathers was $18,000–$25,000, and $10,000–$18,000 for mothers. On the Hollingshead seven-point occupational index (Hollingshead & Redlich, 1958), fathers' mean rating was 3.06, s.d. = 1.80, and mothers' mean rating was 4.22, s.d. = 1.86.

The overall data base comprised families who had originally been recruited between 1981 and 1984 in three counties of the San Francisco Bay Area, for a larger, longitudinal study of divorce. Recruitment was by means of letters sent to parents who had recently filed for dissolution, and by community outreach to professionals and institutions which serve divorcing families (schools, attorneys, social agencies, and the family courts). Both parents and all children in each family had agreed to participate in the research in exchange for brief preventive counseling. Family members were seen for approximately 6 sessions at baseline and 1 session each at the 1- and 2-year follow-ups. Extensive clinical process records were kept of the initial historical material that was gathered and of all subsequent contacts with family members. A clinical summary was completed at the end of the baseline counseling. Follow-up interviews were fully recorded as well. At intake, and again 1- and 2-years later, all family members had been evaluated separately by a battery of psychodiagnostics, described in Huntington (1985), which included written family history questionnaires, structured observation sessions, standardized psychological adjustment measures, and Divorce Apperception Test, and sentence completion projectives.

Research clinicians, who were blind to the hypotheses to be tested in this particular study, undertook clinical ratings of parents, children, and parent-child relationships, using the interviews and psychodiagnostic material described above, after the 1- and 2-year data had been collected. Although the same clinician rated both family process and child outcome, the specific items used in this study were embedded in multiple ratings of various aspects of family life, numbering a total of approximately 800 items per case. Interrater reliabilities were calculated using intraclass correlations (ICC) on randomly selected 1-in-every-8 cases during the coding period. The clinical ratings of the multiple items tapping each concept were reduced by factor analysis. Principal-components analyses with oblique rotation were utilized.

Internal consistency of the new scales was measured by Chronbach's Alpha. Concurrent validity of new measures was evaluated by correlating each with established measures of similar concepts wherever possible. Discriminant validity was assessed by comparing a sample of parents involved in ongoing litigation over custody and visitation with a *normal* community sample of divorced parents. The list of specific measures used in this study, together with sources of information and brief descriptions of items and their psychometric properties, are summarized in Table 9.1.

The process model proposed in Fig. 9.1 was tested using path analyses, with each dependent variable involving a separate analysis. The dependent variables included the child's Interpersonal Competence, Self-Preoccupied/Narcissistic Style, General Aggressiveness, Overly-Responsible/Controlling Style, Emotional Constriction, General Emotional-Behavioral Problems, and Somatic Complaints. A series of simultaneous multiple regression equations were calculated. First, each dependent variable was regressed on all predictors. The predictors included the hypothesized mediating variables (Role Reversal, Role Diffusion [vs. Role Structure], and Rejection/Distancing [vs. Warmth/Acceptance] between parent and child) and the exogenous variables (Gender and Age of Child, Coparental Alliance, and Parental Boundary Problems), none of which was

TABLE 9.1
Summary of Measures

Concept	*Measure*	*Description and Psychometric Properties*[a]
Parental Alliance	Coparental Alliance	Clinical rating, factor derived from parent-parent relationship ratings (6 items, 5-pt. scale, e.g., parent is ideologically committed to shared parenting; respects, trusts and supports other parent; believes other parent has important role in child's life). Correlation with Ahron's (1981) discuss and share decision making r= .56; Ahron's (1981) support scale r= .44; Straus' (1979) verbal reasoning r= .39. Discriminates normal divorced parents from those in litigious custody disputes (t = 4.06, $p < .001$. Alpha = .96 for individual parents and .91 for both parents combined; ICC = .74
Parental Capacity	Parental Boundary Problems	Clinical rating, factor derived from parent-child relationship ratings (9 items, 5-pt. scale, e.g., child must provide approval for parent, used to ward off depression, must share parent's feelings). Discriminates litigious from normal divorced parents t = 7.42, $p < .001$. Alpha = .90 for individual parents and .42 for both parents combined; ICC = .69.
Parent-Child Subsystem (Role) Disruption	Role Diffusion	Clinical rating, factor derived from parent-child relationship ratings (11 items, 5-pt. scale, e.g., irregularity and unpredictability in child's activities; discipline is unclear, inconsistent; little coordination between family members; decisions are made according to parents' needs). Alpha = .91 for individual parents and .62 for both parents combined; ICC = .68.
Parent-Child Subsystem (Role) Disruption	Role Reversal	Clinical rating, factor derived from parent-child relationship ratings (5 items, 5 pt. scale, e.g., parent allows child to discipline parents or sibs; child assumes executive role in family; child is parent's confidant). Discriminates litigious from normal relations t = 6.99, $p < .001$. Alpha = .76 for individual parents and .61 for both parents combined; ICC = .64.
Parent-Child Emotional Relationship	Warm/Accepting vs. Rejecting/Distancing Parent-Child Relationship	Clinical rating, factor derived from parent-child relationship ratings (13 items, 5-pt. scale, e.g., warmth/love, joy/fun, parent views child as great burden, blames child for parental difficulties, anger expressed between child and parent). Alpha = .91 for individual parents and .56 for both parents combined; ICC = .61.
Child Outcomes (a) Social Competence	Interpersonal Competence	Factor from clinical ratings of child's emotional-relational style (8 items, 5-pt. scale, e.g., able to strategically withdraw, able to reason, rationalize own needs in relation to others; moves in and out of peer relationships with security and comfort). Correlation with Social Involvement (clinical rating r= .73; with Achenbach Social Competence T score r= .33 (see Achenbach & Edelbrock, 1983). Alpha = .73; ICC = .61.
	Self-Preoccupied/ Narcissistic	Factor from clinical ratings of child's emotional-relational style (6 items, 5-pt. scale, e.g., preoccupied with own needs, takes care of self first, no inhibitions of own needs/wants, does not worry about others, opportunistic, exploitive). Correlation with Achenbach Aggression r= .38. Alpha = .73; ICC = .61.

(*Continued*)

TABLE 9.1 Continued

Concept	*Measure*	*Description and Psychometric Properties*[a]
	Overly Responsible/ Controlling of Others	Factor from clinical ratings of child's emotional-relational style (4 items, 5-pt. scale, e.g., takes initiative on behalf of others; controls, organizes, directs others; precocious pseudo-adultlike ((not playful). Alpha = .77; ICC = .59.
(b) General Emotional-Behavioral Problems[b]	Total T Score[b] Achenbach Behavior Problems Checklist	Parent rating, general index of child's behavioral and emotional problems (118 items, 3-pt. scale). See Achenbach and Edelbrock (1983) for further discussion of psychometric properties and norms. Intercorrelation of parent's ratings $r = .24$.
	Emotional-Behavioral Problems[b]	One factor derived from clinical ratings of child's behavioral and emotional problems (9 items, 5-pt. scale, e.g., poor self-esteem, powerlessness, (no) age-appropriate responsibility for self, depression, suicidal thoughts, anger, conduct problems). Correlation with Achenbach Total T score r = .52. Alpha = .87; ICC = .71.
	Somatic Complaints	Parent rating, factor for Somatic Complaints. See Achenbach and Edelbrock (1983) for further discussion of psychomatric properties and norms. Intercorrelation of parents' ratings $r = .28$.
	Emotionally Constricted	Factor from clinical ratings of child's emotional and relational style (4 items, 5-pt. scale, e.g., emotionally constricted, apathetic, passive, limited range of emotions). Correlation with Achenbach Depression $r = .25$, Withdrawn/Uncommunicative $r = .21$, Somatic Complaints $r = .25$. Alpha = .82; ICC = .65.
	Aggression[c]	Parent rating, factor for Aggression. See Achenbach and Edelbrock (1983) for further discussion of psychometric properties and norms. Intercorrelation of parents' ratings $r = .30$.
	Hostile-Aggressive[c]	Factor from clinical rating of child's emotional and relational style (5 items, 5-pt. scale, e.g., expresses anger/hostility; imitated aggressor; problems modulating affect, bullying, aggressive or sexual impulses spill over). Correlation with Achenbach's Aggression $r = .56$. Alpha = .88; ICC = .73.

[a]ICC = Intraclass correlation; Alpha = Chronbach's Alpha.

[b]The correlations between the parent ratings on the Achenbach CBCL Total T score and the clinician's ratings of the same concept were sufficiently high to warrant standardizing and combining the two scores to form one composite measure, called General Emotional-Behavioral Problems.

[c]The correlations between the parent ratings on the Achenbach CBCL Aggression factor and the clinician's ratings of the same concept were sufficiently high to warrant standardizing and combining the two scores to form one composite measure, called General Aggressiveness.

predicted by other variables in the model. Next, working backwards, each mediating variable was regressed on all variables antecedent to it. Reduced path models were obtained in a second series of calculations regressing endogenous variables on only those predictors that were significant at the .05 level. Significant direct effects between variables in the model were diagrammed with connecting lines. Standardized regression coefficients (path coefficients) obtained from least squares regression made it possible to compare the relative influence of predictors on the mediating and dependent variables.

RESULTS

The correlations among variables in the path models are shown in Table 9.2 and the correlations among the dependent variables are shown in Table 9.3.

TABLE 9.2
Correlations Among Variables in Path Model (N = 133)

Independent	1	2	3	4	5	6	7
Coparental Alliance	–	-.35***	-.52***	-.10	-.46***	-.09	.09
Parent Boundary Problems	–	–	.49***	.53***	.42***	-.19*	-.12
Role Diffusion (vs. structure)	–	–	–	.17*	.74***	.07	.01
Role Reversal	–	–	–	–	.16+	-.08	-.06
Parent-Child Rejection (vs.warmth/ acceptance)	–	–	–	–	–	.16+	-.02
Age	–	–	–	–	–	–	.03
Gender	–	–	–	–	–	–	–
Dependent							
Interpersonal Competence	.30***	-.41***	-.34***	-.23**	-.38***	.38***	.19*
Self-Preoccupied/ Narcissistic	.01	.03	.19*	-.00	.32***	.02	-.07
Overresponsible (controlling)	-.01	.12	-.02	.44***	-.01	-.03	.08
General Emotional-Behavior Problem	-.28***	.41***	.42***	.19*	.57***	-.13	-.24**
Emotionally Constricted	-.35***	.44***	.41***	.33***	.35***	.04	-.13
Somatic Complaints	-.21**	.21**	.24**	.22**	.32***	.04	-.03
General Aggressiveness	-.16+	.30***	.31***	.17+	.47***	-.09	-.25**

+$p \leq .10$.
*$p \leq .05$.
**$p \leq .01$.
***$p \leq .001$.

TABLE 9.3
Correlations Among Dependent Variables (N = 133)

Variable	*1*	*2*	*3*	*4*	*5*	*6*	*7*
Interpersonal competence	–	-.09	.17*	-.63***	-.51***	-.20*	-.44***
Self-preoccupied/ Narcissistic		–	-.09	.42***	-.16+	.18*	.55***
Over-responsible/ Controlling			–	-.09	.05	-.00	-.04
General emotional-Behavior Problem				–	.29***	.50***	.67***
Emotionally constricted					–	.24**	.08
Somatic Complaints						–	.32***
General Aggressiveness							–

+$p \leq .10$.
*$p \leq .05$.
**$p \leq .01$.
***$p \leq .001$.

Variations in the Children's Functioning

Figs. 9.3 through 9.9 show the reduced path models for each dependent variable. The path coefficients varied minimally from the original to the reduced models. All path models explained significant amounts of variance in the children's functioning, but with different patterns of independent variables, specifically as follows:

Figure 9.3. Interpersonal Competence was predicted directly by Gender (girls $>$ boys), Age (older $>$ younger), and Warm/Accepting relationships with parents ($R^2 = .38$), and indirectly by Age (older $<$ younger), Coparental Alliance, fewer Parental Boundary Problems, and appropriate Role Structure. Role Reversal was not significant in this analysis.

Figure 9.4. Self-Preoccupied/Narcissistic Style was predicted directly by Coparental Alliance and Rejection/Distancing between parents and children ($R^2 = .13$), and indirectly by Age (older $<$ younger), absence of a Coparental Alliance, Parental Boundary Problems, and Role Diffusion. Gender and Role Reversal had no significant effects.

Figure 9.5. Overly Responsible/Controlling Style was predicted directly by parent-child Role Reversal ($R^2 = .19$), and indirectly by Parental Boundary Problems. Age, Gender, Coparental Alliance, and Role Diffusion were unrelated to this outcome.

Figure 9.6. Emotional Constriction was predicted directly by Role Reversal and Parental Boundary Problems ($R^2 = .21$), and indirectly by Parental Boundary Problems. Age, Gender, Coparental Alliance, and Role Diffusion were not predictive.

Figure 9.7. General Emotional-Behavioral Problems were predicted directly by Gender (boys $>$ girls), Age (younger $>$ older), and parent-child Rejection/Distancing ($R^2 = .42$), and indirectly by Age (older $<$ younger), absence of a Coparental Alliance, Parental Boundary Problems, and Role Diffusion. Role Reversal was not associated with behavior problems.

Figure 9.8. General Aggressiveness was predicted directly by Gender (boys $>$ girls), Age (younger $>$ older), Rejection/Distancing between parents and children ($R^2 = .30$), and indirectly by Age (older $<$ younger), lack of a Coparental Alliance, Parental Boundary Problems, and Role Diffusion. Role Reversal was not predictive.

Figure 9.9. Somatic Complaints were predicted directly by Role Reversal and Rejection/Distancing in parent-child relationships ($R^2 = .14$), and indirectly by Age (older $<$ younger), a failed Coparental Alliance, Parental Boundary Problems, and Role Diffusion. Gender was unrelated to this outcome.

It should be noted here that in the analyses undertaken, as illustrated in Figs. 9.3–9.9; mother's and father's scores for each of the independent variables were

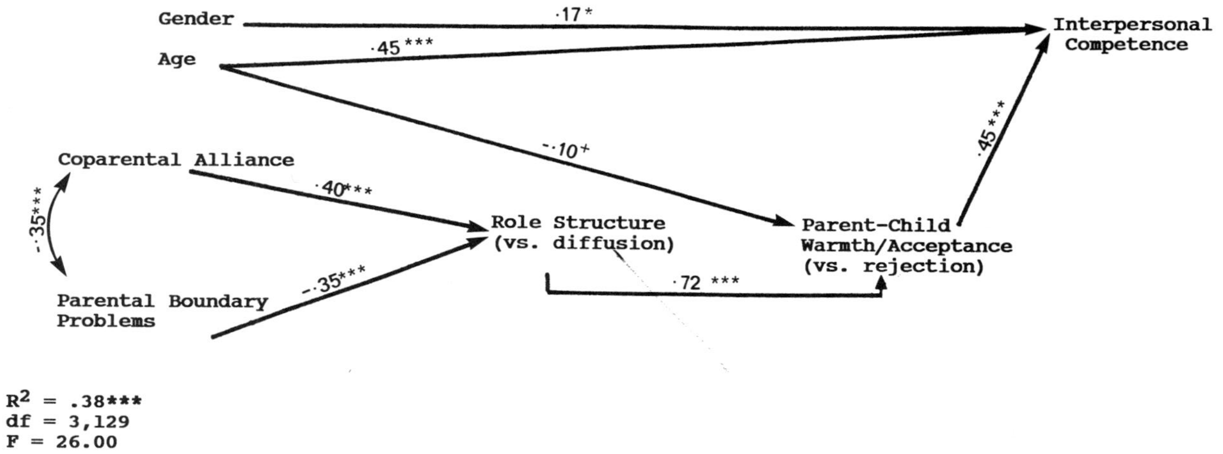

FIG. 9.3. Path model of family process and children's interpersonal competence.

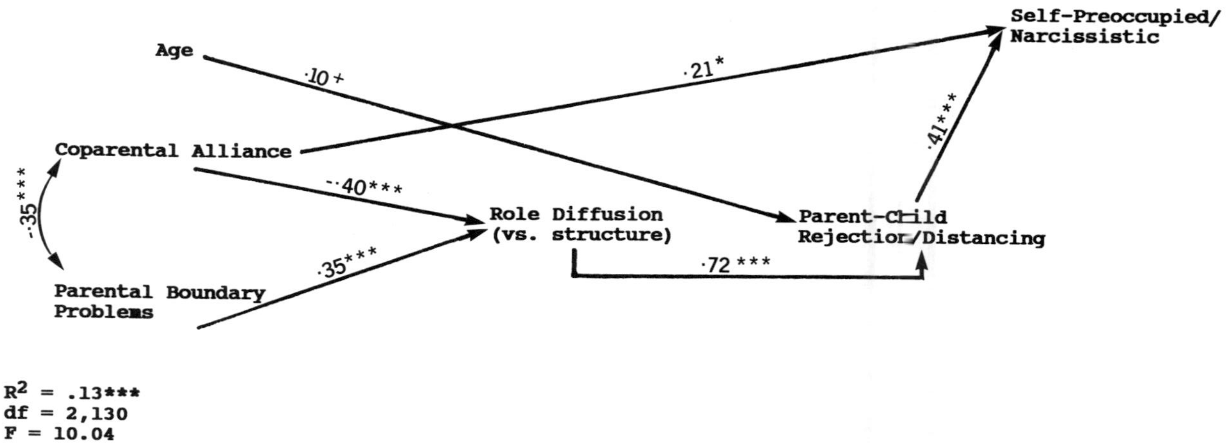

FIG. 9.4. Path model of family process and children's self-preoccupied/narcissistic style.

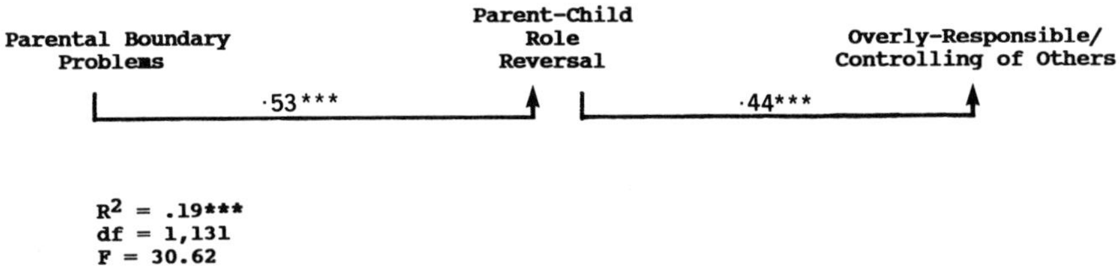

FIG. 9.5. Path model of family process and children's overly responsible/controlling style.

added together to produce a single parental score. Chronbach's Alpha for combining parents' scores was high for Coparental Alliance (.91), only moderate for Role Reversal (.61) and Role Diffusion (.62), barely adequate for Rejection/Distancing (.56), and poor for Parental Boundary Problems (.42), as shown in Table 9.1 above. Because it was possible that important differences between the mother's and father's scores were being obscured by compositing the parental scores, the above analyses were repeated using separate mother and father scores for Rejection/Distancing and Boundary Problems. The overall patterns of results was virtually unchanged, with the added suggestion that Rejection/Distancing between mother and child was more predictive than that between father and child, but that older children were more likely to be Reject(ed)/Distanc(ed) by their fathers than by their mothers. Father's Boundary Problems were also more salient than mother's Boundary Problems. However, both mother's and father's scores on these variables added significantly to the variance, with the same direction of effects, on all dependent variables except Interpersonal Competence and Somatic Complaints (where only mother's scores reached significance). Given the results of the reanalyses, it seems valid to present the combined mother/father ratings on all the independent variables associated with family process.

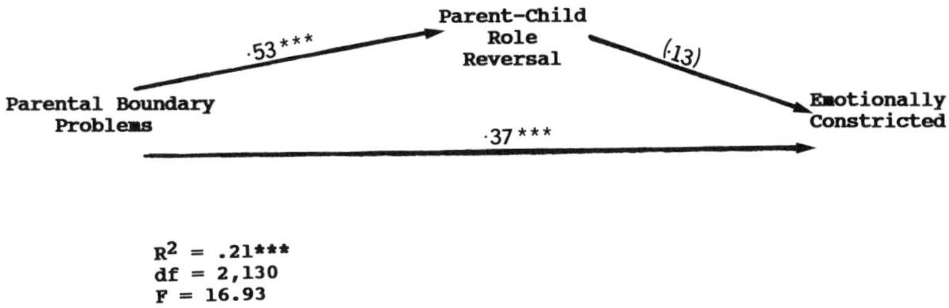

FIG. 9.6. Path model of family process and children's emotional constriction.

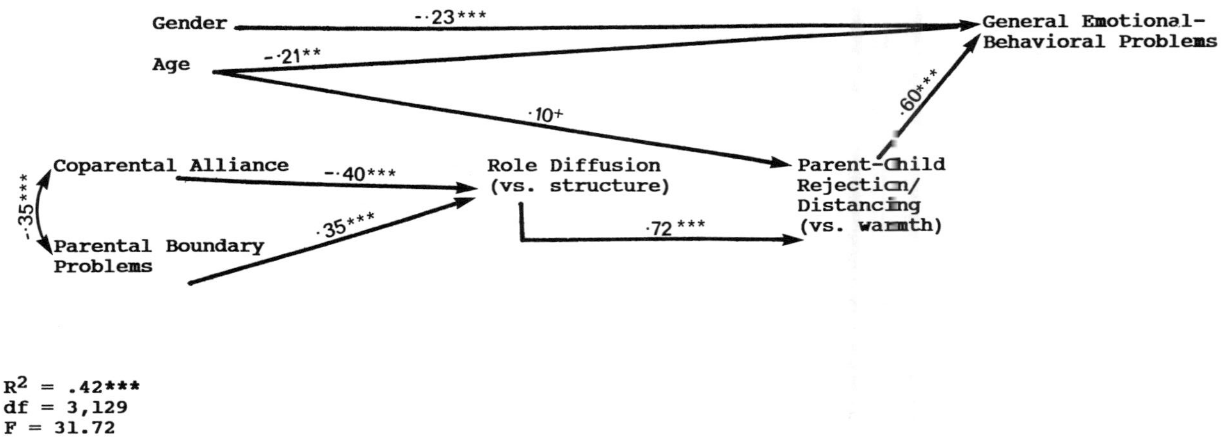

FIG. 9.7. Path model of family process and children's general emotional-behavioral problems.

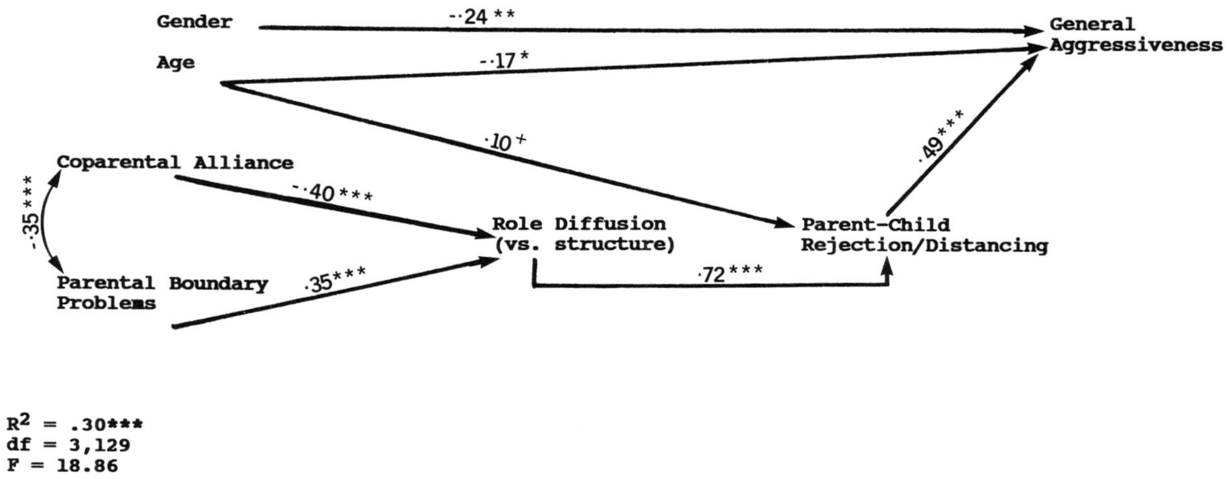

FIG. 9.8. Path model of family process and children's general aggressiveness.

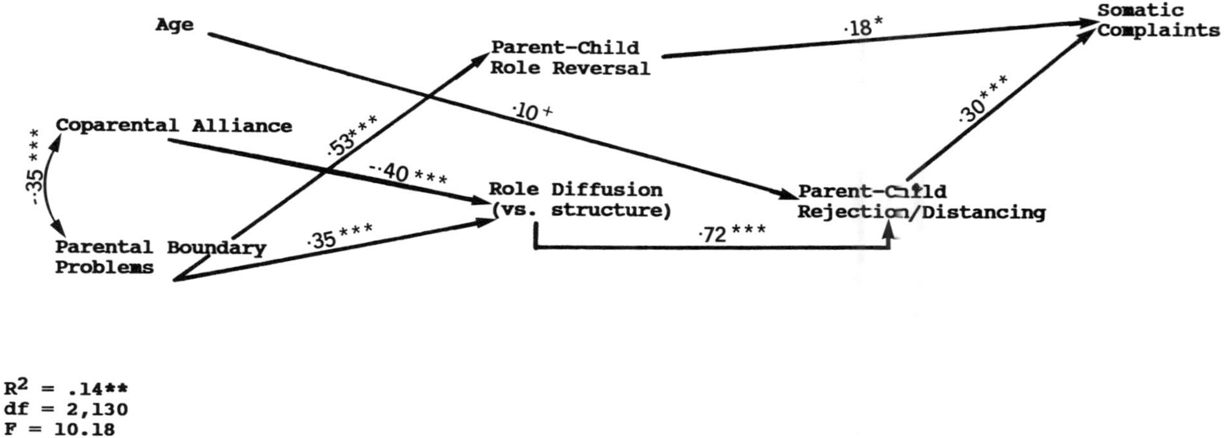

FIG. 9.9. Path model of family process and children's somatic complaints.

DISCUSSION

As shown in Fig. 9.3, interpersonal competence in children (as judged by clinicians) is more likely to be manifest in older children and in girls. Children who are interpersonally competent are more likely to have warm, accepting relationships with their parents. While younger children tend to enjoy warmer parent-child relations, a more important predictor of positive affective relations is appropriate role structure among family members. These results indicate that role structure, which implies consistent management and discipline that is sensitive to the child's needs, coupled with appropriate demands for performance and expectations for coordination of family members' activities, are likely to predict warm and harmonious parent-child relationships. This confirms the extensive research of Baumrind (1971, 1978) on the benefits of *authoritative* parenting and adds the further observation that this kind of parenting is more likely to be achieved in the presence of a better coparental alliance and in the relative absence of parental boundary problems, even in divorced families where parents have been separated 2- to 3-years. That is, where parents remain supportive of each other in their executive capacities and are able to maintain a psychological separation of their own needs from those of their children, family members' roles are more likely to be well-defined and appropriately assigned, and parent-child relations are more likely to be warm and accepting, all of which, in turn, are linked to interpersonal competence in the offspring.

Figures 9.4 and 9.5 show some aberrations in the child's capacity to relate interpersonally. In Fig. 9.4, note that, contrary to the hypothesis, children who are self-preoccupied and narcissistic (in that they take care of their own wants and needs first and tend to be opportunistic and exploitive of others) have parents who are significantly more likely to be supportive of each other in terms of having a coparental alliance. However, in agreement with the predictions of the model, children who are perceived to be self-preoccupied and narcissistic have relationships with parents that are mutually rejecting and distancing. Furthermore, rejection and distancing are more characteristic where children are older and in families that are role diffuse. In turn, role diffusion is a joint product of a failed coparental alliance and dissolution of parents' emotional boundaries with those of the child. In some respects, these observations are contradictory and could be artifacts of the data. However, if these results stand when subject is more rigorous empirical investigation, they may suggest a particular kind of divorced family in which the parents remain ambivalent about the divorce, emotionally preoccupied and attached to each other (thus giving rise to mutual support), but who are at the same time rather neglectful, avoidant, and perhaps rejecting of their children. This kind of family environment appears to be fertile ground for the development of sociopathy. It is interesting to note that Hetherington (1989) has made similar observations about a subgroup of her sample of children from divorced families.

As shown in Fig. 9.5, parental boundary problems (where the parents' capacity for empathy is limited by their own more intrusive emotional needs) are more likely to be associated with a significant amount of role reversal between parent and child. In such cases, the child is more likely to become the parent's confidant(e) and to assume executive and disciplinary functions in the family on behalf of parents and siblings. Children who are involved in role reversal with their parents are likely to be neither rejected nor warmly accepted by their parents. It is possible that there is more ambivalence in these relationships, although this cannot be stated definitively, as the scale does not discriminate ambivalence from neutral affective relations. These children are not likely to manifest typical kinds of emotional and behavioral problems (see Table 9.2). Instead, according to clinical ratings, their style of relating is marked by pseudo-adultlike, controlling, and overresponsible attitudes. It is interesting to note that the correlates of an overly responsible, controlling style include a diminished capacity for playfulness and fantasy. This strong correlation between parent-child role reversal and controlling behavior in the child was also found by George and Solomon (1989).

Figure 9.6 adds to our understanding of the effects of parental boundary problems and role reversal in that both are directly predictive of emotional constriction in children. Clinicians rated such children as less able to experience or express a range of emotions and as more apathetic, passive, and secretive. In a related study, clinicians observed that these children tend to be hypervigilant with respect to their parents' emotional states and to suppress their own feelings, as if they fear being ignored, rejected, punished, or abandoned should they make emotional demands of their own (Johnston et al., 1987). Contrary to the hypotheses, however, the breakdown in the coparental alliance is unrelated to parent-child role reversal. Neither age nor gender is associated with role reversal or with overly responsible, controlling, and emotionally constricted styles. Whereas in this study, boys and girls of different ages are equally likely to assume unusual functions of caring for parents and siblings and can become constricted and burdened by these responsibilities, other researchers investigating generational boundary dissolution between mothers and preschool children have found elevated effects for boys compared to girls (Sroufe, Jacobvitz, Mangelsdorf, DeAngelo, & Ward, 1985). Furthermore, these same authors propose that boundary problems are a function of maternal role relations history rather than the concurrent coparental relationship. Clearly, this intriguing phenomenon of role reversal which has been described in the clinical literature, especially with children of substance-abusing parents (e.g., Brown, 1988), warrants further investigation.

Next, to consider the family processes where children manifest general emotional and behavioral problems, as rated by clinicians and parents: As shown in Fig. 9.7, these patterns are the converse of those children who are perceived as being interpersonally competent (cf. Fig. 9.3). In accord with an extensive body of previous findings (Zaslow, 1988, 1989), boys are more likely to manifest symptomatic behaviors. Young children are also more disturbed. Children with emotional and behavioral problems are likely to experience more rejecting, distancing relationships with their parents. This particular kind of negative parent-child relationship is more likely to occur where children are older, but especially in families that are role diffuse. In these situations, children and parents often act unilaterally in terms of their own egocentric needs. Discipline is inconsistent and insensitive, and is characterized by neglect. There is poorer coordination of activities among family members and less predictability with respect to family affairs. In accord with the principal hypotheses, an absence of coparental alliance and the existence of parental boundary problems are characteristics of role diffuse families. This means that in families marked by structural disorganization, parents are less supportive and appreciative of each other in their parental roles and, indeed, may undermine each other's authority and affection with the children. Additionally, these parents have more difficulty separating their own needs from those of their children. To varying extents, the children are used to meet parents' emotional needs, e.g., to assuage their anger and to ameliorate depression and loneliness. Hence the findings of Hetherington et al. (1982) and those of Wallerstein and Kelly (1980), with respect to the dynamics of divorcing families, are confirmed.

The family environment of children who have problems of undercontrol is illustrated in Fig. 9.8. General aggressiveness (as judged by parents and clinicians) is a product of essentially the same family processes as those described above for children who have general emotional and behavioral problems (cf. Fig. 9.8 with Fig. 9.7). This is in full agreement with the extensive research of Patterson (1980) and associates. Also in accord with previous findings (Block et al., 1988; Block et al., 1981; Emery, 1982; Rutter, 1971), boys are more likely than girls to be overly aggressive.

It is interesting to note that children who have more somatic complaints (as judged by parents) have family environments that show elements of both role diffusion and role reversal. There is also more rejection and distancing between parents and children in these families (see Fig. 9.9). This path diagram is particularly intriguing because it illustrates the full complement of structural breakdown and aberration in family functioning that is the apparent consequence of a failed coparental alliance and parental boundary problems (both of which are significantly correlated with each other). Whereas the absence of a coparental alliance predicts role diffusion, parental boundary problems can lead to either role reversal or role diffusion, or both. In accord with the hypotheses, although role reversal is not associated with parent-child rejection and distancing, role diffusion is strongly linked to this kind of negative parent-child relationship. One could conjecture that children subjected to these kinds of ambiguities in parent-child relationships are particularly stressed and can become somatically symptomatic. Alternatively, there could be two routes to somatic disturbance: one, being over burdened with role reversal; the other, being in a hostile, rejecting relationship with parents. However, the amount of explained variance for this model is relatively small (14%), which suggests that other factors not in the model (perhaps constitutional ones) could also help explain these symptoms. Interestingly, there is no propensity for boys, compared to girls, to manifest more somatic complaints. In general, these findings confirm earlier clinical reports of the family etiology of somatic illness (Minuchin et al., 1975, 1978; Selvini-Palozzoli, 1974).

Although this study constitutes a relatively novel exploration of family role structure and affective relations, it is preliminary and exploratory. There are a number of methodological weaknesses that need to be addressed in future research. First, although many of the theoretical concepts have long been used by structural family therapists (e.g., Minuchin, 1974), they are relatively new to empirical research and hence few established measures were available. Second, because the data had already been collected, the family process measures were largely clinical ratings from case records, albeit from unusually detailed ones. Only a limited amount of data addressing these hypotheses was available directly from parents, and none from the children. Although interrater reliabilities were adequate, agreement could have been achieved because raters were evaluating clinicians' reconstructed views of families rather than family relationships directly. Third, this study was a concurrent analysis of family relationships. Unfortunately, the longitudinal data available for this study did not include variables that would allow for a more definitive test of the causal predictions in this process model. For example, an overly responsible child may make a parent more prone to role reversal, and, of course, a child who is aggressive provokes more rejection, tension, and difficulty in enforcing family rules, and may cause parents to dispute with each other. An interactional model, showing bidirectional influences, is probably a better model to evaluate, although a far more complex one. Fourth, the method of recruitment to the study may have resulted in a nonrepresentative sample. Because we found broad variations within the variables studied, and given the multivariate analyses used, this threat to external validity should be reduced. Fifth, various other demographic variables and social-psychological characteristics of these families might provide alternative explanations for these results. In previous analyses with these data, we found no correlation between child functioning and the following demographic variables: SES, ethnicity, family income, length of separation, custody arrangement, and whether or not the parents were remarried or living with a new partner (Johnston, Kline, & Tschann, 1989; Kline, Tschann, Johnston, & Wallerstein, 1989). Hence, these variables were not included in this preliminary study. However, these factors and other social-psychological characteristics of the family (e.g., social support, quality of new marriage) are hypothesized to be external to and mediated by the intrafamilial processes studied here. For example, it is suggested that stress resulting from low income, minority status, or lack of social supports is likely to induce interparental discord and diminish parental empathy, giving rise to family structural changes such as role reversal and diffusion. The influence of these factors upon intrafamilial processes needs to be explored in future research with larger samples that will allow more variables to be examined simultaneously.

SUMMARY

A principal finding of this study is that family structural breakdown (role diffusion) is likely to be a consequence of coparental discord and diminished capacity to maintain parental boundaries in divorced families. In turn, more negative and distant parent-child relationships result, especially for older children. These family relations are associated with reduced social competence, emotional-behavioral problems and aggression (especially in boys), and somatic symptoms (in boys and girls alike). In addition, a self-preoccupied, narcissistic relational style that is suggestive of the development of sociopathy (in both boys and girls) is a product of family role diffusion in the presence of a coparental alliance. Clearly, despite divorce, the exigencies of the coparental relationship continue to exert an important influence on children via the structural and affective quality of the parent-child relationship, at least 2- to 3-years after the parental separation.

The second principal finding is that family structural aberration (role reversal) is likely to be a consequence of parents' diminished empathy and capacity to maintain appropriate boundaries between their own and their children's needs after divorce. Both girls and boys, and younger and older children, in these family relationships are likely to be emotionally constricted, suffer more somatic symptoms, and have an overly responsible, controlling style of relating to others, with diminished capacity for creative play. Although not identified as having typical kinds of problematic behaviors or interpersonal difficulties, these children appear limited in their capacity for pleasure and for autonomous, intimate relations with others.

This research attempts to link family processes with individual outcomes in children and hence bridge two levels of analysis, the interpersonal and intrapersonal. The theoretical model proposed here is essentially a *process* model that illustrates how parents' individual functioning and coparental functioning affect parent-child relationships, which in turn are linked to specific adaptive or maladaptive interpersonal styles in children and to the manifestation of children's stress symptoms and emotional and behavioral disturbances. It suggests that the structure of family relations, i.e., the pattern of role relationships and the level of disorganization of the family as a group, is reciprocally related to the quality of the emotional relations between family members. Further, it suggests the ecological context for a child's developing style or "internal working model" for relating to others.

ACKNOWLEDGMENTS

Funds for the collection of these data were provided by a consortium of agencies: San Francisco Foundation, Morris Stulsaft Foundation, Van Loben Sels Foundation, Zellerbach Family Fund, Jewish Community Endowment Fund, and Benjamin and Mae Swig Foundation.

REFERENCES

Achenbach, T. M., & Edelbrock, C. (1983). *Manual for the child behavior checklist and revised child behavior profile.* Burlington, VT: Queen City Printers.

Ahrons, C. R. (1981). The continuing coparental relationship between divorced spouses. *American Journal of Orthopsychiatry, 51,* 415–527.

Anthony, E. J. (1987). Risk, vulnerability, and resilience: An overview. In E. J. Anthony & B. J. Cohler (Eds.), *The invulnerable child* (pp. 3–48). New York: Guilford Press.

Bandura, A. (1977). *Social learning theory.* Englewood Cliffs, NJ: Prentice-Hall.

Baumrind, D. H. (1971). Harmonious parents and their preschool children. *Developmental Psychology, 4*(1, Pt. 1), 99–102.

Baumrind, D. H. (1978). Parental disciplinary patterns and social competence in children. *Youth and Society, 9,* 239–276.

Belsky, J. (1980). Child maltreatment: An ecological integration. *American Psychologist, 35,* 320–335.

Belsky, J. (1984). The determinants of parenting: A process model. *Child Development, 55,* 83–96.

Block, J. (1971). *Lives through time.* Berkeley, CA: Bancroft Books.

Block, J. H., Block, J., & Gjerde, P. F. (1988). Parental functioning and the home environment in families of divorce: Prospective and concurrent analysis. *Journal of American Academy of Child & Adolescent Psychiatry, 27*(2), 207–213.

Block, J. H., Block, J., & Morrison, A. (1981). Parental disagreement on child-rearing orientations and gender-related personality correlates in children. *Child Development, 52,* 965–974.

Bond, C. R., & McMahon, R. J. (1984). Relationships between marital distress and child behavior problems, maternal personal adjustment, maternal personality, and maternal parenting behavior. *Journal of Abnormal Psychology, 93,* 348–351.

Bowen, M. (1978). Theory in the practice of psychotherapy. In M. Bowen (Ed.), *Family therapy in clinical practice.* New York: Aronson.

Bretherton, I. (1985). Growing points of attachment theory and research. In I. Bretherton & E. Waters (Eds.), *Monographs of the Society for Research in Child Development.* (Serial No. 209, pp. 3–38).

Brody, G. H., & Pellegrini, A. D. (1986). Marital quality and mother-child and father-child interactions with school-aged children. *Developmental Psychology, 22,* 291–296.

Brown, S. (1988). *Treating adult children of alcoholics: A developmental perspective.* New York: Wiley.

Campbell, S. B. (1979). Mother-infant interaction as a function of maternal ratings of temperament. *Child Psychiatry and Human Development, 10,* 67–76.

Caspi, A., & Elder, Jr., G. H. (1988). Emergent family patterns: The intergenerational construction of problem behavior and relationships. In R. Hinde & J. Stevenson-Hinde (Eds.), *Understanding family dynamics.* New York: Oxford University Press.

Cherlin, A. J., Furstenberg, Jr. F. F., Chase-Lansdale, P. L., Kiernan, K. E., Robins, P. K., Morrison, D. R., & Teitler, J. O. (1991). Longitudinal studies of effects of divorce on children in Great Britain and the United States, *Science, 252,* 1386–1389.

Colletta, N. (1979). Support systems after divorce: Incidence and impact. *Journal of Marriage and the Family, 41,* 837–846.

Coolidge, J. C., & Brodie, R. D. (1974). Observations of mothers of 49 school phobic children. *Journal of the American Academy of Child Psychiatry, 13,* 275–285.

Cowan, P. A., & Cowan, C. P. (1988). Changes in marriage during transition to parenthood: Must we blame the baby? In W. A. Goldberg, & G. Y. Michaels (Eds.), *Transition to parenthood: Current theory and research.* Cambridge, England: Cambridge University Press.

Easterbrooks, M. A. (1987, April). *Early family development: Longitudinal impact of marital quality.* Paper presented to the Biennial Meetings of the Society for Research in Child Development, Baltimore, MD.

Egeland, B., & Sroufe, L. A. (1981). Attachment and early maltreatment. *Child Development, 52,* 44–52.

Emery, R. E. (1989). Family violence, *American Psychologist, 44,* 321–328.

Emery, R. E. (1982). Interparental conflict and the children of discord and divorce. *Psychological Bulletin, 92,* 310–330.

Emery, R. E., & O'Leary, K. D. (1982). Children's perceptions of marital discord and behavior problems of boys and girls. *Journal of Abnormal Child Psychology, 10,* 11–24.

Freud, A. (1966). *The ego and the mechanisms of defense* (rev. ed.). New York: International Universities Press.

Garmezy, N., Masten, A. S., & Tellegen, A. (1984). The study of stress and competence in children: A building block for developmental psychopathology. *Child Development, 55,* 97–111.

Gassner, S., & Murray, E. J. (1969). Dominance and conflict in the interactions between parents of normal and neurotic children. *Journal of Abnormal and Social Psychology, 74,* 33–41.

George, C., & Solomon, J. (1989, April). *Internal working models of parenting and security of attachment at age six.* Paper presented at the Biennial Meeting of the Society for Research in Child Development, Kansas City, MO.

Goldberg, W. A., & Easterbrooks, M. A. (1984). Role of marital quality in toddler development. *Developmental Psychology, 20,* 504–514.

Gottman, J. M., & Krokoff, L. J. (1989). Marital interaction and satisfaction: A longitudinal view. *Journal of Consulting and Clinical Psychology, 57,* 47–52.

Greist, D., Wells, K. C., & Forehand, R. (1980). An examination of predictors of maternal perceptions of maladjustment in clinic-referred children. *Journal of Abnormal Psychology, 88,* 277–281.

Grych, J. H., & Fincham, F. D. (1990). Marital conflict and children's adjustment. *Psychological Bulletin, 108,* 267–290.

Hershorn, M., & Rosenbaum, A. (1985). Children of marital violence: A closer look at the unintended victims. *American Journal of Orthopsychiatry, 55,* 260–266.

Hess, R. D., & Camara, K. A. (1979). Post-divorce family relationships as mediating factors in the consequences of divorce for children. *Journal of Social Issues, 4,* 79–96.

Hetherington, E. M. (1965). A developmental study of the effects of sex of the dominant parent on sex-role preference, identification and imitation in children. *Journal of Personality and Social Psychology, 2,* 188–194.

Hetherington, E. M. (1989). Coping with family transitions: Winners, losers and survivors. *Child Development, 60,* 1–14.

Hetherington, E. M., Cox, M., & Cox, C. R. (1982). Effects of divorce on parents and children. In M. E. Lamb (Ed.), *Nontraditional families* (pp. 223–288). Hillsdale, NJ: Lawrence Erlbaum Associates.

Hetherington, E. M., & Frankie, G. (1967). Effects of parental dominance, warmth and conflict on imitation in children. *Journal of Personality and Social Psychology, 6,* 119–125.

Hollingshead, A. B., & Redlich, F. C. (1958). *Social class and mental illness: A community study.* New York: Wiley.

Howes, P. W., & Markman, H. J. (1987, April). *Marital quality and child attachment: A longitudinal investigation.* Paper presented to the Biennial Meetings of the Society for Research in Child Development, Baltimore, MD.

Huntington, D. S. (1985). Theory and method: The use of psychological tests in research on divorce. *Journal of the American Academy of Child Psychiatry, 24,* 583–589.

Isaacs, M. B., Montalvo, B., & Abelsohn, D. (1986). *The difficult divorce.* New York: Basic Books.

Jacobson, D. S. (1978). The impact of marital separation/divorce on children: II. Interparental hostility and child adjustment. *Journal of Divorce, 2*(1), 3–19.

Jaffe, P., Wolfe, D., Wilson, S., & Zak, L. (1986a). Family violence and child adjustment: A comparative analysis of girls' and boys' behavioral symptoms. *American Journal of Psychiatry, 143,* 74–77.

Jaffe, P., Wolfe, D., Wilson, S., & Zak, L. (1986b). Similarities in behavioral and social adjustment among child victims and witnesses to family violence. *American Journal of Orthopsychiatry, 56,* 142–146.

Johnson, P. L., & O'Leary, K. D. (1987). Parental behavior patterns and conduct disorders in girls. *Journal of Abnormal Child Psychology, 15,* 573–581.

Johnson, S. M., & Lobitz, G. K. (1974). The personal and marital adjustment of parents as related to observed child deviance and parenting behaviors. *Journal of Abnormal Child Psychology, 2,* 193–208.

Johnston, J. R., & Campbell, L. E. G. (1987). Instability in the networks of divorced and disputing families. In E. J. Lawler & B. Markovsky (Eds.), *Advances in group processes: Theory and research, Vol. 4* (pp. 243–369). Greenwich, CT: JAI Press.

Johnston, J. R., & Campbell, L. E. G. (1988). *Impasses of divorce: The dynamics and resolution of family conflict.* New York: The Free Press.

Johnston, J. R., Campbell, L. E. G., & Mayes, S. M. (1985). Latency children in post-separation and divorce disputes. *Journal of the American Academy of Child Psychiatry, 24,* 563–574.

Johnston, J. R., Gonzalez, R., & Campbell, L. E. G. (1987). Ongoing postdivorce conflict and child disturbance. *Journal of Abnormal Child Psychology, 15,* 493–509.

Johnston, J. R., Kline, M., & Tschann, J. M. (1989). Ongoing postdivorce conflict: Effects on children of joint custody and frequent access. *American Journal of Orthopsychiatry, 59,* 1–17.

Jouriles, E. N., Barling, J., & O'Leary, K. D. (1987). Predicting child behavior problems in maritally violent families. *Journal of Abnormal Child Psychology, 15,* 165–173.

Jouriles, E. N., Pfiffner, L. J., & O'Leary, S. G. (1988). Marital conflict, parenting, and toddler conduct problems. *Journal of Abnormal Child Psychology, 16,* 197–206.

Kelly, J. B., & Wallerstein, J. S. (1976). The effects of parental divorce: Experiences of the child in early latency. *American Journal of Orthopsychiatry, 46,* 20–32.

Klein, M. M., Plutchik, R., & Conte, H. R. (1973). Parental dominance-passivity and behavior problems of children. *Journal of Consulting & Clinical Psychology, 45,* 469–474.

Kline, M., Johnston, J. R., & Tschann, J. M. (1991). The long shadow of marital conflict on children's postdivorce adjustment. *Journal of Marriage and the Family, 53,* 297–309.

Kline, M., Tschann, J. M., Johnston, J. R., & Wallerstein, J. S. (1989). Children's adjustment in joint and sole physical custody families. *Developmental Psychology, 25,* 430–438.

Lidz, L., Cornelison, S., Fleck, S., & Terry, D. (1968). Schism and skew in the families of schizophrenics. In N. W. Bell & E. F. Vogel (Eds.), *A modern introduction to the family* (rev. ed., pp. 650–662). New York: The Free Press.

Main, M., Kaplan, N., & Cassidy, J. (1985). Security in infancy, childhood and adulthood: A move to the level of representation. In I. Bretherton & E. Waters (Eds.), Growing points of attachment theory and research. *Monograph of the Society for Research in Child Development* (Serial No. 209).

Milliones, J. (1978). Relationship between perceived child temperament and maternal behaviors. *Child Development, 49,* 1255–1257.

Minuchin, S. (1974). *Families and family therapy*. Cambridge, MA: Harvard University Press.

Minuchin, S., Baker, L., Rosman, B., Liebman, R., Milman, L., & Todd, T. (1975). A conceptual model of psychosomatic illness in children, family organization and family therapy. *Archives of General Psychiatry, 32,* 1031–1038.

Minuchin, S., Rosman, B., & Baker, L. (1978). *Psychosomatic families*. London: Harvard University Press.

Olweus, D. (1980). Familial and temperamental determinants of aggressive behavior in adolescent boys. *Developmental Psychology, 16,* 644–660.

Orvaschel, H., Weissman, M., & Kidd, K. K. (1980). Children and depression: The children of depressed parents; the childhood of depressed patients; depression in children. *Journal of Affective Disorders, 2,* 1–16.

Patterson, G. R. (1980). Mothers: The unacknowledged victims. *Monographs for the Society for Research in Child Development, 45*(5, Serial No. 186).

Pederson, F. (1982). Mother, father, and infant as an interactive system. In J. Belsky (Ed.), *In the beginning: Readings in infancy*. New York: Columbia University Press.

Porter, B., & O'Leary, K. D. (1980). Marital discord and childhood behavior problems. *Journal of Abnormal Child Psychology, 8,* 287–295.

Quinton, D., Rutter, M., & Liddle, C. (1984). Institutional rearing, parenting difficulties and marital support. *Psychological Medicine, 14,* 107–124.

Rosenbaum, A., & O'Leary, K. D. (1981). Children: The unintended victims of marital violence. *American Journal of Orthopsychiatry, 51,* 692–699.

Rutter, M. (1971). Parent-child separation: Psychological effects on the children. *Journal of Child Psychology and Psychiatry, 12,* 233–260.

Rutter, M. (1979). Maternal deprivation, 1972–1978: New findings, new concepts, new approaches. *Child Development, 50,* 283–305.

Rutter, M. (1987). Psychosocial resilience and protective mechanisms. *American Journal of Orthopsychiatry, 57,* 316–331.

Schwarz, J. C., & Getler, H. (1980). Parental conflict and dominance in late adolescent maladjustment: A triple interaction model. *Journal of Abnormal Psychology, 89,* 573–580.

Selvini-Palozzoli, M. (1974). *Self-starvation: From the intrapsychic to the transpersonal approach to anorexia nervosa* (A. Pomerans, Trans.). Human Context Books (London: Chaucer).

Shaw, D. S., & Emery, R. E. (1987). Parental conflict and other correlates of the adjustment of school-age children whose parents have separated. *Journal of Abnormal Child Psychology, 15,* 269–281.

Shaw, D. S., & Emery, R. E. (1988). Chronic family adversity and school-age children's adjustment. *Journal of the American Academy of Child and Adolescent Psychiatry, 27,* 200–206.

Simmel, G. (1955). *Conflict: The web of group affiliations*. New York: The Free Press.

Sroufe, L. A., Jacobvitz, D., Mangelsdorf, S., DeAngelo, E., & Ward, M. J. (1985). Generational boundary dissolution between mothers and their preschool children: A relationship systems approach. *Child Development, 56,* 317–325.

Steinman, S. B. (1981). The experience of children in joint custody arrangements: A report of a study. *American Journal of Orthopsychiatry, 51,* 403–414.

Steinman, S. B., Zemmelman, S. E., & Knoblauch, T. M. (1985). A study of parents who sought joint custody following divorce: Who reaches agreement and sustains joint custody and who returns to court. *Journal of the American Academy of Child Psychiatry, 24,* 554–562.

Straus, M. A. (1979). Measuring intrafamily conflict and violence: The conflict tactics (CT) scales. *Journal of Marriage and the Family, 41,* 75–86.

Swanson, G. E. (1988). *Ego defenses and the legitimation of behavior*. Cambridge, England: Cambridge University Press.

Tschann, J. M., Johnston, J. R., Kline, M., & Wallerstein, J. S. (1989). Family process and children's functioning during divorce. *Journal of Marriage & the Family, 51,* 431–444.

Vogel, E. F., & Bell, N. W. (1968). The emotionally disturbed child as the family scapegoat. In N.

W. Bell & E. F. Vogel (Eds.), *A modern introduction to the family* (rev. ed., pp. 412–427). New York: The Free Press.

Waldron, S., Shrier, D. K., Stone, B., & Tobin, F. (1975). School phobia and other childhood neuroses: A systematic study of the children and their families. *American Journal of Psychiatry, 132,* 802–808.

Wallerstein, J. S. (1985a). The overburdened child: Some long-term consequences of divorce. *Social Work, 30,* 116–123.

Wallerstein, J. S. (1985b). Parent-child relationships after divorce. In E. J. Anthony & G. Pollack (Eds.), *Parental influences in health and disease* (pp. 317–347). Boston: Little Brown.

Wallerstein, J. S., & Kelly, J. B. (1976). The effects of parental divorce: The experience of the child in late latency. *American Journal of Orthopsychiatry, 46,* 256–269.

Wallerstein, J. S., & Kelly, J. B. (1980). *Surviving the breakup: How children and parents cope with divorce.* New York: Basic Books.

Weiss, R. S. (1979). Growing up a little fast: The experience of growing up in a single parent household. *Journal of Social Issues, 35,* 97–111.

Whitehead, L. J. (1979). Sex differences in children's responses to family stress: A reevaluation. *Journal of Child Psychology and Psychiatry and Allied Disciplines, 20,* 247–254.

Wolfe, D. A., Jaffe, P., Wilson, S. K., & Zak, L. (1985). Children of battered women: The relation of child behavior to family violence and maternal stress. *Journal of Consulting and Clinical Psychology, 53,* 657–665.

Wolfe, D. A., Zak, L., Wilson, S., & Jaffe, P. (1986). Child witnesses to violence between parents: Critical issues in behavioral and social adjustment. *Journal of Abnormal Child Psychology, 14,* 95–104.

Wolkind, S., & Rutter, M. (1973). Children who have been "in care"—An epidemiological study. *Journal of Child Psychology and Psychiatry and Allied Disciplines, 14,* 97–105.

Wynne, L. C., Rykoff, I. M., Day, J., & Hirsh, S. I. (1968). Pseudo-mutuality in the family relations of schizophrenics. In N. W. Bell & E. F. Vogel (Eds.), *A modern introduction to the family* (rev. ed., pp. 628–649). New York: The Free Press.

Zaslow, M. J. (1988). Sex differences in children's response to parental divorce: I. Research methodology and postdivorce family forms. *American Journal of Orthopsychiatry, 58,* 355–378.

Zaslow, M. J. (1989). Sex differences in children's response to parental divorce: II. Samples, variables, ages and sources. *American Journal of Orthopsychiatry, 59,* 118–141.

10 The Structuring of Family Decision-Making: Personal and Societal Sources and Some Consequences for Children

Guy E. Swanson
University of California, Berkeley

A family is all that the textbooks say. A man and a woman create it to serve their personal interests. It is also created by a society, the husband and wife serving as agents of that larger social order. It is a household: a special form of localized community (Netting, Wilk, & Arnould, 1984; Parsons, 1959) in which participants' biological requirements—as in eating, sleeping, defecating, copulating, recovering from illness, resting, and motility—are met through a spatial-technological pattern and a moral order. It is the great center of biosocial reproduction. It is, at one and the same time, an interpersonal relationship (in Ernest Burgess' [1926] famous phrase, "a unity of interacting personalities"), a group, a face-to-face group, and a primary group (one in which people have diffusely supportive and personalized relations). It is a center of institutional activities, including those of kinship, and is a focus of interinstitutional relations. Like all social relations, it exists as long as its members continuously recreate and use it. It is constantly adapting to changing circumstances and adapting them to its requirements. And a family is often vastly consequential: both for its members and for the people and groups they encounter.

To explain how given families get organized and operate as they do, and how they have the consequences they have, we need systematic grounds from which to take account of the many arrangements they embody. It is not enough to know that members' interests and resources are important, that the broad societal reasons for people's forming families help to shape what they do, that every group is also an interpersonal relationship. It is not enough to know that, to function well, a family must have arrangements through which it is nurtured as an interpersonal relationship and as a group, and must also have arrangements which integrate the several aspects of its organization. We need, in addition, to identify the *systematics* of relations among these and other features of families: the systematic ways in which they constitute or determine a family's structure, cohesion, adaptability, and impact.

In this chapter, I offer resources and evidence toward our meeting those objectives. I propose that there are systematic relations between the personalities and societal backgrounds of a husband and wife and the way in which a family gets organized as an interpersonal relationship and as a decision-making group and I suggest that these several factors, and the family's organization itself, affect the psychological functioning of the children. These proposals emerge in three new and interrelated studies.

In the first study, I looked for characteristics of wives' and husbands' personalities that are related to the way in which a family is organized. Patterns of family decision making were related to assessments of the spouses' personalities that were made a decade earlier.

The second study developed from the idea that husbands and wives will tend to find comfortable a pattern of family decision-making that fits well with their personal dispositions—with their personalities—but that the family's organization will be based on other grounds if their personalities prove unsuitable. The study tests hypotheses about the conditions under which the family's organization will be shaped more by the parents' personalities than by certain of their premarital status characteristics and conditions under which the opposite pattern will be found.

The third study is based on findings from the first and second. It asks whether there are links between (a) parental personalities and other factors that shape a family's organization, and (b) some aspects of children's psychological functioning that have been shown to be associated with that organization. In the samples I had available, I could look for connections of family decision-making and these other *independent* variables with children's intellectual abilities and with their use of denial as an ego defense.

FAMILY DECISION-MAKING

The place to begin is with ideas about the nature, centrality, and forms of decision-making in families. These are at the heart of all three studies.

Because a family is a group, the center of its organization is found in standing arrangements through which participants do things together: through which they move jointly, if often unwittingly, toward setting objectives and developing implementations. In that broad sense, their process of doing things together is one of collective *decision-making* and, for that reason, differences among families in the way they organize for decision-making prove fundamental for comparative studies.

Family case workers and therapists as well as social scientists have found that a family's arrangements for decision-making are of basic importance (e.g., Constantine, 1987; Walsh, 1982). Variations in patterns of decision-making are associated with distinctive patterns in the way a family develops, in its internal dynamics, and in the nature of its vulnerabilities and of its methods of adaptation. They therefore are useful in interpretations, predictions, and interventions, serving practitioners in the way that structural features of personality serve a therapist who treats individuals: that is, these patterns embody a system's principal components and their interrelations. It is through altering that system, or capitalizing upon it, that the practitioner hopes to have a major and lasting effect.

The patterns of organization for decision-making that I have used appear in Fig. 10.1. They embody the combinations of three features presented in Fig. 10.2: organization for principled or accommodative decision-making, organization as an association or social system, and hierarchical or equalitarian organization. (Discussions of the theoretical grounds for this classification appear in Swanson, 1967 and 1971. Detailed instructions for combining codes in Fig. 10.1 to fit the combinations of Fig. 10.2 are given in Swanson 1974, 1985a, and 1988.)

The three features of a family's organization given in Fig. 10.2 are basic to most typologies of family decision-making (Constantine, 1987; Scanzoni & Szinovacz, 1980) with the exact labels varying from one writer to another. Each feature treats participants in terms of a distinctive relationship they will have when doing things together. I give brief definitions of all three and then an operational definition of each one:

1. Groups organized for principled decision-making are able, organizationally, to take account of diverse points of view and integrate them under common goals.[1] Groups organized for accommodative decision-making are unable, organizationally, to perform one or both of these activities.

2. The distinction between association and social system treats members in their dual roles as (a) creators-users of the group and as (b) its agents. It refers to the degree to which they are able to influence joint undertakings in one or the other of these capacities.

3. The distinction between hierarchy and equality refers to differences among members in their influence on joint undertakings.

Principled vs. Accommodative Decision-Making. A code for principled decision-making as a feature of organizations was derived from G. H. Mead's (1934) suggestion that certain forms of social organization embody and foster what he called "reflective intelligence." As he noted, all groups have something

[1]Systematic grounds for focusing on these and other features of this typology are found in Swanson 1967: 32–43; 1971; 1974; 1986.

Below are nine models of ways families make decisions. We would like your impression about how your family makes its decisions. Read through all nine of the models and choose the one that best describes your family. Put a 1 in the blank beside that model. Then put a 2 beside the model that is the next best description of the family.

Note that each model focuses on the parts the parents play in making family decisions. Models 1-4 describe families in which one parent has final decision making responsibility, if he/she wants, and models 5-9 describe families in which the parents have joint responsibility for most decisions.

___1. In this family, one parent is seen by all as being the "head" of the family. He/she makes the final decisions. However, the other parent has the right to give advice and to expect that his/her advice will be sought and taken into account.

___2. This family is identical with the one just described except that the "head" of the family makes the final decisions on the important issues the family has to decide. In less important family matters, each parent has his/her own areas of responsibility and competence and has considerable freedom to decide what will be done.

___3. In this family, one parent is without question the head of the family. He/she can, if he/she chooses, have the final word in deciding what the group will do, and how it will do it. The other parent does not usually expect to be consulted for advice, even though he/she sometimes is.

___4. This family is identical with the one just described except that the decisions of the head of the family usually apply to the most important issues the family has to decide. In less important family matters, each parent has his/her own areas of responsibility and competence and has considerable freedom to decide what will be done.

___5. In this family, both parents discuss a problem together and agree on a solution before they announce their decision to the family or begin to carry it out.

___6. This family is identical with the one just described, except that "decision" is too strong a word for the parents' standard way of doing business. They talk over the problems, or talk around them, until a sort of common view emerges. This view is then the basis for action.

___7. In this family, the parents often consult together about what the family will do, and agree on a solution before they announce their decision to the family. However, each parent also has the right to make decisions and act on his/her own. If the other parent wishes, he/she then can review this decision, and question and even delay the action, until both parents have consulted together and reached an agreement about the final course of action.

___8. This family is identical with the one just described except that, should the parents disagree on something that is urgent and important, one in particular has the right to break the tie and make the decision.

___9. In this family it is difficult to identify standard procedures of decision making. Things are often done, or not done, pretty much as the moment dictates. The parents may or may not consult together about decisions. If either dislikes what the other is doing, about all he/she can do is to withhold resources (like money, time, encouragement) that are necessary for his/her partner's activities. Similarly, he/she often finds that the best way to get his/her partner moving is to supply some of these resources specifically for the purpose he/she intends.

FIG. 10.1. Patterns of family decision-making.

in the way of goals or purposes and all accommodate their activities to the environment in which they function. Mead suggested that the control of collective action by group goals was better differentiated, hence more salient, in some groups than in others. In that sense, these groups were organized specifically to shape their activities according to their goals: to engage in principled or "reflec-

Principled Rather Than Accommodative Decision-Making	Association or Social System	Hierarchical (+) or Equalitarian (0)	Codes in Figure 10.1
Yes	Association	+	4
		0	7
	Social System	+	1,2
		0	6
No	Association	+	8
		0	9
	Social System	+	3
		0	5

FIG. 10.2. Key to Fig. 10.1.

tive" decision-making. For groups so organized, accommodations to environmental contingencies would have a lesser place than for groups without these features.

As Mead saw it, groups were organized for principled decision-making if they had two features: an organization that (a) assures attention to diverse but complementary points of view and, that (b) subordinates these to control by common purposes. He used athletic teams and team games as illustrations. In baseball teams, for example, the interrelated points of view are structured into complementary roles (e.g., batter, pitcher, catcher). The common purpose is evident in the carrying out of a play or the effort to win a game and is structured into the leadership roles through which plays are chosen and coordinated (e.g., managers, pitchers, and catchers exercise leadership at certain points in the course of a game).

I have proposed elsewhere (Swanson, 1971, 1974) that the patterns of family decision-making in Fig. 10.1 vary in the extent to which they honor and embody diverse points of view or subordinate differences in members' outlooks to a common purpose. Several patterns lack one or the other of these features. Thus Patterns 3 and 5 stress common interests and objectives but make little formal place for specialized concerns. This is so in the pure democracy of Pattern 5 because decisions that require consensus turn primarily upon what it is that participants have in common and therefore do not provide for the fulfillment of special or divergent interests. In Pattern 3, one person can, and sometimes does, make decisions about having to take account of others' views.

Other families make diverse and special interests preponderant and obscure common goals. This is so in Patterns 8 and 9. In Pattern 9, it is hard to see the emergence or pursuit of common objectives or of something like collective decisions. In Pattern 8 the situation is not as extreme, but common interests tend to preponderate only in extreme situations.

The remaining patterns vary in many respects but seem to contain both of the features Mead had in mind. In the consultative arrangements of Pattern 6 or the federal structure pictured in Pattern 7 there is an important role for both diverse and common interests. This is also true in the hierarchical arrangements in Patterns 1, 2, and 4. In these three patterns, special interests have a legitimate place in advising on, or in implementing, the choices that are made on the group's behalf by one or a few individuals.

Association vs. Social System. The next distinction in Fig. 10.2 builds on the one just described. It turns on the *relative importance* given by the pattern of decision-making to personal and special interests as against common interests.

All groups are in some degree both associations and social systems. They are associations in being arrangements through which participants get the things they severally want. In that sense, participants are the creators and users of groups. Groups are social systems in being arrangements through which common interests are defined and served. Participants discover that, to satisfy personal desires, they must support and serve the relationship that the group provides and which gives participants the means for attaining personal objectives. In that sense, participants become the agents of the group. In most cases, they also internalize many common purposes, making them their own.

For reasons presented in earlier reports (Swanson, 1967, 1969, 1971, 1988), it is useful to think of Patterns 1, 2, 3, 5, and 6 as giving greater weight to common interests and, by that criterion, as stressing organization as a social system. It is also useful to think of Patterns 4, 7, 8, and 9 as making a relatively greater place for the pursuit of personal and special interests, and, by that criterion, as stressing organization as an association. Thus, in Patterns 1, 2, and 3, a single individual, although he or she may have to receive advice, has the authority to make decisions for the family. In Patterns 5 and 6, the requirement of consensus makes no legitimate place for members' using the family as a facility through which to pursue interests that diverge from those they have in common. By contrast, the use of the group to pursue special as well as common interests is more strongly supported in Patterns 4 and 8 by the rather narrow limits in which the family's *head* can make decisions and by the members' freedom of individual action outside those limits. Patterns 7 and 9 give even greater weight to the serving of special interests because members are free to *do their own thing* unless challenged by their fellows.

Hierarchical vs. Equalitarian. The final distinction in Fig. 10.2 is that between hierarchical and equalitarian organizations. As is evident, Patterns 1, 2, 3, 4, and 8 are hierarchical, one parent making authoritative choices on behalf of the group. In some cases these choices are made after consulting other members and in other cases without any necessary consultations. The remaining patterns are equalitarian.

Study 1: Parents' Personalities and Family Decision-making

Are there connections between the way a family is organized to make decisions and the personalities of the parents? There seem to be no systematic studies of this question and certainly none that are aimed at all of the features of decision-making given in Fig. 10.2. What is more, there seem to be no theories of personality and family organization that could guide the construction of hypotheses. This being so, Study 1 had to be exploratory. I used data already at hand and drew on suggestions contained in studies of other topics. Fortunately, the data I had enabled a longitudinal exploration: spouses' personalities as measured earlier in a marriage could be related to patterns of family decision-making observed 10 years later.

The three dimensions of family decision making given in Fig. 10.2 had been embodied in an earlier version of the codes given in Figure 1 and used in research on 118 of the families that have been studied longitudinally at the Institute of Human Development (IHD), University of California, Berkeley (Swanson, 1988). These aspects of decision making were coded for each family from interviews with both parents.

One or both parents in these families had been asked to complete the California Psychological Inventory (CPI) in 1958 and, again, in 1968. Scores for the principal dimensions of the Minnesota Multiphasic Inventory (MMPI) were derived for these IHD subjects using the equivalences identified by Rodgers (Megargee, 1972, pp. 255–256). These two broad-spectrum tests of personality—the first designed to catch major dimensions along which laymen assess one another's personalities in everyday life; the second, to measure clinically-relevant symptoms—served as indices of the parents' personalities. (Personality assessments using the California Q-set [Block, 1961] were also available but could not be employed as "independent" measures because they, like the ratings of decision making, were based on the interviews with the parents.)

What connection might we expect between the aspects of personality measured by the CPI and MMPI and the features of decision making in Fig. 10.2? I take up each aspect of decision making in turn.

On Correlates of Principled vs. Accommodative Decision Making (PDM). The family's pattern of principled or accommodative decision making might reflect the intellectual level of the parents. Earlier research on the IHD sample found no association between PDM and the spouses' scores on either conventional or Piagetian tests of intelligence (Swanson, 1974), but an approach predicting from personality to the assessment of intellectual function might have a different result (Scheier & Carver, 1988). It would take greater account of such motivational factors as dispositions toward intellectuality while not slighting intellectual abilities. By this reasoning, one might expect to find significant relations between PDM and the spouses' scores on those scales of the CPI intended as measures of intellectual ability and potential for achievement: Achievement via conformance, Achievement via independence, Intellectual efficiency.

Other features of PDM direct attention to other features of personality. PDM as a decision-making strategy involves people's examining a problem from diverse points of view and then taking them into account in ways that promote specific objectives. Perhaps, then, PDM is more likely if the spouses accept diverse views as deserving serious consideration and are confident of the values from which they appraise them and of their own ability to act upon those appraisals. That pattern strongly resembles the "authoritative" pattern in parents' personalities and in child-rearing that many investigators have found associated with children's intellectual competence (Baumrind, 1975; Maccoby & Martin, 1983, pp. 37–51; Moselle, 1984). Two CPI scales seem related to a person's acceptance of diverse views: Self-control (adequacy of self-regulation and freedom from impulsivity and self-centeredness) and Tolerance (social beliefs and attitudes that are permissive, accepting, and nonjudgmental). A person's being confident of his own values and abilities—but without his tending to be domineering—is described in several scales, notably Social presence (poise, spontaneity, and self-confidence) and Self-acceptance (sense of personal worth, self-acceptance, and capacity for independent thinking and action). Combinations of such indicators of the parents' acceptance of diverse perspectives and of their confidence in their own values may be what one seeks as predictors of PDM.

On Correlates of Association vs. Social System (ASSN). This distinction turns on the extent to which personal and special interests can legitimately be pursued through the group's organization. This pattern suggests that people with relatively strong desires to attain to personal goals and interests as against fostering joint efforts might find a group organized as an association to be more comfortable. Associations are, however, organizations that foster the pursuit of common as well as special interests and it is therefore unlikely that they will be formed by people who are without restraint in their pursuit of personal interests. Many scales of the CPI and MMPI assess some aspects of, on the one hand, self-centeredness, desire for immediate gratification, and impulsivity or, on the other, of concern for others or of conformity to social requirements. Perhaps it is some combination of these ingredients that makes more likely a family's development as an association rather than as a social system.

On Correlates of Stratification (STRAT). Equalitarian and hierarchic arrangements are different points on a continuum of stratification. If the arrangements are hierarchical and a function of the participants' personalities, some participants must be strikingly more forceful or effective as personalities than are the others. Several combinations of several variables on the CPI and MMPI could embody that pattern and there seem no compelling reasons for thinking one more important than another in predicting to family structure.

SAMPLE

The IHD families are described in many places (e.g., Eichorn et al., 1981; Swanson, 1988). One parent in each family has been studied at the Institute since 1928–1930. They were chosen originally by sampling every third infant born in the city of Berkeley and all of the children entering the junior high school that served the northern end of the city of Oakland. These subjects, their parents, and, as they arrived, the subjects' spouses and children have been followed down to the present. They prove to be fairly representative of the geographic areas from which they came (Block & Haan, 1971, pp. 21–30), but well above the national average in income, education, and scores on tested intelligence. They are almost exclusively Caucasians and are preponderantly native-born, of northern and western European antecedents, and of Christian religious affiliation. They include sizeable numbers of persons from all socioeconomic levels except unskilled laborers or people with no more than a grade school education. Careful studies (Eichorn et al., 1981) indicate that the decline over the years in the number of subjects available for study is due primarily to migration from the area and has little or no relationship to the subjects' socioeconomic status, IQ's in adolescence, or their scores on indices of personality. Refusal to cooperate has been rare.

In 1958, the subjects from Berkeley, and their spouses, were seen and were asked to complete the CPI. They would have been married from 6 to 8 years. That same year, the subjects from Oakland (but not their spouses) were seen and were given the CPI. They would have been married about 16 to 20 years.

In 1968–1970, all subjects having a child aged 14- to 18-years who was still living at home were reinterviewed as were their spouses and adolescent children. There were 118 cases in which a subject, his/her spouse, and one or more of their children aged 14 to 18 were interviewed. All the studies I report here include data from those of the 118 families for which appropriate measures were available. Study 1 is based entirely on them.

The 1968–1970 interviews with the parents were coded for the main dimensions of decision-making given in Fig. 10.2. Unfortunately, data on file in the Institute's archives are not adequate for a comparable coding of family decision making for earlier periods.

The re-study in 1968–1970 involved subjects and spouses from both samples and all were asked to complete the CPI. Table 10.1 shows the numbers from each administration who actually completed this test. Some of the numbers are rather

TABLE 10.1
Available Data

1968: Family decision-making		100
1968: CPI/MMPI:	Fathers	88
	Mothers	100
1958: CPI/MMPI:	Fathers	77
	Mothers	65
1968: Family decision-making and CPI/MMPI:	Fathers	81
	Mothers	86
1958: Family decision-making and CPI/MMPI:	Fathers	69
	Mothers	57
1958 and 1968: Family decision making and CPI/MMPI:	Fathers	59
	Mothers	53
	Both	38

small and I have combined the members of the two samples in most analyses. An examination of the data shows no appreciable differences between them on points that are important for my analyses.

FINDINGS

Table 10.2 shows the significant results from step-wise multiple regressions in which the 1958 CPI–MMPI personality variables were used to predict the families' scores on each of the three dimensions of decision making as based on the 1968 interviews. (Each dimension of decision making was dichotomized as described earlier and was analyzed separately. Table 10.2 shows the combination of personality variables that best predicts each aspect of decision making, the associated beta weights, and their levels of significance.) In these analyses, fathers' and mothers' CPI–MMPI scores were run separately, and together, as independent variables. Although the number of cases is sometimes small, the results seem sensible and, as we shall see in Study 2, they appear again in a different and larger sample. (I wait until that study's findings are in hand to consider why, in Table 10.2 and in later tables, we find that two aspects of family decision making are related to the personality of *one,* but *not both,* of the parents in these families.)

Principled vs. Accommodative Decision Making (PDM). PDM is predicted by the four features of the fathers' personalities given in Table 10.2. Three are from the CPI, one from the MMPI. Using standard interpretations of this person-

TABLE 10.2
Stepwise R Between Characteristics of Parents' Personalities and Features of Family Decision Making

Family Characteristics in 1968	*Parents' Characteristics in 1958*	*Data*	*Beta*	*p <*
Principled vs. accommodative decision making	Father's (N = 68, R = .50, p <.001)			
	Tolerance	CPI	.46	.001
	Femininity	CPI	-.31	.01
	Psychological mindedness	CPI	-.27	.04
	Depression	MMPI	-.24	.04
Association vs. social system	Mother's (N = 57 R = .53, p < .01)			
	Hypochondriasis	MMPI	.48	.002
	Sense of well-being	CPI	.30	.05
	Flexibility	CPI	.36	.02
	Social presence	CPI	-.41	.04
	Self-acceptance	CPI	.22	.21
Hierarchic vs. equalitarian stratification	(N = 47, R = .50, p < .01)			
	Father's paranoia	MMPI	-.31	.03
	Mother's achievement via independence	CPI	-.32	.03
	Father's hypochondriasis	MMPI	-.27	.06

ality profile, the fathers whose personalities as of 1958 predict their families' being organized for principled rather than accommodative decision making in 1968 are open to a variety of points of view and are able to deal with the uncertainties involved in resolving them (high score on tolerance). They are enterprising, buoyant, and ambitious (high tolerance, low femininity, low depression). They tend also to work within established social arrangements: to be unassuming, conventional, serious, deliberate (low psychological mindedness).

These indices do not include any of the CPI scales that were designed as measures of intellectual ability and of achievement potential. (But the Tolerance scale shares many items with these scales and correlates with grade-point averages in high school and college (Megargee, 1972, pp. 164, 181).) Rather the indices show a person whose orientations fit well with the style of decision making caught in PDM itself: an able and energetic person who is open to many points of view, helpful in personal relations and group activities, and capable of being decisive. That may be a combination of characteristics that fosters PDM.

It is striking that aspects of the fathers' personalities, and not of the mothers', have significant relations with PDM. I have not found a satisfactory explanation for this and it may not be found in other samples. It does, however, deserve attention. So does the equally striking finding that now follows: features of mothers' personalities, but not of fathers', predict a family's organization as an association or social system.

Organization as an Association or Social System (ASSN). Table 10.2 shows that a pattern of the mothers' personalities predicts whether a family is more likely to be organized as an association than as a social system. Four of the five significant predictors are from the CPI. Taken together, they show that organization as an association is more likely if the mother is socially active and impulsive, especially if these tendencies are tempered with some uncertainty and restraint. Specifically, the profile is one of women who are rather self-oriented, demanding, persistent, and pace-setting and are so in both socially negative and socially positive ways. Thus they are likely to be self-oriented, stubborn, and demanding (high hypochondriasis) and also spontaneous, assertive, self-centered, expressive, and highly active (high scores on sense of well-being, flexibility, and self-acceptance). These tendencies are moderated by some patience and self restraint and by feelings of uncertainty (low social presence). Overall, these women seem energetic, impulsive, and rather self-oriented but in socially controlled ways which suggest that anxieties and inhibitions, and not just commitments, lead to their being socially supportive and productive.

As I have defined it, organization as an association means giving a legitimate place to the pursuit of personal and special interests as well as of common interests. These women seem to press for the former but to be capable of both. The signs of strain may indicate that the two pursuits are not well integrated (Swanson, 1985a, 1986).

Hierarchical vs. Equalitarian Organization (STRAT). Looking again at Table 10.2, we find that a *combination* of features of *both* parents' personalities predicts the families' ratings on this organizational pattern. A family is more likely to be hierarchical if (a) the fathers tend to be alert, ambitious, outgoing, and to have initiative (low hypochondriasis), and to be cheerful, balanced, and decisive (low paranoia) and, if (b) the mothers are inhibited, cautious, submissive, and compliant (low scores on achievement via independence). In this sample, men are almost always the heads of hierarchic families and this combination of spouses' personalities suggests a balance of power based on personal dispositions in which husbands have greater strengths.

Do the profiles of personality in Table 10.2 persist over time? Table 10.3 shows the results from scoring the sample's 1968 CPI's for these profiles using the beta weights obtained in 1958. In each case there are significant continuities across the decade. The table shows that PDM is predicted from the concurrent 1968 CPI–MMPI scores whereas ASSN and STRAT are not. In Study 2 we find conditions under which the correlations between people's scores across time are strengthened and under which the 1968 scores, as well as those from 1958, predict all three aspects of decision making. I return to the findings on this subject from Study 1 when these results from Study 2 are before us.

TABLE 10.3
Intercorrelations of 1958 and 1968 Indices[a]

Indices	*I. 1968 Personality Profiles*			*II 1968 Decision-Making Codes*		
	IA	*IB*	*IC*	*IIA*	*IIB*	*IIC*
I. 1958 Personality Profile from Table 2 Related to:						
A. PDM	.63##			.50**		
B. ASSN		.28*			.53#	
C. STRAT			.46**			.50#
II. 1968 Coding of Organization for Family Decision Making Concerning:						
A. PDM	.43#					
B. ASSN		.07				
C. STRAT			.15			

[a]$p < .05$*, .02**, .01#, .001##.

Study 2: Alternative Bases for Family Decision-Making

There is no mystery in husbands and wives' wanting a style of family organization that fits well with their dispositions, an organization in which the personal and the mutual complement one another. Some couples achieve that sort of organization. Others find it difficult to attain. Some who find it difficult discover that features of their interpersonal relations or of their own or their spouse's personality get in the way. When that happens, and assuming that the problematic conditions are unchanged, the marriage will be stronger if it is organized on some other basis. Certain conventional social roles may serve that purpose.

The problems with personalities that I have in mind are not the gross incompatibilities that destroy a marriage but incompatibilities that a couple can accept as long as they do not have to take them much into account. A wife may be able to overlook her husband's untidiness if outsiders do not know about it; a husband may pass over his wife's obstinancy if she also goes out of her way to please him.

There are, however, personal and interpersonal insufficiencies which, even if not extreme, affect almost everything that a couple does. They do this by preventing the development of workable routines for making joint decisions. Suppose, for example, that a husband and wife are strongly attached to one another but are also rather reserved: they have difficulty in being open; in communicating what they think and feel. That makes is hard for either one to anticipate problems that may arise in their relationship or to propose appropriate solutions. As a result, their decision making will often be too slow, too halting, too little informed. If these personal dispositions continue, and if their marriage is to work, the couple must find some grounds other than intimate awareness on which to routinize a timely and effective decision-making. Whatever they choose, it must be relevant, available, and easy to use.

What are some of the alternative grounds on which family decision making can be organized? There are many possibilities, but I focus here on a societal factor that is known (Sussman & Steinmetz, 1987) to influence the way marriages and families are organized: the social statuses of the husband and the wife at the time they marry. Those statuses embody something of the levels of culture and prestige and, perhaps, of wealth and influence, of the husband and wife (and their friends and relatives) in the larger community and society. In marrying, a couple usually takes account of the socioeconomic level from which each comes, seeing the similarities and differences as grounds for compatibility or as facts that can thereafter be safely discounted. These statuses-at-marriage can serve as grounds for structuring marital and family decision making because they are relatively clear, fixed, and objective, because they are always available, and because, as we shall see, they have implications for the major aspects of any group's organization for making and implementing decisions.[2]

My proposal, then, is that couples tend to organize a family in a way that fits well with their interpersonal relations and personalities but that they will find other grounds for that organization if those interpersonal relations, or one or both of their personalities, are in some way unsuitable. Theories about the levels of social relations that exist in groups help us to identify problems with interpersonal relations and personalities that are especially likely to disrupt the three features of decision-making discussed in Study 1. I describe these connections, suggest how a couple's social statuses at the time of marriage may serve as alternative grounds for organizing family decision making, and examine data from two samples in which these suggestions can be evaluated.

Explanations of group growth and development highlight the fact that any group is both a group and an interpersonal relationship. The features of decision making described in Study 1 can be properties of groups: that is, of arrangements through which people make and implement collective choices (Swanson, 1988, p. 43, 85, 179–199). Two of these features—principled vs. accommodative decision making and organization as an association or social system—are possible *only* if a group exists. The third feature—hierarchical or equalitarian stratification—can arise in a group or in an interpersonal relationship. Figure 10.3 shows these connections.

It is convenient to begin with the relations under *interpersonal relations* at the top of Fig. 10.3. That is where families and other groups have their beginnings and these relations continue as vital aspects of a group after it forms. When

---

[2]Research on juries and other informal groups shows that hierarchic relations are often based on the members' relevant social class positions (Nemeth, 1981).

I. A family is an interpersonal relationship.

- A. As such it is grounded in bonds of interdependence (attachment, trust, intimacy, mutual need).
- B. These, in turn, may become the basis for the development of a network of exchange relations: of giving and getting among dyads or larger aggregates.
- C. Both networks of interdependence and networks of exchange relations involve <u>stratification</u> among members: <u>equalitarian or hierarchic relations.</u>

II. A family is also a group.

- A. As such it is grounded in the development of collective purposes and in leadership roles through which these purposes are represented and promoted: a charismatic center.
- B. Such leadership roles involve <u>stratification</u> among members: <u>equalitarian or hierarchic relations.</u>
- C. They also:
  1. Embody an institutionalized distinction between collective purposes as against the personal or special interests of membvers or subgroups.
     - a. The family is organized as a <u>social system</u> if the pursuit only of collective interests is given a formal and legitimate place. It is organized as an <u>association</u> if personal and special interests also have such a role.
  2. Embody both collective purposes and the social arrangements through which they are examined and implemented.
     - a. The family is organized for <u>principled decision-making</u> if its organization embodies a differentiation between collective purposes and these social arrangements. If they are not so differentiated, the family is organized for <u>accommodative decision-making.</u>

FIG. 10.3. Some foundations of decision-making structures.

people first try to do something together, they are drawn to one another by mutual need. This is noted in Fig. 10.3 as a network of interdependence. If these attachments prove worthwhile and durable, people begin to develop one-on-one connections with those among the other participants who are best able to provide what they want. In Fig. 10.3 that is labeled as a network of exchange.

Stratification is intrinsic in interpersonal relations. The participants may not see it as important, but there is always some distribution of influence or power in networks of interdependence or exchange: Some participants may be more needed or more needy or all may be quite equal as partners. Other things being equal, the routinization of these stratified relations will smooth people's living with one another.

Studies of group development show that a third step in the process occurs when people become aware of having joint or common interests as well as personal interests and when they develop leadership roles (whether equalitarian or hierarchic) through which their joint efforts can be mobilized, directed, and coordinated. Figure 10.3 (section IIA) refers to these leadership roles in labeling this step as organization under a "charismatic center": that is, under persons and roles that give direction and form to collective action. It is when people have that kind of relationship that we begin to think of them as able to act as a group and not as just a collection of interacting individuals. As the figure suggests, these developments make possible all three aspects of a group's decision-making.

A group's organization as an association or social system depends on the prior development of common as against personal or special interests and sets the terms on which both will be served. Therefore, the appearance of common interests and of roles to implement them—that is, of a charismatic center—should precede the clear development of organization as a social system or as an association.

A group's organization for principled or accommodative decision-making also assumes the prior existence of common interests and of some standing arrangements through which they are represented or promoted. As a collective activity, principled decision-making uses common interests and purposes as guides to actions that should be undertaken, as criteria in the making of collective choices, and as conditions to be met in attaining a collective fulfillment. (As we have seen, the role of common interests and purposes is more differentiated in organization for principled as against accommodative decision making.) This activity is impossible without a charismatic center: without arrangements for leadership through which relevant people and resources can be mobilized and a sufficient assent assured.

As is obvious, stratification can be rooted in people's organization as a group as well as in their interpersonal relations. Indeed, it inheres in the very equalitarian or hierarchic arrangements of leadership roles themselves.

Looking at the whole pattern given in Fig. 10.3, we see that the social relations in IA (networks of interdependence) and IIA (a charismatic center) undergird participants' functioning in interpersonal relations or as a group and are therefore essential for the grounding of the three aspects of decision making introduced in Study 1. If participants' interdependence or personalities do not support dependable relations of the sort indicated in IA and IIA, the group will have difficulties in decision making. Some conditions frequently observed in families can serve as illustrations.

If the spouses and children are not close interpersonally, they are more likely to experience one another's bids for influence on decisions as, potentially, efforts to dominate. That will, at best, set limits on their ease in initiating influence or accepting it and therefore on their ability to establish effective routines for carrying on their life together. A finding from Study 1 calls attention to a further consequence. That study showed that hierarchic stratification tends to appear when the wife is not as steady, energetic, and effective a problem-solver as her husband. In a relationship that is close and loving this may not cause great difficulties for either partner. In one that is not close, the constant acknowledgement of the wife's insufficiencies in arrangements (the hierarchy) through which most decisions are made is more likely to be an unrelieved embarrassment to her and an irritation to her husband.

Problems for decision making also arise in families in which one or both spouses lacks the personal qualities required for effective leadership: for the founding and operation of a charismatic center. Research on American and European families (and on families in other societies as well) has shown that strains are especially likely if the husband is not at least his wife's equal in the skills and orientations associated with leadership. The result tends to be ambiguity as to who has the right to what degree of influence over decisions and the appearance of difficulties around principled vs. accommodative decision making or organization as an association or social system.

Illustrative problems can be seen by again referring to findings from Study 1. A family tends to get organized as an association if the wife is rather energetic and impulsive and finds it important to be independent in interests and activities. If a wife with these predispositions has a husband whose personality is not appropriate to the role of a leader in the family, their relations must be very uncomfortable. One spouse, at least, will not be doing his part in defining, representing, and implementing common interests and relating them to personal and special interests. In that context, a relatively impulsive wife with interests of her own provides an added threat to the couple's solidarity and to the family as a collective undertaking.

Similar points can be made concerning the family's organization for principled or accommodative decision making. Both assume effective leadership in identifying and solving problems, in employing resources, and in mobilizing others to implement group objectives. Spouses with role-inappropriate personalities are less likely to provide that leadership. Study 1 shows that organization for principled decision-making tends to be associated with the husband's being a considerate, self-disciplined, tolerant person who is intellectually able and is confident about his masculine identity. If a husband's personality is not appropriate for family leadership and he tries to behave as head of an organization for principled decision making, he is likely only to underline his personal insufficiencies and to impede effective decision making.

To summarize, the three features of organization for collective decision making presented in Study 1 are rooted in a network of interpersonal attachments and interdependence and/or an organization around leadership roles that make it possible for people to do things together as a group. If the spouses have such attachments and have personalities that are role-appropriate, they probably have much to gain from tailoring their organization for decision making to their personalities. If they do not have such attachments and personalities, it will be better for them to base their organization for decision making on some other grounds, thereby gaining a more stable foundation for their relations and not calling attention to their personal and interpersonal insufficiencies.

What might serve as alternative grounds? My focus is on the couple's premarital social statuses. The couple's status backgrounds can serve as alternatives to their personality characteristics as they seek grounds on which to organize their joint decision-making because these statuses are relatively clear, fixed, and objective and because they have implications for each feature of decision making considered in Study 1.

Principled or Accommodative Decision Making. Social status is an index of cultural background and, at least on the contemporary scene, people at higher levels of culture have been trained to seek out diverse points of view on an issue the better to insure that they have taken all important alternatives and considerations into account and have attained a high level of objectivity and comprehensiveness before forming any conclusion (Lehman, Lempert, & Nisbett, 1988). Therefore, if a couple's use of principled or accommodative decision-making is not to be based on their personalities, it can be based on their general cultural level: higher levels making principled decision making more likely.

Association or Social System. Study 1 shows that the likelihood of organization as an association rather than a social system increases if the wife has an agenda of her own and the motivation to pursue it. It seems plausible that a wife from a higher social background than her husband's will be in a better position than otherwise to define interests of her own and to be accorded a social position from which to pursue them. That background may therefore make it more likely that the family will be organized as an association.

Hierarchic or Equalitarian. In Study 1, hierarchic arrangements were more common if the wife was intellectually less able and emotionally less stable than the husband. It seems plausible that a woman from a lower social background than her husband's will be more likely to defer to his judgment and leadership than would otherwise be the case. (Hierarchic arrangements have also been shown in studies of modern families to be more likely in small families than in large, perhaps because control by one parent is easier with fewer people. Family size needs, therefore, to be held constant in our analyses.)

To summarize, the arguments I have given suggest that:

1. People will move toward a pattern of joint decision making that fits well with relevant aspects of their interpersonal attachments and of their personalities (as defined in Study 1), but not if such a pattern would be undependable or threatening.

2. If a pattern grounded on their interpersonal relations and personalities would be undependable or threatening, they may find some other basis for organizing their joint activities: one that will give them a workable relationship. The participants' premarital social statuses may serve that purpose for spouses in modern marriages and families.

3. Given the connections developed in Fig. 10.3, couples that lack personalities appropriate for the exercise of family leadership will tend to base all three features of group decision making on something other than the aspects of their personalities that would otherwise be relevant, and couples who do not have strong interpersonal attachments will base their pattern of stratification in like manner.

SAMPLES, METHODS, FINDINGS

The data from the IHD sample that were used in Study 1 can help us judge the usefulness of these suggestions and so can data from a sample of college undergraduates. The undergraduates (N = 240) were students in introductory sociology who volunteered to participate in a study of "social relations and our personal feelings" by answering a long questionnaire. They described many features of their family and parents including the family's pattern of decision-making, certain of the parents' personality characteristics, the patterns of leadership and closeness in the family, and many of its basic demographic characteristics.

The degree of interpersonal attachment among family members in the IHD sample was indexed by a factor score derived from a varimax factor analysis of the feelings and ties expressed by parents and children when asked, in interviews, about their relations with other members of the family. (More details about its construction appears in Swanson, 1974.) High scores mean that the mother and the children report that they feel close to the father and that the children say their mother is supportive. (This index is based on data for 1968. No comparable rating for 1958 seems possible, if only because the children's reports were not obtained.)[3] The college undergraduates rated their families on these same items and a single score was derived for each family from these ratings (Swanson & Phillips, 1990).

The appropriateness of the personalities of the IHD parents for their role as leaders was estimated from their scores on the CPI. Among the outcomes of a varimax factor analysis of the CPI scales was a well-defined factor that brought together personal qualities that have been associated in previous studies (Megargee, 1972, pp. 120–121) with leadership (high loadings from the CPI scales for dominance, sociability, social presence, and self-acceptance.) Parents were evaluated as being at the same level as their spouse on this factor or as having a score

[3]Dr. Marjorie P. Honzik has developed codes on family relations from the 1958 data for fathers and mothers. These codes are proving useful for many purposes but even the four that most resemble my index of familial closeness have only insignificant correlations with it. (These are Dr. Honzik's codes for compatibility in parent-child views as reported by the parents and codes on the family's "emotional tone.")

that was at least one-half of a standard deviation above or below their spouse's. Undergraduates rated each of their parents on items embodying this factor. They also reported whether their mothers or their fathers led or dominated their families or were equal in influence.

For the IHD sample, the parents' personality profiles as given in Table 10.2 were used again. Hollingshead (Hollingshead & Redlich, 1958) social class ratings were available for the families from which the parents came.

The undergraduates had been asked about the social status of their parents since marriage as compared with that of the families from which each came and the answers provided an indication of their mobility through marriage. Undergraduates were also asked to indicate which of a wide sampling of personality characteristics (Swanson & Phillips, 1990) typified each of their parents. These items enabled the construction of an index corresponding to each of the profiles given in Table 10.2.[4] (Footnote 4 gives some illustrative items.)

Table 10.4 shows the significant results for the families of adolescents and of undergraduates with respect to correlates of PDM and ASSN. The analyses that underlie this table began with explorations to see whether the correlations between spouses' personalities and family decision making as reported in Study 1 would appear in families in which the father and mother were equal in personality characteristics associated with leadership, in families in which the father's characteristics were superior to the mother's, and in families in which the reverse was true.

As Table 10.4 shows, a first significant finding is that the correlations between spousal personalities and PDM and ASSN as found in Table 10.2 appear in families in which the father's leadership characteristics equal or exceed the mother's. (This finding, appearing in both the IHD and undergraduate samples, is consistent with earlier findings on the importance of fathers in the organizational structuring of families. I have suggested possible explanations in previous reports, especially Swanson, 1988). Table 10.4 also shows that, in families in

---

[4]Students were asked to check each item in a set of 62 which characterized their fathers and each which characterized their mothers. In forming indices to match those in Table 2, I looked for items that would catch major correlates reported by Megargee (1972) or Dahlstrom, Welsh, and Dahlstrom (1972, vol. 1) as associated with the variables from the CPI or MMPI that appeared in a particular profile. Thus, Megargee reported that the CPI scale on Tolerance had been found to correlate with tests and ratings showing persons with high scores to be enterprising, tolerant of others' views, and intellectually able and to have broad and varied interests. The undergraduates had used items that seemed to tap each of these correlates, the following being illustrative characterizations: On being enterprising: "Self-reliant, confident, enterprising, planful. . ." On being tolerant: "Thinks of the children in ways that respect their integrity as persons: their disappointments, enthusiasms . . . lets them be themselves." "Listens carefully, wants to understand what you are saying." On being intellectually able: "Effective in analyzing problems, finding solutions." On having broad interests: "Enjoys many interests outside as well as within the family and encourages other members to do the same." A complete list of these items is available from the author upon request.

TABLE 10.4
Role-Appropriateness of Father's Personality as a Mediating Variable in Predictions of PDM and ASSN[a]

Sample	Predictors	*Is Father's Personality Role-Appropriate?* No 1968[b]				Yes 1968[b]			
		IA	*IB*	*PDM*	*ASSN*	*IA*	*IB*	*PDM*	*ASSN*
IHD	I. Parent's 1958 Personality that Predicts:								
	A. PDM	.35		.09		.45#		.42**	
	B. ASSN		.10		.00		.45**		.54#
	II. Parent's Premarital Status Used to Predict:								
	A. PDM			.62##				.12	
	B. ASSN				.41				.18
	III. PDM	.35				.74##			
	IV. ASSN		.21				.46**		
Under-graduates	I. Parent's Personality Profile for:								
	A. PDM			-.004				.30##	
	B. ASSN				.11				.29#
	II. Parent's Premarital Status Used to Predict:								
	ASSN[c]				.43##				-.17*

[a]See Table 10.3, Footnote a.
[b]Parent's 1968 personality scores on the 1958 profile that predicts PDM (IA) or ASSN (IB). The relevant personality profiles are given in Table 10.2.
[c]Data on the premarital status levels of the undergraduates' parents were not obtained. As a result, it is not possible to compute their correlation with PDM.

which the father has a *lower* score than his wife on personality characteristics associated with leadership, PDM and ASSN are based on the spouses' status backgrounds: specifically, (a) the higher the mean of the social class positions from which the spouses came, the more likely that their joint family will be organized for principled rather than accommodative decision making; (b) the higher the status of the wife's family relative to the husband's, the more likely that they will organize their decision making as an association rather than as a social system.

Table 10.5 shows the significant correlates of hierarchic as against equalitarian decision making. They are the same for both samples of families. If the

TABLE 10.5
Family's Closeness and the Role-Appropriateness of the Father's Personality as Mediating Variables in Predictions of STRAT[a]

		Family is Not Close and/or Father's Personality is Not Role-Appropriate[b]		*Family is Close and Father's Personality is Role-Appropriate[b]*	
		I 1968[c]	*STRAT*	*I 1968[c]*	*STRAT*
IHD	I. Parents' 1958 Personality Profile that Predicts STRAT	.01	.29	.60**	.58*
	II. Parental Premarital Status Characteristics that Predict STRAT		.61**		-.05
	III. STRAT	-.05		.76##	
Under-graduates	I. Parents' Personality Profile for STRAT		.14		.46##
	II. Parents' Status Characteristics for STRAT		.39##		.05[e]

[a]See footnote (a) for Table 10.3.
[b]The measure of family closeness is for 1968. Data for 1958 do not enable the construction of a comparable index.
[c]Parents' 1968 personality scores on the 1958 profile that predicts STRAT as given in Table 10.2.
[d]This is the multiple correlation OF STRAT WITH (1) family size (beta = .27*) and (2) the mother's having married up (beta = .30**).
[e]This is the multiple correlation described in Note (d) above.

family is above the sample mean in the closeness of its members' attachments to one another *and is also* one in which the father has a score on group leadership that is at least equal to the mother's, then the relations found in Study 1 between the parents' personalities and stratification are found again. In the other families, decision making is more likely to be hierarchic if the family is small or if the father's family of origin is of higher status than the mother's.

Two other findings emerge from analyses connected with Tables 10.4 and 10.5 but not included in them. First, the patterns of personality associated in these tables with any given feature of family decision making do not correlate significantly with either of the two other features of decision making. Second, depending on the relevant conditions, *either* the couple's personalities *or* the statuses of the families from which they came, *but not both,* tend significantly to predict their patterns of family decision-making. (The one exception is the failure in Table 10.4 of the correlation of .41 in row IIB to reach significance. The number of cases available here was small (N = 15) so perhaps this should not been seen as a true exception.) The findings are consistent with the expectation that status origins are a substitute for spousal personalities as a basis for organizing a couple's joint activities.

DISCUSSION

The findings in Study 2 show that the correlations between personality and decision making uncovered in Study 1 appear only if spouses and families have close interpersonal relations and/or if the husbands have role-appropriate personalities. They also show that it is not the couple's premarital social statuses as such that affect the three features of their joint marital decision making, but those statuses if needed as replacements for interpersonal closeness and/or the role appropriateness of the husband's personality.[5] Both findings are stable across samples and methods.

In Study 1, certain profiles of the spouses' personalities were consistent across the decade under study. Tables 10.4 and 10.5 show that the patterns of personality found important in Study 1 are consistent only if the couple's family relations are interpersonally close and/or if the husband's personality is role-appropriate. This takes us a further step in understanding the findings of Study 1. It also raises a new question: Why are these profiles of personality consistent under these conditions? Do people who tend to have stable personality profiles tend also to be interpersonally close and to have role-appropriate personalities? Or do close relations and role-appropriate personalities, especially in husbands, tend to stabilize personality profiles, converting them from *states* to *traits?* Or do those conditions lead to more stable marriages which, in turn, stabilize the spouses' personalities? Or do people with more stable profiles tend to marry spouses with

---

[5]In Study 2, I worked from the assumption that spouses try to routinize their joint decision-making by basing it on grounds that are relevant and stable. That does not rule out their use of additional criteria. Thus spouses might build on their premarital social statuses if they felt that insufficiencies in their interpersonal ties, or in their capacities for leadership, made it too threatening to build on them. Or they might resort to their premarital statuses because they could serve as "conventional" (Langer, 1983) or "peripheral" (Petty and Cacioppo, 1986; Petty et al., 1987) criteria that can be used for making choices when more "mindful" or "central" processing is not readily possible. I have chosen to base my case simply on the spouses' effort to find stable grounds for decision-making because, first, it seemed sufficient for my purpose and, second, because it was not clear that these alternative arguments applied. (Specifically, it was not clear that a couple's building upon the fact of a spouse's marrying up or down would be less conflictual and threatening than their building upon, say, a relationship that was not close, and it was not clear that people are behaving less "mindfully" (*i.e.*, engaging less in self-regulation) when they work from their respective social backgrounds than when they work from an acquaintance with one another's personalities.)

stable profiles, the married pair reinforcing one another's personal tendencies? These and other possibilities remain to be explored.

Study 3: Some Consequences for Children

I have found in several earlier studies that the way a family is organized for decision making helps us to predict things about the children's personalities and about their styles and levels of cognitive functioning.[6] Two of these investigations employed the IHD sample and uncovered direct, positive correlations: a correlation of PDM with adolescents' scores on Wechsler's tests of intellectual level (WISC or WAIS as appropriate for the subject's age) (Swanson, 1985b); a correlation of an equalitarian family organization with adolescents' use of denial as a defense (Swanson, 1988).[7] Do the links between parents' personalities and premarital social statuses discussed in Study 2 explain these correlations between family decision-making and children's functioning? The question can be explored in the IHD sample, the only one for which I presently have the needed measures.

Tables 10.6 and 10.7 show the chief results. In each case the findings in Study 2 prove important because the same *independent* variables have systematic relations with children's functioning. This time, however, they operate in different combinations. (The cells in these tables give the correlations between an aspect of children's functioning (i.e., IQ scores or use of denial as a defense) and the variables in the left-hand column when the values of the variable in the two right-hand columns [e.g., role-appropriateness of father's personality] are held constant.)

In families in which the fathers have role-appropriate personalities, it is the related features of the parents' social status—and not, as in Study 2, their personalities—that predict children's functioning. In the remaining families, it is relevant aspects of the parents' personalities—not, as in Study 2, their status characteristics—that predict children's functioning. Tracing these connections for children's Wechsler's scores, we find that if the father has a role-appropriate personality, the median scores for the children in the family are associated with

---

[6]In other studies these patterns of decision-making were among the variables that correlated with each of several aspects of children's functioning: with certain other ego defenses (Swanson, 1988), with phobic, hysteric, and obsessive symptoms (Swanson, 1985a), with "pre-genital" tendencies in personality (Swanson, 1987), with tendencies to lose oneself in imagined worlds (Swanson, 1978a, 1978b), and with scores on Kohlberg's test of moral judgment (Swanson, 1985).

[7]I had also found a correlation between PDM and Adolescents' scores on two Piagetian indices of cognitive complexity (Swanson, 1974). Recent analyses show that scores on these measures are high if the family is organized for PDM *or* if the father's personality is appropriate to his leadership role. The small number of cases makes it impossible to investigate likely sources of the small remaining variance.

TABLE 10.6
Correlations With Children's IQ Scores[a]

	Is Father's Personality Role-Appropriate?	
Correlation	*No*	*Yes*
Between median IQ of children in the family and:		
A. Father's personality profile that predicts PDM	.50#	.06
B. Mean of parents' premarital social statuses	.02	.61##

[a]Consult Table 10.3, footnote a.

the mean of their parents' social statuses, whereas if the father's personality is not role-appropriate, the children's median scores correlate significantly with the paternal personality profile shown in Studies 1 and 2 to predict PDM. The results for children's use of denial as an ego defense are formally similar: if the father's personality is role-appropriate and the family is close, the children's use of this defense is predicted by the mother's marital mobility status (the mother did *not* marry down) shown in Study 2 to be associated with an equalitarian rather than a hierarchic organization for family decision making. In other families, children tend to use denial if the profile of fathers' and mothers' personalities is the one shown to predict equalitarian organization in Studies 1 and 2. (When the relations shown in Tables 10.6 and 10.7 are taken into account, the correlations I have *previously* reported between PDM and children's IQ and

TABLE 10.7
Correlations With Children's Use of Denial[a]

	Both of the Following True: Are Relations in this Family Close and Is the Father's Personality Role-Appropriate?[b]	
Correlation	*No*	*Yes*
Between a randomly chosen child's score on denial and:		
A. Parents' personality profile that predicts STRAT	.46#	-.10
B. Mother came from a family of lower status than did father	.03	.33*

[a]Consult Table 10.3, footnote a.

[b]The rating for family closeness is from 1968. Data for 1958 do not enable the construction of a comparable index.

between an equalitarian family and children's use of denial are found to disappear.)

The findings thus answer one question but present a set of unexpected, provocative relations. Assuming that these relationships are not peculiar to the IHD sample or in some way "artifactual," how can they be explained? Why is it that a parental personality profile or some feature of the parents' premarital social status, but not both of these factors, tends to predict these two aspects of children's functioning? I suggest a few plausible arguments:

• Perhaps the connection is social-cognitive. If something about the parents' personalities and also something about their original social statuses is relevant for the organization of an aspect of family decision-making and if, for reasons given in Study 2, the parents ground the family's organization on *just one* of these relevant characteristics, they may find it cognitively simpler to *reserve* that characteristic *for that one purpose* and to use the second suitable characteristic when dealing with such different but related matters as the cultivation of their children's intellectual skills or the patterns of control and support which give rise to their children's ego defenses. (If so, these processes are likely to be "mindless" (Langer, 1983) rather than the results of self-conscious choices.)

• Perhaps the connection is social-motivational. Thus, by building upon both sorts of parental characteristics relevant for a given aspect of family decision making—using one as the basis for that aspect of family organization and the other as the basis for features of the children's behavior that are linked to this aspect of family organization—the fuller reality of the parents' characteristics can be taken explicitly into account: can be expressed and dealt with by all members of the family.

• Perhaps, in a special form of the social-motivational argument, the parental characteristics in a pair that is *not* made a basis for the organization of the family's decision-making is suppressed, even repressed, and the children, becoming aware of this hidden but potent aspect of their parents' relations, accommodate to it or, however *unconsciously,* are seduced into such an accommodation by one or both parents.

• Or perhaps, to make a final suggestion, it is vital for children to gain skills in interpreting both interpersonal relations and status relations and in managing themselves in relation to both. If so, it may be that children, while obtaining relevant experiences with one of these forms of relationship through its embodiment in the organization of the family, will seek, or be encouraged by their parents to seek, experiences with the other form of relationship by dealing with the social statuses embodied in their parents' backgrounds and in their present status positions.

SOME GENERAL CONCLUSIONS

The findings in these studies raise questions and suggest possibilities.

Among the questions: Why is it, in Study 1, that the personality of the father *or* of the mother, but *not both,* predicts organization for PDM or ASSN? (It is not that men and women with these predictive personalities marry spouses with just any profile of personality. Analyses conducted in Study 1 but not presented here show that people with the personality profiles related to PDM or ASSN tended to marry spouses with specific personality profiles. Additional analyses show that these correlations are about the same in marriages that are, or are not, interpersonally close and in those in which the husband's personality is, or is not, role-appropriate. And the taking account of these additional spousal profiles does not improve the predictions of family decision making given in Table 10.2!)

Among the possibilities: Will the associations of spouses' personalities and social backgrounds in Studies 1 and 2 open new possibilities for studying assortative mating based on personality? Perhaps the fact that the profiles in these studies derive from *the relevance of personality characteristics for people's relations in a family or interpersonal relationship* will help to overcome difficulties in previous research on this subject. And such new studies of assortative mating might, in turn, have implications for research on marital satisfaction.

I want, however, to underscore five themes that appear in two or more of the studies just described and that respond to the call for systematic understanding of relations within families and of relations between families and the wider social order. First, three key aspects of organization for family decision making are shaped by the spouses' personalities *or* by their premarital social statuses, but *not equally by both.* Second, the importance of those personalities or premarital statuses in shaping family decision making is determined by the suitability of the husband's personality for a leadership role and/or the closeness of family relations. Third, it is their *relevance for interpersonal relations or group functioning* that gives these several personality, interpersonal, and status variables their role in shaping decision making. Fourth, the personality and status variables have objective properties apart from their role in interpersonal relations and group functioning and it is those *independent* properties that people *put to work* in *constructing* a group or interpersonal relationship. Fifth, Studies 2 and 3 disclose systematic and interrelated patterns which contain unexplained but systematic reversals. The study of such reversals often holds special promise for the extension of our understanding.

REFERENCES

Baumrind, D. (1975). Early socialization and adolescent competence. In S. E. Dragastin & G. H. Elder (Eds.), *Adolescence in the life cycle* (pp. 117–143). New York: Wiley.

Block, J. (1961). *The q-sort method in personality assessment and psychiatric research.* Springfield, IL: Thomas.

Block, J., & Haan, N. (1971). *Lives through time.* Berkeley: Bancroft.

Burgess, E. W. (1926). The family as a unity of interacting personalities. *Family, 7,* 3–9.

Constantine, L. L. (1987). *Family paradigms: The practice of theory in family therapy.* New York: Guilford.

Dahlstrom, W. G., Welsh, G. S., & Dahlstrom, L. E. (1972). *An MMPI handbook* (Vol. 1). Minneapolis: University of Minnesota Press.

Eichorn, D. H., Clausen, J. A., Haan, N., Honzik, M. P., & Mussen, P. H. (Eds.). (1981). *Present and past in middle life.* New York: Academic Press.

Hollingshead, A. B., & Redlich, F. D. (1958). *Social class and mental illness.* New York: Wiley.

Langer, E. J. (1983). *The psychology of control.* Newbury Park, CA: Sage.

Lehman, D. R., Lempert, R. O., & Nisbett, R. E. (1988). The effects of graduate training on reasoning: Formal discipline and thinking about everyday life. *American Psychologist, 43,* 431–442.

Maccoby, E. E., & Martin, J. A. (1983). Socialization in the context of the family: Parent-child interaction. In P. H. Mussen (Ed.), *Handbook of child psychology* (vol. 4, pp. 1–102). New York: Wiley.

Mead, G. H. (1934). *Mind, self and society.* Chicago: University of Chicago Press.

Megargee, E. I. (1972). *The California Psychological Inventory handbook.* San Francisco: Jossey-Bass.

Moselle, K. A. (1984). *Patterns of family moral discussion associated with the coordination of affectiveness and responsibility in children.* Unpublished doctoral dissertation. Department of Psychology, University of California, Berkeley.

Nemeth, C. J. (1981). Jury trials: Psychology and law. In L. Berkowitz (Ed.), *Advances in experimental social psychology* (vol. 14, pp. 309–361). New York: Academic Press.

Netting, R. M., Wilk, R. R., & Arnould, E. J. (Eds.). (1984). *Households: Comparative and historical studies of the domestic group.* Berkeley: University of California Press.

Parsons, T. (1959). The principal structures of community: A sociological view. In T. Parsons (Ed.), *Structure and process in modern societies.* Glencoe, IL: The Free Press.

Petty, R. A., & Cacioppo, J. T. (1986). *Communication and persuasion: Central and peripheral routes to attitude change.* New York: Springer-Verlag.

Petty, R. A., Kasmer, J. A., Haugtvedt, C. P., & Cacioppo. (1987). Source and message factors in persuasion. A reply to Stiff's critique of the elaboration likelihood model. *Communication Monographs, 54,* 233–263.

Scanzoni, J., & Szinovacz, M. (1980). *Family decision-making: A developmental sex role model.* Newbury Park, CA: Sage.

Scheier, M. F., & Carver, C. S. (1988). A model of behavioral self-regulation: Translating intention into action. In L. Berkowitz (Ed.), *Advances in experimental social psychology* (Vol. 21, pp. 303–346). New York: Academic Press.

Sussman, M. B., & Steinmetz, S. K. (1987). *Handbook of marriage and the family.* New York: Plenum.

Swanson, G. E. (1967). *Religion and regime: A sociological account of the reformation.* Ann Arbor: University of Michigan Press.

Swanson, G. E. (1969). Rules of descent: Studies in the sociology of parentage. *Anthropological papers* (No. 39). Ann Arbor: University of Michigan, Museum of Anthropology.

Swanson, G. E. (1971). An organizational analysis of collectivities. *American Sociological Review, 36,* 607–624.

Swanson, G. E. (1974). Family structure and the reflective intelligence of children. *Sociometry, 37,* 459–490.

Swanson, G. E. (1978a). Trance and possession: Studies of charismatic influence. *Review of Religious Research, 19,* 253–278.

Swanson, G. E. (1978b). Travels through inner space: Family structure and openness to absorbing experiences. *American Journal of Sociology, 83,* 890–919.

Swanson, G. E. (1985a). Phobias and related symptoms: Some social sources. *Sociological Forum, 1,* 103–130.

Swanson, G. E. (1985b). The powers and capabilities of selves: Social and collective approaches. *Journal for the Theory of Social Behavior, 15,* 331–354.

Swanson, G. E. (1986). Immanence and transcendence: Connections with personality and personal life. *Sociological Analysis, 47,* 189–213.

Swanson, G. E. (1987). Tricksters in myths and families: Studies in pregenital relations. In D. Leland & J. G. Jorgensen (Eds.), *Themes in Ethnology and Culture History* (pp. 259–308). Berkeley: Folklore Institute.

Swanson, G. E. (1988). *Ego defenses and the legitimation of behavior.* Cambridge, England: Cambridge University Press.

Swanson, G. E., & Phillips, S. L. (1990). *Vulnerability to will surveillance, replacement, and withdrawal: Some social correlates.* Paper submitted for publication.

Walsh, F. (Ed.). (1982). *Normal family processes.* New York: Guilford.

11 Work and Family Dynamics

Martha J. Moorehouse
University of California, Santa Cruz

Developmental research on the connections between work, family life, and children's development has had a very narrow focus. Echoing widespread public concerns, early studies anticipated that the simple fact of mothers' employment would deprive children of the nurturant care necessary for healthy social, emotional, and intellectual development (see reviews by Bronfenbrenner & Crouter, 1982; Hoffman, 1979, 1989). However, the evidence accumulating from studies comparing outcomes for children of employed women to outcomes for children of women who remain at home does not support this social problem perspective on maternal employment. In fact, there has been little evidence of direct associations, positive or negative, between measures of children's well-being and their mothers' employment status per se (Bronfenbrenner & Crouter, 1982; Gottfried & Gottfried, 1988; Hoffman, 1979, 1989). Reviewers have concluded from this lack of evidence that additional comparisons between the children of employed and nonemployed women will be of little use. To provide further insight into the connections between work and family that are important for children's development, research must, as Hoffman (1989) has observed, "examine the relationships between the mother's employment status and the intervening steps that mediate the effects on the child" (p. 283).

In line with Hoffman's recommendation, research efforts are now focusing on how work affects processes operating within the family. One approach simply examines differences in family process variables as a function of maternal employment status. For example, studies have examined whether employed mothers in dual-earner families are able to spend as much time in close one-on-one interactions with their young children as are mothers in traditional single-earner families, who remain at home while their husbands work (see reviews by Hoffman, 1984, 1989).

This approach has been a useful first step in the study of work and family dynamics. It has provided clear evidence that good mothering and healthy child development can be accomplished in a variety of work and family contexts. That is, there are few signs of differences in family processes as a function of maternal employment status per se. Mothers in dual-earner families seem to spend as much time in shared child-centered activities with young children as do mothers who remain at home (Hoffman, 1984, 1989), and dual-earner parents are as effective as traditional single-earner parents in monitoring the behavior and whereabouts of older children (Crouter, MacDermid, McHale, & Perry-Jenkins, 1990).

A second, interactional, approach takes the additional step of examining outcomes for children and investigates whether the same child-rearing practices are equally effective in different earner contexts, or whether child-rearing interactions affect children differently, depending on the work that their parents do (Crouter et al., 1990; Moorehouse, 1991a). This interactional approach thus applies an ecological perspective on family relationships by positing that family processes may operate differently in different contexts of parental work (Bolger, Caspi, Downey, & Moorehouse, 1988; Bronfenbrenner, 1979, 1986; Bronfenbrenner & Crouter, 1982; Crouter, Perry-Jenkins, Huston, & McHale, 1987; Moorehouse, 1991a).

Although the interactional approach represents an important advance in concept and in method, its application has been limited by the pervasive and enduring view of maternal employment as a social problem. That is, much of the research using an interactional approach either searches for the specific conditions under which maternal employment disrupts family processes, or it attempts to identify the factors that buffer maternal employment's potentially disruptive impacts (Crouter et al., 1990; Gottfried & Gottfried, 1988; Greenberger and Goldberg, 1989; Moorehouse, 1991a).

One consequence of this social problem perspective on mothers' employment is that we have gained little insight into the mechanisms through which maternal employment benefits women's own well-being or the well-being of their families. A second consequence of the social problem perspective is that the study of mothers' employment and the study of fathers' employment continue to follow the strikingly different courses that Bronfenbrenner and Crouter (1982) observed nearly a decade ago:

> Research on the impact of work on family life has treated the job situations of mothers and fathers as separate worlds, having no relation to each other and leading to rather different outcomes. . . . For mothers, it was the fact of being employed that was presumed to be damaging to the child; for fathers, unemployment was seen as the destructive force. (p. 41)

A further and ironic consequence of the social problem perspective is that in dual-earner families, where of course fathers are also employed, the employment of mothers has been the sole focus of attention. In contrast, in single-parent families headed by employed women the study of mothers' employment has been seriously neglected.

It is clear that research must move beyond a social problem perspective on mothers' employment to gain further insight into the connections between work and family dynamics that are influential in children's development. A first task for research is to understand how parents' (both mothers' and fathers') experiences at work transfer to family life in positive as well as negative ways. A closely related task is to learn more about how parents themselves are affected by specific experiences at work and about how these work experiences then carry over into family relationships and children's lives. In other words, we need to understand more about how men and women are affected by the work that they do, so that we can understand how children will be affected by the work that their mothers and fathers do. This perspective views work contexts as settings for adult development, and it thus provides an alternative to the social problem perspective.

To address these questions about what aspects of work experiences are important, studies must examine differences among dual-earner families. A result of the social problem perspective on maternal employment has been a focus instead on differences between dual-earner families and traditional single-earner families. This global contrast cannot provide the necessary information about the specific aspects of employment situations that are influential in family life and in children's development. The possibility that the mother's involvement in employment will alter the impact that the father's work situation has on family life must also be addressed. For example, do fathers' positive or negative interactions at work carry over into interactions with children more when mothers are also employed? Thus, a key task for research on two-parent dual-earner families is to examine the combined effects of parents' work experiences.

A final task is to determine whether some kinds of family socialization processes are more affected by parents' work than are other processes. For example, the socialization processes that shape sex roles, motivational orientations, achievement behavior, and knowledge about the world of work may be especially open to influence from what parents do at work and from how work and family roles are coordinated at home.

Overview of Chapter Organization

The chapter is divided into two major sections. The first section reviews efforts to investigate the family processes through which work affects children's development. The studies that are discussed represent the first research approach, which simply examines differences in family process variables as a function of work, and the second interactional approach, which examines whether child-rearing interactions show different relationships to children's outcomes in different contexts of work and family. Three areas of research are examined: (a) the mother-child relationship and recent debates about risks for attachment relationships when mothers are employed, (b) fathers' family participation, and (c) other qualities of child-rearing interactions, especially parenting styles and parental monitoring. The second section of the chapter defines an agenda for new research that will move us beyond a social problem perspective on maternal employment, and it presents some promising lines of inquiry. The three central tasks for new research are: (a) to examine the potential for positive as well as negative spillover from work to family life, (b) to identify the influential aspects of parents' work experiences by taking into consideration the potential for parents' work situations to affect their own well being and development in adulthood, and (c) to study specific links between aspects of parents' work experiences, family socialization processes, and children's competence in particular domains.

LINKS THROUGH FAMILY PROCESSES

Mother-Child Relationships

Early accounts of the effects of maternal employment assumed that mothers who held paid jobs would not have enough energy or time for the warm, stimulating interactions that nurture children's development (see reviews by Hoffman, 1980, 1984, 1989). However, research on mothers' activities with their young children finds no evidence that maternal employment significantly reduces the time children spend in close interaction and shared activities with their mothers (Hoffman, 1980, 1984, 1989). In fact, evidence suggests that the employed mother often sets aside special periods for uninterrupted time with the child (Hoffman, 1980). It is time in other activities, including leisure pursuits, housework, and sleep, that is sacrificed, instead of time in close interactions with children (Hoffman, 1984).

Examining differences in time spent in shared activities as a function of mothers' employment status does not tell us whether shared mother-child activities play a different role in facilitating children's development in different contexts of maternal employment. My own research has examined this possibility and found support for a process model in which differences in the effectiveness of shared mother-child activities are specified as one possible mechanism linking maternal employment patterns to children's outcomes (Moorehouse, 1991a). In this model, when employment conditions occur that would be expected to exacerbate work-family stress, such as changes in work hours, then compensatory mechanisms involving the frequency of shared mother-child activities would come into play. For example, as mothers shift into full-time jobs, it is likely that extra effort must be made to find time for shared activities with children. If this effort is not made, and less time is spent together in shared activities, then children would be expected to be more vulnerable to disruptive effects of their mothers' work status. However, it is expected that maintaining a frequent involvement in shared activities will mitigate potentially disruptive effects of employment and will help transmit possible psychological benefits of mothers' work experiences to children.

This model was evaluated for a sample of 1st graders and their mothers. The data consisted of mothers' reports of stability and change in their work hours, mothers' ratings of time spent in child-centered shared activities, and teachers' assessments of children's school competence. Consistent with the conceptual model, I found that shared mother-child activities had a stronger and more positive association with children's competence when mothers experienced changes in their work hours or worked full-time hours rather than remaining at home. Thus, when shared activities were frequent, children in potentially stressful situations (such as having their mothers work long hours on an ongoing basis or change their work hours, especially increasing to full time), were doing as well or better than children whose mothers were at home all along. These potentially stressful situations were associated with lower social and cognitive scores for children, *only* when shared mother-child activities were infrequent. Although a further assessment needs to be carried out using longitudinal data, these findings suggest that mothers who frequently engage their children in shared activities may effectively buffer children from potentially disruptive features of their employment situations. Equally important is the possibility that these frequent shared mother-child activities transmit the psychological benefits of mothers' work experiences to children. A broader implication of these findings is that family relational processes may operate differently in different contexts of parental employment and that research designs must be sensitive to these possibilities.

The findings from research on mother-child relationships, reviewed earlier, challenge the assumption that maternal employment necessarily deprives children of the nurturant care important for healthy development. However, new concerns about the negative effects of maternal employment on the mother-child relationship have been raised in studies of infants. In a meta-analysis, Belsky (1988) has found that babies who experience extended hours of nonmaternal care (more than 20 hours per week) are more likely to have insecure attachment relationships with their mothers than are the babies of women who remain at home. However, it is premature to conclude that these differences result from mothers' employment status for two reasons. A number of studies find no differences between children of employed and nonemployed women in the quality or stability of attachment relationships (Hoffman, 1989). Furthermore in all studies, the majority of children of employed women have secure relationships (see reviews by Belsky, 1988; Clarke-Stewart, 1988; Thompson, 1988). Thus, mothers' employment status per se does not appear to be the key variable.

Why do some studies nonetheless find an association between extended hours in nonmaternal care and insecurity in infants' attachments to their mothers? An explanation proposed by Clarke-Stewart (1988) is that children of employed women are in fact more independent, and, as a result, are likely to be misclassified as avoidant and insecure in studies of attachment relationships which rely on the Strange Situation procedure. According to Clarke-Stewart:

> The Strange Situation may not be equally stressful for these two groups, [infants of employed and nonemployed mothers]. Consider the features of which the Strange Situation is composed—the infant plays with someone else's toys in a room that is not his or her own, is left during daylight hours with a woman who is not the mother, and plays with and is comforted by that woman in the mother's absence; then the mother returns to pick the infant up. Although at least some infants of nonworking mothers undoubtedly have had experiences like these before their assessment in the Strange Situation, infants of working mothers are more likely to have had them regularly and routinely and therefore be more accustomed to them. (pp. 297–298)

Thus, children of employed women, who have a good deal of experience with other caregivers and possibly other care settings, may not find the procedure "strange enough" to prompt comfort seeking and reassurance on reunion with their mothers. Instead, these children may display independence. If these arguments are correct, Belsky's (1988) conclusion that children in nonmaternal care more than 20 hours per week are at risk for emotional insecurity may stem, at least in part, from a misclassification of the independent behavior of children of employed women in studies using the Strange Situation paradigm.

Weinraub, Jaeger, and Hoffman (1988) investigated whether the relationship between attachment security and independence in children differs as a function of their mothers' employment status. Their findings indicated that when mothers were employed, children who had secure attachment relationships with their mothers were also rated as more independent. This relationship between security of attachment and independence in children's behavior was not observed when mothers were homemaking full-time.

Weinraub et al.'s (1988) findings that the security of mother-child attachment is associated with independence in children of employed women, but not in children of women who remain at home, have several interesting implications for research. First, we need to determine whether the Strange Situation paradigm is as valid a measure of the quality of relationships between employed women and their young children as it is for nonemployed women and their children. To assess validity, we need longitudinal studies to determine whether the quality of mothers' caregiving in the first year predicts children's attachment classifications, both when mothers are employed and when mothers are not employed. When mothers are employed, we also need to establish whether attachment classifications based on children's behavior in the Strange Situation predict children's social competence later in the course of development.

A broader implication of Weinraub et al.'s (1988) finding of different developmental correlates of attachment as a function of maternal status is that different contexts of parental employment may foster different kinds of competencies in children. For example, children in dual-earner families may be encouraged to develop competencies such as independence, which will especially suit them to assume similar nontraditional family role arrangements in adulthood (Hoffman, 1979, 1989). If this is the case, why haven't we seen more evidence of differences in children's outcomes in studies comparing the children of employed and nonemployed women? A first reason is that differences may be subtle, and their detection may require the use of specialized measures. Indeed, when measures of more specific competencies are used, for example of sex-role attitudes or daughters' career aspirations, differences are more likely to be observed (Hoffman, 1989). A second reason is because key mediating or moderating factors may not have been taken into account. For example, Bronfenbrenner, Alvarez, and Henderson (1984) found that the relationship between mothers' employment status and their favorable perceptions of their children depended on the child's sex and the family's social class status. That is, daughters were described in the most favorable terms when mothers were more educated and employed full time. In contrast, sons received more favorable descriptions when mothers remained at home.

Whether or not children's competencies differ as a function of parents' work context, it may be that different processes shape development in different contexts of work. Other findings from the Weinraub et al. (1988) study provide supportive evidence on this point. Specifically, different factors predicted security of mother-child attachments in dual- and single-earner families, even though children in these two contexts were equally likely to have secure attachments to their mothers. In dual-earner families, mothers' satisfaction with child care arrangements predicted child attachment security. In traditional single-earner families, mothers' personal coping abilities predicted attachment security. Patterns of relationships among social support variables, marital adjustment, and mothers' satisfaction with their roles also varied for the two groups, leading the authors to conclude that family processes may indeed vary as a function of maternal employment.

Taken together, findings from studies of early relationships suggest that employment does not interfere with the sensitive caregiving that is a prerequisite for the development of secure ties between mother and child and for the child's emotional security. How is it, then, that "good" mothering is accomplished in different contexts? Perhaps work makes little difference for women who are easily able to provide responsive care, and for those who have untroubled personal histories, strong personal resources, and close relationships that are stable and supportive. However, it is possible that work situations can tip the balance in either direction in terms of the quality of care that mothers are able to provide when they are in more vulnerable situations, less prepared for mothering, troubled by personal problems, or socially isolated.

In more vulnerable personal situations, it may be that difficult work conditions, such as very long hours (Owen & Cox, 1988), will be sources of stress and will impede the quality of maternal caregiving. In contrast, more positive work situations may provide mothers with assistance in managing work-family schedule conflicts or with sources of emotional support. Consistent with this hypothesis, recent studies of qualities of work settings have linked social support in the work environment to well-being (Repetti, 1987) and less role strain in women (Greenberger, Goldberg, Hamill, O'Neil, & Payne, 1989). Opportunities to master work tasks may also affirm a sense of personal competence and self-esteem (Kohn, 1977; Kohn & Schooler, 1983; Mortimer & Lorence, 1979; Mortimer & Finch, 1986). As discussed later in this chapter, we have much to learn about how specific aspects of work affect adult well-being and competence in family roles. What is clear is that good mothering and the healthy development of children can be fostered in a variety of settings. Thus, the key issue for future research is to determine what mechanisms are involved in different settings, rather than to continue to search for the one "good" context for children and their mothers.

Father-Child Relationships

Researchers who have attempted to understand the implications of mothers' employment for family processes and children's development now have begun to examine fathers' roles in dual-earner and single-earner families. There have been two schools of thought about how fathers' relationships with children will be affected by their wives' employment. According to one view, fathers in dual-earner families may spend more time caring for their children, form closer ties, and thus have a more positive influence in their children's lives (see Hoffman, 1989, for a review). This point-of-view has received some support from findings that fathers in dual-earner families spend proportionally more time doing housework and caring for children than traditional single-earner fathers. These differences usually are small, however, and they may arise from decreases in the time that wives spend, rather than from actual increases in time spent by husbands (Pleck, 1984).

A contrasting point-of-view comes from findings that dual-earner fathers who spend more time caring for children also show more irritation towards children (Easterbrooks & Goldberg, 1985), and report more marital dissatisfaction (Crouter et al., 1987). Similarly, Baruch and Barnett (1986) found that fathers' who did more family work were more critical of their wives and that their wives reported less satisfaction with life and with their balance of work and family responsibilities, whether the families were dual- or single-earner. Although these studies did not examine children's outcomes, their results suggest that fathers in more traditional family situations, where wives are not involved in paid work, may in fact have a more positive influence on their children's development.

Findings from my own research are consistent with this hypothesis. I examined associations between measures of fathers' and mothers' shared activities with children and children's social and academic competence in school for a sample of dual-earner and traditional single-earner families with 1st graders. Results indicated that fathers in dual-earner families spent more time in shared activities with their children than did fathers in single-earner families. However, in dual-earner families, these father-child shared activities were negatively related to children's school outcomes. Only in single-earner families were father-child shared activities related positively to children's outcomes (Moorehouse, 1989).

One possible explanation for findings of negative correlates of father involvement in dual-earner families is that there are differences in the amount of support that employed and nonemployed women provide for the relationships that fathers have with their children. Perhaps when mothers are employed, they are no longer as available to operate the family's "emotional switchboard" and to help fathers make close emotional connections with their children. Another possibility is that more of the single-earner fathers who spend lots of time with their children are highly motivated and have chosen to do so. Perhaps in dual-earner families, more fathers feel pressed into service instead, and so they resent the greater responsibility that they have taken on for children. Indeed, qualitative accounts indicate that men feel they are *helping* their employed wives by doing housework or by "baby sitting" their own children (Hochschild, 1989; Lein, 1979). They may feel that child care is women's work, not men's work.

Such findings suggest that we will need to search further to find fathers who are doing a lot of the child-rearing, while avoiding tension in their relationships with their children or spouses. Will we find these fathers among well-educated men in dual-career families who, when asked to fill out surveys of social attitudes by researchers, report egalitarian views? Perhaps not. Hochschild's (1989) case studies vividly illustrate the struggles that some well-educated dual-career couples are having over work and family roles. It could be that men in dual-career families compare their own lot with that of their fathers. They may feel that, compared to their fathers, they are doing a great deal more of the work around the house. And they may be right. However, their wives may be aware of how much more they could be doing. Research comparing the family roles and relationships of men whose own mothers did or did not work outside the home could shed some light on these issues. This question raises the broader issue of how sex role socialization of children is affected by parents' involvement in work and family roles. We turn to this topic later in the chapter when we consider more specific links among parents' work experiences, family socialization processes, and children's development.

In summary, there is no simple correspondence between the work and family role configurations of husbands and wives (Pleck, 1984). That is, husbands do not simply pick up where their employed wives leave off. Researchers need to further examine the possibility that different processes may underlie fathers' family participation in different contexts of work and family. In addition to further investigating the impact that mothers' employment has on fathers' family participation, we need to investigate the impact that men's own work situations have on relationships with their children, especially in families where mothers are also employed. One possibility is that, if their wives are also employed, men will talk more about what has happened at work and their feelings of stress or of satisfaction with their jobs. As a result, children in dual-earner families may be affected more strongly by their fathers' work-related moods.

Parental Control and Parental Monitoring

The studies of mother-child and father-child relationships reviewed in the previous sections focused on aspects of warmth and closeness in parent-child relationships. Other key dimensions of child-rearing interactions, including parental styles of control and parental monitoring, have also been studied. In this work, we continue to see a social problem perspective predominate as researchers examine whether the effectiveness of these child-rearing practices is disrupted in dual-earner families.

Parental Styles of Control. Additional evidence about how parents' work affects child-rearing practices and their outcomes in families with young children comes from a study of family socialization by Greenberger and Goldberg (1989). An important feature of this work is its focus on dimensions of parenting styles that have important implications for children's social relationships, self-competence, and motivation (Baumrind, 1967, 1978; Maccoby & Martin, 1983). Greenberger and Goldberg related both men's and women's investment in work and in parenting to their styles of parental control, demands for mature behavior, and to favorable perceptions of children's behavior. Their data were obtained from a survey of men and women in dual-earner, middle-class families with preschool-aged children. The measure of men's and women's work involvement included parents' hours of work and time spent on work after hours, as well as items that tapped psychological commitment to work (i.e., centrality of work to the self, salience of work relative to other activities, and levels of aspiration).

For both men and women in dual-earner families, it was the degree of investment in parenting that predicted parents' socialization practices and views of their children, rather than their degree of investment in work. These findings thus challenge the social problem perspective that children are most influenced by the absence or work-related fatigue of employed parents. Indeed, the results suggest that there may be special benefits from a high commitment to both work and parenting. Greenberger and Goldberg found that women were most likely to parent in an authoritative manner when their commitments both to work and to parenting were high. These authors suggest that a "zestful" personality may explain this pattern. While it may be correct to attribute this finding to personality factors, it is also possible that situational factors, including qualities of work settings, may be involved. Thus, it would be fruitful for new research to examine whether certain kinds of work environments help engender a high commitment to both work and parenting, and thus facilitate authoritative styles of child-rearing.

Parental monitoring of children's behavior and whereabouts is another key family process variable whose implications for development have been well documented (Patterson, 1982, 1988; Patterson & Stouthamer-Loeber, 1984). In micro-analytic studies of coercive family processes, Patterson and his colleagues have found that poor parental monitoring contributes to the development of conduct problems in children. In turn, the resulting conduct problems further weaken parental monitoring. Over time, children's antisocial behavior generalizes to include interactions in school settings and with peers.

Crouter et al. (1990) examined the effectiveness of parental monitoring in dual-earner and single-earner two-parent families with 4th- and 5th-grade children. Parental monitoring was assessed through separate telephone interviews with children and parents about the child's experiences, whereabouts, playmates, and activities for the day. The effectiveness of parental monitoring was indexed by the number of discrepancies between parents' and children's reports. Consistent with previous research by Patterson and his colleagues, boys who were less well monitored by parents did less well in school and had more conduct problems, according to their own reports and to reports by parents. However, there was no association between earner status and the amount of parental monitoring that children received or children's outcomes. That is, boys and girls in dual-earner families were as well monitored and were doing as well as children in single-earner families.

Crouter et al.'s (1990) results do not rule out the possibility that monitoring plays a different role in single- and dual-earner families, for there may be a different relationship to child outcomes in each of the two contexts. Results from analyses addressing this possibility are intriguing, although not altogether consistent. Results indicated that dual-earner parents of less well-monitored boys perceived their child's conduct to be significantly more problematic than did other parents. This was especially true for dual-earner mothers of less well monitored boys. However, other child outcomes, including children's self-perceptions of conduct and measures of school performance (reported both by parents and children), did not show these differences. The authors reasoned that dual-earner mothers, tired and irritable after a long day of work, housework, and caregiving, may be more reactive to boys' acting-out behavior. Mothers may be more reactive than fathers because mothers do more of the monitoring and because mothers are less likely to view unruly behavior as simply "boys just being boys."

The longitudinal follow-up that Crouter and McHale are now conducting may provide an opportunity to examine whether these patterns have long term consequences for children's achievement and adjustment.

Summary

The few studies that have examined questions about differences in family processes involving parent-child relationships suggest, for the most part, that parents in dual-earner families and parents in traditional single-earner families are likely to follow similar child-rearing practices and orientations. That is, dual-earner parents are as likely as parents in traditional single-earner families to feel a strong commitment to parenting, engage younger children in shared child-centered activities, and monitor the whereabouts of older children. Although parents' engagement in these practices does not seem to depend on their employment circumstances, there is evidence to suggest that these practices can affect children differently, depending on the circumstances of parental employment. For example, there are my findings, discussed earlier, that raise the possibility that the benefits of frequent shared mother-child activities and the costs of infrequent activities are magnified when mothers change their hours of employment (Moorehouse, 1991a). Perhaps the effects of authoritative styles of parenting and other child-rearing practices are also magnified under stressful work conditions, but this is not yet known. Also missing is an understanding of the qualities of work situations that benefit adult well-being, family relationships, or children's development.

DEFINING AN AGENDA FOR NEW RESEARCH

It is clearly important to learn more about the specific qualities of work situations that affect parental well-being and family life for mothers, fathers, and children. This section defines three tasks for new research and presents promising lines of research. A first task has been suggested before: to consider the possibilities for positive as well as negative carryover from work to family relationships and children's lives. A second, closely related, task is to identify the aspects of work that influence adult well-being and family life. We need to understand how women and men are affected by the work that they do so that we can understand how children will be affected by the work that their mothers and fathers do. This perspective views work contexts as settings for adult development (Crouter, 1984), and thus provides an alternative to the social problem perspective.

We need to do more than merely specify the influential aspects of parents' work, however. A third task for research is to examine whether some kinds of family socialization processes are more affected by parents' work than are other processes. For example, are the socialization processes that shape sex roles, motivational orientations, achievement behavior, and knowledge about the world of work especially open to influence from what parents do at work and how work and family roles are coordinated at home? In particular, do daughters derive special benefits from the role models of achievement that their working mothers provide? This idea is evaluated in light of evidence from research on the development of achievement-related attitudes and behaviors during middle childhood and adolescence.

Task 1: Including Positive Possibilities

Spillover involves a direct transfer of skills, moods, or qualities of relationships from work to family or family to work (Staines, 1980; Voydanoff, 1987). Spillover models thus allow for positive as well as negative connections between work and family, although studies have focused more on negative spillover (Baruch, Biener, & Barnett, 1987; Bolger, DeLongis, Kessler, & Wethington, 1989; Small & Riley, 1990). A noteworthy exception is a study of women's perceptions of positive spillover (or enhancement) in combining work and family roles by Tiejde, Wortman, Downey, Emmons, Biernat, and Lang (1990). Perceptions of role conflict were also examined. The sample consisted of married professional women who had young children. Tiejde et al.'s (1990) results support a multidimensional model of spillover, in which enhancement and conflict are essentially independent dimensions, rather than a unidimensional model, in which enhancement and conflict are opposite ends of a single continuum. Additional results raised the possibility that women's symptoms of depression and their satisfaction with parental roles may be a function of their location on each of these dimensions. For example, women experiencing high enhancement and low conflict in combining work and family roles reported fewer symptoms of depression and more satisfaction with marriage and parenting than other groups of women.

We do not yet know how conditions of work contribute to role enhancements and conflicts or how children are affected. To shed light on these issues, the next section reviews promising lines of work on the problems and potentials that stem from two aspects of work situations: job autonomy and social support.

Task 2: Influential Dimensions of Employment

A focus on job autonomy and social support contrasts with the emphasis that is usually placed on women's role satisfaction as the key variable mediating the effects of maternal status on family life and relationships. Findings from studies of women's role satisfaction consistently show that greater role satisfaction is associated with more favorable outcomes for the mother-child relationship and children's well-being (Hock, 1978; Lerner & Galambos, 1985, 1988). Although these studies have made good progress in understanding the subjective side of women's experiences, we have not yet learned much about the objective conditions of work life or of home life that lead women to be satisfied or dissatisfied with their roles. This gap may reflect tendencies to view women's satisfaction as determined more strongly by their own dispositions than by the situations that they experience at work (Feldberg & Glenn, 1979). However, the substantial body of research on job autonomy attests to the influence that conditions of work can have on adult well-being and on family relationships.

Job Autonomy. The program of research by Kohn and his colleagues (Kohn, 1977; Kohn & Schooler, 1983) represents the most impressive effort to elucidate connections between class-associated occupational dimensions of work experience, adult functioning, and socialization of children. In Kohn's model, the structural imperatives of jobs, including the degree of routinization, the amount of autonomy from direct supervision, and the substantive complexity of work tasks, give rise to values of either autonomy or conformity in workers. On the one hand, the greater the freedom experienced on the job and the more complex and challenging the work, the more likely the worker is to place a high value on self-direction. On the other hand, the more constraining and routine the work, the more likely the worker is to value conformity.

The model linking class-associated occupational conditions to adult psychological functioning has been tested successfully for workers of both sexes. Although research on women has been limited to cross-sectional analyses (Miller, Schooler, Kohn, & Miller, 1983), relationships have been demonstrated for men using longitudinal data and causal modeling techniques to establish the direction of effects (Kohn, 1977; Kohn & Schooler, 1983; Mortimer & Finch, 1986; Mortimer & Lorence, 1979).

Kohn (1977) examined the additional link between occupational conditions and parental values only for men. According to his model, working-class fathers, who experience little freedom on the job, were expected to value conformity and encourage obedience in their children. In contrast, fathers in higher occupational classes, who are more likely to be self-directed in their work, were expected to endorse child-rearing practices that would encourage their children to be self-directed, rather than conforming. As hypothesized, men functioned differently in the father role according to whether they experienced job conditions that foster conformity or self-direction. Although outcomes for children were not evaluated, this research gives us a persuasive account of some of the links between men's work and family contexts.

The work of Kohn and others provides an account of how social class stratification will be *maintained* across generations through the effects of class-associated work conditions (particularly conditions constraining or encouraging self-direction) on workers' psychological orientations and parental values. Can the job conditions that are typically associated with working class occupations be *modified* to encourage self-direction in the work place and at home? Research suggests that such modifications may be achieved in participative management settings (Crouter, 1984), as discussed next.

Key features of participative work settings are inclusions of workers at all levels of the organization in the decision-making and problem-solving processes of the company. Crouter (1984) examined participative work settings as contexts for adult development and explored the implications of participative work experiences for individual functioning and for family roles and relationships. Open-ended interviews were conducted with a sample of blue-collar workers employed by a machine company noted for its implementation of a participative style of management. In the interviews, workers provided examples of communication and problem-solving skills that were learned at work and then applied at home, especially in interactions with children. A manager and father of four provides one example.

> I have a 16-year-old son and I use some of the things we do at work with him instead of yelling. We listen better here. We let people tell their side. (p. 81)

A second example comes from a machine operator and mother of an 8-year-old.

> I say things to my daughter that I know are a result of the way we do things at work. I ask her, 'What do you think about that?' or 'How would you handle this problem?' I tend to deal with her the way I deal with people at work. The logic is the same. (pp. 81–82)

These comments bring to mind authoritative styles of child-rearing, which have been found to foster children's social and motivational competence (Baumrind, 1967, 1978). However:

> It is likely that only those employees who experience participative work as a learning process that enhances their own competence will in turn shift towards more authoritative modes of parenting. In contrast, workers who perceive participative work as a demanding, stressful experience may generalize their frustration to their relationships with their children by being short-tempered, authoritarian, and so on—a process described by McKinley (1964). (Crouter, 1984, p. 82)

One implication of this body of work is that we need to attend to variations within contexts of employment instead of focusing so single-mindedly on differences between family contexts where mothers are or are not employed. Furthermore, in dual-earner families, we need to ask how parents' work experiences combine to affect family life and children's development. A second implication is that spillover from work to family is likely to depend both on the objective quality of work conditions and on how these conditions are evaluated by the worker (Crouter, 1984). Workers may gain values of self-direction and skill in communication and decision making that may carry over into family life. Questions of how these experiences are transferred to family life and how children are affected require further systematic study.

Social Support and Work-Related Moods. Studies are finding that the social environment of the work place also has implications for adult well-being. For example, in a study of female bank workers, Repetti (1987) found that the quality of a worker's relationship with a supervisor and the general quality of interpersonal relationships in the work place predicted workers' feelings of depression and anxiety outside of the work setting. Because the work environment was rated both by individuals and by their coworkers, Repetti was able to show that these relationships were not simply a function of individual's response tendencies.

Do work-related feelings of anxiety and depression transfer to family relationships as spillover models would suggest? Or do feelings change or get put aside when workers reach home as compensation occurs? The little evidence available suggests that work moods may affect family life at least some of the time and that both spillover and compensation processes may be involved.

Consistent with a compensation model, a study of male workers by Crouter and her colleagues (Crouter, Perry-Jenkins, Huston, & Crawford, 1989) found that men's high levels of stress and fatigue at the end of the work day were associated with low involvement in housework. A similar connection between work stress and low involvement in home life was found by Repetti (1989) in a longitudinal study of the marital interactions of male air traffic controllers. Repetti found that work overload resulted in social withdrawal and less expression of anger at home. Additional findings of compensation have been reported in a longitudinal study of "stress contagion" by Bolger et al. (1989). Bolger and his colleagues found that male and female workers reduced their housework to compensate for heavy loads at work.

Negative spillover from work to home also occurred in two of these studies. Crouter et al. (1989) found that high levels of stress were associated with more negative marital interactions. Similarly, Bolger et al.'s (1989) research indicated that, after an argument with someone at work, workers were more likely to come home and argue with their spouses. Negative spillover from home to work also occurred, but only for men; after an argument at home, men were more likely to argue with someone at work.

These three studies have found relationships between work stress and home life that are similar to the patterns of energy deficit and negative spillover that Piotrkowski (1979) observed in a small-scale qualitative study of men's work experiences and family lives. For other men, Piotrkowski (1979) observed a contrasting pattern of positive spillover, in which energy, enthusiasm, and other good feelings about the work day carried over into interactions at home. Quantitative evidence of positive spillover, although limited, includes findings from a study of low-income employed women and their adolescent daughters by Piotrkowski and Katz (1983). Mothers' reports of positive job mood correlated with daughters' ratings of their mothers' acceptance and availability. Findings from my own work also suggest that school-aged children are aware of their mothers' and fathers' positive and negative feelings about work. Moreover, perceptions of qualities of parents' work predict children's confidence in their academic abilities (Moorehouse, 1991b; Moorehouse & Sanders, in press).

Although a number of conceptual and methodological issues must be resolved (Crouter et al., 1989), findings thus far underscore the need for a balanced consideration of both the problems and possibilities that can arise from specific conditions of mothers' and fathers' employment. As discussed below, the next step is for research to link conditions of work to specific aspects of family socialization processes.

Task 3: Connecting Parents' Work to Specific Aspects of Family Socialization Processes and Children's Development

A third task for research is to examine whether some kinds of family socialization processes are affected more by parents' work conditions than are other processes. One possibility is that work conditions especially affect the socialization processes that shape sex roles, motivational orientations, achievement behavior, and knowledge about the world of work.

For girls, less rigid sex-role stereotypes, higher aspirations, and greater respect for women's competence are associated with mothers' employment (Hoffman, 1986, 1989). One explanation for these findings is that daughters derive special benefits from the role models of achievement that their employed mothers provide (Bronfenbrenner & Crouter, 1982; Hoffman, 1980, 1986). As intuitively appealing as this idea may be, we do not yet have empirical evidence that daughters' achievement success changes as a result of their mothers' employment. There is also a conceptual problem with this explanation. Most women are employed in female-dominated occupations where pay rates are lower, tasks are routine, opportunities for advancement are meager, and the type of work conforms to traditional gender role stereotypes. The role modeling hypothesis does not give an account of how mothers' employment under these conditions would contribute to daughters' development of the attitudes and behaviors known to affect achievement success (see Dweck & Legett, 1988; Eccles, 1987 for reviews of achievement motivation research). How sons would be affected is also unclear from the role modeling account and from the available empirical evidence. Although earlier studies sometimes found that boys scored lower on achievement tests when their mothers were employed, more recent longitudinal studies have not confirmed these findings (Gottfried, Gottfried, & Bathhurst, 1988; Hoffman, 1989).

One way to address these issues is to build on studies of job autonomy, and examine whether mothers' opportunities for self-direction (in nonprofessional and professional occupations) are associated with mothers' achievement-related interactions with their children, and children's motivational outcomes. Patterns need to be examined for both sons and daughter to determine whether processes are gender specific. Another important dimension to examine further is social support in the work place. Rather than affecting achievement or independence training, social support may have implications for mothers' warmth and availability and, thereby, affect children's confidence in their abilities.

These same aspects of fathers' job situations need to be considered, especially in dual-earner families where spillover from both mothers' and fathers' jobs may occur. Also important to consider is the possibility that fathers' participation in family work and parents' sex-role attitudes may mediate effects of parents' employment on both daughters and sons.

An additional issue to consider is children's own perceptions of the positive and negative aspects of their parents' work. As much as concerns about children's welfare have figured in the study of mothers' employment, we know very little about children's points of view (Piotrkowski & Stark, 1987). My own work suggests that school-aged children feel quite certain about their knowledge of some qualities of their parents' work, and these qualities are associated with children's confidence in their academic abilities and with their vocational interests (Moorehouse, 1991b; Moorehouse & Sanders, in press).

Finally, the kind of influence that parents' work has on family socialization processes is likely to depend on children's ages. Changes in children's competencies with development may determine whether a particular aspect of parents' work is a source of stress or support for further development.

SUMMARY AND CONCLUSIONS

This chapter has argued that an examination of differences in family process variables as a function of maternal employment status has been a useful first step in research on work and family dynamics. The research evidence clearly shows that good mothering and healthy child development can be accomplished in a variety of work and family contexts. That is, there are few signs of differences in family processes as a function of maternal employment status per se. Mothers in dual-earner families seem to spend as much time in shared child-centered activities with young children as do mothers who remain at home (Hoffman, 1984, 1989), and dual-earner parents are as effective as traditional single-earner parents in monitoring the behavior and whereabouts of older children (Crouter et al., 1990). Thus, a single-minded focus on the problems associated with mothers' employment will provide few insights into the connections between work and family life that are important for children's development. To move beyond a social problem perspective will require a shift in methodological approach as well as a shift in conceptual perspective.

The interactional approach represents a promising advance in research strategy. This approach takes the additional step of examining outcomes for children and investigates whether the same child-rearing practices are equally effective in different earner contexts, or whether child-rearing interactions affect children differently depending on the work that their parents do. It has already yielded evidence that family processes may operate differently in different contexts of parental work. For example, although mothers' engagement in shared activities with children does not differ as a function of their pattern of employment, infrequent shared activities seem to affect children differently depending on their mothers' work pattern (Moorehouse, 1991a). Although the interactional approach represents an important advance, its application has been constrained by the pervasive and enduring view of maternal employment as a social problem. That is, studies using an interactional approach have tended to search for the specific conditions under which maternal employment disrupts family processes, or they have attempted to identify the factors that buffer maternal employment's potentially disruptive impacts (Crouter et al., 1990; Gottfried & Gottfried, 1988; Greenberger & Goldberg, 1989; Moorehouse, 1991a).

For researchers seeking to move beyond a social problem perspective on maternal employment, a first task is to identify the positive and negative dimensions of parents' work experiences and to discover how experiences at work transfer to family life. A closely related task is to learn more about how parents themselves are affected by specific experiences at work and about how these work experiences then carry over into family relationships and children's lives. Job autonomy and social support in the work place are two dimensions of work experience that especially deserve further study. To study these and other potentially influential dimensions of work, researchers must go beyond the usual comparisons between dual-earner families and traditional single-earner families and examine variations among dual-earner families.

Research is also needed on single-parent families, most of which are headed by employed women. It is in this group that variations in qualities of work situations may have the most impact on family processes. Thus, studies of this group are needed to fully understand the connections between work and family which are important for children's development.

A final task for research is to determine whether some kinds of family socialization processes are more affected by parents' work than are other processes. For example, the socialization processes that shape sex role attitudes, motivational orientations, achievement behavior, and knowledge about the world of work may be most open to influence from what parents do at work and from how work and family roles are coordinated at home.

In sum, although traditional arrangements (with mother at home and father at work) will continue to suit some families, most two-parent families will find that the employment of both parents is needed to pay the bills, to realize future goals such as a college education for children, or to achieve a sense of adult self-worth. In single-parent families headed by employed women, children may be especially affected by aspects of mothers' employment. Thus, a fuller understanding of the advantages and disadvantages of different work and family arrangements at different points in family life and children's development is urgently needed.

REFERENCES

Baumrind, D. (1967). Child care practices anteceding three patterns of preschool behavior. *Genetic Psychology Monographs, 75,* 43–88.

Baumrind, D. (1978). Parental disciplinary practices and social competence in children. *Youth and Society, 9,* 239–276.

Baruch, G. K., & Barnett, R. C. (1986). Consequences of fathers' participation in family work: Parents' role strain and well-being. *Journal of Personality and Social Psychology, 51,* 983–992.

Baruch, G. K., Biener, L., & Barnett, R. C. (1987). Women and gender in research on work and family stress. *American Psychologist, 12,* 130–136.

Belsky, J. (1988). The "effects" of infant day care reconsidered. *Early Childhood Research Quarterly, 3,* 235–272.

Bolger, N., Caspi, A., Downey, G., & Moorehouse, M. (1988). Development in context: Research perspectives. In N. Bolger, A. Caspi, G. Downey, & M. Moorehouse (Eds.), *Persons in context: Developmental processes.* New York: Cambridge University Press.

Bolger, N., DeLongis, A., Kessler, R. C., & Wethington, E. (1989). The contagion of stress across multiple roles. *Journal of Marriage and the Family, 51,* 175–183.

Bronfenbrenner, U. (1979). *The ecology of human development.* Cambridge, MA: Harvard University Press.

Bronfenbrenner, U. (1986). Ecology of the family as a context for human development: Research perspectives. *Developmental Psychology, 22,* 723–742.

Bronfenbrenner, U., Alvarez, W. F., & Henderson, C. R., Jr. (1984). Working and watching: Maternal employment status and parents' perception of their three-year-old children. *Child Development, 55,* 1362–1378.

Bronfenbrenner, U., & Crouter, A. C. (1982). Work and family through time and space. In S. B. Kamerman & C. D. Hayes (Eds.), *Families that work: Children in a changing world.* Washington: National Academy Press.

Clarke-Stewart, K. A. (1988). "The 'effects' of infant day care reconsidered" reconsidered: Risks for parents, children, and researchers. *Early Childhood Research Quarterly, 3,* 293–318.

Crouter, A. C. (1984). Participative work as an influence on human development. *Journal of Applied Developmental Psychology, 5,* 71–90.

Crouter, A. C., MacDermid, S. M., McHale, S. M., & Perry-Jenkins, M. (1990). Parental monitoring in dual- and single-earner families: Implications for children's school performance and conduct. *Developmental Psychology, 26,* 649–657.

Crouter, A. C., Perry-Jenkins, M., Huston, T. L., & Crawford, D. W. (1989). The influence of work-induced psychological states on behavior at home. *Basic and Applied and Social Psychology, 10,* 273–292.

Crouter, A. C., Perry-Jenkins, M., Huston, T. L., & McHale, S. M. (1987). Processes underlying father involvement in dual-earner and single-earner families. *Developmental Psychology, 23,* 431–440.

Dweck, C. S., & Legett, E. L. (1988). A social cognitive approach to motivation and personality. *Psychological Review, 95,* 256–273.

Easterbrooks, M. A., & Goldberg, W. A. (1985). Effects of early maternal employment on toddlers, mothers, and fathers. *Developmental Psychology, 4,* 774–783.

Feldberg, R. L., & Glenn, E. N. (1979). Male and female: Job versus gender models in the sociology of work. *Social Problems, 26,* 524–538.

Eccles, J. S. (1987). Gender roles and women's achievement-related decisions. *Psychology of Women Quarterly, 11,* 135–172.

Gottfried, A. E., Gottfried, A. W. (1988). Maternal employment, family environment, and children's development: Infancy through the school years. In A. E. Gottfried & A. W. Gottfried (Eds.), *Maternal employment and children's development: Longitudinal research.* New York: Plenum Press.

Greenberger, E., & Goldberg, W. A. (1989). Work, parenting, and the socialization of children. *Developmental Psychology, 25,* 22–35.

Greenberger, E., Goldberg, W. A., Hamill, S., O'Neill, R., & Payne, C. K. (1989). Contributions of a supportive work environment to parents' well-being and orientation to work. *American Journal of Community Psychology, 17*(6), 755–783.

Hochschild, A. (1989). *The second shift: Working parents and the revolution at home.* New York: Viking Press.

Hock, E. (1978). Working and nonworking mothers with infants: Perceptions of their careers, their infants' needs, and satisfactions with mothering. *Developmental Psychology, 14,* 37–43.

Hoffman, L. W. (1979). Maternal employment: 1979, *American Psychologist, 32,* 859–865.

Hoffman, L. W. (1980). The effects of maternal employment on the academic attitudes and performance of school-age children. *School Psychology Review, 9,* 319–336.

Hoffman, L. W. (1984). Maternal employment and the young child. In M. Perlmutter (Ed.), *Parent-child interaction and parent-child relations in child development. The Minnesota Symposia on Child Psychology* (Vol. 17, pp. 101–128). Hillsdale, NJ: Lawrence Erlbaum Associates.

Hoffman, L. W. (1986). Work, family, and the child. In M. S. Pallak & R. O. Perloff (Eds.), *Psychology and work: Productivity, change, and employment* (pp. 173–220). Washington, DC: American Psychological Association.

Hoffman, L. W. (1989). Effects of maternal employment in the two-parent family. *American Psychologist, 44,* 283–292.

Kohn, M. L. (1977). *Class and conformity.* Chicago: University of Chicago Press.

Kohn, M., L., & Schooler, C. (1983). *Work and personality.* Norwood, NJ: Ablex.

Lein, L. (1979). Working couples as parents. In E. Corfman (Ed.), *Families today* (Vol. 1). Bethesda, MD: National Institute of Mental Health.

Lerner, J. V., & Galambos, N. L. (1985). Maternal role satisfaction, mother-child interactions, and child temperament. *Developmental Psychology, 21,* 1157–1164.

Lerner, J. V., & Galambos, N. L. (1988). The influences of maternal employment across life: The New York Longitudinal Study. In A. E. Gottfried & A. W. Gottfried (Eds.), *Maternal employment and children's development: Longitudinal research.* New York: Plenum.

Maccoby, E. E., & Martin, J. A. (1983). Socialization in the context of the family: Parent-child interaction. In E. M. Hetherington (Ed.) & P. H. Mussen (Series Ed.), *Handbook of child psychology: Socialization, personality and social development, 4,* 1–101. New York: Wiley.

Miller, J., Schooler, C., Kohn, M. L., & Miller, K. A. (1983). In M. L. Kohn & C. Schooler (Eds.), *Work and personality.* Norwood, NJ: Ablex.

Moorehouse, M. (1989). *Fathers' and mothers' shared activities with children when mothers are employed.* Paper presented to the Family Research Consortium, Cape Cod, Massachusetts.

Moorehouse, M. (1991a). Linking maternal employment patterns to mother-child activities and children's school competence. *Developmental Psychology, 27,* 295–303.

Moorehouse, M. (1991b). *Linking specific aspects of parents' employment to children's academic attitudes and work interests*. Paper presented to the Society for Research in Child Development, Seattle, Washington.

Moorehouse, M., & Sanders, P. E. (in press). Children's feelings of school competence and perceptions of parents' work in four socio-cultural contexts. *Social Development*.

Mortimer, J. T., & Finch, M. D. (1986). The development of self-esteem in the early work career. *Work and Occupations, 13*(2), 217–239.

Mortimer, J. T., & Lorence, J. (1979). Occupational experience and the self-concept: A longitudinal study. *Social Psychology Quarterly, 42*(4), 307–323.

Owen, M. T., & Cox, M. J. (1988). Maternal employment and the transition to parenthood. In A. E. Gottfried & A. W. Gottfried (Eds.), *Maternal employment and children's development: Longitudinal research*. New York: Plenum Press.

Patterson, G. R. (1982). *Coercive family processes*. Eugene, OR: Castilia.

Patterson, G. R. (1988). Family processes: Loops, levels, and linkages. In N. Bolger, A. Caspi, G. Downey, & M. Moorehouse (Eds.), *Persons in context: Developmental processes*. New York: Cambridge University Press.

Patterson, G. R., & Stouthamer-Loeber, M. (1984). The correlation of family management practices and delinquency. *Child Development*, 55, 1299–1307.

Piotrkowski, C. (1979). *Work and the family system*. New York: The Free Press.

Piotrkowski, C., & Katz, M. H. (1983). Work experience and family relations among working-class and lower-middle class families. In H. Z. Lopata & J. H. Pleck (Eds.), *Research in the interweave of social roles: Families and jobs*. Greenwich, CT: JAI Press Inc.

Piotrkowski, C., & Stark, E. (1987). Children and adolescents look at their parents jobs. In J. H. Lewko (Ed.), *New directions for child development: Vol. 35. How children view the world of work*. San Francisco: Jossey-Bass.

Pleck, J. H. (1984). Men's family work: Three perspectives and some new data. In P. Voydanoff (Ed.), *Work and family: Changing roles of men and women*, Palo Alto, CA: Mayfield Publishing Co.

Repetti, R. L. (1987). Individual and common components of the social environment at work and psychological well-being. *Journal of Personality and Social Psychology, 52*, 710–720.

Repetti, R. L. (1989). Effects of daily workload on subsequent behavior during marital interaction: The roles of social withdrawal and spouse support. *Journal of Personality and Social Psychology, 57*, 651–659.

Small, S. A., & Riley, D. (1990). Toward a multidimensional assessment of work spillover into family life. *Journal of Marriage and the Family, 52*, 51–61.

Staines, G. L. (1980). Spillover versus compensation: A review of the literature on the relationship between work and nonwork. *Human Relations, 33*, 111–129.

Thompson, R. A. (1988). The effects of infant day care through the prism of attachment theory. *Early Childhood Research Quarterly, 3*, 273–282.

Tiedje, L. B., Wortman, C. B., Downey, G., Emmons, C., Biernat, M., & Lang, E. (1990). Women with multiple roles: Role-compatibility perceptions, satisfactions, and mental health. *Journal of Marriage and the Family, 52*, 63–72.

Voydanoff, P. (1987). *Work and family life*. Newbury Park, CA: Sage Publications.

Weinraub, M., Jaeger, E., & Hoffman, L. (1988). Predicting infant outcome in families of employed and nonemployed mothers. *Early Childhood Research Quarterly, 8*, 361–378.

12 Perspectives on Research in the Early Years of Family Life: Costs and Benefits of Nontraditional Variations

Susan Crockenberg
University of Vermont

In the 1980s researchers concerned with the development of children in families addressed three key questions: (a) What is the process by which family characteristics influence developmental outcomes? (b) What contribution do fathers make to this process? and (c) How does the family's social context affect family process, or affect the way in which family process contributes to human behavioral development. Each chapter in this section makes a unique contribution to one or more of these questions. As a collection, the chapters set the stage for family research in the 1990s. A central theme of this stage setting is that family differences that deviate from some normative view of family structure or roles do not in themselves constitute family problems.

Family Process. Family process refers to the dynamics of family interaction that explain patterns of correlations previously reported in studies of family variables and developmental outcomes. To illustrate, Cowan, Cowan, and Kerig replicate the finding that parents treat male and female children differently, but extend earlier work to show that such differential treatment occurs almost exclusively in families in which mothers and fathers differ in parenting style, and is apparent primarily, though not exclusively, in fathers' interactions with girls. Moreover, gender-linked differences in parenting are most clearly evident in parents' reactions to the assertive behavior of boys and girls. This difference may explain, in part, why girls are more likely than boys to develop internalizing reactions, such as depression and anxiety, in response to marital conflict.

Similarly, Janet Johnston expands previous research on conflict in divorcing families to show that parental conflict, by changing the structure and functioning of the family as a working group and the affective relations between members, exposes children to relationships with their parents that have undesirable effects on their development. Simply put, and consistent with considerable research on the correlates of empathy, when the structure of the family fails to support the goals and meet the needs of parents, parents are unable to empathize with and to meet the needs of their children (role diffusion), and may in fact turn to their children to achieve their own goals and needs (role reversal). Johnston argues that the developmental outcomes associated with high conflict vary depending on whether and how conflict affects family structure and on the children's age and temperament-related capacity to understand and cope with the changes that occur in parental behavior. Thus, even high interparental conflict may have no adverse impact on child outcome if it is resolved, or if parents compartmentalize it, limiting the amount of spillover to the parent-child relationship.

Martha Moorehouse adds an important dimension to the focus on family process by indicating that the same process may have a different impact on the child depending on other characteristics of the family. In her study of maternal employment, differences in the amount of shared mother-child activities were more strongly associated with differences in child competence in families with employed mothers than in families with nonemployed mothers. Frequent shared activities were associated with child competence, infrequent shared activities with lack of competence in children of employed mothers. Moorehouse identifies shared activities as part of the process by which employed mothers accommodate to the needs of their children and foster competent child behavior. Similarly, Guy Swanson identifies family decision making as a process by which parents' personality and social-class background may influence the development of differences in children's IQ.

Fathers. During the past 2 decades there has been growing recognition that the father's role in child development has been neglected. With this recognition has come an attempt to rectify the one-sided emphasis on mothers as architects of their children's development. The research reported in these chapters represents the fruits of that endeavor.

As mentioned earlier, the Cowan et al. study of the transition to parenthood indicates that fathers are primarily, though not exclusively, responsible for the sex-differentiated treatment of their children. One implication of this finding is that studies that include only mothers likely underestimate the impact of differential socialization on the development of sex differences, and may lead to the erroneous conclusion that inborn, sex-linked biological differences account for differences between male and female children in behavioral development to a greater extent than is in fact the case.

Johnston's findings confirm that including fathers in studies increases our ability to predict differences in child behavior from differences in the way parents respond to the conflict that accompanies divorce. She found that both mothers' and fathers' scores on the parenting variables predicted child outcomes. Even in instances in which father's or mother's behavior was more salient, both added significantly to the variance in outcome. One of the cautions raised about behavioral research is that associations between predictors and outcomes are significant, but account for a relatively small amount of the observed differences in child behavior. These data confirm that one reason for the low prediction has been sole reliance on differences in mothers to account for differences in the way children respond to family conflict.

Evidence that both fathers and mothers play a critical role in shaping the family interactions that give rise to differences in the child's development comes also from Swanson's data. When fathers had what Swanson describes as "role-appropriate personalities," family decision making was likely to be principled. Mothers' personalities predicted whether a legitimate place was given to the pursuit of personal and special interest in family decision making. Moreover, when the father had a lower score than his wife on personality characteristics associated with leadership, decision-making characteristics were associated with spouse's relative social class positions premaritally. Thus, at least for the cohort that reached adulthood by 1950, father's personality appeared to be a vehicle for circumventing the automatic transmission of class-based decision-making styles across generations.

Moorehouse, too, considers fathers' central role in children's development. She points out that the development of children in families in which mothers are employed outside the home is influenced by fathers' reactions to their own work, as well as by their reactions to spouses' work. Though obvious once stated, this observation is routinely overlooked by researchers who typically infer that differences in child behavior associated with maternal employment are due either to the experiences of children in alternate care settings or to differences in the way their mothers interact with them when they are together. Nor is the possibility of paternal influence merely speculative. Evidence that fathers who do more family work when their wives work outside the home are more irritable with their children suggests that variations in fathers' behavior may well contribute to differences in child outcome typically attributed to other influences.

Social Context. Although all the investigators represented in this section acknowledge that social context affects family process in important ways, Moorehouse argues most explicitly that detailed information about context is necessary in order to understand variation in family process. Her thesis with respect to maternal employment is that knowing a women works outside the home gives us very little information about the impact of that experience on her, and indirectly on the rest of her family. That differences in the work experience exist and likely influence parenting is suggested by the replicated finding that low work satisfaction is associated with less desirable parenting among employed mothers. It is essential, therefore, to know about work conditions, for example, the amount of autonomy in decision-making at work, to understand how a woman's (or man's) experience in the work environment might affect what happens within the family.

Moorehouse calls attention also to the social context in which research is carried out and the impact of that context on the questions researchers ask about the effects of maternal employment. She identifies the pervasive view of maternal employment as a "social problem," even among researchers who anticipate no adverse main effects of employment on parenting and child development. The result of this perspective is that researchers ask under what conditions maternal employment has adverse effects on children or attempt to identify conditions that buffer children from the negative effects of maternal employment presumed to occur in the absence of some positive event that protects the child from the stress of having a mother employed outside the home. Considerably less attention is given to the possibility of positive effects of maternal employment on children. As a consequence, the view of maternal employment as a social problem, albeit only under certain conditions, is perpetuated because the information we acquire bears only on adverse effects.

Implications for Family Research in the 1990s

The researchers whose work is reported in this section identify specific questions that should be pursued in future studies of human development in families. They also identify, often implicitly, the broad conceptual and methodological issues that need to be addressed in family research in the 1990s. It is these issues to which we turn our attention now.

One prescription that emerges from the research reported and discussed in these chapters is the need for greater understanding of the dynamics by which events, structures, and interactions influence human development. To illustrate, from the Cowan et al. chapter we know that fathers are key figures in the differential treatment of boys and girls. Moreover, from Kerig's (1989) analyses, it appears that this differential treatment of girls by fathers is strongly linked to marital dissatisfaction and conflict. As the Cowans point out, however, we can only speculate about the dynamics that underlie these associations. Possibly the differential treatment of daughters by fathers has it origins in the way husbands treat their wives. Husbands who dislike their spouse's assertiveness, may be less satisfied in their marriages, and may dislike and respond negatively to their daughter's assertiveness. This explanation places the locus of influence squarely on the husband/father. Alternately, if men who report more dissatisfaction with their marriages in fact have more assertive spouses, their daughters may learn from their mothers to be assertive with their fathers, and so contribute to the pattern of negative response to assertion that develops between fathers and daughters. The point is that we need more information about what happens over time in families in order to understand the process by which the differential treatment of daughters by fathers develops. Obtaining this information requires both conceptualizations to guide our questions and methodologies appropriate to the questions asked.

A second implication of the research presented in this section is the need to consider a broader range of outcomes than has previously been included in research on families. Janet Johnston draws our attention to the possibility that by limiting the study of the effects of family conflict to externalizing and internalizing behaviors in children we may underestimate the impact of such conflict on children. She documents, for example, that in families characterized by role reversal, children assume the burden of emotional care for parents and siblings and develop "overly responsible, controlling, and pseudo-adult styles of relating to others." Moorehouse suggests a more basic consideration with respect to our choice of outcome. She argues that by focusing on adverse effects, we may miss entirely the benefits of certain family structures. Thus, maternal employment may increase children's ability to function autonomously and to take greater responsibility for family tasks, it may alter their aspirations and expectations concerning adult roles, and it may expose them to different conflict resolution strategies. A related consideration regarding outcome has to do with whose development is of interest. By focusing exclusively on children's development, and considering adult behavior merely as a process variable, we overlook the effect of family structures and interactions on the development of adult family members. It is likely that the developmental needs of adults and children are not always congruent, and that benefits for one group will be achieved at some cost to the other group, at least in the short term. Thus, marital conflict may increase the anxiety of children under some circumstances, but it may be necessary for the adult members of the family to alter their relationships so that each member can continue to grow and develop. Knowing how family processes affect adult and child development allows us to better evaluate their impact on human development.

Another critical need in future research is to expand our study of families to consider the effect of living in family arrangements that deviate from the two-parent, heterosexual family of European background that remains normative in our minds if not in reality. We need to know how adults and children living in single-parent families, in grandparent-grandchild families, in gay/lesbian families, or in first-generation immigrant families develop and how the dynamics of family life support or undermine that development.

Finally, researchers concerned with the impact of family characteristics, interactions, and processes on human behavioral development must forsake the view of differences in families as inherently problematic. This is no easy task because our assumptions about the likely impact of certain family conditions are embedded in both our theories and in the cultural, political, and religious circumstances in which we have been raised and continue to live and do our work. Moorehouse indicates how the failure to question our assumptions has led to an approach to the study of the effects of maternal employment on children that emphasizes adverse effects, and neglects possible benefits. But the need to question our assumptions about likely outcomes is not limited to work on maternal employment. It is critical in the study of the impact of divorce on child development, in the study of the effect of living in a single-parent family, and in the study of the effect of marital conflict between parents. In each of these areas, the assumption has been that the event or structure or type of interaction will adversely affect development unless some other circumstance buffers the child from their full negative impact. This is not to deny the possibility that certain family structures or circumstances increase the risk of pathology or at least of nonoptimal outcome in development. The point is simply that failure to question the assumption of adverse effects directs the research in ways that maintain the assumption without ever having tested it.

REFERENCES

Kerig, P. K. (1989). *The engendered family: The influence of marital satisfaction on gender differences in parent-child interaction.* Doctoral Dissertation. University of California, Berkeley.

III RETHINKING RESEARCH ON FAMILY NETWORKS IN MIDDLE AND OLD AGE

13 An Intergenerational Family Congruence Model

Rosemary McCaslin
California State University, San Bernardino

It is, by now, widely understood that the population of the United States is aging. The social implications of this demographic trend are less clear, however. Aging is not simply an individual occurrence; rather, people age within the same family, community, and other personal systems within which they have spent the earlier years of their lives. By definition, a population with a large proportion of elderly also has a large number of middle-aged adults attempting to care for their parents. Additionally, an aging population will contain children who may benefit from the wisdom and caring of grandparents, but who also may compete with the elder generation for their parents' time and resources. In short, a growing elderly population affects persons of all ages, and it makes necessary a better understanding of family roles and functioning throughout the life cycle.

Considerable empirical data now exist to describe relations and behaviors of family members in adult life (e.g., Troll, 1986). Most important among these findings is that the majority of elderly persons have ongoing relations with their families and that family members provide most of the care needed by dependent elders, regardless of the availability of formal services (Brody, 1985; Brody, Poulshock, & Masciocchi, 1978; Cantor, 1975; Hooyman, Gonyea, & Montgomery, 1985; Horowitz & Dobrof, 1982). In fact, it appears to be nearly universal for at least one adult child to remain in close enough proximity to aging parents for routine contact to occur (Shanas, 1979; Shanas et al., 1968). In the United States, at present, persons over age 65 average one or two contacts per week with their children (Kovar, 1986).

Most existing theoretical models of the family are inadequate to guide analyses of such adult family relations. Often, the interactions of only two generations are considered, usually dependent children and their parents. Functional views of the family tend to emphasize procreation and socialization and, in consequence, they provide little insight into the reasons why families continue to be important after those early-life tasks are complete.

Additionally, family models commonly assume that one central generation or event drives and determines the responses of all other family generations and members. Family stages most often are defined by the developmental stages of dependent children and by the concomitant changes in parents' relation to their offspring from birth to adulthood (e.g., Rhodes, 1980). The few family development models that focus on later life (e.g., Greene, 1986) also tend to define the family narrowly, in this case according to the changing needs of its frail elderly members.

Family developmental tasks or stages are determined by more than simply the presence or absence of young children or frail elderly, or by the degree of dependence that either of those generations may exhibit. Certainly, the comings, goings, successes, or failures of an individual can affect any or all of the other members of a family. However, the needs of one generation, be it children or elderly, do not fully determine the behaviors of other family members. In reality, critical events and developmental tasks may occur simultaneously in the lives of various family members, and families often must struggle to meet the competing needs of various members.[1]

Such internal family conflicts are sufficiently common in midlife that the terms "sandwich" generation (Miller, 1981) and "women in the middle" (Brody, 1981) have been coined to refer to prototypic situations. Middle-aged women are described as struggling with their own developmental tasks while, at the same time, trying to meet the needs of both older and younger generations who depend on their care, resources, and energy. In such situations, the needs and the life-events of all three generations may interact, and such interactions can affect the possibilities available to each generation.

A family's response to the needs of a particular generation or individual must be considered with reference to the competing needs and resources of the other generations and individuals who constitute that family. Further, the circumstances of individual family members change as each moves through time, and these individual changes create continual alterations in the set of interactions that define "the family."

In sum, the circumstances and problems faced by families in an aging society

---

[1]Steinglass (1980) comes to similar conclusions regarding the inadequacy of most conceptual models for viewing alcoholism from a family perspective. He criticizes the tendency of some researchers to emphasize family composition and their failure to view families from a developmental perspective. Steinglass also stresses the need for interactive models, and he notes that there will be wide variations from any *typical* family pattern. However, the model he proposes is focused narrowly on the alcohol-related reciprocal behaviors of abuser and family system and, therefore, the entire family is defined according to changes in only one designated individual (the alcoholic).

tend to be multigenerational, interactive, and complex. Accordingly, family researchers need to broaden their perspectives to consider the changing pressures and opportunities through which individuals remain connected to their families throughout the life cycle.

REQUIREMENTS FOR A MODEL OF LATE LIFE FAMILIES

A family model that is adequate for research on families in late life should be equally useful for studying any family constellation, regardless of the ages (or other individual attributes) of its members. Such a model should be able to guide clinical interventions with specific families and to inform policy decisions that affect families of a particular type, as well as to shape empirical efforts to understand the nature of family lives.

The Intergenerational Family Congruence Model, which is presented here, is designed to achieve those goals by being applicable to any specific family or to any general type of family. It is intended to depict the changing potentials for interaction over time among the individuals who constitute a particular family. Four basic assumptions underlie this approach.

1. *The family is a focal point for individual development throughout the life span.* Family interactions have frequently been viewed as an initial context for growth and learning in childhood. Parents are assumed to play an important role in their children's development, whether viewed as being the earliest love objects, as the primary shapers and reinforcers of learned behavior, or as representatives of the larger community's norms.

Some theorists of adult development likewise view childhood experience as being carried forward in life, to be utilized and refined in newly created natal families and in continuing ties to the family of origin (e.g., Erikson, Erikson, & Kivnick, 1986). Childrearing, for example, may provide vicarious opportunities for parents to relive and rework earlier developmental stages from their own childhoods. Similarly, the aging of their parents may allow adults to anticipate and to prepare for their own aging.

2. *Family members' ability to be helpful to each other is a function of the relative congruence between the current needs and resources of each.* Individuals typically look to their relatives as a primary source of both affective and instrumental support (Brody, 1985; Cantor, 1975; Johnson & Catalano, 1981; Shanas, 1979). Family members' ability to respond effectively to each others' needs, however, may be constrained by a wide range of life circumstances, including health, finances, job demands, and the concurrent needs of other family members.

For example, middle-aged adults, members of the "sandwich" generation, may lack the time and energy needed to provide for the personal care needs of both frail parents and dependent children. Likewise, this middle generation may have insufficient financial resources to augment their own caregiving with the services of paid helpers. In the affective realm, the frailty and impending death of parents may remind the middle-aged offspring of their own aging and may lead to denial of parental dependency. Similarly, a "woman in the middle" experiencing menopausal changes may find that she does not always react objectively to her teenage daughter's emerging sexuality.

At other times, the needs and interests of different generations can facilitate mutually supportive relationships. For example, when elderly grandparents have teen-aged grandchildren, the two generations can be valuable resources for each other. Erikson (Erikson et al., 1986) has suggested that late-life psychosocial issues include a need to reevaluate the sense of personal identity that was originally forged in adolescence and to develop a new sense of self that includes the future of younger generations. Similarly, grandchildren may represent their grandparents' legacy; a grandchild's successes can serve as evidence that the grandparent's contributions will continue to guide the family beyond their own individual lives. Elders who can see their values and their accrued wisdom passing on to future generations are enabled to attain a sense of immortality that facilitates acceptance of their own impending mortality (Spikes, 1980). The adolescent grandchildren may be searching for their own sense of separateness, and they frequently look to adults other than their parents for the guidance they still require (e.g., Konopka, 1976). Grandparents can provide a point-of-view that is different from that of parents while, at the same time, promoting continued identification with the family.

3. *Potentials for interaction among family members may be supportive, conflictual, or benign, and these potentials will change over time and circumstances.* Families are no more static than are the individuals of which they are constituted. The same relatives who are unable to be helpful in one situation may later, as circumstances and perspectives change, become optimal sources of assistance. For example, a middle-aged couple who are overwhelmed today by the concurrent needs of their parents and children may have more time for the parents after the last child leaves home (though perhaps less money if children are in college). Or, an adult daughter may initially experience her mother's decline emotionally, as a threat of abandonment; but with time and with an increased awareness of mortality gained from her mother's aging, the daughter may refine her own career goals to better reflect the time remaining before her own retirement. Once these personal issues are addressed, the daughter may better be able to understand and respond to her mother's growing dependence.

Intergenerational divergence can also occur between a parent and a young child. For example, some mothers return to paid employment when their children begin school, and hence are occupied and supervised during the school day. These changes can be conflictual both for mother and for child. The child still needs individual attention during his hours at home, and the mother may find her time and energy stretched between career concerns and parenting. Additionally, since the latency-age child seeks sameness in her environment as a stable backdrop from which to move into the world, it may be upsetting for the child to realize that her mother is no longer at home, and therefore not potentially available at all times.

4. *A family continues to exist even if one particular generation is not represented by living members.* The absence of a specific generation does not necessarily cause families to dissolve; and in some cases such absence can strengthen family bonds. A couple may marry, in part, out of a desire to have children, yet the marriage often continues as a childless unit if childbearing proves impossible. Families who have lost entire generations through historical disaster often cherish their remaining family members. Likewise, in some families, ancestors are maintained as symbolic members long beyond their historical presence.

BENEFITS OF A DEVELOPMENTAL PERSPECTIVE

A model that describes the complex and dynamic nature of families must focus attention on circumstances in which individual life changes are most likely to occur and to affect family functioning. Both external events and the internal motivation of developmental tasks can lead to *transitional* behaviors (Hamburg & Adams, 1967). During periods when individuals are actively working on a specific developmental issue, they are sometimes referred to as being "in transition" between life stages (Rapoport, 1963). By definition, at such times a person is meeting new demands for which the previously developed patterns of behavior are inadequate; thus, the motivation to enlarge his or her behavioral repertoire is higher than at other times. Similarly, changes in individual variables, such as role performance, expectations, availability, or emotional investment, require reciprocal adjustments, and often new behaviors, from other family members.

Life cycle theories can be used to identify the individual developmental transitions that create potentials for family change. Erik Erikson's (1950) model, in particular, has several benefits: it is widely recognized and understood, it has some empirical validation, and it is naturalistic and nonpathological (Monk, 1990).[2] Accordingly, Vaillant and Milofsky's (1980) expansion of Erikson's model is utilized in the Family Congruence Model that is proposed here.

In Erikson's (1950) original model, individual development is described as an epigenetic process of growth that follows a predetermined sequence of critical steps. Specific developmental stages are defined by a succession of seemingly

[2]Competing views of individual development do exist, and others of these theoretical perspectives could be used within this general family model.

contrary, polar predispositions which demand attention and, hopefully, resolution. A different set of syntonic and dystonic possibilities frame the growth-producing tension of each stage, and these poles are the common designation for each stage.

The developmental tasks that frame childhood in Erikson's perspective are widely recognized. These begin with the task of developing Trust (versus Mistrust). The infant acquires an inner certainty of the parent's external existence and, from this beginning, develops a basic confidence that the self and the world will remain predictable. Next, the toddler searches for a sense of Autonomy (versus Shame and Doubt) by exploring both the possibilities and the dangers of his or her newly found mobility. This beginning capacity for autonomous action, in turn, enables the young child to develop sufficient Initiative (versus Guilt) to enjoy the excitement of new activities in spite of their dangers. As children enter school, they must struggle to master the task of Industry (versus Inferiority): the freedom of play gives way to the gratification of working on a task until it is completed. During adolescence, the psychosocial issues of Identity (versus Role Confusion) become the central focus of development. Young people search for an inner sense of sameness and continuity to guide them through the rapid and often unsettling changes that occur both in their physical bodies and in their social roles.

In contrast to the relatively fine developmental increments described for childhood in Erikson's (1950) original model, only three broad stages were posited for the far more numerous years of adulthood and old age. These three have been documented and expanded by Vaillant and his collaborators (Vaillant, 1977; Vaillant & Milofsky, 1980), using quite dissimilar data sets: a select group of psychologically healthy college-educated men, and a sample of undereducated men from high-crime, inner-city neighborhoods. Similar patterns were identified in each study group, in spite of the differences in their circumstances.

Erikson (1950) described the developmental task of young adults as that of achieving Intimacy (versus Isolation): ". . . the capacity to commit . . . to concrete affiliations and partnerships and to develop the ethical strength to abide by such commitments. . . ." (p. 263). Vaillant and Milofsky (1980) further identified this stage as a critical boundary between youth and adulthood. Those persons in each of their study groups who did not master this developmental task tended to be unsuccessful in the remaining developmental stages.

Vaillant and Milofsky (1980) also found evidence of the stage described by Erikson (1950) as Generativity (versus Stagnation): the investment of one's time and energy in productivity, creativity, and guidance of the next generation. Furthermore, Vaillant and Milofsky identified two additional adult stages. Career Consolidation (versus Self-absorption), hypothesized to emerge between Intimacy and Generativity, involves the mature refinement of one's career goals or other life commitments. Keepers of the Meaning (versus Rigidity), said to appear after Generativity, is defined as a type of general mentoring: "[p]assing on the torch and exposure of civilized values. . . ." (p. 1350).

Finally, Vaillant and Milofsky (1980) documented the developmental task Erikson (1950) attributed to old age, Integrity (versus Despair). Successful negotiation of this stage involves a complex, individual reevaluation of one's life that results, on balance, in "the acceptance of one's one and only life cycle as something that had to be and that . . . permitted of no substitutions . . ." (p. 232).

The developmental stages defined by Erikson (1950) and by Vaillant and Milofsky (1980) are used in the Congruence Model to focus attention on the complex and changing connections between individuals and the families of which they are members. Because individual transitions can produce change and accompanying stresses for the entire family system, clinical problems frequently surface during periods when one or more family members are struggling with a newly emerged developmental task (Rapoport, 1963). Steinglass (1980) succinctly describes these dynamics.

> New demands are placed on the family, and existing resources or patterns of behavior are inadequate to meet these demands. These transitional periods also frequently highlight competing developmental needs either of separate individuals within the family or competing needs of an individual and the family itself. (p. 213)

It should be emphasized, however, that transitional periods also create potential for growth, both for individuals and for their family systems. Roles, attitudes, and expectations that have outlived their usefulness can be more easily examined and altered during times of discontinuity. Furthermore, positive developmental steps taken by one family member often impact other family members to the extent that previous interactive patterns involving that individual are no longer possible.

THE CONGRUENCE MODEL

Figure 13.1 presents the Intergenerational Family Congruence Model in its most general form. The basic components of the model are described next, along with a discussion of their utility for analyzing families. Following this overview, the model is applied to illustrative family situations.

For heuristic purposes, the general model depicted in Fig. 13.1 describes families in terms of selected variables that will be applicable to most situations. When applied to an existing family, the actual individuals in each generation or involved in a specific situation would constitute the most basic level of data. Pertinent individual characteristics including gender should be added, and overarching contexts such as historical time (Hareven, 1977), and cultural background should be examined as well.

For illustrative purposes, in Fig. 13.1 the partial life line of one individual is

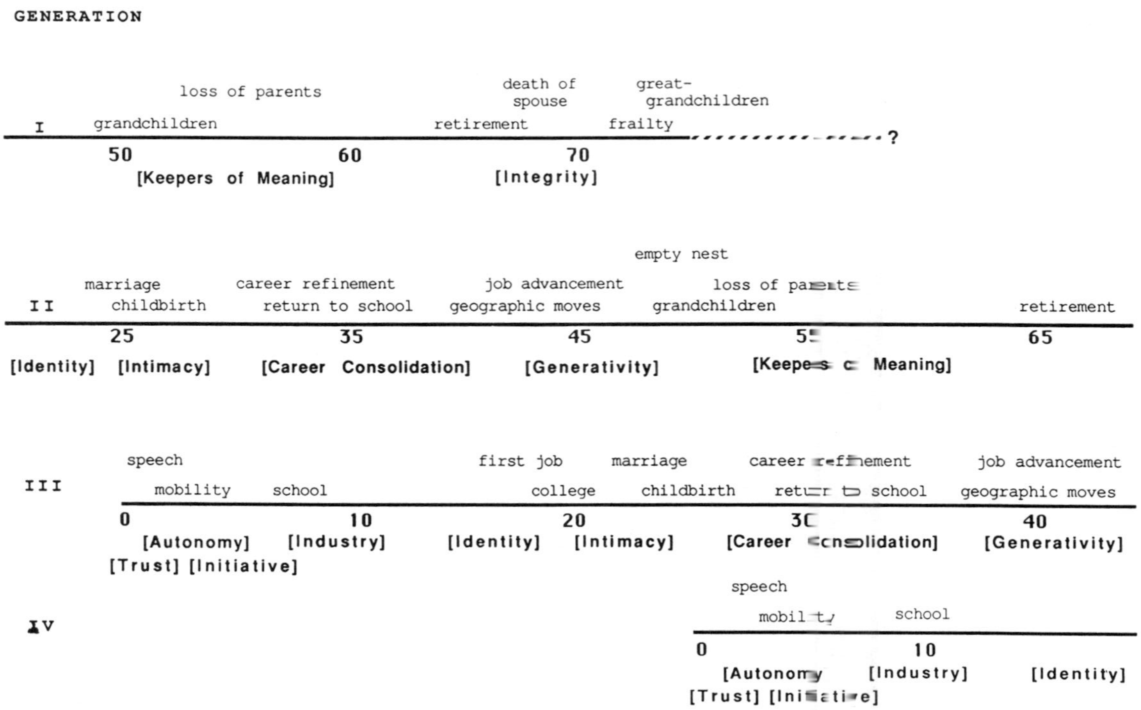
GENERATION
I
grandchildren
loss of parents
retirement
death of spouse
frailty
great-grandchildren
?
50
60
70
[Keepers of Meaning]
[Integrity]
II
marriage
childbirth
career refinement
return to school
job advancement
geographic moves
empty nest
grandchildren
retirement
25
35
45
65
[Identity]
[Intimacy]
[Career Consolidation]
[Generativity]
III
speech
mobility
school
first job
college
marriage
childbirth
job advancement
geographic moves
0
10
20
40
[Autonomy]
[Industry]
[Identity]
[Intimacy]
[Generativity]
[Trust] [Initiative]
IV
speech
school
0
10
[Industry]
[Identity]
[Trust]

FIG. 13.1. The intergenerational family congruence model.

included for each of four generations in a hypothetical family. Each life line begins at the same calendar year (not specified here) and continues marking calendar time. Three essential types of information are presented for each family member: (a) the age of the person is indicated by the solid line; (b) likely life events are noted above the age lines; (c) life stages, as defined by Erikson (1950) and Vaillant (1977) are indicated below the age lines. The latter two types of information are placed at ages of typical occurrence.

Before turning to applications of the model, the rational for including each of these three types of information is worthy of note. Each is discussed, in turn, next.

Ages

The age of each person is noted below the lifelines as basic information and as a guide to life events and developmental issues likely to be pertinent at a given point in time. To simplify the illustration, each person depicted in Fig. 13.1 is assumed to have been born when his or her parent was aged 25. In an actual family, of course, the years between each generation might be many more or many fewer and would vary among individual members. This information alone may be important: A child born to a 15-year-old mother will reach adolescence at a very different point in his mother's life (age 30) than will a child born to a 45-year-old mother (age 60). Likewise, the family experiences of siblings can vary considerably if their births are spaced over a large span of time.

Life Events

Common, empirically observable life events are noted above each life line in Fig. 13.1. Those chosen for illustration are usually considered to be major life events; they tend to create shifts in an individual's interests, and they may alter the allocation of personal resources. Such events often affect more than one generation. For example, the birth of the first child in a generation initiates parental responsibilities and at the same time confers grandparental status on the preceding generation.

Knowledge of life events that have been experienced provides important information about potential demands on each individual's time and resources and about the likely availability of one individual or generation to provide assistance to others. These data also are useful in assessing the developmental stages of individual family members.

Life Stages

Individual life stages, as defined by Erikson (1950) and by Vaillant and Milofsky (1980), are noted below each life line in Fig. 13.1; they are placed at ages typical for their occurrence. This presentation of the Congruence Model follows the convention of referring to each stage by its positive pole, except in those cases where maladaptive stage resolution is pertinent to the discussion. In assessing families, however, it is important to remember that each developmental stage in an individual life can result in either growth-producing resolution or can lead to a range of maladaptations.

The developmental stage attained by each individual can suggest issues arising from family interactions that are likely to be especially meaningful or particularly difficult for that person. For example, middle-aged adults who are in the Keepers of the Meaning stage may readily offer advice on a wide range of life issues; their unsolicited helpfulness may be rejected by an adolescent who is focused on defining her identity for herself. Similarly, life stages may predict the aspects of life in which an individual's energies will be most vested, and predict that individual's ability to understand the issues and events of particular concern to other family members. For example, a woman who is dealing with Career Consolidation issues by returning to college after her children are grown may resent the needs of an adult child who asks to move back into the parental home.

Typical age ranges in which developmental tasks take place can be used to exemplify prototypical family experiences. In childhood, biological age is often a good predictor of developmental stage, since physical maturation is vital to cognitive, social, and emotional development. In adulthood, however, life stages are no longer constrained by age and perhaps do not occur in a set order. In fact, there is evidence that the timing of common events in the adult life cycle is becoming increasingly flexible (e.g., Hareven, 1977; Hirschorn, 1977; Neugarten, 1970). For example, colleges now must plan for the needs of a growing group of students who return to school as adults, as well as planning for traditional students in their late teens and early 20s.

Yet in spite of such increased variability in life cycles, the timing of an event may affect its meaning for individuals and for families. Neugarten (1979) has argued persuasively that life events are especially likely to create crises if they are "off time," that is occurring either earlier or later than social norms would dictate. For example, a 15-year-old parent is likely to need considerable assistance with childrearing from family members, and these family members are likely to react emotionally to such a situation.

APPLICATIONS OF THE CONGRUENCE MODEL

The general Intergenerational Family Congruence Model described earlier is now applied to a range of family situations. This model can be used to assess the potential for various relations among generations, either for particular families or for families of a specified type. Such assessments can be used (a) to determine the circumstances within which a particular family is currently functioning, (b) to anticipate future possibilities for stress or change within the family, and (c) to understand a family's previous development and the continuing impact of this development on the family and on the individuals within it. Each of these temporal assessments is illustrated, in turn, in the following case examples. The family dynamics involved in each situation have been simplified to underscore particular issues.

CURRENT FAMILY CIRCUMSTANCES

Figure 13.2 illustrates the use of the Congruence Model to describe the dilemmas that may confront a family with elderly members. Discussions of the "sandwich" generation typically focus on middle-aged women confronted with the competing demands of frail parents and adolescent children (e.g., Brody, 1981; Miller, 1981). In fact, caregiving women are frequently in late middle-age and may themselves already be grandmothers, suggesting that there may be competing needs among four or five generations, rather than just three. In fact, given the tendency for men to marry women younger than themselves, the caregiver's responsibilities actually may be split between parents and spouse, rather than between parents and children.[3]

Figure 13.2 illustrates a common "woman-in-the-middle" situation. An extended 5-generation family is depicted, within which the primary caregiver is a 75-year-old woman (Mrs. A), attending to the needs of her frail 85-year-old husband (Mr. A) and her ailing 95-year-old mother (Great-great Grandmother). Because Mrs. A, herself, is reaching the age at which frailty becomes common, she is likely to require increasing assistance from her eldest daughter (Daughter #1), who can be defined as the secondary family caregiver.

Following the pattern established in Fig. 13.1, these four family members are depicted in Fig. 13.2 by parallel life lines, along with life lines for one female member of the two succeeding generations (who will become pertinent in further discussion). The age of each person is noted below their life line in 10-year increments, facilitating comparison of the relative ages of family members at various points in time. Similarly, likely life events and developmental stages are noted for each person at the ages when they are most likely to occur. Information about all of these family members enables a fuller assessment of each individual's situation as well as assessment of the family as a whole.

For example, at age 55 and with her own young grandchild, Daughter #1 exemplifies the common depiction of a woman-in-the-middle. Yet, the potential demands on her time and energy go far beyond obligations to her parents and to

---

[3]The author is indebted to Corinne Nydegger for her insightful clarification of this midlife family issue and for the example utilized here.

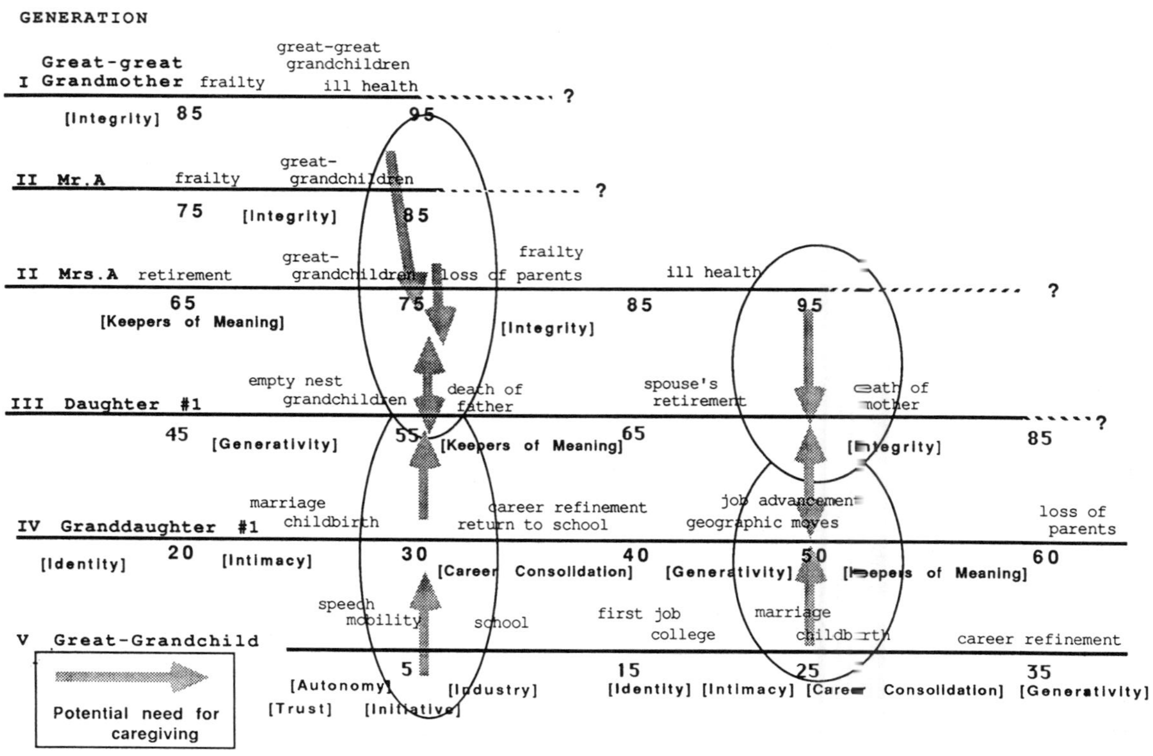

FIG. 13.2. Family caregivers.

her children. She may be called upon to assist two generations older than herself and two generations younger. Daughter #1's responsibilities for her mother could easily continue (and increase) for another 20 years; by this time Granddaughter #1 may be needed as secondary caregiver, thus replicating the current situation. Additional demands on Daughter #1 and Granddaughter #1 may also arise from the needs of their own spouses, their parents-in-law, or their careers outside the home.

Considering resource allocation alone, this family is likely to find itself stretched to the limit, with little capacity to absorb additional stresses. Should either Mrs. A or Daughter #1 become ill, for example, the demands on the other would greatly increase. The next generation (Granddaughter #1) may then be pressed into service as a caregiver for her elders while, at the same time, she is raising her own young children.

With so many potentially dependent members, this family may soon experience the dilemmas of an aging society as a series of personal problems. At 95 years-of-age, Great-great Grandmother is likely to need considerable assistance in managing routine daily activities. She will be able to continue living independently only if sufficient help is available. Family members have competing obligations, however, and at the same time, community-based long-term care programs are underdeveloped, publicly underfunded, and privately expensive. If the necessary assistance cannot be pieced together, Great-great Grandmother's only viable option may be nursing home placement. Institutional care is likely to be even more expensive than home care, and public funds will cover the cost only after Great-great Grandmother's personal resources are depleted (U.S. Congress, 1987). As a result, the family as a whole will have reduced financial resources for meeting the needs of other elderly members, as well as the needs of growing children. Additionally, Great-great Grandmother's move to a nursing home will not necessarily reduce the stress on Mrs. A. She will likely still feel the need to see her mother frequently and to augment institutional care with more personalized attention. If changes in the health and vitality of other family elders occur, it may create a series of resource allocation problems that would replicate and exacerbate the scenario outlined here.

FUTURE FAMILY POSSIBILITIES

In Figure 13.3, the Congruence Model is used to describe the potential effects of teen-aged pregnancy on family function. Information available about a family's current (and past) circumstances can be used to anticipate the problems and possibilities they are likely to encounter at a future time. It is, of course, impossible to predict the exact timing of future events, much less to predict how a given individual will react to events they have not yet encountered. However, reasonable expectations can be drawn from information about individuals' reactions to

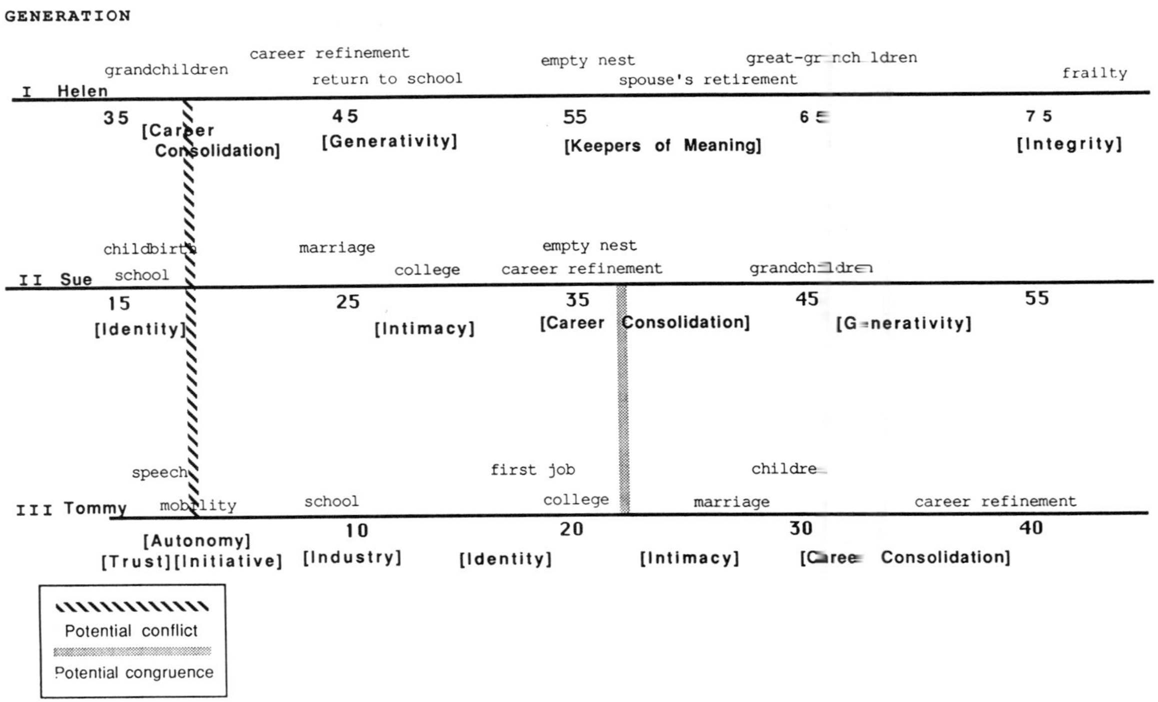
GENERATION
I Helen
career refinement
grandchildren
return to school
empty nest
spouse's retirement
frailty
35
45
55
75
[Generativity]
[Keepers of Meaning]
[Integrity]
II Sue
marriage
college
empty nest
career refinement
school
15
25
35
45
55
[Identity]
[Intimacy]
[Career
Consolidation]
III Tommy
speech
school
first job
college
marriage
career refinement
10
20
30
40
[Autonomy]
[Trust][Initiative]
[Industry]
[Identity]
[Intimacy]
Consolidation]
Potential conflict
Potential congruence

FIG. 13.3. Teenage parenthood.

past experiences and about the likely future circumstances of various family members. Such predictions may assist individual family members to make realistic life plans, and may also guide social planning.

For example, public concern about our society's relatively high rate of teenage pregnancies focuses not only on the immediate costs of supporting these immature parents and their children, but also on the potential needs of mother and child for support in the future. These global concerns might be rendered more manageable by anticipating particular future family stages that are likely to be difficult for family units begun earlier than average.

As an example, Fig. 13.3 illustrates some predictable developmental sequences for a teenaged mother (Sue), her child (Tommy), and her mother (Helen). When Tommy is born, his mother (Sue) is 15 years old and in the early stages of identity formation. Her own developmental tasks focus attention on herself and on the behaviors of other people as reactions to her actions. This self-absorption, although age-appropriate, will make it difficult for Sue to provide the consistent attention and empathic responsiveness that Tommy needs to develop a healthy sense of trust. Similarly, Sue's adolescent needs for experimentation are not likely to match well with Tommy's needs for predictable rules against which his autonomy can be tested. As Fig. 13.3 shows, the possibility of conflict between Sue's and Tommy's needs is high.

Tommy's initial developmental needs (along with his needs for adequate physical care) necessitate the involvement of other adult caregivers. As is often the case, it is his grandmother, Helen, who will augment and correct his mother's parenting. At age 35, it is likely that Helen has resolved issues of identity and intimacy sufficiently well that when necessary she can put the needs of her infant grandson above her own. However, caring for Tommy (while continuing to guide Sue through adolescence) may well require that she delay the next stage of her own development. Figure 13.3 also illustrates this potential for conflict that exists between Sue and her mother, Helen.

Before Tommy was born, Helen was ready to confront the set of issues that Vaillant and Milofsky (1980) identified as Career Consolidation, a mature clarification of career commitment. For many women, this stage occurs as their children are approaching adulthood, and it involves the choice of and training for an occupation outside the home. However, the need to assist with Tommy's care is likely to foreclose some of Helen's future options, such as returning to school or testing her skills in paid employment. The resolution of this developmental stage, however, is also possible through a commitment to her grandchild and to continued nurturance of her family.[4]

[4]In Erikson's formulation, nurturance and care of subsequent generations is posited as the essence not only of adult generativity, but also of the generational cycle, "irrevocably binding each generation to those that gave it life and to those for whose life it is responsible" (Erikson et al., 1986, p. 73).

Figure 13.3 also indicates that Grandmother Helen will be aged 55 at the time when Tommy leaves home and Sue returns to her own interests. If she has devoted the intervening years entirely to raising her grandchild, she may find herself with a stereotypic "empty nest" and few other responsibilities or interests to occupy her time. It is likely that she will find it difficult to enter the employment market or to return to school at this point in her life. On the other hand, volunteer opportunities may be readily available to her. If she is married to a man somewhat older than herself, his retirement may give the couple increased time for leisure activities. However, if the health of her husband fails (or that of her parents or parents-in-law), she may find herself moving into the next tasks in a career of family caregiving. Helen's resolution of her remaining mid- and late-life issues will depend on a combination of her available opportunities, her choices among these, and the meaning she ascribes to her chosen activities.

Looking at other possibilities in the family's future, it is possible that Sue and Tommy may experience a greater congruence between their developmental needs than is typical when children are born during the parents' 20s. Figure 13.3 shows that when Tommy reaches late adolescence and is ready to leave home, Sue will be aged 35. If all has gone well, she will have finished school and may have married; both identity and intimacy issues may have been addressed through these life events. As Sue approaches the developmental tasks of Career Consolidation, her responsibilities to her eldest child will be decreasing. Unlike Helen, Sue may have numerous options for midlife redefinition of her goals and commitments.

Sue's potential situation at age 35 is in striking contrast to that depicted in Fig. 13.1 for a woman who becomes a mother at age 25. When childbirth occurs at a more normative age, parents will be middle-aged (45) during the notoriously difficult years of raising teenaged children. At this time, adults are often reassessing their achievements and future possibilities; they may find themselves ill equipped to tolerate rejection from adolescents who are attempting to create their own unique identities. Additionally, emergent adolescent sexuality can conflict with the parent's adaptation to mid-life changes in reproductive functioning.

PREVIOUS FAMILY DEVELOPMENT

A final example of the Congruence Model, depicted in Fig. 13.4, illustrates how a family's past life experiences and their reactions to these events can play a major role in shaping the behavioral patterns and resources that will be available to respond to subsequent events. The Congruence Model can be used to assess developmental influences occurring earlier in a family's history that may have an impact on the subsequent development both of the family as a whole and of its individual members. For example, children of alcoholics have been identified as prone to difficult childhoods and problematic adult outcomes (Cotton, 1979;

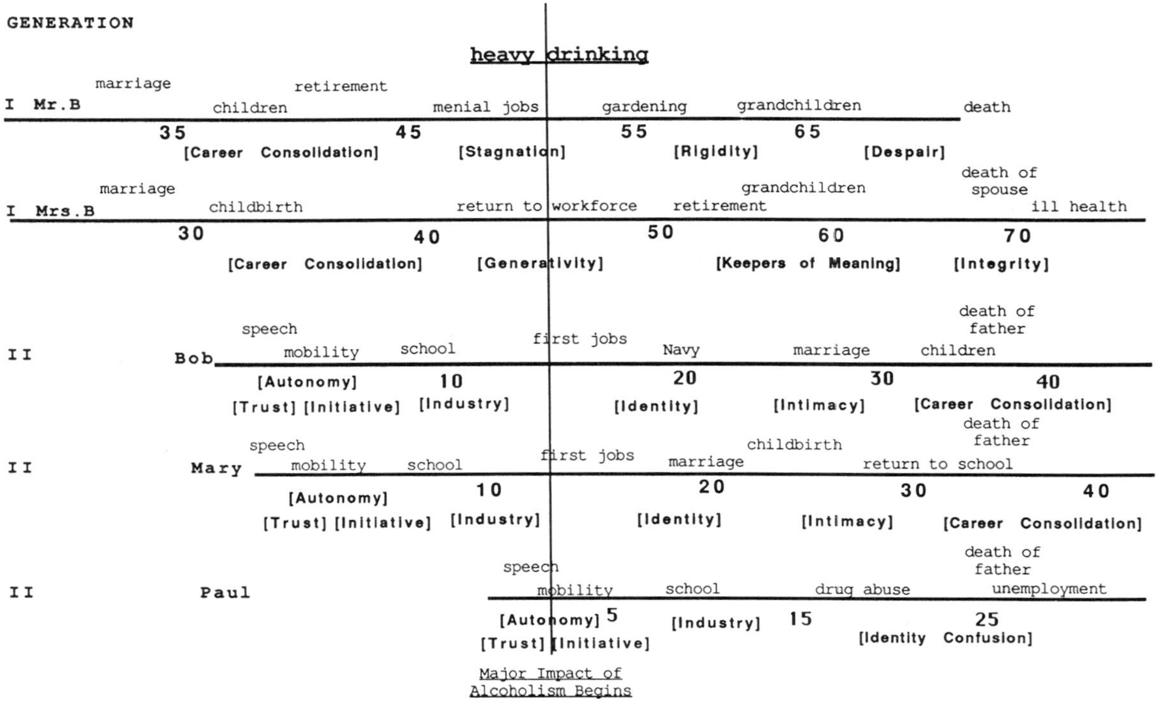

FIG. 13.4. Alcoholic family.

Miller & Jang, 1977; Werner, 1986). Yet, the family dynamics that create difficulties for children in alcoholic homes have not been fully identified (El-Guebaly & Offord, 1977). Children in alcoholic homes may be at risk for successful negotiation of early developmental stages, and parental alcoholism may have differential impact on several siblings in the same family, depending on their stages of development at the time that the parental alcoholism surfaces (Ackerman, 1983).[5]

Figure 13.4 depicts an alcoholic family that includes children with notable differences in their ages. Mr. B was a career military man who served as a surgical technician; he was a moderately heavy social drinker. Mrs. B had served as a military nurse, but she became a full-time homemaker after her marriage. Two children, Bob and Mary, were born 16 months apart, in the early years of the B's marriage. The youngest child, Paul, was born 10 years later.

Mr. B's mid- and late-adult life had a pronounced effect on the other members of his family. He retired from military service at the age of 45, and discovered that he was not qualified for civilian employment equivalent to his highly skilled military career. After several years of working at menial jobs, he retreated to a life consisting of gardening and continual, daily drinking. In Fig. 13.4, Mr. B's life stage for this period of time is labeled by its dystonic pole, Stagnation, indicating his failure to resolve the developmental task of "assuming sustained responsibility for the growth, well-being, and leadership of others" (Vaillant & Milofsky, 1980). In the remaining years until his death (from alcoholism) at age 72, Mr. B continued to be unsuccessful in his attempts to master the developmental issues of later adult life. Vaillant's definition of the Keepers of the Meaning versus Rigidity stage is somewhat tentative, but suggests an active mentoring role in late middle-age that has also been described by others (e.g., Levinson, Darrow, Klein, Levinson, & McKee, 1978). There being little evidence of such activity in Mr. B's life, this part of his life cycle is shown in Fig. 13.4 as characterized by Rigidity. Likewise, Mr. B was unable to achieve a satisfying summation of the life he had lived, and is shown as approaching his death with Despair rather than with a sense of Integrity.

Figure 13.4 shows that Mrs. B returned to full-time employment as a nurse when the cost of Mr. B's alcohol consumption began to exceed his meagre retirement pay. Thus assuming primary responsibility for the well-being of herself and her children, she was able to successfully negotiate her remaining developmental tasks. In contrast to her husband's, the last three stages of Mrs. B's life are shown in Fig. 13.4 as Generativity, Keepers of the Meaning, and Integrity.

At the time their mother returned to work, Bob was aged 14, Mary was 13,

---

[5]The author is indebted to Marjorie E. Hunt for a critical summation of the empirical literature on alcoholic families and for the example utilized here.

and Paul was 3. This established family pattern continued until the two eldest children left the home: Bob at age 18 to join the Navy, and Mary at age 18 when she married. Thus, at age 10, Paul became the only child in the home. By the age of 14, Paul was heavily involved in drug abuse; as a 25-year-old adult, he has not married nor settled on a career. He is depicted in Fig. 13.4 as continuing to struggle with Identity Confusion. Bob, on the other hand, subsequently married, and both he and Mary have established stable, nonalcoholic families. As Fig. 13.4 indicates, these two elder siblings have achieved satisfactory resolution of the developmental tasks they have confronted in their lives to date.

Much of the difference in these three siblings' adult lives can be traced to differences in their childhood exposure to alcoholism. As young children, Bob and Mary experienced a family in which the father worked productively, the mother cared for home and children, and drinking did not create major problems. During adolescence, however, they had to learn to contend with their father's frequent drunkenness, and its accompanying mood swings and unpredictable behavior. The situation did create difficulties for the teenagers: they avoided bringing friends home, and they worried that people thought badly of them because of their father's drinking. Their early family circumstances, however, had enabled their successful psychosocial development throughout childhood and had given them internal resources sufficient to surmount a difficult adolescence.

Paul, on the other hand, was affected by alcoholism from a very early age. During his earliest years, his father's drinking was increasing, along with his anger and frustration at not being able to establish a civilian career. By the time Paul was aged 3, his family consisted of a mother who worked away from home and returned exhausted, an unpredictable father who was usually at home and often drunk, and only his teenaged brother and sister to rely on for his daily needs. At age 10, he lost the protection, assistance, and alternate role modeling provided by his siblings. In virtually every stage of development, Paul had less than optimal support and guidance from his family. In adolescence, following his father's example, he gave up and turned to self-medication for his internal pains. His future is unknown.

IMPLICATIONS FOR RESEARCH

The three foregoing examples provide only a sampling of the individual and family dynamics that can be identified and analyzed using the Intergenerational Family Congruence Model. Such a model, which is based on shifting congruence among individual members, allows a broad range of family circumstances to be studied and directly compared. The model's capacity to describe families of all ages draws attention to important issues that are often overlooked in research based solely on child-rearing families.

This model focuses attention on the need to understand some of the specific strengths and weaknesses of different types of families. At the present time, considerable societal attention is focused on changes in American families. The family forms about which concern has been raised are varied, and they include extremely young and unusually late parenting, as well as single-parent families. It is commonly assumed that *nontraditional* families are necessarily inferior to those that better approximate the social ideal (Nydegger, 1983). Yet, it is unlikely that various types of nontraditional families would endure over time if they did not have their own advantages.

Social concern about particular family forms often contains the implicit assumption that it is possible to classify families as *good* and *bad*. The Intergenerational Congruence Model can be a valuable tool for reframing these questions. The dynamic, ever changing nature of all families can be emphasized, and particular life stages and events can be identified as likely to be more or less difficult for specific types of families. Thus, the question changes from "how functional" is a family to "how useful can family members be to each other under particular circumstances?"

The ubiquity and strength of postparental family ties requires that research on the family must take into account all family functions and roles, not merely the roles of procreation and socialization. It is important to remember that the aging of each individual family member increases the likelihood of changes in family composition over time. For example, family members may be added through birth and marriage, while other members may be lost through death and divorce.

In spite of such accumulating changes in membership, families continue to exist as critical support systems for their individual members, throughout the life span. It may well be productive, then, for family researchers to question how families are able to maintain their supportive functions in spite of changes in membership. The possibilities for substitution in family membership and roles may be an especially pertinent avenue of inquiry. Are family functions necessarily lost if a particular generation or member is absent? Can some family functions be carried out by substitute members? If certain roles and functions can be delegated, are other family members the only possible substitutes? Or can families incorporate non-relatives to assure that all necessary functions will be fulfilled? The Intergenerational Congruence Model can be used to guide these inquiries, since it can describe changes that take place in families over time and can identify the types of membership substitutions that do occur.

Recognition that most adults hold simultaneous membership in families of origin and in families of procreation leads to additional research questions. For example, the reality of multiple family membership suggests that the way a family perceives itself and its members may provide a more meaningful basis for defining families than do conceptual approaches based on academic perceptions of form or function. Indeed, it is likely that those persons who are considered to constitute the relevant family may vary over time. It is also likely that individual family members may expand or contract their family ties, in accordance with the changing needs and circumstances of themselves and of their families.

Thus, most basically, the Intergenerational Congruence Model directs attention to the processes by which individuals are bound to families. This is a critically important but extremely difficult area of family research. Its goal is better understanding of the complex and fluid networks of interrelations that constitute families.

REFERENCES

Ackerman, R. J. (1983). *Children of alcoholics* (2nd ed.). Holmes Beach, Florida: Learning Publications.

Brody, E. (1981). "Women in the middle" and family help to older people. *The Gerontologist, 21,* 471–480.

Brody, E. (1985). Parent care as a normative family stress. *The Gerontologist, 25,* 19–29.

Brody, S. J., Poulshock, S. W., & Masciocchi, C. F. (1978). The family caring unit: A major consideration in the long-term support system. *The Gerontologist, 18,* 556–561.

Cantor, M. (1975). Life space and the social support system of the inner city elderly of New York. *The Gerontologist, 15,* 23–27.

Cotton, N. S. (1979). The familial incidence of alcoholism: A review. *Journal of Studies on Alcohol, 40,* 89–116.

El-Guebaly, N., & Offord, D. R. (1977). The offspring of alcoholics: A critical review. *The American Journal of Psychiatry, 134*(4), 357–365.

Erikson, E. H. (1950). *Childhood and society.* New York: W. W. Norton.

Erikson, E. H., Erikson, J., & Kivnick, H. (1986). *Vital involvement in old age.* New York: W. W. Norton.

Greene, R. R. (1986). *Social work with the aged and their families.* New York: Aldine de Gruyter.

Hamburg, D. A., & Adams, J. E. (1967). A perspective on coping behavior: Seeking and utilizing information in major transitions. *Archives of General Psychiatry, 17,* 277–284.

Hareven, T. K. (1977). Family time and historical time. *Daedalus, 106,* 57–70.

Hirschorn, L. (1977). Social policy and the life cycle: A developmental perspective. *Social Service Review, 51*(3), 434–450.

Hooyman, N., Gonyea, J., & Montgomery, R. (1985). The impact of in-home services termination on family caregivers. *The Gerontologist, 25,* 141–145.

Horowitz, A., & Dobrof, R. (1982). *The role of families in providing long-term care to the frail and chronically ill elderly living in the community.* New York: Brookdale Center on Aging, Hunter College.

Johnson, C. L., & Catalano, D. (1981). Childless elderly and their family supports. *The Gerontologist, 21*(6), 610–618.

Konopka, G. (1976). *Young girls: A portrait of adolescence.* Englewood-Cliffs, NJ: Prentice-Hall.

Kovar, M. G. (1986). Aging in the eighties, age 65 years old and over and living alone, contacts with family, friends and neighbors. *Advance data from vital health statistics,* No. 116. Hyattesville, MD: National Center for Health Statistics, May 9.

Levinson, D. J., Darrow, C. N., Klein, E. B., Levinson, M. H., & McKee, B. (1978). *The seasons of a man's life.* New York: Alfred A. Knopf.

Miller, D. (1981). The "sandwich" generation: Adult children of the aging. *Social Work, 26,* 419–423.

Miller, D., & Jang, M. (1977). Children of alcoholics: A 20 year longitudinal study. *Social Work Research and Abstracts, 13*(4), 23–29.

Monk, A. (1990). Gerontological social services: Theory and practice. In A. Monk (Ed.), *Handbook of gerontological services* (2nd ed., pp. 3–26). New York: Columbia University Press.

Neugarten, B. L. (1970). Dynamics of transition of middle age to old age. *Journal of Geriatric Psychiatry, 4,* 71–87.

Neugarten, B. L. (1979). Time, age and the life cycle. *American Journal of Psychiatry, 136,* 887–894.

Nydegger, C. N. (1983). Family ties of the aged in cross-cultural perspective. *The Gerontologist, 23,* 26–32.

Rapoport, R. (1963). Normal crises, family structure, and mental health. *Family Process, 12,* 68–80.

Rhodes, S. L. (1980). A developmental approach to the life-cycle of the family. In M. Bloom (Ed.), *Life span development: Bases for prevention and interventive helping* (pp. 30–40). New York: Macmillan.

Shanas, E. (1979). The family as a social support system in old age. *The Gerontologist, 19,* 169–174.

Shanas, E., Townsend, P., Wedderburn, D., Friis, H., Milhøj, P., & Stehouwer, J. (1968). *Old people in three industrial societies.* New York: Atherton.

Spikes, J. (1980). Grief, death and dying. In E. W. Busse & D. G. Blazer (Eds.), *Handbook of geriatric psychiatry* (pp. 415–426). New York: Van Nostrand Reinhold.

Steinglass, P. (1980). A life history model of the alcoholic family. *Family Process, 19,* 211–226.

Troll, L. (Ed.). (1986). *Family issues in current gerontology.* New York: Springer.

United States Congress, House of Representatives, Select Committee on Aging. (1987). *Long-term care and personal impoverishment: Seven in ten elderly living alone are at risk.* Washington, D.C.: U.S. Government Printing Office, October.

Vaillant, G. E. (1977). *Adaptation to life.* Boston: Little, Brown.

Vaillant, G. E., & Milofsky, E. (1980). Natural history of male psychological health IX: Empirical evidence for Erikson's model of the life cycle. *American Journal of Psychiatry, 137,* 1348–1359.

Werner, E. E. (1986). Resilient offspring of alcoholics: A longitudinal study from birth to age 18. *Journal of Studies on Alcohol, 47*(1), 34–40.

14 The Prolongation of Life and the Extension of Family Relationships: The Families of the Oldest Old

Colleen Leahy Johnson
University of California, San Francisco

> Though many facts of life extension are familiar, their meanings for the personal life of family members are elusive. . . . . . Indeed an exciting new family literature is beginning to map and interpret these unparalleled changes; it is beginning to move beneath the surface for the subjective implications of the protracted and intimate interplay of family relationships. (Riley, 1983, p. 440)

A new age category has emerged in aging research which reflects dramatic changes in our age structure. Whereas we previously thought of the oldest age group as 75 years and older (Neugarten, 1974), a new age marker of 85 years is now being used to identify "the oldest old." The population increase after age 85 is traced directly to declining mortality rates in the 8th and 9th decades in life. This age group, in fact, is the fastest growing segment of our population; between 1960 and 1980, the oldest old increased by 141% (Rosenwaike, 1985; Rosenwaike, Yaffe, & Sagi, 1984). In Soldo and Manton's view (1985), this recent prolongation of life is already exerting profound changes in our understanding of aging.

Until recently virtually nothing was known about this population, because most researchers made no finite age distinctions after age 75. In this previously uncharted area, new epidemiological data indicate that these "true survivors" in our culture differ in their health and functioning from younger older people (Manton & Soldo, 1985; Rosenwaike, 1985; Soldo & Manton, 1985). Less well understood is the impact that the protracted life span is having on the American family system.

This chapter reports on a current research project that is exploring the implications of these demographic changes among 150 San Franciscans who are 85 years and older and who are still living more or less independently in the community. The research is examining adaptation in late late life, with a special interest in how individuals manage their social environment and maintain some level of social integration. One major objective is to explore the extent that their family relationships enhance their adaptation. I outline here the conceptual frameworks needed to analyze the families of the oldest old and illustrate the variations in family structure and functions at that stage of life. This project was undertaken to provide much needed information on the more dynamic aspects of family functioning, information that will augment the demographic material now emerging from large-scale surveys.

Background

Family structure is affected by the fact that, among those age 85 and older, there are only 44 males for every 100 females (Rosenwaike et al., 1984; Verbrugge, 1984). For example, of the approximately 12,000 people in San Francisco who are 85 years of age and older among whom our sample was drawn, only 3,000 are men. The late-life family thus is a unit predominantly headed by women, so despite the prolongation of life, the numbers in late-life marriages have not risen, and the length of time married has not reached the potential span provided by the extension of life (Watkins, Menken, & Bongaarts, 1987).

In regard to family structure as assessed by marital status, household structure, and the presence of children, surveys indicate that the oldest old have more depleted family resources than the general population, 65 years and older (Shanas, 1979a, 1979b). The 1980 census finds that of the noninstitutionalized oldest old, only 9.8% of the women and 53.1% of the men are married (Rosenwaike, 1985). Where children are available, members of this age group are likely to have children who are also in old age and thus to have some functional impairment themselves (Brody, 1977). Also, women in advanced old age today have fewer children than did their counterparts in 1900 (Treas, 1977), a mean of only 1.0 daughters in comparison to 3.3. Except for the 20% of the oldest old who are in institutions, there has been an increased trend for the oldest old to maintain independent households. In combination, these factors can result in an abbreviated network for many in this age category. Because living arrangements in old age are directly associated with earlier fertility rates, the high numbers living alone today may be a direct result of the numbers of children and not because of cultural values supporting the independence of the nuclear household (Hauser & Wisler, 1984).

Even with the paucity of findings on the late late life family, it is possible to explore other implications of these demographic changes. Certainly, declines in mortality have made it possible for many Americans to spend more time in families. Using simulated models, Watkins and her colleagues (1987) have found that despite declines in fertility and increases in the incidence of divorce, individuals spent more years as parents, as currently married spouses, and in conjugal family units than did earlier cohorts. They spend about 27 adult years with a spouse and surviving child, 4 more years than did parents in 1800. The time spent as an adult child with a surviving parent, 65 years and older, has risen, so that the proportion of an adult lifetime spent in this status has risen from 15 to 29% (Watkins, Menken, & Bongaarts, 1987). Couples with dependent children, in fact, have more surviving parents than they have children, a mean of 2.7 parents as compared with a mean of 1.7 children (Preston, 1984). Moreover, the number of years spent as children of older parents is greater than the years spent as parents of dependent children.

Over the past 2 decades, the government has increasingly taken over responsibility for the care of the elderly (Shanas & Maddox, 1985). The impact of this policy change means that the prolongation of life has not necessarily resulted in increased economic burdens for the elderly or their families. While needs for family support increase with advanced old age because of the higher incidence of chronic impairments, recent research suggests that such responsibilities do not rest solely upon children, at least on a full-time basis. Dependent elderly, 65 years and older, are usually cared for by a spouse, while children function as primary caregivers of only one-quarter of the impaired elderly (Stone, Cafferata, & Sangl, 1987). Moreover, fewer than 20% of individuals age 70 and older, who live alone and have impairment on their activities of daily living, receive assistance on these activities from a son or daughter (Kovar, 1986). Instead, offspring are more often mediators between their parent and formal social service agencies (Johnson, 1983; Johnson & Catalano, 1983).

The Study of the Family in Late Late Life

Given these demographic facts, the structure of the family as a physical or domestic unit is less commonly encountered among the oldest population. Many in this age group have outlived the family as a household; they have outlived the family as defined by its nuclear form; and some have outlived the family as a unit of social organization in which various tasks are performed and social interactions take place. Thus the study of roles and relationships within a given family is not always possible.

Other family researchers in gerontology have reached similar conclusions (Troll & Bengtson, 1979), and they suggest that positive family relationships do not necessarily rest upon face-to-face contact. Even researchers on family supports to older people do not consider face-to-face social contact an essential prerequisite for the provision of support (Litwak, 1985). Consequently, emotions and sentiments about the family rather than contact and aid from them may provide intangible supports even with physical and social distance among its members.

When the nuclear family cross-culturally is given small functional value, meaning that it fulfills few basic survival needs, it tends to disappear below the conjugal unit of parents and children or even the elemental dyad of mother and child (Adams, 1960; Levy-Strauss, 1956). When the family is given great functional value, however, this unit takes on a much more complex form than that of the nuclear unit. Thus one would expect that the late-life family potentially could have great functional value because many older members need social supports. Such functioning is usually not the case in our society, however, because of realistic social and cultural obstacles (Bellah, Madsen, Sullivan, Swidler & Tipton, 1985; Lasch, 1979).

With marriage, adult children rarely live in the same household or often even in the same community as their parents. Consequently, parents and adult children are not intimately involved with each other's lives on a daily basis. In keeping with American values, moreover, norms of obligation are deemphasized, and instead personal autonomy and independence from kin are endorsed (Johnson, 1988; Kluckhohn & Strodtbeck, 1961; Quinton, 1983). These personal freedoms are also reflected in the American kinship system, where relationships outside the nuclear unit are noted for their flexibility and for the freedom granted to individuals to define to whom they are related (Furstenberg, 1981; Schneider, 1965).

I suggest and I hope to illustrate in what follows that when faced with the adaptive challenges of advanced old age, our family system permits family members to sort out relationships, define what constitutes family membership, and essentially play with its structure to determine the type of kinship relations that best meets their needs. Given the individual's freedom to define the family as he or she chooses, it becomes necessary to ask, what maintains the family? If we assume that the family in late late life is characterized by a "latent web of continually shifting linkages that provide the opportunity for activating and intensifying close family relationships" (Riley, 1983, p. 439), then there is a need to identify the mechanisms used for activating and deactivating these relationships over time. Are bonds formed on the basis of sentiments, on the need for social support, or on a more general sense of obligation?

I also suggest that there are both cultural and social mechanisms operating that determine the nature of family life for the oldest old. The social mechanisms rest upon objective demographic factors that determine family structure—marital status, household structure, the numbers and location of children and kin, and the potential personnel who can perform family roles. Potential family resources come from two sources: the family of orientation consisting of parents, siblings, and relatives in the family in which one was born, and the family of procreation, consisting of the spouse, children, grandchildren, and other relatives created with marriage. Moreover, structural resources may decline over time, either by the loss through deaths or through conscious decisions to distance oneself from some relatives.

One common source of depletion in family resources comes from the loss of relations with members of the family of orientation after the deaths of parents. If bonds between siblings are weak, these relationships are not sustained after the parents die, and usually no relationships with nieces and nephews form. The proximity of children and other relatives also determines whether family relations are conducted face-to-face or by telephone and letters. Social mobility and intermarriage also may create greater subjective social distance among kin, and subsequently, these factors may affect relationships. Consequently, these structural factors can impose either constraints or facilitators to family integration.

Given the presence of structural resources, family relationships are culturally constructed through a matrix of values, norms, and meanings, which define the level of commitments one has to maintain family relations. Families vary a great deal in these norms and values, which regulate their relationships and define the optimal degree of attachment to the family. These norms concern the relative value placed upon dependence, interdependence, or independence, upon self-interest versus family interest, and upon voluntary versus obligatory bonds. There also are varying degrees of normative pressure for reciprocity among family members, and these also influence the helping patterns.

These norms also serve to shape the emotional component of family relations. In the emotional domain, individuals do not necessarily need face-to-face contact and reciprocal interactions in order to invest intense sentiments of love and affection in their family relationships. The social patterning of sentiments defines how priorities and loyalties are assigned. Emphasis can be placed upon marital relations over filial loyalties, or upon work commitments over family loyalties. Such differing priorities ultimately determine the family status of the older generation.

Thus in the study of families of the oldest old, one needs to analyze both the structural and the cultural factors that determine the nature of their family life. In a later section, family types are described which range from an actively functioning family, to the family as an abbreviated vestige of a former time.

THE STUDY

The ongoing anthropological research reported here combines both quantitative and qualitative methods. We are exploring longitudinally the physical and social resources of community-dwelling individuals, 85 years and older in San Francisco, with a special focus on the types of competencies needed to manage the physical environment and to maintain an optimal level of social integration. Most of the 150 respondents interviewed were selected from public voting records, and each individual interviewed was asked to refer us on to an age peer. By intention, all respondents are White, all are cognitively alert, and all possess the stamina to participate in a 2-hour interview. The interview was open-ended, with respondents being permitted to range freely in their discussions. In addition, standard instruments were used to measure perceived health status, functioning on the activities of daily living (Duke University, 1978) and mood (Bradburn Affect-Balance Scale; Bradburn, 1969).

A demographic profile of this sample indicates that these individuals do not differ greatly from the national population in gender distribution and marital status. A large majority are women and few are married, although most had been married at some point. Only 19% are currently married, and 58% of the sample live alone, a higher portion than reported nationally (Kovar, 1986; Rosenwaike, 1985). A surprising number, 46%, still live in a single family dwelling rather than an apartment or more protected senior housing. Almost one-third have no surviving child, a proportion similar to the White population in New Haven, 85 years and older (Cornoni-Huntley et al., 1986). Of those with children, 32% have lost at least one child. Over one-half have at least one child in the vicinity. While two-thirds have grandchildren, less than one-half have a surviving sibling. Only 5% have no surviving family members, but an additional 19% have no spouse, child, or other relative with whom they are in contact. Thus almost one-quarter of the sample do not maintain any ongoing family interactions.

Respondents come from all echelons of our socioeconomic structure and religious backgrounds. Most describe their health as excellent or good and feel their health is better than most in their age group. Nevertheless, over two-thirds report some restrictions in their activities, self-reports that agree with our assessments of their performances on the activities of daily living. Over one-half have some problems with their eyesight or hearing, and a similar proportion report some difficulty in sleeping.

Even with high levels of functional impairment, most individuals maintain their independence from members of their primary family network. Only 37% have a family caregiver. If in need of someone to grocery shop or to assist them in household tasks, fewer than one-quarter could call upon a child. For those who have children, few report they have expectations of assistance from children. Although children are a source of sociability, few use their children as confidants or sounding boards when they are troubled. In fact, 70% have no confidant they can turn to if they are feeling "down in the dumps," either out of preference, "I wouldn't want to burden others," or because those relatives and friends who would be potential confidants are dead. Despite the high level of impairment, however, 59% of the sample still maintain reciprocal relations by helping others and 8% perform the caregiving role for another.

Certainly these distributions differ from the prevailing surveys of the families of the overall population, 65 years and older (Shanas, 1979a, 1979b), largely because many of the oldest old have lost some family resources over the passage of time. Nevertheless, Field and Minkler (1988 and this volume) report on the Berkeley Older Generation Study, of whom 27 individuals are 85 years and older and all of whom have children. They found the only significant changes occurring among the oldest old over a 14-year period are fewer contacts with the "least-seen child" and with siblings (Field & Minkler, 1988). Their reports of a higher family involvement most likely results from a sample in which only one-third are among the oldest old and all of whom have children. In another report (Johnson & Troll, 1990), we found that family integration rests upon the presence of children, which in turn links individuals to grandchildren, great grandchildren, and their in-laws.

Despite the numbers who are not actively involved in family life, nonetheless, a large majority do not experience the mental health problems commonly associated with social isolation. Most are able to maintain their sense of well-being with half of the respondents saying they are very happy or mostly contented. In response to the Bradburn Affect-Balance Scale, over one-half say they are never lonely, angry, depressed, bored, uneasy, or restless. In fact, in responses to questions on self-concept, one-third describe themselves as more comfortable with their self-image now than in the past. Most think about their death without trepidation and have made practical and mental preparations for it.

In summary, these respondents are quite competent in maintaining their mood or morale in the face of functional impairment and considerable depletions in their social networks. In the absence of longitudinal data for this sample, we are unable to determine whether their remarkable skills in the face of diminishing social and physical resources are of long duration or whether they developed in response to living to advanced old age. By their own interpretations, however, it would appear that living so long entails, not dependence upon family, but instead the development of both practical and subjective coping skills to deal with the problems of long-term survivorship.

FAMILY TYPES IN LATE LATE LIFE

As the profile of family structure indicates, many of the oldest old have abbreviated family structures because of age-related losses of spouses, children, and other relatives. In other words, there are some oldest old who have outlived their families. The sheer age of family members is also prominent. The oldest generation's ages range from 85 to 104. Their children's ages range from their 50s to 70s. Some marriages have lasted for more than 65 years. Most grandchildren and in a few cases, great grandchildren, are already forming families of their own. For example, one woman was describing the assistance she was receiving from her nephew; we were surprised to learn that the nephew was 80 years old!

Moreover, the usual conceptions of the family do not always apply, for the boundary of the late-life family is continually shifting, and often it surrounds an idea or a system of meanings rather than an easily identifiable unit. Consequently, in research with the oldest old, it is useful to establish a system of classification that can be used for comparative purposes. Four types have been identified in this research: (a) the functioning family, (b) the potential family, (c) the family as a vessel of sentiment, and (d) the attenuated family.

First, *the functioning family* of the oldest old has an observable structure and a well-defined set of statuses and roles. Members are in frequent contact, and relationships are characterized by patterns of reciprocity and interdependence. Family relationships are in a manifest, rather than a latent form. It is an ongoing, functioning unit rather than a potential one. Generally, there are explicit norms in regard to family responsibilities, and family interests are expected to take priority over individual interests. Approximately one-quarter of the families are of this form, and the respondents are generally active with their children and in some cases they are still married.

Mrs. O., age 92, best illustrates the roles and relationships in an active functioning family. With the assistance of her 64-year-old daughter, she is caring for her 96-year-old husband, who is impaired both mentally and physically. In her family of origin, her 94-year-old brother and her 89-year-old sister are still alive. Her sister lives down the street and comes daily, not to help out, but to pay a social call. Her visit takes place after Mr. O. goes down for a nap, a time when the two sisters reminisce about the past. This interlude is a positive experience for both of them, and their relationship of 89 years' duration is much closer now than at anytime since childhood. Always temperamentally different, their lives took different directions in earlier adulthood. Only now have leveling effects occurred which have minimized differences and restored intimacy and interdependence to their relationship. The widowed, childless sister ameliorates the loneliness and restrictions imposed on Mrs. O. because of her husband's poor health. The sister in turn receives rewards by being included in all of Mrs. O.'s activities with her children and grandchildren.

Mrs. O.'s marital role is of 67 years' duration, and the marriage was reported to have been quite successful. This relationship has changed dramatically since Mr. O.'s stroke last year. The couple can no longer go out together or share activities and interests in the home. His dependency upon her has currently transformed the relationship into something akin to a parent-child relationship. She describes his behaviors as a mother would discuss an errant child. Her only time to herself is when he naps, and she does not leave him alone except for brief periods.

In her parenting roles, Mrs. O. is a particularly good example of the extensions and modifications of family roles and relationships over time. She and her husband had planned an early retirement 35 years ago. They sold their house and moved to an easy-maintenance apartment complex. While getting settled, however, a divorced son received custody of his young children because of his ex-wife's illness. Due to their son's financial and professional difficulties, he was forced to take a position in the East, leaving his young children in the care of his parents. The O.'s gave up their apartment, bought a house in a neighborhood with young children, and began a renewed round of parenting activities, PTA, music lessons, and medical and dental appointments. These parenting activities continued until their son remarried 12 years later.

As grandparents, they also became surrogate parents, and not surprisingly until this day, they have maintained a close parent-like relationship with these particular grandchildren. Their grandchildren, of course, are now approaching middle age and their father is in his mid-60s and now retired. He lives in a nearby community and is in weekly contact with his parents. Even now, the O.'s parenting roles are continually being redefined and changing. Thus Mrs. O. has not outlived her worries about her children and grandchildren. She also has had to revise her expectations in regard to how their lives have turned out. Mrs. O. is particularly worried about her divorced daughter, age 64, who came home 4 years ago to recuperate from surgery. Since her daughter has never left to reestablish an independent life, Mrs. O. is concerned about how her daughter will manage without her parents.

In all, this respondent has a complex web of family relationships which, unlike most in the sample, has not diminished in its composition in late late life. Such strong bonds are perhaps associated with the strong norms of commitment and loyalty to her family which Mrs. O. espouses.

The second type, *the potential family,* in contrast to the functioning one, is one that is dynamic and changeable. It consists of what Riley (1983) calls "continually shifting linkages." Roles are flexibly defined and usually latent in form, only to be activated in times of need or for special ritual celebrations. With an illness, death, or accident, members may mobilize their resources and provide concrete assistance as well as social and emotional benefits. When needed, the norms of reciprocity are activated, and feelings of attachment serve to consolidate the actions of family members. Once the crisis is passed, however, roles return to their latent form, and few functions are performed. Given the dynamic nature of relationships in this kind of family, it is difficult to give exact percentages, but we estimate that 30 to 40% of the respondents have such a family form, making it the most common type in the sample.

The roles, relations, and helping patterns in these families exist in their potentialities, rather than in continuous interactions. Usually members express norms of independence over dependence, yet feelings of commitment and affection are also endorsed. Geographic distance among relatives may be the factor that makes the family a unit of potentialities rather than a functioning unit. For example, Mrs. W. is an active widow who is proud of her independence from a devoted son who lives 500 miles away. She traces her particularly close bond to her son to the fact that as a young widow, she raised him alone. Nevertheless this bond is sustained with only intermittent contact. On his occasional business trips to the city, he stays with her rather than at a downtown hotel. He sends her a plane ticket so she can visit him and his family twice a year. In between, they telephone each other several times a month.

Her only relative in the area is a sister who is caring for her terminally ill husband. After her car was stolen several years previously, Mrs. W. gave up driving and thus is now unable to get to the suburb where her sister lives. In the meantime, she is leading an active social life, going to numerous senior citizen meetings and socializing with her neighbors.

During the course of the year after our first contact, Mrs. W. fell and broke her leg. She spent a week in the hospital, and since then she has never recovered her stamina. She also complains of serious memory problems. Her son responded to her accident with alacrity, hiring helpers for her and looking around for senior housing near his home. When an earthquake damaged her apartment, she moved to senior housing in her son's city.

Other very old persons opt for independence even when children live in area. For example, when Mrs. L. was widowed while living on the East Coast, her daughter and son in the Bay Area insisted that she move to be near them. They even picked out a condominium for her to purchase, so Mrs. L. finally acquiesced and moved here. Throughout her married life, her husband's job had necessitated 20 moves, so she was quite accustomed to relocating and making new friends. After a period of adjustment to the city, she made friends through a church and a senior center. She is most emphatic about her social preferences. For ordinary social needs, she prefers spending her time with her new friends rather than her children, particularly because she is not fond of her son-in-law. She even passes up holiday meals with her family if she has a more attractive invitation. On a daily basis, her attachment to her family is weaker than her attachment to her friends. When she had a bout of pneumonia, however, her children were the ones who saw that she got prompt medical attention and arranged for hired help during her period of recovery.

Her two surviving siblings live out of state, and both are too impaired to sustain contact. Nevertheless, her kitchen door is covered with pictures of her nieces and nephews, whom she saw at a recent wedding. Not surprisingly, this independent woman preserves her options to decide how much involvement she will have with her family.

The third type, *the family as a vessel of sentiment,* functions mainly in the meanings that individuals assign to family relations. In this family type, no instrumental functions are performed, roles have become inactive, and reciprocity is absent. Even when feelings of attachment persist, contacts are usually confined to intermittent letters and telephone calls. Thus most of the time, the family persists primarily in the memories of the surviving members. Some individuals prepare family genealogies to reaffirm the personal significance their family has for them. Others dwell in the past, relive their childhood, and sentimentalize their parents and their way of life. Approximately 10 to 15% of the respondents fall into this category.

For example, Mrs. S., who has been widowed for many years, never had children. Now she lives in a downtown, single-room occupancy hotel and is impoverished financially. Except for contacts with the manager and a woman in the next room, she is quite isolated. She is vague about her past and the series of events which led to her current status of being without visible family resources. She is proud of the fact, however, that she has "a whole county full of relatives in Wisconsin." She has no telephone, but she calls her niece collect from a nearby store three times a year. Relatives have not visited her for some years, and she has not had the money to visit them. She has their pictures prominently displayed, however, and she thinks much about the past and her happy childhood on a large farm. In fact, when asked about her worries, she said, "Now that all my sisters and brothers are in the cemetery, I have nothing left to worry about." She went to elaborate steps to be assured she would be buried with them, using all of her savings to make arrangements with undertakers both in California and Wisconsin.

Another respondent, Mrs. T., also loves to reminisce about her parents and her happy childhood on a Montana ranch. Her father was a gold miner, while her mother homesteaded some miles away and cared for the children. As to her childhood, she said, "I was never unhappy. There was never any hurt in my family—not a sad eye among the eight of us." She was proud of her parents as immigrants and pioneers. Now at 90 years-of-age, it is surprising to find that even with such strong family sentiments, she is "free of her family." Over the years, she has lost contact with all of her siblings. "I had too many things to do and too much to see. Once my parents died, there was no reason to go back." Such a strong endorsement of her independence and autonomy has resulted in few family resources in late late life. Presently her only family contact is with one widowed, childless daughter, who is very ill with cancer.

The fourth type, *the attenuated family,* refers to those cases where individuals have outlived their families. These individuals usually are unmarried and childless. Some came without their family as refugees from Europe, and many of these lost most family members during the Holocaust. Others had weak or conflictual relationships with siblings and other members of their family of orientation, so those relationships broke down after their parents' deaths. Presently, even though a few remote cousins or nieces and nephews have survived, those with attenuated families maintain no ongoing relationships with them. In other words, no family structure remains, and there are no family roles to perform.

Mrs. L. is a 90-year-old woman who has been widowed for many years, after two unhappy marriages. Her daughter died in a car accident at age 26, 40 years ago, and Mrs. L. still thinks of her all the time and often dreams of her. Her sibling's death many years ago had no impact on her family resources, for they had never been close. "Her husband made lots of money and she thought she was better than the rest of us." As a consequence, she has no contacts with her sister's two daughters. Thus, in reality, Mrs. L. has no family. Apparently, emotional bonds were weak in her family of orientation and few norms of attachment were enforced, so with the passage of time, all relationships in her family of orientation ceased. With her daughter's premature death, no family resources remained.

CONCLUSIONS

Like families in any stage of the developmental cycle, the late late life family exhibits great variation in family structure and functioning. Nevertheless, there are certain realities at this stage of life which have a major impact on family structure and functioning. Namely, in living to advanced old age, individuals risk outliving the family as a functioning unit. In this analysis, I have explored the interactions between the structural resources and the cultural domain, the norms, the meanings, and the sentiments these oldest old assign to their family.

Four family types have emerged from a content analysis of the interviews, types that reflect differing norms, values, and sentiments that shape the strength of attachments to the family. First, there are actively functioning families with ongoing role relationships and strong patterns of reciprocity. Second, the family can also exist in its potentialities. In this most common type, supportive relationships are activated only in times of need or on special occasions. A third type of family is the family as a vessel of sentiment, where contacts and interactions are not sustained, yet sentiments remain high. Finally, the attenuated family is one with no structural resources remaining, a situation characterizing almost one-fourth of the sample.

These respondents vary in their norms on the optimal degree of attachment to their families. On the one hand, those who espouse norms of independence and personal autonomy usually had long ago loosened their bonds to their siblings and other relatives in their family of orientation. Even though their attachment and commitment to their parents remained strong in the past, patterns of reciprocity among siblings did not continue after the deaths of the parents. With such weak ties to members of their family of orientation, for all intents and purposes, relationships ended over time. The independent oldest old could compensate by developing strong bonds with their descendants in their family of procreation. If they lost these relationships and were widowed, however, their family life ended. On the other hand, those with actively functioning families are likely to espouse strong norms of interdependence and attachment not only with descendants but with members of their family of orientation. In late late life, they could still activate these norms by having a strong sense of responsibility to family members. In contrast to those with less active families, continuities in family relations are pursued well into late late life.

These findings suggest the need to make more finite distinctions in the study of the families of our oldest population. With the prolongation of life, we need new conceptual approaches to better understand how family resources and relationships change after age 65. Obviously, analyses that make no such age distinctions overlook the dynamic events taking place in the last 20 or 30 years in the lives of the oldest old. With such omissions, we are unable to determine the prevalence of various family types in late late life.

ACKNOWLEDGMENTS

The research reported here has been funded by National Institute on Aging, 1R37 AG06559. This research is still in process so this discussion comes from the first round of interviewing. The analysis was illuminated by many discussions with Lillian Troll, Leonard Pearlin and Barbara Barer.

REFERENCES

Adams, R. (1960). The nature of the family. In G. Dole & R. Carneiro (Eds.), *Essays in the science of culture* (pp. 30–49). New York: Crowell.

Bellah, R., Madsen, R., Sullivan, W., Swidler, A., & Tipton, S. (1985). *Habits of the heart.* Berkeley and Los Angeles: University of California Press.

Bradburn, N. (1969). *The structure of psychological well-being.* Chicago: University of Chicago Press.

Brody, E. (1977). *Long-term care of older people.* New York: Human Sciences Press.

Cornoni-Huntley, J., Brock, D., Ostfeld, A., Taylor, J., & Wallace, R. (Eds.). (1986). Established populations for epidemiologic studies of the elderly. *National Institute of Health Publication No.86-2443.* Washington, DC: USDHHS.

Duke University Center for the Study of Aging and Human Development. (1978). *Multidimensional Functional Assessment: The OARS Methodology.* Durham, NC: Duke University.

Field, D., & Minkler, M. (1988). Continuity and change in social support between the young old and the very old. *Journal of Gerontology: Psychological Sciences, 43,* 100–106.

Furstenberg, F. (1981). Remarriage and intergenerational relations. In R. Fogel, E. Hatfield, S. Keesler, & E. Shanas (Eds.), *Aging: Stability and change in the family.* New York: Academic Press.

Hauser, R., & Wisler, A. (1984). Living arrangements of older women: The ethnic dimension. *Journal of Marriage and Family, 46,* 301–309.

Johnson, C. (1983). Dyadic family relations and social supports. *The Gerontologist, 23*(4), 377–38.

Johnson, C. (1988). *Ex-famlia: Grandparents, parents and children adjust to divorce.* New Brunswick, NJ: Rutgers University.

Johnson, C., & Catalano, D. J. (1983). A longitudinal study of family supports. *The Gerontologist, 23,* 612–618.

Johnson, C., & Troll, L. (1990). Families and social networks among the oldest old. *Journal of Gerontology: Social Sciences, 47*(2), 5566–5672.

Kluckhohn, F., & Strodtbeck, F. (1961). *Variations in value orientations.* New York: Harper & Row.

Kovar, M. G. (1986). Aging in the eighties. *Advanced data.* U.S. Department of Health and Human Services (No. 115), May 1.

Lasch, C. (1979). *Haven in a heartless world; The family beseiged.* New York: Norton Press.

Levy-Strauss, C. (1956). The family. In H. Shapiro (Ed.), *Man, culture and society.* New York: Oxford University Press.

Litwak, E. (1985). *Helping the elderly: The complementary roles of informal networks and formal systems*. New York: Guilford Press.

Manton, K., & Soldo, B. (1985). Dynamics of health changes in the oldest old: New perspectives and evidence. *Milbank Memorial Fund Quarterly, 63,* 206–285.

Neugarten, B. L. (1974). Age groups in American society and the rise of the young-old. *The Annals of the American Academy, 2,* 187–198.

Preston, S. (1984). Children and the elderly in the United States. *Scientific American, 251,* 44–49.

Quinton, A. (1983). Culture and character. *New Republic,* October 17, pp. 26–29.

Riley, M. (1983). The family in an aging society: A matrix of latent relationships. *Journal of Family Issues, 4,* 439–454.

Rosenwaike, I. (1985). A demographic portrait of the oldest old. *Milbank Memorial Fund Quarterly, 63*(2), 187–205.

Rosenwaike, I., Yaffe, N., & Sagi, P. (1984). The recent decline in mortality of the extreme aged: An analysis of statistical data. *American Journal of Public Health, 70*(10), 1074–1080.

Rytina, S., Blau, P. M., Blum, T., & Schwartz, J. (1988). Inequality and intermarriage: A paradox of motive and constraint. *Social Forces, 66,* 645–675.

Schneider, D. (1965). American kinship terms for kinsmen: A critique of Goodenough's componential analysis of Yankee kinship terminology. *American Anthropologist, 67,* 288–319.

Shanas, E. (1979a). Social myth as hypothesis: The case of family relations of old people. *The Gerontologist, 19,* 3–9.

Shanas, E. (1979b). The family as a social support system in old age. *The Gerontologist, 19,* 169–174.

Shanas, E., & Maddox, G. (1985). Health, health resources and the utilization of health care. In R. Binstock & E. Shanas (Eds.), *Handbook of aging and the social sciences* (pp. 697–726). New York: Van Nostrand Reinhold.

Soldo, B., & Manton, K. (1985). Changes in health status and service needs of the oldest old: Current patterns and future trends. *Milbank Memorial Fund Quarterly/Health and Society, 63,* 286–323.

Stone, R., Cafferata, G., & Sangl, J. (1987). Caregivers of the frail elderly: A national profile. *The Gerontologist, 27,* 616–626.

Treas, J. (1977). Family support systems for the aged: Some social and demographic considerations. *The Gerontologist, 17*(6), 486–491.

Troll, L., & Bengtson, V. (1979). Generations in the family. In W. Burr, G. Nye, R. Hill, & I. Reiss (Eds.), *Contemporary theories about the family* (pp. 127–161). New York: The Free Press.

Verbrugge, L. (1984). Longer life but worsening health: Trends in health and mortality of middle-aged and older persons. *Milbank Memorial Fund Quarterly/Health and Society, 62*(3), 475–519.

Watkins, S., Menken, J., & Bongaarts, J. (1987). Demographic foundations of family change. *American Sociological Review, 52,* 346–358.

15 The Importance of Family in Advanced Old Age: The Family is "Forever"

Dorothy Field
Meredith Minkler
University of California, Berkeley

Research on family dynamics and family processes has usually focused on young families, those including infants and young children, or sometimes adolescents. This is not surprising, for, as the readers of this volume are well aware, the majority of interactions between the generations, and the greatest amount of influence across the generations, occurs during the earlier years. Nevertheless, we are coming to understand that a family is "forever" in many important ways. As soon as researchers began to look at the dynamics of the empty nest family, they found that family interactions continue virtually unabated throughout the adulthood of the second generation, so long as the first generation is alive (Troll, Miller, & Atchley, 1979). Although individual differences are great, of course, stability of family interactions is the rule.

The early years of a family can be considered to constitute only the opening act of the family drama: The drama continues across time, adding and sometimes deleting characters. The many scenes are played out on a variety of stage sets. Because of recent demographic changes, vast and important differences have appeared in the continuing family drama. Some of the players are remaining on stage far longer than in previous epochs, while at the same time, fewer new players seem to be appearing to augment the cast.

For the first time in history, American adult couples are finding that they have more living parents than they do children (Preston, 1984). In fact, those persons aged 85 and over are members of the fastest-growing age group in the United States (Longino, 1986; Siegel & Taeuber, 1986). As a result, the parent/adult child relationship is likely to be maintained over many years. For many (indeed, for most) families, *forever* is lasting much longer than it used to do. It is more crucial than ever, therefore, to understand some of the ways in which parents and their adult children interact and to understand the dynamics of the family throughout life.

Both cross-sectional and longitudinal research have shown us that families maintain their ties throughout life. In spite of media portrayals to the contrary, research has consistently shown that adult children do not abandon their parents, nor do they "warehouse" them in nursing homes (Brody, 1981; Doty, Liu, & Weiner, 1985). In fact, some 80% of all care is given by families (Shanas & Maddox, 1976)—by the spouse, if available, otherwise by daughters, and, less often, by siblings or grandchildren (Brody, 1985; Johnson, 1983; Stone, Cafferata, & Sangl, 1987; Troll et al., 1979). Old persons are in contact with one or another of their children on average once or twice a week (Kovar, 1986; Troll, 1986). By conservative estimate, 9% of men and 18% of women over 85 years old live with children (Rosenwaike, 1985), yet other studies suggest that over a quarter may do so (Bould, Sanborn, & Reif, 1989).

It is likely that during advanced old age the amount of family contact will change for several reasons. For example, health will become more closely associated with extent of contacts with family, for as health declines, the old person may need more instrumental support. But there are other changing aspects of the family that are likely to be important as well. For example, we know that in earlier adult years, socioeconomic status (SES) is a predictor of family contacts: lower-SES groups see more family members than friends (Lowenthal & Robinson, 1976), and have higher expectations of filial responsibility (Rosenthal, 1986; Seelback & Hansen, 1978). Whether this remains the case in advanced old age is an important research question. Similarly, women have been shown to be the "kinkeepers" (Rosenthal, 1985), and in the earlier adult years, women are more involved with family than are men (Abel, 1991). Whether the greater involvement of women continues during the later years, or whether there are changes resulting from retirement among the second generation or increasing dependency among the first, again constitutes a critical avenue for study. Recent demographic changes, in which many potential female caregivers are now employed and many more caregivers' families are shattered by divorce, also suggest that there may be major changes in the care of the very old (Suzman & Riley, 1985). In addition, although age itself is only a poor predictor, age- or time-related events such as widowhood, loss of siblings, and dispersion of grandchildren are likely to lead to changes in the composition of family contacts during advanced old age (Troll et al., 1979).

The qualitative dimensions of family process are also important. How do old people feel about their families? Will satisfaction and involvement with spouse, children, siblings, or grandchildren change in old age? If so, will satisfaction increase as contacts increase? Or will increasing dependency lead to dissatisfaction, based either on family responsiveness or on the old person's increasing dependency?

These questions can be answered only through longitudinal study, for cross-sectional studies can only compare members of different age cohorts, and thus are unable to capture the changes that may occur across time within individual persons. Few of the longitudinal studies of aging have examined social support in old age, but those that have, for example, the Duke Longitudinal Studies of Aging (Cutler, 1977), the Bonn Longitudinal Study of Aging (Lehr, 1987; Olbrich & Lehr, 1976), and the Berkeley Older Generation Study (Field & Minkler, 1988), have demonstrated that most elders maintain their social networks, and within these networks they tend to continue a level of social involvement consistent with that which characterized their earlier lives. Social support, however, includes support derived from friends, church and club activities, and work involvements, as well as family. To understand late-life change within family relations requires more information, both quantitative and qualitative, than most longitudinal studies have collected. Until recently, only the Bonn Study had examined longitudinal change in quantity and quality of family interactions (Olbrich & Lehr, 1976). In that study, although decline in beyond-family roles occurred in advanced old age, the spousal and grandparental roles declined only slightly, and the parental role not at all (Lehr, 1987). Now, the Berkeley Older Generation Study is yielding similar results: Although there is decline in beyond-family participation and involvement, there is very little change in the old person's within-family roles (Field & Minkler, 1988).

This chapter discusses some findings from the Berkeley Older Generation Study, specifically, the longitudinal study of emotional and instrumental or tangible family support in advanced old age (Field & Minkler, 1988; Field, Minkler, Falk, & Leino, in press). We have been particularly interested in how changing health can affect social support systems, for in advanced old age, health is a central issue. As one participant put it, "At my age, health is everything!" Health is indeed important; but more important, we have found, is the continuity of the family itself. It is hoped that the observations contained in this chapter will help to draw attention to new perspectives on the family to be gained by more differentiated examination of the later end of the life span.

This study focuses on the critical transition period between young-old and old-old age. The young-old are usually considered to be between ages 60 and 75 (Neugarten, 1974), and they are more like middle-aged persons in personal and social resources, whereas the old-old, defined as those 75 and over, are said to face much more difficult problems of health, constricting social relationships, and increasing dependency.

We hypothesized that the amount of contact old people have with family and the quality of their feelings for family members would be influenced by health, socioeconomic status, gender, and age. In addition, based on the research described earlier, we expected that there would be longitudinal change in the associations between these predictors and the observed family contacts and subjective feelings toward family during the years of advanced old age. We also expected, of course, to find significant interrelationships and interconnections between these various dimensions. It was essential, therefore, to adopt a method of analysis that could take into account the interrelatedness of the questions of interest. Our results do show evidence of significant influence, particularly of health and socioeconomic status, on both family contacts and family feelings, but these sometimes occurred in directions contrary to those we had hypothesized.

THE BERKELEY OLDER GENERATION STUDY

Subjects

The Berkeley Older Generation Study consists of all surviving parents of the Guidance Study and the Berkeley Growth Study children. These studies have been sponsored by the Institute of Human Development, University of California, Berkeley, since 1929 (Bayley, 1933; Maas & Kuypers, 1974; Macfarlane, 1938). The survivors among the sample of parents are described in detail in Field, Schaie, and Leino (1988). The results presented here are gleaned from analyses of the two most recent data collections, carried out in 1969, when the parents were on average 69 years old, and in 1983, when they were 83, with a range of 73 to 93. Seventy-four of the survivors were interviewed both in 1969 and in 1983; of these, complete data on all 38 family support variables that are included in our model are available for 84% of the sample: 42 women and 20 men. All study members have at least one living child (the mean is 2.2); and 1 to 16 grandchildren (the mean is 5.9). In 1969, 24% were widowed; this rose to 55% in 1983. Only 4% of the group were divorced. Berkeley participants were originally selected because they were parents of young children; therefore they do not represent the approximate 7% of the national cohort who never married. In other ways, however, these proportions are similar to those of the national cohort (Longino, 1986).

Interviews

The 1969 and 1983 interviews were intensive, structured but open-ended, and covered a wide variety of topics; they usually lasted 4 to 6 hours. Each interview was coded by two raters. All coding discrepancies were resolved by discussion between the raters, and the resulting scores were conference-agreed. All raters were "blind"; that is, no rater was familiar with a participant's records from another time period, nor did the same rater judge a spouse's interview. The two time periods, then, were rated independently, but by the same team of judges.

The Measures

The Family Constructs. The target constructs, family feelings and family contacts, are each represented at each measurement point by 6 measured variables. The six family contacts variables are the following: how frequent were the contacts with the most-seen grandchild; how often the most-seen child was seen; how often all grandchildren were contacted; how often siblings were contacted; whether married or no longer married; and how often all children were seen. The six family feelings variables are: a judgment of the participant's feelings of satisfaction with all children; self-report of satisfaction with children; self-report of satisfaction with grandchildren; a judgment of whether the participant would like to have things different with his/her children; an overall rating of involvement with family; and an overall rating of marital adjustment.

The Predictor Constructs. The predictor constructs are socioeconomic status (*SES*), measured by Hollingshead ratings of education and occupation (Hollingshead & Redlich, 1958), *age,* represented by chronological age, *gender,* represented by sex, and *health,* measured by five variables at each measurement period. These variables are: how often participant saw a doctor; extent of dependency; self-reports of overall health; raters' judgments of overall health; and how much trouble was experienced with the activities of daily living.

Method of Analysis

The primary analysis uses latent variable path analysis with partial least squares (PLS), also known as "soft modeling" (Falk & Miller, 1992; Lohmoeller, 1989). This is a structural equations modeling procedure that is well suited to data from the behavioral sciences, most of which do not conform to the assumptions of the better-known LISREL-type path modeling (Deal, Wampler, & Halverson, 1989). The approach is appropriate for small samples and for variables with correlated error terms, and it can contain both interval and categorical variables in the same model. It has been shown to work with longitudinal data (Falk & Miller, 1992; Ketterlinus, Bookstein, Sampson, & Lamb, 1989). The estimation procedure is an iterative partitioned principal components analysis for reduction of the many manifest (measured) variables. Each construct is estimated separately, and the interrelations of the constructs, as specified in the model (see Fig. 15.1), are then considered. Because of the sophistication of the PLS modeling procedure, the interrelatedness of all the constructs is taken into account. The method is described in greater detail in Field et al. (in press).

One of the advantages of the PLS procedure is that the investigator can (indeed, must) specify the relationships between the constructs. The straight arrows in Fig. 15.1 signify our hypotheses that health, SES, age, and gender all impinge upon the amount of family contacts and the positiveness of family feelings at each time period. We will, therefore, describe these relations as "influences," rather than using the more conservative designation of "associations." Furthermore, this is a time dependent longitudinal modcl, in which Time-1 occurred some 14 years before Time-2. As a result, we feel justified in asserting that Time-1 constructs influence Time-2 outcomes.

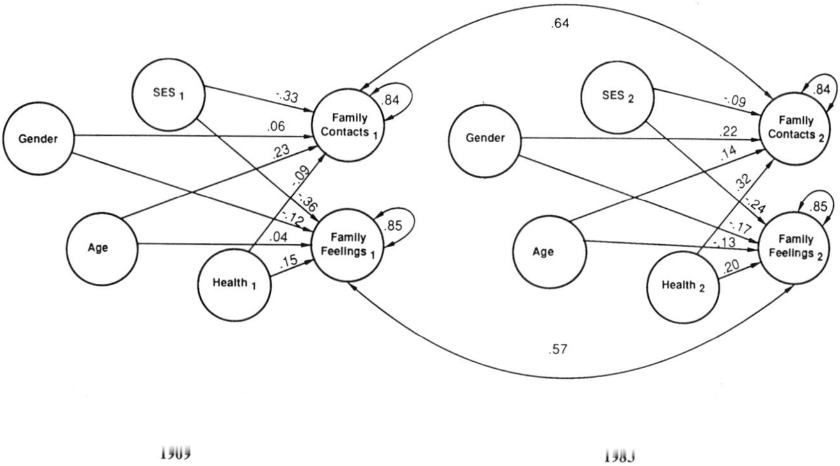

FIG. 15.1 The interrelationships of the latent variables over time. Note: For ease in comparing the two measurement points, gender and age are represented twice; gender is, of course, identical at both times. Age is equivalent at both times ($age_{1983} = age_{1969} + 14$). Adapted from Field (1990).

RESULTS

Overview

Strong consistency over time, both for family contacts and for family feelings, was found. Yet, at the same time we found longitudinal change in the makeup of these two constructs. At the first measurement period, when the average age of participants was 69, SES was the most important predictor of contacts, and health was inconsequential; at the second measurement period, however, when the average age was 83, the relative importance of these predictors was virtually reversed. For subjective positive feelings toward family, the changes were not as great: SES was the strongest predictor of good feelings, and health was second at both times. These findings demonstrate that it is crucial to distinguish between what we have earlier referred to as the social *behaviors* of old persons—extent of contact with family members, etc.—and their level of *commitment* or feelings with respect to family relationships (Field & Minkler, 1988).

The Longitudinal Model

Figure 15.1 illustrates our longitudinal model. We have postulated a time-related model in which the four predictor constructs (*gender, age, SES,* and *health*—listed in the order in which their effects presumably occur) influence the two target constructs (*family contacts* and *family feelings*) at each of two measurement periods (1969 and 1983). As noted, the study is longitudinal; therefore each of the four predictors and the two targets occurs twice in the model.

Note the considerable consistency over 14 years in family contacts (r = .64) and in family feelings (r = .57). That is, families whose members contacted each other and had positive feelings for each other when the parents were 69 tended to be in contact and to have positive feelings 14 years later. Before discussing the other results presented in Fig. 15.1, the makeup of each of those constructs (shown in Fig. 15.2) is described.

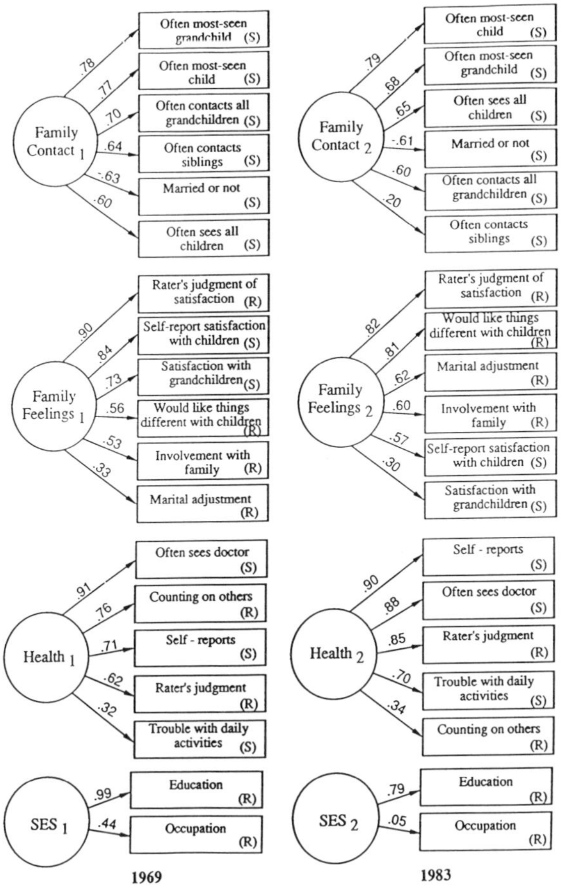

FIG. 15.2. The manifest variables that comprise the latent variables at each measurement point. Note: (S) indicates self-reports; (R) indicated raters' judgments, based on a reading of the entire interview.

The Make-up of the Family Constructs

The family construct variables are shown in Fig. 15.2; they are listed in order of their loadings at each measurement period. The loadings indicate the relative importance of each of the variables in the makeup of each construct. In 1969, when most of the study members were young-old, the most important influence on amount of contact with other family members was whether the respondents were still married. The married people saw other family members less often than the no-longer married. The second most influential factor in determining amount of contact with family members was the extent of interaction with siblings, followed by that with the most-often-seen child and most-often-seen grandchild.

By 1983, however, change was evident. Significantly fewer persons were still married, and many siblings had died. For those who still had siblings, however, there was no change in amount of contact: declining health or mobility problems did not prevent these old people from contacting their siblings (Field & Minkler, 1988). As a result of the changes in these two variables, their relative importance in the family-contact construct declined. At Time-2, the most-seen child is pre-eminent, but the most-seen grandchild is not far behind. Note that it is not the total contact with all children or grandchildren; rather, it is the amount of contact with one member of each generation that carries the most influence in the later family construct.

There was more longitudinal consistency in positive feelings about the family than was found for family contacts. Although five of the variables contribute to the feelings construct at each measurement period, two are most critical. These are raters' judgments of the study participants' general and specific satisfaction with their children. As for feelings about grandchildren, we showed earlier that although contact with grandchildren declined, feelings about them did not (Field & Minkler, 1988). These subsequent analyses reveal, however, that although feelings about grandchildren did not themselves decline, their relative strength in predicting variance in the family feelings construct definitely did.

Change in the Relations Between the Constructs

Now we return to the results shown in Fig. 15.1. Here we describe the relative weights; the relative impacts are described later. Note that at both measurement points, 16% of the variance in family contacts and 15% of the variance in family feelings was explained by the predictors SES, health, gender, and age. This information is contained in the model as looped, double-pointed arrows, or "spans," that show the squared multiple correlations of .84 for contacts and .85 for feelings at each measurement point. We submit that this is a quite satisfactory amount of explained variance, given that so many aspects of old people's lives, many of which were not included in this model, can influence the extent of family contacts and involvement. Similarly, the correlational stability in the family constructs across 14 years of advanced old age described earlier (*r*s of .64 for family contacts and .57 for family feelings) occurs despite the fact that there is also longitudinal change in the relative importance of the predictor constructs. Both of these findings are noteworthy, considering that many other changes very likely had occurred (e.g., in the numbers of and availability of friends, in ties with voluntary clubs and religious organizations, in geographical location of family members, and in mobility), any of which could be expected to exert a strong influence on the lives of these old persons during those years.

Family Contacts. In this section and the one following, we describe the percentage of explained variance in each target construct that is contributed by each of the predictor variables. The total explained variance was 16% at each of the two measurement periods. Of that variance, a proportion was contributed by each of the predictor constructs, which proportion changed over time. In 1969, SES was by far the strongest predictor of contact, contributing 64% of the total explained variance. Age contributed 25%, with only 7% contributed by health and 4% by gender. Those persons of lower SES, older persons, those in poorer health, and women had more frequent contact with their families.

In 1983, however, persons in better health, women, and (to a small extent) older and working-class persons had more family contact. In 1983, health contributed 63% of the total explained variance (up from only 7% in 1969); the relative importance of SES declined to 9% (down from 64% in 1969); gender increased to contribute 22%; and age declined to account for only 6% of the total explained variance. The increase in the importance of gender is no doubt related to the increase in numbers of widowed women: widowed persons see family members more than do the married. With respect to health, and contrary to our expectation, it was *better* health, not worse, that led to more contacts. Possible explanations for this finding are discussed next.

Family Feelings. The weighting of the four predictors was not the same for family feelings as it was for family contacts. At both measurement periods, persons of lower SES had more positive feelings for family members; SES accounted for 80% of the total explained variance in 1969 and 40% in 1983. Health was the second strongest influence at both times (14% in 1969 and 34% in 1983), and once again, it was good health that was associated with good feelings. Gender and age each increased their explanatory power from only 3% to 13%, still a small proportion of the total explained variance. The older persons and the men enjoyed stronger feelings of satisfaction and involvement with family. Although women saw more of family, it was the men who were more satisfied with family.

Longitudinal Association of the Constructs. Among other influences on each of our target constructs is the other target: Good feelings are likely to

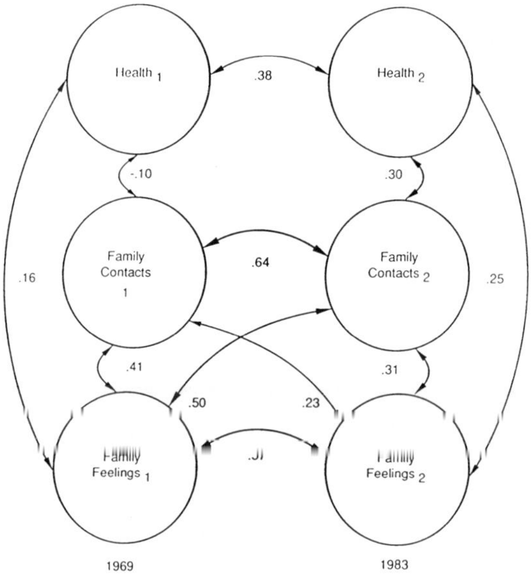

FIG. 15.3. Correlations of the family contacts, family feelings, and health constructs.

promote greater contact, and, one might hypothesize, greater contact will engender good feeling. In fact, however, as Fig. 15.3 shows, we found only a moderate correlation between contacts and positive feelings in 1969 ($r = .41$) or in 1983 ($r = .31$), indicating that these influences are not necessarily direct. There was also a cross-time correlation of .50 between 1969 feelings and 1983 contacts, showing that feelings for family do predict later contacts with family. The cross-time correlation between 1969 contacts and 1983 feelings, however, was only .23, indicating that the opposite is not true: Earlier contacts are poor predictors of later feelings toward family.

DISCUSSION

These results bolster our argument that a life-span orientation must be a part of any comprehensive theory of family dynamics. There appears to be no time during the life course when family is not central, and the literature makes it clear that in advanced old age family is paramount.

The Bonn Longitudinal Study of Aging found results similar to ours. Examining all aspects of social roles, they found some longitudinal change. The Bonn study members seldom gave up any of their social roles, but when this did happen, peripheral roles such as citizen or club member were the first to go.

Sometimes friend or neighbor roles were relinquished, but if this occurred, there was a strong loss of satisfaction. The most important finding was that family roles were maintained (Olbrich & Lehr, 1976). The most recent (1982) Bonn follow-up revealed a decline in the spouse role (as a consequence of bereavement) and the grandparental role (since grandchildren had grown up and typically married and moved away). There was, however, no change in the parental role (by which Lehr means both physical contact and emotional involvement with one's children) for most persons. When an individual increase in the parental role was observed, it "apparently was a way of coping with many problems in daily life," such as poorer health, housing problems, and a negative attitude toward the future (Lehr, 1987). This suggests that the old people sought out their children only when help was needed.

The Berkeley results parallel those from the somewhat younger Bonn group. Although the Berkeley men and those persons aged 85 or more declined significantly in amount of contact with friends and in desire for friendship (Field & Schaie, 1985), there was no significant change in any of the measures of involvement with family (Field & Minkler, 1988). We have not yet examined individual differences among the Berkeley participants, but we expect results similar to those from Bonn when we do so. Individual differences, the importance of which is well understood by family researchers but by few gerontologists, must be considered in research of this kind.

It is interesting that the correlations between strength of family feelings and amount of contact are so modest at each time period. Troll and Bengtson (1979) found that perceived feelings of closeness are independent of actual involvement, and this finding holds for the older Berkeley parents, as well. Clearly, it is possible to maintain considerable contact in spite of moderate or cool feelings for family; alternatively, it is possible to have strong positive feelings about family despite lack of opportunity for contact. The very interesting cross-time correlation of .50 between earlier (1969) feelings and later (1983) contacts, however, suggests that there is a voluntary aspect to amount of contact, and that those persons with strong positive feelings somehow manage to arrange greater frequency of contact in the long run.

We were surprised that those participants in better health saw family members more often than did those who were in poorer health, for our expectation was that failing health would lead to more contact with children. That good health was associated with family contact at the first measurement period (1969) is not hard to understand, since participants by definition were in good enough health to live for at least 14 more years, and this generally good health meant that they probably had adequate mobility to see family often. However, we expected that as health declined, an increase in contact with the most-seen child, at least, would be observed, for the old persons would begin to rely more upon that child for various forms of instrumental support. Research has consistently demonstrated that within the family, the spouse is the major caregiver, but adult children and other relatives provide significant support, and the amount of assistance increases as the health of the old person deteriorates (Abel, 1987; Johnson & Catalano, 1983; Stone et al., 1987), and of course after bereavement. Cantor (1980, 1983) indeed has demonstrated the "hierarchical compensatory" nature of informal networks, within which, in time of need, support is activated first from the closest, most intimate source (spouse and/or children) and only if necessary from the most distant.

Our finding that participants in better health saw family members more often than those in poor health may be explained in part by the fact that this group of survivors is well-favored. The health of the group as a whole, of course, declined significantly between 1969 and 1983. However, when we examined individual differences in self-reported health, using the Standard Error of Measurement (Dudek, 1979; Schaie, 1984), we found that only about 30% had declined reliably in health (Field et al., 1988). In other words, most persons were stable, even though the health decline of the minority was so great that it significantly affected the group means. This is in agreement with Nowlin's (1985) finding that health was remarkably stable for the participants in the Duke Longitudinal Study of Aging; however, when decrement occurred, the drop was abrupt and often profound. It appears that many of the Berkeley people are still in good health. As a result, caregiving is not yet a pressing obligation for most of the potential caregivers. In addition, the 10% of our study members who were most seriously ill happened to be married, and in most of these cases the spouse was providing the great majority of caregiving, with only minor help from other family members. Based on earlier research, we can anticipate that in the future this overall picture will change dramatically.

The finding that study members in better health had more feelings of closeness to and involvement with family than those in poorer health is easier to understand. The literature indicates that as health declines, social relationships, including those within the family, may be characterized by increasing asymmetry, in which elders receive more tangible aid but find themselves unable to give as much in return (Kahn, 1979). This may be problematic, because *reciprocity* is an important element in a relationship, and each partner must feel that he/she is contributing to the relationship. Recent studies have demonstrated the pivotal role of reciprocity in maintaining satisfaction with social relationships (Antonucci & Akiyama, 1987; Ingersoll-Dayton & Antonucci, 1988; Rook, 1987). Yet others (e.g., Lee & Ellithorpe, 1982) have found little association between the elderly's interactions with kin and their general emotional well-being. In particular, a number of studies (cf. Conner, Powers, & Bultena, 1979; Lee, 1985) have demonstrated that although frequency of interaction with friends is positively associated with morale and life satisfaction in the elderly, no such relationship exists for frequency of interaction with children. This finding may reflect the elders' interpretation of kinship interactions as motivated primarily by feelings of obligation, rather than by affection or love (Lee, 1985). For example, Thompson and Walker (1984) found that among older mother/daughter pairs, mothers were more attached than daughters, yet when relationships were highly reciprocal, there was greater attachment in both generations. There is growing evidence that parents who need considerable assistance may see their children's attitudes change from love and affection to obligation and duty (Abel, 1991; Baruch & Barnett, 1983; Troll et al., 1979; Weishaus, 1978). If the elderly parent senses such changes in the attitudes of their caregiving children, this, coupled with losses in reciprocity, may result in a lessening of feelings of closeness by the older person.

Additional support for this hypothesis is provided by Thomas' (1988) study of the predictors of elderly parents' satisfaction with their children's help. In that study, the parents' relatively good health was among the key factors associated with higher levels of satisfaction with their children's help. Thomas (1988) suggested that "receiving assistance necessitated by failing health might arouse dissatisfaction, not because of the quality of the assistance but because that assistance meets needs arising from unwelcome dependency" (p. 513). This is a potentially powerful explanation of our own observation of a strong positive association between good health and feelings of closeness toward children.

The finding of a strong inverse relationship between socioeconomic status and family contacts and good feelings in 1969, with a lessening of the intensity of this relationship in 1983, is also of interest. As noted, previous studies have shown that among the upper- and middle-SES groups, friendship ties and beyond-family involvements predominate, whereas persons from working class groups are more likely to associate with their children than with their friends (Lowenthal & Robinson, 1976). Moreover, elderly persons of lower SES tend to expect and receive more instrumental assistance from their children than do their higher-SES counterparts (Seelbach & Hansen, 1978). Our own earlier research supports these findings, yet we did find longitudinal change (Field & Minkler, 1988). In 1969, working-class participants saw their most-seen child significantly more often than did members of the middle class, but by 1983 there was no longer a difference between the groups. There are several possible explanations for this change. It may be that as friends have died, the old people have become more interested in their children as sources of social interaction. Or this change may reflect the changing circumstances of the older generation: their real needs for assistance at the latter time may have made impossible the subtle distancing that the higher SES groups had previously practiced. It may be that no longer could the older generation choose involvement with friends over family contact, or that no longer could the younger generation maintain the primacy of their separate activities. Unfortunately, our data do not allow us to discover which generation was more likely to be responsible for the distancing. We do know that working-class parents did not live significantly closer to their children, nor did geographical distances separating parent and child change significantly between measurement times.

Note, however, that there was far less diminution of the influence of SES on family feelings: The lower-SES participants continued to have stronger feelings of satisfaction with their families than did higher-SES persons. In part, this may reflect earlier findings that lower-SES persons have higher expectations of filial responsibility in terms of tangible aid and extent of contacts (Rosenthal, 1986; Seelbach & Hansen, 1978). For such persons, the increase in assistance from children as health deteriorates would be associated with feelings of satisfaction, since such an increase would represent not that the parents are "becoming a burden," but rather that the children are carrying out expected roles. It should be noted, however, that such perceived fulfillment of filial roles does not lead to greater happiness or life satisfaction—indeed the opposite may be true! For example, Lee's (1985) research among elderly White residents of Washington state revealed that among those with the highest expectations of assistance from their children, the more contact they had with these offspring, the less happy they were. Other studies have lent support to this finding, in part by suggesting that heavy reliance on children as primary caregivers tends to increase family conflict (Johnson, 1983).

The finding that the women are in greater contact with family than are the men is in accord with the literature. Women usually are the "kinkeepers" (Abel, 1991; Rosenthal, 1985), and this role necessitates regular contacts. We did not expect the results we obtained regarding gender and positive family feelings, however. Although the strength of the association was slight in 1969 (only 3% of the total explained variance), it was considerable (22%) in 1983, and it was consistent: Men expressed more satisfaction and involvement with their families than did women. We suspect that this results from the general optimism that we have noted about the men. As Skolnick (1981) and others (e.g., Bernard, 1973) have suggested with respect to younger marriages, there is a "his" and a "hers," and his is usually seen to be better. This was true for these very old men, as well. They reported happier marriages than did their wives, with more pleasure in shared activities and closer affectional ties (Field & Weishaus, 1992).

The present study's finding of greater marital satisfaction among men than among women is of special interest because these results came from a group of intact marriages that had lasted for at least 50 years. Other investigators have often found that the more satisfied men were those in second marriages (Bernard, 1973). The Berkeley men's feelings of marital satisfaction were echoed in their greater life satisfaction (Field & Schaie, 1985) and greater satisfaction with their financial status (Field & Weishaus, 1992), as well. We came away from our interviews with the strong sense that these men were *survivors;* they knew it, and they took real pride in their accomplishments.

It is also possible that because women are among the "vulnerable groups" (Seelbach & Hansen, 1978) of elderly who tend to expect more filial assistance, they may be less easily satisfied than men with the quantity and quality of support received from their children. Older men, who may have lower expectations to begin with, may express greater satisfaction because the level of contact and assistance received exceeds what they had hoped for.

It is interesting that at both measurement periods the role of the primary (most-seen) child and of the primary grandchild are more influential in the contact construct than are the total contact with all children or all grandchildren. Like Kivett and Atkinson (1984), who looked at rural elders in the Southeast, we found that those parents who had more children also had more total contact, but our model makes it clear that the importance of one primary member is basic. This supports the old adage in the social support literature that the most important difference in number of contacts is the difference between 0 and 1 (Granovetter, 1973).

The role of age in influencing either family contacts or family feelings and involvement, particularly at the first measurement point, is relatively minor. Although age itself is not linked with family contacts or feelings, time- (or age-) related changes, such as changes in health or marital status, do have an impact. The greatest longitudinal changes in the makeup of the target constructs are time-related, not age-related. The decline in importance of contact with siblings, for example, reflects the fact that so many sibs had died between measurement periods. Similarly, the decline in the importance of satisfaction with grandchildren in the family feelings construct reflects the fact that between 1969 and 1983, most of these grandchildren had grown up, gone off to college, married, and so on. The likelihood of this explanation is further supported by the finding that while contact with grandchildren declined, feelings of closeness toward them did not (Field & Minkler, 1988). All these findings suggest the need for a more careful look at those concomitant or time-linked developments (e.g., decreased functional health status and increased reliance on family as a consequence of widowhood, etc.) that do appear to influence family feelings and/or frequency of contact in the elderly, but which are not a simple function of increasing age.

The findings of this study can help to shatter the still-common myth that families abandon their elders. The great majority of studies show that, in truth, old persons see one or another of their children on average once or twice a week (Kovar, 1986; Shanas, 1979). The Berkeley and Bonn longitudinal studies can take this finding further, for both have examined the possibility of change over time in the same families. These studies show no decrement in contact with children. The data show clearly that for almost all old people the family is right there when it is needed, or at least is perceived by the old people to be there. Indeed, a recent national survey of the elderly who live alone found almost three-quarters reporting that a child could "be there within minutes," if needed (Kovar, 1986).

The foregoing data can help illuminate the role that feelings for and commitment to family members play in the family drama. These feelings and commitments were built up over lifetimes measured in the 80s of years (for siblings), 60s of years (for spouses), 50s of years (for children), or 20s of years (for grandchildren), and they remain strong and vital.

CONCLUSION

The family drama motif is a useful metaphor for considering the continuing, vital role of the old within the context of society's most enduring institution. The principal actors in this drama have been the elderly parents in the Berkeley Older Generation Study, who have appeared in many scenes, in which they have played many roles. The centrality of their roles has waxed and waned as the scenes have shifted. We can imagine periods of less intense involvement after they themselves left home but before they began their own families, and after their own children left home but before they became grandparents. Yet they have shown us clearly that, although both stability and change influence the later acts of the family drama, the family is indeed "forever."

The Bonn and Berkeley Studies agree: Family roles maintain their importance in the lives of old persons. Moreover, those changes that are observed, such as decreased contact with spouse, siblings, or grandchildren, tend to reflect role exit by the other party due to death, geographical moves, etc., and therefore do not reflect any loss of desire for contact.

Where changes in the subjective feelings toward other actors in the family drama occur, these seem to reflect factors such as changes in role reciprocity, as described before. A key finding of our study was that older persons in poorer health felt less close to and involved with family than did those in better health. This illustrates again the importance of viewing the health and social well-being of the oldest members within the context of the total family drama.

For the majority of Berkeley parents, good health and mobility have functioned together to make possible the independence they cherish, while enabling them to continue fulfilling roles as parent, grandparent, sibling, and friend or neighbor. Although functional independence is the rule rather than the exception, about a third of the community-based elderly nationwide need some regular assistance with transportation, shopping, or other activities (Shanas, 1979), and Berkeley Study members are no exception.

Particularly for the oldest old, those aged 85 or more, these ongoing needs for instrumental support may influence the family drama in yet another way, through the often-profound influence that caring for the old may have on younger players. Significant role conflicts and pressures are faced by middle-aged and older daughters and daughters-in-law who are caught between the competing demands of their elderly parents, their spouses, their jobs, and often their college-age children (Brody, 1985; Stone et al., 1987).

Variously termed *women in the middle* or the *sandwich generation,* this large cohort of women and their life experiences can best be understood when it is realized that their caregiving responsibility expands across generations in two directions (sometimes simultaneously), and that their roles in the paid labor force, their retirement decisions, and so on, all are dramatically affected by their unpaid roles as family caregivers of the old.

The extent of the latter responsibility has only recently begun to gain the attention it deserves. For example, Traveler's Insurance Company recently discovered that 20% of its employees had major caregiving responsibilities for elders, spending on average 10 hours a week in this activity (Lewin, 1989). This discovery was greeted with considerable surprise and media attention. Subsequently, similar findings by other major employees have resulted in widespread discussion of what a Newsweek cover story nicknamed "The Daughter Track" (Beck et al., 1990). By 1989, *parent care* was being heralded as the next major job benefit, with some predicting that employer-sponsored elder care would eventually be more common than child care (Scharlach, Lowe, & Schneider, 1990).

The use of terms like the *sandwich generation* implies that today's working women are unique in the extent of their job and caregiver conflicts, yet this is not the first generation to experience such competing demands. With the exception of a brief period following World War II, women's labor force participation rates have risen steadily in the United States since the late 1800s. And although only 4% of the U.S. population lived to be 65 or older in 1900, that picture changed markedly over subsequent decades (Siegel & Taeuber, 1986), with the care of elderly Americans falling disproportionately on their daughters. The role conflict engendered by these concomitant trends can, of course, be expected to worsen in the years ahead. Estimates suggest, for example, that 75% of all women aged 45 to 60 will be in the labor market by the year 2000 (Creedon, 1988). Already, 20 to 30% of workers over age 30 are involved in caregiving, and these figures are likely to increase as life expectancy continues to climb (Creedon, 1988). Epidemiologists recently projected, for example, that in 50 years, women in the United States will live to an average age of 92, and men to 86 (Guralnik, Yanagishita, & Schneider, 1988). Placed in sociohistorical perspective, then, the increasing demands on informal caregiving to the elderly may be seen as part of decades-long trends in life expectancy gains and in increased female labor force participation, trends that are expected to continue well into the future.

We have argued that most of the observed changes are time-related, not age-related, but are these changes also history-related? It is always difficult in longitudinal research to separate out the effects of age and cohort (Schaie, 1989). Here we do not mean the early historical experiences that distinguish a cohort, such as their birth during the Victorian/Edwardian era, the effects of World War I, and their experiences as young adults in the Great Depression. Instead, we refer to the effects of recent societal changes, such as increasing proportions of old people, increasing prevalence of divorce, or the *apparent* decline in the importance of the family in U.S. society, coupled with the increasing need of old people for emotional ties and instrumental support within the family. As noted earlier, one of the most salient phenomena considered—the often-conflicting roles of family caregivers—appears in sociohistorical perspective to be part of a long-term trend, rather than a temporary historical aberration. Similarly, studies dating back several decades have supported our findings of greater network involvement of women, class differences in extent of interaction with family and friends, etc. (Lee, 1985; Lowenthal & Robinson, 1976). In short, while sociohistorical developments play a significant role in influencing families and social support of the elderly over time, stability, rather than change, appears a dominant theme in many of the areas we examined.

The media have given extensive attention to the *needs* of family caregivers for the old. This picture has been useful in pointing up the importance of supporting the families and individuals who are engaged in this critical task. Even so, such news coverage may have a downside, because it underplays the fact that elderly family members also remain vital *givers* of care and support in their own right. In fact, in intrafamilial transfer of fiscal and related resources between young and old, from three to four times as much help flows from elderly parents to their adult children and grandchildren as flows in the opposite direction (Troll, 1986).

Ethnicity may also play a role, and more research is needed on ethnic differences. For example, in Black families, well over a quarter of grandparents take a grandchild in to live with them for long periods of time, and in other ways also play a vital caregiving role for younger family members (Burton & Stack, this volume). The study of the often selfless roles of the Black grandparents would be of particular value in counteracting the popular impression of the old as "greedy geezers" who have "mortgaged their children's future" (Longman, 1987). The importance of examining the positive and supportive roles played by elders in the unfolding family drama cannot be overstressed.

ACKNOWLEDGMENTS

This research was supported in part by grants from the National Institute on Aging, AG04041 and AG05869. The authors wish to thank Frank Falk for his advice about the PLS modeling and Victor Leino for carrying out the analyses. We also wish to acknowledge helpful discussions with Lillian Troll. Finally, we are most grateful to the members of the Berkeley Older Generation Study, whose patient and understanding cooperation with several generations of IHD investigators has made this study possible.

REFERENCES

Abel, E. (1991). *Who cares for the elderly? Public policy and the experience of adult daughters.* Philadelphia: Temple University Press.

Antonucci, T. C., & Akiyama, H. (1987). Social networks in adult life and a preliminary examination of the convoy model. *Journal of Gerontology, 42,* 519–527.

Baruch, G., & Barnett, R. C. (1983). Adult daughters' relationships with their mothers. *Journal of Marriage and the Family, 45,* 601–606.

Bayley, N. (1933). Mental growth during the first three years: A developmental study of sixty-one children by repeated tests. *Genetic Psychology Monographs, 14,* 1–92.

Beck, M., Kantrowitz, B., Beachy, L., Hager, M., Gordon, J., Roberts, E., & Hammill, R. (July 16, 1990). Trading places. *Newsweek,* 48–54.

Bernard, J. (1973). *The future of marriage.* New York: Bantam.

Bould, S. S., Sanborn, B., & Reif, L. (1989). *85+: The oldest old.* Belmont, CA: Wadsworth.

Brody, E. M. (1981). "Women in the Middle" and family help to older people. *The Gerontologist, 21,* 471–480.

Brody, E. M. (1985). Parent care as a normative family stress. *The Gerontologist, 25,* 19–26.

Cantor, M. H. (1980). The informal support system: Its relevance in the lives of the elderly. In E. Borgatta & N. McCluskey (Eds.), *Aging and society* (pp. 131–144). Beverly Hills, CA: Sage Publications.

Cantor, M. H. (1983). Strain among caregivers: A study of experience in the United States. *The Gerontologist, 23,* 597–604.

Conner, K. A., Powers, E. A., & Bultena, G. L. (1979). Social interaction and life satisfaction: An empirical assessment of late-life patterns. *Journal of Gerontology, 34,* 116–121.

Creedon, M. A. (1988). The corporate response to the working caregiver. Washington, DC: U.S. Government Printing Office.

Cutler, S. J. (1977). Aging and voluntary association participation. *Journal of Gerontology, 32,* 470–479.

Deal, J. E., Wampler, K. S., & Halverson, C. F. (1989). *Structural equations modeling in family science; A comparison of LVPLS and LISREL.* Presented at the meetings of the National Council on Family Relations, New Orleans.

Doty, P., Liu, K., & Weiner, J. (1985). An overview of long-term care. *Health Care Financing Review, 6*(3), 69–78.

Dudek, F. J. (1979). The continuing misinterpretation of the standard error of measurement. *Psychological Bulletin, 86,* 335–337.

Falk, R. F. & Miller, N. (1992). *A primer for soft modeling.* Akron, OH: University of Akron Press.

Falk, R. F., & Miller, N. B. (1991). A soft models approach to transitions. In P. Cowan & M. Hetherington (Eds.), *Advances in family research: Vol. 2* (pp. 273–301). Greenwich, CT: JAI Press.

Field, D. (1990). Longitudinal studies of families in advanced old age: The family is "forever". In R. Schmitz-Scherzer, A. Kruse, & E. Olbrich (Eds.), *Altern—Ein lebenslanger Prozess der socialen Interaktion* (pp. 345–355). Darmstadt: Steinkopff Verlag.

Field, D., & Minkler, M. (1988). Continuity and change in social support between young-old and old-old or very-old age. *Journal of Gerontology: Psychological Sciences, 43,* P100–P106.

Field, D., Minkler, M., Falk, R. F., & Leino, E. V. (in press). The influence of health on family contacts and family feelings in advanced old age: A longitudinal study. *Journal of Gerontology: Psychological Sciences.*

Field, D., & Schaie, K. W. (1985, August). *Life satisfaction and intellectual functioning: Continuity between young-old, old-old, and very-old age.* Presented at the meetings of the American Psychological Association, Los Angeles.

Field, D., Schaie, K. W., & Leino, E. V. (1988). Continuity in intellectual functioning: The role of self-reported health. *Psychology and Aging, 3,* 385–392.

Field, D., & Weishaus, S. (1992). Marriage over half a century: A longitudinal study. In M. Bloom (Ed.). *Changing lives: Studies in human development and professional helping* (pp. 269–273). Columbia, SC: University of South Carolina Press.

Granovetter, M. S. (1973). The strength of weak ties. *American Journal of Sociology, 78,* 1360–1380.

Guralnik, J. M., Yanagishita, M., & Schneider, E. L. (1988). Projecting the older population of the U.S.: Lessons from the past and prospects for the future. *Milbank Quarterly, 66,* 283–308.

Hollingshead, A. B., & Redlich, R. C. (1958). *Social class and mental illness: A community study.* New York: Wiley.

Ingersoll-Dayton, B., & Antonucci, T. C. (1988). Reciprocal and nonreciprocal social support: Contrasting sides of intimate relationships. *Journal of Gerontology: Social Sciences, 43,* S65–S73.

Johnson, C. L. (1983). Dyadic family relations and social support. *The Gerontologist, 23,* 377–383.

Johnson, C. L., & Catalano, D. J. (1983). A longitudinal study of family supports to impaired elderly. *The Gerontologist, 23,* 612–618.

Kahn, R. L. (1979). Aging and social support. In M. W. Riley (Ed.), *Aging from birth to death: Interdisciplinary perspectives* (pp. 77–92). Boulder, CO: Westview Press.

Ketterlinus, R. D., Bookstein, F. L., Sampson, P. D., & Lamb, M. E. (1989). Partial least squares analysis in developmental psychopathology. *Development and Psychopathology, 1,* 351–371.

Kivett, V. R., & Atkinson, M. P. (1984). Filial expectations, associations, and helping as a function of number of children among older rural-transitional parents. *Journal of Gerontology, 39,* 499–503.

Kovar, M. G. (1986, May 9). Aging in the eighties, age 65 years and over and living alone, contacts with family, friends and neighbors. *Advance data from vital health statistics.* No. 116. Hyattsville, MD: National Center for Health Statistics.

Lee, G. R. (1985). Kinship and social support of the elderly: The case of the United States. *Ageing and Society, 5,* 19–38.

Lee, G. R., & Ellithorpe, E. (1982). Intergenerational exchange and subjective well-being among the elderly. *Journal of Marriage and the Family, 44,* 217–224.

Lehr, U. (1987, July). Consistency and change in social participation and personality: Findings from an 18-year longitudinal study. In D. Field & E. Olbrich (Conveners), *Continuity in personality in the later years: Findings from four longitudinal studies.* Symposium at the biennial meetings of the International Society for the Study of Behavioral Development, Tokyo.

Lewin, T. (November 14, 1989). Aging parents: Women's burden grows. *New York Times,* A1, B12.

Lohmoeller, J.-B. (1989). *Latent variable path modeling with partial least squares.* New York: Springer.

Longman, P. (1987). *Born to pay: The new politics of aging in America.* Boston: Houghton Mifflin.

Longino, C. F., Jr. (1986). The oldest Americans: State profiles for data-based planning. *Final Report for the A.A.R.P. Andrus Foundation.* Coral Gables, FL: Center for Social Research in Aging.

Lowenthal, M. F., & Robinson, B. (1976). Social networks and isolation. In R. H. Binstock & E. Shanas (Eds.), *Handbook of aging and the social sciences* (pp. 432–456). New York: Van Nostrand Reinhold.

Maas, H. B., & Kuypers, J. A. (1974). *From thirty to seventy.* San Francisco: Jossey-Bass.

Macfarlane, J. (1938). Studies in child guidance: 1. Methodology of data collection and organization. *Monographs of the Society for Research in Child Development, 3,* (Whole No. 19).

Neugarten, B. L. (1974). Age groups in American society and the rise of the young-old. *The Annals of the American Academy, 2,* 187–198.

Nowlin, J. B. (1985). Introduction. In E. Palmore, E. W. Busse, G. L. Maddox, J. B. Nowlin, & I. C. Siegler (Eds.), *Normal aging III* (pp. 1–4). Durham, NC: Duke University Press.

Olbrich, E., & Lehr, U. (1976). Social roles and contacts in old age: Consistency and patterns of change. In H. Thomae (Ed.), *Patterns of aging* (pp. 113–126). Basel: Karger.

Preston, S. (1984). Children and the elderly in the U.S., *Scientific American, 251*(6), 44–49.

Rook, K. S. (1987). Reciprocity of social exchange and social satisfaction among older women. *Journal of Personality and Social Psychology, 52,* 145–154.

Rosenthal, C. J. (1985). Kinkeeping in the familial division of labor. *Journal of Marriage and the Family, 47,* 965–974.

Rosenthal, C. J. (1986). Family supports in later life: Does ethnicity make a difference? *The Gerontologist, 26,* 19–24.

Rosenwaike, I. (1985). A demographic portrait of the oldest old. *Milbank Memorial Fund Quarterly, 63,* 187–205.

Schaie, K. W. (1984). Midlife influences upon intellectual functioning in old age. *International Journal of Behavioral Development, 7,* 463–478.

Schaie, K. W. (1989). Introduction: Social structure and behavior. In K. W. Schaie & C. Schooler (Eds.), *Social structure and aging: Psychological processes* (pp. 1–10). Hillsdale, NJ: Lawrence Erlbaum Associates.

Scharlach, A. E., Lowe, B. F., & Schneider, E. L. (1990). *Elder care and the work force: Blueprint for action.* Lexington, MA: Lexington Books.

Seelbach, W. C., & Hansen, J. (1978). Correlates of aged parents' filial responsibility expectations. *Family Coordinator, 27,* 341–350.

Shanas, E. (1979). Social myth as hypothesis: The case of the family relations of old people. *The Gerontologist, 19,* 3–9.

Shanas, E., & Maddox, G. (1976). Aging, health, and the organization of health resources. In R. H. Binstock & E. Shanas (Eds.), *Handbook of aging and the social sciences* (pp. 592–618). New York: Van Nostrand Reinhold.

Siegel, J. S., & Taeuber, C. M. (1986). Demographic perspectives on the long-lived society. *Daedalus, 115,* 77–117.

Skolnick, A. (1981). Married lives: Longitudinal perspectives on marriage. In D. H. Eichorn, J. A. Clausen, N. Haan, M. P. Honzik, & P. H. Mussen (Eds.), *Present and past in middle life* (pp. 269–298). New York: Academic.

Stone, R., Cafferata, G. L., & Sangl, J. (1987). Caregivers of the frail elderly: A national profile. *The Gerontologist, 27,* 616–626.

Suzman, R., & Riley, M. W. (1985). Introducing the "oldest-old." *Milbank Memorial Fund Quarterly, 63,* 177–186.

Thomas, J. L. (1988). Predictors of satisfaction with children's help for younger and older elderly parents. *Journal of Gerontology: Social Sciences, 43,* S9–S14.

Thompson, L., & Walker, A. J. (1984). Mothers and daughters: Aid patterns and attachment. *Journal of Marriage and the Family, 46,* 313–322.

Troll, L. E. (1986). Introduction: Parent-adult child relations. In L. Troll (Ed.), *Family issues in current gerontology* (pp. 75–83). New York: Springer.

Troll, L. E., & Bengtson, V. (1979). Generations in the family. In W. Burr, G. Nye, R. Hill, & I. Reiss (Eds.), *Contemporary theories about the family* (pp. 127–161). New York: The Free Press.

Troll, L. E., Miller, S. J., & Atchley, R. C. (1979). *Families of later life.* Belmont, CA: Wadsworth.

Weishaus, S. (1978). *Determinants of affect of middle-aged women towards their aging mothers.* Unpublished doctoral dissertation, University of Southern California, Los Angeles.

16 Perspective on Research With Older Families: Contributions of Older Adults to Families and to Family Theory

Laura Carstensen
Stanford University

Family relationships play a powerful role in the lives of the elderly. In old age, most people maintain regular contact with family members (Shanas, 1979); older siblings seem to experience renewed emotional closeness (Cicerelli, 1989, 1982), and, in times of ill-health or crisis, relatives are more likely than anyone else to come to one's aid (Brody, 1978, 1980). However, the literature on aging and the literature on the family have remained largely distinct and had very different foci. The focus in gerontology has been primarily on the *needs* of the older individual and the ability of the family to provide emotional and instrumental assistance. In this arena, little consideration has been given to the impact these relationships have on the larger family system. Family researchers, on the other hand, have focused traditionally on procreation and the socialization of young children. Only recently have some social scientists begun to consider the family as a system that lasts a life-time and involves multiple generations.

This section of chapters makes it exceedingly clear why the time has come to conceptualize the family more broadly as an intergenerational system. It is not that families are only now beginning to consider older members part of the family unit. Historically, many families have incorporated older relatives into their lives. However, current demographic trends, specifically the rapidly growing number of older people and the declining birthrate, are reshaping the prototypical family (see Skolnick, this volume). More families than ever before are including older relatives in their day-to-day lives. Not just grandparents, but great-grandparents are coming to be expected players in young children's lives. In addition to the increasing number of older people, the elderly population is changing. Older people are better educated, healthier, and more physically fit than previous generations. Morbidity compression, i.e., the minimization of morbidity before death (Fries, 1990), is increasing and subsequently healthy older relatives are assuming active, instrumental roles until shortly before death. In the following discussion, I comment briefly on each of the chapters and then return to some more general thoughts about possible directions for research in the 1990s.

McCASLIN

McCaslin's congruence model provides an interesting framework for thinking about the ways that individual developmental trajectories interact with the broader family system. She elucidates well the bidirectional forces within the family. Students of child development recognized years ago that parents not only influence children, but children influence parents. In adulthood, such reciprocity continues. The gerontological literature has traditionally focused on the ways that the attention and support of adult children affects older generations, with little consideration afforded to the ways that older generations influence younger ones. The congruence model makes explicit the obvious, yet often neglected, fact that one generation does not drive all events in the family unit.

I like the fact that McCaslin's model shows the ways that older people contribute to the family, not simply place demands on it. Again, the gerontological community has focused much more on the needs of the frail elderly than the contributions they make and subsequently constructed a literature that disproportionately portrays the weaknesses rather than the strengths of older people.

The primary reservation I have about the proposed congruence model involves its predictive utility, which is only as strong as the life stage framework on which it is built. Although McCaslin cites some evidence in support of stage theories, there is considerable evidence that adulthood stages are not reliable periods in most people's lives (Schulz & Ewen, 1988). On the contrary, many efforts to validate stages using large, representative, samples have failed to support the idea of reliable change in adulthood (Costa & McCrae, 1984). Thus, while there is an intuitive appeal to the idea of predicting psychological dispositions based on age, support for the practice is equivocal.

Nevertheless, the model does provide a way of considering the complementarity of relationships across generations. Intergenerational interactions may be enhanced by the perspective that time provides. Grandparents, for example, can provide a unique opportunity for grandchildren to interact with adults who are highly invested emotionally, but more instrumentally detached than parents. This may be particularly valuable during adolescence and young adulthood when tensions can run high between parents and their children.

JOHNSON

Johnson's chapter presents a very important, qualitative analysis of the family in advanced old age that both augments the available demographic literature and challenges popular myths about the family in old age. These myths include both the desolate abandoned older family member and the happily-ever-after family. Based on interviews with 150 people over the age of 85, Johnson offers a four category typology of the family in very old age: (a) the functioning family, (b) the potential family, (c) the family as a vessel of sentiment, and (d) attenuated family. Perhaps the most important message in this work is that the family takes many different forms in late life, forms that are motivated by very different factors. In reading this chapter, my initial assumption was that "functioning families" represent those that have always been emotionally close and "potential families" have probably been more instrumental, but on further reflection I am not at all convinced that this is true. Rather some families may feel the "success" of a family can be measured by the dispersion of grown children who pursue lives of their own, whereas other families tacitly measure success by the maintenance of close relationships with parents and siblings. Moreover, psychological variables alone do not predict family form in old age. Rather life events, like deaths, and structural factors, like economic resources, contribute considerably to family form in old age. Thus, one cannot *plan* for family form with much assurance.

Johnson's typology reveals a fundamental difference between families in early and late life. Late life families are, in large part, "volitional" in contrast to young families where influence is virtually inevitable. Although young families vary tremendously, they unfailingly exert powerful influences on young children; that is, the question is not *whether* they influence the socialization of children, but *how*. For example, neglectful parents influence young children as much, if not more, than attentive parents. But in old age, it appears that families can influence or fail to influence an individual. Families may be "forever," as Field and Minkler observe, but they are forever in very different ways. For some, family members will be people who are obliged to help when no one else will. For others, families will function as the central source of emotional support. For still others, "family" will come to comprise a collection of distant memories.

This chapter also makes it clear that gender makes a difference in old age. One does not have to extrapolate too far from findings about basic gender differences in morbidity and mortality to conclude that females are far more likely than males to experience the "attenuated family," after having outlived all of their relatives, including, in many cases, their children.

FIELD AND MINKLER

Field and Minkler describe the transition from young-old age to old-old age, based on longitudinal analysis of interviews with subjects from the Berkeley Older Generations Study (BOGS). The subjects in the BOGS joined the study in the late 1920s as the *parents* of the young children who were the target of the study. Today, information about these parents' lives constitutes one of a few longitudinal data bases in the world that include people of this age. Their sample is small (with particularly few men) and generalizability to the national population is limited by the factors that plague all longitudinal data sets. Nevertheless, the sample offers the rare opportunity to examine intraindividual change in social networks throughout a time in life where very little is known.

Field and Minkler showed convincingly that, when considering social relations in late adulthood, consistency is the rule. Interestingly, the one change they did note involved the interaction of health status and social contact. Health predicts social contact differentially by age. In the 60s, *poor* health leads to increased contact with family members, but by the eighth decade, *better* health is associated with more family contact. This is the type of finding (very common in the gerontological literature) that forces us to question "obvious" assumptions about the role of the family in old age. At first, it seems intuitively obvious that older people gradually come to need more assistance and younger family members gradually increase the assistance they provide. No doubt, this is true in many cases, but the literature suggests that alternative scenarios are also likely. One possibility is that families provide help early on in a health crisis, but, as the chonicity of the problem becomes apparent, they delegate responsibility to professional health service providers. If so, the relationship of health and contact may be curvilinear as opposed to linear. It is also possible that these findings reflect selective attrition. People who succumb to illness in their 60s may represent a more needy and infirm group than those who remain healthy until their 80s and 90s. Such an argument is consistent with Johnson's observations about the impressive competence of her very old subjects.

Again, Field and Minkler's work shows that gender matters. Married people see family members less often than unmarried people. Since women are more likely than men to be widowed, they are more likely to come to depend on family members other than a spouse. Most men will live out their lives living with a wife who provides emotional and instrumental support. The same will not be true to most women.

SUMMARY AND FUTURE DIRECTIONS

A consistent theme running through these chapters is that older people hold the potential to contribute a great deal to the family in the future—in sharp contrast to the popular, pessimistic view of aging that portends that the graying of America will place a massive drain on precious family resources. Perhaps, as more older people survive into old age, they will provide a much-needed and stabilizing force for 20th (and 21st) century families.

One is struck by the paucity of information about the extended family structure. Many questions need to be addressed. How do older families function optimally? Can families be "typed" for a life-time or do families evolve and transcend types? Which family types are most beneficial and for whom? Very likely, one form of family will not be uniformly "best" for all its members. Just as having a child can increase closeness to parents, but place distance between spouses, introducing an older relative to a nuclear family setting may hold benefits for a grandchild but present problems for an adult child.

One caveat—asking empirical questions that are based on faulty assumptions and myths about aging hold the potential to reify them. For example, the bulk of gerontological research on intergenerational contact has focused on the burdens older people place on their younger relatives. Subsequently, the current literature comprises a disproportionately large number of articles on burden; and considerable media attention has been given to such problems. Yet, empirical research is mounting that suggests that older social network members *receive* no more assistance than younger support network members (Antonucci & Akiyama, 1987); and despite popular concerns about the financial cost of older relatives, financial aid flows down through the generations more than up (Johnson, 1988). In part, these findings are surprising because so few researchers are asking what older people contribute to the family.

Another domain sorely in need of further research is successful aging. We must begin to ask how older people contribute to society and to their families. Existing evidence suggests that although older people may retire from some walks of life, they rarely withdraw from the family. Thus, when considering successful aging, the family domain must not be overlooked. Older people serve multiple roles, from instrumental keepers of children to more recondite keepers of family history. It appears, also, that older family members frequently serve as central communication centers for the family, contributing to the maintenance of emotional closeness among siblings and extended family members.

The research reported by both Johnson and Field and Minkler was based on Caucasian populations. One cannot help but think about the difference ethnicity makes. Whether we look cross-culturally or at ethnic groups within the United States, we see that models built on middle-class Whites are not generalizable to all people. Burton, Stack and others (e.g., Jackson, Antonucci & Gibson, 1990) make it eminently clear that the family takes very different forms in different ethnic groups. Important questions about ethnicity remain, not simply documenting differences, but addressing why they exist. It is not clear, for example, that variability in family interactions are necessarily due to differing cultural beliefs. On the contrary, differences are often driven by economic need more than desire. For example, Hispanic-, Black-, and Asian-Americans are more likely than Caucasian-Americans to live in extended family households, but they are frequently dissatisfied with their circumstances. Weeks and Cuellar (1981) found that although Hispanic-American elderly were much more likely than their Caucasian counterparts to live with relatives, they were less likely to view families as emotional resources. They also found that among Asians living with adult children, loneliness and dissatisfaction were common. Assumptions about harmonious coexistence may become increasingly inaccurate due to a growing schism between the values of minority group cultures and the *ability* of minority families to care for their aging relatives (Sokolovsky, 1985).

The fact that social class and minority status are confounded can lead to misguided conclusions about the effects of ethnicity. When socioeconomic status is controlled, interactional patterns among different ethnic groups are much more similar than different. For example, although older Black women are more likely to live with younger relatives than their Caucasian counterparts (Tate, 1983), when social class is controlled, interaction patterns are highly similar (Cantor, 1979).

To the extent that minority status compounds the negative effects of age — referred to as double jeopardy or, when referring to females, triple jeopardy—it influences income, health care, housing quality, and social opportunities. These corollaries of minority status demand serious practical considerations for social policy. That is, when membership in a minority group entails increased risk to health and welfare, special efforts need to be made to circumvent potential problems. Thoughtful consideration of planning to accommodate differences in a wide spectrum of domains, from diet to language, is necessary. However, in theoretical discussions it is essential to acknowledge that cultural norms about interaction and filial responsibility are frequently not adhered to by ethnic minority groups once they are assimilated into mainstream culture (Rosenthal, 1986). Last but not least, it is important that we do not misattribute to ethnic *preferences* outcomes that are, in fact, driven by dire economic demands. Living with relatives provides a good example. Many people assume that Black families reject institutional care as a viable option for very frail relatives, when in fact cost is often the prohibiting factor.

Research on the extended family holds the potential to make important contributions to the refinement of theories about emotional and social aging. Early models aimed at explaining reduced contact in old age viewed older people outside of a family context and tacitly considered contact with all types of social partners equivalent. The age-related decline in the frequency of social interaction was interpreted as evidence of a general emotional and social withdrawal (Cumming & Henry, 1961) or, alternatively, of evidence of limited access to social partners (Havighurst & Albrecht, 1953; Maddox, 1970). A more recent theoretical model that considers individual change within a life-span context—socioemotional selectivity theory (Carstensen, 1987, 1991)—led to findings that instead suggest that older people are more discriminating than younger people in their choice of social partners and that they base choices on different factors (Fredrickson & Carstensen, 1990). Similarly, a recent analyses of longitudinal data suggest that while emotional disinvestment does occur in peripheral relationships, increasing emotional closeness to a select group, *usually comprised of family members,* is also typical (Carstensen, in press).

As the population of older people grows at an unprecedented rate, the effects of this demographic shift will profoundly influence the family. Broadening our views of aging and the family to include a life-span perspective will, no doubt, inform us about roles that older people play in the lives of younger relatives and the roles younger relatives play in the successful aging of their elders. Communication among family researchers, life-span developmentalists and gerontologists holds the potential to lead to important advances in theory and research.

REFERENCES

Antonucci, T. C., & Akiyama, H. (1987). An examination of sex differences in social support in mid and late life. *Sex Roles, 17,* 737–749.

Brody, E. (1978). The aging of the family. *Annals of the American Association of political and social science, 438,* 13–27.

Brody, E. (1980). Women's changing roles and care of the aging family. In J. P. Hubbard (Eds.), *Aging: Agenda for the eighties* (pp. 11–16). Washington, D.C.: Government Research Corp.

Cantor, M. (1979). The informal support system of New York's inner city elderly: Is ethnicity a factor? In D. Gelfand & A. Kutzik (Eds.), *Ethnicity and aging* (pp. 153–174). New York: Springer.

Carstensen, L. L. (1987). Age-related changes in social activity. In L. L. Carstensen & B. A. Edelstein (Eds.), *Handbook of clinical gerontology* (pp. 222–237). New York: Pergamon Press.

Carstensen, L. L. (1991). Socioemotional selectivity theory: Social activity in life-span context. In K. W. Schaie (Ed.), *Annual review of gerontology and geriatrics* (pp. 195–217). New York: Springer.

Carstensen, L. L. (in press). Change in emotional and social patterns in adulthood: Support for socioemotional selectivity theory: *Psychology and Aging.*

Cicerelli, V. (1982). Sibling influence throughout the life-span. In M. E. Lamb & Sutton-Smith (Eds.), *Sibling relationships: Their nature and significance across the life-span,* Hillsdale, NJ: Lawrence Erlbaum Associates.

Cicerelli, V. (1989). Feelings of attachment to siblings and well-being in later life.*Psychology and Aging, 4,* 211–216.

Costa, P. T., & McRae, R. R. (1984). *Emerging lives, enduring dispositions: Personality in Adulthood,* New York: Little, Brown.

Cumming, E., & Henry, W. H. (1961). *Growing old: The process of disengagement,* New York: Basic Books.

Fredrickson, B. L., & Carstensen, L. L. (1990). Choosing social partners: How old age and anticipated endings make us more selective. *Psychology and Aging, 5,* 335–347.

Fries, J. S. (1990). Medical perspectives upon successful aging. In P. Baltes & M. Baltes (Eds.), *Successful aging: Perspectives from the behavioral sciences* (pp. 35–50). Cambridge, England: Cambridge University Press.

Havighurst, R., & Albrecht, R. (1953). *Older people.* New York: Longmans, Green.

Jackson, J. S., Antonucci, T., & Gibson, R. C. (1990). Cultural, racial and ethnic minority influences on aging. In J. E. Birren & K. W. Schaie (Eds.), *Handbook of the psychology of aging.* San Diego: Academic Press.

Johnson, C. L. (1988). *Ex Familia.* New Brunswick, NJ: Rutgers University Press.

Maddox, G. L. (1970). Themes and issues in sociological theories of human aging. *Human Development, 13,* 17–27.

Rosenthal, C. J. (1986). Family supports in later life: Does ethnicity make a difference? *The Gerontologist, 26,* 19–24.

Schulz, R., & Ewen, R. (1988). *Adult development and aging: Myths and emerging realities* (pp. 205–206). New York: Macmillan.

Shanas, E. (1979). Social myth as hypothesis: The case of the family relations of old people, *The Gerontologist, 19,* 3–9.

Sokolovsky, J. (1985). Ethnicity, culture and aging: Do differences really make a difference? *Journal of Applied Gerontology, 4,* 6–17.

Tate, N. (1983). The Black aging experience. In R. McNeely & J. Colen (Eds.), *Aging in minority groups* (pp. 95–106). Newbury Park, CA: Sage.

Weeks, J., & Cuellar, J. (1981). The role of family members in the helping networks of older people. *The Gerontologist, 21,* 338–394.

IV CASE STUDIES: THEIR ROLE IN THEORY AND RESEARCH

17 Developmental Process: Mother-Child and Father-Child Interaction During the Second Year of Life*

Calvin F. Settlage, M.D.
Daniel H. Silver
Joseph Afterman, M.D.
Kent Hart, M.D.
Kristin Nelson

Our research is focused on how the child-parent interaction serves the development of mental functions and regulatory structures in the child. Mental functions and structures result from the experience of the biologically maturing individual in interaction with the surrounding familial, sociocultural, and physical environment. Those elements of mental make-up that are not biologically-rooted are developed through human interaction and developmental process involving internalization and identification (Hartmann, 1939/1958; Hartmann & Kris, 1945; Settlage, 1980/1989).

The initial study in this evolving series explored the relationship between mother-child interaction during the second year of life and the child's concurrent independent functioning in a play group (Settlage, Rosenthal et al, 1990). The second study addressed the phenomenon of the appeal cycle in early mother-child interaction (Settlage, Bemesderfer et al, 1991). The third study examines the regulation of aggression in the child-parent interaction and its role in developmental process and in pathogenic process.

In this chapter, an overview of theoretical considerations and our research approach and methodology will be followed by the case study of Walt and his parents in illustration of our methods and findings.

From the Child Development Research Group of the San Francisco Psychoanalytic Institute.

*A research-in-progress version of this paper was presented at the Meetings of the American Psychoanalytic Association, New York City, May 12, 1990.

THEORETICAL CONSIDERATIONS

Our research is grounded in psychoanalytic developmental theory and influenced in particular by separation-individuation theory (Mahler, 1979a, 1979b; Mahler, Pine, & Bergman, 1975). Separation-individuation theory details a phasic progression during the first 3 years of life whereby the child individuates and achieves psychological separateness from the mother: differentiation, practicing, rapprochement, and object constancy. The rapprochement subphase spans the second year of life, the period under study.

The rapprochement subphase (Mahler, 1972) takes its name from the observation that the child now becomes highly preoccupied with mother's whereabouts and actively seeks and approaches her, demonstrating new skills and sharing newly found objects. This behavior is understood to reflect a phase-specific, heightened separation anxiety due to a full cognitive awareness of psychological separateness and therefore of dependency and relative vulnerability and helplessness. The consequent intense need for and fear of losing mother cause the child to seek repeated assurance of her continued interest and availability.

During this subphase, the child moves from the mutual, relatively comfortable psychological dependence on the parent during the first year of life to a significant degree of psychological independence and autonomy of function. This achievement requires the formation of self-regulatory structures (McDevitt, 1975).

Developmental Process

Developmental process is the function- and structure-forming mental process that parallels the interaction between the individual and the environment. As the primary developmental relationship, the child-parent interaction is the prototypical vehicle for developmental process (Settlage, 1980/1989; Settlage, Curtis et al., 1988). With Sander (1964), we view mother-child interaction as a developmentally crucial, reciprocal, regulatory interchange. With the mother, or the father, in the role of auxiliary ego (Spitz, 1959), the interaction serves the regulation of the child's urges, impulses, and feelings, and provides the model for internalization and identification. Internalization transforms the parental and mutual regulatory actions and the governing values of the parent into inner regulations and self-governing values (Schafer, 1968).

Object and Self-Constancy

A major outcome of early developmental process stemming from family interaction is the formation of libidinal or emotional object and self-constancy in the child. Object and self-constancy are pivotal mental structures whose adequate development provide sound underpinnings for all subsequent development (Settlage, 1980). On the other hand, their impairment contributes to the pathology of the more severe mental disorders (Settlage, 1964, 1977).

These structures enable separation without disruptive separation anxiety and serve the regulation of human relationships and the sense of self (Settlage, 1980, 1989). Initially, these structures comprise the integrated representations of the self on the one hand and of the mother on the other. Their ongoing formation includes representations of experience with the father and other significant love objects, and with mother and father in interaction with each other.

Representations of self and other are first organized by the child's subjective sense of emotionally charged, pleasurable and unpleasurable, or good and bad experiences in the mother-infant interaction. At this early level of cognitive development, the child is seen to have a disjunctive sense of unintegrated good and bad representations of the mother and of the self. It is the subsequent amalgamation of these sets of good and bad representations that results in a unified image of the mother and the self as separate entities each having good and bad features.

Effective integration of the contrasting good and bad representations into reasonably stable object and self-constancy structures requires a predominance of loving over angry feelings in the child-parent interaction (McDevitt, 1975). Loving feelings provide the cohesion of the unified representation. Angry, rageful, hostile feelings interfere with this cohesion and with the stability of the constancy structures. The structuring process can also be impaired by conflicting experiences with different love objects, as occurs, for example, in the divorce situation.

RESEARCH APPROACH AND METHODOLOGY

Our research approach is motivated by the aim of retaining the complexity and potential insights of psychoanalytic theory and method while working toward the formulation of empirically testable hypotheses. Our choice of a clinically oriented methodology has the purpose of providing clinically relevant findings. We have found that a clinically focused research approach promotes thinking about the observational material of parent-child interaction in ways that could be useful to parents, caregivers, and clinicians working with young children. A long-range objective of our research is a reduction in the incidence, prevalence, and severity of mental and emotional disorders, through parent-education and preventive-intervention.

Our studies of child-parent interaction all employ a semistructured observational situation (SSOS). Our laboratory setting is a 10 × 12 foot room containing a play area and an interview area. A screen effects a partial separation between the two areas and allows the child and parent to be either outside or within each other's direct view. The play area contains a low table and age-appropriate toys.

The interview area is equipped with two chairs and a telephone resting on a small table. The child and parent are observed and videotaped through a one-way mirror.

The SSOS has 6 phases, each of which is 3- to 5-minutes in length except for the interview phase of 25 to 30 minutes:

Phase 1 Parent and child alone together.
2 Phone call to parent.
3 Parent and child alone together.
4 Researcher enters room and interviews parent.
5 Parent leaves and interviewer remains.
6 Parent returns and interviewer leaves.

The phone call to the parent (Phase 2) and the interview (Phase 4) are experimental stimuli that place increasing demands on the parent's attention. The resultant decrease in the parent's involvement with the child invokes psychological separation. The parent is informed in advance about these procedures. The only instruction to the parent is to behave in whatever way seems natural. The decreased parental involvement stimulates separation anxiety and related feelings of distress and anger in the child, and evokes the coping and regulatory capacities of the child-parent pair.

Because our research and attachment theory research share similarities in objectives and methodology, we take note of certain similarities and differences in our approaches. The primary experimental stimulus in our SSOS and in the *strange situation* of attachment research (Ainsworth & Wittig, 1969; Ainsworth, Blehar, Waters, & Wall, 1978) is separation from a parent. The strange situation and the last two phases of the SSOS involve physical separation and reunion. However, our primary focus is on the first four phases of the SSOS, involving emotional rather than physical separation.

Both research paradigms are concerned with some of the same basic phenomena, such as the child's exploratory and relational behaviors. In the strange situation, the parent's behavior is controlled. The classification of the infant's quality of attachment is based solely on the infant's patterns of behavior during separation from and reunion with the parent. In our research, the parent's behavior is not controlled and our assessments of the quality of the child-parent interaction are based on the behavior of both parent and child.

The studies by Ainsworth and her colleagues, which included extensive in-home observations of parent-child interaction (e.g., Ainsworth, Bell, & Stayton, 1971), were focused on the first year of life. The strange situation employed in Ainsworth's laboratory research was first and most extensively applied to one-year old children. In our studies, we observe parent-child interaction during the second year of life in the laboratory setting of our SSOS.

Bowlby (1969) originally described the set goal of the "attachment behavioral system" as proximity to the attachment figure. Sroufe and Waters (1977) suggested that the set goal needed to be reconceptualized as "felt security." This necessitated a shift in emphasis away from attachment behavior toward the inner world of the child. Main and her colleagues (e.g., Main, Kaplan, & Cassidy, 1985) have led the move to study mental representation of the self in relation to attachment. Coming from different but, we think complementary theoretical and methodological perspectives, attachment research and separation-individuation research now have in common an interest in the formation of mental structure.

The First Study

The initial study in the series (Settlage, Rosenthal, et al., 1990) postulated that the quality of the mother-child interaction as measured in the SSOS would correlate with the child's functioning in a concurrent play group observational situation (PGOS). Seven, 5-point scales were used to assess theoretically relevant aspects of the mother-child interaction in the various phases of the SSOS. Ratings on all scales were ordered along a continuum of least (1) to most (5) effective functioning. All scales included detailed descriptions anchoring each scale point. Examples of SSOS scales are *Maternal Empathy, Maternal Capacity for Split Attention,* and the *Child's Response to the Diminished Availability of the Mother.* Eight similarly constructed scales, designed to reflect the child's age-characteristic ego capacities, were used to assess the child's functioning in the playgroup. Examples of PGOS scales are *Capacity for Curiosity and Exploration, Capacity for Play,* and *Capacity for Social Relations.* We found a strong overall correlation ($r = .84$, $p < .01$) between the composite SSOS and PGOS assessments.

The Second Study

Our second study delineated and conceptualized the developmental function of the *appeal cycle,* a natural, regularly-occurring phenomenon of child-parent interaction (Settlage, Bemesderfer et al., 1991). The paradigmatic appeal cycle has four phases: adaptation, distress, appeal, and interaction. In *Phase 1,* the child employs the developing self-regulatory capacities and attempts to adapt to the diminished involvement with the parent by engaging in more or less independent, self-initiated play and exploration. In *Phase 2,* the child shows mounting signs of distress. In *Phase 3,* the child makes either a *direct* or an *indirect* appeal to the parent. In a direct appeal, the child seeks to engage the parent physically or verbally. In an indirect appeal, the child behaves in a way difficult for the parent to ignore—for example, reaching for a forbidden object such as an electrical outlet. In *Phase 4,* the parent responds to the appeal, and the ensuing interaction relieves the child's distress and reestablishes self-regulation. The child returns to the independent activity of the adaptive phase and the cycle is repeated.

In our view, the paradigmatic appeal cycle is a model for regulatory child-parent interaction serving developmental process. The timing and nature of the parental response involves empathy with the child's feelings and attuned assessment of the balance between the child's distress and the child's still-operative self-regulatory capacities. An appropriate parental response and the ensuing interaction affirm the developmental relationship and reinforce the identification-derived functions and structures. The interactional phase is thus considered to be an instrumental event in the formation of mental structure.

In contrast to the paradigmatic appeal cycle in which sensitive parental responses lead to reintegration, readaptation, and function and structure formation in the child, we have observed the following variations in the appeal cycle, which we hypothesize to be less developmentally effective: (a) the unanswered appeal; (b) appeal with discrepant response; (c) continued appeal and interaction; (d) the unanswered continual appeal; (e) the self-managed appeal; (f) distress without appeal.

Where there is a characteristic pattern of unanswered appeals, one would expect anger to rise in the child as a result of continuing frustration of the basic desire for contact. Where the characteristic pattern is distress without appeal, the distressed child's failure to seek contact and comfort from the parent may be based on a history of untoward parental responses to the child's overtures when the parent is engaged in an activity that does not include the child. Although further research is needed to understand the precursors and sequelae of these patterns, our clinical impression is that a relative absence of paradigmatic cycles in a given child-parent pair suggests difficulty in that relationship.

The Third Study: Regulation of Aggression in the Early Child-Parent Interaction

Within the literature on aggression, there is a lack of agreement about a specific definition of aggression. Among psychoanalytic theorists, some see aggression and assertiveness as unrelated lines of development that can become intertwined when the parent misperceives and reacts to assertive behavior as being hostile behavior (e.g., Stechler & Halton, 1987). Others believe that the term *aggression* should be limited to hostile destructive behavior (e.g., Brenner, 1982). Still others believe that aggression includes nonhostile, assertive aggression and hostile destructive aggression. Spitz (1965), for example, pointedly emphasizes that he does not mean hostility when he speaks of aggression. Parens (1979) does not see aggression as being inherently hostile and destructive. McDevitt (1983) defines aggressive behavior as the forceful prosecution of one's ends, including exploration, coping, and mastery. This definition of aggression would appear to embrace assertiveness.

In our current exploratory study, we are viewing aggression as a continuum ranging from nonhostile, assertive behavior to hostile, destructive behavior. Our aim is to continue the effort to contribute to the theory of aggression through the observation of behavior not circumscribed by a limiting definition (Parens, 1980/1989). However, as we proceeded with this study, we came to believe that the term *regulation of aggression* was too broad to be applied to the phenomena under study. We therefore focused our study on the *regulation of anger*. Because a lack of modulated control of anger, including its defensive inhibition, commonly plays a role in pathogenesis, our focus on anger is in keeping with our dual interest in studying both normal developmental and pathogenic processes.

With children's anger as a focus, we will be studying the proposition that anger can impel both nonhostile, assertive and hostile, destructive behavior. We believe that anger, in analogy to the concept of *signal anxiety* (Freud, 1926), is a signal from within that something has gone wrong in a relationship. The recognition, causal exploration, and mutual regulation of anger in the child-parent interaction could prevent its mounting to hostile, destructive and potentially pathogenic proportions.

From the perspectives of both psychosexual and separation-individuation theory, a major developmental confrontation with aggression and anger takes place during the second year of life (Settlage, 1980/1989). Aggression can be mobilized in the child by separation experiences which entail the threat of loss of relationship, by disciplinary experiences, including toilet training, which entail the threat of loss of love and frustration of the child's developing sense of autonomy, and by self-frustration. The child-parent interaction entails similar threats of loss for the parents which can mobilize their anxiety and aggression. As emotion reverberates from child to parent and back again (or vice versa), aggression and anger can become focal issues in the child-parent relationship.

The effective regulation of anger by both parent and child assuages the threats of loss. In so doing, regulation of anger maintains the developmental interaction and developmental process. Parental participation in the regulation provides the child with a model for identification in the development of self-regulation. Successful modulation of anger in the child-parent relationship insures the predominance of loving over angry feelings and furthers the integration of mental structure.

Methodology

Our method is closely related to traditional psychoanalytic, clinical observation but differs from it in the following respects:

1. our method involves the direct observation of developmental interaction;
2. both mother-child and father-child interactions are assessed;
3. observations are made in a standardized observational situation;
4. because subjects are videotaped, repeated observation of the same behavior is possible in global, narrative, and microanalytic modes of analysis; and

5. confirmation of preliminary findings and impressions can be sought through consensus, based on individual and group study of the same videotaped and transcribed data.

In keeping with the preceding theoretical discussion of anger in reaction to threats of loss, anger can be stimulated by several factors in our observational situation:

1. the threat of loss caused by separation, both emotional and physical;
2. self-frustration experienced by the child in independent play;
3. parental intrusion on the child's autonomous functioning, as in seizing the initiative or giving excessive instructions for play; and
4. the frustrating intrusion of parental discipline.

In addition, internal factors such as the anger aroused in the child and the child's fantasies influence and often augment the negative aspects of the child's subjective experience.

We currently are working with an organizing framework involving two distinct forms of regulation of anger. One type prevents too great a degree of anger from arising in the child by avoiding excessive frustration of the child's needs. The other type keeps anger from spiralling in intensity once it is aroused. Both types of regulation involve parental attunement and regulatory responsiveness to the child's needs and feelings. Centrally, the second type involves not responding to the child's anger with overly strong parental feelings of anxiety or anger, or with excessively punitive or rejecting attitudes.

Subjects

The subjects are 10 children ranging in age from 17- to 21-months and their mothers and fathers. The sample is evenly divided between *normal* and *identified problem* families. The identified problem group is made up of five families with children selected by a preschool director as having an adjustment or symptomatic problem, mild to moderate in degree and not reflective of a serious disorder. The normal group is made up of five families with children in the same preschool who are not identified as having problems in that setting.

Procedure

Videotaping. Each child is videotaped separately with each parent in our semistructured observational situation. The interval between tapings is 3- to 4-weeks. The order of mother or father first is randomly determined. The tapings yield 20 parent-child pairs.

Selection of Segments for Detailed Study. One member of the research team, blind to whether the subject pair is in the normal or identified problem group, views each tape several times and delineates three segments for transcription. For purposes of comparison between subject pairs, the phone-call segment is transcribed for each taping. In order to allow greater insight into the interactions of each pair, with particular regard to the regulation of anger, two other segments, each 3–5 minutes in length, are selected on the basis of the pair's characteristic style of regulating overt and more subtle instances of expression of anger.

Descriptive Transcripts. The selected segments are transcribed and commented upon by another member of the research team, also blind to the pair's group membership. The transcription of the segments is preceded by a brief description of the child-parent interaction when they are alone together during Phase 1 of the observation. This provides a baseline for later observations. Each segment is introduced by a brief statement of the immediately preceding context.

Each transcript has three levels of exposition set forth by the transcriber:

1. a detailed description of the pair's overt behavior;
2. a first level of inference offering observation-close ideas about the apparent situational and affective-cognitive determinants of the described behavior;
3. a second level of inference offering ideas about the possible internal dynamics, defenses, motivations, and meanings of the behavior.

The tapes and transcripts are studied by other members of the research team and discussed in a group meeting. The aim is to discern patterns, modes, and styles of individual and interactive behavior.

The Parent's Perspective. Within a few weeks of the taping, the parent is shown the selected segments of videotape and invited to comment on what he or she sees, on the reasons for the child's and the parent's behavior, and on how the parent experienced the observational situation. As deemed appropriate in relation to the parent's observations and feelings, the interviewer seeks clarification of behavior important to the research. Questions from the parent are answered, as far as is possible and appropriate. The debriefing session is audiotaped, transcribed, and studied in a process similar to the one described for the videotape transcripts. The purpose of the debriefing is to gain clarification of the observed behavior through access to the parent's understanding of the observed behavior and interaction.

WALT AND HIS PARENTS

Taken from our study of the regulation of aggression, the case of Walt and his parents is presented and discussed in illustration of our methods and findings.

The descriptive and inferential data in these examples of interactions are presented in summary form rather than in the full and detailed form of the transcripts. Although the mother–child segment begins during the phone call phase and the father–child segment during the interview phase, the behavior is representative for each pair.

Mother and Walt (18 months)

During Phase 1, Walt and his mother engage in mutual exploratory play. Mother's style is to take the initiative, verbally and in action, and lead Walt into play with a toy. She also interrupts activities to which she had previously directed him. Walt appears to explore and play happily, readily accepting mother's leads and interruptions. At one point Walt squeezes a cloth-covered foam block, and mother comments, "Squishy block." The significance of this particular activity, which takes place in a different way with the father, is discussed later in illustration of the integrative aspect of developmental process.

In the period immediately preceding the segment under study, while mother is talking on the phone, Walt engages in the following activities: (a) he places the rings over the tail of the duck pull-toy and struggles to keep the toy upright, doing so without apparent frustration even though a missing wheel causes it to fall over repeatedly; (b) he circles directly in front of mother, pulling the airplane pull-toy; (c) he goes to the door, faces toward mother, and quietly rocks back-and-forth on his feet while sucking on the pull-toy string; (d) he again pulls the airplane in front of mother, and then goes to the toy chest and explores its content.

Segment. Walt picks up a toy from the toy chest, examines it, and drops it back into the chest. He slowly picks up and squeezes a cloth-covered foam block and drops it. Picking up and squeezing another block, he throws it onto the floor. With an angry tone, he methodically throws the blocks out of the chest, one-by-one.

After exploring the toy box, Walt takes out a string of popbeads, bites them, and takes them to mother. She affectionately touches his back, lightly with one hand.

He leaves her and goes to the large ball which he bites and holds in his teeth. He returns to mother, hesitating at the room divider, and places the ball in her lap. She taps him gently on the head with it. He looks up, with a seemingly pleased smile.

Going to the plane, he pulls it in front of mother. He walks to the corner of the room, where a floodlamp is mounted on the wall, and tugs on the cord hanging from it. Mother wryly says, "He's going to dismantle your research lab." In a moderately strong voice, she calls out, "Hey, Wally" and smiling, shakes her head in a No-No gesture, adding "Go play with your airplane." He does so and she approvingly says, "That's it." Busy with the airplane, he ignores mother when she offers him the ball as a play object. She tosses it away. Shortly afterward, Walt shifts his attention to the air conditioner.

When mother hangs up the phone, she turns to Walt and says, "That was [interviewer's name] on the phone, Walt." Referring to the air conditioner, mother asks, "What's that?" and says, "There's air coming out." She laughs in an exaggerated way. Saying, "Watch this," she demonstrates how a kleenex tissue is blown into the air. Walt laughs imitatively. Mother suggests, "Put one up." He does so and laughs. After mother again laughs in an exaggerated way, he laughs loudly and similarly. The play has the quality of mounting excitement.

Mother calls attention to Walt's hair blowing in the air current and then puts her head over the air conditioner, saying, "It makes Mom's hair fly, too." Walt reaches for mother's hair while she is withdrawing her head. She lowers her head. Walt grabs her hair and forcefully pulls her head down to the air conditioner. Undoing his grip on her hair, mother gently says, "Don't pull my hair, just dry it." He readily accedes. Mother affectionately tousles his hair and he lays his head on the air conditioner. She caresses the back of his head, saying, "It's cool, it's cool."

Comment. Walt's circling in front of mother while she is on the phone is understood by our research group to be an inhibited approach reflecting a conflict between his desire for contact and his worry about mother's possible negative reaction to being interrupted. Distress is suggested by the regressive behavior of sucking the string while rocking back-and-forth by the door. The arousal of anger and its expression is suggested by the squeezing and throwing of the foam blocks. His doing so in a methodical manner reflects self-regulation of his anger.

Self-regulation can take adaptive and maladaptive forms. Excessive demands on a child's capability for regulating her or his own intense needs, desires, and feelings tend to call forth pathogenic defensive processes. Under sufficient stress, Walt's very controlled, methodical manner might shift from adaptive regulation toward maladaptive obsessive-compulsive behavior.

In response to Walt's direct appeal of placing the ball in her lap, mother affectionately, but briefly interacts with him. His distress continues to mount. Anger now is indicated by the biting and "dismantling" activity, the latter also being an obvious indirect appeal. Mother responds to this appeal with warm and effective disciplinary action, and Walt returns to independent play. Although he accepted mother's action without overt protest, Walt's lack of response to Mother's tossing the ball suggests that his angry feelings have been only partially assuaged.

Upon completion of the phone call, Mother actively sets about restituting the relationship. The reference to the interviewer acknowledges the intrusion of the phone call. It is of interest, though, that mother does directly acknowledge Walt's feelings. The exaggerated quality of her laughter and the mounting excitement of the air conditioner play suggest that she seeks to divert Walt from angry feelings by arousing other feelings. Her keyed-up, stimulating, "having fun" style provides a playful context and sanction for Walt's aggressive act of pulling her head down to the air conditioner. At the same time, we understand this act to be driven by his anger over the phone call disruption of the relationship. Mother responds to his act not with anger or anxiety, but with gentle limit setting followed by affectionate contact. She dampens rather than amplifies his anger.

The *debriefing* confirmed that mother was aware of Walt's wanting her attention and involvement. Her understanding is that he turns to her out of boredom, having consumed everything of novelty in the room. She indicates her awareness, though, that he does not like to be isolated from her or to play by himself for a long time. She distinguishes between his bringing things to her, which is an acceptable claim for attention, and his "just interrupting," which is not. Even so, she "somehow decided not to weed out" all of his interrupting bids for attention. She notes that he feels safe with "my mental attention" on him.

Mother understands Walt's bringing things to her as manifesting generosity and a wish to please her. She sees his flinging blocks around as evidence of boredom, not of frustration and anger over the disrupted relationship.

It is noteworthy that Mother does not have the concept that Walt's bids for attention reflect a need to restore the relationship in the service of his developing self-regulatory functions. She is aware that he is mimicking her behavior and pursuing her leads and interests, but she has no explicit understanding that his development is progressing through interaction with her.

Father and Walt (21 months)

The 3-month rather than 3 to 4-week interval between the tapings of Walt with each of his parents was due to an unavoidable scheduling problem.

During Phase 1, father tends to let Walt take the initiative and then to interact with him in a directing, somewhat competitive way. This is demonstrated after Walt squeezes the foam block as he did with mother. Father takes the block and forcefully squashes it flat on the play table several times calling attention to the slow reinflation and rising of the block.

In the period immediately preceding the segment under study, Walt engages in the following activities: (a) he repeatedly pulls the airplane in circles in front of father and the interviewer; (b) in father's eyeshot, he dismantles the artificial floral display (there is no response from father); (c) he pulls the duck pull-toy in circles in front of father; and (d) gets the big ball from the toy chest and takes it to father.

Segment. The segment occurs midway through the interview phase. Walt grabs and tugs on father's hand as if to pull him out of his chair. He says, "Ball" and places the ball in father's lap. Referring to his conversation with the interviewer, Father says, "Hey, we're talking, Walt." Father starts to toss the ball to Walt but instead throws it hard on the floor, saying, "That one doesn't bounce very much." Walt tosses the ball and it bounces on the floor. He looks up at father who looks sidelong at him and laughs lightly in a forced manner. Walt bounces the ball again and father suggests, "Try kicking it." In further play with the ball, father arranges for Walt to kick it away from the interview area toward the play area.

Walt picks up the string of the airplane and pulls it first toward the far wall and then toward father until he is close to him but facing away with head down, looking at the floor.

Walt returns to the play area. While holding the pull-toy string in one hand, he squashes a foam block with the other hand. He bites the block hard, squeezes it between his knees, and quickly looks up to the corner of the room. With the block held in his hand, palm up, he opens his hand and fully extends his fingers in the opposite of a grasping gesture. The block rolls off of his hand with no impetus from him. After staring fixedly at the block, he forcefully squashes it against the floor. As it reinflates, he touches it delicately, then squashes it and glances in father's direction.

With the block in his hand, Walt moves toward father but stops short, looks up at the ceiling where the microphone hangs, and again lets the block roll off of his hand. With head thrown back, he rotates himself in a tight circle, facing toward and away from father. He rises slightly on his toes and lets out a sort of yell, "Aiii!-ah." He goes to the chairs in front of the one-way mirror. With his back to father and appearing disconsolate, he lays his head on a chair seat. Father observes but ignores this behavior.

Walt looks into the mirror, smiling and pointing at his image. He makes faces while vocalizing softly to himself. He glances toward the corner of the room where the flood lamp is mounted. He is drooling. He squeezes himself between and then behind the chairs where his view of father is blocked by the back of a chair.

Comment. During Phase 1, father carries Walt's squeezing of the foam block into a more forceful squashing. He also introduces humor in relation to the block's slow reinflation. In the period just before the segment, Walt expresses inhibited appeals in pulling the toys in circles in front of father and an indirect appeal—dismantling the floral display.

In the segment, father attempts to fend off Walt's direct appeal with the ball by admonishing that he and the interviewer are talking. His actions with the ball nevertheless engage Walt, as is evidenced in Walt's showing father that the ball does bounce and looking to father for an acknowledging response. Father discourages interaction by getting Walt to kick the ball away from them.

Conflict about making another direct appeal to father is evident in Walt's moving close to father but looking down while standing with his back to him.

Walt's anger is expressed in play with the foam block. Repeatedly, he squeezes and forcefully squashes the block, emulating father's play in Phase 1 that introduces and sanctions this behavior. His mounting frustration and sense of helplessness at not being able to involve father are suggested by his impotent gesture of letting the block roll from his unclenched, graspless hand.

A further progression in Walt's conflictual need for interaction with father is indicated in the abruptly ended approach which turns into rotation toward and away from father while looking up at the ceiling. His frustration and anger seem to be expressed in the stifled yell. Walt pointedly moves away from father, hangs his head, and regressively drools. His reaction to the state of the relationship is suggested by the interposition of a chair-back between father and himself.

In the period following the end of this segment, Walt achieves a degree of reintegration and engages in mirror play with his own image.

The *debriefing* revealed that father sees boys as being *physical.* "It's fun to watch how they play . . . the way they attack objects . . . he's smashing the block."

Father did not see Walt as seeking his attention: " . . . he seemed to solicit my attention very little . . . quite happy to be by himself regardless of what I was doing." Yet, father also noted that Walt spent most of the time on father's and the interviewer's side of the room, and that Walt " . . . dogged my tracks here more than any other place, but it wasn't even very much." In response to the debriefer's observation that Walt tugged on his hand, father says, "Yeah, that's the game we play at home. He respects the fact that two people are talking and realizes that ball playing is not in the cards now, so he'd better find something to do on his own. He has an incredible ability to go back to pleasurable things."

Father volunteers that he "just read an article about the hole that blew in that airplane. Nasty thing to have happen. Good Lord!" The debriefer observes, "You chuckled when Walt bit that block." Father responded, "There's something that intrigues him—to make it collapse and watch it pop back." In relation to Walt's hanging his head over the chairs, father says, "Period of boredom here." Later, father observes that Walt is "feeling tired and bored." It seems likely that father's association to "the hole that blew in that airplane" is stimulated by awareness at some level of Walt's anger, and perhaps his own in reaction to what he felt to be a difficult situation (see next paragraph). But he interprets Walt's aggressive and regressive behavior as manifestations of boredom.

With regard to discipline, father observes, "you can affect behavior by being forceful and not giving in. If you seem wishy-washy, he will take his cue from that and won't accept correction or restraint." At an earlier point, father noted, "during my conversation with you, I had a lot of tension over what Walt was doing, hoping I suppose that he would continue to amuse himself and not come over and become demanding." Although father stresses the importance of firmness in discipline, he did not act firmly. He tended to delay disciplinary action, take ambivalent action, and not follow through on his admonitions. As is suggested by father's hoping that Walt would continue to amuse himself, the impression is that father preferred to avoid disciplinary confrontations.

Father's view that Walt understood that he is not to intrude on adult conversation and could capably amuse himself, may explain why he saw Walt as bored rather than distressed and angry. It also might be that father preferred to acknowledge boredom rather than anger. In any case, father does not have the concept that Walt was seeking to restore the disrupted relationship and get help with regulation of his feelings. He seems to be less aware than mother of Walt's emulation of him, for example in the squashing of the blocks, and does not evidence understanding that Walt is developing through interaction with him.

The Integrative Aspect of Developmental Process. Following the described, selected research segment, Walt engages in play that appears to link the tissue play with mother and the block play with father.

The lack of regulatory interaction between Walt and his father continues. Several minutes later, Walt moves toward father but stops and again rotates himself while looking at the ceiling. He then takes notice of the box of Kleenex and engages in air conditioner play with single tissues as he did with his mother. He makes many trips between the Kleenex box and the air conditioner. The expended tissues accumulate on the floor. Father notes this behavior and says, "That box is getting very important to somebody," and laughs. The interviewer replies, "He's pulling a lot of kleenex." Under his breath, father says, "We'll see—I'll try to put an end to it." More loudly and directed toward Walt, he says, "Whoops! Uh-oh!" Walt ignores him and proceeds with the tissue play.

However, Walt now engages in a new activity with the tissues. Instead of floating them on the air current, he crumples and squeezes them, and squashes them against the air conditioner in an attempt to stuff them in the vent. This activity very much resembles the squeezing and squashing of the foam blocks.

Our understanding of this sequence is that Walt, deprived of self-affirming, supportive, and regulatory interaction with father, invokes and reenacts the memory of the pleasurable and exciting but regulated tissue play with mother. In so doing, he juxtaposes experience with father and experience with mother. The play with the tissues and the play with the blocks are brought together and condensed by the act of squeezing and squashing. It can be postulated that Walt's behavior reflects the parallel internal, developmental process of amalgamation and integration of representations of disparate experiences with the parents into the object constancy structure.

DISCUSSION

Our study of the regulation of anger is still underway. At this time, the work is focused on the delineation of individual and interactive regulatory functioning in the child-parent pairs in a given family. Comparisons between families and between the normal and the identified problem groups are still to be made. Because the regulation of anger study is ongoing, we cannot reveal whether Walt's family is in the normal or the problem group. Our findings are tentative and do not permit the kind of generalization and hypothesis formation that may result from the completed study. But we do want to share some of our preliminary impressions.

The interaction between Walt and mother has a fairly comfortable tone and involves some aggressive, moderately angry interactions followed by active modulation into playful exchanges. These exchanges, for the most part, involve directly expressed feelings and overt behavioral manifestations of anger. Metaphorically, Walt and his mother seem to be operating in a somewhat tough, but loving, playground.

Mother is fairly successful in both of our posited forms of regulation of anger. She prevents too great a degree of anger from arising in Walt by maintaining emotional contact with him, for example, in tapping him affectionately on his head with the ball in response to his appeal during the phone call. And she keeps his aroused anger from spiralling in intensity, for example, in her gentle and nonpunitive response to Walt's pulling her hair.

The interaction between Walt and his father, although friendly, seems strained, and the more limited exchanges do not result in modulation of Walt's feelings. In comparison with mother and Walt, the relationship between father and Walt seems less supple. Father seems to have difficulty responding effectively to Walt's needs or Walt's anger, particularly when father is involved with the interviewer. For example, during Walt's repetitive and somewhat defiant kleenex pulling episode, father seems unable to use either firm limit setting or playful, distracting tactics to regulate Walt's behavior.

There is a good deal of inhibition of anger and its direct expression in Walt's interaction with father. Father's behavior may have been influenced by the *tension* he felt in being a subject of observation. From the research data alone, we cannot know whether his style of interaction also reflected his personality and involved an internal conflict over the expression of his own aggression. Regardless, Walt's interaction with father seems to be more problematic than his interaction with mother.

Whether Walt's contrasting experience with mother and with father poses a significant problem for the integration of his object and self-constancy cannot be predicted on the basis of these single, brief observations.

Other Regulatory Phenomena and Modes

It interests us that parental restitution of the disrupted child-parent relationship often does not include empathic acknowledgment of the child's angry feelings. The communication of empathy would in itself be regulatory in that the validation and labeling of feelings helps the child define, and regulate and gain mastery over them through identification with the parent. It also affirms the sense of self through the experience of shared subjectivity with the parent. In addition, the empathic exchange can be internalized in the service of self-regulation. One reason for nonacknowledgment might be the parent's concern that doing so will augment the child's claim for involvement and intensify rather than moderate the anger. In this regard, we have observed, as with Walt's mother, that some parents attempt to divert and override the child's angry feelings by stimulating other feelings such as those associated with pleasure and excitement.

In self-regulatory and adaptive functioning, the child has a dual relationship with the parent. One relationship is the actual, immediate relationship and the other is the remembered relationship involving internal representations of experience with the parent. In Walt's case, the remembered relationship is illustrated by his squeezing and squashing the foam blocks when he is not interacting with father, and by his air conditioner play with the tissues in the absence of mother.

We think the importance of the toy or activity to which the child returns lies in its being imbued with relationship with the parent. These *imbued objects and activities* resemble but are distinct from Winnicott's (1953) concept of the transitional object. According to Winnicott, transitional objects derive from the child's oral and contact needs,which are predominant in the first year of life. Imbued objects, as we are conceiving them, arise from reciprocal interactions more characteristic of the second year of life. The similarity between the two phenomena has to do with the holding function that each can perform as a temporary substitute for the parent-in-the-flesh during transitions in the separation-individuation process.

Self-regulation clearly includes inhibition of anger and the urge to reach out to the parent. This inhibition is reflected in the phenomenon of the indirect appeal as contrasted with a direct appeal. As illustrated by Walt's behavior, it is also reflected in the child's moving or turning toward and then away from the parent. The child may look toward the parent and then deflect the look to the corner or ceiling of the room in a form of gaze aversion (Fraiberg, 1982; Stern, 1974). Children may engage in circling or body-rotating behavior in the space in front of the parent. In this behavior, the child repetitiously faces toward and away from the parent. In the context of separation-individuation theory, the child can be thought of as resisting or defending against the urge for rapprochement.

Because the formation of mental structure is very much in process in children at the age under study, temporary regression in level of organization, integration, and function is common. This is evidenced, for example, in self-soothing actions such as sucking, in drooling, and in marked changes in physical competence such as uncharacteristic clumsiness or falling down.

Here, there is the question of whether regression may serve the preservation of the sense of self. The loss of relationship with the parent and the aroused anger disrupt the integration and integrity of the developing sense of self. Regression could function to counteract the loss of sense of self through a psychological return to earlier representations of the self in a less conflicted, affectively more harmonious relationship with the parent. This possibility is suggested by our impression that a child under stress tends to move from the higher level, abstract, symbolic mode of remembering to the more palpable, sensorimotor, action mode of remembering and reenactment. Conceivably, the temporary, regressive dissolution of recently developed mental boundaries between self and other could alleviate feelings of anxiety and helplessness engendered by the threat of loss of relationship. These feelings stem from the full awareness of both separateness and dependency characteristic of the rapprochement subphase.

Limitations of the Current Study and Directions for Future Research

One limitation of this study is the lack of longitudinal data. Observations of parent-infant interaction during the first year of life would permit study of the emergence of mutual regulatory patterns of anger and aggression and their possible consistencies or transformations during the second year. It also would allow observation of the precursors of the appeal cycle as it is seen in the second year of life. Similarly, observations during the third year of life would reveal whether the delineated issues and patterns of anger continue or abate, or are subject to further transformation.

Another limitation is our lack of information about the relationship of the parents with each other. The couple relationship has been found to contribute to development beyond the contribution of the relationship of each parent with the child (Cowan, Cowan, Heming et al., 1985).

As is suggested by the difference between maternal and paternal behavior in the case of Walt and his parents, there is the dual question of whether parental interactional behavior is related to the parent's own gender, and whether it is different with girls than with boys. We anticipate that further study may reveal such gender-related differences in appeal cycles and patterns of regulation of anger.

Education for Prevention: The Appeal Cycle

Walt's parents do not have a clear understanding of how their interaction with him serves the regulation of his urges and feelings and his mental and emotional development. This has been true for most of the parents in our studies. Parents, and child caregivers generally, commonly do not understand that a child's bid for attention may be seeking a supportive response to a legitimate developmental need. Instead, they may believe that the child is seizing the opportunity to engage in provocative behavior when the parent's attention is diverted, or is seeking unnecessary and unwarranted attention. They fear that responding to the child's bid for attention will *spoil* the child.

The issue of how the child learns and develops is crucial. Traditional learning theory would hold that if the child is positively reinforced for seeking contact, he or she will seek more and more contact. Psychoanalytic theory and attachment theory take the position that parental responsiveness to the child's signals will result in less demanding and less clingy behavior. Attachment research (Bell & Ainsworth, 1972) found that when mothers were responsive to their infant's crying during the first year of life, crying decreased over the course of the year, and when they were unresponsive, crying increased. This finding is in accord with psychoanalytic developmental theory which holds that the child's internal sense of security and trust is born of responsive parenting and develops over the first 3 years of life into object and self-constancy. As internalization proceeds and these structures become integrated, the need for immediate involvement with the parent lessens. In terms of the appeal cycle, a satisfactory interactional phase will enhance, rather than detract from the child's developing capability for independent function and adaptation.

We suspect that study of nonparental, child-caregiver interactions (which we plan to undertake) will confirm that the appeal cycle is a phenomenon of those relationships as well. If so, we believe that the development of children would be greatly enhanced by imparting a full understanding of developmental process and the appeal cycle to parents and child caregivers.

We believe that the observation and assessment of child-parent interaction in the context of the appeal cycle has the potential to detect developmental difficulty and thus permit timely intervention. Because the formation of normal and pathogical functions and structures is in process and therefore quite malleable during the second year of life, preventive-intervention should be effective. In an intervention study, research findings suggesting the possibility of developmental difficulty would be followed up by a clinical evaluation. Clinical evaluation would include a full review and appraisal of the family relationships and the child's development and behavior from birth to the present. The aim would be to determine whether the detected signs of difficulty reflect pathological processes warranting intervention or processes within the range of normal development.

In closing this presentation and discussion of research on child-parent interaction and developmental process, we emphasize that the appeal cycle is a *process* model of mental and emotional development, both within a given cycle and across repeated cycles. Breaks in parental attunement and assessment of the child's developmental needs are inevitable (Tronick & Gianino, 1986). The regulatory function of a given appeal cycle may not take place. But the process model of ongoing development permits restoration of the relationship and regulation of the child's emotional equilibrium in subsequent cycles.

ACKNOWLEDGMENTS

We are indebted to Philip M. Spielman, M.D. for his contributions to the research and his thoughtful help with this paper. We also are indebted to Jane Welker, M.A., Director of the Early Childhood Laboratory, Human Development and Family Studies Unit, University of California, Davis, for her consultation to our *Regulation of Aggression* study and her help in obtaining the subjects and making arrangements for the videotaping facility.

Funded in part by the Fund for Psychoanalytic Research of the American Psychoanalytic Association.

REFERENCES

Ainsworth, M. D. S., & Wittig, B. A. (1969). Attachment and exploratory behavior of one-year-olds in a strange situation. B. M. Foss (Ed.), *Determinants of infant behavior* (pp. 111–136). London: Metheun.

Ainsworth, M. D. S., Bell, M. V., & Stayton. (1971). Individual differences in strange-situation behavior of one-year olds. In H. R. Schaffer (Ed.), *The origins of human social relations* (pp. 17–57). London: Academic Press.

Ainsworth, M. D. S., Blehar, M. C., Waters, W., & Wall, S. (1978). *Patterns of attachment: A psychological study of the strange situation*. Hillsdale, NJ: Lawrence Erlbaum Associates.

Bell, S., & Ainsworth, M. D. S. (1972). Infant crying and maternal responsiveness. *Child Development, 43,* 1171–1190.

Bowlby, J. (1969). *Attachment and loss, Vol. 1: Attachment*. New York: Basic Books.

Brenner, C. (1982). *The mind in conflict*. New York: International Universities Press.

Cowan, C. P., Cowan, P. A., Heming, G., Garett, E., Coysh, W. S., Curtis-Bowles, H.,& Bowles, A. J. (1985). Transitions to parenthood: His hers, and theirs. *Journal of Family Issues, 6,* 451–481.

Fraiberg, S. (1982). Pathological defenses in infancy. *Psychoanalytic Quarterly, 51,* 612–535.

Freud, S. (1926). Inhibitions, symptoms and anxiety (pp. 87–156). *Standard Edition, 20*. London: Hogarth Press.

Hartmann, H. (1939/1958). *Ego psychology and the problem of adaptation*. New York: International Universities Press.

Hartmann, H., & Kris, E. (1945). The genetic approach in psychoanalysis. *Psychoanalytic study of the child* (Vol. 1, pp. 11–30). New York: International Universities Press.

Mahler, M. S. (1972). The rapprochement subphase of the separation-individuation process. *Psychoanalytic Quarterly, 41,* 487–506.

Mahler, M. S. (1979a). *Infantile psychosis and early papers: Selected papers 1.* New York: Jason Aronson.

Mahler, M. S. (1979b). *Separation-individuation: Selected papers 2.* New York: Jason Aronson.

Mahler, M. S., Pine, F., & Bergman, A. (1975). *The psychological birth of the human infant: Symbiosis and individuation.* New York: Basic Books.

Main, M., Kaplan, N., & Cassidy, J. (1985). Security in infancy, childhood, and adulthood: A move to the level of representation. In I. Bretherton & E. Walters (Eds.), *Growing points of attachment theory and research. Monographs of the society for research in child development, 50,* (pp. 66–104) (1–2, Serial No. 209).

McDevitt, J. B. (1975). Separation-individuation and object constancy. *Journal of the American Psychoanalytic Association, 23,* 713–742.

McDevitt, J. B. (1983). The emergence of hostile aggression and its defensive and adaptive modifications during the separation-individuation phase. *Journal of the American Psychoanalytic Association, 31,* 273–300.

Parens, H. (1979). *The development of aggression in early childhood.* New York: Jason Aronson.

Parens, H. (1980/1989). Toward an epigenesis of aggression in early childhood. In S. I. Greenspan & G. H. Pollock (Eds.), *The course of life, Vol. 2: Early childhood* (pp. 129–161). New York: International Universities Press.

Sander, L. W. (1964). Adaptive relationships in the early mother-child interaction. *Journal of the American Academy of Child Psychiatry, 3,* 231–264.

Schafer, R. (1968). *Aspects of internalization.* New York: International Universities Press.

Settlage, C. F. (1964). Psychoanalytic theory in relation to the nosology of childhood psychic disorders. *Journal of the American Psychoanalytic Association, 12,* 776–789.

Settlage, C. F. (1977). The psychoanalytic understanding of narcissistic and borderline disorders: Advances in developmental theory. *Journal of the American Psychoanalytic Association, 25,* 805–833.

Settlage, C. F. (1980). Psychoanalytic developmental thinking in current and historical perspective. *Psychoanalysis & Contemporary Thought, 3,* 139–170.

Settlage, C. F. (1980/1989). The psychoanalytic theory and understanding of psychic development during the second and third years of life. In S. I. Greenspan & G. H. Pollock (Eds.), *The course of life, Vol. 2: Early childhood.* New York: International Universities Press.

Settlage, C. F. (1989). The interplay of therapeutic and developmental process in the treatment of children: An application of contemporary object relations theory. *Psychoanalytic Inquiry, 9,* 375–396.

Settlage, C. F., Bemesderfer, S., Rosenthal, J., Afterman, J., & Spielman, P. M. (1991). The appeal cycle in early mother-child interaction: The nature and significance of a finding from developmental research. *Journal of the American Psychoanalytic Association, 39,* 987–1014.

Settlage, C. F., Curtis, J., Lozoff, M., Lozoff, M., Silberschatz, G., & Simburg, E. J. (1988). Conceptualizing adult development. *Journal of the American Psychoanalytic Association, 36,* 347–369.

Settlage, C. F., Rosenthal, J., Spielman, P. M., Gassner, S., Afterman, J., Bemesderfer, S., & Kolodny, S. (1990). An exploratory study of mother-child interaction during the second year of life. *Journal of the American Psychoanalytic Association, 38,* 705–731.

Spitz, R. A. (1959). *A genetic field theory of ego formation.* New York: International Universities Press.

Spitz, R. A. (1965). The evolution of dialogue. In M. Schur (Ed.), *Drives, affects, and behavior, Vol. 2* (pp. 170–190). New York: International Universities Press.

Sroufe, L. A., & Waters, E. (1977). Attachment as an organizational construct. *Child Development, 48,* 1184–1199.

Stechler, G., & Halton, A. (1987). The emergence of assertion and aggression during infancy: A psychoanalytic perspective. *Journal of the American Psychoanalytic Association, 35,* 821–838.

Stern, D. W. (1974). Mother and infant at play: The dyadic interaction involving facial, vocal, and gaze behaviors. In M. Lewis & L. A. Rosenblum (Eds.), *The effect of the infant on its caregiver* (pp. 187–213). New York: Wiley-Interscience.

Tronick, E. Z., & Gianino, A. F. (1986). The transmission of maternal disturbance to the infant. In E. Z. Tronick & T. Field (Eds.), *Maternal depression and infant disturbance* (pp. 5–11). *New directions for child development, 34.* San Francisco: Jossey-Bass.

Winnicott, D. W. (1953). Transitional objects and transitional phenomena. *International Journal of Psychoanalysis, 34,* 89–97.

18 Continuity and Change in the Transition to Parenthood: A Tale of Two Families

Isabel S. Bradburn
Joan A. Kaplan
University of California, Berkeley

In the past decade, a number of longitudinal research projects have documented the experiences of men, women and their marriages during the transition to parenthood (Belsky, Gilstrap, & Rovine, 1984; Cowan & Cowan, 1992; Feldman & Aschenbrenner, 1983; Grossman, Eichler, & Winickoff, 1980; Heinicke, Diskin, Ramsay-Klee, & Oates, 1986; Lewis, Owen, & Cox, 1988). Analyses of group data demonstrate that becoming a family entails dramatic shifts in personal identity and family life. In addition to provoking a rearrangement of work and family roles and reducing the time and energy for the marital relationship, the process of family formation alters the central aspects of men's and women's self-concepts and their relationships to spouses, parents, friends, and the society at large (For reviews of research of the transition to parenthood, see Berman & Pedersen, 1987; Cox, 1985; Michaels & Goldberg, 1988; Palkovitz & Sussman, 1988).

Studies of the process of becoming a family highlight the interconnections among societal, familial, and individual factors that shape the development of family members and their relationships with one another. Recent changes in women's participation in the workforce and in ideologies concerning the sharing of family labor have led to uncertainties about who will perform what childrearing and household tasks. Wives and husbands often engage in complex negotiations both at home and at the workplace in order to arrange and provide acceptable care for their children. Couples with more traditional work arrangements—where husbands are the sole wage-earners—experience dilemmas about whether and when wives should return to or begin work outside the family. Fathers and mothers who are struggling to create new, less traditional kinds of families have few models available from their growing up years to shape their beliefs and behavior. Shifting norms in the larger society, conflicting aims and goals for men and women within families, and conflicts and uncertainties within each spouse combine to make the transition to parenthood a stressful and challenging time in the life of a family.

From the research on the transition to parenthood, it is possible to paint an overall picture of change and continuity during this pivotal time in family development. What is missing from these group snapshots taken in late pregnancy and again after the birth of a child is a portrayal of the mechanisms or processes that individual families adopt to cope with the complex demands of bearing and rearing children. In this chapter, we explore the interior of family life using case studies of two contrasting but representative families who participated in the Becoming a Family Project (Cowan & Cowan, 1988). The families' participation in the project allows us to interpret their experiences in light of the group trends. This type of case study, we suggest, can be particularly useful in guiding future research and intervention in family processes.

The two families were chosen for detailed analysis because of their contrasting role arrangements and their similarity in family structure. The McLeans[1] represent a relatively traditional American family, with an employed father and a mother who puts her professional aspirations on hold to stay home and care for their first—and later their second—child. The Swenson family illustrates a more contemporary configuration. In this couple, the mother enters pregnancy with the stronger career focus in the couple, and the father, at least in the early years of family formation, has a stronger identity as a parent than he does in his work outside the family. Both couples initially give birth to a daughter and then have a second child by the time the older child has entered Kindergarten. The ways in which these individual, marital, and family factors interact in the couple's early adaptation to family life, along with the dramatic changes and underlying consistencies exhibited by each family, are the foci of this chapter.

The Study: Sources of Information About the Family

Descriptions of the design and methods used in the larger study appear in this volume (see chapter by Cowan, Cowan, & Kerig) and in more detail elsewhere (Cowan & Cowan, 1990). Participants included men and women who, at the beginning of the study, ranged in age from 21 to 48 and had incomes that ranged from $7000 to $72,000 in 1979–80. They were recruited from 28 communities in the San Francisco Bay Area.

The information for the case studies came from material gathered over a 6-year period. It included interviews by a staff couple when the couples were in late pregnancy and again at 6, 18, 42, and 66 months postpartum, and an extensive

[1]The names and many details have been changed to protect the privacy of the families.

battery of questionnaires filled out by each partner at each assessment period. In the course of our family portraits, we describe a few of these questionnaires. We have organized our descriptions of the families using the five-domain model of family life proposed by Cowan and Cowan (1988, 1992). The model emphasizes the interaction among five interlocking subsystems of the family:

1. the individual family members (mother, father, children);
2. the couple relationship;
3. each of the parent-child relationships;
4. the relationships—both historical and current—between each spouse and his or her own parents;
5. the balance between the life stresses impinging on the family and the social supports available to buffer them.

The model assumes that each subsystem affects and is affected by all of the subsystems in the family, an assumption supported by the analysis of group data (e.g., Cowan & Cowan, 1988). Study questionnaires and interviews were designed to elicit information about each of these subsystems.

We turn now to the stories of two families, the McLeans and Swensons, as they make the transition from being partners to being parents and partners.

THE McLEANS

Michael and Gail were in their middle thirties when Gail became pregnant with their first child. When the research staff team first met with them, they were in the midst of another major transition: After several years away, Michael and Gail had recently moved back to the San Francisco Bay Area. Michael had just started in a new position as a medical researcher at a local hospital, and Gail had recently stopped looking for work due to her pregnancy. Both were excited to be back among old friends and were in the process of reestablishing themselves in the community.

The McLeans had been married 12 years by the time they decided to have a child. They described their relationship as having undergone many phases, including estrangement and a brief separation several years before Gail became pregnant. The early years of their marriage were characterized by frequent moves in support of Michael's career advancement. Due to their time spent together plus a period of couples therapy in recent years, Gail and Michael felt that they knew each other well, and had well-established patterns—some that they enjoyed, others that they were working to change.

As was the case for many couples in the longitudinal study (see Cowan & Cowan, 1992), the decision to have a child had involved a long and complex process. Early in their marriage, the McLeans felt that Michael's career and financial status did not provide enough stability in which to raise children. The marital difficulties they then experienced put off the question of a family still further. The choice to start a family now represented to both partners a renewed commitment to their relationship after rocky times. For Michael, having a child fulfilled a long-held dream; for Gail it was a more recent wish, one about which she still felt some what ambivalent.

Each of the McLeans grew up in intact families, the eldest of two children. Michael grew up in Australia at the end of the Second World War; much of his postwar childhood was financially difficult, and he and his family lived with his paternal grandparents for many years. Michael's parents were religious and brought up their children strictly, with many rules and little encouragement to express feelings. Michael described his father as solid, calm and protective, a shy man who worked long hours and with whom he discussed the pragmatic affairs of life. Michael's mother was "more volatile" and exciting; she took her son places and engaged him in "conversations about life." The McLeans senior had a solid, if quiet, marriage, in Michael's view. Despite tensions that arose mainly over family rules, Michael grew up feeling relatively positive and unconflicted about his relationship with his parents.

As a young man, Michael came to the United States for medical training. His career was important to him and he devoted most of his youth to its development. At the same time, Michael built strong friendships with other men that he maintained throughout the years. Michael especially valued spontaneously "going out and doing things," and having time alone to think and dream. Occasionally, he suffered depressive bouts that seemed to stem from not meeting his expectations of himself.

Gail's family was more financially secure than was Michael's. Her parents both had careers that occupied much of their time, and Gail remembered often being left with relatives while her parents went out at night. Like Michael's parents, Gail's mother was talkative and "emotional," while her father took care of practical aspects of family life. They sometimes had marital difficulties, and Gail's father left the family for one 6-month period when Gail was a child. Gail was often sick as a child, and generally it was her father who took her to the doctor and administered her medicine. As an adult, Gail seemed to maintain a more "hot–cold" relationship with her parents. She felt close to them, but preferred not to spend extended periods of time with them. In particular, Gail had a complex relationship with her mother that developed new intensity as she herself was becoming a mother.

Gail had worked at various jobs but, to her disappointment, felt no strong sense of vocation. She had obtained a master's degree in Russian studies, but was unable to find work in this field. In her free time, Gail enjoyed socializing with friends and acquaintances. Gail described herself as "insecure," and battled feelings of depression, usually brought on by feeling that other did not value her.

Unlike many of the couples in the Becoming a Family project, Gail and Michael felt rich in emotional support for their impending transition. Most of their old friends were also expecting children, and Gail's sister and her family lived nearby. Gail's parents were also only a few hours away, although Gail was not sure how much involvement she wanted them to have with the birth, commenting, "The same people who are a source of support are in some ways a source of tension." Michael also felt ambivalent about his parents' involvement. Although he would have liked them to share the experience of his child's birth, his parents lived too far away for a short visit, and a long stay threatened to add stress rather than alleviate it. Because he knew his parents were particularly excited about the birth of their first grandchild, the decision not to invite them was all the more difficult for Michael.

Pregnancy: The Early Transition to Parenthood

The Project staff couple first met with Gail and Michael 1 month before the baby was due. Both were eagerly anticipating the birth, although Gail worried about the baby's and her own health during labor. Michael had no such concerns, believing that all would go smoothly. According to the couple, this pattern—of Gail envisioning catastrophes and Michael being optimistic—characterized many of their interactions. In Gail's estimation, Michael was often unrealistic with "his head in the clouds," whereas Michael felt Gail worried too much. Each partner agreed with the other's assessments, at times appreciating and at times feeling irked by the other's point-of-view.

The month before they became parents, Michael and Gail independently rated themselves as very happily married on the Locke-Wallace Short Marital Adjustment Test (Locke & Wallace, 1959). Each described the other in many positive ways on the Adjective Check List (Gough & Heilbrun, 1980), including finding the other supportive, understanding, attractive, and sexy. Their marriage occupied a large portion of Michael's and Gail's emotional life, as shown through a pie-shaped chart that each drew to depict their central roles in life. This exercise, called *The Pie* (Cowan & Cowan, 1990 and in this volume), allows each partner to describe the relative salience of their major roles in life right now—partner, lover, parent, worker, son/daughter, and so on.

According to both Michael and Gail, the experience of pregnancy changed their relationship as a couple. They spent less time with friends and more alone with each other. Michael described the pregnancy as "a shared intimate experience that brought us closer together." He anticipated this closeness taking a different form after the baby's birth, requiring a lot of energy and ". . . a change in emotional focus. It's going to be less directly between the two of us. More between us and the child." Gail also anticipated similar, substantial changes in their well-developed patterns and routines, but felt that their familiarity with one another would ease the transition.

In addition to changes they anticipated in their marriage, Gail and Michael each voiced some concerns about managing both parenthood and work outside the family. While noting her confidence in Michael's involvement in child rearing, Gail said,

> I've been concerned about how we're going to cope, how long I'll stay home. What kind of job can I get, how difficult is it going to be—how guilty am I going to feel not working, how guilty am I going to feel working? How are we going to arrange childcare, and all that . . .

Michael sounded a similar theme:

> I want to give the child as much attention and love as I can give . . . my job is a fairly intense involvement. And I've got to be very careful not to let that take time away . . . which I can easily do. I've made that resolution . . . I want the child to be uppermost.

Both parents echoed questions voiced by many couples in the study: How do we manage traditionally male and female tasks, work outside the home, and childcare in our new family? Both parents wanted a balance between the two major roles but recognized how difficult it would be to achieve their goal.

Because Michael and Gail believed that they were fairly compatible in outlook, neither anticipated many problems in their attitudes toward raising children. And indeed, we found few discrepancies between their views on a set of scales describing their ideas about parenting (Heming, Cowan, & Cowan, 1990). However, two items on which the parents differed would prove to play a substantial role in their future family life. Whereas Gail believed that (a) parents should cancel plans to go out if a child protested, and (b) preschoolers were best taken care of almost entirely by their parents, Michael disagreed. Perhaps most importantly, both believed their partner's views matched their own, when in fact they differed markedly.

Infancy to Toddlerhood: "Everything is Extreme."

When their staff couple visited Gail and Michael approximately 6 months after the birth of a daughter, they found the new parents exhausted but exhilarated. Sarah was a healthy infant, responsive and curious. "I can't get over how much love I feel towards her," said Gail. Michael was surprised at his continuous delight with Sarah, and at how protective of her he felt.

Like many couples in the longitudinal study, Gail and Michael had expected that an infant would change their lives dramatically, but they felt unprepared for the degree of work a baby entailed. Most of the specific changes they predicted did in fact occur, but unanticipated difficulties also presented themselves. One major jolt to their childcare plans was Sarah's refusal to feed from a bottle. Michael and Gail had planned to breast- and bottle-feed Sarah so that both parents could share the work. As it was, only Gail got up in the night, and she was chronically exhausted.

As they had planned beforehand, Michael did as much as he could in the mornings and on weekends, while Gail took on the bulk of the baby tending and housework. This arrangement mirrored those of a majority of the couples in the longitudinal study (Cowan & Cowan, 1988)—although not, as we shall see, of the second family presented, the Swensons. The McLeans were generally satisfied with this set-up, although juggling the demands of home with work created tension for Michael and in another way, for Gail, too. These tensions sometimes surfaced as resentment towards the other partner: for Gail, that she carried the heaviest load of caretaking; for Michael, that he could no longer work in the evenings.

As he had predicted, managing responsibilities of family and work created a good deal of stress for Michael. He worked an estimated 65 hours a week, and work pressures increased at the same time that demands at home intensified. Michael's feelings about his situation were mixed. He both appreciated and regretted the fact that he was not home during the day: He felt less burdened than Gail did by the minute-to-minute demands of an infant, but he missed watching Sarah's daily growth and development. He wanted to spend more time with his daughter, yet he also wanted to devote more time to his work. Time spent with friends or alone—something Michael particularly valued—was extremely rare.

Gail also felt conflicts between work within the family and outside of it, but unlike her husband, her concerns centered less on her actual work load than on whether she should have a major work role outside the family. She felt restless being at home all the time and wanted to obtain a part-time job, believing it would "be good for me . . . to do something practical and something else other than being a mother." At the same time, she felt guilty at the thought of leaving Sarah with strangers; as she had noted before the baby's birth, Gail believed that children should stay at home with at least one parent. Michael had no such qualms about putting Sarah in part-time daycare. He felt satisfied being the family's sole source of income, but supported Gail's decision to seek work for her own satisfaction. As many new parents reported, the family could have used an additional paycheck, but childcare payments would have consumed most of Gail's earnings. This way of thinking about the issues of women's work and the cost of child care was echoed by the majority of the couples in the study. Gail's ambivalence about this issue would continue for many years.

An important resource for Gail was a mothers' support group that she began attending when Sarah was born. With her group she could discuss practical problems—which is the best car seat?—or more personal concerns—should she get a job? Gail described her group as a "lifesaver." Although Michael did not have an organized support group, he derived support from and was able to talk about family issues to several colleagues at work. Michael also felt supported by several long-distance friendships.

Like many of the couples in the larger study, Michael and Gail both experienced shifts in their attitudes and feelings towards their own parents after starting their family. Initially both felt a new appreciation for the struggles their parents underwent in raising them. Michael began increasingly to admire his father's "strength and stability" and actively tried to emulate that model in his own household. His urges to protect his child from harm and discomfort led him to a new understanding of the devotion his parents had given him and his brother, which at times had felt smothering to him. As Sarah became a toddler, however, Michael began to question and reject many of the ways in which he had been raised, most obviously by minimizing the number and importance of family rules. He also felt liberated by the everyday "naturalness" of taking care of a young child, which seemed in sharp contrast to the physical modesty that had characterized his childhood family.

Gail, who as a child had been closer to her father than to her mother, drew nearer to her mother as she came into her own motherhood. In the process, she discovered that many of the ways she related to Sarah mirrored the ways her mother had related to her when she was a child. Gail's mother apparently had also felt guilty about leaving her children. Gail felt "more tolerant" and understanding of her parents, particularly her mother, as she coped with the strain of taking care of Sarah: She also became more comfortable with her in-laws.

The couple's relationship had undergone substantial changes since the baby's arrival. Generally, both partners described their mates as supportive. Again like many couples in the study, Gail and Michael felt they had grown closer, but also more distant since the birth of their child. In order to cope with the continual demands of caring for an infant, the parents "had to share, draw together." Yet they also grew further apart: "Her life is the baby, mine is work," Michael wrote. Gail felt the closeness to and distance from Michael more acutely: "Everything is just more extreme."

Michael and Gail had time to themselves only in the evenings, after Sarah had gone to sleep, and by then they were usually exhausted. Due to their fatigue, financial stress, and Gail's hesitation to leave Sarah with a babysitter, they did not take planned time away from their baby. This state of affairs was described by most couples in the first 2 years of parenthood. As Gail had predicted before Sarah's birth, most of the couple's relationship centered around their child. The partners felt supported by each other, mainly in their attempts to help each other with child care. This pattern persisted as Sarah became a toddler. Through their mutual involvement in parenting, Michael believed that he and Gail had developed a deeper commitment to one another: "There's another person that links us together now."

When Sarah was 18 months old, the McLeans again rated themselves as happily married, although their marital satisfaction scores had declined between pregnancy and the first 18 months postpartum. This pattern was typical of a majority of couples becoming first-time parents (Cowan & Cowan, 1988).

Transition to a Two-Child Family: "More Like a Family"

When Sarah was nearly 3 years old, Michael and Gail had a second child, Jason. The arrival of another child further enriched the family, at the same time creating additional complications for Gail and Michael and their marriage. Gail commented that she felt closer to Michael after Jason's birth, "more like a family." Michael also felt that the "teamwork of raising two small children has drawn us together." Yet the partners also felt that their stress level had increased "drastically"; most of their energy was spent coping with necessary chores and tasks, and their relationship as a couple continued to center primarily around the children.

For Michael and Gail individually, the difficulties each experienced earlier in maintaining any sense of themselves independent of their family and work roles had become even more entrenched. Michael's struggle to balance his work and home life intensified, especially as he attempted to gain promotion and become more financially secure. Until now the couple had been relying on monetary help from Gail's parents to supplement their income. This irked Michael, and was partly why he was working so hard to become financially independent.

As Sarah reached the age of 3½, Michael was occupied more and more with his work, which now took up almost two-thirds of his psychological life, as he depicted in his *Pie*. He felt he had less control over his life than he had had earlier, and his roles as a husband and father had become blurred so as to be indistinguishable. Whereas in previous assessments he had separated out different aspects of his family life—husband, lover, father—he now collapsed them into one "slice" of his *Pie,* which occupied less psychological space overall than his career slice. In his ideal picture of his life, Michael's world was more differentiated; he reduced his work life by half, making room for other aspects of himself:

> Work and parenting take essentially all my time and energy. Self-expression has to be channelled into these activities—there's no time otherwise. [In the ideal picture] the . . . 'selfish' segments seem too big but that's probably because right now, they hardly exist at all.

For Gail, having a second child meant even greater psychological involvement in her role as a mother, as she reflected when Sarah was a preschooler:

> I felt mired in motherhood. I really felt absolutely committed, committed and buried . . . when [Sarah] was two and a bit, I started to feel like I was coming out

> of it. And now I feel absolutely submerged again . . . physically . . . and emotionally and intellectually submerged.

Gail's *Pie* diagrams over the years reflect a steady increase in the proportion of her psychological involvement as a mother, representing three-quarters of her sense of herself by the time Sarah was 3½ years-old. The other aspects of herself that she included were wife, daughter, cook, and cleaner—all family or house-related pursuits. Reflecting on her reactions to making these pie-charts, Gail wondered whether "I have any other identity besides being a mother." Having a second child intensified this feeling. As she immersed herself in the minutiae of babyhood once again, she wondered, "Can I cope again outside in the real world as a grown-up?" Gail said she was actively looking for part-time work, but not finding many opportunities for the limited number of hours she felt she could manage. Interestingly, at the pre-school age follow-up, for the first time Gail included a sliver called, "myself," in her *Pie*. In Gail's "ideal" pie-chart, she enlarged this sliver for "myself" and drew "mother" half as large as it featured in her "real life" *Pie*.

When she was 3½, Sarah attended nursery school most of the day and Jason was in daycare several mornings a week. Although this arrangement allowed Gail time to search for a job, get household chores done, and have a brief respite for herself, sending Sarah to preschool was a continuing struggle. Gail had difficulty separating from her daughter, and worried that Sarah did not like being away from home. Sarah's teachers assured Gail that once she was alone at school Sarah appeared engaged and content, but Gail continued to worry. She described how she saw her children—and particularly, her daughter—as an extension of herself.

> I think I'm Sarah. I think I'm Jason. And I think they're me—I think [Sarah]'s exactly like I am and with all my anxieties and I think I deal with her that way . . . it's like I turned into her and she turned into how I was as a kid . . . I can't step away from [them].

One consequence of the lack of psychological separation between Gail and her children can be seen in her urge to protect her children from life's difficulties. Although she believed that children need to learn how to handle frustrations and problems themselves, Gail noted that in practice she often intervened unnecessarily in their affairs.

Michael, on the other hand, saw himself as almost too detached from his family. Rather than as an extension, Michael viewed his children as quite different from himself, and marveled at their individuality and accomplishments. Having a family changed his opinion about the relationship between parents and children. Originally, he had assumed he and Gail would "mold" their offspring, asserting their values and personalities on them. Once he became a father, he realized that the children had their own personalities from the start.

The addition of another child changed both parents' relationship with Sarah; for Gail, change happened even before Jason's birth. While she felt "in the long run" the family would benefit from another child and Sarah from a sibling, Gail had the sense of betraying her oldest child and of losing a special relationship with her.

> I really mourned the last 2 months of my pregnancy, my relationship with Sarah. That it would never, ever be the same again, and it hasn't been, and it won't be . . . obviously [since the baby's birth] the whole dynamic has changed.

The way most parents commonly interacted with one another at this stage in their family's development was through looking after children, and Michael and Gail were no exception. In their taut schedule of feeding and clothing the children, getting them to and from their respective childcare placements, playing with them—especially Sarah, the preschooler—managing limit-setting and the relations between their preschooler and infant, Gail and Michael saw themselves operating as a team who could ill afford to spend time and energy disagreeing about childcare decisions. Michael reflected,

> We have these roles which we've each adopted which fully complement each other. Which together just about cope with the situation, so there's no time to be disagreeing and arguing and discussing about what we're doing. We're just trying to do it.

Both Michael and Gail felt their team-work style worked well for them, yet their independent ratings of their beliefs about childrearing indicated a growing disparity between them. Of perhaps even greater significance, each partner now had a less realistic view of the other's beliefs.

As was typical of most couples in the larger study, 3½ years after their first child's arrival, taking an hour or two alone together away from the children was a novelty. Michael described a recent lunch with Gail:

> We were sort of bemused by the whole thing. We were sitting there—it was like talking to somebody you never talk to. Remaking a relationship which is sort of dormant at the moment, because the relation that we had, the relationship we really had with each other is completely submerged by this relationship we each have with the children. So that, it's, we're really both sort of partners in a job right now. It feels like that.

Even in the sexual arena, parenting intruded. Not only were Michael and Gail usually exhausted by bedtime, but nursing made intercourse painful for Gail, and they reported having gone for more than a year without having sexual intercourse.

Beyond Early Childhood: Crisis and Opportunity

Their staff couple visited the McLeans and their family for the last time when Sarah and Jason were 7 and 4, respectively. The family was readjusting to life in the Bay Area after a year spent in another state, again in connection with Michael's work. Although the children had flourished, the time away had been difficult for Gail and for the McLean's marriage. Moving had interfered with Gail's attempts at establishing job connections and had removed her from her mothers' group, an important source of support. Both parents continued to feel acutely stressed by parenting two young children, and communication between them had grown increasingly strained. At the time of the staff visit, the McLeans were trying to mend their relationship with the help of marital therapy.

As individuals, Gail and Michael felt they remained "on hold." The struggle to balance work with family life continued for Michael, although with less intensity. He had achieved his promotion, and felt more financially secure and in command of his schedule, working regular circumscribed hours and conscientiously "being a parent" during other times. He still had little time to himself, but he resolved some of his frustration by including his family in activities he loved, such as hiking. Gail was working part-time as a translator and "half-heartedly" looking for other work; her fears about her ability to "be anything besides a mother" had intensified the longer she remained at home, adding to her ambivalence about seeking jobs.

Despite feeling overwhelmed by parenting, Michael and Gail continued to express deep pleasure in their children. Each felt they were close to being the kind of parent they wanted to be. "Of course, I want to be perfect, right?" said Gail. "I'm not that, but the bottom line is, I'm there for them." At the same time, both noted some deficiencies in their parenting. Gail wanted to be on an emotional even keel, and Michael wanted to be more consistent with discipline and limit-setting. Both said that they treated their two children differently, based on their developmental ages and on the distinct relationships each had built with each child. At this point in their family's development, both parents felt their interactions were easier with Jason than with Sarah, who in Gail's eyes, was becoming "a proto-teenager." Gail in particular struggled with her daughter, observing, "I'm too involved with the kids . . . so enmeshed."

Some of the difficulties that Gail and Michael experienced in being parents appeared to stem at least in part from their own childhood histories. The ways in which Gail felt overly involved with her children, and especially, with Sarah, echoed themes of Gail's relationship with her own parents. Gail's fears of leaving her children appeared to be one manifestation of this attempt, which she traced back especially to her distress at her father's 6-month absence when she was young. Michael was also struggling to give his children a better experience than he felt he had had in aspects of his upbringing. He identified his difficulty in setting consistent limits as a reaction against the emotional constriction and strictness of his childhood. Whereas he felt he had received automatic consequences regardless of his actions, Michael was determined that his children "have recourse to discussion" about their discipline, even though he conceded that this was not always what young children needed.

The conflicts each partner experienced in relation to their parenting also showed up in their marriage. Just as many parents in the study described, Michael and Gail continued to communicate with each other mostly through or in reference to the children. Moreover, the pattern that Gail and Michael had identified earlier as a coping strategy necessary to handle the stress of parenting—that of action-parenting, without much discussion between them—they now viewed as a risk to their relationship. Michael said,

> We don't communicate well . . . I anticipate how she is feeling and act according to that before she says anything. We're good at disguising our real feelings from each other.

Whereas before their first child's birth the partners believed that they knew each other well, 7 years later they felt they did not "know each other at all." Cumulative stress and frustration that had built up over the years made Michael less responsive to Gail's increasing need for his support, which left both partners feeling badly. By the time they met with their staff couple the last time, Michael and Gail reported that they were working on identifying their communication patterns in marital counseling and as a result, both felt more optimistic about their marriage than they had in several years.

Summary

As Gail and Michael so eloquently describe their experience, we can see how the five domains affecting family life intersect with one another in the McLean family. Parenting young children was a source of delight and pride, a shared experience that drew Gail and Michael together. At the same time, Gail and Michael's lives grew more separate, as Gail's revolved almost exclusively around the children and family, while a large part of Michael's life involved his career. As the McLeans struggled with the complex demands of raising children, they had less time and energy to give to themselves and to one another, and their relationship began to suffer. Their short-term coping strategy, of minimizing communication between them in the service of child-tending, led to increased distance between them.

As individuals, Michael and Gail felt bolstered but also beleaguered by their development as parents. Both felt a sense of well-being in their identity and skills as parents, but simultaneously felt they had to put themselves "on hold." This feeling spilled over into their marriage, which became, like their psychological pictures of themselves, subsumed by their parenting roles so that they functioned as mutual helpmates. No longer able to do even that effectively, each began to resent the ways in which the other was not able to meet their needs. Eventually, having reached a point of crisis, they were in the process of working to recapture their former closeness through the help of couples therapy.

The process of becoming a family also spurred Gail and Michael toward new reflections on and feelings about the families in which they grew up. Both gained renewed appreciation for the struggles their parents went through, and Michael in particular found himself trying to emulate his father in some ways, while consciously rejecting aspects of his upbringing in others. In her relationship to her daughter, Gail found links with her past history with her parents: her own difficulty separating from Sarah mirrored her mother's trouble separating from her, and long-suppressed feelings surrounding her father's absence when she was a child surfaced for Gail in her interactions with her children.

Gail's difficulty with separating from her children may also have had ramifications for the marriage, as the couple did not leave their children for regular—or even infrequent—time together for themselves. At the same time, real financial constraints and limited family support made babysitting, at least in the earliest years, a luxury, and leaving the children with extended family was not a readily available option.

One major source of support for Gail was her mothers' group, to which she could bring her concerns and share experiences with other mothers. Michael too relied on same-sex friendships, though in less organized fashion. Later on, Gail and the couple sought extra support and help through therapy. These resources appear to have helped bolster the couple in this stressful time period.

We turn now to the Swensons, a less traditional family in which the wife's career was the more established of the pair as they approached parenthood. The similarities and differences between these two couples show how the 5-domain model illuminates both the changes and the continuities that take place as partners become parents.

THE SWENSONS

At the time of their initial interview with their staff couple, Natalie Swenson was 29 and in her 5th month of pregnancy and her husband Victor was 34. They both had a long history in the Bay Area, living in the same suburban town since their marriage 6 years earlier and having both families nearby. In their interview there was a relaxed manner in which they often spoke together, and the conversation was punctuated with laughter. Here and in the questionnaires about their relationship (e.g., Locke & Wallace, 1959), Natalie and Victor characterized themselves as happily married, and they described their roles as partners with each other as being the most important in their lives. Victor explained that the primary reason the couple had "waited so long to have children" was their strong desire to have time for their relationship together and for their individual needs. They had devoted much effort to these and were now ready to integrate a child into their life.

In contrast to the McLeans, prior to the birth of their first child, the Swensons each contributed equally to the household finances. They also divided their various household chores equally, according to each person's strengths and preferences. As Natalie commented, "He hates cleaning bathrooms, and I hate laundry, so we both feel like we're justified in how we share it. We take care of each other."

Victor and Natalie felt they could talk with each other about everything. As Natalie said, "If he does something I don't like, I'll let him know it, and he always will listen to me if I'm very upset." They could also communicate during more difficult times, when one partner was feeling unfulfilled in the marriage. Natalie described how:

> we feel that we both can give each other that time apart from one another that we need. I think that whenever he's been depressed or I've been depressed, we say to each other, "Well, I don't really feel that good right now. I don't want to talk to you." And we both respect that.

Victor added, "The good thing about Natalie and I is we pick up on a problem, and we know when to leave it alone and when we can discuss it." Unlike many of couples in the longitudinal study, both Natalie and Victor described a flexibility in their relationship that incorporated an expectation of the ups and down inherent in marriage. We found it unusual for partners at this early stage of family development to be as tolerant of and as able to address these marital ebbs and flows as Natalie and Victor seemed to be.

Interestingly, this strong couple relationship was created by two individuals who recounted quite different backgrounds and characterized themselves as "total opposites." Natalie was the only girl, the youngest of four children quite close in age. Natalie felt close to all the members of her family and frequently referred to the warmth and affection they had for one another. Her parents had come to the United States as adults in the 1940s after escaping from Eastern Europe during the Second World War. Natalie's mother was a homemaker, and her father a retired businessman who had been a professor in Europe. She identified with her father's struggles as an immigrant who had never been able to achieve the same professional status in the U S as he had in Europe, more than with her mother's struggles as a housewife. Recently, her father had become disabled from Parkinson's disease and now relied heavily on his wife for support.

Victor was the oldest of three children. His brother and sister were substantially younger, and Victor had "played a major part in taking care of them when they were babies." He had been born in Europe, and his family had come to the Bay Area when he was a school child. Victor had a close relationship with his mother and maternal grandmother from whom he had received comfort and support throughout his life. His feelings toward his father were more mixed, bearing the scars of difficult early childhood experiences.

> I never liked my dad . . . He used to be a very, very heavy drinker, and when I was a little kid, he used get very drunk and come home and eat me alive, taking out his frustration on me . . . I'd have bad reactions—welts—I think I was about 6 or 7.

Perhaps not surprisingly, Victor described himself as a child with "lots of anger." In his early school years, he fought frequently with other children and had been suspended for his behavior. He remembered his move to the U S as difficult, often being teased by classmates because he could not speak English and was unfamiliar with American customs. During childhood and adolescence, he felt that "the Boy Scouts and sports in high school really saved me; I had lots of friends and people who really cared for me." His entrance into military service also proved to be a pivotal experience:

> It wasn't until I went into the marines . . . that my dad and I really started getting close . . . I think my fear had stopped. I was finally able to tell him how I felt about things . . . [It was] right before the marines that I found out that he really cared for me. He started crying the day I left for the service. The first time I ever saw that. He was letting me out of the car and I was walking across the street to go to the building and he couldn't even drive, he was crying so hard. That really got me.

Victor's feelings of closeness for his father continued to grow from this point on, with a new understanding of his father's limitations and affection, though, of course, there were still struggles between them.

Natalie described their differences as adults: "Victor just seems to take things more in stride than I do . . . once any situation happens, I usually get into it fine. It's just initially the problems—I tend to dwell on them much more than he does." Victor characterized himself as "quick to adapt" and did not see the need to discuss or worry about issues before they happened. His personal philosophy seemed to stem from the hurdles he had tacked in his childhood and adolescence.

At the time of his wife's pregnancy, Victor was working as the assistant manager of his father's electrical repair shop, though earlier in their marriage, he had earned a bachelor's degree in occupational therapy. In general, he did not talk much about his work, and this seemed to reflect its relative importance in his life. In his description of himself using *The Pie,* his "worker" slice was significantly smaller than those representing any of the other roles in his life. As he said, "Job . . . that's a tiny slice." In his ideal description of his life, no worker slice existed.

In contrast to her husband, Natalie's job occupied a slice of her *Pie* equal in size to the other two significant slices, those of "partner" and "mother." Natalie was actively pursuing a career in business as a sales manager for a large corporation. She had begun the job a year earlier and characterized it as quite rewarding. She acknowledged that though she had "come around," it had been more Victor's idea to have a child, "I started working [years ago] because I didn't like kids; he always knew he wanted to be a father." In these attitudes towards work, Victor and Natalie, respectively, were quite different from Michael and Gail.

Pregnancy: The Beginnings of Family Formation

In their initial interview, Natalie and Victor both described the upcoming birth of their child as "the natural extension" of their relationship as a couple. As Victor said, "I don't think we could ask for anything more beautiful in life than having a baby and sharing it with each other." They had been ready to expand their family for some time and had felt quite disappointed when a year earlier Natalie had a miscarriage in her first trimester. In contrast, this pregnancy seemed "smooth, better than expected."

The Swensons entered pregnancy as a "shared experience." They had some expectations of the changes the baby's birth would bring to their life. Like many other couples in the study, Natalie worried that she and Victor would have less time and energy for their relationship and that it "wouldn't be as spontaneous as before." During the pregnancy, Victor and Natalie said that they had experienced both more distance *and* more closeness. Initially, Natalie's fatigue and fears of another miscarriage created a distance emotionally and sexually, but from this came a closeness through nonsexual expressions of affection and frequent conversations about upcoming parenthood.

Both wondered how their lives as individuals would be changed with parenthood. As Victor said, "I'm just used to doing what I want to do, but I'm not going to be able to." He anticipated reductions in his personal recreation time yet also looked forward to sharing it, "having the baby on my back in a backpack—taking it on trips." Victor believed that he "had a feel for fatherhood," and he looked forward to his active participation in the raising of their child. He felt strongly that he would not be the kind of uninvolved, abusive father that his father had been.

Natalie anticipated that her adjustment would include physical exhaustion, possible depression, and internal conflicts when she returned to work. She had arranged a 3-month maternity leave before her return to full-time work, but acknowledged, "It's much easier to say, 'Oh yeah, I'm going back.' I'm sure it will be very hard." Natalie described her feelings about her two roles as caretaker and worker, saying that she had confidence in her abilities to do her job, but felt uncertain about whether she would be a good mother.

Beyond her comments, Natalie's omissions and casual remarks in conversation suggested how difficult it was for her to recognize consciously the depth of her work–family struggle. During her first pregnancy, she had been under a tremendous amount of stress, looking for a new job and anticipating difficulties when she told future employers that she was expecting a child. She described both her miscarriage and the job search as stressful but did not suggest any link between them. In another instance, when talking with their staff couple about the larger study, Natalie spontaneously asked them whether there were large numbers of families in which one parent did not want a child. Though it took yet another form, Natalie, like Gail and Michael, was struggling to establish and incorporate identities of herself as both a worker and a parent.

Victor and Natalie felt supported by each other and those around them as they began their new family. Victor's involvement had eased many of Natalie's concerns about pregnancy and parenthood, "Because of him I feel like I can handle it. I have so much support. If I had a husband who said, 'You're having the baby, you take care of it' . . . I probably would not have the child." Both of their families talked excitedly of grandchildren and offered to help with childcare—each taking a full day per week or more if necessary. In addition, one of Natalie's closest friends was expecting her first child a month after Natalie. The two women had helped each other through pregnancy, and Natalie hoped that they would similarly share the experience of raising a child. At work, she felt quite supported by those coworkers, mostly males, who were already parents themselves and empathized with her work–family dilemmas.

Early Months and Years of Parenthood

When their daughter Kim was 6 months old, Natalie and Victor, in contrast to their own expectations and to Gail and Michael's experience, were surprised at how smooth the transition to parenthood had been. Victor believed that "our life hasn't really changed that drastically. Kim has just been incorporated in . . . I am head over heels in love with this girl—I don't even want her to go out on a date!" Natalie felt that the bond begun in pregnancy had deepened and she and Kim had gradually "fallen in love."

Both Natalie and Victor distinguished between the first 3 months in which they experienced difficulties and the time thereafter, when their joy finally overwhelmingly outweighed their frustration. Despite his new infatuation, the beginning months were disappointing for Victor because he did not "get a reaction" from his daughter. In contrast, Natalie didn't need any sort of reaction, "Once I started breastfeeding and getting involved with her, I realized how intimate a relationship it is between a mother and her baby." Her stress came from fatigue and the constant demands of a newborn—"My whole schedule revolved around her." Imbalances in each partner's roles at home during the first 3 months, created largely by Natalie's maternity leave, also led to some strains in their relationship. Natalie and Victor both believed very strongly that it wasn't fair to let one person "carry the burden [of childcare] completely," and Victor did help during evenings and weekends, yet Natalie felt more responsible for those tasks because she was at home full-time. This scenario, which mirrored that of Gail and Michael, was especially common for formerly working and soon-to-be-working-again mothers in the study.

After 3 months at home, Natalie did return to work, and Kim was cared for by either a sitter or her grandparents. By the time Kim was 6 months old, Victor and Natalie's routines around the house had returned to "the same [ones] we've always had . . . whoever's available to do it," including the new duties of caring for Kim. Victor described how the couple began and ended their day:

> In the mornings, Natalie needs more time to get ready for work than I do. So we have an understanding that I pick up the baby, I change her, I feed her, I get her bags ready. And we, you know, flow along . . . When we come home from work after picking up the baby, because I do it in the morning, then Natalie without saying anything will change and feed her and put her to bed.

We can see that up to this point, Natalie and Victor are sharing more of the burden of Kim's care than Gail and Michael did, but even with that, the quality of their relationship had also suffered during their transition to parenthood. Like a majority of the couples in the study, their marital satisfaction had declined from late pregnancy, although less so than the average. Overall the Swensons actually described themselves as closer than they had ever been in the past. Their move to start a family had solidified and renewed their commitment to each other. They did argue more, mostly about Kim and the adjustment to her. Natalie got angry at some of the ways Victor was going about child care tasks and saw Victor as shirking responsibilities at home in order to spend time with friends and in recreation. Like Michael, Victor's friendships were a support to him, and he believed that rather than shirking his home responsibilities, he was recognizing his own need to "take a break" from family tasks and encouraged Natalie to recognize her individual needs as well.

In the midst of these tensions, Natalie and Victor had less time together to discuss difficulties and resolve their disagreements. Nevertheless, the communication skills and patterns established earlier in their marriage smoothed many of the bumps in their transition to parenthood. As Kim grew to be a toddler, many of the positive feelings and patterns established at 6 months continued. Victor and Natalie felt they and their family were doing "really exceptionally well." They talked to each other even more than in the past, had dinners out regularly and were even planning their first vacation as a couple since Kim was born.

Victor and Natalie's pictures of themselves and their lives as individuals had changed in ways they saw as both positive and negative since becoming parents. Natalie observed:

> a greater change in myself than there is in [Victor]. Kim has allowed the kid in me to come out again . . . The intensity that I feel for her was a real shock. And

> watching her move, and just each small day's development, I'm awestruck by her. I think, "I've worked all my life to develop a career, but it's nothing compared to this, to having her." And I was really surprised by that, it's changed me a great deal.

These comments echoed sentiments Michael McLean had expressed about fatherhood, yet unlike Michael, Natalie found her return to work "the hardest thing I ever had to do." She had trouble leaving Kim on Mondays and felt like a stranger by the weekend. Soon after returning, she drafted a proposal to solve her dilemma—she wanted to shift from full time employment to a four-day 80% time work week. These changes had implications for their income and their family, and ultimately, Natalie and Victor decided to make the necessary financial sacrifices so Natalie could manage all the roles in her life.

As Kim got older and more independent, Natalie continued to work a 4 day week, but now exercised more and even took business trips "without feeling guilty." She began to be able to do things for herself again. In contrast to some return-to-work mothers, Natalie's adaptation to her mother and worker roles seemed quite quick and full. In another respect, however, her reactions were quite typical of women in our study. Natalie talked about feeling both "brave" and "guilty" for having altered her work schedule: Brave for doing what she needed, and guilty for not putting in enough time and effort at work *and* for leaving Kim with a sitter. This feeling of not being quite comfortable at home or at work was mentioned by almost every new working mother in our study. Perhaps so she could feel better about her performance in both arenas, Natalie looked forward to Kim's entrance into nursery school, when she could return to a full-time position.

During Kim's infancy, Victor became increasingly frustrated with his job at his father's shop and wanted to find work that was more related to his interests. In his *Pie,* work continued to be absent from his ideal life. By the time Kim was 18 months, he had shifted to a 4-day week because he "couldn't stand it anymore." He enjoyed fatherhood, but partly because of his job frustration, he needed and wanted to be more involved in athletics—the piece of his individual life that gave him the most satisfaction. This became increasingly easy to do as Kim grew, and he was even able to take weekend backpacking trips with friends.

Victor and Natalie saw themselves as having opposite styles of parenting, but they appreciated each other for their respective contributions. Natalie described herself as "interested in developing Kim's mental" capacities, buying books and reading with her. Victor, on the other hand, was developing Kim's physical, experiential side. As he said, "I like to put her on my bicycle and go for a ride real fast. I like the thought of the wind hitting her face, and I like the thought of her eyes watering . . . the rain hitting her face." Natalie initially had concerns about Victor's "crazy" play, but, "Now I think a lot of the things that Victor wants to do for her, like have her walk in the rain are okay because I trust him . . . I know he would never do anything that would endanger her."

Relative to other couples, the Swensons held high expectations for Kim. They wanted her to feel very independent and also worked hard to foster a sense of responsibility in her. At 18 months she had the "job" of feeding the cat. They characterized their daughter as a "strong individual." Natalie had recently become concerned that Kim seemed to be preferring her father. On the one hand, Natalie and Victor considered this a phase, but on the other, Natalie felt envious of Victor and wondered whether Kim "really liked him better." This sensitivity to their child's choosing one parent over the other was mentioned by many parents in the study—from birth through the Kindergarten period.

Kim's birth, according to Victor, had "affected everybody"—himself, Natalie, all the grandparents, and Victor's and Natalie's relationships with their parents. Natalie's mother felt "like a mother again," and Natalie saw "a tremendous change" in her father, who had mentally and physically withdrawn since developing Parkinson's. Becoming a mother made Natalie feel much closer to her mother than ever before because she gained more understanding and sympathy for her mother's struggles and life as a homemaker. Victor's mother loved Kim deeply; but his father had difficulty adjusting to being a grandfather—he was jealous of his wife's feelings for the baby. Consequently, Kim's birth deepened Victor's feelings of closeness with his mother, but it increased the feeling of tension with his father until Victor confronted his father about the changes. He accused his father of feeling jealous and displaced by Kim, and helped him recognize that his wife could care for both him and her granddaughter. Following this, Victor's father's love for his granddaughter continued to grow as did Victor's feelings of closeness to his father.

The support the grandparents had given during the first 2 years was substantial, each eagerly taking Kim for a full day a week. According to Natalie, this support eased her return to work and allowed her and Victor time together as a couple, to have dinner or play tennis. The support and contact with her friend, who had given birth a month after Kim was born, had also eased Natalie's transition, as she had someone with whom she could share her joys and frustrations. Both women hoped to have their second child "together" as well. While Victor and Natalie believed they gave more attention to Kim than either of them had received as children, they felt fortunate that their parents contributed so much love and energy to their new family. This family support had become a natural piece of their lives, and it appeared to be facilitating their growth as individuals, a couple and a family.

At this point, the Swensons began to discuss whether and when to have a second child. Though they both wanted to expand their family, for now they were putting it off. Natalie felt reluctant because having a second child "might hold my career back even longer." Victor too was not yet ready to give up his recreation and had trepidations about altering the delicate balance they had achieved.

Preschool: A Time of Crisis and Reevaluation

The years following Kim's second birthday brought many changes to the Swensons' lives—changes that affected all levels of their developing family. For couples in the larger study, the period when their child entered preschool often brought unexpected hurdles, even for those who made a fairly smooth transition to parenthood.

In their interview when Kim was 3½ years-old, Natalie described how crises in both her and Victor's individual lives strained their ability to communicate with each other such that neither one could draw the other back into the relationship:

> We were both under a lot of stress at work . . . we were so distant from each other. He has a tendency not to talk when he's having problems, until it just gets to the point where he isn't talking to me at all . . . normally it happens at different times. I'm up, and he's going through something that is hard for him or vice versa. This was the first time we were both going through a difficult period at the same time . . . We just kept—Oh God—fighting with each other.

Their old ways of communicating that allowed for withdrawal seemed less effective during this "longer and more intense" period of stress, and each partner worried that they "couldn't bring their relationship back." Eventually, when both almost simultaneously recognized the importance of their marriage, Natalie and Victor made attempts to strengthen their relationship, even while their work tensions remained high. By the time their staff couple visited with the Swensons, Victor and Natalie had transformed the period of extreme distress into one of reassessing their needs and goals as individuals, more certain of their bond as a couple.

When Kim entered preschool, Natalie returned to full-time employment and was promoted soon thereafter. Natalie was glad to be back at work full-time but now had to "fight for getting off early—or on time—to be at home with my family." At the same time, Victor and Natalie continued to consider whether to have another child. Natalie was unsure she could "go through that again" when there were so many stresses at work. She was facing a difficult transition point in her feelings about the balance of work and family roles in her life, and felt unable to share her worries with Victor because of his withdrawal and the strain between them. With their marriage solidified, Natalie did become pregnant again. Though she could still not picture herself leaving a career entirely to stay at home with her children, Natalie was now questioning earlier assumptions about herself and entertaining the possibility of starting her own business or climbing "a less structured corporate ladder."

Meanwhile, Victor's work situation had become even more dissatisfying for him. He felt "locked in" to work at his father's shop. His frustrations mounted and peaked during his period of withdrawal from his wife and family. His father retired a couple of months after Kim turned three, and Victor began to realize that his anger and frustration at work had stemmed not from the job itself but from being unable to separate from his family of origin: "I had initially begun working for my dad because he had a major heart attack—he was ill, and I felt guilty. I realize now that I resented it throughout."

Less than a month after his father's retirement, Victor quit his job, "for my sanity mainly." He was now searching for the career that would suit his work and family needs:

> My family comes first, not my career. I want to be able to go to work and come home and enjoy my kids and spend time in the yard on Saturday and Sunday . . . I would also like to give Natalie the opportunity to not work for a while so that I could take the brunt of the financial matters.

Now, able to feel more separate from his parents, Victor was actively seeking ways to fulfill his own needs and provide for his growing family.

Victor and Natalie were both quite affectionate with Kim, but they also continued to instill in her a sense of responsibility and of individuality, as a person and a female. They both appreciated Kim's sense of whimsy and mischief, but she had duties around the house and was expected to act politely by, for example, saying "excuse me" before interrupting her parents' conversations.

Some of Natalie's beliefs about raising Kim seemed to be linked to her own sense of herself and her work-family struggles. She hoped that Kim would become "the kind of person that makes her own decisions . . . able to say 'no' to situations she feels are not good for her." Both Victor and Natalie worked against any sex-stereotyped treatment of their daughter. Natalie wanted her daughter to be able to grow up "without being fearful, without anxiety about being a woman . . . the way I've been anxious in the working world," and Victor was very conscious of not doing "girl things" with her all the time.

Natalie recognized that she was more of a disciplinarian than Victor, and she had begun to get Victor to discipline Kim more "so it's not just me who's doing it." Victor had become aware that though he tried discipline his child, he sometimes held back because "I am a lot more volatile than Natalie." He was likely to punish Kim more severely and compensated by "trying to be a little more flexible" about how frequently he punished her. Victor feared losing his relationship with her because of her punishment, much like his father did by disciplining him so severely. As was often the case with new parents in the study, becoming a parent had brought to the surface issues and struggles from the past that had not been fully worked through. For Victor, these mainly concerned his childhood and ongoing relationship with his father.

Throughout their difficult times, the caregiving and support the Swensons received from their families was a mainstay in their life. Natalie saw their families' support as integral to her having been able not just to return to work but to stay:

> It's interesting when you make a decision like we did not to go away from the family, it works out to be a benefit . . . so we aren't pulled away from work when the kids are sick or whatever as much as some other people might be who've moved away from their families. We have a real safety valve.

Ultimately their "safety valve" helped sustain a stability within their family from which Victor and Natalie could resolve their personal crises and their difficulties as a couple using their ability to communicate with each other. One outcome of their reevaluation was the recognition that, as Natalie put it, "Our marriage is too important to us. I really believe in fighting for our relationship."

The Family Expands: The Resolution of Role and Identity Struggles

When their staff couple visited the Swensons during Kim's Kindergarten year, they found a bustling household: Kim was an active 6-year-old, playing in the house with the neighbors' children, with her sister Stephanie, now a young toddler, tagging along. In the midst of this "chaos," Victor and Natalie described and experienced a comfort with each other and their lives that had been absent earlier. They talked about changes in where they lived, what they did and the way they thought. They had moved to a larger home in the same town and had both changed jobs and career directions. They seemed comfortable with their new lives and confident in their ability to master future changes, separately and together as a couple.

Though both Victor and Natalie recognized that their time alone together had been limited, even more so since Stephanie was born, they seemed to have accepted that for now and saw it as another stage of their family's development. They felt that the difficult times had ended and things were not "coming at them" to the point that they could not handle them. As Natalie reflected,

> We've definitely gone through some difficult times together. But it's weird, it's like below all that we know that we'll be okay. But we know that we have to go through that process, to talk it out, think it out, and eventually we'll find resolution together.

They excitedly told their staff couple that their lives outside of their relationship had become the "total opposite" of what they had been 2 years prior. After spending 6 months at home with Kim, supported almost solely by Natalie's income, Victor had begun work as a real estate broker in a small firm. For the first time during the study, he reported in questionnaires that he considered his work a career and that his ideal view of his life (reflected in his *Pie*) included a slice for "career." His job suited many of the needs he had articulated 2 years earlier: He worked close to home and could therefore spend less time commuting and more time with his family, and the office environment was not stressful.

Conversely, Natalie was now out of an office and based at home raising her children and developing a small business with a friend. Late in her second pregnancy, Natalie's entire division was laid off, and with her severance pay, she was able to stay at home for a year after Stephanie was born, a time which she thoroughly enjoyed. With some distance, Natalie was now able to recognize the enormity of the tensions she had experienced earlier between work and family roles:

> I always felt on a fence between both worlds. But I never really felt more a part of one than the other. And when I decided I wanted another baby, I just wanted more flexibility to be with my children.

In her *Pie,* the size of her slice for mother and for career had not changed drastically since the time of her first pregnancy. However, in her comments about her *Pie,* Natalie now noted "I finally feel resolved about the size of the piece that is mother."

Both Victor and Natalie expressed confidence in their parenting. They believed they were able to be affectionate and give a sense of limits to their children, applying a philosophy that typifies Baumrind's (1989) authoritative style of parenting. The Swensons felt that

> responsibility breeds independence . . . whether that is from a sense of self esteem or confidence. It also incorporates having to do chores . . . we are both very independent people even though we rely heavily on one another.

Kim's responsibilities at home had expanded to include putting away her books, dinner dishes, and laundry.

Unlike the McLeans, Victor and Natalie felt they had even more unified values regarding childrearing since Stephanie's birth. Though Natalie recognized that she was still "stricter" than her husband, she felt that their styles as parents were "meshing." Both girls, it seemed, had a "special relationship" with their father, but Natalie acted less concerned about this and clearer about her own role as a parent to her daughters than she had been in the past.

Natalie and Victor still seemed in close contact with their parents, but they had consciously moved further away from them psychologically in order to concentrate on the family they were building. Both Natalie's and Victor's fathers had continued to decline in health, and the stress was difficult for their mothers. However, as Natalie remarked,

> I used to take on a lot of the anger and fear and upset that my mother was going through. I've learned to try and listen to her and let it pass through me because I will not let anything affect *our* family. I used to.

Looking back on the changes that had occurred since they decided to have children, the Swensons realized that there had been many that had affected all the relationships within their family. At this point, both Victor and Natalie expressed an overwhelming sense of unity in their household and their life together. Victor described it:

> The more tests you're put through . . . the more difficult situations that you go through, finances or having the children. And the way that you adapt together, in the end result, you become stronger

Summary

Though Victor and Natalie were less traditional in their family arrangements before and after the birth of their first child, all five domains of family life were still clearly affected in their transition to parenthood. They continually struggled with issues central to being a family in our culture—the integration of life inside and outside of their nuclear family. Their relationship with each other changed over time, and they had less time than before to discuss these changes and other concerns that arose. Though they were unique in their ability to communicate with each other even during difficult times, their communication was strained considerably by the stresses of combining family and individual life.

As an individual, Natalie's ambivalence about work and family roles was not fully resolved until Kim was almost 6 years old. When Kim was young, Natalie found ways to limit her time at work in order to develop her sense of herself as a mother, and therefore kept her "two selves" separate from each other. Crisis and the threat to the equilibrium of her marriage pushed her to make some adjustments, which ultimately led to a more comfortable and integrated resolution of these two roles. Victor had a clear commitment to fatherhood and uncertainty about the presence or direction of his career goals. During the early years of parenthood, while Victor felt frustrated about his job, he seemed unable to make steps to change it. It took Victor's recognition of his job's link with his father to help him separate and develop an individual career identity.

The raising of their own family brought to the surface conflicts that stemmed from Victor and Natalie's own childhoods. As she became a mother, Natalie gradually became able to accept her own identification with her mother. For Victor, becoming a father both brought his ambivalent feelings for his father to the surface and provided him the strength to resolve them in some way. Their parents' instrumental and emotional support was crucial to the success of their early transition to parenthood. However, as their family grew, Victor and Natalie began to pull away from their close connection with their parents to concentrate on themselves both as a result of their personal changes and as a way of coping with their changing personal and family needs. In the final visit with the Swensons, they felt a renewed commitment to their relationship and seemed more aware of the ways in which their relationship was connected to the other domains of their life. This commitment and recognition allowed them to feel comfortable and look excitedly toward the future.

THE McLEANS AND THE SWENSONS: SIMILARITIES, CONTRASTS, AND CONCLUDING THOUGHTS

The couples presented in this chapter, the McLeans and the Swensons, typify some of the general trends reported by the Becoming a Family Project. As they made the transition from a couple to a family, all partners experienced marked upheavals in the central domains of family life—their marriages, their sense of themselves, their parenting and their relationships with their own parents.

The two couples represent approaches to family formation that differ from each other in ways that seem to mirror the kinds of choices and dilemmas facing families in the United States today. The McLeans exemplify the more traditional household arrangements of the nuclear family, in which the husband is sole provider, the wife is a full-time homemaker, and there is little regular contact with extended family. The Swensons are more atypical: Not only were they dual wage-earners, but the wife felt more established in and valued her career more than the husband did his, and they also divided household roles equally. Also less typical in this historical period is the Swensons' regular contact with and support from their local extended families.

On the more personal, individual level, marked differences existed between the two wives and the two husbands at the time when they were expecting their first child. Natalie Swenson was on an established career track (although she later gave it up), whereas Gail McLean, not yet clear about her vocation, struggled with feelings of insecurity and depression. Michael McLean had launched himself onto a high-powered professional course, whereas Victor Swenson was only beginning to seek a career direction of his own. As their children grew, each of the four individuals struggled to redress the conflicts they felt between work and family responsibilities: for Michael McLean and Natalie Swenson, this entailed eventual cutting down of psychological investment in and actual hours spent at work; for Gail McLean and Victor Swenson, this meant eventual increased attention to and focus on their own goals and work identity.

Just as the four adults struggled to balance family concerns with the rest of their individual lives, each couple worked hard to sustain their marital relationship in the face of what at times felt like overwhelming personal and external stress. Both couples felt less satisfied with their marriage after the birth of their first child, and at times, both felt that their union was in jeopardy. The Swensons reached this point sooner than the McLeans, when both Natalie and Victor experienced simultaneous crises in their sense of themselves and their work. They resolved their tension through a longstanding productive communication pattern and an underlying belief in their ability to resolve their own problems. They kept some distance from each other until each felt less vulnerable, and then initiated a series of discussions about their individual stressors. The McLeans' marital crisis appeared to have been longer in the brewing: it was the manifestation of both partners feeling that they had put themselves and their relationship "on hold" to manage the multiple demands of childrearing, and in the process, they had communicated less regularly and grown estranged. With Gail focusing on some of her own needs and "issues" from her family of origin, and with her and Michael placing a priority on their marriage, the McLeans were beginning to mend their relationship.

In many ways, the approach each couple took to parenting reflected the problems that ultimately beset their respective marriages. The McLeans put their commitment to childrearing above all else, believing that this was necessary in order to parent their children as they would like. As a result, they had little time and energy to devote to themselves as individuals or as a couple, and eventually their marriage suffered. Their actual parenting reflected their devotion and attention to Sarah and Jason, at times at the expense of separation and limit-setting. While this parenting strategy helped nurture appropriate dependency and capacity for emotional intimacy in the children, it may ultimately present Sarah and Jason with some difficulties with individuation and autonomy as they grow older.

The Swensons put a premium on maintaining individual pursuits as well as their relationship, independent of the children; although they were devoted parents, they did not permit their children to "take over" the rest of their lives. It was when each partner was unable to do what he or she wanted for him or herself within the constraints of their family and work situations that the Swenson marriage became shaky. Characteristically, Victor and Natalie each handled their emotional turmoil alone, and allowed the other to do so too, before they talked together. The Swensons' parenting strategy, which also characterizes much of their marriage, appears to be warm and responsive *and* to encourage structure and the development of independent competence. It would be interesting to see whether this emphasis would lead to some discomfort for Kim and Stephanie in expressing their needs for dependency in the future.

In large part, the ability of the Swensons to take time and energy for themselves and their marriage apart from the children rested on the ready availability of extended family support. Both grandmothers regularly took care of the children, thereby providing steady emotional support for the parents. The Swensons helped create this situation by refusing job offers that would take them away from the extended family. In contrast, the McLeans' extended families lived far away, and Michael and Gail had comparatively little direct contact with them.

The close relationship between the Swensons and their own parents was not without its difficulties, especially in the case of Victor and his father. Victor was actively differentiating himself from his father and had to effect a break in order to move on with establishing his own work direction. In ways, this mirrors some of Gail McLean's feelings toward her natal family, whom she described as a source of both support and tension. Gail, too, struggled with distinguishing herself from her mother and with transferring some of her relational patterns with her mother to her relationship with her daughter, just as Victor had to work to keep his discipline of Kim from mirroring his father's intensity with him.

Case Studies and the Methodological Agenda for Family Research

In our view, qualitative case studies of participants in quantitative family research projects serve a number of important functions. First, they help bring the data to life and remind us of the real people behind all the measures, variables, and patterns of results. Second, case studies graphically demonstrate why there is likely to be continuity and predictability across time. Although circumstances—and roles, feelings, and relationships—change, Michael and Gail and Victor and Natalie remain essentially the same people over time, using their characteristic styles of dealing with the world to react to new and more complex problems.

Case studies also demonstrate that there is more fluctuation within a broad band of continuity than group data curves indicate. Often the staff couple would be told that if they had come for the follow-up interviews two, or six, months earlier, they would have received a very different picture, for example, when the staff couple met with the Swensons *after* the resolution of their marital crisis. During that interview, Natalie told interviewers that "you would have heard a totally different story if you'd been here 6 months ago." Clearly, the data would have looked different if the Swenson interview had taken place in the midst of their crisis. The common observation that each new parent has his or her "ups and downs" and that marital temperatures fluctuate markedly over time is a reality that often gets obscured by the big picture formed on the basis of aggregate group data.

Case studies, then, serve two important and necessary functions. They help us to validate and refine our theories of family adaptation, and they suggest new and more differentiated questions for future research agendas. As we consider the McLeans and the Swensons, we become more confident that the general conclusions derived from the large-scale research on the transition to parenthood are close to the mark in describing the dynamics of family life during this period. But we also have the sense that particularities of individual, marital, family and societal conditions affect the pace and quality of each couple's adaptation.

We have learned from the McLeans and the Swensons that longitudinal studies following families at fixed intervals are bound to miss some of the most important events related to our understanding of family transitions. It will be necessary to make different and more flexible arrangements with our research subjects if we are really going to follow them through a major life change. Case studies also make it impossible to forget a vital research principle that is only now being rediscovered: families that do not follow majority trends should not be treated as "noise" in the system. Rather, they pose essential questions that will lead us ultimately to a better understanding of the different pathways that propel families toward relative adaptation or dysfunction.

The two couples presented here were both devoted to their families and willing to struggle to make their marriages work. The McLeans represented a common pattern in which husbands and wives lose sight of their own needs, as individuals and in relation to each other as partners, in the intense demands of managing childrearing and a high-pressure career. The Swensons, in contrast, showed the more unusual ability to maintain their own needs and their marriage as a high priority in the face of high stress. Both of these couples experienced a period of prolonged marital distress at different times in the life of their own family. Group data on the decline of marital satisfaction during the transition to parenthood obscure the fact that the declines were caused by very different factors and that each couple drew on different resources to cope with the serious challenge of raising a family. Case studies provide the opportunity to examine in depth the processes associated with relative adaptation and dysfunction in different couples. In the richness of their detail, case studies not only stimulate differentiated questions for future research, but also suggest that interventions must be tailored to the particular circumstances, strengths and weaknesses of specific families.

ACKNOWLEDGMENTS

Each of the authors contributed equally to the manuscript, and authorship was determined by chance. This research was supported by NIMH grant # MH 31109. We would like to thank all of the families who participated in the Becoming a Family Project, especially the two described in this case study, for their cooperation and enthusiasm throughout the study and for allowing the Project to have a glimpse into the complex and personal changes that occurred in their lives as they became parents. We also greatly appreciate the helpful comments Phil Cowan, Carolyn Pape Cowan, and Marc Schulz provided on earlier drafts of the manuscript.

REFERENCES

Baumrind, D. (1989). Rearing competent children. In W. Dam (Ed.), *Child development today and tomorrow*. San Francisco: Jossey-Bass.

Belsky, J., Gilstrap, B., & Rovine, M. (1984). The Pennsylvania infant and family development project, I: Stability and change in mother-infant and father-infant interaction in a family setting at one, three, and nine months. *Child Development, 55,* 692–705.

Berman, P., & Pederson, F. (Eds.). (1987). *Men's transition to parenthood: Longitudinal studies of early family experience.* Hillsdale, NJ: Lawrence Erlbaum Associates.

Cowan, P. A., & Cowan, C. P. (1988). Changes in marriage during the transition to parenthood: Must we blame the baby? In G. Y. Michaels & W. A. Goldberg (Eds.), *The transition to parenthood: Current theory and research.* Cambridge, England: Cambridge University Press.

Cowan, P. A., & Cowan, C. P. (1990). Becoming a family: Research and intervention. In I. Sigel & G. Brody (Eds.), *Family research, (Vol. I).* Hillsdale, NJ: Lawrence Erlbaum Associates.

Cowan, C. P., & Cowan, P. A. (1992). *When partners become parents: The big life change for couples.* New York: Basic Books.

Cox, M. (Ed.). (1985). The transition to parenthood. Special issue of *Journal of Family Issues, 6,* Number 4.

Feldman, S. S., & Aschenbrenner, B. (1983). Impact of parenthood on various aspects of masculinity and femininity: A short-term, longitudinal study. *Developmental Psychology, 19,* 278–289.

Gough, H. H., & Heilbrun, A. B. (1980). *The Adjective Checklist Manual.* Palo Alto, CA: Consulting Psychologists Press.

Grossman, F., Eichler, L., & Winickoff, S. (1980). *Pregnancy, birth, and parenthood.* San Francisco: Jossey-Bass.

Heinicke, C. M., Diskin, S. D., Ramsay-Klee, D. M., & Oates, D. S. (1986). Pre- and postbirth antecedents of 2-year-old attention, capacity for relationships and verbal expressiveness. *Developmental Psychology, 22,* 777–787.

Heming, G., Cowan, P. A., & Cowan, C. P. (1990). Ideas about Parenting. In J. Touliatos, B. F. Perlmutter & M. S. Straus (Eds.), *Handbook of family measurement techniques.* Newbury Park, CA: Sage.

Lewis, J. M., Owen, M. T., & Cox, M. J. (1988). The transition to parenthood: III. Incorporation of the child into the family. *Family Process, 27,* 411–421.

Locke, J., & Wallace, K. M. (1959). Short Marital Adjustment and predictions tests: Their reliability and validity. *Marriage and Family Living, 21,* 251–255.

Michaels, G. Y., & Goldberg, W. A. (Eds.). (1988). *The transition to parenthood: Current theory and research.* Cambridge, England: Cambridge University Press.

Paklovitz, R., & Sussman, M. B. (Eds.). (1988). Transitions to parenthood. Special issue of *Marriage and Family Review, 12,* Nos. 3 & 4.

19 The Life and Family of Karl Schulz

John A. Clausen
University of California, Berkeley

In tracing lives through longitudinal research, one is unlikely to find that both members of a married couple are contained in a sample that was selected prior to adolescence. If marital partners are subsequently included in the research, however, the researcher can not only present a developmental picture of one person antecedent to the marriage but the views of both as to how the marriage has run its course over time. This opportunity was available for many of the subjects of the three longitudinal studies conducted at the Institute of Human Development from 1928 (Berkeley Guidance Study and Berkeley Growth Study) or 1931 (Oakland Growth Study) to date.

The case history I present is of a family deemed to have been highly successful—rewarding and sustaining to the married couple and to their children through their years at home. The degree to which serious problems were avoided is unusual for the total population studied, and the marriage ranked very high in the mutual satisfaction of husband and wife at every period of study. The success of this couple is not adventitious; it is illustrative of a tendency that received strong statistical support in the larger study: the tendency for successful marriages and child-rearing and for personality stability to be rooted in the acquisition by late adolescence of a high degree of individual maturity, and more specifically, what I have elsewhere characterized as "planful competence" (Clausen, 1991).

The stability of a marriage depends on the attitudes, temperaments, and everchanging role relationships of two persons. It may seem unreasonable to expect that the adolescent personality orientations of either spouse will markedly affect the stability of the marriage except in the instance of psychopathology or deviance. We know, however, that very early marriages and marriages made with minimal acquaintance tend to be much more short-lived than those based on longer acquaintance between persons reasonably mature at the time of marriage. One might anticipate that most planful, competent young men and women will not marry until they feel that they know what they are getting into and are ready to work out their relationships. Obviously, one partner may be much more planful than the other, and either one may change or turn out to have attributes that make a stable marriage unlikely. Nevertheless, adolescent competence should pay off for both men and women; it will not only influence marital choice, but should make the chooser a better candidate for a successful marriage. Mutual choice under such circumstances should predict a lasting marriage (or at least a more lasting marriage in a period when there is much instability in marital ties).

This perspective and these hypotheses have led to the preparation of histories of persons who in adolescence scored high on an index of planful competence and those who scored low. By way of statistical support for the hypotheses, 82% of the senior high school males who scored in the highest third on planful competence and 94% of the senior high school girls who scored in the highest third on dependability had only one marriage, but this was true of only 55% of the males and 50% of the females who scored in the lowest third. No one in the top third had more than two marriages, but 14% of the males and 19% of the females in the bottom third had three or more marriages. The importance of early competence is, of course, only a part of the story. The rest is worked out through the interaction of two unique personalities, each of whom brings somewhat different expectations to the marriage; together they build up a new set of expectations and shared meanings.

Why this History

Much of the data collection for the Adolescent (Oakland) Growth Study took place at the school from 1932–1938. Karl Schulz seldom missed school during his adolescent years and he participated in every follow-up (at ages 37, 43, 48 and 61). The record of his life is therefore unusually complete.

During his early adolescent years Karl struck the research staff as being a sad and lonely boy. At the age of seven he had lost his father, with whom he had been close, and the staff felt that that loss had very much blighted his early years. Karl was obviously very bright but he seemed embarrassed in social situations and was characterized as being largely silent in group settings; he avoided being the center of attention. Commenting on the youth's appearance when he was 15, a staff psychologist stated: "He is, and probably will continue to be, a homely fellow." But she then added, "Seems surprisingly well-liked for one so unresponsive." Nearly 50 years later, the interviewer who conducted a clinical interview with Mr. Schulz when he was 61 years old characterized him as "a rugged-looking man, very masculine in appearance; could be considered handsome." In adolescence he was often characterized as unkempt; in his later years he was seen as "very neat, clean, and well-groomed."

There appear, then, to be some rather considerable differences between Karl the adolescent and Karl the retired scientist-engineer. There were indeed many changes, especially in his social presentation of himself. At the same time, there were remarkable stabilities. At every period he was seen as highly dependable, very intelligent, productive, and straightforward. As we shall see, the most substantial changes appear to take place between adolescence and the first adult follow-up, when Karl was 37 years old. Since then there has been some additional mellowing, perhaps related to his retirement at age 58, but on the whole there has been remarkable stability in his personality over the adult years. His history has been chosen for presentation because it illustrates so well how personal strengths and a supportive environment can overcome what clinicians may perceive as serious vulnerabilities. The most important supportive element in Mr. Schulz's life was clearly his wife. Substantial detail about his marriage and family life has been included because the family has been the core of Karl's life—and because Mr. and Mrs. Schulz have been willing to share their life very fully with us.

A first draft of the account that follows was sent to Mr. and Mrs. Schulz and was discussed, with an effort to clear up ambiguities, correct errors, and add further clarification, at a subsequent session in their home. This session is described late in the account, but corrections or points at which the information obtained in the early years proved discrepant with Mr. Schulz's recollections are noted as we proceed.

KARL SCHULZ'S CHILDHOOD

Karl was an only child. Both of his parents were offspring of Western European Protestants who had migrated to the United States in the latter half of the 19th century. Karl's father was a college graduate and an engineer on the staff of a large chemical company. His mother had graduated from high school and attended business college for a year. Then she had worked for a number of years. Both parents appear to have had strong intellectual and cultural interests. Karl's mother mentioned that prior to her husband's death, they had attended the opera as well as enjoying outdoor interests together.

From all that we have learned about them, they appear to have been loving parents. When Karl was 7, however, his father died of a heart attack. Karl and his parents had been out for a walk, and suddenly his father collapsed and was carried home. Karl is not sure whether he died immediately or within the next day. The event left him with a great feeling of loss.

Upon the death of her husband, Mrs. Schulz was apparently able to manage for a year or so on the proceeds of insurance and investment income, but she then took a job selling real estate. The stock market had crashed and the Great Depression was beginning. It was the worst of times for entering the labor market, but Karl's mother had no alternative. At this time, or shortly before, her own mother and her divorced sister came to live with Karl and Mrs. Schulz. By pooling resources, it was possible to make mortgage payments and hold on to the house that Karl's parents had been buying. This also assured that someone would be there when Karl returned from school, and he reported that his grandmother had been primarily responsible for his supervision during the daytime.

When Karl entered the study at age 11, his mother was characterized by the study staff as energetic, restless, excitable, and inclined to worry. Later, at the tea held for parents of the senior class, she was described as being at ease, poised, and vivacious. Mrs. Schulz was seen as having considerable concern over her son's development and as interested in getting helpful suggestions from the study staff. She was always a willing participant when interviews were requested.

Mrs. Schulz's principal concern in the early years was her son's sleep difficulties. She reported that he would frequently lie awake until very late at night and was resistant to going to bed when she thought he should. He himself indicated on research inventories that he had trouble sleeping, and it would appear that his reading after going to bed was perhaps the major issue of discipline for his mother. Later, she wished that he would be more sociable.

Karl spent a good deal of time in solitary activities, reading and building things in his workshop, but he also participated in sports and appears to have been accepted by other boys. He was always tall for his age, and in the childhood years quite thin. He had been seen as sickly in his preschool and early school years, and underwent three operations, including an appendectomy, before he reached age 8. Despite this, he did so well in school that he skipped a grade. His mother regarded him as overly conscientious. It would appear that she communicated to him her need for emotional support and for his cooperative behavior, and he strove to meet her expectations. Although it was she who put him to bed each night and who instructed him in moral values, the mother's real estate sales job took her away from home at the very times when parents and children would usually be able to spend time together, on weekends. Karl was one of the minority of children who checked as typical of his situation the inventory items: "I wish my mother were not so busy," and "I wish my mother could be happier."

His mother reported that Karl had slept in the same room with her until he was 10 years old, possibly as a consequence of the size of the augmented household. We do not know when his sleep difficulties began, but they persisted long after he had his own room. His mother also indicated that she was still participating in brushing his teeth and bathing him when he was 11. She stated that "He would never wash his face, would wear that same shirt and socks for weeks." At this period he was rated by the study staff as somewhat more unkempt than most of his peers.

Karl attended Sunday School regularly between the ages of 6 and 15 but by the latter age he preferred to sleep later on Sunday morning and to attend church. He had strong religious attitudes: He saw God as making us want to do good things, and as the creator of all things. He saw Jesus as a great example and hell as a feeling of misery in one's self. He saw death as everlasting sleep and he indicated that he prayed to do what his parents had taught him.

Karl always scored high on IQ tests, his scores ranging from 119 on a group test to 142 on the Stanford-Binet. Scores improved over the high school years; he had been seen as not able to mobilize his full capacity at age 13. His school grades were mostly A's with the exception of B's in English, though occasionally he received A's there as well. He was seen by teachers and staff as being quite independent in his thinking but highly conventional and inhibited in his behavior.

Although he was viewed by his peers in junior high school as silent and embarrassed before the class and as anxious and somewhat unattractive, he was not only accepted but initially viewed as slightly more popular than the mean. Karl characterized himself as unattractive on early inventories. He also indicated that he worried a good deal about bad things happening. He was most often seen as inhibited and somewhat withdrawn through the junior high years. He was described as going off by himself with a basketball and apparently working to improve his skills as a basketball player. At home he occupied himself with woodworking and reading. He also cut lawns and worked at other jobs to earn spending money.

Several months before his 15th birthday, Karl took the Rorschach test, that series of inkblots that, like summer clouds, may call to mind a menagerie of beasts or evidence of hidden fears. He was described as "much interested in the test, enjoying fantasy, slightly excited." His responses were characterized as "sensitive, reactive, decidedly introverted, active fantasy [with] much originality and unique thought trends. Anxiety, worry, and unhappiness are indicated in a small degree." Karl was clearly not inhibited in his imagination.

Toward the end of junior high school it appeared that Karl was having a particularly difficult time, perhaps brought on by pubertal development. Late in his last semester in junior high, his mother reported that he and the two boys who had been his close friends seemed unable to get along, and Karl became more solitary. Staff observers also commented at this time that he seemed more self-conscious and shy, and less confident of himself. He was characterized as "very inhibited and shy with adults." Yet an observer of Karl's participation with his friends a few months earlier had noted that "in a situation with friends, [Karl] is communicative, accepted, and shows initiative," unlike his behavior in larger groupings. On one of the inventories, during the difficult period, he acknowledged feeling "very unhappy without knowing why"—not a terribly atypical admission in mid-adolescence.

Note: In reviewing this account, Mr. Schulz could not recall any falling-out with his friends or any special unhappiness toward the end of his junior high years. He thought that perhaps he had shifted from being involved primarily with neighborhood boys to being more involved with friends from school. It is quite possible that this was the case and that his mother was aware only of the neighborhood situation.

Judges who reviewed all of the materials relating to Karl's junior high years characterized him as more adult- than peer-oriented. He was seen as selective in his choice of friends, respectful of his parents, and not at all likely to claim the rights and privileges of adolescence. Prior to attendance of senior high school, then, we have a boy who was somewhat withdrawn socially but clearly not rebellious, one who seemed often sad but also able to manage his school work and his activities in a fruitful manner, and an exceptionally dependable boy.

THE SENIOR HIGH SCHOOL YEARS

Karl's first year in senior high school found little change either in his self-perceptions or in the ratings by others, but in his last 2 years he seemed to become more sociable and somewhat less inhibited. In his first year he joined the chess club and the model airplane club and occasionally participated in group activities with other members of the study sample, but by and large he made little use of the clubhouse that was available to study members. He became more involved in playing basketball, and also received more respect from his peers by virtue of his academic performance.

Throughout his high school years, beginning in junior high, Karl indicated that his occupational goal was to become an engineer. He apparently always had before him the idealized image of his father and his father's occupation, and his superior intellectual ability and superior performance in mathematics and science suggested that engineering was a logical choice.

Karl was determined to learn to "do things right." Although he said that he did not like to dance, he attended a remedial class in dancing so that he would become more skillful, as he apparently did by his senior year. His conscientiousness and dependability stood out. At the same time, by his senior year he was seen as being able to relax and to acknowledge feelings denied previously. Whereas in most earlier years he had responded to an annoyance inventory indicating that almost nothing annoyed him, in his senior year he mentioned many annoyances. By then he also became involved in many more social events, participating more fully in events sponsored by the research program. On one weekend trip, a staff psychologist who had observed him noted that he had addressed staff members more familiarly than previously, asked questions, kidded a girl about her ping pong and then took her on for a game: "His whole manner was changed into a rather light-hearted, wisecracking mood, and I thought he got along very successfully." At the senior year graduation party, he brought a tall, bright but not very popular girl and appeared to be having a lot of fun. Nevertheless, he dated very little and on the whole seemed uninterested in girls.

Psychologists who read over all the senior high school materials exhibited a high degree of consensus in their assessment of Karl's dominant traits. He received the highest possible rating on the traits "ambitious" and "values independence," and was only a shade lower on "prides self on objectivity," "dependable," "intelligent," and "productive." At the other extreme, he received the lowest possible score on the item "deceitful," and very low scores on "self-dramatizing," "talkative," and "poised."

Our index of "planful competence in adolescence," made up of three components, showed Karl to be at the edge of the upper third of study group males. He was very near the top on "dependability" and "intellectual investment," but somewhat below the mean on "self-confidence." The latter measure probably reflected his social presentation of self rather than his confidence in his abilities. In any event, he was clearly more aware than many of his peers of his own strengths and weaknesses, seemed remarkably undefensive, and had the discipline and ability needed to make mature choices, though his lack of experience with the opposite sex might make him vulnerable to a misstep when it came to marriage.

A staff member who wrote a detailed assessment of all of the adolescent material prior to the first follow-up predicted that Karl Schulz would indeed become an engineer or go into some other closely allied vocation. Further, she noted, "I would not expect that he would have gone into the administrative aspects of the field but rather some aspect of it which would have allowed him independence but not great responsibility for others. For instance, research in this area would fulfill these requirements." It was also predicted that he would marry but probably would marry late and that he would lead a fairly conventional and comfortable life. At the same time, this psychologist surmised that fatherhood might be "a somewhat more difficult problem because of his need for autonomy and his tendency toward inhibition."

KARL SCHULZ AT 21

Three years after Karl's graduation from high school, Karl was interviewed by Miss Chaffey, a staff member who had been his counselor when he was in junior high school. The interview was not guided by any theoretical perspective or directed toward the systematic collection of data, but simply sought to find out "how things were going" with former study members. Miss Chaffey characterized Karl as "more free and talkative than usual." America was now at war, and Karl was about to enter his senior year at the University of California. He indicated that he was doing well in engineering school and would enter the Army upon graduation, to receive further electronics training and then enter the Signal Corps.

Reading this interview nearly 50 years later, one becomes vividly aware of social change. Karl was interested in the prospect of further training because, as he reported, they were "working out a new method of detecting the presence of airplanes." Radar was not yet widely known, but Karl hoped to be able to go to England "because the men who invented this system are working it out there." Karl also looked forward to traveling and seeing some of the world, so he did not seem apprehensive about entering the service.

As of 1942, his grandmother and one aunt still lived with his mother, but his other aunt (who had presumably lived with them for a while) had gone to Guatemala. Karl's mother and grandmother had planned to visit her there until the war intervened. Mrs. Schulz was still heavily involved in her job. Karl said that she was essentially running the real estate office, since her boss was often away and seemed indifferent about managing. He described his mother as "too much identified with the business now" to think of leaving, even though she sometimes talked about leaving. Karl was living at home during his college years, and since tuition was free for state residents, apparently his college attendance was not a financial problem.

Asked if he was sorry he hadn't joined a fraternity, Karl replied that quite the opposite, he was glad because he wouldn't have had time. He reported that he had to work pretty hard but was in the top fifth of his class and hoped to become a member of Tau Beta Pi, the national honorary society for engineering students. He had gone skiing a few times and apparently participated in a square dancing group. He was still in touch with and getting together with several of his friends from the study group, and he asked about others in the group, both men and women. Asked what he thought about the number of his peers who were marrying before going into the service, he though there was some danger in this "since a boy might change a lot," but that it probably depended on the circumstances. He mentioned that he was going to a different church, because he liked both its minister and the social activities of the young people there better than at the church he had previously attended. It was the church that the Institute Director's daughters, who were roughly his age, were also attending.

Karl's observations about the kinds of governmental controls that might be necessary after the war suggested a very conservative (keep government out of business) outlook, yet one that was on the whole quite realistic.

Miss Chaffey noted that "his only sign of embarrassment was at first when we were talking about him. He kept looking away from me. So I changed the subject and told him what I was doing and he immediately looked directly at me and continued to do so." Karl seemed to be moving toward much greater self-acceptance and ease and was looking ahead with interest and enthusiasm.

KARL SCHULZ AT 37

Nearly 20 years intervened between high school graduation and the first adult follow-up. The interviewer, who conducted a series of three interviews with Mr. Schulz, characterized him as a "refreshingly undefensive, good-natured, intellectual and interesting person. He is a good-looking man who dresses casually but is well-groomed. I found (him) to be a very easy person to interview not only because of his involvement in and positive evaluation of the study, but also because he is sufficiently relaxed to be able to accept the questions without feeling threatened by them. He is somewhat shy and reserved but he related easily in the interview situation."

The initial interview dealt with recollections of adolescence, and the picture that Mr. Schulz presented was consonant with what we already knew, though presented rather tersely. He noted that he had been more academically than socially inclined and had been extremely shy. He remembered with pleasure playing chess with members of the chess club, playing basketball and learning how to drive. He noted his earlier ambivalence about dancing: "Once a week they had dances that we sort of wanted to go to but always tried to avoid." He commented on the change in his attitude toward girls in his senior year: "I realized it was foolishness not to go out, and I gradually got to feeling more interested in them. . . They didn't seem quite so strange."

Mr. Schulz remembered himself as feeling reasonably well satisfied during his adolescent years. At the same time, when he filled out a life chart, indicating on a year to year basis the level of life satisfaction, the lowest point was the year of his father's death, when he rated satisfaction at 3 on a 9-point scale, and life satisfaction gradually increased during the junior and senior high school years, rising to 7 in the senior year.

Asked how well he thought he had understood himself in adolescence, Karl replied in some detail:

> I thought I knew all about myself at that time. I understood the direction I was going, educationally and vocationally. As far as emotions and feelings, I didn't have too good an understanding of them, although I can't think of times of real confusion. We had lots of talks about the meaning of life, and religion.
>
> I think I knew my assets and limitations reasonably well. I thought I was reasonably intelligent. . . I did my best in math and science. I thought I was healthy and capable of taking care of myself. Felt fairly confident in myself in most situations, certainly not all. My limitations were in keeping too much to myself. I was sort of an introvert. I had close friends but I was shy with others. I didn't have too good an ability to express myself.

He felt that his mother and grandmother had respect for his judgment and he for theirs, though they were not always in agreement.

When he was asked whether there were any experiences or people that had been especially influential in his life or anyone on whom he had tried to model his own life, he replied, "No, not really, other than the projection of my father . . . what he might have been like . . . This was always kind of a guide for me and I try to do what he would have done." Thus he formulated explicitly the inference that the staff had drawn from early observations of the youth.

The 1958–59 follow-up focused much more on the early years than on what had happened since, and it was especially deficient in getting at educational and occupational histories. To fill in the picture, data are available from a questionnaire designed for this purpose in 1964.

Karl had graduated from the University of California with a degree in engineering and had immediately entered military service. He was sent to Officer Candidate School and not long thereafter sent overseas. The Army years brought his first prolonged period of life outside the family home, and he felt that this had been a useful experience, though he had not been enthusiastic about Army regimentation.

While in the service, stationed on the East Coast, he met Kathleen, the woman who would become his wife. Their meeting was described in several of the subsequent interviews as having occurred at a dance for young officers, held in a large New York hotel. The future Mrs. Schulz was tall, like her husband-to-be, and the two gravitated toward each other in the course of a Paul Jones (a square dance in which men move in one direction and women in another, and then are told to "grab a partner."). They saw a good deal of each other in the brief period before Karl went overseas, and they corresponded very frequently thereafter. Upon his return from the service in 1946, Kathleen flew west for a visit, and before the visit ended they had set the date for their wedding, a month or two later. By then, Karl had secured a promising job in the field of aeronautical engineering. We turn first to his occupational career.

Early Occupational History

At the time of the first follow-up, Karl was still with his initial employer. He was also taking graduate courses at a prestigious university, part time, to prepare him for more technical work. He was about to become a scientist in the field of aeronautical research. There had been several promotions, and Karl Schulz expressed a high degree of satisfaction in his job. Not only did he find the work entirely suitable to his interests but he appreciated the freedom to develop ideas and use his imagination, and the use of his skills and abilities. Unlike many professional jobs, his was apparently strictly an 8 to 5 job, which did not require his being under great pressure. Indeed, among the things he liked best about the job were its general convenience for the family and the amount of leisure time that it provided. The only respects in which he was less than fully enthusiastic were that his job apparently entailed some supervision of others, not quite as much opportunity for advancement as he would have liked, and a relatively lower income than he felt was merited. However, he had acknowledged at the time of the previous interview that he was earning more than he had expected to be earning.

Karl indicated that on the average he devoted 40 hours a week to his job, a respect in which he was highly unusual in that non-manual workers among those in the study reported working an average of 51 hours a week. The only thing that might induce him to change jobs, he thought, would be "a tremendous salary increase for the same sort of work." The income he reported for the year was well above the national average, and about equivalent to the higher levels of Federal civil service or a full professorship in all but the top universities.

The questionnaire sent in 1964 inquired into the priorities accorded among work, marriage and the family, church, and community affairs. Mr. Schulz indicated a very high level of involvement and of satisfaction in his family roles. He rated family activities as those that he enjoyed most, as well as those on which he was now spending the most time. He also rated family activities second among those to which he would like to devote more time, first being recreation and leisure. Family activities were also rated second in providing him with the greatest sense of accomplishment. Here work and work-related activities rated first. Not given high priority in any of these choices were community affairs and church activities.

Marriage and Early Parenting

Although we did not learn the details of their early married life until later, it was evident that Karl and Kathleen had a very happy life together. Despite their brief episode of relationship (2 months) before Karl was shipped overseas, they apparently felt very comfortable and in touch through what Karl later characterized as "thousands of letters." Asked many years later about factors influencing their marriage, Kathleen Schulz mentioned her immediate positive response to Karl: "He seemed like an old friend—easy to talk to, comfortable to be with." Above all, she had been impressed with his character. In response to the same question, Karl said he "knew immediately she was the one." They had been married for 10 years at the time of the 1958 follow-up.

In a later interview we learned more about their early married life. Demobilization of the armed forces brought an acute shortage of housing. There had been very little construction of residential dwellings during the depression and war years, and the Schulzes had to settle for a furnished room near Karl's place of work. They were still in that furnished room when their first child was born.

There had also been an acute shortage of automobiles, no new ones having been available for private purchase from the end of 1941 until the war's end in 1945. It was many months before the Schulzes could acquire a car. So the early years were a struggle, but the Schulzes managed to put money aside and 3 months before their second child was born they were able to build a house.

Asked in 1958 what sort of person his wife was, Mr. Schulz replied, with a warm laugh, "She is delightful. She is a very good-natured person . . . sentimental, easygoing, and kind . . . she has a good memory . . . she's intelligent . . . quick . . . she is more interested in people than I am . . . she is more extraverted . . . she even wondered whether she would be interviewed. . . she'd love it and it would be easier for her than it is for me, I think."

Although many of the details of his wife's background did not come out until the next follow-up, when Mrs. Schulz did indeed participate in an interview, it is relevant to note that her background was quite different to that of her husband. She came from an Irish Catholic family in which she had experienced a happy childhood and had a very close, loving relationship with her mother. Karl rather glossed over the extent to which his own mother was disappointed in his marrying a Catholic, though he alluded to this when asked if he had ever disappointed his mother. It appears that what was most problematic for her was the likelihood that the children would be raised as Catholics (as indeed they were).

To interject a note about Mrs. Schulz not derived from the interview with her husband, two staff members made separate visits to the Schulz home within a year of the first follow-up interview and administered intelligence tests to the children. Both mentioned being cordially received by Mrs. Schulz, and one added, "I was introduced to all the children who appeared an eager, enthusiastic group, anxious to do their tricks for me." She went on to state that "as long as the children stayed within what appeared to be fairly firm rules about their conduct, [Mrs. Schulz] was content to let things go, but if they stepped outside the boundaries, they were greeted by a yell from her and a general admonition to behave themselves. However . . . the children acted in a spontaneous and friendly manner both to their mother and me." The second test administrator found Mrs. Schulz composed and pleasant. Both commented on the large, modern home, nicely furnished, into which the Schulzes had moved relatively recently.

Returning now to Karl's characterization of his wife, he could think of nothing specific when asked what about her irritated him. He made it clear that any irritations were trivial. He reported that decisions were usually mutually agreed to but that each deferred to the other in areas where they were most competent. For the most part, he said, "our minds seem to run in the same channel and we usually come to similar decisions. There really aren't too many causes for disagreement."

At the time of the interviews, there were four children in the family, ranging in age from 3 to 11, the oldest and youngest being girls and the middle children boys. Mr. Schulz felt that the first and third children tended to resemble him, in being somewhat less social and more stubborn than the others, while the second and fourth children were more like his wife, "easy to get along with."

The final interview in the series dealt largely with parenting. His characterization of his strong and weak points as a parent were somewhat similar to his characterization of himself as an adolescent:

> I know some of my faults . . . I tend still to have a temper and have to consciously work at it . . . I get excited too easily when the kids do something they shouldn't do. Possibly I'm a bit too strict in terms of rules . . . and I'm a little bit fussy,

> maybe." [Then, on the positive side, he noted] "I spend as much time as I can with them and it is hard to give each one a share of individual attention. I like to play with them . . . teach them to do things . . . also teach them attitudes, like right and wrong and fair play. I try to give them help in school work and in their scouting when it is needed. I think I probably am giving them a liking of the outdoors . . . we go camping, picnicking, hiking . . . try to stimulate their interests in many things.

He felt that it was necessary to discipline children, but one should not do this harshly. "After a certain age I think you gain less by spanking and then it is best to deprive them of their privileges." He commented that sometimes it is desirable to give in to the children when they have strong feelings, and he noted that each child should be treated in terms of his or her own needs. "You have to use common sense and try to be reasonable."

In his discussion of childrearing, he frequently touched upon the importance of such matters as tending to the children's health, providing them with attention and love, helping to develop their capacities and, perhaps above all, giving them a feeling for the rights of others. The interviewer noted that in talking about his children his responses were more spontaneous and free and much longer than those given in the initial interview in the series.

When asked to compare the ways in which he had been raised with those in which he was raising his own children, he noted, rather surprisingly, that his children were more closely supervised than he had been. And he pointed out that "a larger family makes a difference." But in general he felt that the basic aims he and his wife had were not different from those of his own mother and grandmother.

The only child about whom he expressed any apprehension was his 11-year-old daughter, feeling she might have a difficult time because she didn't easily make friends and didn't take advice easily. The expression of his concerns was very similar to that of his own mother when he was 11, at the start of the research project.

From the 1964 questionnaire, we learned more about the marriage and parenting. He reported almost no significant disagreements with his wife on a large number of areas of family life where disagreements are fairly frequent. Those that were mentioned at all, with an indication of "very little" disagreement, were religious training for the children, where to go on vacation, in-laws—whom to see and how often—the use of birth control, and how strict to be with the children.

Asked about decision making, he indicated that he would more often make decisions on selecting and buying a car, on how the children should be disciplined, and how money is spent, but his wife would more often make the final decision relating to religious training for children, getting together with friends, and the use of birth control.

Karl's rating of his marriage was just below the "almost perfect" level. He saw mutual understanding of each other's problems and feelings as the most important element of marriage for him, with a chance to have and rear children second in importance. He surmised, however, that companionship and husband and wife doing things together might be most important to his wife, and he rated this as third in importance to himself. Standard of living, sexual relations, and the security and comfort of a home were rated lower in importance. Asked to choose the attributes most to be desired for a youngster in his or her early teens, when given a list of 17 parental values, Mr. Schulz chose the same items for a boy as he chose for a girl—that the child be happy, be honest, and be dependable.

He felt that the children's preschool years had been the period in which he had enjoyed them most, because they could take care of their own physical needs, yet were very dependent on their parents, and their problems were relatively few and relatively unimportant. The senior high school years were seen as the greatest problem, with the note that "their problems get more serious and far-reaching." He acknowledged that occasionally he felt inadequate as a parent in not being able to understand the child's attitude or to get across to them what seemed to him to be right. He felt that having children "brings parents together and keeps you interested in many things that would not touch your life otherwise. They can present a real challenge to help them achieve the most to which they are capable."

The chart on which Mr. Schulz recorded his year to year life satisfaction, from early childhood to his current age, showed the first year of army life to be the low point beyond adolescence and the next year, when he met his wife, to require two checks, one for the exhilaration he felt after meeting her, and a second, much lower, for military life, now overseas. The high, reaching "absolute tops" on the scale, was the year of his marriage, and the subsequent years dropped off slightly, though generally one or two categories from the top. The family had acquired their first new home when he was 29 and their second when he was 36, and both of these enhanced the evaluation of those years.

Several clinical psychologists and psychiatric social workers completed a personality Q-sort for Karl Schultz at 37, based on all material collected in the follow-up, including the comments of the interviewer and those who administered psychological tests, the life chart, and other available materials. This time the sorters were in complete agreement on four of the five most salient features of his personality, which were seen as "dependable," "straightforward," "values intellectual matters," and "arouses liking." They again agreed that his least typical attribute was "self-dramatizing," and he also received extremely low scores on the items, "self-defeating" and "feels victimized." He was now seen as substantially more introspective than he had been, as somewhat less overcontrolled, as more physically attractive, cheerful, and poised but as placing less value on independence and also less likely to think unconventionally. He was still seen as productive, intelligent, and ambitious, though on all of these attributes he had dropped a couple of notches from the extraordinarily high initial ratings. Verbal fluency and initiation of humor had come up substantially, but Karl Schulz still scored relatively low on satisfaction with self, perhaps because of his impressive ability to discern the respects in which he wished to improve. The correlation between his senior high school Q-sort profile and that at age 37 was .55, suggesting substantial stability yet considerable change as well. Karl Schulz now was well up in the top third of the study group in the measure of competence.

The relatively young age of the children at the time of the first adult follow-up made it difficult to assess just how smoothly family relationships were developing. There was no evidence in any of the interviews of any tension between husband and wife over childrearing, though Mr. Schulz reported that his wife was somewhat more lenient than he was and he indicated some problems in the responsiveness of his eldest daughter to parental guidance. It is difficult to know when a person reports on their perceptions of themselves as parents the extent to which self-awareness on the one hand and self-protectiveness on the other influence the report. The most perceptive and skillful parents are often more aware of the respects in which they fall short of their objectives in childrearing than are neglecting or harsh parents, for the latter almost always deny the existence of problems. Karl Schulz was clearly more self-aware than self-protective, and the picture he gave was of a somewhat overly controlling, occasionally critical but generally supportive and never harsh father who enjoyed his children. It seemed clear that rules were very important in this family, as indeed they tend to be in larger families. There was no indication of parental tensions over discipline, but some suggestion that Karl was stricter than his wife as well as a suggestion of anxiety involving the oldest child.

By the time of the 1964 questionnaire a fifth child had been born. The one place where it appeared that husband and wife were not closely together was with reference to church attendance. Karl reported that his wife attended church at least once a week, while he attended less than once a month. This did not appear to be a problem for either one. One might have anticipated some tensions over the issue of religion, but this couple seems to have coped very well with what might have been a serious stumbling block.

THE SCHULZES IN 1970

When Karl Schulz was next interviewed in 1970, at age 48, his wife and two of the children also participated in the follow-up. The Vietnam War was in its most brutal phase. The interviewer's introductory comments to the transcription of the interview described Mr. Schulz as more reserved and highly controlled than had the interviewer who saw him at 37. The latter was the mother of several children and nearer to her respondent in age than was the interviewer at 48. Although positively impressed by her respondent, the current interviewer felt that Mr. Schulz had shown acute discomfort when attention was focused on aspects of his own personality, and that the interview had been fairly stressful for him. She commented: "His way of approaching life is on a more objective, rational, intellectual basis, yet he shows warmth and genuine concern for others, but is not intuitive and as comfortable with people as he is with ideas." She noted that he seemed to take considerable satisfaction from his roles as father and husband as well as his occupational role and that "he is successful in all these roles, knows that he is, and is appropriately self-confident." She felt he had a good awareness of his strengths and weaknesses and that husband and wife appeared to counterbalance each other's personality with ease and comfort. A second rater of his personality characterized him as "the personification of the silent majority." Both saw him as conflict-free, stable, and able to provide his children with many of the gratifications he lacked as a child.

The Interview With Mr. Schulz

The initial questions in the interview were about parents, but of course Karl had lost his father very early in life. His mother was now in her 70s and age had taken its toll. She had had a series of mild strokes which left her unable to drive and markedly limited in her activities, though she was not bedridden. Her sister, who had lived with the family when Karl was small, was now looking after her. Karl was in touch with them and visited about once a month, but his mother's memory was so impaired as to make meaningful communication difficult.

The interview then turned to discussion of the children. It became apparent that the oldest daughter, Fran, now 22, had had a difficult few years when she headed off to college. Mr. Schulz did not volunteer any details about the problem other than saying that they had seemed to be at odds in everything during her first couple of years in college. He did not tell why she had dropped out of college to take a job. He focused instead on his feeling that more recently "her attitudes in general have changed, mellowed, and she's found things aren't quite as idealistic or black and white as she had believed." His major satisfaction with his daughter was that "she's adjusting finally to the world or the community as it is, not expecting all her dreams to come true overnight."

The oldest son, John, was now in college, and seemed to be doing reasonably well, though it was suggested that perhaps too much of his time was going to sports and hiking and fishing. As before, this son was characterized as much more like his mother, easygoing and comfortable with people.

The second son, Scott, on the other hand, was still seen as more like Mr. Schulz himself had been in adolescence, quiet, a little less self-confident and less sociable. By everyone's accounts, the older boys enjoyed each other and did a good deal together; their father had indeed transmitted to them an interest in fishing and in the out-of-doors. It did not appear that there were any particular tensions between father and sons, as there obviously had been with the oldest daughter.

The youngest daughter, Sara, fourth child in the family, was again characterized as being like her mother, enthusiastic about things and sociable. She had just been selected as one of the cheerleaders at high school, and appeared to be doing reasonably well in school. Her father summed up his feelings with the statement: "She just seems to be a very delightful girl at the moment." He added, however, that "it's once they get beyond this stage that the problems start coming out, you know."

The youngest son, George, seemed to be coming along very well. His father noted, "He tends to be at the top, as far as leading or ability at playing things . . . so he's, I think, a little overconfident sometimes." But again the boy was characterized as easy to get along with. Mr. Schulz felt that the younger children had learned from "taking in" all the discussions with the older children and hearing them "yelled at" from time to time. The two younger children were in parochial school, the daughter a senior, and the son probably in the 5th grade. It developed that each of the children shifted to a public high school after graduation from the 8-year parochial school.

The interview next turned to family interaction, and a discussion of how disagreements are handled. Despite the national furor over Vietnam, Mr. Schulz indicated that national and international political and social issues were not generally discussed with the children. "There's always something else we're taking about, of lower family-type levels. I'm not sure that we agree politically." He went on to indicate that he and his wife did not try to influence the children one way or another with reference to political issues. "There are probably disagreements, but they're not really discussed very thoroughly or brought out to any extent. We've had some disagreements on what the kids thought they should be able to do. Particularly I think when they get to the driving age this has been the most noticeable." Staying out late at night was again an issue in the family, though Mr. Schulz felt that "as long as we feel we're being reasonable about it, they seem to accept it pretty well."

Karl felt that his wife would definitely tend to be the confidante of the children, particularly because she was available to them when they came home from school or from other activities that they would want to talk about. He did not feel that there were significant differences between himself and his wife in the rearing of the children and noted that they present a united front both because they usually agree and to preclude having the children play one parent against the other. He expressed their primary aims as being to produce "decent human beings basically who would contribute to the general society and at the same time be happy individuals." Asked for a basic principle of his moral philosophy, he replied with the Golden Rule of treating one's neighbor as one would want to be treated.

The interviewer asked whether any issues such as opinion about birth control were voiced by the children as challenges to their parents in this family in which mother and children were Catholic. Mr. Schulz felt that the children had their own views, but said that there had not been any challenge as such. Again it appeared that such issues are simply not discussed, at least not with the father in this family. The fact that the youngest child was still preadolescent would suggest that if such discussions took place, they would be confined to the older offspring and would not be topics of table conversation.

Discussing parenting in general, Karl felt that the first-born child tended to be more difficult at every stage, but especially in the college years. He noted, "We didn't realize these problems existed until we got involved with them, then you learn to deal with them one way or another." He felt that being a parent had made him more tolerant and had made life richer, but of course it also meant that one's time is not really one's own, quite often.

Mr. Schulz did not feel that there had been much change from his own adolescence to that of his children in terms of getting a job, or independence, or sexual attitudes. He thought that he and his wife probably understood their children a little better than his mother and grandmother had understood him as an adolescent, pointing out that his mother had had to be heavily involved in her job. Basically he felt that he had had somewhat more freedom than he and his wife were permitting their children, but this was primarily because of his mother's work involvement. He did indicated that his mother and perhaps his aunt as well had at times suggested that they thought Karl and his wife should be somewhat more permissive with their children, but apparently this was not a major issue.

When the interview turned to the marital relationship, Mr. Schulz responded very similarly to the way he had more than a decade previously, in characterizing his wife as easy to get along with, goodnatured, reasonable, fair, enthusiastic. He felt that she kept the family organized and running smoothly and that they were able to discuss things completely freely. His only irritation, a minor one, was that his wife was a little less tidy than he would have liked, but he said that he now understands that this is primarily a matter of her sense of priorities, when she's busy doing other things. He thought the two had grown together over the years, each influencing the other in desirable ways.

He saw his wife as less restrictive with the children and acknowledged that both were a little on the conservative side and somewhat old-fashioned. He saw his wife as more religious than himself as well as being more friendly and interested in social activities.

Asked how his wife might see him, his reply was basically as a partner in the maintenance of the family and a good provider. It was difficult for him to say in what respects his wife might be irritated with him.

Questions about decision making evoked almost identical answers to those given a decade previously—that they tended to think somewhat alike and there were seldom problems, but then he added, "If one of us feels very strongly one way or another, this might settle it, but there's usually little difference between us on most of the items I can think of." He felt his wife had helped him become a more considerate person.

Asked for his definition of love within marriage and whether it had changed over the years, Karl replied that he felt it was basically the same, though tempered with time. "As you have gotten to know a person really well, it's sort of a deeper sense of companionship, if you will, or sort of rely on the other more, because you've developed this way, you've worked together."

Karl's personality Q-sort at age 48 reflects the somewhat less enthusiastic response to him by the interviewer at this period. There was also less consensus among the raters as to certain of his attributes; they agreed completely on only one of his most salient traits—"dependable." In addition, he was still seen as valuing intellectual matters, as straightforward and as valuing independence. And, as in adolescence, he was seen as priding himself on his objectivity, and to even a greater degree than in adolescence, as "aloof." But he was now seen as much more "giving," much more satisfied with himself, and more masculine. He had dropped from the extraordinarily high rating on "arouses liking" received at the previous follow-up to a slightly above average rating on this attribute and had also dropped to average on introspectiveness. Ratings at this period correlated more highly with those for the adolescent years than had those for the previous follow-up ($r = .61$), suggesting more stability than had the earlier assessment, and there was a closer relationship between the two adult Q sorts ($r = .66$) than existed between either and the adolescent evaluations.

The Interview With Mrs. Schulz

Like her husband, Mrs. Schulz made a very positive impression on the interviewer, who saw her as "a warm, compassionate, humorous woman . . . [with] good judgment and good common sense . . . I find her one of the most pleasant women I have seen." It was from this interview that we learned about Mrs. Schulz's own family background, and as previously noted, hers appeared to have been a happy childhood in which she had a close relationship with her mother, even though at times she may have felt somewhat rebellious in the adolescent years.

In general, it can be said that the picture Mrs. Schulz communicated about the marriage was entirely consonant with her husband's characterization of it, but she gave somewhat more detail, especially in discussing the children. What quickly became apparent, however, was a much higher level of emotional concern with the problems of her oldest child. She noted something that we had not previously registered, that Frank had been born less than a year after they were married, before their lives had achieved very much stability. Kathleen had wanted to breast feed Fran, but this didn't work out, and apparently this was very traumatic for the mother. She reported an early comment by her husband that in the first 6 months she had cried more than her daughter had. It will be remembered that Kathleen had come from the East Coast to marry Karl and had given up all of her own ties there to move into a new community and take on a totally new role. For more than 20 years, Kathleen had been faced with childrearing, and she was just beginning to contemplate greater freedom for herself. Fran had been the "pioneer" among the children, and Kathleen felt that this had been very hard on the girl. It was she on whom her parents tried out "all the midnight rules" and she who in a sense educated them in how to become more comfortable parents.

Kathleen Schulz agreed with her husband that Fran had definitely matured in the last couple of years, but the first 2 years of college had been a terrible wrench for both mother and father. Fran had gone to the University of California campus that spawned the student rebellion of the 60s, and had arrived there when turbulence was at its height. She had joined a sorority but relatively early had established a liaison with a male student who ultimately persuaded her to quit college at the end of her sophomore year and to take a job. The relationship had broken up some months thereafter, with the boy having indicated that he was not really interested in a permanent kind of relationship. This had been extremely traumatic to Fran, though it appeared that she had mobilized herself well and was now working toward the completion of her college in addition to holding a job.

Mrs. Schulz described her oldest son, John, as very different from Fran—friendly, athletic, popular. He was now a junior in a small college several hundred miles from his home and had had some discomfort in going from being an important figure at high school to being an unknown person on the college campus. John apparently had little trouble in confiding in his mother and she found him a joy. She felt that he would be like his father, whom she characterized as "about as steady a husband as anyone could find anywhere . . . Karl really is a soft-spoken tremendous father." But she was a bit apprehensive because John seemed to be easily led and she wondered whether he might be induced to try drugs. She thought, though, that neither of her older sons needed a crutch or to prove something and that therefore they would stay away from drugs.

Both parents had been very active in attending school functions such as basketball games and other activities that their children took part in. Although the children were reported to have sometimes chided their parents for being "up tight" about marijuana, Mrs. Schulz retained a strong aversion to drug experimentation.

The second son, Scott, now 17 and a high school junior, was characterized by his mother as quiet and much more like his father than John was. He was highly selective in his choice of friends and much less sociable. But he was an excellent athlete and a good student, and as his mother laughingly reported, "He's a good kid . . . was easy to raise." He had tagged along a good deal with John before his older brother had gone to college and was then forced to find his own friends. In a period when long hair and adolescent rebellion were most fashionable and were problematic for many parents, neither boy had presented any problems and both had received leadership and scholarship awards in the community where they went to school.

The younger daughter, Sara, was described by her mother as a friendly, popular girl who, in the 8th grade of the Catholic school she was attending, was now not only taller than the boys and girls but taller than the teachers. She was both a cheerleader and captain of the girls' volleyball team. Unlike her brothers, she seemed to be questioning many of the school's restrictions, including a dress code that suggested that girls didn't wear trousers to the movies. Her mother opined that high school would probably be a merry chase with her. She saw Sara as being a good deal more aggressive than the other children and wished that that aggressiveness might have been spread more evenly through the family. Sara could at times get "awfully mad" at her parents but "in 2 minutes she's your best friend and kind of sorry that she's got such a quick temper."

Mrs. Schulz regarded Sara as contributing a great deal of humor to family gatherings. One of the teachers had commented that Sara's compositions in English were "hilarious." But Mrs. Schulz was clearly anticipating that when Sara got to high school she would be testing the limits, particularly as they related to what time she was to come in at night.

George, the youngest son, was described as "just the ever-loving spoonful in the house . . . He's a great little kid and he's the neatest child I've ever had; he makes his own bed, picks up his own clothes . . . it really makes you sit and wonder whether this kid got, you know, ten times more love than anybody else and certainly a very relaxed mother and father. I mean, you don't climb the walls, because you know this, too, will pass." She went on to note that they tried to be somewhat more lenient on things that weren't terribly important.

In general, Mrs. Schulz expressed herself as very pleased with the way the children had turned out. She felt that Fran would "make a very fine wife and mother" and that she had turned out extremely well.

Although there was no mention of the Vietnam War, Mrs. Schulz did indicate that the older boys resented the prospects of being drafted and one assumes that they may have strongly disapproved of what was happening in Vietnam. There was no indication, however, that the Vietnam War was a matter of strong disagreement within the family.

Data From Questionnaires in 1970

In addition to the interviews conducted with the study members and their wives and with children between the ages of 14 and 18, questionnaires were distributed at the time of the second follow-up. The questionnaires touched upon job attitudes, political and social participation, and perceptions of the marital partner, identified children between the ages of 14 and 18, and objectives and assessments of parenting. Neither Karl nor Kathleen Schulz claimed to understand the children "very well" but both felt that they understood them fairly well in most respects. Asked to indicate the degree of agreement with the children in a number of areas that were frequent sources of intergenerational disagreement, especially in the 1960s, Mr. Schulz indicated that he did not know his children's political attitudes or where they stood on civil rights and race relations, while Mrs. Schulz checked that she did not agree with the children's views in these two areas. Both parents reported that they discussed issues of right and wrong to help their children become good persons, but, as Mr. Schulz had already reported in the interviews, political issues and issues of race relations were not part of such discussions. It may be, however, that the children were freer discussing these issues with their mother than with their father.

Both parents saw themselves as middle-of-the-road, but more conservative than their children. (One wonders if the children had been adolescents in the climate of the 80s rather than the 60s, might the parents have seen themselves as less conservative than the children.) It is highly relevant to recall that a major issue of the 1960s was the "generation gap," yet neither of the children who were questioned felt that such a gap existed in their experience.

Both parents indicated that they had enjoyed the children most in the earlier school years when the problems they posed were relatively easy to handle. As a consequence of their experience with Fran, both reported that after high school was the most difficult period, noting that once the children were away from home, parents could have only slight influence upon them.

The Schulzes showed substantial consensus in the values they chose as most important attributes for an adolescent child, both feeling that being dependable ranked first for boys and girls and both also chose considerate as one of the three most important attributes of a girl. Mr. Schulz rated ambition somewhat higher than did his wife, who chose self-control as extremely important for a boy, and for both boys and girls Mrs. Schulz chose being a good student as extremely important, while her husband chose popularity.

In indicating the frequency of various responses to the children when the children did or were about to do something wrong, Mr. Schulz indicated somewhat greater use of control although both indicated that they would point out how others would be affected and would attempt to teach what's right and wrong. Mrs. Schulz reported that the children "very often" challenged her about what's right and wrong, while Mr. Schulz felt that this occurred only "fairly often," and Karl said that he "sometimes" changed his mind in response to their challenges but his wife said that she "often" changed her mind.

In their perceptions of each other, the Schulzes showed a good deal of consensus, agreeing that Karl was more often somewhat critical but also more likely to keep his feelings to himself in expressing their feelings for each other. Moreover, both agreed that they are very similar in expressing feelings toward the children and that they were seldom angry but moderately critical. The biggest disagreement was on the openness of expression of displeasure, something acknowledged by Karl with reference to his own behavior but not seen as such by his wife. Both rated the marriage as very happy.

Because it would be inappropriate to reveal the specifics of the children's responses to their questionnaires and interviews, it will suffice to say that on the whole the two children who were seen had high respect for their parents and considered their parents, and especially their mother, to have had the strongest influence on them and to be the people whose ideas and opinions meant most to them. Yet neither parent had seen himself or herself as being that influential. Moreover, while Mrs. Schulz had felt that she understood her children only "fairly well," both children felt that she knew them "very well." This reverses the more usual finding in which parents thought they understood their children very well but the children felt differently. This is not to say that the children viewed their parents as perfect models to follow, but rather that whether they agreed or disagreed on various issues, their parents mattered very much to them and both children saw their parents as strongly supportive of them.

Subsequent to the 1969–70 follow-up, Eliane Aerts carried out a study of whole families, drawing upon the interviews with husband, wife, and children in all families where both parents and at least one child had been interviewed. Codes and scales were developed to relate to closeness of family bonds, communication within the family, decision making as it related to parents and children, and relationships between the family and members of the external community. The Schulz family was seen as somewhat above average in solidarity and openness of communication, but somewhat below average in personal acceptance of members and in rational problem solving. The preparer of this history would disagree with the below-average ratings in personal acceptance and rational problem solving. The difference in assessments may reflect differences in perspectives and experience in rearing a family as well as the additional source of data on which I drew. The questionnaires completed in 1969–70, especially those of the children, provided substantial evidence beyond that available in the interviews. The parents' references to reliance on rules, not only for younger children but for older adolescents, with little evidence in their interviews of rational renegotiation of rules, probably resulted in the lower placement on rational problem solving. However, the children's and parents' questionnaires indicated, as noted before, a good deal of success on the part of the children in negotiations on rules, as well as strong indications of personal acceptance within this family.

In terms of decision making, the family was seen as somewhat parent-dominated, but not strongly so. The raters agreed that the best characterization of the family, from a list of eight possible types (adapted from Swanson, 1974) was as follows:

> Parents, or one of the parents, has authority to decide on individual and on family matters. The children are expected to seek the parents' advice concerning their own

> life plans, and are expected to follow them. Parents decide in terms of general standards of what the members' duties are, and what is right for the parents and children to do. One parent, however, gets spontaneous allegience and influences all the other members on family matters. That parent acts as mediator and interprets the rules.

Mrs. Schulz was clearly the mediator for this family.

Note: When Mr. Schulz read this statement, he took it to mean that the parents tried to influence their children's career plans, and he noted that they made no attempt to influence the children in this respect. I explained that "life plans" here meant day-to-day activities and adventures for younger children and not the life plans of adolescents.

As the family was approaching the "empty nest" stage, then, it appeared to be functioning well but with some parental apprehension as to what would happen when other children left home. Among the study families, this one rated exceptionally high in marital satisfaction and consensus between the parents, showed no appreciable coalitions, and there was very high parental involvement in the lives of the children. What would the next decade bring?

THE SCHULZES IN 1982

We saw both Mr. and Mrs. Schulz again some 13 years later. Again the interviewers were enthusiastic in their descriptions of the Schulzes as extremely pleasant, competent persons. In the interval since our previous contact, both of their mothers had died. Karl had retired 3 years before the interview at age 58. He had advanced in his field of engineering research to the top level that he could occupy without having major administrative responsibilities. His whole career had been spent with a single employer, and it had been a highly satisfying career, both intrinsically and extrinsically. Asked in what ways his job had been important in determining his sense of self, Karl Schulz replied: "It was a good part of it. It gives you an identity in terms of what you're contributing and where you fit into the picture of the world aside from your family." Yet when asked which aspect of life had *most* influenced his sense of self, it was not the job or career but rather family relationships and activities. The job took second place.

In retirement, he missed some of the long-term relationships with his former associates, whom he characterized as a friendly group. Yet he did not feel any different sense of self since retiring, for he had the satisfaction of knowing what he had contributed. And what pleased him most about not working was not having to get up early in the morning, noting that he was "a night person."

The Schulzes had been in complete agreement on when he would retire and what they would like to do. They had been making good progress toward their objectives, but unfortunately in the previous year Mrs. Schulz had had a fall and suffered a broken leg, and more seriously, a detached retina. Karl was very much concerned about his wife's sight, as indeed she was, for efforts to repair the retinal damage resulted in the loss of sight in the affected eye.

Fran, the oldest daughter, was now 34, and George, the youngest child, was, at 21, a senior in college. He had been away but was about to spend 6 months at home on an internship arrangement that would bring him back to the Bay Area. The intermediate children had graduated from college, though only the oldest son, John, had married. Scott was working at a job that he very much enjoyed, one for which his college education had specifically prepared him, and he was living several hundred miles away. Sara had a job in the publishing business and had an apartment in a city fairly near to her parents' home, so she could visit frequently. Although Sara's life style was not entirely to her mother's liking, on the whole the Schulzes were very pleased with the way their children had turned out. But Mrs. Schulz would have liked to have some grandchildren on the way, and was beginning to wonder how long she would have to wait.

The 1982 follow-up was designed in several segments, with both a structured interview to get at certain data systematically and a clinical interview to reveal what was most salient in the lives and current thoughts and emotions of the study members. The clinical interview afforded an opportunity to learn more about Karl's earliest experiences in the family and a bit more about his parents' marriage. Among his early memories were going camping with his parents (apparently from infancy), going fishing with his father and sitting on his father's lap, holding the steering wheel of the car while driving out in the country. Karl said that his mother had been an adventuresome young woman who went to Alaska at a time when Alaska constituted the last frontier. It appears that she may have gone with a friend from the midwestern state where she had grown up. At a time when very few young women would have ventured to Alaska, there was apparently a demand for their services, and both took jobs in a bank. It was in Alaska that Karl's parents had met. His father was there on an engineering assignment. We don't know how long it was before his parents married, but it was not until after they had returned to the contiguous 48 states that they married, in San Francisco. Perhaps, like Karl and his wife, his parents had corresponded and deepened their knowledge of each other. In any event, there is every indication that theirs had been a happy, rewarding relationship and that they were competent and caring parents. Karl's distant memory of his father was vague, but beyond his own memories his mother must have presented a very positive picture of the father he knew for so short a period.

Karl's mother became a very involved businesswomen, whose success was apparently sufficient to provide her with a comfortable income in later life. She had, however, suffered further strokes beyond the previous follow-up, which made it very difficult to communicate with her, and there had not been a great deal of interaction between his mother and the children as they grew older.

Although he felt that he had missed his father's guidance, companionship, and teaching, Karl thought that in some ways he became more independent, "probably because I had to." He noted that his mother had given him a great deal of freedom rather than being overprotective as might have been expected under such circumstances. He felt that both his mother and his grandmother had given him a lot of encouragement. "You can do this, you can do that." His mother encouraged him to go to college and to set his sights high, but he did not feel that she had really pressured him. Thinking back on what it had meant to be an only child, he had not felt particularly deprived. Here again he felt that having to play by himself and come up with his own activities had not been all bad, although it did not enhance his social skills.

From Mrs. Schulz's clinical interview we learned more about her enduringly close relationship with her own mother, a strong independent woman. Kathleen's mother had died only a few years before, having outlived her husband by 25 years. Mother and daughter had been in close touch right until the end, and indeed Kathleen had been with her mother on the East Cost during the last few weeks of her illness, until she entered a hospital and it was necessary for Kathleen to return to her own family commitments on the opposite coast.

We learned a bit more about their early married life in California. Mrs. Schulz described with considerable humor the problems of living in a furnished room through one's initial pregnancy. When she had the baby, there was nowhere for her mother to come and stay, so she and Karl managed on their own. Looking back she commented: "There were tears and gnashing of teeth, but you survived. And you look back and think, 'gee, maybe this is where you get your strength'." They not only survived, but as she noted, their coping together brought them closer.

In their interviews, both the Schulzes commented on the relatively meager social life in the early years of their marriage. For both of them, the community into which they moved was one in which they had no previous contacts, and except for social activities connected with Karl's employment, it took some time before they acquired local friends with whom they would get together socially. But because both were highly autonomous persons and were fully available to each other, it does not appear that there were major strains at any time.

Asked some rather searching questions about their marriage in the structured interview, both Karl and Kathleen again reported in very similar terms how they had gravitated toward each other across a lot of short people at the dance in 1943. Both remained as enthusiastic about their marriage as they had been on earlier occasions. As Mrs. Schulz put it: "I think we've had just a tremendous marriage . . . we enjoy the same things . . . I think we balanced each other out well." Karl indicated that he had quickly felt that Kathleen was the person he wanted to marry, though both had felt that no decisions should be made before his return from service. He noted that they had both wanted to have a family and "it seemed like we just jelled." Above all, Karl had been able to talk freely to

Kathleen. With her he was at ease; she had a good sense of humor and wasn't demanding. He used the term "terrific" to characterize the marriage. Neither had ever thought seriously of divorce nor had they every been separated. Asked what had kept them together, both gave rather similar replies: Karl's—"willingness to share and confront problems and take care of the children. . Because we still love each other;" Kathleen's—"Our commitment when we married, our attitudes and expectations." Both would like their children's marriages to be like theirs. Kathleen commented, "I would hope that they would marry someone who would cherish them." Karl's formulation: "To have the same support, family life. I think it's been great."

Both Karl and Kathleen felt that their level of satisfaction in the marriage had remained constant over the years. There were differences in emphasis over the years, but both found it hard to say when the marriage was at its best or worst. Karl summed up his feelings:

> When you're young its romantically wild and then you have children, which is fun, and then you have yourselves, which is fine, too. Probably when we were first having our family, probably the first child was most exciting. Doing things together.

On each of the occasions when she was seen, Mrs. Schulz was characterized as warm, competent, humorous, and very pleasant to interview. She could be emotional, but she could also master her emotions. She had learned to "roll with the punches," as she once put it, and the difficult times never got her down. There was little evidence of personality change from age 48 to 61, and there is good reason to suppose that Kathleen Schulz was in adolescence a competent, warm person who had benefited from having a loving, caring and competent mother.

The personality assessment of Karl at 61, based on another round of Q-sorts, suggested minimal change over the adult years. He again received the highest possible score on "dependable," and was only a shade lower on "straightforward," "productive," "has wide interests," and "warm." Again, the attributes deemed least applicable to him were "deceitful" and "feels victimized." Equally inapplicable was the statement, "disorganized and maladaptive when under stress or trauma." Both of the Schulzes were effective copers. The stability of Karl's personality over the adult years is attested to by the correlation coefficient between his age 37 and age 61 profiles—.75, which is as high as the average reliability of the Q-sort composite at any given period.

A Further Interview With Karl

At the time of the last full follow-up, study members were asked to indicate the degree to which they were willing to have materials gathered in the past used in reconstructing sequences in the life course. Specifically, they were asked to indicate whether they would give approval only for statistical use of their data, whether we might use brief excerpts for illustrating particular life-course phases, or whether the study member would be willing to collaborate with a staff member in constructing a full life history. More than four-fifths of the study members indicated that they would be willing to share their life stories. From among a random subsample of this group, living within 50 miles of Berkeley, 60 members were selected for intensive life history interviews. Karl Schulz was one of this group. He was interviewed in 1984.

The writer conducted this interview at Mr. Schulz's home, the home that the Schulzes had acquired in their mid-30s. It was in a pleasant upper-middle-class community, on a block of very well-maintained homes on relatively spacious grounds. We reviewed recollections of adolescence, as had been done nearly 30 years earlier, at the time of the first intensive follow-up. Asked how well he knew himself and understood himself—his goals, his needs, and his values—at the end of adolescence, Karl Schulz again noted that he knew both where his problems lay and what his strengths were. When the interviewer explained his interest in trying to ascertain how lives get organized, Karl noted that his early goal of going into engineering "was a big help in making decisions and getting things organized . . . you were not floundering around."

We discussed his playing basketball, which he did in high school but not in college. He noted that he "felt pretty intense about studying": "I guess I felt that it would pay off later and I didn't have that much feeling of doing social things. Sort of one thing at a time, you might say."

The interviewer observed that is was unusual for a man to be as successful as Mr. Schulz had been and at the same time not to be so involved in the job that he had to stint on the family's time. He commented that there was very little pressure in his job to work overtime and that his being in a carpool had helped to define his hours of work. One aspect that he liked was that there was a good deal of leeway in setting his own schedule for tasks that needed to be accomplished. He noted that his research-oriented job was very different from production engineering: "It wasn't pure science, but you had a lot of personal choice of what you could do or how you could do things."

Asked when he felt he had become fully mature—intellectually and emotionally mature—Karl Schulz thought that this occurred a few years after he had married. His wife had brought new perspectives and the children had made him aware of aspects of life that he had really not been aware of before. He saw his military service as also having contributed to making him mature. Asked to define what maturity meant to him, he replied: "[Being] able and willing to take charge of your life and taking responsibility for your actions whatever you do."

Karl Schulz did not think he had ever experienced any period of depression, and certainly no midlife crisis. His life, he said, had been "pretty even." Asked to look back over his life and say whether he had remained pretty much the same person that he had been or whether he might have changed, he said that he did indeed think that he had changed. "Hopefully you grow and change and adapt a little bit." On the other hand, his general moral values had not changed though he might have different attitudes than he had held earlier. Asked in what respects he felt he had changed, he replied: "I think I am more understanding of people and their problems. After you've been through some yourself, you realize how people have to behave or do things in certain cases." He felt that he had become more comfortable with people and friendlier than he had appeared earlier. His philosophy of life, however, was little changed: "You try to be a good person and do what is morally right and try to bring your family up that way."

How would he most like to be remembered? "As a good husband and father, I guess. Maybe a good neighbor and someone who has made a little contribution toward the good of mankind in the work you've been doing, although I don't think any of my efforts have been that overwhelming. . . . Basically, that you have lived a good life."

A REVIEW SESSION WITH THE SCHULZES

When a draft of Karl Schulz's life story up to 1970 had been prepared, a copy was sent to Mr. and Mrs. Schulz with an indication that his life story had been expanded somewhat, drawing upon Mrs. Schulz's interviews, and a request for permission to use the interview for a seminar on family dynamics and ultimately for our conference. The Schulzes were asked to suggest any corrections, modifications to preserve anonymity, or other changes that they deemed desirable and an appointment for an interview at their home was arranged at this time. Karl and Kathleen Schulz received the writer cordially and we entered into a wide-ranging discussion that continued for more than 4 hours, with lunch at midsession. Mr. Schulz suggested dropping a few descriptive phrases that would tend to identify him but otherwise did not so much suggest changes to indicate where his memory was not quite consonant with certain details presented. These have been specified in the foregoing account.

All of the children had completed their transition to full adult status, and the Schulzes brought the interviewer up to date on the status not only of their children, all of whom were now married, but of their grandchildren. Their oldest daughter had indeed married and was now happily at home with two youngsters. Two of the sons had wives who were employed full-time, but they had taken time off to have children and then returned to the job. Their husbands were apparently sharing child care and home duties on an equitable basis. Moreover, the data we had secured from two of the children in the past 3 years (by mail questionnaire) suggested happy marriages and high job satisfaction. Although only one of the children now lived within an hour's drive of the parents, all five were bringing their families to their parents' home for Christmas.

The offsprings' family patterns are different from those of Kathleen and Karl. There are fewer children, wives tend to be employed, husbands and wives share in the same tasks rather than having a sharp division of labor. Despite such changes, the several types of information that we have about the offsprings' families that they shared attributes that Kathleen and Karl valued in their own marriage—cherishing their partners, providing mutual support, and feeling strongly committed to each other.

In the course of the interview, we discussed in some detail the early years of the marriage. The interviewer noted that the early years of childrearing tend to be difficult for many young couples and not infrequently lead to tensions between them. The Schulzes did not recall significant tensions. There were difficult days, they recalled, but they shared whatever problems existed. Karl commented his wife was never demanding, that she was willing to put up with a modest style of life. Moreover, "we depended on each other; if either had blown our tops, we wouldn't have lasted." Each knew that the other could be depended upon. Kathleen commented that if she had had a bad day, she knew that shortly after 4:30 Karl would be home, and that he would take over. He would feed the little ones, he would play catch with the older ones, and generally take charge so that Kathleen could retire to read a book or rest or do whatever else she felt like doing.

Because Karl had to be at work very early in the morning, Kathleen generally tended the children if they needed attention at night, but she regarded this as appropriate. Although at the start they had relatively little, once they managed to rent a small house, life was much more pleasant, and they managed almost immediately to begin saving. They both noted that when things were roughest, they knew that their general progress was going to be "always up." Kathleen observed that rough going prepares one for future coping and wondered whether the lack of struggle of the current generation of young adults would not make it harder for them to cope if they ran into difficulties subsequently. As she noted, their children had many more possessions when they got married. She and Karl had each other and a determination to build a family and a life together. She also noted that although there had been rough going in terms of living arrangements initially, "we never had any emotional rough going."

When the interviewer asked whether either Karl or Kathleen had ever experienced a period of depression in those early years, both immediately said "No." The only period of depression for Kathleen was when she fell and broke her leg and suffered a detached retina, which led to the loss of sight in one eye.

Because several early interviews had suggested relatively little discussion of current social issues at home, the interviewer inquired as to whether social issues were not ever discussed in the family during the 1960s and 70s when there was so much turmoil. Karl said that of course major crises and news stories would be discussed but that more often dinner conversation related to what was going on at the school or in the activities of various family members. He noted that the family had on one trip passed near Selma, Alabama, and that they had explained to the children the struggle for civil rights there. Mrs. Schulz remembered a local issue that related to a school board member in which she had expressed strong feelings and found that the children disagreed with her views. She reported a "knock-down, drag-out battle" as they discussed this issue. There was no indication that she felt the children were wrong but merely that there would at times be vigorous discussions of social issues. Further, the Schulzes urged their children to "get out and vote for what you think is right" when they became of age. Neither Karl or Kathleen Schulz regarded themselves as having been an activist in any area, nor had their children been activists. As Mrs. Schulz put it, "None of ours ever carried a banner."

The Schulzes could think of no major issue that had been especially difficult for them, though one candidate that came to mind was the question of whether they needed a larger house in the early years of family growth. They built their second, larger house only 7 years after having built their first house, and Karl had been rather reluctant to take on this financial burden. However, Kathleen had pushed for the house, and he acceded. As they both noted, it was the best investment they had ever made.

The interviewer inquired about Karl's retirement, which had come when he was only 58. He reported that he was finding work less exciting and that he was enjoying getting up early in the morning less and less. It was not that there was anything he specifically wanted to do, but there were rumors that the retirement program would be changing for the worse, and apparently a substantial number of Karl's colleagues decided to retire at the same time. Since retirement income would be reasonably adequate, and since Kathleen had qualified for social security by working the six quarters that were necessary for her to qualify, there were no financial constraints requiring continued employment.

The Schulzes plan to stay in the area as long as they can. They enjoy their home (they had just remodeled several rooms) and their yard, and they noted that their closest friends were here in the community. Asked how they had made these friends, Kathleen commented that some were neighbors, some had come through the church and some through work but the largest number were through the activities of their children. Parents of the children's friends often became their friends. It was clear that they are strongly rooted in the community and that they are good citizens of that community. Thus the Schulz family might be considered not a "haven in a heartless world" but a haven in a warm and friendly world where there are opportunities for one to shape one's own life.

Overview

Karl and Kathleen Schulz retain a traditional view of the family, especially in their emphasis on the importance of children and relatively traditional gender relationships. In many traditional families, however, husbands have not been as fully available to their wives and children as Karl has been. And in many families of their age peers, women who were raised to espouse traditional values have been influenced to a substantial extent by the women's movement and have re-evaluated the childrearing years, when they were confined to the home, often with considerable resentment. One finds no such resentment in Kathleen Schulz. One finds rather the satisfaction of having raised five children who are competent, decent human beings. Relatively few of our study members have managed to bring large families through the 60s without suffering at least one casualty to the "drop out, turn on" generation.

Perhaps the most important part of the traditional orientations of Karl and Kathleen Schulz has been their commitment to each other. They did not marry with the idea that they might get divorced. Both were highly competent persons and both believed they could cope together with whatever lay ahead. Moreover, despite having very different personalities, neither was self-centered or defensive, nor was either a particularly critical person. They respected each other's judgment and integrity. Starting with similar values and objectives, they forged a set of mutual expectations and confidence of support that prepared them for cooperation rather than conflict when problems arose.

One might wonder how a man who had been a somewhat inhibited adolescent, not at ease in social situations, could establish so thoroughly intimate a marital relationship as Karl and Kathleen share. One answer, of course, is Kathleen, who could at once put Karl at ease. Another is that Karl had enjoyed close friendships with several of his classmates. He was not lacking in the ability to relate closely, even if his emotional expression had seemed constricted. Certainly his emotional expression where Kathleen was concerned was not constricted. There had been, in his words, a "mad romantic phase" to the early years of marriage, and each partner always expressed genuine enthusiasm in talking about the other. Above, all, they were best friends from the start.

In an era before children were regarded as burdens and seen by many feminists as a source of oppression of women, both Karl and Kathleen looked forward to the opportunity to nurture a family. They were willing to take on the responsibilities of parenthood even though they knew that their own freedom would be limited; they had strong convictions that parenthood was an essential part of the lives they wanted to live.

From all the data reviewed, they appear to have been warmly accepting of their children, but they set limits for the children and held them to those limits, perhaps being a bit overly strict in the earlier years but relinquishing controls and encouraging the children in a wide variety of acceptable activities. From questionnaires received from three of the children, and from the Schulzes' most recent reports, all seem to be doing well and all regard their parents with considerable affection. The values they espouse for their own children are very close to those espoused by Karl and Kathleen. In their 30s, they still see their parents as having been highly supportive and their own developmental years in the family as not at all stressful.

In considering this family history, we cannot ignore the importance of potentialities and proclivities genetically acquired. The patterns of personality resemblance within the family show amazing consistency from early childhood to the most recently available data. Two of the children most clearly resemble Karl, in being less socially outgoing and two more clearly resemble their mother, with the youngest child less clearly similar to either parent. All had superior intelligence, as evidenced by testing in the early years and more recently. The boys' tall stature made them obvious recruits for a basketball team, and they were successful athletes, not only in basketball but in other sports as well. Throughout their childhood and adolescent years, they received love and guidance from parents who had sufficient resources to provide them with intellectually stimulating opportunities. All were assisted to go away for their college experience. Finally, all seem to have been imbued with motivation to do something significant with their lives.

SOURCES OF DATA FOR HISTORY OF THE SCHULZ FAMILY

Karl's adolescence

Interviews with mother on "Habits and regimes," 1932, 1936.

Annual physical exams, 1932–1938.

Annual administration of California Adjustment Inventory, 1932–1938.

Observations of Karl at dances, on playground, on field trips.

Ratings of Karl by psychology staff, every fall and spring, 1932-1938.

Ratings of Karl's mother on dominant traits.

Intelligence tests—Stanford Binet, ages 12 and 17.

Peer ratings, junior high years.

And dozens of inventories, opinion ballots, etc., 1932 to June 1939.

Adulthood - Karl

1958 (Age 37): Four sessions averaging 2 hours each, using structured interview schedule dealing with recollection of adolescence including social skills, dating, sources of satisfaction and dissatisfaction, plans, relations with parents; description of spouse, marital relations, socialization practices; social issues; personal habits and view of self (dictated by interviewer from notes, 41 pages).

1964 (Age 44): Current status survey - 12-page structured, largely precoded questionnaire on career, marriage, parental values and socialization practices.

1969 (Age 48): Two tape recorded interviews using schedule of open-ended questions, dealing with relations with parents, siblings, children, spouse, and with occupation, finances, self views, recreation and health (fully transcribed, 40 pages), plus 13-page questionnaire.

1982 (Age 62): Tape recorded fully transcribed clinical interview on relationships with parents, spouse, children and life history (44 pages). Structured interview (taped, transcribed with some cuts) dealing with social supports, life review, occupation, marriage, satisfaction with children (17 pages). Series of questionnaires on marriage, retirement, health, etc.

1984 (Age 63): Tape recorded "life history" interview dealing with recollections of adolescence; early life interests; values, plans; effects of Depression and World War II; turning points in the life course; sense of identity and overview of life (fully transcribed, 16 ss. pages).

Interviews with Mrs. Schulz

1969: Tape recorded interview, largely on marriage and family relationships (61 pages).

1982: Tape recorded, fully transcribed clinical interview (67 pages) and partially transcribed structured interview (14 pages) similar to husband's.

Interview with Mr. and Mrs. Schulz

1988: Review of history prepared from archives and further questions about early years of marriage and family developments - tape recorded, not transcribed except for excerpts.

Material from children of Karl and Kathleen Schulz

1970: Interviews with two older sons (fully transcribed) and questionnaires relating to current interests, plans, family relationships, values.

1982–83: Questionnaires on current status (occupation, marriage, relations with parents) of two older sons and youngest daughter.

Note: Interview materials provided the basis for personality Q sorts at each period and for ratings of marriage, parenting, etc. Ratings at each period were done without knowledge of or reference to other periods. All interviews except those with children were conducted by fully qualified psychologists, social workers or sociologists.

REFERENCES

Clausen, J. A. (1991). Adolescent competence and the shaping of the life course. *American Journal of Sociology, 96,* 805–42.

Swanson, G. E. (1974). Family structure and the reflective intelligence of children. *Sociometry, 37,* 459–490.

20 Perspectives on the Use of Case Studies: All it Takes is One

Nancy J. Chodorow
University of California, Berkeley

As one might imagine, since every social science and humanities field has something to say about families, there are many different approaches to family study. We can look at families historically or ethnographically, we can report group or aggregate data (on 1, 10, 1,000, or 10,000 families), we can clinically interview family members, we can observe family interaction. Any particular approach to families will be a product of the interaction of theory, method, and empirical claim, and the relations among these three are also variable. This section of *Family, Self and Society* presents case studies of families. Calvin Settlage and his coworkers, Isabel Bradburn and Joan Kaplan, and John Clausen, all, in providing case material, give us a sense of the people behind, or within, their studies. We learn from them about the potential contribution of case material, and they indicate for us how differently and for what different purposes case material can be presented. We see three particular instances of the intertwining of theory, method, and result.

Settlage et al. come from a psychoanalytic perspective. They are interested in psychic structure formation in children and in how the microdynamics of parent-toddler interaction contribute to this. Their theory seems to come from researchers like Mahler (1975) and from their own, in particular, Settlage's, previous writing: They argue that parent responses are crucial to the child's ability to form self and object constancy, which in turn depends—and this is the subject of their chapter—on the ability to modulate and regulate anger. Psychoanalysis has been criticized for not being sufficiently based on empirically testable hypotheses. This group hopes to confront and mitigate that criticism: Study of interactions among identified "problem" and "normal" families should help to elucidate more definitively how parents contribute to structure formation and self and object constancy.

"Developmental Process: Mother-Child and Father-Child Interaction During the Second Year of Life" is not a report of findings but is written in response to a request for case material from the editors of this volume. The chapter provides exemplary evidence of the kinds of data the Settlage group draws upon "in illustration of our methods and findings (p. 371)." The case, then, is not meant in itself to illustrate or demonstrate conclusions: We could not, without at least one case each from a *problem* and a *normal* family, ourselves conclude what parental behavior may be criterial.

Yet even one case example gives us much information. It indicates the kinds of systematic observation that might substantiate psychoanalytic developmental hypotheses. It gives us a sense of the remarkably fine-tuned level of clinical and behavioral detail a trained observer might find in parent-toddler interaction. When we read about "affect modulation," "regulatory interchanges," or "separation anxiety," it is especially useful to know what everyday behaviors are summarized in such experience-distant terms. Psychoanalysis presents particularly acutely a dilemma of inference and representation found in all social science research: Unconscious and structural concepts like "self-object constancy" and "self and object representation" are inferred from behavior, and therefore a demonstration of researchers' inferential processes and "raw data" is particularly helpful.

At the same time, this chapter reveals a kind of theoretical saturation that may be more characteristic of psychoanalytic case presentation than that of many other studies of family behavior or dynamics. It is not clear how this research group could *change* its theoretical understanding from such research. Rather, given previously formulated theoretical understanding of the requisites of development, their research can demonstrate how parents look who meet these requisites more and less successfully.

In "Continuity and Change in the Transition to Parenthood: A Tale of Two Families," Bradburn and Kaplan report to us on two families studied by the "Becoming a Family" project, which we also read of elsewhere (Cowan, Cowan, and Kerig, this volume). The authors are particularly concerned to distinguish aggregate group data from individual cases, and note that individual case data does not necessarily conform to group norms. They point out that these cases, drawn from quantitative rather than clinical or qualitative studies, have been discussed in terms of "data . . . measures, variables, and numbers" (p. 413), in terms of aggregate group fluctuations and trends.

However, Bradburn and Kaplan have chosen two cases that specify, rather than challenge, generalization: "What is missing from these group snapshots taken in late pregnancy and again after the birth of a child is a portrayal of the mechanisms or processes that individual families adopt to cope . . . " (p. 386). These couples are "similar" to other couples in the study: "we could interpret the specific information . . . in light of what we already knew from the group trends" (p. 386).

Though they do not demonstrate the potential lack of fit between group and individual data, these cases do give us in a direct way the source of research conclusions. As Bradburn and Kaplan point out, study findings demonstrate some continuity and predictability across time, but described as correlations between a large sample, this is an assertion. By reading cases, we are able to see how continuity works—what it is made up of in individual personality and patterns of relationship.

These cases, like cases in general, do not simply confirm hypotheses and trends. They exemplify how most cases are what I would call "leaky": that is, as anyone puts together a narratively coherent case, there are always elements that must be included that are not directly theory relevant, or that demonstrate the theory in an interesting and novel way. Leakiness is rewarding for the reader, and generously risktaking for the writer or writers, who, giving us qualitative, descriptive data, allow us to form our own conclusions or to stress aspects of the study that the writers themselves might not have stressed. A case study enables a reader to make different conclusions, or simply to focus on other aspects of the case than those upon which the writer has chosen to focus. In this case report, we get a rich sense of the individuality of each member of the two couples and of their sense of the progress (and retrogress) of their selves and relationships from before becoming parents to being "real" families, with two children. We can evaluate what *we* think of each couple as parents and as people, what *we* consider a successful transition to parenthood. We can interpolate from other methods, imagining, for example, members of the Settlage group studying or assessing the McLeans and the Swensons as parents and focusing on and finding relevant parts of the data presented that Bradburn and Kaplan do not find notable or central.

In "The Life and Family of Karl Schulz," Clausen provides us one of the fullest cases possible: a life history and a family history, or several family histories, as we learn of Karl Schulz's family of origin, his own marriage and family, and the beginnings of his children's families. Such a case study gives us a rich sense of what it means for even one person to live his or her family life. This theoretically infused account unpacks the sequelae and nature of planful competence in an individual life and presents a wide range of data in so doing. Clausen makes one kind of sense of the Schulz family and of Karl Schulz, but because he gives us a case study, with complex, leaky, empirical detail, he also invites the reader to rethink for him or herself.

Clausen suggests that the success of Karl and Kathleen Schulz is "illustrative of a tendency that received strong statistical support in the larger study: the tendency for successful marriages and child-rearing and for personality stability to be rooted in the acquisition by late adolescence of a high degree of individual maturity, more specifically . . . 'planful competence' " (p. 417). Karl's own life demonstrates "how personal strengths and a supportive environment can overcome what clinicians perceive as serious vulnerabilities" (p. 419), in this case, early loss of a father and a rather sickly, shy, asocial, sleep-disordered childhood. Here is an adolescent boy characterized by researchers as "sad," "lonely," "homely," and "unkempt" (p. 418) and by peers as "silent," "embarrassed," "anxious," "somewhat unattractive," "inhibited," and "somewhat withdrawn" (p. 421), who ends up a successful, happily married engineer and father of five successful children. According to Clausen, "planful competence"—continuing dependability, responsibility, and conscientiousness, ranked high by researchers throughout this longitudinal study—provides the central explanation for Karl Schulz's many successes, for his successful marriage, family and professional life, for his late adolescent maturity, for his thinking through choices, and for his knowing his strengths and limitations, all contributing to what would be for many people an enviably successful and fulfilling life. By giving us a case study, Clausen shows not only that planful competence works, but also how it interacts with, and indeed overcomes, more negative clinical criteria.

Two aspects of this case seem particularly important. First, we note how closely Clausen's account parallels Karl Schulz's own self-description. Unlike the other two case reports, and especially in contrast to the psychoanalytically described research case presented by Settlage et al., Clausen puts forth a phenomenologically meaningful interpretation that he has checked with Karl Schulz, in Schulz's terms as much, perhaps, as in Clausen's own categories. Schulz and Clausen see Schulz and his wife as "copers." We see how they respond to major life changes and crises—coping with Karl's father's death and with the rough going with their first child. Although Clausen wants to correlate "planful competence" with later life success, we see the internal logic to this, as "copers" actively shape their world and its meanings. *Competence* here is not a trait, as we might be led to believe by psychometric rater reports, but an actively engaged practice, which we see through the ongoing, changing case. Clausen has engaged in what Laslett and Rapoport (1975) call "collaborative interviewing," which they deem essential to family research that takes seriously family members' subjectivity. In so doing, Clausen the symbolic interactionist breaks down the distance between researcher as expert and producer of categories and interpretations and people as objects of study. He takes seriously the symbolic interactionist claim that people construct their own lives, not only by reporting on how Schulz constructed his life but also by allowing Schulz to participate in the report.

Second, this case study demonstrates particularly well one of the great strengths of the case method, what I have pointed to as its narrative openness or "leakiness," in which data enable the reader to go beyond the presented interpretation and theory. One can read the account from the perspective of the writer, but one can also construct an alternate interpretation. My own view of Karl Schulz, for example, was not as favorable as John Clausen's. I saw more contradictions, or faultlines, in the life story—a thread of denial of politics and of adolescent and young adult problems in his children, tendencies toward overrigid childrearing, a need to keep conflict and uncertainty out of his life—that speak to greater psychological constriction throughout life than Clausen suggests, and I would have a somewhat different explanation for Schulz's success.

To begin, I would include historical time as part of the explanation. Given his personality, Schulz was fortunate to be part of the 1950s family-forming cohort. Part of the answer to how a lonely, shy, anxious, withdrawn boy became a loved husband and successful father of 5 children, I believe, was the environment of cultural expectations. We cannot know if Karl Schulz would have formed this kind of marriage, given his personality and relational history, in an era less facilitative of and favorable to marriage and family. His success as a research engineer, by contrast, seems more predicted by his planful competence and personal history. To what extent was *this* family a response to a social-historical-cultural context? Ann Swidler (forthcoming) suggests that love and marriage practices and beliefs draw upon cultural availability. Not many people today create successful long-term marriages with 5 children who themselves all go on to successful marriages.

I would also put more explanatory weight on Kathleen. Karl, it is true, did drift toward her and she toward him, but to borrow from a more psychoanalytic perspective, I would see the marriage itself more directly as a transformative and reparative relational experience for Karl. Psychoanalysts note, as Settlage et al. suggest, that facilitating relationships from infancy onward help form psychic integrity and self and object constancy. In a similar fashion, deep, meaningful relationships in adulthood can help overcome, transform, or mitigate early developmental difficulties and trauma. Karl Schulz struck me as somewhat flat: dependability, competence, responsibility, and pleasantness indicate a life with few postchildhood valleys, but also few vibrant peaks. But vibrancy and aliveness do come across in Karl's and Kathleen's description of their marriage. Reading between the lines of what appears to be the jargon of marital satisfaction rating scales, ones senses a deeply rewarding and mutually meaningful relationship, in Berger and Kellner's (1974) classic view a nomos-building relationship that gives meaning to life. This man who rushed home at 4:30 to take care of children bubbles over with affection and praise for his wife.

I bring these examples up not in order to oppose my interpretation to Clausen's but to suggest that the narrative openness of a case study like this enables multiple interpretations, and I believe this is one of its strengths. I suggest that Schulz may have benefitted by his "planful competence" but that he also benefitted from cohort opportunities and serendipity: It is not clear how his planful competence went into meeting or choosing his wife, though he clearly was relationally adept enough, and competent enough, not to mess up a good opportunity.

Like other presentational forms, case presentations and case studies promise a particular window of understanding on phenomena. Among other contributions, their virtues are in specificity, complexity, narrative cohesion, leakiness, and the immediate sense we get of actual people as we read them. I think we can further understand the contribution and potential contribution of case study and case report if we elucidate cases further. Case studies, I suggest, arrange themselves on a spectrum that is on the one end more ethnographic, narrative-historical, hermeneutic—"inductive"—and on the other more quantified, hypothesis demonstrating or testing—"deductive." "Inductive" case studies are those in which a researcher follows up leads and, in a sense, follows the case—ethnographic or psychoanalytic cases are potential models here. Such approaches are certainly theory-infused. This is particularly apparent in psychoanalytic cases as these are traditionally presented—as demonstrative or confirmatory vignettes, rather than as complex and contradictory wholes. But I believe that these inductive approaches—this "following the case"—have the possibility of discovering new theory and findings. Theoretical transformation and discovery are at a potential maximum, as the researcher (and reader) learns things about family structure and process that they did not know before.

Two examples will help illustrate my point, as I believe that the cases in this volume range themselves more on the other end of the spectrum. I think of new ways of conceptualizing family structure, of seeing not only the nuclear family and its "breakdown," but also ways of conceptualizing positively nonnuclear patterns. Carol Stack's *All Our Kin* (1974), in implicit and explicit debate with Moynihan and others who argued that the black family had disintegrated, showed the multiple relationships and coherent interactional and exchange patterns in the African-American families she studied by following kin networks instead of trying, as had previous researchers, to see the Black family through a nuclear family lens. Similarly, Judith Stacey's *Brave New Families* (1990), bringing a feminist interest in gender to working class family study, shows us the remarkable kin networks, combinations, and recombinations that characterize at least some modern working class families. As Stacey puts it, her "n of 2" can never be used to generalize about how "the family" *is,* or how "the family" is changing. But we would never have known of the potential depth, complexity, and changeability in modern White working class kinship structures if Stacey had stayed with her original sociological intention to find a comparative "sample" of unrelated Silicon Valley women and their (previously defined and delineated, by Stacey's expectations and those of the sociologists who helped provide her with family theory) "families," meaning spouses and children. Moreover, because answers and questions were not precategorized in these studies, the researchers were also able to see that the same family can be a different family, depending on whose point-of-view is taken, indirectly confirming D. H. J. Morgan's symbolic interactionist claim (1975) that families are different projects for different people, that members of the "same" family also live in different families.

In both these examples, the cases took the lead, indeed *are* the study, though this does not mean that conclusions are not drawn or theory not formed out of them. For example, whereas we know in each book much about the historical, economic, and social conditions in which the finely detailed interactions described take place, and much about how family members construe meaning, we do not know psychodynamic details about family interaction, identity, or conflict. We can guess at family members' personality structure, but assessment is not provided; we can compare family members, but systematic comparison along particular dimensions is not made.

On the other end are "deductive" or "illustrative" case studies, where the research has been done with a more predetermined template of questions. These are cases done with a sense of data collection and research questions that "go beyond" the cases themselves, where cases help more to *fill out,* or *illustrate,* research, or where they provide the variety that goes to make up a group–normative conclusion. Because they are garnered in terms of predetermined categories, such studies lead to empirical conclusions but are not as likely as more inductive case investigations to lead to new theoretical understandings. While they are leaky, they are not as likely to lead beyond themselves.

The case presentations in this book are more deductive, and they are extremely rich and interesting. They document the variety of cases potentially shaped by larger studies, from observation, parental report and self-rating, and multiple interview and observation. Of the three, Clausen's report is furthest in the inductive direction. He seems to want to show, in the symbolic interactionist tradition, how Karl Schulz constructed the meanings of his life and marriage. He is constrained, however, by data gathered largely along more quantitative, prescripted, lines, lines that stressed personality assessment, clinical interviews, observer ratings, and preset, codable questionnaires, rather than asking Schulz in the first instance to define and react to the terms of the research. We have a real density to the psychological findings reported by Clausen but some theoretical thinness to the account as sociology, say, or history. Settlage et al. come from a tradition of narrative case method that stresses individual difference and uniqueness, though often seen through a rather tight, experience-distant theoretical lens and a variety of cultural assumptions about how *normal* families are put together. They are to be lauded for gathering systematic data on psychoanalytic hypotheses, but in their attempt to be more scientific, the case they present may lose the potential openness of psychoanalytic cases. Bradburn and Kaplan come from a quantitative, academic psychology research tradition and see their cases as more illustrative than individually theory constructionist, although we could read constructionist aspects in them as well.

Yet, were it not for the many and varied research protocols and instruments from the Berkeley and Oakland Guidance Studies, we would be immeasurably poorer in our understanding of life history, family history, cohort effect, the relations between early childhood and later life, and many many other important questions. Similarly, without the Becoming a Family Research, we would not be able as systematically to document how parenthood differentially transforms mothers' and fathers' lives, for example, or the many ways that parent interactions and parent self-feelings affect childhood tendencies and patterns. Without psychoanalytic clinical insight, followed by psychoanalytic child developmental research, we would not know that there was an appeal cycle or how it worked, what the processes of separation and individuation were like, how affect attunement between caretaker and child develops and what are its effects.

This volume provides us with rich examples of what I have called deductive case materials, whose contributions to our understanding of families certainly stand on their own. I pay some attention here to the potential contributions of inductive case studies as well, in order to give us a more complete picture. As families today are in such flux, and as we become more aware that our categories of understanding have been partially shaped by our own ethnic, class, and intellectual histories, I would suggest that it becomes especially important to encourage inductive cases—letting people tell their family stories in their terms. Ideally, of course, there needs to be an interaction between these two kinds of research, in which each gets its full due. We must avoid the notion that the inductive enables and leads to "hypothesis formation and testing," as if this latter is a truer science or gives us more objective findings. At the same time, we must avoid a tendency on the part of interpretive social scientists to argue that quantification, precoded categories, and demonstrative cases do not allow complex understandings of phenomena. Rather, more deductive case investigations and reports—systematic research according to predetermined categories—lead to a kind of sureness about the relations among previously defined factors or elements, and more inductive case studies lead to new factors or elements to see. In one approach, we can find out in great detail about particular individuals or families and make reliable generalizations about group trends, in the other we may radically revise our views about what there is to find out.

Case study in family research accomplishes a number of goals, and each of these studies achieves some of these goals better than others. All—but most clearly Settlage et al. and Bradburn and Kaplan, who show more how their cases *fit* into empirical generalizations and theoretical conclusions—demonstrate the substance, the empirical actuality, of theoretical claims and generalizations. All—but most clearly Clausen, who has so extensively let his data, with its contradictions and lack of expected results, speak to him—remind us of the great individuality of individuals and families, and of the problematic nature of generalization.

Cases enable us to evaluate writers beyond their intentions, to excavate their perspective and pretheoretical assumptions, so crucial in any family research and writing. A comparison of Settlage et al.'s and Bradburn and Kaplan's perspectives helps demonstrate this point. Settlage et al., on the one side, are clearly sensitive to the delicate interactions between parent and child, but they also write as if any break in parent-child connection is problematic. Their text, even as it reports on parental experience and subtle parent-child interactions, is full of terms like *distress, disruptions* of interaction or psychic integrity, *failures, frus-*

tration, helplessness, and *lacks* in interaction, in response to as everyday an event as a parent's talking on the telephone. They point to the "interest," or "noteworth[iness]," of Walt's mother and father's lack of direct acknowledgment of Walt's feelings and their apparent lack of knowledge that Walt uses them to develop his own self-regulation and structuralization. Their theoretical assumptions, their psychoanalytic focus on pathogenesis, and their near-exclusive child-centered perspective, leave little room to acknowledge that being human *means* that a child will not always feel perfect gratification of her or his felt needs for a parent, or that a child's needing to cope and face challenges is also potentially growth-producing: Clearly, at least some members of this research team might approve of a mother's "failure" to respond to an "appeal" to nurse on the part of her 3-year-old, but maintaining the language of child disappointment and child perspective lessens their and our ability to do so.

On the other side, we have Bradburn and Kaplan, whose *families* are seen exclusively from the point-of-view of parents. Family success, or family process, in the transition to parenthood, here means success or process for the individual members of the couple and for the couple as a unit. The Swensons, we are told, have an "unusual ability to maintain their own needs and their marriage" (p. 414). Children in themselves are of almost no interest, and "limit-setting" (precisely that disruption and distress creation that Settlage et al. describe) is taken for granted as a desirable parental goal.

We can see the unwritten assumptions in each study: Where Settlage et al. see a potentially traumatic disruption of interaction, psychic integrity, and structure formation resulting from the parental independence expressed in a phone call, Bradburn and Kaplan convey an unproblematic acceptance of a parental perspective that the children of Victor and Cindy Swenson are little adults—autonomous, individuated, "contributing to the household" at 19 months, being raced on a bicycle with wind hitting their faces until their eyes water. In the Bradburn and Kaplan case presentations, children have individuality and personality not on their own, or as the researcher takes their point-of-view, but exclusively when *parents* see them that way: Gail McLean describes her "Ms. Mature and Sophisticated" daughter putting two fingers in her mouth, and we have an immediate sense of Sarah.

What is smothering and what child abandonment? Both these studies have pathology prevention and family support as a partial goal, but we can see, especially from the untheorized assumptions that emerge in the language of case writing, the very different goals each preventive intervention might have. In the "expert" society in which generations of parents have felt guilty and inadequate, we might worry about the effect—especially on mothers, who tend to be more self-blaming in these matters—of Settlage et al.'s "education for prevention." What would happen if mothers educated for prevention tried sensitively to assess their every response to a phone call or family need for dinner, let alone a financial need or emotional desire to go back to work, in terms of their child's ability to build regulatory structures and self and object constancy? But if we were concerned about our society's radical neglect of children and seeming policy assumption that children will somehow get taken care of while both parents work full time and *fulfill* themselves, we might worry about parent counseling by Bradburn and Kaplan that assessed a successful transition to parenthood solely in terms of the (adult) individual and the couple's relationship.

One central role for case studies are as cases in themselves. As Runyan (1982) suggests, life histories—I would suggest, case studies more generally—can be used as supplements to other forms of inquiry, but they can also be the focus of interest themselves. Along with generalization, "in-depth understanding of particular individuals is also a legitimate objective of intellectual inquiry" (p. 13). Here, it is uniqueness, complexity, and individual variability and unpredictability that are of interest. Cases can be used to support previous theories, as in the Settlage et al. study, and they can be generated within the context of previously framed questions, as we see the narrativized checklists, multiple choice inventories, assessments, and closed–answer self-reports in the Bradburn and Kaplan and the Clausen studies.

But even with previous theoretical saturation and shaping, cases enable us to see multiple levels of information, give us some access to the richness and depth that form any family structure and process and any individual life history, whether as seen in the microdynamic context of a short interaction between a toddler and his parents or across the life span of a retired engineer and his family. Cases destabilize, and I would say, thereby enrich, any conclusions we wish to draw about the family now or in the future, and they point us, in their labyrinthine complexity, to new ways of seeing and understanding families.

REFERENCES

Berger, P., & Kellner, H. (1974). Marriage and the construction of reality. In R. L. Coser (Ed.), *The family: Its structures and functions* (pp. 157–174). New York: St. Martin's Press.

Laslett, B. & Rapoport, R. (1975). Collaborative interviewing and interactive research. *Journal of Marriage and the Family,* 968–977.

Mahler, M. (1975). *The psychological birth of the human infant.* New York: Basic Books.

Morgan, D. H. J. (1975). *Social theory and the family.* London: Routledge & Kegan Paul.

Runyan, W. M. (1982). *Life histories and psychobiography.* New York and Oxford: Oxford University Press.

Swidler, A. (forthcoming). *Talk of love.* Chicago: University of Chicago Press.

Stacey, J. (1990). *Brave new families.* New York: Basic Books.

Stack, C. (1974). *All our kin.* New York: Harper.

V
TOWARD A NEW AGENDA FOR FAMILY RESEARCH

21 Issues in Defining a Research Agenda for the 1990s

Philip A. Cowan
Donald A. Hansen
Guy E. Swanson
Dorothy Field
Arlene Skolnick
University of California, Berkeley

The chapters in this book suggest that family research has come a long way in the 20th century. And yet, with many unresolved issues and much that we do not yet know about how families function, there is still a long way to go. In the process of writing some of the chapters and reading all of the others, the editors have begun to see that new agendas grow organically out of old ones, rather like the development of families themselves. The big questions about families in the past remain the big questions today. What is needed now is a reconsideration of the traditional answers. This reconsideration must be accompanied by a special effort to avoid static, a-contextual, method-bound depictions of the family in which a small detail in the corner of the mural is presented as the complete picture of family functions and dysfunction.

An agenda for family research in the 1990s overflows with potential items—enough to occupy the attention of researchers for decades to come. Here we propose 6 major items to be placed on a family research agenda for the remaining years of the current decade:

1. We must reconsider our definitions of families and what they do.
2. We must create a better balance between the need to generalize about families and the need to consider particularities of historical and cultural context as they play out in the lives of individuals.
3. We must place on the mainstream family agenda a central issue from feminist family research: the role of gender in shaping the quality of life inside and outside the boundaries of the nuclear family.
4. We must move beyond the methodological imperialism that has dominated

family research in the greater part of this century. No single method can be allowed to delimit the meaning and reality of our knowledge about families. It is necessary to consider how information from clinical and phenomenological studies, ethnographic qualitative studies, theoretical-explanatory quantitative studies, historical analyses, cross-cultural comparisons, and case studies can be articulated and integrated.

5. We must develop more explicit pictures of the mechanisms linking (a) the structure and function of the family system with the development of its individual members, (b) social context with family structure and development, and (c) societal norms and arrangements with the development of the individual self.

6. We must confront the fact that values shape our science. In our tendency to compare the families we study to some, often ill-defined, "ideal" of family functioning, family research often moves from a descriptive search for understanding to a prescriptive moral enterprise. Some family forms and functions are valued while others are regarded not only as dysfunctional but as undesirable and unworthy of societal support. We need to make these values more explicit and open to discussion, debate, and empirical examination.

WHAT FAMILIES AND KINSHIP ARE AND WHAT THEY DO

The first item we would place on a new agenda for family research is a consideration of the subject matter we study. Textbook writers and researchers have for too long referred to *the family* without describing what families are and what they are not, and without considering the variety of viable family forms. Skolnick (1991) has argued that we should think of *the family* as a term like *the economy*. When we hear someone speak of the economy we do not think of the grocery store down the street or a General Motors assembly plant, but as the array of organizations and activities having to do with the production and distribution of goods. Following this analogy, *the family* has to do with the organization of sexual relations, marriage, parenthood, childrearing, kinship, inheritance, and coresidence.

Let us take a brief look at where the field has been on this issue. In a wide-ranging survey of marriage, family, and kinship in both simple and complex societies, anthropologists Beth Dillingham and Barry Isaac (1975) concluded that *marriage* is in all cases a societally approved relationship between persons of opposite sex, at least one of whom is allowed to have exclusive right to sexual intercourse with the other; a relationship that can (in principle if not in practice) lead to the participants' engaging in sexual reproduction and also to their caring for any children of their union. In every society, *family* is an approved relationship in which one or more adults are formally responsible for socializing children because these children are united with them by ties of descent or adoption. For this reason, the children have claims to inherit property and possessions from the adults. *Kinship,* Dillingham and Isaac note, consists everywhere of relations among persons linked by marital or family ties. She suggests that these relationships are universally privileged and societally underwritten because they insure a society's future.

Such conceptions of marriage, family, and kinship are what Aerts (Chap. 1, this volume) calls "institutional." They not only guide the daily lives of family members, but they also shape the research questions and methods of those who study family life. They appear, if only implicitly, in every chapter in this book. Without some institutional definitions of family, it is hard to imagine how we could draw useful comparisons among societies or historical periods or groups within societies. It would be impossible to distinguish figurative usages from literal meanings (e.g., describing a church or nation as a *family* or the relationship of a nun to Christ as *marriage).*

The institutional meanings of marriage and family help us understand what protagonists may feel is at stake in current social disputes over extensions of these symbols to domestic partners or homosexual couples. In a word—everything. Couples living together and not married are able not only to raise children but also to have the financial protection of common law if and when the relationship terminates. The exchange of legal marriage vows between homosexual partners raises questions about whether societal approval of the marital bond is necessary for couples to maintain their longterm intimate relationships, and whether the approval of a community within the society is sufficient to provide both social and legal sanction to the couple. Grandmother–mother–child household units perform many family functions and are increasingly common. Each of these arrangements violates some of the essential attributes included as essential ingredients of the contemporary definition of what it means to be a family.

The fact that men and women in these nontraditional arrangements are putting strong bids for social and legal recognition and support of the designation *family* raises a dilemma for researchers. Do we declare their claims invalid because they fail to meet the test of traditional definitions? This is what currently happens in the political arena; as a consequence, all but the traditional family forms tend to be treated as deviant or immoral. The most prevalent solution for social scientists in recent years has been to acknowledge, sometimes with reluctance, that nontraditional families now comprise a substantial proportion of the population, with the exact percentage depending on the definition of *traditional.* This approach represents a step along the road to the contextualization of family studies, but it continues to maintain a deviance model of the family. Nontraditional families differ from what is explicitly described as a social norm and implicitly represented as an ideal; the implication in most family studies is that difference = deviance = dysfunction.

What are we to do? Aerts provides a new, minimalist definition of the family unit as an adult responsible for a developing child, a dyadic definition that encompasses most but not all variations on existing families both heterosexual and homosexual as long as the parenting adult can be either male or female. Is Aerts premature, perhaps, in assuming that the changes in family life in the past 50 years, especially in women's roles, will continue at the same pace and in the same way and thus make this minimalist definition the statistical norm? Will the mother–child unit become societally normative in the sense of being prescriptive or will we see a dramatic increase in males as active parents in the coming decades? And will Aerts' new definition be useful in the analysis and understanding of families in different cultures and at different historical periods?

Aerts' solution is to pare down the definition of family to the smallest and most universal unit of analysis. Another approach is to think of the traditional definition of the family as a prototype, with other groups being considered a family if they share one or more of the prototypic features—that is we would shift from multiplicative definition (marriage *and* child, mother *and* children) to a disjunctive definition (marriage or child). The fewer features a given example shares with the prototype, the harder the example would be to categorize and the less consensus we would see among observers. Thus, the definition of family would not be a matter of yes or no, but a matter of more or less.

The central theoretical issue raised by all of these definition strategies is whether we should reformulate our definition of the family to accord with contemporary realities, or whether we can use the traditional definition as a useful standard of comparing families and evaluating family functioning. This latter alternative can work only if we forego our usual tendency to treat the new and unusual with pejorative descriptions.

We should note that family researchers are not the only ones involved in the business of defining families. The public and the legal system are also engaged in sorting out this issue. According to one 6-year-old, "family is when you knock on the door and they have to let you in." With the advent of palimony suits and trials over the issue of surrogate parenthood, judges and juries are now engaged in a high-stakes process of determining who is in and who is out of a family. Family researchers can adopt any definition that seems fruitful, but they should keep in mind that common-sense definitions held by family members and by the legal system help to determine family members' expectations and shape the form and quality of family relationships. Although we would be foolhardy to propose a single answer to these questions of definition, we would be remiss if we did not view this issue as a central concern for a new family research agenda.

Balancing Generality and Particularity in the Study of Families

The variety of existing family or family-like organizations poses problems for family researchers that go beyond the task of defining which social unit are appropriate to study. The heterogeneity of our subject matter makes it clear that we must open up new and detailed discussions about the relation of specific data to general theory development. No single data set can truly represent *the family*.

One of the most currently popular theoretical statements about families is that they are *systems*. But we do not really know whether the same laws of system structure and function are applicable to a nuclear family, a divorced family, a mother-child family, and a four-generational matrilineal household (see McCaslin, Chap. 13, this volume). In our search for general conclusions about families, it is critical that we recognize the historical and cultural multiplicities that affect researchers' definitions and understandings of contemporary families.

As an example of how contemporary family life has changed in the past 50 years, consider the contrast between the family of Karl Schulz who was the primary breadwinner in his family when his family began in the 1940s (Chap. 19, this volume), and the dual-worker Swenson family of the 1980s (Chap. 18, this volume) who represent only one of many examples of how contemporary family life has changed in the past 50 years. Aerts describes the recent shifts in Western societies toward marriage as optional, the legitimation of working motherhood, and the erosion of fatherhood. Sometimes, though, trends are moving in two directions simultaneously. While some fathers are disappearing others have become more active both as members of nuclear families and as primary custody parents. It is still possible that the parent role may become *less* gender specific than it is now.

Family structures then, tend to be different and more varied than they used to be. Changes in birth control technology and patterns of residence have led to smaller families living at removed distances from their kin, often in isolation from their neighbors. With the new, increased tempo of divorce and remarriage, families are also extending in new ways. Children today often have multiple sets of grandparents, parents, aunts, and uncles, all bidding for a role in their socialization and control. Some children never live with or know their fathers. Increasing numbers experience a *series* of parents: mother and father, mother alone, mother-stepfather; or, perhaps mother, grandmother, aunts, and cousins. And for some children, movement from one parent to another and then back again is so fluid and recursive that it can hardly be thought of as a series. Yet we and the child may retain a sense of *family* (Burton & Stack, Chap. 4, this volume).

One of the potentially revolutionary changes in family life results from the increased longevity of both men and women that has occurred in recent years. Four-generation families are becoming common; even five and more generations can often be found. This historical shift changes the meaning of *generations* and changes relationships across generational lines. The 70-year-old second generation may be taking care of aged parents and looking after their great grandchildren. Meanwhile, the 50-year-old third generation is sandwiched between raising adult children (or even young children, a consequence of later marriage and childbirth patterns) and concern for their parents and grandparents. As multigenerational families increase, there are more frequent reversals of parent-child roles in which the mature child becomes the parent to the older generations.

Heterogeneity in family forms is increased further when we consider cultural and ethnic variations in household arrangements, marriage, and kinship networks. As Carstensen (Chap. 16, this volume) notes, extended families operate very differently in White American, African American, Hispanic, and Asian American cultures, and, within the same ethnic group extended families operate differently from country to country, or even region to region.

The increased variety of childrearing environments has made it more difficult for a family researcher working with one population to assume that what he or she finds can be generalized to others. It also means that individuals growing up in today's families may have a more complex, and perhaps more confused idea about the meaning of family life. Increasing divorce rates signify not only that the structure of the family is less stable, but also that the *meaning* of family for someone about to get married now may be quite different than it was a few decades ago, or different than it is in another region or ethnic community. Similarly, all of the concepts describing family roles and relationships—spouse, parent, child, grandparents, sibling, uncle, cousin—change in meaning over time, place, and culture.

Although the quest for general laws and universal principles remains one of the highest and most demanding goals of family research, we must recognize that it is only one goal. It may have been overemphasized to the neglect of the particular, that is, the specific family in its unique temporal and cultural context. Recognizing that a great deal of family life cannot, at present, be represented in universal statements opens new possibilities for theory development. But we need to explore ways to link particularistic research findings with the development of general family theories.

One avenue for future exploration is what Chodorow (Chap. 20, this volume) calls the "leaky"ness of case studies. When we find that theories or *facts* don't apply to an individual family, we should not simply argue that principles derived from group data will never fit single cases perfectly. Instead, we need to take the discrepancy between general theory and this family seriously, viewing it as a challenge to formulate more differentiated and integrated questions. As Chodorow suggests, the study of cases is an ideal way to generate family theory through induction rather than deduction.

But particularity need not be studied only through the analysis of single cases. We must begin to account not only for the *rules* but also for the exceptions to the rules. The epidemiological concepts of risk and resilience, popularized by Rutter and Garmezy (1983) are finding their way into family research. Why is it that some families are more resilient than their life circumstances would suggest? Why are other families that appear to be in the category that we would label advantaged, vulnerable to what seem like mild stressors? Attempts to answer these questions force us to pay more attention to the specificity and particularity of family life. As part of a new agenda for family research, then, we believe that it would be wise to struggle more actively and explicitly with the tensions between formulating universal (general) and contextual (more specific) theoretical statements.

BRINGING BACK TO CENTER STAGE THE STUDY OF GENDER ISSUES IN FAMILY LIFE

Issues of how gender affects the dynamics of family life are already at the top of the feminist family research agenda. Ironically, the concern with gender in feminist research on the family arose, in part, in reaction to the writings of Talcott Parsons and Sigmund Freud, both of whom were accused of creating theories that justified the enduring subordination of women to men.

Several chapters in this book focusing on treatments of gender roles in family life include appraisals of Parsons' or Freud's influence on family theory. The evaluative tone of our authors is strongly negative, centering on Parsons' and Freud's endorsement of *traditional* gender roles as in some respects immutable and necessary for adequate family functioning. Parsons is chastised for seeing gender-linked roles as unavoidable products of human biology and massive social trends. Freud has elicited disapproval for his view that mothers' and fathers' family roles are the product of biological characteristics as modified through historical experience of the human species. These views fly in the face of contemporary egalitarian ideology. They are challenged, too, by the less frequent, but still significant, numbers of men who are actively involved as primary caretakers of their children.

Parsons' (1955) paper on the American family gets the most attention. His expectations were extrapolated from census reports for the period 1900 through 1950. Although he assumed that social trends would insure the predominance of families headed by both fathers and mothers, and of families in which the father was the chief breadwinner and the mother primarily a housewife, his general expectations were disconfirmed by trends in the decade that followed.

Our authors hint, however, that some of Parsons' expectations are not so readily dismissed. In fact, while denying the assumption that traditional gender roles are more adaptive, evidence presented in this volume supports the notion that these traditional roles are still pervasive in the families that we study. As Aerts and DeVos report, there are many institutional supports in all advanced industrial societies that expressly encourage what have come to be called the traditional family role arrangements that Parsons expected. Despite the prevalence of egalitarian ideology, women do most of the household maintenance and child care even when both partners work outside the home full time (Cowan & Cowan, 1988). Studies find, as Parson expected, that marital strains are likely if wives earn more than their husbands or have more prestigious occupations (Becker, 1981; Ferree, 1990; Greenstein, 1990). Although good mothering and healthy child development can be accomplished in a variety of work and family arrangements, Moorehouse (Chap. 11, this volume) finds partial support for Parsons' arguments for the importance of the maternal care of very young children. And many of our authors concur in Parsons' judgment that the increased importance of marriage relative to that of the parent-child relationship is a major source of strain in family relations.

As Fass (Chap. 6, this volume) puts it, we need to "free ourselves of the tyranny, not of Parsons, but of our disillusionment with Parsons." Research on gender issues in the dynamics of family life, and on how instrumental and expressive roles are played out *both* by males and females, are central to our understanding of how families operate. We need to know the consequences in today's world for families arranged just as Parsons described them, and for other kinds of arrangements as well.

Similarly, to reject some of Freud's assumptions about the superiority of men's development over women's, especially in the moral realm, should not cause us to reject his conclusions that gender plays a central role in the dynamics and development of family relationships and in the development of the self and personality. Psychoanalytic writers are actively assessing and enlarging Freud's theory as it focuses on early object relations (e.g., Chodorow, 1978, 1989; Greenberg & Mitchell, 1983). Jeanne Block (1983) and others in developmental psychology have highlighted the fact of gender differences in parenting style and explored the complex behavioral mechanisms by which boys and girls receive different and unequal treatment. Despite such exemplars, however, issues of gender have not received the attention they deserve from family scholars. Neither has Freud's emphasis on the specifically erotic relations of family members, relations that loom even larger following the sexual revolution of the 1960s and the contemporary rise of interest in understanding familial child abuse. It is time to correct the mistake of ignoring Parsons and Freud's questions because we do not believe in all of their methods or answers.

THE OVERTHROW OF METHODOLOGICAL IMPERIALISM

The study of families as both personal and collective projects requires improved interpretive frameworks that capture more of the systematic arrangements and processes through which people do things together. We can no longer afford to let any single method hold dominion over the enterprise of understanding family life. The challenge is to go beyond assertions that a family is a system and to spell out the structures and processes through which people jointly transact their relations with one another and with a wider social order. Beyond asserting that families have such wider social relations we need to specify in a theoretically orderly way what those relations are and how they operate.

Two broad approaches have emerged for reaching these objectives. Each of our chapters tends to stress one or the other. The first—the ethnographic approach—tries, above all, to be faithful to the whole complex of projects in which members of given families are involved and to the chance events that prove important for those projects and their interrelations. The second—the theoretical-explanatory approach—looks for theoretically general relations that can be found in one or more of those family projects and stresses the formulation and testing of statements about causal relations. In addition to these two approaches, we show that historical/cultural comparisons and single case studies provide additional methodological perspectives on the understanding of family life.

The Ethnographic Approach. One approach to understanding families is often referred to as "humanistic," or "contextual," or "grounded" or, as the authors here do, "ethnographic" or "interpretive." They remind us that people have many projects under way at once. Adult family members are simultaneously making a living and being kinsmen. They are forming and abandoning personalized ties and friendships. They have one or more roles in the governance of their society or in implementing societal choices. Most of them participate in a social community. All are pressed to do what is normatively expected of persons of a particular age, sex, class, and birth rank. The advocates of the ethnographic approach note that family projects change in nature and importance over time, sometimes unexpectedly, and that these projects tend both to complement and to conflict with one another.

Ethnographic investigators assert that all projects in which people engage are in some sense interdependent parts of a whole. Therefore, to understand any one project requires that we understand its place in the whole system and also its distinctive characteristics. In practice, this means that we observe people carrying out one or a few projects—running a household, perhaps, or rearing children, or participating in specific community activities—and discover the ways in which they take account of other essential interests as they do this. We need to learn what those other interests are. (The training of psychotherapists or field ethnographers typically includes consideration of the major projects in which people engage and of a range of diverse cases in which possible connections among those projects are brought to light.)

The ethnographic method tends to be associated with qualitative analysis, though it is possible to adopt a highly quantitative approach to ethnography as well. Open-ended questions are formulated. Observations are gathered in the form of field notes. On the basis of these observations questions are reformulated and new questions are raised. Tentative conclusions are usually discussed with the participants. This process is repeated until the need for further revisions of questions and conclusions is ended. Usually, few quantitative data are reported outside a proportion of people in the sample displaying a particular behavior pattern. Although exceptions to the general rule are noted in this approach, the emphasis in the ethnographic approach is on normative description and not on the understanding of individual differences.

What can we hope to gain from careful and informed work along these lines? Ethnographic investigators think that we can come to understand how the meaning of the projects on which we focus affects what we do. Such understanding can then become the basis for causal explanations, for predictions, and even for interventions. Hansen (Chap. 3, this volume) documents the possibilities for a young woman's career in school (Kimberly), Burton and Stack (Chap. 4, this volume) for the cycles of life in some multigenerational Black families, and Johnson (Chap. 14, this volume) for the role of kin in the lives and fulfillment of old-old people. Each of the case studies in Part III offers even wider-ranging explanations for events in given families.

The Theoretical-Explanatory Approach The second approach to studying families as projects differs from the ethnographic approach more in emphasis and procedure than in principle. Its advocates emphasize the presence of systematic variability within their samples and between their subsamples. They believe that useful and important information can be obtained by describing and explaining that variability, preferably in causal terms, and from testing these explanations against further evidence. As in the ethnographic approach, the theoretical-explanatory approach relies on the investigator to determine which variations are important to understand, and which antecedents or causes must be taken into account for interpretations to be meaningful.

Researchers who work from this approach say that it enables them to account for phenomena on the basis of a modest array of general premises. The identification of causal pathways, they claim helps to shape the directions of theory formation, which ultimately informs planned social change and intervention by members of the helping professions.

This approach guides the work of the majority of our authors. For example, the Cowans show that the authoritarianism of fathers tends to vary with the sex of their children, being higher with daughters, and that, longitudinally, couples in which husbands are more authoritarian than their wives were more likely to be unhappy before the baby comes along. Swanson suggests that family structure consists in part of layers of social relationships that differ in developmental complexity. He tests predictions about the consequences that disruptions of relations at given levels will have for the family's organization and ability to make decisions. Johnston (Chap. 9) deals with layers in the organization of families, showing that a breakdown in the "groupier" aspects of family relations (role reversals, role diffusion) is related to symptoms of disturbance in which children display more advanced levels of cognitive and affective development (e.g., constricted behavior, overly responsible behavior, psychosomatic complaints). By contrast, disruptions at more interpersonal levels of family relationships are associated with symptoms at less advanced levels of personal development (e.g., narcissism, general emotionality, aggressiveness). Moorehouse shows us how various familial arrangements and practices can serve as ways of coping with varied forms of a mother's working outside the home, and interprets the consequences of each for the mother, father, and children. Field and Minkler (Chap. 15, this volume), using a longitudinal approach, show that although there is continuity in activity and emotional involvement in the family in old age, there is a change over time in the importance of variables that predict this involvement.

Aerts and DeVos work on even larger canvases but with no less specificity. Aerts identifies political and economic changes that shape the contemporary family as an institution and shows how public policies and familial responses have shaped the dynamics of the family and the personal lives of its members. DeVos sees Japanese society as one in which people are trained to be "agents" or "trustees" of the family and other groups, and expected to be ardent, energetic, and creative in these roles (always disciplined by the group's judgment of its own longterm interests).

In contrast with the ethnographic approach, the theoretical-explanatory approach tends to rely heavily on quantitative methods, statistical tests, and, increasingly, on path models of the complex chains of connections between independent and dependent variables. Despite the contrasts, however, the approaches are similar in that both involve description and "understanding" of families in context and both are typically employed as parts of the process of explaining and predicting. The two approaches are complementary. Ethnographic accounts, however fascinating, are likely to be only a series of vignettes until placed in a framework in which we can compare and contrast families from differing environments or from different situations within the same community. And ultimately, no account of the relationships among variables is likely to have much explanatory power unless it is fleshed out—and perhaps shaped by—a description of the social and cultural contexts in which the families we study live out their lives.

Although ethnographers tend to favor qualitative methods, and researchers with a theoretical-explanatory bent tend to rely on quantitative methods, it would be consistent with a new agenda for family research to assume that both strategies could be useful. Ethnographers would do well to include statistical analyses of group trends and individual differences in their studies, and theoretical-explanatory investigators could pay more attention to the qualitative features of the environments in which individual and between family variation occurs.

Historical and Cross-Cultural Perspectives. In the 1960s Marshall McLuhan (1964), commenting on the need for a more global perspective on contemporary culture and mores, observed: "I don't know who discovered water, but I'm damn sure it wasn't a fish." Discoveries are often made by viewing phenomena from vantage points at some distance from the ones we usually "swim around in." Both ethnographic and theoretical-explanatory methods of studying families in one place at one moment in time can and should be enriched by historical and cross-cultural frames of reference.

Historical studies of family life are invaluable in helping researchers test the limits of generality of their theories and evaluate the impact of changing times on family structure and interaction processes. The historical approach need not be restricted to comparisons between now and decades or centuries ago. Each generation of a family is a product of a different historical time; there is always a confounding of generation (age) and cohort effects whenever we attempt to understand the principles by which behavior patterns and personal values are transmitted from one generation to another.

Similarly, cross-national, cross-cultural, or cross-community comparisons help us to evaluate the extent to which principles of individual and family adaptation can be generalized across social contexts. We should admit that both historical and cross-cultural family studies raise as many problems as they solve. Because the connections between being married and becoming parents, or the links among kin networks vary from one time to another and one culture to another, it is difficult to know just how different families can be compared. What does divorce mean, for example, in a society in which one spouse is expected to die before the couple lives in an empty next, as compared with a society in which the couple may face 40 years together after the children leave home? How do we compare the function of kin networks in Caucasian and Asian families when so many aspects of family life differ between groups?

The Case Study Method. The use of multiple perspectives ranging across cultures and across time helps us test the limits of generality that can be achieved in our family theories; it pushes us to pay attention to the contextual and specific factors that make families different from each other. Paradoxically, the use of case studies from past and present and from various cultural groups helps us to test the limits of specificity by pushing us in the direction of generality. With all due respect to Tolstoy, neither happy nor unhappy families are different from each other in all their details. As we focus on the particularities of a single family, and then another, inescapable generalizations begin to emerge inductively. But unlike the generalizations from group data, theoretical principles based on aggregating cases are likely to take qualitative variations among families more seriously.

There is a dynamic tension involved in the contrast between group and individual methods of gathering and analyzing data. Findings at one level need have no relation at all to findings at the other. A correlation between variables, statistically significant in the group data, may not apply directly to any of the individuals in the sample. Clinical predictions based on odds derived from populations are never applicable to the individual case. Our enthusiasm for the case study in family research is based on the considerations outlined in Chodorow's spirited defense of it (Chap. 20, this volume). The case study provides us with stringent tests or proposed generalizations, and suggestions for corrections when generalizations go too far. It draws our attention to exceptions to the rule, and to the possibility that there are alternative pathways to development. The corrections and possibilities suggested by the individual case can then be tested with larger, but better-defined samples.

Our final agenda item is concerned with issues inherent in family research. Here we simply provide two cautionary notes to our support of methodological pluralism. First, while we see almost limitless opportunities to become more differentiated in our view of families by adopting different perspectives, we recognize the potential dangers inherent in comparative research whether it uses large group or single case sources of data. It is much too easy to jump from the observation of historical, cultural, or between-family differences to conclusions about the superiority of a particular example of family life.

Second, we must identify more clearly the sociohistorical and sociocultural contexts that shape the questions we choose to answer and the theory and language we use to characterize the phenomena we study. Lawson's discussion (Chap. 7, this volume) speaks to the time- and space-bound contexts of how we define the issues in our investigations of the generation gap, the problem family, the culturally "deficient," adolescence, and maternal employment. To anticipate the last agenda item on our list, if we study family-work interrelations by asking about the potentially negative effects of mothers working outside the home, without asking about the potentially negative effective of fathers working outside the home, we have let time and culture impose limits on the kinds of information our studies can yield.

ESTABLISHING LINKS BETWEEN SOCIETY, FAMILY, AND SELF

The need to pay attention to sociocultural and temporal contexts of the family is crucial not only in establishing the limits of generality of family theory, but also in discovering the mechanisms by which societies, families, and individuals influence each other.

Family–Individual Development. The authors in Part II of this volume pay particular attention to the interplay of family structure, role performance, and family process (e.g., decision-making, parenting style) on children's development. Not in evidence in this volume, but increasingly important in family studies, is the reciprocal impact of the child's temperament and personality on the relationship with his or her parents. Untangling the direction of effects is a complex business; one way of determining what comes first is to begin a study of family development before the child's birth and follow the family into the early childrearing years (e.g., Cowan, Cowan, & Kerig, Chap. 8, this volume).

With increased interest in the notion that development occurs throughout the lifespan, questions about the links between family-level variation and individual development can be extended to the study of older families (see McCaslin's Intergenerational model, Chap. 13, this volume). For example, what is the relative importance of family and nonfamily to old people? Although longitudinal studies of German and American old persons have found a high correlation between activity with family members and satisfaction with family in both countries (Field, Fooken, & Rudinger, 1991) it has also been shown that life satisfaction is much more affected by amount of contact with friends (Ishii-Kuntz, 1990) than by contact with families. Other aspects of individual development, such as how current relationships between middle-aged men and women and their aging parents influence the level of ego-development of both generations have yet to be studied.

Society-Family. Attending to differences in family structure and function across country, region, social class, ethnicity, and other demographic indices of culture is necessary but not sufficient for the development of family theories. We need to know a great deal more than we do about the underlying processes and mechanisms by which these differences come into being. For example, it is obvious that families with economic advantage are different from families of poverty, but how does the income level transform the psychological realities of family life?

More specifically, we need to identify the interplay of the family as a system with the social systems operating outside the family (e.g., work-family; school-family). Note that we are not asking how the society influences the family, as if the impact is all one-way. In fact there is a great deal of reciprocity; family realities and roles both affect and are affected by the transactions between family members and social systems. The fact that mothers are still primary caretakers in most families is both a product of societal values and has an impact on the operation of the workplace. As women are increasingly needed in the labor force, a few businesses have begun tentatively to make working conditions more attractive to mothers of young children, with flexible working hours and child-care benefits. (The Swedish system of childcare or the Israel Kibbutz provide important comparative cases.)

Society–Individual. There is no doubt that social and cultural forces shape the development of individuals both in their behavior patterns and in their conception of themselves. There is speculation that culture also determines the kind of self that individuals contemplate when they reflect on their own mental and physiological processes, and how that self is both connected with and differentiated from the external world. The question for study is how that influence occurs.

Society–Family–Individual. Very few investigators try to link society, family, and individual systems empirically. At most, they focus on the connections between society and family, society and individual, or family and individual. The authors in this volume tend to assume, either explicitly or implicitly, that the family mediates the impact of culture on the individual. Social values and norms dictate family roles which, in turn, affect family relationships and children's development. To the extent that families play a brokering role society and self, we need to know more about the processes governing these transactions and how they operate.

We also need to investigate other possible models of linkage. Societal arrangements and norms can have direct effects on the individual (e.g., through television) that are not necessarily mediated by family relationships. And both families and individuals have a guiding force than can function as a historical and cultural influences on future generations.

Theoretical models and research designs quickly grow complicated. Ethnicity and social class are often confounded (Carstensen, Chap. 16, this volume). For example, family effects that we attribute to ethnic group membership may often be better explained by social class. Psychological effects that we attribute to aging may be better explained by cohort differences, physical health, or social isolation. It is difficult, then, to identify clearly the societal effects we are studying, Furthermore, these variables have complex effects on the interior dynamics of family life. The goal of attempting to disentangle society, family, and self in order to study their linkages will often be illusory. But the effort to do so ought to pay off in the utility and power of more differentiated and integrated family theories.

FAMILY RESEARCH AS A MORAL ENTERPRISE

We have noted the tendency of social researchers to assume that the *normative* is nonproblematic and that *nonnormative* or difference is deviant or pathological. Family researchers tend to focus on the negative effects of major life changes including marriage, divorce, maternal employment, single parenthood, older parenting and aging families, and remain relatively blind to evidence of positive effects (see Crockenberg, Chap. 12, this volume). Conversely, by focusing on the benefits of family stability and traditionality, researchers tend ignore the potential costs to individuals and relationships.

Carstensen points out that research based on faulty assumptions and myths can reify those assumptions and myths. When researchers report the negative impact of divorce on children without investigating the positive effects, they are communicating to their peers and to the general public that "divorce is a bad thing." When they study the effects of mothers' behavior on children, they imply that what mothers do is centrally important and what fathers do is irrelevant to their children's development.

The controversy over how to define normality and psychopathology in individual development has been raging for many decades, but the controversy over how to define family adaptation and pathology is just beginning. Until very recently, clinically based theory and research (cf. Walsh, 1982) implied: that nuclear mother–father–child families are more adaptive than single parent families; that high conflict, especially in marital relationships is a risk factor both for couples' satisfaction and for children's development; and that individuation of children from parents is the proper developmental task of adolescent and young adult children. There has been little consideration of the possibilities that other family forms (single parent, grandmother–mother–child) can be equally adaptive, that family conflict can promote growth, or that connectedness between the generations is as important as individuation.

Our argument here returns to our discussion of generality and particularity in family research. In an almost unswerving devotion to establishing general laws, researchers investigating family psychopathology have focused on trends and ignored the exceptions. In the study of adaptation and mental health, many of the exceptions to the general rule that negative circumstances and conflictful family interaction patterns produce problematic outcomes lie in the realm of nonnormative family patterns. Unless we pay more attention, for example, to families of poverty, or ethnic families, or nontraditional families whose members all develop well in their eyes and ours, we are likely to keep sending the message that the mainstream is the only stream flowing toward mental health. The risk and resilience approach to the study of psychopathology in family life (e.g., Rutter, 1987) not only provides a more differentiated picture of what makes for adaptation and dysfunction, but it also provides an important corrective to the traditional middle class values approach to the study of individual and family mental health.

In formulating our new agenda for family research, then, we face two major issues. First, as we have been arguing, implicit value assumptions have been biasing the questions we ask. Second, we tend to ignore the exceptions to the rule that could inform us more fully about family strengths and resilience, especially in the face of what would otherwise be considered high risk of distress or dysfunction (e.g., Werner & Smith, 1982). Both issues require that we recognize family research as a moral enterprise. This means that we need to consider the ultimate goals of our specific research projects. At present, family research is devoted almost entirely to description, with only peripheral emphasis on treatment and preventive intervention. It is one thing to describe the negative consequences, if any, of dual career couples or divorce or single parenthood; it is another to wonder how negative consequences can be minimized and positive consequences can be promoted.

Intervention is not the only route for family researchers to improve the lot of families. We need to rethink the prevailing pessimistic belief that family research and theory has been ignored by policy-makers and by families themselves. It is true that there are few examples of dramatic, pervasive applications of family research findings or theories analogous to the technological applications of research from the physical sciences. Still, ideas and concepts from the social sciences permeate everyday discourse: discussions of the unconscious, bonding, family dysfunction, and stress reactions probably occur more frequently among laymen than they do within the walls of mental health centers.

Taylor (1983) argues that social research and theory transform family life, schooling, medicine, and therapy in subtle and complex ways. Giddens (1984) agrees:

> The social sciences necessarily draw upon a great deal that is already known to the members of the societies they investigate and supply theories, concepts and findings which become thrust back into the world they describe . . . Viewed from a technological standpoint, the practical contributions of the social sciences seem, and are, restricted. However, seen in terms of being filtered in the world they analyze, the practical ramifications of the social sciences have been, and are, very profound indeed. (p. 351)

Because family research tends to carry a moral meaning and message, researchers have an obligation to consider the potential uses of knowledge when they formulate their questions, and the potential application of their findings to social policies relevant to family life. What we say the family is will increasingly define what the family ought to be (Fass, Chap. 6, this volume). This alone gives family researchers more power than they are accustomed to having and more responsibility than they are accustomed to shouldering.

These, then, are the six items we would place on an agenda for family research as we approach a new century. The form and content of this volume is based on our assumption that family research will benefit from more interchange, not simply on the level of theories, methods, and findings, but also on the issues of what the field of family research is contributing to the world and where it should be heading. Whatever theories we give allegiance to or see as most useful, whatever changes we have yet to find in the form and function of family life, whatever challenges family researchers choose to pursue, we expect the field to remain united in one belief: Families mattered in the past; they continue to matter in the present; and they will matter still, in the uncertain years of our future.

REFERENCES

Becker, G. S. (1981). *A treatise on the family.* Cambridge, MA: Harvard University Press.

Block, J. H. (1983). *Sex role identity and ego development.* San Francisco, CA: Jossey-Bass.

Chodorow, N. J. (1978). *The reproduction of mothering*. Berkeley, CA: University of California Press.

Chodorow, N. J. (1989). *Feminism and psychoanalytic theory*. New Haven, CT: Yale University Press.

Cowan, C. P., & Cowan, P. A. (1988). Who does what when partners become parents: Implications for men, women, and marriage. *Marriage & Family Review, 13,* 105–132.

Dillingham, B., & Isaac, B. (1975). Defining marriage cross-culturally. In D. Raphael (Ed.), *Being female: Reproduction, power, and change* (pp. 55–63). The Hague: Mouton.

Ferree, M. M. (1990). Beyond separate spheres: Feminism and family research. *Journal of Marriage and the Family, 52,* 866–884.

Field, D., Fooken, I., & Rudinger, G. (1991, November). *Health and family relationships in old age: Findings from the Bonn Longitudinal Study of Aging and the Berkeley Older Generation Study*. Paper presented at the meetings of the Gerontological Society of America, San Francisco.

Giddens, A. (1984). *The constitution of society: Outline of the theory of structuralism*. Berkeley, CA: University of California Press.

Greenberg, J. R., & Mitchell, S. A. (1983). *Object relations in psychoanalytic theory* Cambridge: Harvard University Press.

Greenstein, T. N. (1990). Marital disruption and the employment of married women. *Journal of Marriage and the Family, 52,* 657–676.

Ishii-Kuntz, M. (1990). Social interaction and psychological well-being: Comparison acros stages of adulthood. *International Journal of Aging and Human Development, 30,* 12–36.

McLuhan, M. (1984). *Understanding media: The extension of man*. New York: McGraw-Hill.

Parsons, T. (1955). The American family: Its relation to personality and to the social structure. In T. Parsons & R. F. Bales (Eds.), *Family socialization and interaction processes* (pp. 3–33). Glencor, IL: The Free Press.

Rutter, M. (1987). Psychosocial resilience and protective mechanisms. *American Journal of Orthopsychiatry, 57,* 316–331.

Rutter, M. & Garmezy, N. (1983). Developmental psychopathology. In P. Mussen (Ed.), *Handbook of child psychology* (Vol. IV). New York: Wiley.

Skolnick (1991). *Embattled paradise: The American family in an age of uncertainty*. New York: Basic Books.

Taylor, C. (1983). Political theory and practice. In C. Loyd (Ed.), *Social theory and political practice*. Oxford: Clarendon Press.

Walsh, F. (Ed.). (1982). *Normal family processes*. New York: Guilford.

Werner, E. E., & Smith, R. S. (1982). *Vulnerable but invincible: A longitudinal study of resilient children and youth*. New York: McGraw-Hill.

Author Index

A

B

C

F

G

I

J

K

L

M

P

Q, R

S

Subject Index

G

O

P

R

S